Lev Tolstoy

was born in 1828 at Yasnaya Polyana, some 130 miles from Moscow, the son of a Count and a Princess. Both parents died when he was young, and in 1841 he moved with his guardian to Kazan where he briefly attended the university. A dissolute life and the inheritance of the Yasnaya Polyana estate led to his abandoning his studies in 1847. For the next four years he divided his time between estate management in the country and a round of pleasure in Moscow and Petersburg, accumulating large debts, but also feeling his way as a writer. In 1852 he joined the army and saw action in the Caucasus, Silistria and the Crimea, where periods of drinking, gambling and womanizing alternated with the writing and publication of his semi-autobiographical *Childhood* and his Sevastopol stories. Returning to Petersburg in 1856, he frequented its literary salons and explored its demi-monde. He paid two long visits to Western Europe, opened a school for peasant children on his estate, and published several stories of limited success, while a passionate liaison with a peasant woman resulted in the birth of a son. Marriage to Sofya Behrs in 1862 was a turning point in his life, and in 1863, when the first of their thirteen children was born, he completed *The Cossacks* and began work on *War and Peace* which was to occupy him intermittently for six years. *Anna Karenina* followed in the 1870s, but an increasing preoccupation with religious problems culminated in a spiritual crisis, lucidly recounted in his *Confession*. An unconventional Christian, he studied Greek and Hebrew, translated the Gospels, wrote a critique of dogmatic theology and was eventually excommunicated by the Orthodox Church. A stream of articles inveighed against urban squalor, the private ownership of land, many state institutions and above all war. His yearning for 'self-improvement' led him to give up alcohol, tobacco, blood sports and the eating of meat. He renounced his title and the copyright to all his works since 1881, simplified his dress and cobbled shoes (badly). Many of his later stories were moralistic and didactic, including the notorious *Kreutzer Sonata* and the harrowing *Death of Ivan Il'ich*, but *Hadji Murat* and parts of *Resurrection* showed that he never quite lost his outstanding gifts as a novelist. Towards the end of his life he found himself the focus of attention of much of the world, and Yasnaya Polyana became a place of pilgrimage; but the friction created by his unorthodox views in a family largely unsympathetic towards them was such that after 48 years of marriage he finally left home for good in 1910, only to die on an obscure railway station at Astapovo.

continued over

R. F. Christian

was born in Liverpool in 1924 and educated at Queen's College, Oxford, where his classical studies were interrupted by wartime flying duties in the RAF. On his return to Oxford in 1946 he took up the study of Russian, graduating with first class honours in 1949. After a spell in the British Embassy in Moscow he left the Foreign Office for an academic career, eventually becoming Professor of Russian at Birmingham and St Andrews Universities, and holding visiting professorships in North America and the USSR. His particular interests are in nineteenth-century Russian literature, especially Tolstoy, and his publications include *Tolstoy's 'War and Peace'. A Study* (OUP), *Tolstoy. A Critical Introduction* (CUP) and comprehensive editions of Tolstoy's letters and diaries (Athlone). He is also the joint author of *Russian Syntax* (OUP). Since retiring in 1992 he has been appointed Honorary Professor of Russian at St Andrews University.

INTRODUCTION

TOLSTOY'S DIARIES GREATLY EXCEED in length and scope those of any other Russian author. They are usually divided into two categories. The diaries proper are written for the most part in exercise books, and are dated chronologically. The so-called 'notebooks' consist of various kinds of scribbling pads, desk calendars and loose sheets of paper, some dated, some not. Some notebooks are virtually identical with diaries in the normal sense and contain entries, usually dated, for periods when Tolstoy did not keep a regular diary. Others contain random notes and observations, lists of popular expressions and a variety of ephemeral matter. Others again, especially those of the last twenty years of his life, were essentially first drafts of what were later to become entries in his diary proper. Tolstoy's diaries and notebooks taken together occupy thirteen volumes of the ninety-volume Soviet edition of his works (the Jubilee Edition 1928–58), and it is most unlikely that they will ever be translated in full. For the purposes of this edition I have confined myself almost entirely to the diaries proper, and have only very occasionally included an extract from a notebook or sheet of paper where the content seemed to justify it. When this has been done, I have indicated it in a footnote.

Tolstoy's diaries span a period of sixty-three years. The first entry is dated 17 March 1847, when Tolstoy was aged eighteen and a student at Kazan University. The last entry was written on 3 November 1910, as he lay dying at the railway station at Astapovo. There are unfortunately considerable gaps in the record, of which the first is the three-year period from June 1847 to June 1850. It was once argued that Tolstoy had destroyed his diaries for these years, but there is no evidence to support this contention and it is no longer seriously maintained. For the period 1850 to 1865 Tolstoy kept his diary fairly regularly in the sense that there are at least some entries for every year, but those for the late 1850s and early 1860s are comparatively short. Then there is a gap of thirteen years from 1865 to 1878 when Tolstoy was wholly absorbed in writing *War and Peace* and *Anna Karenina* – in some respects surrogate diaries – while from 1878 to 1888 there are relatively few entries except for two sustained six-month periods in 1881 and 1884. From 1888 to 1910 Tolstoy kept his diary regularly and the older he grew the longer it became. Roughly speaking, one half of it covers the period up to 1894 when Tolstoy was already sixty-six, while the other half is devoted to the last sixteen years of his life when his greatest literary

achievements were behind him and his writing became increasingly didactic
and moralistic. I have deliberately included a higher proportion of what he
wrote in his younger days, but even so the balance of any selection must
inevitably be weighted towards the years of his decline as an artist and his
rapidly growing reputation as a moral and spiritual guide.

To translate all Tolstoy's diaries into English would be a daunting task,
and it is not surprising that it has never been undertaken. A beginning was
made in 1917 with *The Diaries of Leo Tolstoy. Youth, 1847–1852, translated
from the Russian by C. J Hogarth and A. Sirnis*. It was an unsatisfactory
beginning, and the book has long been out of print. The year 1917 also saw
the appearance of *The Journal of Leo Tolstoy; First Volume, 1895–1899*,
translated by Rose Strunsky, but this translation also left much to be
desired, and there was no second volume. Ten years later Louise and
Aylmer Maude published *The Private Diary of Leo Tolstoy, 1853–1857*, a vast
improvement over any previous translation of any portion of the diaries, but
despite their great experience and intimate knowledge of Tolstoy and his
family they were unable to avoid some errors in deciphering the
manuscripts, while certain passages were omitted for reasons of propriety.
Finally the fiftieth anniversary of Tolstoy's death in 1960 was marked by the
publication in America of *The Last Diaries of Leo Tolstoy*, translated by Lydia
Weston-Kesich, an accurate translation but confined to the year 1910. With
the exception of Strunsky's unsatisfactory version there are no English
translations in whole or part of the years between 1857 and 1909, although
individual entries have of course been quoted in English by biographers
with access to Russian sources.

After publishing my edition of Tolstoy's letters in 1978, the Athlone Press
invited me to produce a companion edition of his diaries, also in two
volumes and of roughly comparable length. My choice of what to include
was made first of all on the basis of a careful reading of volumes 46–58 of the
Jubilee Edition of Tolstoy's works. I then compared the passages I had
chosen with the choice made in volumes 19 and 20 of the more recent
edition of N. N. Akopova and others, Moscow, 1965, and made a number of
changes in order to reduce the amount of my own material and make it
approximate more closely to their judicious and carefully balanced
selection, while retaining certain passages of a politically sensitive or
indelicate nature, as well as entries which present Tolstoy in a less than
favourable light and which for that reason are sometimes conveniently
overlooked. In making my selection I followed the same general principles
as I followed when preparing my edition of Tolstoy's letters. First of all I
chose passages to do with Tolstoy the writer, his views about his own works
and the works of other writers; secondly – those which concerned Tolstoy
the thinker in a broader sense and expressed his attitude to the times he
lived in, contemporary social problems, rural life, industrialization,

education, and more especially in later life, religious and spiritual questions; and thirdly – those which recorded the main stages of his biography, his relations with his family and friends, and the growth and development of his own personality. In making this one-volume abridgement, I have been guided by the same general considerations.

Tolstoy's diaries are an invaluable mine of information about his life and thought, his restless, complex, contradictory nature and his unrelenting quest for 'self-improvement' and a rational answer to the question of the purpose of existence. They are the fullest and frankest record of his dissolute bachelor days, his eventful career as a soldier, his first, faltering steps as a writer, his disoriented years divided between the capital cities and his country estate, his hesitant and fruitless courtship of Valeriya Arsenyeva, his travels in Europe, and his eventual wooing and winning of Sofya Behrs. They are an indispensable source (together with the diaries of his wife) for the story of a most exceptional marriage, and they record his considered thoughts and ill-considered prejudices on the great variety of subjects to which he applied his powerful and unorthodox mind. They are the germ out of which his earliest 'fiction' grew, and although they tell us disappointingly little about his two great masterpieces, they reveal a lot about his literary tastes and practices. They cannot by any stretch of imagination be called works of literature. The language in which they are written is decidedly unpolished, at times ponderous and repetitive, at times laconic and abrupt. The syntax can be awkward and involved, the grammar not impeccable. The diaries abound in abbreviations, misspellings and lapses of the pen. The punctuation is unorthodox. The handwriting defies description. To charges of stylistic inelegance, Tolstoy would certainly have replied that he was only concerned with what he wished to say, not how he said it, and that he was not writing with one eye on the public (not, at least, until very late in life). It does not follow, however, that the form is always redeemed by the content. It would be foolish to pretend that there are not many trivial, tedious and jaundiced entries, or that the thoughts which take up a disproportionate amount of space in later years have not been more cogently expressed in one or other of his numerous books and articles. Nevertheless the diaries are an unparalleled record of the stages of development of a unique personality. Tolstoy himself attached the greatest importance to them. He often referred not merely to the pleasure he got from reading and rereading them, but also to their significance for understanding him. Towards the end of his life he frankly acknowledged 'The diaries *are* me.' They are the story of his life told by himself and when read consecutively they reveal the process of his evolution as no other document can do.

The Honourable Gwendolyn Fairfax once remarked to Miss Cecily Cardew: 'I never travel without my diary. One should always have something sensational to read on the train.' If not sensational, the first entry in Tolstoy's diary was sufficiently unusual for parts of it to be omitted from Hogarth's translation, being written at the age of eighteen in a university clinic where Tolstoy was recovering from venereal disease, and it immediately strikes a note of candour and self-preoccupation. At this stage of his life Tolstoy had no audience in mind except himself and there is no reason to doubt the truthfulness of what he wrote. He began by asking himself what his motives were for keeping a diary at all and acknowledged that one comprehensive purpose was to monitor the development of his faculties, draw up tables of rules for cultivating those faculties and define the nature and scope of his future activities. One of his first rules for developing his intellectual faculties was to evaluate and make extracts from important books he was reading, and since as a young law student at Kazan University he had been set the task of comparing Catherine the Great's *Instruction* to the commission charged with preparing the new Code of Laws with Montesquieu's *De l'esprit des lois*, it seemed appropriate for him to record in his diary his views about the Empress's manifesto. In reducing the diaries to a single volume, I have omitted these ponderous and unremarkable views, while retaining the conclusions which Tolstoy reached while still a teenage undergraduate. In addition to registering the growth and development of his faculties, his diaries were also intended to record his frequent dissatisfaction with himself, his many falls from grace and subsequent remorse and his constant striving towards moral self-improvement. It is Tolstoy himself and not the world about him that is the centre of attention of these early entries, and the picture which emerges from them is of a young man over-addicted to self-analysis and self-reproach, vain, egotistical, prone to show off, lazy, irresolute, fond of gambling and abnormally sensual. He is convinced that he is 'a remarkable person', an exception. At the same time he recognizes that he must be a difficult, even an 'unbearable' man, hard to get on with, difficult to understand, 'somehow unlovable', for all the love he claims to feel towards other people. He desperately wants to be loved, to be accepted, to earn the praise of his fellow men, while being at the same time uneasily aware of his superiority over them. On at least one occasion he admits to wishing to 'influence other people's happiness', to be useful to them, but for the most part it is his own personality, its shortcomings and the need to remedy them that are his main preoccupation. As well as tabulating his weaknesses, the early diaries contain some succinct generalizations about life and death, religion and various aspects of human behaviour – as, for example, that 'the most offensive form of egoism is self-sacrifice' or 'unhappiness makes man virtuous, happiness makes him vicious'. They also include observations on the books he is reading and occasional extracts from literary or philosophical works which have impressed him. Having moved to the Caucasus in 1851 he begins to record details of army life, military actions and the officers and men with whom he lived. His entries become more self-consciously literary and he confesses to wishing to use his diaries 'to form his style', to serve in fact as trials of the pen. He seems now at times to be writing with an imaginary audience in mind and to be drafting out material which will form the basis of short stories firmly grounded in his own experience. 'I'll try and sketch Knoring's portrait', he writes of an officer colleague, adding significantly that 'it's impossible to *describe* a man, but it is possible to describe the effect he has on me'. He tried his hand too at natural descriptions and recorded conversations which would reappear in revised form in his earliest fiction. He painstakingly formulated generalizations on human virtues and vices – on courage, for example, or cowardice – and on national characteristics. He also made notes about his literary plans and outlined the ideas for his early Caucasian stories and his first major work of fiction *Childhood*. It was in his diaries that he spoke for the first time about his love of history, his wish 'to compile a true, accurate history of Europe', and the need of the historian to explain every historical fact *in human terms*. Tolstoy never realized his characteristically unrealizable ambition as a historian, but his extensive historical reading and his overriding concern with the role of the individual in the historical process provided much of the stimulus to write a full-scale novel on a major historical theme.

Scattered throughout the early diaries are numerous *obiter dicta* about writers and works of literature – interesting more for what they tell us about Tolstoy than about the authors themselves. They include references to Pushkin, Lermontov, Griboyedov, Turgenev, Pisemsky and Ostrovsky, as well as Rousseau, Balzac and George Sand, Goethe and Schiller, Dickens and Thackeray. They confirm his belief in the moral purpose of literature; they venture the opinion – welcome for him – that in contemporary works of fiction interest in the details of *feelings* is replacing interest in events themselves; and they reveal that it is the character and personality of an author as reflected in what he writes that interests him most as a reader. They also contain, incidentally, some unflattering remarks about women authors which ill accord with his later admiration for George Eliot, Mrs Gaskell, Mrs Henry Wood and others.

At this early stage in Tolstoy's life one already finds in his diaries an anti-militaristic strain, a tendency to venerate the common people at the expense of his own class of society and an orientation towards the practical and the useful which are such typical features of the mature Tolstoy – whether in his resolve to edit a journal to propagate morally useful writings or his desire to found a religion 'purged of faith and mystery, a practical religion which does not promise a future bliss but provides bliss on earth'. It was also becoming clear to him that literature was to be his true vocation; 'literary fame', as he expressed it, 'and the good which I can do by my writing'.

His writing, however, did not immediately prosper after his return to

St Petersburg in 1856, and the next few years until his marriage in 1862 were difficult and unsettled ones, punctuated by travels in Western Europe, estate management and educational experiments at home, and the determination to find a wife before it was too late. His diaries give a clear, if incomplete, picture of his mental and spiritual development during his late twenties and early thirties when, although he moved in the circles of the Moscow and Petersburg intelligentsia he was not himself an 'intellectual', and while he had certain convictions and beliefs, they did not tally with any recognizable conservative, liberal or radical viewpoint. His views altered with the company he kept. He liked upsetting other people's convictions. Although hostile to 'progress' in the sense of industrialization, capitalist expansion or the building of railways, and to a system of priorities which put telegraphs, roads and ships before literature, he criticized the Slavophiles for their backwardness and expressed the fear that he might himself lag behind his age. Indifferent or hostile to constitutional government and unimpressed by what he saw of parliamentary democracy in the West, he noted that 'all governments are alike in their extent of good and evil: the best ideal is anarchy'. Nationalism he regarded as 'a unique obstacle to the development of freedom', although he had his moments of jingoism during the Crimean War and again during the Polish insurrection of 1863. Contemptuous of aristocratic privilege and indolence, he could also write, in a positive sense: 'Aristocratic feeling is worth a lot.' Congenitally hostile to the dogmas of Orthodoxy, he still classed himself as a believer and found inspiration, though not rational satisfaction, in the ritual of the Orthodox Church. 'The nearness to death', he wrote, 'is the best argument for faith . . . Better to accept the old, time-honoured, comforting and childishly simple [faith]. This is not rational, but you feel it.' Instinct and intuition counted for much with him. His powerful mind seemed able to demolish any logical theory, but only to throw him back on irrational hunches, faith, or the activity of the heart, which by their very nature defy logic. Elsewhere he confessed to himself, 'The sort of mind which I have and which I like in others is the sort which does not believe in any theory . . .' Caught between the Scylla of faith and the Charybdis of reason, he lived in a state of constant turmoil, unsure of himself and deeply suspicious of people who subscribed to any man-made philosophy. It was bad enough, no doubt, to have to believe in God when all your reason revolted against it; but it was much better than believing in Chernyshevsky.

The single most important event in Tolstoy's life was his marriage to Sofya Behrs in 1862, the prelude to and immediate aftermath of which are recorded in his diary for that year. On the one hand his wife brought him a sense of stability which he had not previously known and created an atmosphere in which he could work with the maximum encouragement and support; on the other hand her strong personality and quick temper, and the fact that her views on many fundamental issues differed widely from his own led to increasing friction and animosity as time went by and his attitudes became more extreme. Shortly before he was married Tolstoy gave his fiancée his bachelor diaries to read and the shock which she – a sheltered girl of eighteen – experienced on learning about his sexual promiscuity was one from which she never perhaps fully recovered. Both husband and wife had recourse to their diaries at times of bitterness and tension. Each had access to what the other wrote and both said things which they bitterly regretted afterwards. 'She will remain a mill-stone round my neck and round the children's until I die,' he wrote in 1884. On another occasion he wrote that it was fortunate for his daughter Masha that her mother did not love her, while his son Seryozha is described as having 'the same castrated mind' as his mother. Needless to say, these were uncontrollable outbursts which later caused him great remorse. 'Some three days ago,' he observed in 1894, 'I read through my diary for 1884 and was disgusted with myself for my unkindness and the cruelty of my opinions about Sonya and Seryozha. Let them know that I take back all the unkind things I said about them.' The following year he wrote *'When reading through my diary I found a passage – there were several of them – where I repudiate those angry words which I wrote about her. These words were written at moments of exasperation. I now repeat this once more for the sake of everybody who should come across these diaries* [Tolstoy's underlining]. I was often exasperated with her because of her hasty, inconsiderate temper, but, as Fet used to say, every husband gets the wife he needs. She was – and I can see now in what way – the wife I needed. She was the ideal wife in a pagan sense, in the sense of loyalty, domesticity, self-denial, love of family – pagan love – and she has the potential to become a Christian friend.' Likewise his wife had occasion to regret her more intemperate utterances – provoked by Tolstoy's absurd jealousy of the composer Taneyev she once allegedly shouted at him 'you're evil, you're a beast' – although she did not actually repudiate them in writing in the same way as her husband. A reading of both their diaries is absolutely essential to an understanding of their long, loving, but at times unhappy and turbulent marriage; yet considerable allowance must be made for the fact that when things were running smoothly, as they often were, they seldom found the need to say so.

From the early 1880s onwards, after Tolstoy's so-called 'conversion', his diaries came to be used more and more as a vehicle for his religious, moral and social philosophy, and to include raw material which was subsequently processed into articles, letters and even works of fiction. Towards the end of his life they were written in the knowledge that they would be read outside the family (at times, indeed, in the hope that they would be) and increasingly they became the subject of bitter family

altercations, especially with the appearance on the scene of Tolstoy's
dedicated but dictatorial disciple Vladimir Chertkov. The story of the
struggle for their possession and publication and the bitterness it created
between those most closely involved – Tolstoy and his wife, their daughter
Alexandra and Chertkov – has been told many times. Every entry made was
certain to become public property, if not immediately, at least in the not very
distant future, not excluding the so-called 'secret diary' of 1908 and the
'diary for myself alone' of 1910. In the circumstances it is not surprising that
the more intimate side of Tolstoy's life is less in evidence – though frank
enough when it is – and that the prevailing tone of the later diaries is
pedagogical and moralistic. The constant harping on certain themes is
bound to be tedious at times, but that does not mean that there are not many
shrewd observations on a wide range of subjects of universal interest. There
are, for example, some pertinent remarks on social and political theories,
some of which were withheld from circulation in the Soviet Union. 'It
doesn't follow,' he wrote, 'that, as Marx says, capitalism leads to socialism.
Perhaps it will do, but only to socialism by force.' And again: 'Even if what
Marx predicts were to happen, then the only thing that would happen would
be that despotism would be transferred. Now the capitalists are in power,
then the workers' bosses would be in power.' The argument that the end
justifies the means never weighed in the least with Tolstoy. Indeed on one
occasion he referred disparagingly to what he called 'the socialist, Marxist
idea that if you do something wrong for a very long time it will come right of
itself'. His views on economics were concerned primarily with an answer to
the question of the ownership and redistribution of land, and he believed
that it was to be found in the writings of the American economist Henry
George and in his Single Tax system. The most important factor in the
economic equation for him was the agricultural labourer, but no economic
or political changes, he reiterated, could be of lasting value as long as people
remained the same. Only religion, he believed, had the power to transform
people's lives and eliminate the need, inherent in all political systems, for a
quite unacceptable degree of coercion. His views on religion take up many
pages of his later diaries, especially his insistence on religion as a moral code
of practice whether sanctioned by Christ or by one of the Eastern faiths to
which he became increasingly attracted. His diaries reveal that he was a
most unorthodox Christian and in one entry he went so far as to write: 'Read
an interesting book about Christ never having existed, that it was a myth.
There is as much to be said *for* the likelihood that this is true as there is
against.' What one believed, however, or which of the great religious
teachers of the world one turned to for support, was ultimately less
important than how one lived. There was no reason why a Christian
should live a better life than, say, a Hindu; but Tolstoy for his part found that
the essence of Christ's teaching as he interpreted it, especially its

emphasis on turning the other cheek, non-resistance to evil by force, loving one's neighbour and forgiving one's enemies, provided him with the best prescription for a happy and worthwhile life – if only he could follow it! Another theme which constantly recurs in the diaries is that of the meaning and purpose of art, an activity which he, like many other people, regarded as essentially the expression and communication of feelings. But, more than most people, he was acutely aware of the *power* of art – its power for evil as well as good – and therefore the nature and quality of the feelings communicated by the artist must be the paramount considerations, and what was good art must ultimately be a question of ethics, not aesthetics; a quasi-religious activity with a clear moral purpose. Tolstoy's attitude to art as a necessary ingredient in his recipe for the moral and spiritual progress of mankind obviously conditioned his views about what he was reading and what he would write. Of course in later life he never wrote anything to compare artistically with *War and Peace* and *Anna Karenina*, but he did continue to produce stories, plays and one major novel which are still widely read all over the world today. There are many references in the diaries of the last two decades of his life to *Resurrection, Hadji Murat, The Kreutzer Sonata, Father Sergce* and *The Fruits of Enlightenment* and also to many other minor works. They include draft plans and modifications to them, as well as various seemingly trivial details which are nevertheless important to the student of Tolstoy's literary methods and practices. He also confided to his diaries some terse, laconic pronouncements about his fellow authors, especially Russian, which, although influenced naturally enough by his general philosophy of art, were often shrewd. He praised Gorky for his great talent and knowledge of the people, but did not admire him as a psychologist and found his attribution of heroic thoughts and feelings to his characters arbitrary and exaggerated. Gogol had, in his opinion, 'an enormous talent, a wonderful heart and a weak, i.e. unadventurous, timid mind'. He acknowledged that Chekhov, like Pushkin, had made important advances in form and was enthusiastic about some of his short stories, but was disappointed by what he saw as a lack of content, more particularly in his plays. He found much to admire in *The Brothers Karamazov*, especially the Grand Inquisitor legend and the Father Zosima episode, but criticized Dostoyevsky for his 'slipshod manner of writing' and 'unnatural conversations'. Of Andreyev he said: 'His denominator is disproportionately big compared with his numerator.' Of Bernard Shaw – 'He has got more brains than is good for him'!

If Tolstoy's observations about his fellow writers are unlikely to give offence, the same is not true of some of the derogatory things he said about women. 'For seventy years,' he wrote in 1899, 'I have been lowering my opinion of women more and more, and I need to lower it still further.'

Or again: 'If men knew all women as well as husbands know their wives they would never argue with them and would never value their opinion.' He admitted to finding it difficult to love a Jew, adding that he 'must try hard'. He had some rude things to say about doctors and was capable, like most people, of contradicting himself – which certainly does not mean that Bertrand Russell was right when he remarked that it was the greatest misfortune for the human race that Tolstoy had so little power of reasoning. But it is not so much the prejudices and occasional logical inconsistencies that dominate the diaries of his old age as the personal tragedy of a man who tried to live – and to love his neighbours – in an environment from which he was growing increasingly alienated, while continuing to be surrounded by a loving family and the veneration of men and women throughout the world. These diaries record his sense of loneliness and isolation, his anguish at being continually misunderstood and on numerous occasions his wish to die. 'Living is dying,' he wrote. 'Try to die well.' The tragic events of 1910, his wife's hatred of Chertkov, her attempts at suicide and his own departure from home in the middle of the night make painful reading. The very last entry in his diary shortly before he lost consciousness ends with the words: 'Here is my plan. *Fais que dois, advienne que pourra* [Do what you must, come what may]. And all is for the good of others and above all for me.' Perhaps significantly, the last word he wrote was – me.

In translating the diaries I have kept as closely as possible to the sense of the original, while smoothing over some of the syntactical roughnesses and correcting obvious slips of the pen. To facilitate reading I have inserted the first person pronoun in a number of contexts where Tolstoy omits it and I have also taken liberties with the punctuation. My transliteration system and general editorial policy follow the principles set out in the preface to my edition of Tolstoy's letters. In a few cases, however, I have retranslated the titles of articles by Tolstoy, so that what was previously *A Circle of Reading* is now called *A Cycle of Reading* and *The End of an Age* has been renamed *The End of the World*. *Letter to an Indian* has been preferred to the earlier *Letter to a Hindu*, while the word *zapiski* has been consistently translated as 'notes' instead of 'memoirs' in the stories *The Notes of a Billiard Marker*, *The Notes of a Madman* and *The Posthumous Notes of Fyodor Kuzmich*. The spelling of the Cossack village where Tolstoy was first stationed has been standardized as Starogladkovskaya (different variants exist), and I have regularly used the forms Vanechka and Kostenka (not Vanichka and Kostinka) where Tolstoy's own spelling is erratic. I have used the hybrid combination Nicholas Pavlovich (not Nikolay Pavlovich) when the Tsar Nicholas I is referred to by Christian name and patronymic, but Nicholas in all other contexts. With newspaper titles I have kept the widely used *Notes of the Fatherland* to translate *Otechestvenniye zapiski* and have used *The Herald of Europe* for *Vestnik Evropy* and *The Russian Herald* for *Russky vestnik*. *Sankt-Peterburgskiye vedomosti* is rendered as either *The St Petersburg Gazettte* or the *Petersburg Gazette*, depending on whether Tolstoy uses the full or abbreviated form. *Versta* (3,500 feet), *arshin* (28 inches) and *vershok* (1¾ inches) have not been translated. *Dvoryanstvo* has normally been translated as 'gentry', except in the standardized phrase 'Marshal of the Nobility'. I have generally preferred to translate *khudozhestvenny* (artistic) as 'literary' or 'fictional' in a literary context; both 'hunting' and 'shooting' have been used to render *okhota* and its derivatives. Generally speaking, I have tried in my translations, as I did in the *Letters*, to recapture Tolstoy's habit of repeating the same word rather than employing a synonym, and the observations I made in my preface to that edition are applicable to this one also.

The footnotes and critical apparatus are intended to be self-sufficient, but cross-references have been made to the *Letters* in cases where more detailed information might be desired, particularly where a person mentioned has a biographical entry in that edition as one of Tolstoy's family circle or a frequent correspondent. The short narrative account of Tolstoy's life, divided chronologically into periods, follows the same lines as the one originally written for the *Letters*.

St Andrews, 1993   R. F. CHRISTIAN

1847–1855

LEV NIKOLAYEVICH TOLSTOY was born on 28 August 1828 at Yasnaya Polyana, his mother's estate some 130 miles to the south west of Moscow. His mother, born Princess Marya Volkonskaya, died before Tolstoy was two years old, and his father, Count Nikolay Tolstoy, a retired Lieutenant Colonel and veteran of 1812, only survived her by seven years. Tolstoy, who was the fourth of their five children, was left an orphan at the age of nine, and was brought up by two married aunts, the second of whom lived in Kazan, which was to become the Tolstoys' home from 1841 to 1847. In 1844 he succeeded with some difficulty in passing the entrance examinations to Kazan University, and began to study Oriental languages with the intention of becoming a diplomat. A year later he transferred to the Law Faculty, but his initial enthusiasm for the subject soon wore off, and although he passed his first-year examinations well enough, his erratic attendance in his second year coupled with a somewhat dissolute life and an attack of venereal disease led to his withdrawing from the university on grounds of 'ill health and domestic circumstances'. The circumstances referred to in his letter of withdrawal concerned the final division of his parents' estates between himself and his brothers and sister, as a result of which Tolstoy inherited Yasnaya Polyana and four other estates, a total of some 5,400 acres of land together with 330 male serfs and their families. His diary for 1847, as well as expressing at length his views about Catherine II's *Instruction* to the commission engaged in drafting a new Code of Laws, which had been a special subject of study at Kazan University, also records the first stages of his new life as a landowner at Yasnaya Polyana and his determination to define the nature and scope of his future activities and to draw up rules of behaviour which would enable him to develop his mental, physical and moral faculties along the lines he desired. As a boy, he later recalled, he had been greatly impressed by reading the story of Joseph in the Bible, various tales from the Arabian Nights, the Russian *byliny* or heroic poems and the poetry of Pushkin. In his teens he became an avid disciple of Rousseau. Among other foreign authors he greatly admired Dickens, Sterne, and Schiller, while nearer home he singled out Pushkin, Gogol and the early Turgenev as writers who had made a great impact on him. He also acknowledged the enormous influence on him at the time of St Matthew's Gospel and especially the Sermon on the Mount.

In autumn 1848 Tolstoy left Yasnaya Polyana for Moscow, and spent the winter in frivolous society pursuits. Early in 1849 he moved to Petersburg, but after spending a few weeks preparing to take the entrance examinations for the Law Faculty at Petersburg University and at the same time losing considerable sums of money at cards, he returned to Yasnaya Polyana and opened a school for the peasant children on his estate. For the next two years he continued to live in the country, with occasional excursions into Tula and Moscow society, devoting much time to music, cards and gymnastics and taking his first tentative steps as a writer. In 1851 he wrote the unfinished and unpublished *A History of Yesterday*, a Sternean, digressive, self-conscious analysis of the life of a single day. He also translated most of Sterne's *A Sentimental Journey* and began work on his own autobiographical novel *Childhood*. There are no diary entries for the period June 1847 to June 1850, although a few letters have survived from these years. The diaries for 1850–51 single out what he felt to be his greatest failings – vanity, irresolution, sensuality, cowardice and laziness; they also reveal his growing dissatisfaction with his way of life and the wish to make a fresh start. The opportunity came in April 1851 when his brother Nikolay was due to return from leave to his army unit in the Caucasus, and Tolstoy decided at short notice to accompany him. Soon after arriving in the Caucasus Tolstoy took part as a volunteer in an expedition against a local village (Georgia had been annexed by Russia in 1801 but the mountain tribes living in the north were still proving troublesome), and towards the end of 1851 he moved to Tiflis in order to prepare for examinations which would qualify him to join the army as a cadet.

Tolstoy entered the army proper in 1852 and for the next two years he was attached to an artillery brigade stationed in the Cossack village of Starogladkovskaya in the North Caucasus. He took part in a number of expeditions against the Chechen tribe led by the redoubtable Shamil, in the course of which he narrowly escaped death and capture. He received his commission in 1854 and was soon transferred to active service on the Danube, where hostilities had broken out between Russia and Turkey the previous autumn. He reached Bucharest in March 1854, but saw little fighting, serving for most of the time as a staff officer and being generally in poor health, as a result of which he underwent two operations before returning to Russia in September 1854, in the same month as British and French troops landed in the Crimea. He immediately applied to be posted there and reached Sevastopol in November when it was already under siege by the Allies. He spent the next year in the Crimea and was briefly in charge of a gun battery on the outskirts of Sevastopol during some of the heaviest fighting of the war. After the town had fallen he was despatched as a courier to Petersburg, but soon afterwards he sent in his resignation from the army, which became effective in 1856.

Tolstoy's army service was by no means a full-time occupation. There was ample time for reading, writing, travel, music, gambling, womanizing and many other activities. Reading for pleasure meant mainly fiction and history, with a little poetry thrown in, and with the exception of Rousseau it was largely confined to the nineteenth century, although embracing English, French and German authors no less than Russian. Tolstoy's growing urge to be a writer himself was stimulated not only by what he read, but also by what he lived through in the Caucasus and Crimea and the unexpected amount of leisure time at his disposal. His first published story, *Childhood*, appeared in 1852, followed by *The Raid* in 1853 and *Boyhood* in 1854. In 1855 he published *Sevastopol in December*, *Sevastopol in May* and *The Wood-felling*, all drawing heavily on his own experiences as an army officer, and *Sevastopol in August* followed in 1856. As he said many years later when recalling his military career: 'I didn't become a general in the army, but I did in literature.'

Tolstoy's diaries for the years 1851–55 take on a more conscious literary flavour as he comes to realize that literature was to be his true vocation. That they were the germ of his early fiction is a commonplace which nobody now would seriously dispute.

1847

17 March, Kazan It's now six days since I entered the clinic,[1] and for six days now I've been almost satisfied with myself. *Les petites causes produisent de grands effets* [little causes produce big effects]. I caught gonorrhoea where one usually catches it from of course; and this trivial circumstance gave me a jolt which made me mount the step which I had put my foot on long ago, but had been quite unable to heave my body on to (probably because, without thinking, I put my left foot on instead of my right). Here I'm completely alone, nobody disturbs me, I haven't any servants here, nobody helps me – consequently nothing extraneous has any influence on my reason or memory, and my work must necessarily make progress. But the chief advantage is that I've come to see clearly that the disorderly life which the majority of fashionable people take to be a consequence of youth is nothing other than a consequence of the early corruption of the soul.

Solitude is just as good for a man who lives in society as social intercourse is for a man who doesn't. Let a man withdraw from society, let him retreat into himself, and his reason will soon cast aside the spectacles which showed him everything in a distorted form, and his view of things will become so clear that he will be quite unable to understand how he had not seen it all before. Let reason do its work and it will indicate to you your destiny, and will give you rules with which you can confidently enter society. [. . .] It's easier to write ten volumes of philosophy than to put one single principle into practice.

18 March I've been reading Catherine's *Instruction*,[2] and since I've generally made it a rule when reading any serious work to think about it and copy out any remarkable thoughts from it, I'll write down my opinion here about the first six chapters of this remarkable work [. . .]

19 March A passion for the sciences is beginning to manifest itself in me; but although it is the noblest of all man's passions, I shall never surrender myself to it in a one-sided manner, i.e. completely destroy feeling, not concern myself with application, and only endeavour to educate my mind and fill my memory with facts. Onesidedness is the main cause of man's unhappiness.

24 March I have changed a lot; but I still haven't achieved the degree of perfection (in my studies) which I would like to achieve. I don't carry out what I prescribe for myself; what I do carry out, I don't carry out well; I don't exercise my memory. Therefore I'll write down some rules here which, it seems to me, will help me a lot if I follow them. (1) What is required to be carried out without fail, carry out in spite of everything. (2) What you do carry out, carry out well. (3) Never refer to a book if you forget something, but try to remember it yourself. (4) Make your mind work constantly with all possible vigour. (5) Always read and think aloud. (6) Don't be ashamed to tell people who interrupt you that they are interrupting you; first of all let a person feel it, but if he doesn't understand, apologise and tell him outright. In accordance with my second rule I intend without fail to finish my commentary on the whole of Catherine's *Instruction* [. . .]

26 March [. . .] Generally speaking the following may be said about the Empress Catherine's *Instruction*. As I have already said before,[3] we find two contradictory principles everywhere in it – the revolutionary spirit, to the influence of which the whole of Europe was then subject, and the spirit of despotism which her vanity would not allow her to renounce. Although she was aware of the superiority of the former, it is nevertheless the latter that prevails in her *Instruction*. The republican ideas borrowed for the most part from Montesquieu [. . .] she used as a means of justifying despotism, but for the most part unsuccessfully. Hence we often find in her *Instruction* ideas which are deficient in proofs or lack them altogether, republican ideas side by side with the most despotic ones and, finally, deductions which are often completely opposed to logic.

From the first glance at the *Instruction* we recognize that it was the intellectual fruit of a woman who, despite her great intellect, her exalted feelings and her love of truth, was unable to overcome her petty vanity which obscures her great merits. Generally speaking we find in this work more pettiness than soundness, more wit than reason, more vanity than love of truth and, finally, more self-love than love of the people. This latter tendency is apparent throughout the *Instruction*, in which we find only ordinances concerning public law, i.e. relationships of state (Catherine's own relationships as its representative), and not civil law, i.e. relationships between private citizens. In conclusion I would say that the *Instruction* brought more fame to Catherine than benefit to Russia.

7 April, 8 am I have never kept a diary before, because I could never see the benefit of it. But now that I am concerned with the development of my own faculties, I shall be able to judge from a diary the progress of that development. The diary should contain a table of rules, and it should also define my future activities. In exactly a week's time I shall be leaving for the country. What should I do during that week? Study English and Latin, and Roman law and ordinances: to wit, read *The Vicar of Wakefield*,[4] learning all the unfamiliar words, and go through the first part of the grammar; read the first part of the *Institution*[5] both for the sake of the language and for the sake of Roman law; finish the rules for my inner education; and win back what I lost at chess.

8 April, 6 am   Hope is bad for *a happy man* and *good for an unhappy one.*

Although I have gained a lot since I began to study myself, I am still very dissatisfied with myself. The more progress you make in self-improvement, the more you see the faults in yourself, and Socrates rightly said that the highest state of a man's perfection is the knowledge that he knows nothing.

9 April, 6 am   I am quite satisfied with myself as regards yesterday. I am beginning to acquire physical will-power, but my mental will-power is still very weak. With patience and application I am sure that I shall achieve everything I want.

17 April   I have not behaved all this time as I wished to behave. The cause has been, first, my return home from the clinic; and secondly the company which I have begun to associate with more often. I conclude from this that with every change of situation I shall need to think very seriously what external circumstances will influence me in the new situation, and how this influence can be eliminated. If my return home from the clinic could have such an influence on me, what influence will my transition from the life of a student to the life of a landowner have?[6] [. . .]

I would be the unhappiest of men if I could not find a purpose for my life – a purpose both general and useful – useful because my immortal soul when fully mature will pass naturally into a higher existence and one that is appropriate to it. So now my whole life will be a constant and active striving to achieve this one purpose.

Now I ask myself, what will be the purpose of my life in the country for the next two years? (1) To study the whole course of law necessary for my final examination at the university. (2) To study practical medicine, and some theoretical medicine. (3) To study languages: French, Russian, German, English, Italian and Latin. (4) To study agriculture, both theoretical and practical. (5) To study history, geography and *statistics*. (6) To study mathematics, the grammar school course. (7) To write a dissertation. (8) To attain an average degree of perfection in music and painting. (9) To write down rules. (10) To acquire some knowledge of the natural sciences. (11) To write essays on all the subjects I shall study.

18 April   I wrote down a lot of rules all of a sudden[7] and wanted to follow them all, but I wasn't strong enough to do so. But now I want to set myself one rule only, and to add another one to it only when I've got used to following that one. The first rule which I prescribe is as follows: No.1. *Carry out everything you have resolved must be carried out.* I haven't carried out this rule.

14 June, Yasnaya Polyana[8]   After nearly two months I'm taking up my pen again in order to continue my diary. [. . .]

16 June   Shall I ever reach the stage of being independent of all extraneous circumstances? In my opinion that would be the greatest perfection; for in a man who is independent of all extraneous influence, spirit will necessarily of its own need take precedence over matter, and then he will attain his destiny. I am beginning to get used to the first rule which I prescribed for myself, and today I will prescribe another one, namely the following: regard the society of women as a necessary unpleasantness of social life, and avoid it as much as possible. From whom, indeed, do we derive sensuality, effeminacy, frivolity in everything and a multitude of other vices, if not from women? Who is to blame for the fact that we lose our innate feelings of boldness, resolution, judiciousness, justice, etc., if not women? A woman is more receptive than a man, and therefore women were better than us in virtuous ages; but in the present depraved and corrupt age they are worse than us.

RULES FOR DEVELOPING THE PHYSICAL WILL

General rule. All actions should be resolutions of the will, and not the unconscious fulfilment of bodily needs. [. . .]

Rule 1. Each morning plan everything that you ought to do during the whole day, and carry out everything planned, even if carrying it out involves some harm. Apart from developing the will, this rule will also develop the mind, which will determine the actions of the will more judiciously. 2. Sleep as little as possible (sleep, in my opinion, is a state in which a man's will is completely non-existent). 3. Put up with all bodily discomforts without giving outward expression to them. 4. Stick to your word. 5. If you once start anything at all, don't give it up without finishing it. 6. Always keep a table in which to define all the most trivial circumstances of your life, even how many pipes to smoke a day. 7. If you do a thing, harness all your bodily faculties to what it is you are doing. But if your way of life changes, change these rules too.

RULES FOR DEVELOPING THE EMOTIONAL WILL

The source of all feelings is love in general, which can be divided into two sorts of love: love of ourselves or self-love, and love of everything around us. [. . .] These two basic feelings mutually interact on each other. A general rule: all emotional acts should be, not unconscious fulfilments of emotional needs, but resolutions of the will. All feelings which have love of the whole world as their source are good; all feelings which have self-love as their source are bad. Let us look at each category of feeling separately. What feelings derive from self-love? (1) love of fame, (2) love of gain, and (3) love (between a man and a woman).

Now let us see what the rules ought to be for making the will prevail over each of these feelings.

Rules for subordinating to the will the feeling of self-love

Rule 8. Don't worry about the approbation of people you either don't know, or else despise. 9. Concern yourself more with yourself than with the opinion of others. 10. Be good, and try not to let anyone know that you are good. (Love of fame is sometimes good for others, but not for oneself.) 11. Always look for the good side in other people, and not the bad. Always tell the truth. If, when you are acting for yourself, your actions seem strange, don't try to justify them to anyone. The following rule needs to be added to the ones for subordinating the feelings to the will. 12. Never express your feelings outwardly.

Rules for subordinating to the will the feeling of love of gain

Rule 13. Always live less well than you could live. 14. Don't change your way of life, even if you become ten times richer. 15. Use any increase in your estate not for yourself, but for society.

Rules for subordinating to the will the feeling of love

First rule. Keep away from women. Second rule. Mortify your desires by hard work.

The feelings which derive from love are: (1) love of all creation, (2) love of one's country, (3) love of individual people.

Rules for subordinating to the will the feeling of universal love

Rule 16. Sacrifice all other feelings of love to universal love, and then the will will demand only the fulfilment of the needs of universal love, and will prevail over it. 17. Sacrifice a tenth part of all you might have at your disposal, for the good of others.

Love yourself and others equally, and give help rather to those who are less fortunate than you, and whom you can more conveniently help.

Rules for subordinating to the will the feelings of love of one's country and love of individual people

Rule 18. All these feelings are to be subordinated to one another in the order in which they stand here.

RULES FOR DEVELOPING THE RATIONAL WILL

Rule 19. Decide on all your intellectual occupations at the beginning of the day. 20. When you are studying a subject, try to direct all your intellectual faculties to that subject. 21. Try not to let anything external, physical or emotional, influence the direction of your ideas, but let the ideas determine their own direction. 22. Try not to let any pain, physical or emotional, influence your intellect.

Whatever intellectual occupation you begin, don't give it up until you have finished it. Since this rule could lead to great abuses, it must be limited here by the following rule: have a purpose for your life as a whole, a purpose for a certain period of your life, a purpose for a certain time, a purpose for a year, a month, a week, a day, an hour and a minute, sacrificing the lower purposes to the higher ones.

RULES FOR DEVELOPING THE MEMORY

Rule 23. Draw up a plan of everything you are studying, and learn it off by heart. 24. Learn some poems each day in a language you are weak at. 25. Repeat in the evening everything you have learned during the day. Every week, every month and every year examine yourself in everything you have been studying, and if you find you have forgotten anything, begin again from the beginning.

RULES FOR DEVELOPING ACTIVITY

Activity is of three kinds: physical, emotional and intellectual activity. Accordingly, rules for developing activity can also be divided into rules for developing physical, emotional and intellectual activity.

Rules for developing physical activity

Rule 26. Think up as many occupations as possible for yourself. 27. Don't have any servants. 28. Don't ask for helpers for a job which you can finish on your own.

Rules for developing emotional activity

Since we have already said that all feelings which derive from self-love are bad, it follows that we ought only to give rules here whereby the activity of feelings which derive from love in general might be developed. 29. Feelings which concern love in general. Let your love for the whole human race be expressed in some form every day. 30. Feelings which concern love of one's country. Be as useful to your country as you can. 31. Feelings which concern love of individual people. Try to find as many people as possible whom you can love more than all your neighbours.

Rules for developing intellectual activity

Rule 32. Don't build *châteaux en Espagne* [castles in Spain]. 33. Try to give your intellect as much food as possible.

RULES FOR DEVELOPING THE INTELLECTUAL FACULTIES

We have five main intellectual faculties: the faculty of imagination, the faculty of memory, the faculty of comparison, the faculty of drawing conclusions from these comparisons and, finally, the faculty of putting these conclusions in order.

Rules for developing the faculty of imagination

Rule 34. All games which require reflection are very good for developing this faculty.

I have already spoken about rules for developing the faculty of memory.

Rules for developing the faculty of drawing conclusions

Rule 35. Study carefully the objects you are comparing. 36. Compare any new idea you come across with the ideas you already know. Justify all abstract ideas by examples.

Rules for developing the faculty of drawing conclusions

Rule 36. Study mathematics. 37. Study philosophy. 38. Make critical notes when reading any philosophical work.

Rules for developing the faculty of putting conclusions in order

Rule 39. Study your own being and its structure. 40. Reduce to one general conclusion all your information about any one branch of knowledge. 41. Compare all conclusions with each other, so that no one conclusion should contradict any other. 42. Write compositions which are not trivial, but scholarly. [. . .]

1850

14 June, 1850 Yasnaya Polyana   Once again I have taken up my diary, and once again with new fervour and a new purpose. How many times is that? I can't remember. Never mind, perhaps I'll drop it again; but it's a pleasant occupation and it will be pleasant to re-read it, just as it was pleasant to re-read my old ones. There are lots of thoughts in one's head, and some of them seem very remarkable, but when you examine them they turn out to be nonsense; others on the other hand seem sensible – and that's what a diary is needed for. On the basis of one's diary it's very convenient to judge oneself.

Then again, since I find it necessary to determine all my occupations in advance, a diary is necessary for that too. I'd like to get used to determining my way of life in advance, not just for a day but for a year, for several years, or even for life; it's too difficult, almost impossible. But I'll try; first for a day, then for two days – for as many days as I remain true to my resolutions, for that many days I shall plan ahead. By these resolutions I mean not moral rules independent of time and place, rules which never change and which I draw up specially, but resolutions which are temporal and local: where to live and for how long, what to study and when.

Occasions may arise when these resolutions may be alterable; but I will only permit such deviations when they have been determined by *the rules*; and so in case of any deviations, *I will explain their causes* in my diary. [. . .]

The last three years which I have spent so dissolutely sometimes seem to me very interesting, poetical and, in part, useful; I'll try to recall and record them as frankly and in as much detail as possible. This will be a third purpose for my diary.

17 June   Got up before 8, did nothing till 10, read and wrote my diary from 10 to 12; from 12 to 6 – lunch, a rest, a few thoughts about music, dinner; 6 to 8 – music; 8 to 10 – the estate.

This is the second day I've been idle, and haven't carried out what I intended. Why? I don't understand it. However, I don't despair; I'll force myself. Yesterday, apart from not carrying out what I had intended, I also broke my own rule. But now I won't break my rule again of *not having a woman* in the country, except on certain occasions which I won't look for, but won't let pass either.

When I'm in an apathetic mood, I've noticed that any philosophical work greatly stimulates me to activity – I'm reading Montesquieu now. It seems to me that I've become idle because I've started too many things, and so in future I won't move on to another occupation till I've carried out what I intended to do. So as not to be able to make the excuse that I haven't managed to draw up a system, I'll enter in my diary some general rules, and also some rules with regard to music and the estate.

Some general rules. Don't put off what you propose to do on the pretext of some distraction or diversion, but start the job at once, if only superficially. Ideas will come. For example, if you propose to write out rules, take out an exercise book, sit down at a table and don't get up until you've started and finished. Rules with regard to music. *Play every day: (1) all twenty-four scales, (2) all chords and arpeggios in two octaves, (3) all the inversions, (4) the chromatic scale. Learn one piece and don't go on as long as there is a passage where you have to stop. Transpose all cadenzas into all keys and learn them. Play at least four pages of music each day, and don't go on until you have found the proper doigté* [fingering].

With regard to the estate. *Think about every order from the point of view of its usefulness or harmfulness. Personally supervise every part of the estate each day. Don't be in a hurry to give orders, to scold or to punish,* but remember that on the estate patience is needed more than anything else. *Only cancel an order you have given, even one that has proved harmful, on the basis of your own judgement and in case of absolute necessity.*

Notes The winter before last I lived in Moscow, and lived in a very disorderly manner, without a job, without any occupations and without a purpose; and I lived like this, not because, as is often said and writtten, everyone in Moscow lives like this, but simply because I liked this sort of life. But it is partly the case too that the situation of a young man in Moscow society disposes him to idleness. I mean a young man who combines certain qualifications, namely education, a good name and an income of some ten or twenty thousand. The life of a young man who combines these qualifications is very pleasant and completely carefree if he is not employed, i.e. not seriously, but only on paper, and if he likes being idle. All drawing rooms are open to him and he is entitled to aspire to any marriageable girl; no young man could stand higher in the general opinion of society. But let this same gentleman go to Petersburg, and he will fret about why S. and G. Gorchakov were at court, and he wasn't; or how to get into Baroness Z's soirées or Countess A's reception, etc.; and he won't get in unless he can rely on the help of some countess to gain entry to their *salons.* Or unless he has grown up there, or unless he can endure humiliations, exploit every opportunity, and worm his way in with difficulty, but without honour.

19 June Yesterday went quite well, I carried out almost everything; was only dissatisfied with one thing: I can't overcome my sensuality, the more so since this passion has now become a habit with me. [. . .]

8 December, Moscow[1] I wrote in my diary for five days and haven't touched it for five months. I'll try to remember what I did during that time and why I evidently got so behind with my occupations. During that time a great revolution took place in me: a quiet life in the country, my old follies and the need to busy myself with my affairs have borne fruit. I have stopped building castles in Spain and making plans which are beyond any human strength to carry out. But the chief factor, and the one most favourable to this change of beliefs, is that I no longer rely on my reason alone to achieve anything, and no longer despise the forms generally accepted by all people. Previously everything ordinary seemed unworthy of me; but now, on the contrary, I hardly accept any belief as good and just until I have seen it applied and carried out in practice, and applied by many people. It's strange how I could have despised what constitutes man's chief asset – the faculty of understanding other people's beliefs and seeing them put into practice by other people. How could I have given my reason a free rein, without testing it and without applying it at all? In a word – and a very simple one – I've sown my wild oats and I'm a little older.

My self-love contributed a lot to this change. Having plunged into a dissipated life, I noticed that people who were inferior to me in all else were far superior to me in this sphere; I was hurt, and I convinced myself that this was not my destiny. Perhaps two shocks also contributed to this. The first was my losing money to Ogaryov,[2] which threw my affairs into such complete disarray that it even seemed that there was no hope of putting them in order again; and then there was a fire which forced me against my will to act. Winning money back put a brighter complexion on these acts. One thing I do think, and that is that I've become too cold. Only rarely, especially when I'm going to bed, do I have moments when feeling craves expression. Also in moments of drunkenness. But I've promised myself *not to get drunk*. I won't continue my notes now because I'm busy with affairs in Moscow, but if I have any free time I'll write a story about gipsy life.[3]

I've noticed another important change in me: I've become more self-assured, i.e. I've stopped feeling shy; I suppose that's because I have only one purpose in view (my interest), and in striving towards it I have been able to evaluate myself and have acquired an awareness of my own worth, which does so much to facilitate relations with people. [. . .]

Rules for society. Choose difficult situations, always try to control a conversation, speak loudly, calmly and distinctly, try to begin and end a conversation yourself. Seek the company of people higher in the world than yourself. Before seeing people of this sort, prepare yourself for the sort of relations you are going to have with them. Don't be embarrassed about speaking in front of strangers. Don't continually change the conversation from French to Russian or from Russian to French. Remember that when you find yourself in company where you feel embarrassed you must put pressure on yourself, especially at first. At a ball, ask the most important ladies to dance. If you feel shy, don't become flustered, but carry on. Be as cold as possible and don't betray any impressions. [. . .]

13 December   Although I made no entry in my diary for 12 December, I spent the day well – i.e. not in idleness. I visited the authorities and the clubs, and as a result became convinced, first, that I'll be a success in society the way I'm going at the moment, and that as for gambling I think I'll give it up altogether. I think I no longer have a passion for gambling, but I won't answer for it: I need to put it to the test. I won't look for an opportunity, but I won't let a suitable one pass. [. . .]

15 December   I'm very dissatisfied with yesterday. First because I did nothing about the Trustee Council;⁴ secondly, because I wrote nothing; and thirdly – I began to weaken in my beliefs and to yield to other people's influence. [. . .]

   Rules for society. Don't call a person by different names, but always address him in the same manner.

   Don't tolerate the slightest unpleasantness or sarcasm from anyone, without paying it back twofold.

17 December   Get up early, work on the story and a letter to Dyakov,⁵ go to mass at 10 o'clock at the Zachatyevsky convent, call on Anna Petrovna and Yakovleva.⁶ Then on to Koloshin's,⁷ send for some music, draft a letter to the office, dine at home, work at music and my rules, and go to the wenches and the club in the evening. [. . .]

21 December [. . .] *Must not read novels.*

24 December [. . .] *Rules.*   Only play cards in emergencies. Talk as little as possible about myself. Speak loudly and distinctly. *Rules.* Take exercise every day. In accordance with the laws of religion, don't have any women.

26 December   Spent the day badly; went to the gipsies.

29 December   I'm living a completely brutish life; although not completely dissolute, I've abandoned nearly all my occupations and am in very low spirits. Must get up early, receive nobody before 2 o'clock and not go out; at 2 o'clock go to Chulkov's and the Dyakovs', have dinner and then to the Prince[8] to ask for a post. Must think at leisure about my future actions in any new post. In the morning write my story, read, play the piano or write about music; in the evening – rules or the gipsies.

1851

1 January, Yasnaya Polyana   Visited Pokrovskoye[1] on 1 January, and saw Nikolenka;[2] he hasn't changed, but I've changed a great deal, and I might have had some influence on him if he wasn't so strange; either he doesn't notice anything and doesn't love me, or he's trying to pretend that he doesn't.

17 January, Moscow   Since the 14th I've behaved unsatisfactorily. Didn't go to the Stolypins' ball; lent some money and so am left without a bean; and all because of my weakness of character. *Rule. Don't play eralash[3] for less than twenty-five copecks a time.* I've no money at all; the time for paying many promissory notes has already passed; I'm also beginning to notice that my stay in Moscow is of no advantage to me in any respect, and that I'm living far above my income. [. . .]

Of the three methods which have occurred to me for putting my affairs in order, I've neglected nearly all, namely: *(1) joining a gambling circle and playing while I have the money. (2) entering high society and marrying under certain conditions. (3) finding a profitable place to serve.* Now a fourth method occurs to me – namely borrowing money from Kireyevsky. No one of these four things contradicts any other, and I must *act*. I must write to the country and get them to send 150 silver roubles, go to Ozerov's and offer to sell him a horse and give instructions to have it advertised in the papers too. Must call on the countess[4] and bide my time, find out about invitations to the Zakrevskys' ball and order a new frockcoat. *Must think and write a lot before the ball.* Must visit Prince Sergey Dmitriyevich[5] and talk about a post, and also Prince Andrey Ivanovich[6] and ask for a post. *Must pawn my watch.* [. . .]

18 January   [. . .] Write the story of my day.[7]

25 January   I've fallen in love or imagine that I have; went to a party and lost my head. Bought a horse which I don't need at all. [. . .]

28 February   I've lost a lot of time. At first I was attracted by worldly pleasures, but then I felt empty at heart again; and I've given up my occupations – i.e. occupations which had my own person as their object. For a long time I was tormented by the fact that I had no heartfelt thought or feeling to determine the whole direction of my life – I took everything *just as it came*, but now, I think, I have found a heartfelt idea and a permanent aim – the development of the will – an aim towards which I've been striving but which I only now recognized, not simply as an idea, but as one which is close to my heart.

Programme for tomorrow. Get up at 9 o'clock. Work on the encyclopaedia[8] and write a synopsis. Go to a funeral, then gymnastics, have dinner, and from 6 to 12 work alone or with Koloshin. *Don't smoke. Remember that carrying out what I've proposed to do constitutes the whole happiness of my life, and vice versa.*

1 March   Rule. *In difficult circumstances always act on first impressions.* [. . .]

2 March   I've begun to weaken a bit, mainly because it was beginning to seem that however hard I work on myself, nothing will ever come of me. And this thought occurred to me because I was exclusively occupied with exerting my will, and not bothering about the form in which it manifested itself. I'll try to correct this mistake. Now I want to prepare for my master's examination; consequently this is the form in which my will must manifest itself; but it's not enough to take up a notebook and read; it's necessary to prepare oneself for it, necessary to study systematically; it's necessary to get hold of questions on all subjects and compile synopses on them. It's necessary to try and find a student who can give instruction and explanations.

First of all tomorrow morning, from 8 to 12, read the 'Encyclopaedia',[9] with Nevolin's comments; at 12 go and find a student; at 2 – gymnastics; from 6 till night time work at the 'Encyclopaedia' or something else, with an hour for music. *Rule. Remember that in any affair the first and only condition on which success depends is patience, and that the thing which causes most hindrance, and which has done great harm to me especially, is haste.*

7 March   I've found a useful purpose for my diary apart from defining future activities – to give an account of each day from the point of view of those weaknesses which I'd like to correct.

Today. Took a long time to get up this morning, shrank from it, and somehow tried to deceive myself. Read novels when there were other things to do. Said to myself: 'You must have a drink of coffee', as though it was impossible to do anything without first drinking coffee. With Koloshin I'm not calling a spade a spade; although we both feel that preparing for the exam is a waste of time, I didn't tell him so openly. Received Poiret[10] over-familiarly and allowed myself to be influenced by our not being well acquainted, the presence of Koloshin and a misplaced *grand-seigneur*-ism. Did my gymnastics hurriedly. Didn't knock long enough at the

Gorchakovs' out of *fausse honte* [self-consciousness]. Made a bad exit from the Koloshins' drawing-room; was in too much of a hurry, tried to say something very polite – it didn't come off. At the riding-school I succumbed to *mauvaise humeur* [bad temper] and forgot what I was doing because of a young lady. Tried to show off at Begichev's and, to my shame, tried to imitate Gorchakov. *Fausse honte*. Didn't remind Ukhtomsky about the money. At home I rushed from the piano to a book, and from a book to a pipe and a meal. Didn't give the peasants a thought. Can't remember whether I lied. Probably I did. Didn't go to the Perfilyevs' and the Panins' due to thoughtlessness. All today's mistakes can be put down to the following propensities: (1) *Indecision*, lack of energy, (2) *Self-delusion*, i.e. anticipating the bad in something, and not thinking about it carefully. (3) *Haste*. (4) *Fausse honte*, i.e. a fear of doing something unbecoming, resulting from a one-sided view of things. (5) *Bad frame of mind*, resulting for the most part (i) from haste, (ii) from a superficial view of things. (6) *Muddleheadedness*, i.e. a tendency to forget near and useful aims in order to give oneself airs. (7) *Imitativeness.* (8) *Inconstancy.* (9) *Thoughtlesness* [. . .]

8 March   Took a long time to wake up again, but got the better of myself eventually. Wrote a letter to Nikolenka (*thoughtlessly and hurriedly*), and one to the office, in the same stupid form which I've now adopted (*self-delusion*). Did my gymnastics carelessly, i.e. took too little account of my strength; this weakness I'll call *arrogance*, a retreat from reality. Frequently looked at myself in the mirror. It's stupid, physical self-love, which can only lead to something bad and ridiculous. Was shy again with Poiret (self-delusion). Acted feebly at the stud, bowed first to Golitsyn instead of walking straight on, the way I was going. *Day-dreaming*. Praised myself at gymnastics (self-praise). Wanted to give Kobylin my real opinion about myself (petty vanity). Ate too much at dinner (gluttony). Went to Volkonsky's without finishing what I was doing (lack of persistence). Ate too many sweet things, sat up too late. Told lies. *Occupations for the 9th.* [. . .] Keep a journal of my weaknesses (a Franklin journal).[11] [. . .]

20 March   [. . .] The two chief passions which I've noticed in myself are a passion for gambling and vanity, which is the more dangerous because it assumes a countless multitude of different forms: a desire to show off, thoughlessness, day-dreaming, etc. This evening I must re-read my diary from the day I arrived in Moscow, make some general notes and check my financial expenses and debts in Moscow.

I came to Moscow with three aims. (1) To gamble. (2) To marry. (3) To obtain a post. The first is base and mean and, thank God, after reviewing the state of my affairs and renouncing my prejudices, I've decided to remedy my affairs and put them in order by the sale of part of my property.

The second, thanks to the wise advice of my brother Nikolenka, I've put aside until I'm forced to it either by love or reason or even fate, which cannot be entirely resisted. The last is impossible until after two years' service in the Province, and to tell the truth, although I'd like it, I'd like many other things which are incompatible with it; and so I'll wait for fate itself to place me in that situation.

During this time I've had many weaknesses. The main thing is, I've paid little attention to moral rules, being distracted by rules which are necessary for success. Then I've been taking too narrow a view of things: for example, I've been setting myself a lot of rules which could all be reduced to one thing – not to be vain. I've been forgetting that a necessary condition for success is self-assurance, and a contempt for trivialities which can only come about as a result of moral superiority.

22 March   Worked quite well except for lack of firmness and a desire to show off. Dined at home. Did nothing about the money and didn't think about it.[12] *Self-delusion*. Wrote extracts,[13] notes and my diary, all too hurriedly. I could write a good book: a life of Tatyana Alexandrovna.[14] [...] Gymnastics is necessary for the development of all faculties. Gymnastics of the memory. *Learn something by heart every day. English.*

23 March   [...] *Rule.* Try to form a style: (1) in conversation, (2) in writing. [...]

24 March   [...] *Occupations for the 25th.* From 10 to 11 – yesterday's diary and reading. From 11 to 12 – gymnastics. From 12 to 1 – English. *Beklemishev and Beer* from 1 to 2. From 2 to 4 – riding. From 4 to 6 – dinner. From 6 to 8 – reading. From 8 to 10 – writing. Translate something from a foreign language into Russian to develop memory and style. Write an account of today with all the impressions and thoughts it gives rise to.[15]

27 March   [...] Marya called for her passport. I feel I refrained from ... only out of shame and the fact that she had pimples on her face. So I must note down *sensuality*.

6 April, Pirogovo[16]   Got nothing done. *Lied and bragged a lot, was casual and absent-minded in my preparation for communion.* [...] Want to write some sermons.

8 April   Wrote a sermon, *was lazy, weak and cowardly.*

15 April   Got up late, at 8 o'clock – *laziness and irresolution.* Did my gymnastics well. Played the piano *too hurriedly* – read *likewise.* Dined and argued with Auntie. *Too little fierté* [pride]. Roamed about the whole evening after dinner and had *sensual desires.*

17 April   Wrote nothing – laziness got the better of me!! Today I want to begin a story of a day's hunting. Had a long talk with Auntie. She's very kind and very high-minded, but very one-sided. She feels and thinks in one groove only, and beyond that groove there's nothing. I'm tormented by sensuality. Not so much sensuality as force of habit. I'm sure that anywhere else I wouldn't even have looked at the woman who is now making me struggle violently with passion and succumb to it more and more often, just because I've already had her here. There's no better way of finding out whether you are making progress in anything than by testing yourself on your former way of doing things. To find out whether you have grown or not you need to measure yourself against an old mark. After four months' absence I'm back in the same frame. As far as laziness is concerned I'm almost the same. Sensuality too. In the ability to deal with subordinates, I'm a bit better. But where I have made progress is in my frame of mind.

18 April   I couldn't refrain; I beckoned to something pink which, in the distance, seemed to me very nice, and opened the door at the back. She came in. I couldn't see her, it was vile and repulsive, I even hate her because I've broken my rules on her account. Generally speaking you nurse a feeling very like hatred for people to whom you can't indicate that you don't like them, but who are entitled to assume that you are well disposed towards them. A sense of duty and of revulsion spoke against it; lust and conscience[17] spoke in favour. The latter won.

Terrible remorse; I've never felt it so strongly before. That's a step forward.

19 April   Nikolenka, Valeryan and Masha arrived.[18] Tomorrow I'll go to Tula, decide about the service,[19] and give up Vorotynka[20] for 16,000 roubles. I've become even more religious in the country.

20 May, En route from Saratov to Astrakhan.[21]   [. . .] The recent time I spent in Moscow was interesting because of the direction I was taking, my contempt for society and my incessant inner struggle. [. . .]

30 May, Starogladkovskaya[22]   I'm writing at 10 o'clock at night on 30 June[23] in the village of Starogladkovskaya. How did I get here? I don't know. Why? I don't know either. [. . .]

March–May, 1851[24]

[. . .] Lamartine says that writers neglect literature for the people, that the number of readers is greater among the masses of the people, that all those who write do so for the circle in which they live, but that the people in whose midst there are men and women craving for enlightenment do not have any literature and will not have until writers begin to write for the people.

I won't speak about books which are written with the purpose of finding many readers – they are not literary works, but products of their authors' craft – nor about academic books or textbooks which don't come within the province of poetry. (Where the boundaries are between prose and poetry I shall never be able to understand; although there is a question about this subject in *literature*, I can't understand the answer. Poetry is verse. Prose is not verse. Or poetry is everything except business documents and textbooks.) In order to be good, all works of literature ought to be sung from the soul of their author, as Gogol says about his farewell tale ('it was sung from my soul').[25] But how could anything accessible to the people be sung from the souls of authors who for the most part stand on the highest pinnacle of development? The people wouldn't understand them. Even if an author were to try to descend to the popular level, the people still wouldn't understand him. Just as a sixteen-year-old boy, when he reads a scene in a novel about the seduction of the heroine, isn't roused to a feeling of indignation by it and doesn't put himself in the unfortunate woman's position, but involuntarily transfers himself to the role of the seducer and delights in a feeling of sensuality – so too would the people understand something completely different from what you wanted to say to them. Could the people understand *The Hapless Anton*[26] or *Geneviève?* The words would be accessible as expressions of thought, but the thoughts themselves would be inaccessible. The people have their own literature – beautiful and inimitable; but it is not counterfeit, it is sung from the heart of the people themselves. They have no need of higher literature, and they have none. But try and put yourself on exactly the same level as the people, and they will only despise you. [. . .]

How your view of life changes when you live not for yourself, but for others! Life ceases to be an end and becomes a means. Unhappiness makes man virtuous – virtue makes him happy – happiness makes him vicious. [. . .]

One should not say that life is an ordeal, or that death is a blessing which removes us from all sorrows. This is neither a comfort when one loses one's nearest and dearest, nor a moral precept. To sympathize with such a view is impossible except in a state of despair, and despair is a weakness of faith and of trust in God. As a moral precept this idea is too painful for a young soul, and is bound to shake its faith in virtue. If a man loses a creature he has loved he can love another; if he does not, it is because he is too proud. The source of evil is in each man's soul. [. . .]

Elderly aunts and uncles consider themselves bound to pay for the right to have nephews by issuing exhortations, however useless they may be. They are even displeased when their nephews' behaviour is such that their advice is not appropriate; they think they have been robbed of their due.

There is nothing more painful than to see sacrifices made for you by people with whom you are connected and have to live with, especially sacrifices which you don't ask for, and from people you don't love. The most offensive form of egoism is self-sacrifice. [. . .]

Everyone describes human weaknesses and the ridiculous sides of people by transferring them to fictitious personalities, sometimes successfully, according to the writer's talent, but for the most part unnaturally. Why? Because we know human weaknesses from ourselves, and in order to display them truthfully we need to display them in ourselves, because a given weakness only goes with a given personality. Few people have the power to do this. They try to distort the personality to which they transfer their own weaknesses as much as possible, so that they themselves should not be recognized. Would it not be better to say straight out: 'This is the sort of man I am. If you don't like me I'm very sorry, but God made me this way.' But nobody wants to take the first step in case people might say, for example: 'You think that if you are evil and ridiculous, we must be so too.' And so everyone remains silent. It's like going to a ball in the provinces: everyone is afraid of arriving first and so they all arrive late. If only everyone would show himself as he really is, then what was weak and ridiculous about him before would cease to be so. Surely it would be an enormous blessing to be rid, if only in part, of that terrible yoke – fear of the ridiculous. How many, many true pleasures do we lose because of that foolish terror? [. . .]

2 June My God, my God, what sad and depressing days! And why am I so sad? No, not so much sad as hurt by the awareness of being sad, without knowing what I'm sad about. I used to think it was because of inactivity, of idleness. No, it's not because of idleness, but of the situation I'm in that I can't do anything. The main thing is that I can't find anything like the sadness I feel anywhere at all – neither in descriptions, nor even in my own imagination. I can imagine that it's possible to be sad about a loss, a parting, a disappointed hope. I can understand that it's possible to be disillusioned: that everything begins to pall and that one is disappointed so often in one's expectations and that there's nothing left to look forward to. I can understand, when one's soul harbours love for all that is beautiful, for men and women, for nature, and one is ready to express it all and ask for sympathy but finds nothing but coldness and ridicule and secret malice against people – that sadness can result. I can understand the sadness of a man whose lot is hard and who is oppressed by a painful, venomous feeling of envy. All this I can understand, and from one aspect there is some good in all such sadness.

But the sadness which I feel is something I cannot understand or imagine to myself. I have nothing to regret, almost nothing to wish for, no reason to be angry with fate. I can understand how wonderfully I could live on my imagination. But no. My imagination paints nothing for me – I have no dreams. There is a certain gloomy delight in despising people – but I am not even capable of that; I don't give them a thought at all; sometimes I think that such and such a man has a kind, simple soul; then I think: no, better not seek to know, why make mistakes! I'm not disillusioned either – everything amuses me, but the trouble is that I turned to the serious things in life too early, turned to them when I was not yet ripe for them, but could feel and understand; and so I have no strong faith in friendship, love or beauty, and have become disillusioned about the important things in life; and yet in trivial matters I am still a child.

Now I think, as I recall all the unpleasant moments of my life which are the only ones which come into my head when despondent, that there are too few pleasures and too many desires, and that man is too apt to picture happiness to himself, and that fate too often buffets him painfully for no reason and touches him too painfully on the raw for him to love life; and then there is something especially sweet and grand about indifference to life, and I rejoice in this feeling. How strong I seem to be in the face of all this, in the firm conviction that there is nothing to look forward to here except death; and yet I can now think with pleasure of the fact that I have ordered a saddle on which to ride in my Circassian coat, and that I shall run after Cossack women and be reduced to despair because my left moustache is worse than my right, and spend two hours in front of the mirror putting it straight. But I can't write either, judging by this – it's stupid. [. . .]

8 June, Stary Yurt[27]   Love and religion – these are two feelings which are pure and elevated. I don't know what men call love. If love is what I have read and heard about it, then I've never experienced it. I used to see a boarding-school girl called Zinaida,[28] and I liked her; but I hardly knew her (ugh! what crude things words are! how stupid and vulgar do feelings appear when once expressed). I stayed in Kazan for a week. If I had been asked why I stayed in Kazan, what I enjoyed there or why I was so happy, I wouldn't have said it was because I was in love. I wasn't aware of it. I think that it's precisely this unawareness which is love's chief feature and which constitutes its whole charm. How morally unencumbered I was at the time. I didn't feel all that burden of trivial passions which spoils all the pleasures of life. I never said a word to her about love, but I am so sure that she knew my feelings that if she did love me, I attribute it only to the fact that she understood me. All impulses of the soul are pure and elevated to begin with. Reality destroys their innocence and charm. My relations with Zinaida have remained at the stage of the pure yearning of two souls for one another. But perhaps you doubt that I love you, Zinaida? If so, forgive me; I am to blame; I could have assured you with a single word.

Shall I really never see her again? Shall I really find out one day that she has married some Beketov or other? Or, sadder still, shall I see her looking cheerful in her little cap, with those same clever, open, cheerful and loving eyes? I won't abandon my plans in order to go and marry her; I'm not quite convinced that she can constitute my happiness; but still I'm in love. If not, why these joyous memories which cheer me up, why this way of looking that I always have whenever I see and feel something beautiful? Should I write her a letter? I don't know her patronymic, and perhaps because of that I shall be deprived of happiness. It's ridiculous. We forgot to bring a pleated shirt with us, and because of that I'm not doing military service. If we had forgotten to bring a peaked cap, I wouldn't have thought of presenting myself to Vorontsov[29] and getting a post in Tiflis. It would have been impossible in a fur cap! Now God knows what is in store for me. I surrender myself to His will. I don't know what is necessary for my happiness or what happiness is. Do you remember the Archbishop's Garden, Zinaida – the side path? It was on the tip of my tongue to declare my love, and on yours too. It was up to me to begin; but do you know why, I think, I said nothing? I was so happy that I had nothing to wish for, and I was afraid to spoil my happiness . . . not mine, but ours. That sweet time will always remain the best memory of my life. But what an empty and vain creature is man! When I am asked about the time I spent in Kazan I reply in an offhand tone: 'Yes, for a provincial town the society was very decent, and I spent a few quite happy days there.' You rogue! People make fun of everything. They laugh at the idea that with one's loved one even a hut would be paradise, and they say it's not true. Of course it's true. And not only a hut, but Krapivna, Stary Yurt, anywhere at all. With one's loved one even a hut would be paradise, and that's true, true, a hundred times true.

11 June, The Caucasus. Stary Yurt, the camp. Night time I've already been here for about five days and I'm already in the grip of long-forgotten laziness. I've given up my diary completely. Nature, on which I pinned my hopes most of all when planning to come to the Caucasus, has not so far produced anything to attract me. And the high spirits which I thought would break out in me here aren't in evidence either.

The night is clear, and a fresh breeze is blowing through the tent and causing the light from the tapering candle to flicker. I can hear the distant barking of dogs in the village and the challenging of sentries. There is a smell of damp oak and plane wattling of which the hut is made. I am sitting on a drum in the hut which adjoins a tent on either side, the one covered in, where Knoring [30] (an unpleasant officer) is sleeping, the other open and completely dark except for a patch of light falling on the end of my brother's bed. In front of me is the brightly lit side of the hut on which a pistol, sabres, a dagter and some underpants are hanging. All is still. I can hear the wind soughing, an insect flying past and circling round the fire, and a soldier whimpering and sighing nearby.

I don't feel like going to sleep; as for writing – there's no ink. Till tomorrow. Then I'll write some letters on the basis of the impressions of the day. Occupations for the 12th: From 5 to 8 – bathe and sketch. From 10 to 12 – read. From 12 to 4 – rest. From 4 to 8 – translate from English.[31] From 8 until night time – write. Continue to do gymnastics. Do my accounts book and the Franklin journal.

12 June   Got up late – Nikolenka woke me up coming back from hunting. I keep searching for a frame of mind, a view of things, a way of life which I can neither discover nor define. I would like more order in my mental activity, more activity itself, and at the same time more freedom and less restraint. I hardly slept at all last night. After writing my diary I began to pray to God. It's impossible to express the sweetness of the feeling I experienced at prayer. I recited the prayers I usually do: Our Father, the Mother of God, the Trinity, the Doors of Mercy, an invocation to my guardian angel – and still I remained at prayer. If a prayer is defined as a petition or a thanksgiving, then I wasn't praying. I longed for something exalted and good, but what exactly it was I cannot express, although I was clearly aware of what I longed for. I wanted to merge with the one all-embracing being. I asked it to forgive me my sins; but no, I didn't ask for that, for I felt that if it had granted me this moment of bliss, it had already forgiven me. I asked, and at the same time felt I had nothing to ask for, and that I couldn't and didn't know how to ask. I gave thanks, yes, but not in words or thoughts. In my feeling alone I combined everything, both supplication and thanksgiving. The feeling of fear had completely disappeared. Not one of the feelings of faith, hope or charity could I single out from my general feeling. No – the feeling I experienced yesterday was the love of God. It is an exalted love which combines in itself all that is good, and rejects all that is bad.

How terrible it was for me to look at all the petty, vicious side of life. I was unable to conceive how it could have attracted me. With a pure heart I asked God to receive me into His bosom. I was not aware of the flesh; I was pure spirit. But no! The flesh, the petty side of life got on top again, and before an hour had passed I half-consciously heard the voice of vice, vanity and the empty side of life; I knew where this voice came from, I knew it would destroy my blissful state, I struggled against it and succumbed. I went to sleep dreaming of fame and women; but it's not my fault, I couldn't help it.

Everlasting bliss is impossible *here*. Suffering is necessary. Why? I don't know. Yet how dare I say I don't know? How did I dare think that the ways of Providence could be known? Providence is the source of reason, and reason tries to comprehend it . . . Mind gets lost in these depths of great wisdom, while feeling is afraid to offend it. I thank it for the moment of bliss which revealed to me my insignificance and my greatness. I want to pray, but I don't know how; I want to comprehend, but I dare not – I surrender myself to Thy will! Why have I written all this? How commonplace, feeble and even meaningless is this expression of my feelings; and yet they were so exalted!!

I spent this morning quite well; I was a little lazy and told a lie, but an innocent one. Tomorrow I'll write a letter to Zagoskina, at least in rough. I sketched half-heartedly. In the evening I admired the clouds. The clouds were wonderful as the sun was setting. The west was red, but the sun was still a few feet above the horizon. Massive crimson-grey clouds hovered over it. They seemed to be merging together uneasily. I spoke to someone and looked round again; along the horizon stretched a dark greyish-red streak, tailing off into an infinite variety of shapes, some converging on one another, others drifting apart with bright-red ends.

Man was created for solitude – solitude not in a literal, but in a moral sense. There are some feelings which ought not to be confided to anybody. Even if they are beautiful, exalted feelings, you sink in the estimation of the person you confide them to, or even allow the possibility of guessing at. When confiding them, a person is not fully aware of them, but is only expressing his aspirations. The unknown has the greatest power to attract. My brother and I are now living among the sort of people where it is impossible for us not to be aware of our joint superiority over the others; but we don't say much to each other, as though afraid that if we did say something we might enable people to guess at what we wanted to conceal from them all. We know each other too well.

Three things have struck me here. (1) The officers' talk about bravery.[32] When they start talking about whether a person is brave they say: 'Yes indeed. Everyone's brave.' Ideas of this sort about bravery can be explained like this. Bravery is a state of mind in which the mental powers act in the same way with everyone whatever the circumstances might be. Or it is an intensification of activity which makes one lose the awareness of danger. Or there are two sorts of bravery: moral and physical. Moral bravery is the kind which stems from an awareness of duty, or generally speaking of moral inclinations, and not from an awareness of danger. Physical bravery is the kind which stems from physical necessity without making one lose the awareness of danger, as well as the kind which does make one lose that awareness. Examples of the former are men who voluntarily sacrifice their lives for the safety of their country or of another man. (2) An officer who is serving for gain. (3) The Russian soldiers in the Turkish campaign who flung themselves into the arms of the enemy simply in order to get a drink. That's just an example of physical bravery on our side. [. . .]

13 June I continue to be lazy, although I'm satisfied with myself, except for my sensuality. Several times when the officers have been talking about cards in my presence I've wanted to show them that I like playing. But I've always refrained. I hope that even if they invite me I shall refuse.

3 July I wrote the above on 13 June, and I've wasted all the time since, because on the very same day I got carried away and lost 200 roubles of my own, 150 of Nikolenka's and 500 I borrowed – a total of 850. Now I'm restraining myself and thinking what I'm doing. Rode over to Chervlennaya, got drunk and slept with a woman; it's all very bad and troubles me a great deal. I still haven't spent more than two months well – in such a way that I could be satisfied with myself. Wanted a woman again yesterday. Luckily she refused. How loathesome! But I'm writing it down to punish myself.

Took part in a raid.[33] Acted badly again: acted without thinking and was afraid of Baryatinsky. However, I'm so weak, and so depraved, and so seldom do what is sensible, that I'm bound to succumb to the influence of every Baryatinsky . . . Tomorrow I'll write my novel,[34] do some translating and tell Knoring to wait and I'll try and get some money. On Wednesday I'll go to Groznoye.[35] [. . .]

I've just been lying down outside the camp. A marvellous night! The moon was just climbing up from behind a hillock and shedding light on two small, thin, low clouds; behind me a cricket was chirping its endless, melancholy song; in the distance I could hear a frog, and from near the village came the sound of Tartars shouting and a dog barking; then all was still, and again I could hear nothing but the chirping of a cricket, and see a light transparent cloud drifting past near and distant stars.

I thought: I'll go and describe what I can see. But how can I write it down? I'll have to go and sit at an ink-stained table, take out some drab coloured paper and ink, get my fingers dirty and draw letters on the paper. Letters will make words and words – sentences; but can one really convey feelings? Is it ever possible to transmit to another person one's own views when contemplating nature? Description is not enough. Why is poetry so closely allied with prose, happiness with unhappiness? How ought one to live? Should one try to combine poetry and prose together, or enjoy the one and take to living at the mercy of the other?

A dream has a side which is better than reality; reality has a side which is better than a dream. Complete happiness would be a combination of the two.

4 July I'm almost satisfied with myself, except for the fact that I've been somehow empty of late. I haven't any thoughts; or if I have, they seem to me so worthless that I don't want to write them down. I don't know why this is. Either I've made progress critically, or I've fallen back creatively. Tomorrow I'll go to the village and to Groznoye. I'll talk to my brother about money and decide about a trip to Dagestan. I can write absolutely nothing, although there are characters here worth describing.

How worthlessly the days go by! Take today. Not a single recollection, not a single strong impression. I got up late, with that unpleasant feeling which always affects me on waking up: that I've behaved badly, that I've overslept. When I oversleep, I feel what a cowardly dog feels in the presence of its master when it has done wrong. Then I thought how fresh a man's moral powers are on waking up, and wondered why I can't always keep mine in that condition. I'll always say that consciousness is the greatest moral evil that can befall a man. It's painful, very painful to know in advance that in an hour's time, although I shall be the same man with the same images in my mind, my outlook will have changed independently of myself, and at the same time I shall be conscious of it. I've been reading *Horace*.[36] My brother was right when he said that this person is like me. His main features are: nobleness of character, exalted ideas, love of fame – and complete lack of aptitude for any hard work. This lack of aptitude stems from lack of habit, and lack of habit from upbringing and vanity. [. . .]

As usual, three of us dined together: my brother and I and Knoring. I'll try and sketch Knoring's portrait. It seems to me that it's actually impossible to *describe* a man; but it's possible to describe the effect he has on me. To say of a man that he's original, kind, clever, stupid, consistent, etc. – these are words which give no idea about the man yet purport to depict him, whereas they often simply mislead one. I knew that my brother had lived with Knoring somewhere, had come to the Caucasus with him and was a good friend of his. I knew that he had kept an account of their joint expenses on the journey and was therefore a meticulous man; also that he owed money to my brother and was therefore a rather frivolous one. From the fact that he was friendly with my brother I concluded that he was not a society man, and from the fact that my brother said little about him I concluded that he was not noted for his intelligence. One morning my brother said to me: 'Knoring will be coming today; how glad I'll be to see him.' 'So now we'll see this dandy,' I thought. From behind the tent I heard my brother's joyful cries of greeting, and a voice which responded to them just as joyfully: 'Hello, you ugly old mug!' Not a respectable person, I thought, or one with much understanding of things. No relationship can impart charm to such a mode of address. My brother, as was his wont, introduced me to him; but being already unfavourably disposed towards him, I bowed coldly and went on reading where I lay.

Knoring is a tall man, well-built, but devoid of charm. I can recognize expression in a person's build as much as, if not more than, in his face: there are people who are attractively or unattractively built. His face is broad, with prominent cheekbones, with a certain softness about it – what is called in horses a 'fleshy head'. His eyes are hazel coloured and large, and have only two variations: laughter and a normal condition. When laughing, they remain fixed in an expression of obtuse inanity. The rest of his face is like a passport picture. He was subdued in my presence, I noticed. When the first moments of greeting were over and when the questions 'Well, how are you?' and the replies 'As you see, I'm fine' had been repeated several times, amid pauses, he turned to me and asked: 'Are you here for long, Count?' I again replied coldly. I have a way of immediately recognizing people who like to have an influence over others – probably because I like to myself. He is one of those people. He has an outward influence on my brother. For example, he makes him come to see him. I would like to know whether it's possible for a man consciously to try and acquire influence over other men. It seems as impossible to me as playing music *à livre ouvert* [at sight] used to seem. However, I've tried it; and why shouldn't people who are persistent succeed with practice? Such people have ulterior motives of this sort in everything they do. There is room for so many thoughts simultaneously, especially in an empty head.

10 August, Starogladkovskaya It was a wonderful night the day before yesterday, and I was sitting by the window of my hut in Starogladkovskaya and revelling in nature with all my senses except touch. The moon had not yet risen, but in the south-east the night clouds were already beginning to turn red and a light breeze was bearing with it a scent of freshness. Frogs and crickets merged together into one vague, monotonous night-time sound. The horizon was clear, and studded with stars. I love to gaze at night at the star-covered horizon; behind the big clear stars you can make out little ones merging into white patches. You look hard and admire them, and suddenly everything is hidden again – the stars seem to have come nearer. I like this optical illusion.

I don't know how other people day-dream, but from what I've heard and read, not at all the way I do. People say that as you look at beautiful nature, thoughts arise of the greatness of God and the insignificance of man;

lovers see the image of their beloved in the water. Other people say that *the hills seemed to say this, and the leaves to say that, and the trees to beckon them somewhere.* How can such thoughts arise? One must try to drive home the folly of it. The longer I live the more reconciled I become to various affectations in life, conversation, etc., but this affectation I can't get used to, despite all my efforts. When I indulge in what is called day-dreaming, I can never discover a single sensible thought in my head; on the contrary, all the thoughts which roam around in my imagination are always the most trivial ones – the sort which cannot arrest the attention. But when I do light on a thought which leads on to a series of others, the pleasant state of moral indolence which constitutes my day-dreaming disappears, and then I begin to think.

I don't know how recollections of nights of gipsy revelling have strayed into my roving imagination. Katya's songs, eyes, smiles, breasts and tender words are still fresh in my memory, so why write them down? I want to tell a story about something quite different, after all.[37] I notice that I have a bad habit of digressing, and that it's actually this habit, and not an abundance of thoughts as I used to think, that often prevents me from writing, and makes me get up from my desk and think about something quite different from what I had been writing about. It's a pernicious habit. In spite of my favourite writer Sterne's enormous talent for story-telling and clever prattle, even his digressions are wearisome. [. . .]

22 August   The 28th is my birthday, I shall be twenty-three; from that day I want to live in accordance with the purpose which I have set myself. I'll think it all out carefully tomorrow, but just now I'll take up my diary again, with a list of future occupations and a shortened Franklin table. I used to think that this was just pedantry, which did me harm; but that's not where the fault lies, for no table can constrain the bold movements of the mind. If such a table *can* affect me, it can only be in a useful way, by strengthening my character and accustoming me to activity; and so I'll continue my old system.

At sunrise, set about putting my papers, accounts, books and occupations in order; then put my thoughts in order and start copying out the first chapter of my novel. After dinner (don't eat much), the Tartar language, sketching, shooting, exercise and reading.

25 August   Yesterday I had a Cossack girl at my place. I hardly slept all night. [. . .]

26 August   [. . .] Did nothing all day. Sado[38] was in the way. Roamed around the village in the evening, eyeing the wenches. The drunken Yepishka[39] told me yesterday that the Salamanida business is going well.

I'd like to take her and clean her up. Meant to go hunting the next day, but hadn't made arrangements the night before.

In the morning – write my novel, do some trick riding, study Tartar and go wenching.

29 November, Tiflis[40]   I have never been in love with women. The only strong feeling like love which I did experience was when I was thirteen or fourteen, but I don't want to believe that it was love because its object was a fat chambermaid (with a very pretty face, it's true), and moreover the years from thirteen to fifteen are the most disorganized time for a boy (adolescence); you don't know what to throw yourself into, and sensuality has an unusually strong effect at that period.

I have very often been in love with men; my first love was the two Pushkins, then the second – Saburov, then the third Zybin and Dyakov, the fourth Obolensky, Blosfeld, Islavin, then Gautier and many others.[41] Of all these people I still love only Dyakov. For me the chief sign of love is the fear of offending or not pleasing the object of one's love; simply fear. I fell in love with men before I had any idea of the possibility of *pederasty*; but even when I knew about it, the idea of the possibility of coitus never occurred to me. A strange case of inexplicable sympathy was Gautier. Although I had absolutely no relations with him except for buying books, I used to be thrown into a fever when he entered the room. My love for Islavin spoilt the whole eight months of my life in Petersburg for me. Although not consciously, I never bothered about anything else except how to please him. All the people I loved felt this, and I noticed how hard it was for them to look at me. Often, if I couldn't find that moral understanding which reason required in the object of my love, or after some unpleasantness with him or her, I would feel hostility towards them; but this hostility was based on love. I never felt this sort of love for my brothers. I was very often jealous of women. I can understand ideal love – complete self-sacrifice to the object of one's love. And that is what I experienced. I always loved the sort of people who were cool towards me, and only took me for what I was worth. The older I get, the more rarely I experience this feeling. If I do experience it now, it's not so passionately, and it's towards people who love me – i.e. the opposite of before. Beauty always had a lot of influence on my choice; however, there is the case of Dyakov; but I shall never forget the night when we were travelling from Pirogovo, and, wrapped up underneath a travelling rug, I wanted to kiss him and cry. There was sensuality in that feeling, but why it took that course it's impossible to decide because, as I said, my imagination never painted any lubricious pictures; on the contrary, I have a terrible aversion to all that.

I observe in myself a tendency to squander, which expressed itself in my youth in the destruction of everything that came to hand, and expresses itself now in the destruction of Vanyushka's[42] peace and quiet and the squandering of money without any cause or pleasure. For example. I often ask Vanyushka for a pipe, not because I want to smoke, but because I like him to keep on the move, and I love to squander money. Today I caught my imagination at work; it was painting for itself a picture which showed that I had a lot of money, and that I was losing it gambling and squandering it, and this gave it great pleasure. I don't like what can be acquired in exchange for money, but I do like having it and then not having it – the process of squandering. I'll be careful in future; this tendency has already done me a lot of harm. [. . .]

22 December   I had a terrible dream about Mitenka.[43] On 21 December this year, at midnight, I had something like a revelation. The existence of the soul, its immortality (eternity), the duality of our existence and the essence of free will were revealed to me. Freedom is comparative: in relation to matter man is free, in relation to God he is not.

1852

2 January   When I sought happiness, I used to sink into vice; but when I understood that in this life it is enough simply not to be unhappy, I found fewer vicious temptations in my path – and I am now convinced that it's possible to be virtuous and also not unhappy.

When I sought pleasure, it evaded me, and I would sink into a depressing state of boredom – a state from which one can pass into any other state, good or bad; but more likely the latter. Now that I only try to avoid boredom, I find pleasure in everything. [. . .]

Two observations for the writer of belles-lettres. If a shadow is lying on the water it is very seldom possible to see it, and when you do see it, it doesn't strike you at all.

Every writer has in mind for his own work a special category of ideal reader. It is necessary to define clearly to oneself the demands of these ideal readers, and if there are indeed even two such readers in the whole world – to write *for them only.* When describing characters or landscapes which are unusual for the majority of readers, one should never lose sight of the characters and landscapes which are usual – one should take them as the basis, and describe the unusual ones by comparison with them.

5 February   (Nikolayevka[1] – I'm travelling with the detachment). I am indifferent to life, in which I've experienced too little happiness to love it; and so I'm not afraid of death. I'm not afraid of sufferings either, but I am afraid of being unable to endure sufferings and death well. I am not completely at ease, and I notice this because I keep passing from one state of mind and one view of many situations to another. It's strange that the view of war I had as a child – bravado – is the most comforting one for me. I am going back a lot to a child's view of things.

28 February   With the detachment (near Teplikichu).[2] I have never in real life justified the expectations made for me by my imagination.

I wanted fate to place me in difficult situations for which strength of mind and virtue were needed. My imagination loved to present these situations to me, and an inner feeling told me I should have enough strength and virtue for them. My self-love and confidence in my strength of mind have grown through not meeting rebuttals. Occasions when I might have justified my confidence but didn't I excused on the grounds that the difficulties facing me were too few and that I hadn't employed all my strength of mind.

I was proud, but my pride rested not on actual deeds, but on the firm hope that I would be capable of anything. Because of this my outward pride lacked assurance, firmness and constancy, and I would pass from extreme arrogance to excessive modesty.

My condition in time of danger opened my eyes. I liked to imagine myself completely cool and calm in danger. But I wasn't so in the actions of the 17th and 18th.[3] I haven't the excuse which I normally used that the danger wasn't as great as I had imagined. It was a unique opportunity for displaying all my strength of mind. Yet I was weak and therefore dissatisfied with myself.

I have only now come to understand that confidence in one's future actions is deceptive, and that one can only rely on oneself in the case of something one has already experienced [. . .]

20 *March, Starogladkovskaya* I have just re-read my old diary from July 1851 and something else written in that book. The pleasure I got from reading it makes me continue the diary in order to pave the way for the same sort of pleasure for myself in future. Some thoughts written in that book struck me by their originality, others by their correctness. It seems to me that I have now lost the ability to write and think so readily and boldly. Such boldness, it's true, was often combined with paradoxicality; but on the other hand there was more assurance about it.*

I must confess that one of the main aspirations of my life – to be certain about a thing – is steadfast and unwavering. Can it be that doubts also grow as one grows older? I discovered many pleasant memories in my diary – pleasant simply because they are memories. The whole time that I was keeping the diary I was a very bad person, the direction I was taking was quite false; because of that there isn't a single moment from all that period which I would like to have back exactly as it was; and all the changes which I would like to make I would like to make in myself.

My best memories concern dear Volkonskaya.[4]

Throughout my diary one main idea and desire can be seen – to be rid of the vanity which was oppressing me and ruining all my pleasures, and to search for ways to rid myself of it.

It is nearly seven months since I stopped writing my diary.[5] September I

---

* *Footnote by Tolstoy.* I have now become too lazy to think and be convinced of anything. However, I neither believe nor doubt any less than before. There is equilibrium in everything. I have become too lazy to convince myself of anything, but I am also too tired to undermine my faith, and I carefully preserve those beliefs which my restless mind has left in peace, and I'm afraid to become disenchanted with them or even to think about them.

spent at Starogladkovskaya, and in visits to Groznoye and Stary Yurt; I went hunting, ran after Cossack women, drank, wrote a little and did some translating. In October I went to Tiflis with my brother to look for a post in the service. I spent a month in Tiflis, uncertain what to do, and with foolish and vain plans in my head. From November onwards I was having treatment, and spent two whole months, until the New Year, at home: although it was dull, I spent the time quietly and usefully – I wrote the whole of the first part.[6]

January I spent partly travelling and partly at Starogladkovskaya, did some writing, polished up the first part, made preparations for the expedition and felt well and at ease. February I spent on the expedition – and was satisfied with myself. At the beginning of March I prepared for communion; now I'm bored and idle. When I set off for the expedition I prepared myself for death to such an extent that I not only gave up but quite forgot my previous occupations, so that it's now more difficult than ever to get down to them again.

Although I have thought very little about myself all this time, the idea that I have become far better than I used to be has somehow wormed its way into my mind – and even become a conviction. Have I really become better? Or is it only the same arrogant confidence in my reformation which I always had when I used to plan in advance my future way of life?

So far as I have been able to get to know myself, it seems to me that three evil passions predominate in me: gambling, sensuality and vanity. I have long been convinced that virtue, even in the highest degree, is the absence of evil passions; and so if I have really eliminated to any extent my predominating passions, I can confidently say that I have become better.

I'll examine each of these three passions. The passion for gambling stems from a passion for money, yet most people (especially those who lose more than they win), having once begun to gamble from having nothing to do, or from imitating others or from a desire to win, have no passion for the winnings, but acquire a new passion for gambling itself – for the sensations. Consequently, the source of this passion is habit alone: and the way to eliminate the passion is to eliminate the habit. This is what I have done. The last time I gambled was at the end of August – consequently more than six months ago – and now I don't feel any impulse to gamble at all. At a gambling party in Tiflis I started playing with a marker and lost something like a thousand games; at that moment I might have lost everything. Consequently, having once acquired the habit, it might easily be revived; and so although I feel no wish to gamble, I must always avoid any opportunity to do so, which I am doing without feeling any deprivation.

Sensuality has a completely antithetical basis: the more you refrain, the stronger the desire. There are two causes of this passion: the body and the imagination. It is easy to withstand the body, but very difficult to withstand the imagination which affects the body. The remedies against both causes are hard work and occupations, both physical – gymnastics – and moral – literary composition. But no. Since this inclination is a natural one and one which I find it a bad thing to satisfy only because of the unnatural position I am in (a bachelor of twenty-three), nothing will help to rescue me from temptation except strength of will and prayer to God. I had a woman at the end of September, and again in Tiflis four months ago.

Vanity is an unintelligible passion, one of those evils like epidemics – famine, locusts or war – with which providence punishes human beings. The source of this passion can't be discovered, but the causes which foster it are inactivity, luxury and the absence of cares and privations.

It's a sort of moral sickness like leprosy – it doesn't destroy any one part but disfigures the whole – it insinuates itself gradually and imperceptibly and then develops throughout the whole organism; there is no manifestation of life which it doesn't infect; it's like venereal disease – if it's driven out of one part it appears with greater force in another. The vain man knows neither true joy, nor grief, nor love, nor fear, nor despair, nor hatred – everything about him is unnatural and forced. Vanity is a sort of immature love of fame, a sort of self-love transferred to the opinions of others – a vain man loves himself not as he is, but as he appears to others to be. This passion is developed to excess in our age; people laugh at it, but they don't condemn it because it does no harm to others. But on the other hand, for the man possessed by it it is worse than all other passions – it poisons his whole existence: An exceptional feature of this passion, common to leprosy too, is its extreme contagiousness. It seems to me, however, that while discussing this, I have discovered the source of this passion – love of fame.

I have suffered a lot from this passion – it has spoilt the best years of my life and deprived me for ever of all the freshness, boldness, cheerfulness and enterprise of youth.

I don't know how, but I have suppressed it, and even gone to the opposite extreme: I am on my guard against any manifestation of it, and think carefully in advance for fear of relapsing into my old failing. I don't know whether, through chance or providence, this passion has been so seldom satisfied that I have experienced only the sufferings which it affords; or whether it was the influence of my brother, who hardly understands at all what vanity means, or whether it was my remoteness from vain circles and a way of life which made me look at my situation from a serious point of view – but I completely eliminated this passion during my illness in Tiflis. I can't say that the passion has been completely eliminated, because I often miss the delights it used to afford me; but at least I can understand life without it and have acquired the habit of keeping it at a distance. I have only recently experienced, for the first time since childhood, the pure delights of prayer and love. It is obvious already from my diary of last winter that I wanted to extirpate this passion; but I only attacked those manifestations which were disagreeable to me, not understanding that it was necessary to uproot the passion entirely in order to be rid of it. It seems to me that I have done this now; but I still have leanings towards it, and so I must be on my guard against a new infection.

20 March   Got up after 8. Severe toothache before daybreak. Partly through laziness, partly through illness didn't attend drill. Read my old diary and wrote the new one till dinner. [. . .] It's a long time since I've been as cheerful as today, and that's because I've been working. How many advantages there seem to be in work, while in idleness there is neither benefit nor pleasure; and yet it usually gets the upper hand. [. . .]

Read Thiers[7] and am going to bed at 11.30.

Tomorrow I'll get up earlier and try to spend the day as fully as possible. Damned laziness! What a wonderful person I would be if that didn't impede me. I worry about my brother, and miss him – nasty thoughts on that score keep coming into my head.

21 March   I got up before 8 and read a chapter of Thiers while having tea; then I went for a walk with Dmitry and the dogs. [. . .]

My brother arrived, and I told him how unpleasant it was to write an untruth in a written answer required of me,[8] in the hope that he would completely reassure me on that score, and say it didn't matter at all; but on the contrary, he thought I had done wrong. It's strange how he, with his chivalrous code of honour to which he is always faithful, can get on with and even enjoy himself with the officers here. Why am I somehow ill at ease with him since I came back from Tiflis? Is it because we were too fond of each other, idealized each other while apart, and expected too much of each other?

The order of occupations which I have adopted, i.e. – translation in the morning, correcting after dinner and the story in the evening – is a very good one. The only thing is I don't know when to do gymnastics, and that's absolutely necessary – some exercise every day. [. . .]

22 March   Got up after 9 because I had toothache in the night – so badly that I groaned and cried out in my sleep. Drank two glasses of coffee to counteract the camphor which I'd swallowed a lot of because of the toothache, and sweated the whole morning after it. My brother and Yanovich[9] came round; they disturbed me a bit, but I went on translating. Dined at home; after dinner I was rather idle; I worked, but not as hard as yesterday. I'm convinced that the camphor hasn't destroyed my procreative powers. I haven't done as much correcting as yesterday, nor as carefully; and this is mainly so as not to get bored with the work. Lost two games of chess to Yanovich – without the queen; that shows how modest he is. Didn't go on with the story, partly because I didn't have time, but partly because I'm seriously beginning to doubt the merits of the first part. It seems to me too detailed, long-winded and lifeless. I'll think about it.

Sensuality is beginning to flare up very much – I must be careful. I've had almost no exercise; it's impossible to go out because of the wind, and it's dull indoors.

It's now 11.10, I'm going to bed – I'm satisfied with my day.

23 March Got up at 7, the weather was marvellous; went out hunting, rode up and down the undulating country till one. Killed two ducks. Late for dinner and ate at home. Khilkovsky[10] and Yanovich came after dinner – did gymnastics. I like Khilkovsky very much, but somehow he has a disagreeable effect on me; it's embarrassing for me to look at him, just as it used to be embarrassing to look at people I was in love with. I've received my enlistment papers. I did my gymnastics rather badly. Khilkovsky put me to shame, mainly because I was in too much of a hurry. After gymnastics I played two games of chess, had a wonderful blissful sleep till after 9, and went out to supper. [. . .]

24 March [. . .] A prayer: 'Father, Mother of God, remember my relatives, living and dead'; then: 'Save me, O Lord, from vanity, indecision, idleness, sensuality, illness and mental disquiet; Grant me, O Lord, that I may live without sin and suffering and die without fear and despair – with faith, hope and love I surrender myself to Thy will.'

'Mother of God and Guardian Angel, pray to the Lord for me.'

27 March, 12 o'clock at night Although not quite well, I did corrections until 11 o'clock – not altogether carefully or neatly; had dinner, read a bit and went on with the same work; my brother came and I read to him what I'd written in Tiflis.[11] He thought it wasn't as good as my earlier writing, and I thought it was no good at all. I wanted to lighten my labours, but the copyists can't cope, and consequently I'll have to work on my own.

Apropos of an article by A. Dumas on music,[12] I remembered what enormous pleasure I'm deprived of here. Almost all my dreams of happiness have been destroyed in my imagination by reality, except for the happiness of the artist. I experienced this in the country in 1850,[13] although in a very imperfect form.

Tomorrow I'll do some copying, write a letter to Seryozha and think over the second day:[14] can I revise it or must I abandon it altogether?

I must ruthlessly eliminate all passages which are unclear, long-winded or out of place – in a word, unsatisfactory – although they may be good in themselves.

Persistence and resolution – these are the two qualities which guarantee success in any matter. [. . .]

29 March   [. . .] For some time remorse at the loss of the best years of my life has begun to torment me very much. And it has done so ever since I began to feel that I could do something good. It would be interesting to describe the course of my moral development, but not only words, but even thoughts would be inadequate for that.

Great thoughts have no frontiers, but writers long ago reached the impassable frontier of their expression. Played draughts, had supper and am going to bed. I'm tormented by the pettiness of my life – I feel that it's because I'm petty myself – but I still have the strength to despise both myself and my life. There's something in me that makes me believe that I wasn't born to be the same as other people. But where does this come from? Is there some discord or lack of harmony in my abilities, or am I really superior to ordinary people in some respect? I am old – the time for development has passed, or is passing; but I'm still tormented by thirst . . . not for fame – I don't want fame and I despise it – but to have a big influence on people's happiness and usefulness.

Shall I simply die with this hopeless wish? There are thoughts which I don't voice even to myself; but I value them so much that without them there would be nothing left for me. I wrote the story with enthusiasm; but now I despise the very labour, and myself, and those who will read the story; and if I don't abandon this labour, it's only in the hope of dispelling boredom, acquiring the habit of work and giving pleasure to Tatyana Alexandrovna. If there is a touch of vanity of thought here, it is so innocent that I excuse it in myself, and it confers the advantage of activity.

I have always been afraid of vanity and despise it so much that I don't hope that its satisfaction will afford me any pleasure. But I must hope for this, because otherwise what will be left – what will be my motive force? Love and friendship! Even these two feelings I involuntarily take to be the infatuation and illusion of my youthful imagination. Have they brought me happiness? Or perhaps I have just been unfortunate? This hope alone supports my desire to love and to endeavour. If happiness and useful activity are possible and I experience them, at least I shall be in a position to take advantage of them. Lord have mercy on me.

30 March, Easter Day   Slept well and got up late, at 10 o'clock. I am sometimes stupid enough to eat a lot of hot things with the purpose of testing whether my reproductive powers have been destroyed or not; I did this yesterday and so I had diarrhoea and was upset all day. *I must try to arouse sensuality as little as possible.* [. . .]

Went coursing hares, and only saw one – did gymnastics, drank tea and went round to my brother's, having learned from Buyemsky[15] that everyone there was indecently drunk. The news was correct. [. . .]

I think that I'll go out of my mind with boredom. I despise all passions and despise life, and yet get carried away by petty little passions and distracted by life.

31 March Woke at 6 o'clock and roused everyone; but was too lazy to get up and slept on till 9. [. . .] Arrived at Alexeyev's[16] when everyone was already at table, and my brother was in a pathetic state. I found it so unpleasant to look at him that I left straight after dinner and started writing. Put the finishing touches to one chapter. Nikolenka arrived in the same condition. I went out hunting and learned later from Balta that he had caused a scandal in the square. A pity he doesn't know how much it grieves me to see him drunk; I'm sure that since it affords him very little pleasure, he would refrain from it. The most unpleasant thing of all for me is the fact that he is judged and pitied by people who are not worth his little finger; but they are entitled to pity him. [. . .]

1 April Woke up before 8 again, but went back to sleep and slept till 10. Read *The Contemporary*; all very bad. It's strange that bad books indicate my failings to me more than good books. Good ones make me lose hope. Wrote a chapter *on prayer*; slow going. [. . .] Wrote and wrote, and finally began to notice that my discourse on prayer has pretensions to logicality and profundity of thought; but it isn't consistent. Decided to finish it somehow or other before getting up and immediately burnt half of it – I won't include it in the story, but I'll keep it as a souvenir. My brother has a story about some wench he knocked down yesterday in the square. It's stupid! Things appear in a false light to people who look at them with the aim of writing them down; I've experienced this myself. [. . .]

4 April [. . .] Dined at home; read and slept for two hours; then read again and set off for a walk round the village with evil intentions. My energy flags and my passions get stronger. I haven't any constant energy; but it rises and slumps almost periodically. What causes my energy to rise and fall? The nature of my pursuits, or the people I see, or physical causes? I don't know; but it's interesting and would be useful to know. [. . .] Met Baumgarten and Verzhbitsky at supper. I wasn't very shy, but went to the opposite extreme – I talked a lot. It's silly that the presence of the most insignificant man makes me change; the main thing is to notice this change in me and to try to prevent it. [. . .]

5 April [. . .] O shame! I went and knocked at Kasatka's window. Fortunately for me she didn't let me in. Got a letter and 100 roubles from Tatyana Alexandrovna. I can only redeem this escapade by intensive work and energy. [. . .]

7 April, 11 o'clock at night Although I woke up before 7 I couldn't overcome laziness and only got up at 9. Read over and made final corrections to the first day.[17] I'm absolutely convinced that it's no good at all. The style is too careless and there are too few ideas to make it possible to forgive the emptiness of content. However, I've decided to finish correcting the whole of the first part and tomorrow I'll start on *the second day*. Shall I send off this work or not? I haven't decided. Nikolenka's opinion will decide the matter. I'm very worried about him, and my heart is somehow heavy and apprehensive. I very much want to begin a short Caucasian story,[18] but I won't allow myself to do so until I've finished the work already begun. [. . .]

8 April [. . .] Translated a chapter of Sterne in the morning. [. . .]

10 April Got up before 8. Idled about a bit – attended drill; then got down to the novel, but stopped after writing two pages because it occurred to me that the second day can't be good if it lacks interest, and that the whole novel is like a drama. I'm not sorry; tomorrow I'll cut out all that's superfluous. [. . .]

11 April [. . .] Went to knock at Kasatka's, but fortunately for me a passer-by interrupted me. I'm not well – haemorrhoids and varicose veins – probably the result of abstinence. [. . .]

12 April [. . .] I think Nikolenka seems sorry for me and regrets that he inveigled me into the service. I don't know whether it's a good thing or a bad, but we are very secretive with each other. I'm getting the bad habit of thrusting myself on people to read my story to them. [. . .]

14 April, Kizlyar[19] Got up at 7, went hunting, caught nothing, reached Kizlyar at 12. Read, drank tea and dozed off. The doctor woke me. As far as I can see he's an ignoramus who tries to show off his knowledge and so is brash and dangerous. I'll stay till Sunday, and if I'm no better I'll treat myself at Starogladkovskaya according to the prescriptions. Tomorrow I'll send Dmitry away. Bought some raisins and made my teeth sore. Was very ashamed of myself for it. Read Sterne. Wonderful. 'If nature has so woven her web of kindness, that some threads of love and desire are entangled with the piece – must the whole web be rent in drawing them out?'[20]

I feel a bit easier about my illness. Read *Histoire d'Angleterre*,[21] and not without pleasure. I'm beginning to love history and to understand its usefulness. And this at twenty-four! That's what a bad education means. I'm afraid it won't last long. [. . .]

16 April   Got up at 9. Read *The Wandering Jew*,[22] Yermak[23] and a legend about Peter the Great. There's a certain peculiar pleasure in reading stupid books; but an apathetic pleasure. [. . .]

19 April   [. . .] A man who always speaks the truth can't be a chatterbox.

When you get a letter from a person you love, you want to know not so much what has happened to him as how he regards what has happened. [. . .]

21 April, Oreshinka[24]   [. . .] Killed a hare; I think I'm beginning to like shooting. Wrote a bit, but what I wrote seems poor. I don't know whether going out was good for my health, but it was very good for my pleasure. I spent the whole day in the open air and on the move. Spring and time are passing, but my illnesses will never pass. If I had money, I would buy an estate here, and I'm sure that I would be able to manage it profitably – not as in Russia. [. . .]

22 April, Shandrakovskaya Harbour[25]   [. . .] After dinner and a rest I went shooting and thought about serfdom. I'll think carefully at leisure whether I can make a pamphlet out of my thoughts on the subject.[26] [. . .]

10 May   [. . .] I want to stop reading. *Aquiline noses*[27] are driving me mad; all a person's strength of character and happiness in life seem to lie in them. I'm also tormented by the thought that I've completely lost my cheerful spirits, and, I think, for ever. I'm bored with everyone, and everyone, even Nikolenka, is bored with me. Tomorrow I'll start work on the continuation of *Childhood* and perhaps on a new novel.[28] [. . .]

11 May   Got up early, but can't get out of the habit of reading. Wrote a little, without any self-love and with great ease. It occurred to me that in the direction my writing has taken this year I've been very like certain people (especially young ladies) who try to see in everything a certain special subtlety and complexity. [. . .]

16 May, Pyatigorsk   [. . .] The music in Pyatigorsk, the people promenading and all those things which used to seem so foolishly attractive have made no impression on me. Only one thing disturbed me. The cadets, their dress and the ridiculous saluting for half an hour. I mustn't forget that the main purpose for my coming here is to be cured; and so tomorrow I'll send for the doctor and take a flat *on my own* in the suburbs. Going to bed at 9.15. I've been intemperate these last two days: drank wine and beer and even wanted . . .

18 May　Got up early, got on with *Childhood*; it's become extremely repulsive, but I'll continue with it. The doctor came; I'll start the baths on Tuesday. Walked to the Alexandrovskaya Gallery and did some shopping; had dinner and after dinner had an exceptionally refreshing and pleasant sleep for 2½ hours. Drank the waters. Saluting is unpleasant because there are occasions when it's absurd. Wrote *A Letter from the Caucasus*[29] – tolerably, I think, but not well. I'll continue (1) studying, (2) my working habits, (3) perfecting my style. [. . .]

22 May　Got up at 4.15, drank the waters, took a bath; my head ached and I felt very weak. Didn't write anything, but chatted with Buyemsky about mathematics and told him about Plato's *Symposium*, which he had forgotten. I'd very much like to do mathematics again, only I don't know whether I'm capable of it now. Buyemsky has become less caustic and is beginning to listen. Had dinner, slept, drank the waters, and copied out the *Letter*, the second part of which will need thinking about. Re-read the chapter 'Sorrow'[30] and wept with all my heart. There really are some fine passages in it, but there are bad ones as well. I'm becoming extremely careless about everything. I must put pressure on myself. I'm going to bed, it's 11 o'clock.

23 May　[. . .] *Childhood* seems to me not altogether bad. If I had enough patience to copy it out a fourth time, it would even be good. [. . .]

25 May　Got up before 4, woke up myself, feel fine, the same routine, didn't write much because of pondering over a mystical, rather stupid phrase which I wanted to express eloquently. Wasted the whole morning over it and am still not satisfied. Visited Protasov. Why are all people – not only those whom I don't like or respect and who are of a different bent from me, but all people without exception – noticeably ill at ease with me? I must be a difficult, unbearable person. [. . .]

30 May　Usual routine; wrote a letter to Tatyana Alexandrovna[31] which I didn't send and which I'm dissatisfied with. I'm doing nothing and thinking about the landlady. Have I the talent to compare with our modern Russian writers? Decidedly not. Sitting down to supper at 10.30.

31 May　Got up early, drank the waters, had a bath, drank tea and did nothing before dinner. Didn't sleep, but wrote about courage.[32] The ideas are good, but because of laziness and bad habits the style is unpolished. Drank the waters and was in a cheerful frame of mind. The copyist came and I handed over and read aloud the first chapter. It's definitely no good at all. Tomorrow I'll revise the second chapter; I'll revise it as I copy it out.[33] In the morning I had a strong erection, and when I came home alone I found my young landlady in the kitchen and said a few words to her. She's definitely flirting with me: she ties bunches of flowers underneath the window, waits for the bees to swarm, and sings songs, and all these endearments are destroying my peace of heart. Thank God for the bashfulness He gave me: it's saving me from corruption.

2 June [. . .] Had the old weakness after dinner, and on top of that, I couldn't refrain from eating three glasses of ice cream. In the evening I read, thought, drank the waters at home, but did nothing. Although there will be spelling mistakes in *Childhood*, it will still be tolerable. My only thought about it is that there are worse stories; I'm still not convinced, however, that I lack talent. I think I lack patience, experience and clarity, and there is nothing great about my style or my feelings or my thoughts – I still have doubts, however, about the latter. [. . .]

3 June [. . .] I notice in myself the signs of age. I feel and regret my ignorance and I say with all my heart the phrase which I have often heard elderly people use and which always used to surprise me: 'I now regret that I didn't study, but it's too late!' It's sad to know that my mind is uneducated, imprecise and feeble (although supple), that my feelings lack constancy and strength, that my will is so wavering that the least circumstance destroys all my good intentions – and to know and feel that the germ of all these qualities is or was in me and only needed developing. How long have I endeavoured to educate myself! But have I improved much? It's high time I despaired; but I still hope and count on chance, and sometimes Providence. I hope that something may yet arouse my energy and that I shall not for ever wallow, with lofty and noble dreams of fame, usefulness and love, in the dull slough of a petty, aimless life. I'm going to bed. It's 9.10.

4 June Usual routine; got on with *A Letter from the Caucasus* – not much, but well. I feel fine. At first I was too much addicted to generalization, then to triviality, but now, if I haven't found the mean, at least I understand the need for it and want to find it. Read *Hours of Devotion*,[34] a translation from the German – a book which I would once have read without attention, or would either have enthused about or read with a sneer; but now it made a real impact on me. It confirmed my ideas about ways of improving my affairs and putting an end to quarrels. And I have now firmly decided to go to Russia at the first opportunity and *coûte que coûte* [whatever the cost] to sell part of my estate and pay my debts, and on my first encounter with people to put an end, peaceably and without vanity, to all former hostilities and to try in future by kindness, modesty and a benevolent outlook towards people to overcome my vanity. Perhaps this is the best way to rid myself of my inability to get on with people. [. . .]

5 June   [. . .] It is well known that in a whole forest you can't find two leaves exactly alike. We recognize the difference in the leaves, not by measuring them, but by intangible features which spring to the eye. The difference between people, as more complex beings, is greater still, and we recognize it in just the same way by an ability to combine in one image all their features, both moral and physical. This ability forms the basis of love. From a collection of shortcomings one can sometimes form such an intangible but fascinating character that it inspires love. [. . .]

7 June   [. . .] Feel proud, I don't know what about. But I'm satisfied with myself morally. I've still got a rash, but I'm sure it's venereal disease, the mercury or the gold, despite the fact that the doctor says it's nettle rash. [. . .]

11 June   [. . .] I had dinner, and read about Charles I in Hume's *History*. *History is the best expression of philosophy.* [. . .]

13 June   [. . .] There's too great a friendship between the landlady and me. I'm distracted by everything and vain about everything. I used to be vain about my wealth and my name; now it's my kindness and simplicity of manner. [. . .]

21 June   Got up early, had a bath, drank the waters, did some writing. Behaved well except for the fact that I couldn't refrain from telling Buyemsky that he's stupid. Didn't do much work after dinner; chattered away to everybody at the waters and for no reason at all lied that I was a law school graduate. This circumstance so upset me that I began to walk along the boulevard aimlessly, like a man possessed. Busy at home getting my accounts and linen in order. Three roubles are missing; the landlady accused Ivan Moiseyevich, but I defended him warmly. Masha talked to me and sent me two roses by a little girl. I don't like her any more, but I'm worried simply because I'm a man and she is a woman, and we live in the same yard. I've just discovered the expression 'to contribute one's mite'. [. . .]

22 June [. . .] I notice that conversation is beginning to have a great fascination for me – even stupid conversation. [. . .]

24 June [. . .] Ate Turkish delight and couldn't sleep till morning. Drank the waters, had a bath, drank tea, read; the doctor came; I obtained some tickets, stayed a while at Buyemsky's, got some books and began to read *Confessions*,[35] which unfortunately I can't help criticizing. [. . .]

29 June Got up at 9. The doctor came. He's sending me to Zheleznovodsk. Copied out the latest chapters. Had dinner, did some writing, drank the waters, had a bath and came home very weak. Read *Profession de foi du Vicaire Savoyard*.[36] It's full of contradictions; unclear – abstract – passages and things of exceptional beauty. All that I've derived from it is a conviction that the soul is not immortal. If the idea of immortality requires the idea of the recollection of a former life, we were not immortal. But my mind refuses to understand infinity from one side only. Somebody said that clarity is the sign of truth. Although one may quarrel with this, nevertheless *clarity* will remain the best sign, and one must always use it to check one's judgements.

Conscience is our best and surest guide, but where are the signs which distinguish this voice from other voices? The voice of vanity speaks with equal force. An example – an unavenged insult. The man whose aim is his own happiness is bad; the man whose aim is the good opinion of others is weak; the man whose aim is God is great. But does the man whose aim is God find happiness in that? How foolish! And yet how fine these thoughts seemed to be. I believe in goodness and love it, but I don't know what can show me the way to it. Is the absence of personal advantage not a sign of goodness? Yes, I love goodness; because it is pleasant, it follows that it is useful. What is useful to me is useful for a purpose, and is good only because it is good for me and in harmony with me. This is a sign which distinguishes the voice of conscience from other voices. But isn't this a subtle difference – that what is good and useful (and where shall I put what is pleasant?) has the sign of truth – clarity? No. It is better to do good, without knowing how one knows what it is, and not to think about it. One can't help saying that the greatest wisdom is the knowledge that wisdom doesn't exist.

What is bad for others is bad for me. What is good for others is good for me. That is what conscience always says. The wish or the deed? Conscience reproaches me for actions committed with good intentions but which have bad consequences. [. . .] Is any amusement or pleasure which brings no advantage to others an evil? My conscience does not reproach me for them; on the contrary it approves them. This is not the voice of conscience. Conscience sooner or later reproaches me for every minute

used to no advantage (even though harmlessly). *Variety of work is pleasure.*
I'm going to bed, it's 10.45.

30 June   [. . .] Yesterday I dwelt on the question: are pleasures which
bring no advantage bad? Today I assert that they are. [. . .]

2 July   Got up at 5. Went for a walk, finished *Childhood* and revised it.
Had dinner, read *Nouvelle Héloïse*[37] and wrote a draft letter to the editor.[38]
*Justice is the least degree of virtue obligatory for everyone. Above it are the steps to
perfection; below it – vice.*
  Is *prayer necessary and useful?* Only experience can convince one. Does
God answer our prayers, and can this urge to pray be observed in all men?
Here are two proofs of its usefulness, and there are no proofs to the
contrary. It is useful because it isn't harmful, and also because it is moral
solitude. [. . .]

7 July, Zheleznovodsk[39]   [. . .] I must be quick and have done with the
satire in my *Letter from the Caucasus*, for satire isn't in my nature.[40] [. . .]

8 July   Got up at 8. Drank the waters, had a bath and got on reasonably
well with *A Letter from the Caucasus*. Teeth ached; read the *Confessions* with
great pleasure. [. . .]

9 July   Got up at 8. I've been suffering from toothache, but it's better
now; read the *Confessions* all day. The second part is completely new to me.
Alexeyev came and said that I have to serve for two years. If that's so I shall
resign. My failures lead me to despise people's opinions. Thank God for
them. [. . .]

10 July   [. . .] Here are two possible and delightful ideas – but too good to
come true (1) To live *à trois*: Nikolenka, Masha and I. Valeryan, of course,
would be in the way, but these three people are so good that they would
make even him good. (2) To hand over Yasnaya to Nikolenka and receive
600 silver roubles a year. If I stay on in the service here I'll do that. [. . .]

13 July   [. . .] *The desire of the flesh is personal good. The desire of the soul is
the good of others.* [. . .] I have seen that the body dies; therefore I suppose
that *mine will die too; but nothing can prove to me that the soul dies, and
therefore I say that it is immortal – according to my concepts. The concept of
eternity is a disease of the mind.* [. . .]

15 July   [. . .] I'm reading Rousseau and feel how much higher he is than
me in education and talent, but lower in self-respect, firmness and good
judgement. [. . .]

18 July [. . .] I'm thinking out a plan for a Russian landowner's novel with a purpose.[41]

This is how I pray: *O God, deliver me from evil, i.e. deliver me from the temptation to do evil, and grant me good, i.e. the possibility of doing good. Am I to experience evil or good? – Thy will be done!* Shall I never be able to conceive of the idea of God as clearly as the idea of virtue? That is now my strongest desire.

Punishment is an injustice. Retribution can never be determined by man; he is too narrow – he is a man himself. Punishment as a threat is unjust because man sacrifices a certain evil for a doubtful good. Banishment – even death – is just. Death is not an evil, for it is an undoubted law of God. The idea of God stems from man's awareness of his weakness. [. . .]

20 July Couldn't sleep all night, got up at 6, drank the waters at home, went to see Roger.[42] Moved into No. 8. Health seems better, but am still not doing anything. I'm stopping smoking from today. Tomorrow I'll begin to revise *A Letter from the Caucasus* and replace myself by a volunteer. I'm going to bed. It's 9.30.

22 July Got up at 6. Weather vile, drank the waters at home and was sure that I'd got syphilis again. God's will be done! All is for the best. All my illnesses have brought me an obvious moral advantage, and for this I thank Him. [. . .]

23 July Roger told me that I haven't got syphilis. I'm doing nothing; still smoking. [. . .]

3 August, Pyatigorsk [. . .] Read the *Politique*.[43] In my novel I'll expound the evil of Russian government, and if I find it satisfactory, I'll devote the rest of my life to drawing up a plan for an aristocratic, elective government, combined with the monarchy, on the basis of existing elections. There's an aim for a virtuous life! I thank Thee, Lord; give me strength.

17 August, Starogladkovskaya Was present at the inspection. The best thing I can look forward to from the service is retirement. Came back from the inspection and slept till 9 o'clock. Head very clear. Causes of the decline of literature: reading light works has become a habit, and writing them an occupation. To write one good book in one's lifetime is more than enough. And to read one. [. . .]

18 August Here are four rules by which people are guided: (1) Live for your own happiness. (2) Live for your own happiness while doing the least possible evil to others. (3) Do for others what you would wish them to do for you. (4) Live for the happiness of others. Spent all day on duty or with my brother and the officers. The plan of my novel is beginning to take shape.

25 August   Killed a snipe. Twice attended drill. No one can demand of himself the possibility of complete innocence. How often has the whole human race turned its back on justice? I must work with my brain. I know I would have been happier if I hadn't known this sort of work. But God set me on this path: I must follow it.

26 August   Shooting. Five snipe. Drill. Invited Pakunka round. A good thing she didn't come. I won't walk down her street. I'm somehow afraid of my thoughts – I try to forget myself. Why force myself? I'm happier that way than when I think barren thoughts.

28 August   I'm twenty-four, but have still done nothing. I feel that it's not for nothing that I've been struggling with doubts and passions for eight years now. But what am I destined for? The future will disclose. Killed three snipe.

29 August   Went shooting with Nikolenka; killed a pheasant and a hare. Had a sleep and got a letter from Petersburg from Islavin (a vile letter which I'll answer, not with sarcasm as I was intending to do, but with true contempt – silence) and from the Editor," which made me absurdly happy. Not a word about money. [. . .]

2 September   Mounted drill. Killed three pheasants in the evening. What a delightful thing *David Copperfield* is."

19 September   Went shooting. The plan for my novel is now sufficiently advanced, I think. If I don't get down to it now, it means I'm incorrigibly lazy.

22 September   [. . .] Read a *History of the War of 1813*." Only an idler or a person with no ability at all can say that he can't find an occupation. To compile a true, accurate history of Europe in this century – there's a task for a lifetime. There are few periods in history so edifying as this and so little discussed – discussed truthfully and impartially in the way we now discuss the history of Egypt and Rome. Such wealth and freshness of sources and unprecedented impartiality – it would be perfect. Before thinking of writing anything, another condition of beauty" occurred to me which I hadn't thought of before – the sharpness and distinctness of the characters.

30 September   Unwell, pains in my leg and cheek-bones. Wrote a bit and went shooting. Got a letter from Nekrasov – praise but no money.

5 October   [. . .] I think that here in the Caucasus I won't be able to describe peasant life. This troubles me.

8 October   Spent all day until evening in a strange state of insurmountable apathy; could neither read nor write. Read some rubbish, then wrote 1½ sheets. I must abandon for ever the idea of writing without revising. Three and four times is still not enough. Sent Vanyushka to the barracks yesterday for insolence. I'm more than ever resolved to retire, no matter what the conditions. The service is a hindrance to the only two vocations which I am conscious of within me, especially the better, nobler and more important one, and the one in which I am more certain to find peace and happiness. Everything will be decided by whether Brimmer has recommended me or not.[48] If he has, I'll wait to write to Petersburg, but if not, I'll apply to retire at once.

13 October   [. . .] I want to write some Caucasian sketches to form my style and for money.[49]

19 October   Simplicity is the main condition of moral beauty. *For readers to sympathize with a hero, they must be able to recognize in him their weaknesses as much as their virtues; virtues are possible, weaknesses inevitable.* I have thought of studying music. From tomorrow I hope to begin work unremittingly, either at that or something else. The idea for my novel is a happy one – it may not be perfect, but it will always be a good and useful book. And so I must work and work at it unceasingly [. . .]

  Basis of 'The Novel of a Russian Landowner'. The hero seeks in rural life the realization of his ideas of happiness and justice. Not finding it, and being disillusioned, he wishes to seek it in family life. His friend, a woman, suggests to him that happiness lies not in an ideal, but in regular, life-long work, the aim of which is the happiness of others.

  There is no love: but there is the physical need for intercourse and the rational need for a companion for life. *A proof of the immortality of the soul is its existence. Everything dies, I shall be told. No: everything changes, and this change we call death, but nothing disappears. The essence of every being – matter – remains. Let us draw a parallel with the soul. The essence of the soul is self-awareness. The soul can change with death, but self-awareness, i.e. the soul, cannot die.*

26 October   A sore throat and toothache. Read *Histoire des Croisades.*[50]

28 October   From today I must calculate afresh the period of my exile. My papers have been returned; accordingly I can't hope to return to Russia before the middle of 1854, i.e. before July, or to retire before 1855. I shall be twenty-seven. How old! Three more years' service. I must use them to advantage. I must train myself to work. I must write something good and prepare myself for – i.e. draw up rules for – life in the country. O God, help me! Wrote very little, went shooting and chatted at Nikolenka's. He's an egoist.

31 October   Wrote a little yesterday and today. I've got toothache. Read through my story, extremely mutilated.[51]

13 November   [. . .] Nikolenka grieves me very much; he doesn't love me or understand me. The strangest thing of all about him is that his great mind and kind heart have produced nothing good. Some connection is lacking between these two qualities. Yepishka put it very well when he said that I am somehow *unlovable*. This is certainly what I feel – that I can be no pleasure to anyone, and everyone is a burden to me. When I speak about anything, I involuntarily say with my eyes things which are no pleasure for anyone to hear, and I feel ashamed of myself for saying them.

14 November   [. . .] Drew up a short formulation of my creed: *I believe in one, incomprehensible, good God, the immortality of the soul and eternal retribution for our acts; I don't understand the secret of the Trinity and the birth of the son of God, but I respect and do not reject the faith of my fathers.*

17 November   [. . .] I must get used to the fact that nobody will ever understand me. This fate must be common to all people who are very difficult to get on with.

26 November   Went shooting with Ogolin and stayed a while at my brother's. After dinner I began to write well, and got a letter from Nekrasov. They're giving me fifty silver roubles a sheet,[52] and I intend to write some stories about the Caucasus without delay. Started today. I'm too proud to write badly, but I doubt whether I'm capable of writing another good thing. My whole body itches. [. . .]

28 November   [. . .] The time has passed for me to mill the wind. I definitely can't write without a purpose or the hope of being useful. [. . .]

30 November   Thought a lot, but did nothing. Tomorrow morning I'll get down to revising the description of war,[53] and in the evening to *Boyhood*, which I've finally decided to continue. *Four Periods of Life*[54] will be *my* novel up to Tiflis. I can write about it because it is a long way away from me. And as the novel of a clever, sensitive man who has lost his bearings, it will be edifying though not dogmatic. *The Novel of a Russian Landowner*, however, will be dogmatic. I'm beginning to regret that I've broken with my solitude; it was very sweet. My brother's influence used to be very good for me, but now it's more harmful, making me lose the habit of activity and careful consideration. All this is for the best. That is so clear in my life. Great God, I thank Thee. Do not abandon me.

1 December Spent all day writing the description of war. I don't like anything satirical, and since it was all written in a satirical spirit, it will all have to be revised. [. . .]

3 December Wrote a lot. I think it will be good. And without satire. Some inner feeling speaks out strongly against satire. I even find it disagreeable to describe the bad sides of a whole class of people, let alone an individual. Kochkin and Buyemsky will be on the expedition. My sores are healing. I'm sure they were meant to stop me trying to seduce Pakunka. I thank Thee, God; do not abandon me.

6 December Went to mass; settling accounts with Nikolenka made me angry; stayed at home and wrote a couple of sheets. Drank hot punch, porter and champagne, and played cards. [. . .]

11 December [. . .] Feel positively ashamed to be devoting my time to such follies as my stories when I've begun such a wonderful thing as *The Novel of a Landowner*. What use is money or foolish literary fame? Better to write something good and useful with conviction and enthusiasm. One never tires of that sort of work. And when I finish – as long as I still have life and virtue – something else will turn up.

23 December Out shooting, killed a pig, a wild cat and a hare. Merry-making at my place all evening.

24 December Christmas Eve. Finished the story.[55] It's not bad.

26 December *Reading Lermontov for the third day.* [. . .]

27 December Slept late; began writing my novel, but some officers interrupted me. Went for a ride, and read when I got back and wrote some poems.[56] They came quite easily. I think they will be very useful for forming my style. I can't help working. Thank God! But literature is rubbish, and I would like to have written down some rules here and a plan for the estate.

1853

*1 January, Chervlennaya*¹   Took the field with the division:² cheerful and well.

6 January, Groznaya   A stupid parade. Everyone drinks – especially my brother – and it's very unpleasant for me. War is such an unjust and evil thing that those who wage it try to stifle the voice of conscience within them. Am I doing right? Oh God, teach me and forgive me if I'm doing wrong.

7 January   The morning was a muddle; in the evening Knoring arrived drunk with Gesket and brought some porter; I had a lot to drink. Some officers of the Tenginsk regiment and some wenches turned up from somewhere. I got drunk. Yanovich was drunk and started trying to break my finger and said I was being a fool. The physical pain and the wine made me furious, and I called him a fool and a child. With tears in his voice and a childish³   he started saying rude things to me. I said I didn't want us to abuse each other like troopers, and that the matter couldn't end there.

8 January   I told him this morning that I'd been drunk and apologized for what I'd said to him; but he was so ridiculous that he replied: 'I pardon you; you were to blame.' Tomorrow morning, as soon as I've said my prayers, I'll ask him once more to apologize, regardless of who is there, and if he won't, I'll call him out. He'll have the first shot and I won't fire. I acted stupidly and badly. Yanovich is a good fellow, and I could do him a lot of harm by this affair. Nikolenka has left, but it was sad and painful for him to see this affair and not know how it would end. He's an egoist; but still I love him and it worries me to have distressed him. Several times during these last two days I've thought of leaving the service; but on thinking it over carefully I see that I ought not to abandon the plan I've made – to go on the last expedition this year – in which, it seems to me, I'll be killed or wounded. May God's will be done! Oh Lord, do not forsake me. Teach me. Give me strength, resolution and wisdom.

9 January   I've carried out my intention. Yanovich readily apologized. But if only people could know what an effort it cost me to approach him once again. [. . .]

21 January   Wrote a little, but so carelessly, so superficially and so little that it's as good as worthless. My mental faculties are so blunted by this aimless and disorderly life and the company of people who don't wish to and can't understand anything that's at all serious or noble. I haven't a bean, and this state of affairs makes me fear that people will think badly of me, and that suggests that I might actually do something bad. I don't want to play cards any more; I don't know how God can help. A fat lot of good the Caucasus is doing me when I'm leading such a life as this here. [. . .]

20 February, Camp on the Kachkalykov ridge   We marched from Groznaya to Kurinskoye without any action. Stayed there a couple of weeks, then camped on the Kachkalykov ridge. On the 16th there was an artillery action during the night and on the 17th during the day. I behaved well.[4] I've been winning at cards all this time, but now I haven't a bean, although people owe me money. In that respect I've been too weak-willed, but in general I behaved well. Today Ogolin told me I would get a cross. God grant it – but only for Tula's sake.

10 March, Camp by the river Gudermes   Didn't get a cross, but was confined to the guard room thanks to Olifer.[5] And so service in the Caucasus has brought me nothing but difficulties, idleness and bad acquaintances . . . I must put a stop to it soon. [. . .] The fact that I didn't get a cross distressed me very much. Evidently I'm not lucky. But I confess, this foolish thing would have been a great consolation to me. [. . .]

16 April, Starogladkovskaya   Haven't written my diary for a long time. Having arrived at Starogladkovskaya on 1 April, I've continued to live the same way as I lived on the expedition – like a gambler who's afraid to count how much is chalked up against him. Lost 100 silver roubles effortlessly to Sulimovsky. Went unsuccessfully to Chervlennaya to get a medical certificate. Wanted to resign; but a false sense of shame at returning to Russia while still a cadet is definitely restraining me. I'll wait for promotion, which is hardly likely – I'm already used to failures of all kinds. In Novogladkovskaya, if I didn't sin on the Tuesday of Easter Week, it was only because God saved me. I want to get back into my old rut of solitude, orderliness, and good and wholesome thoughts and occupations. Help me, God! I'm now experiencing for the first time an exceedingly sad and painful feeling – regret at a youth wasted without profit or pleasure. And I feel that my youth has passed. It's time to bid it farewell.

18 April   [. . .] I've just had an explanation about money matters – unpleasant as always – with my brother. After dinner I went to see Yepishka and talked to Salamanida; her breasts have grown ugly, but I still like her very much. However, anything young has a powerful effect on me; every woman's naked foot, it seems to me, belongs to a beauty.

19 April (Easter Day) Didn't go to church, and having broken my fast, ate some *kulich*⁶ which had been blessed. Did nothing all day. Played prisoners' base⁷ with some officers and young lads; sent Vanyuskha to Pakunka without success. Didn't get drunk, nor did my brother, which pleased me very much. [. . .]

20, 21, 22, 23, 24, 25 April Spent all these days almost the same way as the first: played prisoners' base, admired the wenches and got drunk once at Zhukevich's. Finished *Christmas Night*⁸ in rough. I'll start correcting it. Today was a very unpleasant day. It started with my having diarrhoea in the morning, then nothing came from Kizlyar, then a horse was stolen. My present wishes are: *to get a military cross and a commission on the spot, and for both my stories to be successful.* [. . .]

4, 5, 6, 7 May Nothing special. Received forty roubles for the story by post. Wrote quite a lot today, altered and shortened some of it and gave the story its final form. I must have a woman. Sensuality doesn't give me a moment's peace.

8, 9, 10, 11, 12, 13, 14, 15 May I've done nothing these seven days. Went to Kasatka's – continued to drink in spite of the fact that I wanted to stop several times. My brother left today. I've received letters from Nekrasov, Seryozha and Masha – all about my writing, and flattering to my self-esteem. I've fully thought out my story *Christmas Night*. I want to set to and get back into the rut of an orderly life – reading, writing, orderliness and self-restraint. Because of the wenches I don't have and the cross I won't get, I live here wasting the best years of my life. Lord, grant me happiness!

15, 16, 17, 18, 19, 20, 21, 22 May Twice had Kasatka. It's bad. I've let myself go very much. I've given up the story and am writing *Boyhood* with the same enthusiasm with which I wrote *Childhood*. I hope it will be as good. My debts are all paid. A brilliant literary career is open to me; I ought to get a commission. I'm young and clever. It would seem there's nothing else to wish for. I must work hard and restrain myself, and I may yet be very happy.

22, 23, 24, 25, 26, 27 May Nothing special at all. Didn't write much, but have finally thought out *Boyhood, Youth* and *Early Manhood*, which I hope to finish. Today Alexeyev sent me a paper in which Brimmer promises to discharge me with a civil commission. When I think of my service I can't help losing my temper. [. . .]

29 May [. . .] Having looked through article 56, I've decided to leave the army and have asked Alexeyev about this. Went to Kasatka's; a good thing she didn't let me in.

23 June Haven't written anything for nearly a month. Went to Vozdvizhenskaya during that time with my *kunaks*. Played cards and lost Sultan.⁹ Was almost taken prisoner,¹⁰ but on that occasion I behaved well, although too sentimentally. On getting back, I decided to spend a month here to finish *Boyhood*, but I've behaved in such a disorderly manner for a whole week that I've become very sad and depressed, as always happens when I'm dissatisfied with myself. Yesterday Grishka was saying that I was pale after the Chechens had nearly captured me, and that I didn't dare to flog a Cossack who had struck a woman because he would have hit me back. All this so upset me that I had a very vivid and depressing dream and, on waking up late, read about how Aubrey endured his misfortune and how Shakespeare says that a man comes to know himself in misfortune.¹¹ It suddenly became incomprehensible to me how I could have behaved so badly all this time. *If I'm to wait for circumstances in which I can easily be virtuous and happy I shall wait for ever; I'm convinced of that.* Wenches have led me astray. [. . .]

25 June Got a letter today from Seryozha in which he writes that Prince Gorchakov wanted to write about me to Vorontsov, and also a paper about my resignation. I don't know how all this will end, but I intend to go to Pyatigorsk in a few days' time. I lack perseverance and persistence in everything. As a result I've become unbearably repulsive to myself recently since I began to pay attention to myself. Had I persisted in the vainglorious mood in which I came here I would have been successful in the service and would have had reason to be satisfied with myself. Had I persisted in the virtuous mood I was in in Tiflis, I could have despised my failures and once again been satisfied with myself. In small things and in great, this failing is destroying the happiness of my life. Had I persisted in my passion for women, I would have had successes and memories; had I persisted in abstention, I would have been at peace with myself and proudly so. This damned detachment has completely led me astray from the true path of goodness on which I had just made such a good start, and on which I want to start again in spite of everything because it is the best one. Lord, teach and instruct me!

I can't write. I write too sluggishly and badly. But what is there for me to do except write? I've just been thinking over my position. Such a crowd of motley thoughts went round and round in my head that for a long time I couldn't understand anything except that I was bad and unhappy. After that period of painful reflection, the following thoughts took shape in my head: the purpose of my life is known – goodness – which I owe to my subjects and to my fellow-countrymen; I owe it to the former because I own them, to the latter because I possess talent and intelligence. The latter duty I am able to fulfil now, but in order to fulfil the former I shall have to use all the means in my power.

The first thought I had was to draw up rules of life for myself, and now I'm returning to it perforce. But how much time have I wasted in vain! Perhaps God organized my life like this in order to give me more experience. I would hardly have understood my purpose so well had I been happy in satisfying my passions. To determine my actions in advance and to verify their performance was a good idea, and I return to it. As from this evening, whatever circumstances I am in, I give my word to do so every evening. False shame has often hindered me from doing so. I give my word to try and overcome it as much as possible. *Be straightforward, even abrupt, but be frank with everyone – but not childishly, needlessly frank. Refrain from wine and women.* The pleasure is so slight, so blurred, but the remorse is so great. *Give yourself up completely to everything you do. Refrain from action in response to every strong feeling, but think carefully and then act resolutely, even if mistakenly.* I didn't finish my prayers today, having a guilty conscience about A . . .[12] Wrote little and without reflection. Ate too much, fell asleep from laziness, stopped writing on account of Arslan Khan's arrival. Boasted of my connection with the Gorchakovs. Insulted Yepishka for no apparent reason. Wanted to have women. Boasted about my writings to Groman, to whom I read *Karl Ivanich's Story.*[13] [. . .]

26 June [. . .] Went several times to Yepishka's; with regard to Salamanida things are making no progress, and Mikhayla, it seems, is determined to be on the watch. I've decided at all costs to have her. This enforced abstinence, it seems to me, gives me no rest and hinders my work; and the sin is petty, for the unnatural position in which fate has placed me excuses it. [. . .]

29 June Behaved well in the morning, but after dinner I did nothing. The plan I had thought out so well for the *Notes of an Officer in the Caucasus*[14] seemed bad to me, and I spent all the afternoon with the boys and Yepishka. Threw Grishka and Vaska into the water. Not a good thing. I must always write, whether well or badly. If you write, you get used to work and form your style, even though there is no direct advantage. But if you don't write, you get distracted and do stupid things. *One writes better on an empty stomach.* After supper I did the rounds of all the wenches, but no luck anywhere. Tomorrow I must write from morning till evening, and use every means to get a wench.

2 July [. . .] Salamanida has gone away for good, and Fedosiya, with whom I seem to be in love, won't agree on the pretext that I'm going away. Wrote a letter to Nikolenka. Tomorrow I must overcome my shame and take decisive action with regard to Fedosiya. Write *Boyhood* morning and evening.

8 July Got up late. Began to write but couldn't get on. I'm too dissatisfied with my aimless, disorderly life. Read *Profession de foi du Vicaire Savoyard*, and, as always when I read it, it awakens a great many sensible and noble thoughts in me. Yes, my chief misfortune is my great intelligence. [. . .]

I can't prove to myself the existence of God; I can't find a single sensible piece of evidence, and I find the concept unnecessary. It's easier and simpler to understand the eternal existence of the whole world with its incomprehensibly beautiful order than a being who created it. [. . .] I don't understand the necessity for God's existence, but I believe in Him and ask Him to help me to understand Him.

9, 10, 11, 12, 13, 14, 15 July (Pyatigorsk) Left Starogladkovskaya without the slightest regret. [. . .] Yesterday I was tempted by a gipsy beauty, but God saved me. [. . .]

18 July [. . .] Why does nobody love me? I'm not a fool, not deformed, not an evil man, not an ignoramus. It's incomprehensible. [. . .]

23 July I've rewritten the first chapter[15] reasonably well. Didn't stay long at Masha's. Work, work! How happy I feel when I'm working.

24 July Got up at 8, revised the first chapter and wrote nothing all day. [. . .] Must get up early and write, without stopping over what seems weak, as long as it makes sense and runs smoothly. One can revise, but one can't recover time wasted unprofitably.

25 July Worked all day, apart from three hours spent on the boulevard, but only rewrote one and a half chapters. The *New View* is forced, but *The Storm* is excellent.[16] Chatted with Teodorina. My smile is hesitant; this sometimes disconcerts me. [. . .]

27 July [. . .] Read Turgenev's *A Sportsman's Sketches*, and it's somehow difficult to write after him. I must write all day.

31 July Did nothing, went to the fair, bought a galled horse for twenty-four roubles, slept, went to the fair again, walked along the boulevard and took a wench to the Yermolov baths. Looks as if I'll be ill. [. . .]

4 August, Zheleznovodsk 1, 2, 3, 4 August Arrived at Zheleznovodsk, exchanged the horse, drank the first day with Felkersam and Valeryan. Teodorina is in love with me. [. . .] How much company and books mean to me. With good people and bad people I'm quite a different person. [. . .]

11 August, Zheleznovodsk [. . .] Tried to touch Teodorina several times during the evening; she greatly excites me. I've got a sore throat. But tomorrow I'll do some writing. Kasatka has rewarded me with a dose of mercury, which I'm very cross about.

13 August Ill all day, read *Madeleine*[17] and was bled.

26 August Did nothing. Decided to give up *Boyhood*, but to continue the novel and write the Caucasian stories.[18] The cause of my idleness is that I can't write with any enthusiasm.

28 August, Pyatigorsk [. . .] Began a Cossack story[19] in the morning, then because of Nikolenka's arrival and Teodorina's departure and my birthday I went to the shooting-gallery, rode to the colony and took Masha to the boulevard. Didn't enjoy it. Only work can afford me pleasure and profit. I'm going to bed to read.

13 September Felt terribly melancholy in the morning; after dinner I went for a walk, called at Bukovsky's and Klunnikov's, and picked up a repulsive wench. Then got the idea for *Notes of a Billiard Marker*[20] – wonderfully good. Wrote, went to see the assembly hall, then wrote *Notes of a Billiard Marker* again. It seems to me that I'm only now beginning to write with inspiration, and that's the reason why it's good.

14 September [. . .] Teodorina is sulking, and I won't go and see her any more.

18, 19 September Did nothing; began writing today but laziness overcame me; went to Smyshlyayev's in the evening and wrote some verse. [. . .]

29 September In the morning I wrote a good chapter of *Boyhood*. After dinner I went riding from 6 to 8. Went to Aksinya's. She's pretty, but I don't like her as much as before. Offered to take her with me. I think she'll agree. [. . .]

13 October, Starogladkovskaya Went shooting, wrote letters to Maslov and

Barashkin. Killed two pheasants. Read a literary description of genius today,[21] and this work aroused in me the conviction that I'm a remarkable person as far as abilities and eagerness for work are concerned. From today I'll get down to it. In the morning I'll write *Boyhood*, and after dinner and in the evening *The Fugitive*. Thoughts of happiness.

14 October   Did nothing of what I intended, but was lazy and read. Wrote ¼ of a sheet of *The Maid's Room*.[22] Want to make it a rule, having once begun a thing, not to allow myself to do anything else; but so that thoughts which occur to me shouldn't be lost, to note them down systematically in a book with the following subdivisions: (1) *Rules*, (2) *Information*, (3) *Observations*. Today for example: *Observations*: on singing and on Yepishka; *Information*: on the missions in North Ossetia and Georgia; and *Rules*: not to allow myself to be distracted by anything else before finishing the work I've started.

23 October   I woke up very late today and in the same dissatisfied mood. [...] My bad mood and anxiety prevented me from working. I read Zhukova's story *Nadenka*.[23] Formerly it was enough to know that the author of a story was a woman for me not to read it, because nothing can be more ridiculous than a woman's view of a man's life which women often undertake to describe, while on the contrary a woman author has an enormous advantage in the woman's sphere. Nadenka's environment is very well described, but her person is too lightly and imprecisely sketched in, and it's obvious that the author had no single idea to guide her.

I'm taking up my exercise book of *Boyhood* with a sort of hopeless aversion, like a workman compelled to labour at a thing which, in his opinion, is hopeless and no use at all. The work is going unsystematically, feebly and sluggishly.

When I've finished the last chapter I'll have to revise it all from the beginning and make notes and do the final alterations in rough. Much will have to be altered: the character 'I' is colourless; the action is long drawn out, and too consistent in time but not consistent enough in thought. For example the device of describing past events in the middle of the action for the sake of the clarity and sharpness of the story has been sacrificed, given my division of the chapters. [...]

'*Be content with the present!*' This rule which I read today struck me with extraordinary force. I vividly recalled all the occasions in my life when I hadn't followed it, and it seemed to me very surprising that I hadn't followed it. For example, in the most recent case of my own service, I wanted to be a count-cadet, a rich man with connections, a remarkable man, whereas the most useful and convenient thing for me would have been to be a soldier-cadet. How much of interest I could then have learned during this time, and how much unpleasantness I would have avoided. [...]

24 October   Got up earlier than yesterday and settled down to write the last chapter. A lot of thoughts had accumulated, but some insuperable aversion prevented me from finishing it. As in everything in life, so in writing too, the past conditions the future – it's difficult to resume a neglected work enthusiastically, and therefore well.

Before dinner I read a criticism of a description of the war of 1799 between France and Russia,[24] and after dinner went off without any particular enthusiasm to shoot at a range with Groman. The beautiful weather tempted me, and I went off shooting, and killed a hare and chased a jackal till late at night. After supper I played cards till 12 o'clock. How easily bad habits are formed! I'm already in the habit of playing after supper.

When reading a work, especially a purely literary one, the chief interest lies in the character of the author as expressed in the work. But there are works in which the author affects a point of view of his own, or changes it several times. The most agreeable are those in which the author tries, as it were, to hide his own personal view, and yet at the same time remains constantly true to it wherever it does show. The most insipid are those in which the view changes so often that it gets lost altogether.

Milyutin's book seems very well constructed; in spite of the flattery I have often heard and the partial opinions of people who timidly prostrate themselves before everything to do with royalty, it seems to me that Paul I's character, especially his political character, was really noble and chivalrous. [. . .]

26 October   [. . .] Absence of body, passions, feelings, recollections and time (i.e. eternity), is that not the absence of any life at all? What comfort is there in a future life if it is impossible to imagine it?

The description of the struggle between good and evil in a man who is attempting to do, or has just done, an evil act has always seemed to me unnatural. Evil is done easily and inconspicuously, and only much later does a man become horrified and amazed at what he has done.

The common people are so far above us by reason of their lives filled with toil and privations that it is somehow wrong for the likes of us to look for and describe what is bad in them. There *is* bad in them, but it would be better to say only what is good about them (as about the dead). This is the merit of Turgenev and the shortcoming of Grigorovich and his *Fishermen*.[25] Who can be interested in the faults of this pathetic but worthy class? There is more good than bad in them; therefore it is more natural and more noble to look for the causes of the former than of the latter.

In the old days I used to think that having once adopted a rule to be thorough and punctual in my occupations, I could follow it; then these frequently repeated and never accurately observed rules began to convince me that they were useless; but now I'm convinced that these attacks, constantly getting weaker and then recurring again, constitute the normal condition of the periodic scrutiny of oneself.

One must accustom oneself always and in everything to write clearly and distinctly, otherwise one unconsciously conceals from oneself obscurity or inaccuracy of thought by unnatural turns of speech, crossings out and flourishes. [. . .]

28, 29, 30, 31 october and 1 November, Khasav-Yurt[26] [. . .] On the 29th went shooting all day, chatted with Yepishka, played cards and read a biography of Schiller written by his wife's sister.[27] What is especially noticeable in it is the superficial view of a great man by a sentimental woman and a person too close to the poet, and therefore influenced by trifling domestic shortcomings, who had lost proper respect for the poet.

31 October [. . .] I read *The Captain's Daughter* and, alas, I must admit that Pushkin's prose is now old-fashioned – not in its language, but in its manner of exposition. Now, quite rightly, in the new school of literature, interest in the details of feeling is taking the place of interest in the events themselves. Pushkin's stories are somehow bare. [. . .]

Schiller quite rightly considered that no genius can develop in isolation; that external stimuli – a good book or conversation – do more to promote thought than years of solitary toil. An idea must be born in company, but its elaboration and expression take place in solitude. [. . .]

One of the main reasons for the mistakes made by our wealthy class is the fact that we take a long time to get used to the idea that we are grown up. Our whole life up to the age of twenty-five and sometimes beyond runs counter to that idea; quite the reverse of what happens in the peasant class where a youngster marries at fifteen and becomes complete master of himself. I have often been struck by the independence and assurance of a peasant lad, who, in our class, even if he were a very clever boy, would still be a nonentity.

It's strange that we all conceal the fact that one of the main springs of our life is money, as though it were shameful. Take novels, biographies, stories: they all try to avoid money matters, whereas that's where the main interest (or if not the main, the most constant interest) of life lies and where a man's character is best of all expressed.

There is a category of kind, noble people (though for the most part unfortunate in life, and not respected) who seem to live only in order to wait for an opportunity to sacrifice themselves for someone else or for honour's sake, and who only live from the time that sacrifice begins.

I have often had occasion to be surprised at and to envy the sound and clear-cut outlook of people who have not read much.

To look over every work that has been completed in draft, striking out everything superfluous and adding nothing – that is the first process.

When reading a story by an English lady,[28] I was struck by the naturalness of her way of writing – something which I lack, and to acquire which I must work hard and take note. [. . .]

There are people, such as myself and such as I try to portray in the hero of *The Novel of a Russian Landowner*, who feel that they must appear proud, and the more they try to assume an expression of indifference on their faces, the more haughty they appear.

I am often pulled up in a work of literature by routine methods of expression which are not quite correct, sound or poetic, but the habit of meeting them so often makes me write them myself. These ill-considered, conventional mannerisms in an author, the inadequacy of which one feels but which one forgives because of their frequent use, will be for posterity a proof of bad taste. To tolerate these mannerisms means to follow the times: to correct them means to be in advance of them.

2, 3, November   [. . .] Yesterday an argument arose between myself and some of the officers about the value of the conferment of titles; whereupon Zuyev, quite inconsistently, expressed envy of my title. At that moment the thought that he considered me vain about my title hurt my self-esteem; but now I'm heartily glad that he allowed me to notice this weakness in myself. How dangerous it is to trust thoughts that arise in the heat of an argument.

Always to live alone: that's a valuable rule which I shall try to observe.

Almost every time I meet a new person I experience a painful feeling of disappointment. I imagine him to be like myself, and I apply that standard as I study him. Once and for all I must get used to the idea that I'm an exception; that I'm either in advance of my age or that I'm one of those incongruous, unaccommodating natures that are never satisfied. I must take a different standard (lower than my own) and measure people by it. I won't be mistaken so often.

For a long time I deceived myself in imagining I had friends – people who understood me. Nonsense! I've never yet met a man who was morally as good as me, or who was willing to believe that I can't remember one instance in my life when I wasn't attracted by the good, and wasn't prepared to sacrifice everything for it.

For that reason I don't know any society in which I would be at ease. I always feel that the expression of my intimate thoughts will be regarded as falsehood, and that people won't be able to sympathize with my personal interests.

Moved into lodgings yesterday. If I'm forced to spend a month here, I'm sure I'll use it usefully. Already yesterday evening I felt that disposition towards genuine usefulness, the influence of which I experienced in Tiflis and Pyatigorsk. There's no evil without good. Yesterday, at the thought that my nose might cave in, I imagined to myself what an enormous and beneficial stimulus that would give me in the direction of moral development. I pictured to myself so vividly how noble I would be, how devoted to the common good and how useful to it, that I almost wanted to experience what I used to call a calamity justifying suicide.

However, this base thought, i.e. of suicide from the shame of being ugly, which I had heard expressed so well and eloquently by Islavin, I repeated without conviction. How often it happens that one repeats things without thinking about them, merely because they have been well expressed. [. . .]

4 November [. . .] There are some faces, especially those with shining eyes and broad, perspiring features, which, when animated, continually change their expression to such an extent that it is difficult to recognize them. [. . .]

5 November [. . .] I'm absolutely convinced that I'm bound to achieve fame; it's actually because of this that I work so little: I'm convinced that I only need to have the wish to work upon the materials which I feel I have within me. [. . .]

7, 8, 9, 10, 11, 12, 13, 14, 15 November, Starogladkovskaya [. . .] I lost forty-two roubles to Sokovnin and left Khasav-Yurt owing about ten roubles. Visitors didn't give me a moment's rest there, with the result that I was thrown into complete confusion. I liked the fourteen-year-old girl who worked for the landlord very much. I've done hardly anything all these days. Since arriving in Starogladkovskaya I've been shooting once, solicited timidly and unsuccessfully for wenches and chatted with Yepishka and Olifer, whom I dislike very much. Borrowed twenty-five roubles from him. This morning I did such a vile thing that it made me come to my senses. [. . .]

The laughter of people talking *tête à tête* has a completely different, more sincere and attractive character than laughter in a large company. [. . .]

I am replacing all the prayers which I have made up myself by the Lord's Prayer alone. Any requests I can make to God are expressed more loftily and in a way more worthy of Him by the words 'Thy will be done on earth as it is in Heaven'.

I have never made a declaration of love, but when I remember the terrible nonsense I talked to people I liked, with a subtle, meaningful smile, I blush at the mere recollection. The conversations one reads in our high society novels *pour tout de bon* [in all seriousness] are as like as two peas to what I said. [. . .]

17, 18 November Got up early yesterday, but wrote little. Two chapters,

'The Maid's Room' and 'Boyhood', which I've been unable for so long to put into final shape, held me up. Had dinner, played chess badly and boasted again. After dinner Lukashka announced that there would be a wench for me at dusk. I was stupid enough to give her the gold rouble she had been promised, and two silver roubles to him, although she turned out to be a repulsive old woman.

Got up late today. Wrote quite diligently, so that I finished 'The Maid's Room' and 'Boyhood', though only in rough. [. . .] I borrowed Karamzin's history and read bits of it. The style is very good. The foreword[29] aroused a host of good thoughts in me. Beat Alyoshka today. Although he was to blame, I'm dissatisfied with myself for having lost my temper. [. . .]

Someone told Yepishka that I had had a man conscripted because he had killed my dog. Such a terrible slander confirms me in the noble thought that to do good is the only way to be happy. If one looked at life from any other point of view whatsoever, such a slander would be enough to destroy all the happiness of life. [. . .]

19, 20, 21, 22 November [. . .] One of my chief and, for me, most unpleasant vices is lying. The motive for it is usually boasting – the desire to show myself off to advantage. Therefore, so as not to allow my vanity to reach a stage of development in which there is no time to stop and reflect, I set myself a rule: *as soon as you feel the tickling sensation of self-love which precedes a desire to say something about yourself – reflect.* Keep silent and remember that no fabrication can give you more weight in the sight of other people than the truth, which has a tangible and convincing character for everyone. Every time you feel vexation and anger, beware of all relations with people, especially those dependent on you. Avoid the company of people who like getting drunk, and don't drink wine or vodka.

Avoid the company of women you can have easily, and try to exhaust yourself by physical labour when you feel strong desire. Note down every day, from today, violations of these rules. [. . .]

The majority of men demand from their wives qualities which they themselves don't deserve.

Sermons are one of the best and simplest means of the religious education of our lower classes, if only preachers would sacrifice their self-esteem as authors for the sake of the benefit which a consistent, simple and clear exposition of Christian principles in the course of their sermons would provide, or if they would take pains in composing them.

When composing them it is necessary to avoid pomposity (which results in obscurity), as well as excessive simplicity which arouses doubts. [. . .]

The tone of a man I am talking to is always involuntarily reflected in me; if he speaks pompously, so do I; if he mumbles, so do I; if he is stupid, so am I; if he speaks French badly, so do I.

The common people are used to being spoken to in a language not their own, especially with religion, which speaks to them in a language they respect all the more for not understanding it.

There are thoughts (such as these, for example) which have meaning in a general connection, but lose it altogether in isolation.

23 November to 1 December   I've been out shooting several times, and killed some hares and pheasants. I've hardly read or written anything all these days. The expectation of a change in my life disturbs me;[30] while the grey overcoat is so repulsive that it's painful (morally) for me to put it on, which wasn't so before. [. . .]

Discipline is necessary for the existence of a military class and drill is necessary for the existence of discipline. Drill is a means of bringing men to a state of mechanical obedience by means of petty threats. As a result, the cruellest punishments don't produce the sort of subordination which is produced by the drill-habit. [. . .]

The more a man grows used to what is pleasant and refined, the more deprivations in life he stores up for himself. Of all such habits, deprivation of the habit of associating only with refined types of mind is the hardest to bear.

Vladimir was able to convert his people to the faith he had adopted only because he was on the same level of education as they were, though higher than them in social importance. The people trusted him. No ruler of an educated nation could have done the same.

2 December   [. . .] There are two desires, the fulfilment of which can constitute a man's *true* happiness – to be useful and to have a clear conscience.

I have decided, having finished *Boyhood*, to write some short stories, sufficiently brief for me to be able to think them out all at once, and of a sufficiently elevated and *useful* content for them not to weary or disgust me. Apart from that, I'll draw up in writing in the evenings a plan for a big novel and sketch some scenes from it. [. . .]

3 December   Got up early but couldn't begin anything. My Cossack story both pleases and displeases me. Read *The History of the Russian State* till dinner. [. . .]

I have a great defect – an inability to narrate simply and easily the circumstances in a novel which connect the poetic scenes together. [. . .]

I have been undecided which of four ideas to choose for a story: (1) *The Diary of an Officer in the Caucasus*,[31] (2) *A Cossack Poem*,[32] (3) *A Hungarian Girl*,[33] (4) *A Man who Came to Grief*.[34] All four ideas are good. I'll begin with the one that seems the least complicated, easiest and first in order of time – *The Diary of an Officer in the Caucasus*.

11, 12, 13, 14, 15, 16 December   [. . .] Started *Notes of a Bombardier*[35] yesterday, but have written nothing today. I've finished Karamzin's *History*.

For some reason the idea of power is involuntarily associated for me with the shape of a hand – especially a beautiful one. Sometimes when looking at a beautiful hand one imagines: 'What if I were to be dependent on that man?' [. . .]

Read Pisemsky's story *The Wood-Demon*.[36] What affected language and what an improbable subject! [. . .]

As I was being shaved today I vividly imagined to myself how a mortal wound inflicted on an already wounded man must instantly change his state of mind – from desperation to gentleness. [. . .]

17 December   [. . .] Read *The History*[37] all day. [. . .]

Ustryalov names as characteristics of the Russian people: devotion to their faith, bravery, and the belief in their own superiority over other peoples, as though these were not the general characterisitcs of all peoples, and as though the Russian people had no distinctive characteristics of its own. [. . .]

Every historical fact needs to be explained *in human terms*, and routine historical expressions avoided.

As an epigraph to a work of history I would write: 'I will conceal nothing.' It's not enough not to lie directly; one must try not to lie negatively – by keeping silent. [. . .]

19, 20 December   [. . .] Reading Karamzin's[38] philosophical foreword to the journal *Morning Light* which he published in 1777 and in which he says that the aim of the journal is the love of wisdom, the development of man's mind, will and feeling by directing them towards virtue, I was surprised that we could have lost the idea of the one and only aim of literature – the moral aim – to such an extent that if you were to speak nowadays of the necessity for morality in literature, nobody would understand you. But really it would not be a bad thing in every work of literature – as in fables – to write a moral, expressing its aim. *Morning Light* published reflections on the immortality of the soul, the destiny of man, Phaedo, the life of Socrates, etc. Perhaps this was going to extremes, but nowadays we have gone to a worse extreme.

Here is a noble aim, and one within my powers – to edit a journal whose aim would be solely to disseminate (morally) useful works of literature, and for which works would only be accepted on condition that they were accompanied by a moral, the printing or non-printing of which to depend on the author's wishes. Apart from the fact that polemics and the ridiculing of anything at all would *without exception* be excluded from such a journal, it would not conflict with other journals in the line it took. [. . .]

For a work to be attractive, it is not enough for it to be governed by a single thought; it must be wholly imbued with a single feeling. That wasn't so with my *Boyhood*.

21 December [. . .] *Boyhood* is woefully weak – it lacks unity and the language is poor. [. . .]

29, 30, 31 December On the 29th went shooting all day and didn't kill a thing. Yesterday I got on with *The Novel of a Russian Landowner* in the morning; in the evening I suffered from charcoal fumes and slept. This morning I got on with *The Novel of a Russian Landowner*, and in the evening went shooting and to the baths. [. . .]

The manner adopted by me from the very beginning of writing short chapters is the most suitable one.

Each chapter should express only one thought or only one feeling.

1854

2 January, Starogladkovskaya. [. . .] Must copy into my diary only thoughts, information or notes relating to proposed works. When starting each work, look through the diary and copy out in a separate exercise book everything relating to it. Copy out rules from my diary each month. Recall each day and note down in pencil all infringements of the rules, and copy them into the diary.

5 January [. . .] I'm often held up when writing by the wish to insert some good or well expressed thought; therefore if a particular thought should prove difficult to insert somewhere, copy it down in the diary without being delayed by the wish to introduce it at one particular point. The thought will find its place of its own accord.

7 January [. . .] A Russian – or generally speaking any ordinary person – loves in a moment of danger to show that he feels, or actually does feel, more fear of losing things entrusted to him or his own things than of losing his life. [. . .]

8 January In the morning 'The Novel of a Russian Landowner'. Couldn't get on with the writing somehow. Must follow the rule of cutting out and not adding. Dined early. *Go for a walk.* Went for a walk after dinner. *In the evening write 'Notes of a Bombardier'.* Wrote quite a lot, but began late because of the cold. Lay on the stove for a couple of hours in the twilight. *Must be alone.* Nobody called. The terrible cold has been hindering me a lot for two days now.

　　Must write a rough draft without thinking about the right place for the thoughts or their correctness of expression. Copy it out a second time, cutting out everything superfluous and giving each thought its proper place. Copy it out a third time, concentrating on the correctness of expression. [. . .]

12 January In the morning go for a walk and get on with 'The Novel of a Russian Landowner'. Got up very late. Warmed myself by the stove – almost poisoned myself with the fumes – but my cold got worse. Then Ogolin came and I wrote nothing. *Go for a walk.* Did so. *After dinner, thoughts and rules.* Got back home, lay on my bed and fell asleep. Woke up, opened my exercise book and thought about a basic idea, but didn't write it down. *In the evening 'Notes of a Bombardier'*. Opened my exercise book again but instead of writing, dreamed about the Turkish War and Kalafat.[1] Learned at supper that I've been transferred to the 12th Brigade,[2] and decided to go home. [. . .]

16 January [. . .] I was struck today by the poetic beauty of the winter weather. In the sky a mist got up and the pale sun shone through it. On the roads the dung is beginning to thaw and there is a damp moisture in the air. [. . .]

17 January Revise 'Boyhood'. In the morning I didn't have time to say my prayers before the officers arrived. Went to chapel with them. [. . .]

Avoid unnecessary frankness.

Avoid the familiarity and favours of people you are not sure of.

In moments of indecision act promptly, and try to take the first step even though it may prove superfluous. [. . .]

19 January, Shchedrinskaya[3] (Tuesday) Finish 'Boyhood' and leave. Did so. Got up early and wrote or was busy until the moment I left. Had a church service held – out of vanity. Alexeyev took leave of me very kindly. He and Zhukevich shed tears. Got as far as Shchedrinskaya. Re-read *Boyhood* and decided not to look at it again until I get home, but to write my 'Caucasian' *Notes of a Bombardier* on the journey. [. . .]

Today, while thinking of the fact that I've become fond of people whom I previously didn't respect – my fellow officers – I remembered how strange Nikolenka's affection for them had seemed to me. And I explained my change of view by the fact that in the Caucasian service and in many other close-knit circles of people one learns not to pick people out, but to see what is good even in the bad ones. [. . .]

20 January, Stary Yurt Got up early. Reached Nikolayevskaya and Stary Yurt. The news that I hadn't got a cross distressed me very much; but strange to say – an hour later I had calmed down. [. . .]

21 January, Galyugayevskaya [. . .] Here is a fact which needs to be remembered more often. Thackeray spent thirty years preparing to write his first novel, but Alexandre Dumas writes two a week.

You shouldn't show your writings to anyone before they are published. You'll hear more harmful opinions than useful advice. [. . .]

22, 23, 24, 25, 26, 27 January On the road. Was lost all night at

Belogorodtsevskaya, 100 *versts* from Cherkassk, and the idea occurred to me of writing a story *The Snowstorm.*[4] [. . .]

I'm too sociable – I'm fond of people and because of this I waste time, relax my rules and sometimes forfeit people's respect.

Nothing on the road cheered me so much and so reminded me of Russia as a baggage horse which laid back its ears and despite the speed of my sledge tried to overtake it at a gallop. [. . .]

28, 29, 30, 31 January, 1, 2 February, Yasnaya Polyana Was exactly two weeks on the road. The only striking thing that happened was the snowstorm. Behaved quite well. My mistakes were: (1) Weakness with other travellers, (2) Lying, (3) Cowardice, (4) Got angry a couple of times. [. . .]

3 February Woke up early with a sore throat, despite which I rode to the mill and looked at a site for stables. Talked more and more about farming, sent a letter to Shchelin. They say I've been promoted.[5] [. . .]

4 February [. . .] The chief defect and peculiarity of my character is that I remained morally young for too long, and only now at the age of twenty-five am I beginning to acquire a man's independent outlook on things which others acquire well before twenty. [. . .]

5 February [. . .] Was lazy all day. Gave three roubles to a poor woman. Have twenty-six roubles thirty copecks left. Am 240 roubles in debt. [. . .]

13 February, Yasnaya Polyana [. . .] Got a letter from Nekrasov; he's dissatisfied with *Notes of a Billiard Marker.* [. . .]

16, 17, 18 February, Moscow Don't remember anything except that I reached Moscow. I'm physically and morally in disarray, and have spent too much money. [. . .]

14 March 1854, Bucharest[6] I'm beginning my diary in a new exercise book after nearly a month's interval, during which I've felt and experienced so much that I haven't had time to think, still less to make notes. From the Caucasus I went to Tula, saw my aunts, my sister and Valeryan, and learned of my promotion. All my three brothers and the Perfilyevs came to see me and took me off to Moscow. From Moscow I went to Pokrovskoye and said farewell there to my aunt Pelageya Ilinichna, Valeryan, Masha and Seryozha. These two farewells – especially the latter – were among the happiest moments of my life. From there I went to see Mitenka, who, chiefly on my advice, has left Moscow, and the day before yesterday I arrived in Bucharest via Poltava, Kishinyov, etc. *I have been happy all this time!*

My official position here is uncertain and for the past week or so my health has been suspect again. Can this be the start of a new period of ordeals for me?

However, I myself am to blame; good fortune has spoiled me. I've let myself go and have much to reproach myself with from the day of my departure from Kursk right up to the present moment. It's sad to have to believe that I've been as unable to bear good fortune as I was to bear misfortune. Today I'll go to corps headquarters to see the commander of the division, make a few purchases, have a bit of a walk and go home to write letters and have dinner. After dinner I'll do some work and towards evening go to the baths. In the evening I'll stay at home and get on with *Boyhood*.

15 June Exactly three months' interval. Three months of idleness and a life which I can't be satisfied with. I spent about three weeks with Scheidemann[7] and regret that I didn't stay. I would have got on with the officers and could have come to terms with the battery commander. Moreover the bad company and my latent resentment at my undistinguished position would have had a good effect on me. I would have been angry and bored, would have tried to raise myself morally above the position I was in, and would have become better – I would have worked.

My posting to the Staff[8] came just at the time when I had quarrelled with the battery commander, and it flattered my vanity. My illness, during which I couldn't even get back into my old rut of activity and honest work with goodness as its only aim, proved to me how far I had degenerated. The higher I rise in public opinion, the lower I fall in my own. I've had several women, told lies, boasted, and – most dreadful thing of all – I didn't behave under fire in the way I hoped I would.

The siege of Silistria has been raised;[9] I haven't yet been in action; my position among my comrades and my superiors is good; despite the after effects of . . .[10] and the sores my health is reasonably good, and morally speaking I have firmly resolved to devote my life to the service of my neighbour. For the last time I say to myself: 'If three days pass without my doing anything of service to others, I shall kill myself.'

Help me, Lord. [. . .]

23 June During the move from Silistria to Maia[11] I went to Bucharest. I gambled and was obliged to borrow money. The position is humiliating for anyone, but especially for me. [. . .]

24 June Sat down to work in the morning, but did nothing, and was glad when Gorchakov[12] came to interrupt me. After dinner at the General's[13] I read Béranger, went to the doctor, who told me I would have to undergo an operation and have treatment for six weeks or so, and chatted till night fall with Shubin[14] about our Russian serfdom. It's true that serfdom is an evil but an extraordinarily nice evil.

25, 26, 27, 28, 29 June   Put off my operation from day to day waiting for a move to Bucharest, and have put it off here, waiting for lodgings and a doctor. There's been action at Giurgevo[15] in which I might have taken part if I'd been well. I've got no money, not a bean, and I'm in debt. [. . .]

30 June   Was operated on today under chloroform – was a coward. Did nothing because I couldn't. There's hope that I'll recover.

3 July   Read the whole day; my work simply refuses to make progress. [. . .] As soon as I'm on my own and think hard about myself, I can't help going back to my original idea – that of self-improvement; but my chief mistake, and the reason why I wasn't able to go quietly along that road, was that I confused self-improvement with perfection. One must first of all get a proper understanding of oneself and one's defects and try to remedy them, and not set oneself the aim of perfection, which is not only impossible to attain from the low point at which I stand, but the mere conception of which destroys the hope of the possibility of attaining it. It's the same as it was with my estate, my studies, literature and life. With my estate I wanted to attain perfection and forgot that it was necessary first of all to remedy the imperfections, of which there were too many; I wanted to make a correct division of my fields when I had nothing to manure or sow them with.

I must take myself as I am, and try to remedy those defects which can be remedied, and my good nature will lead me on towards the good without a *notebook*, which has been my nightmare for so long. Mine is one of those characters which desire, seek out and are receptive to all that is beautiful, and which for that very reason are incapable of being consistently good.

4 July   My chief defects are: (1) Superficiality (by which I mean irresolution, lack of perseverance and inconsistency). (2) An unpleasant, difficult character – irritability, excessive self-love and vanity. (3) The habit of idleness. [. . .]

5 July   Read during tea, dinner and dessert, and spent all morning writing a single letter to my aunt, which I'll send despite the fact that I don't at all like the French style of it.[16] From day to day it becomes more difficult for me to express myself and to write in French; what need is there for this stupid custom of writing and speaking in a language one knows badly? And how much trouble, waste of time, obscurity of thought and imperfection in one's native language result from this custom, and yet it has to be so!

In the evening I wrote a chapter or so of *Notes of a Bombardier* enthusiastically and reasonably well. [. . .]

6 July Spent all day reading Lermontov, Goethe and Alphonse Karr[17] and couldn't settle down to work. However often I say that I'm not ambitious, and however much I try to be sincere about it, *le bout de l'oreille se montre malgré moi* [the cloven hoof shows in spite of me]. It was unpleasant for me to learn today that Osip Serzhputovsky had been shell-shocked and that the Emperor had been informed about it. Envy . . . and over such a trivial thing, and of such a worthless fellow! [. . .]

7 July I lack modesty! That's my great defect. What am I? One of four sons of a retired lieutenant-colonel, left an orphan at seven years of age in the care of women and strangers, having received neither a social nor an academic education and becoming my own master at the age of seventeen, without a large fortune, without any social position, and, above all, without any principles; a man who mismanaged his affairs to the last degree, who spent the best years of his life without purpose or pleasure, and who finally banished himself to the Caucasus to escape from his debts and above all his habits, and from there, by seizing on to connections which had existed between his father and the Commander-in-Chief of the army, was transferred to the army of the Danube at the age of twenty-six as an ensign, almost without means except his pay (because what means he has he must use to pay his outstanding debts), without patrons, without the ability to live in society, without knowledge of the service, without practical talents – but with enormous self-love! Yes, that is my social position. Let us see what sort of person I am.

I am ugly, awkward, untidy and socially uneducated. I am irritable, boring to other people, immodest, intolerant (*intolérant*) and bashful as a child. I am almost an ignoramus. What I know I have somehow learned myself in snatches, piecemeal, unsystematically, and it amounts to very little. I am intemperate, irresolute, inconstant, stupidly vain and passionate like all people who lack character. I am not brave. I am unmethodical in life, and so lazy that idleness has become for me almost an insuperable habit. I am intelligent, but my intelligence has never yet been thoroughly tested by anything. I have neither practical, social nor business intelligence. I am honest, i.e. I love goodness and have made a habit of loving it; and when I deviate from it I am dissatisfied with myself and return to it with pleasure; but there are things which I love more than goodness – for example, fame. I am so ambitious, and this feeling has been so little satisfied, that as between fame and virtue, I fear I might often choose the former if I had to make a choice.

Yes, I am not modest; and that is why I am proud at heart, but bashful and shy in society.

Wrote this page in the morning and read Louis Philippe.[18] Began writing *Notes of a Bombardier* very late after dinner, and by evening had written quite a lot, despite the fact that Olkhin and Andropov came round to see me. After Andropov left I leaned on the balcony rail and gazed at my favourite street lamp which shines so wonderfully through the tree. Moreover, after the few storm clouds which had passed over and moistened the ground today, one large cloud remained covering the whole southern part of the sky, and there was a pleasant lightness and moisture in the air.

The landlady's pretty daughter was reclining at her window, leaning like me on her elbows. A barrel-organ passed along the street, and when the sounds of a good old waltz receding further and further into the distance had completely died away, the girl gave a deep sigh, got up and quickly moved away from the window. I felt so sad, yet happy, that I couldn't help smiling and long continued to look at my street lamp, whose light was sometimes obscured by the branches of the tree swaying in the wind, and at the tree itself, the fence and the sky, and all these things seemed to me even better than before. [...]

8 July [...] Today I discovered still more poetic things in Lermontov and Pushkin: in the former *The Dying Gladiator* (that dream of home before he dies is wonderfully good) and in the latter, Yanko Marnavich,[19] who accidentally killed his friend. Having prayed long and earnestly in church he went home and lay down on his bed. Then he asked his wife whether she had seen anything from the window, and she replied that she hadn't. He asked again, and then his wife said that she saw a light beyond the river. When he asked a third time, his wife said that she saw the light getting bigger and coming nearer. He died. It's marvellous! But why? Try and explain poetic feeling after that!

9 July Spent the morning and all the rest of the day, first writing *Notes of a Bombardier*, which, by the way, I've finished, but which I'm so dissatisfied with that I can hardly avoid re-writing it all afresh or entirely abandoning it – abandoning not only *Notes of a Bombardier*, but abandoning literature altogether – because if a thing which seemed admirable as an idea turns out to be worthless in practice, the man who undertook it has no talent; and then reading Goethe, Lermontov and Pushkin. The first I don't understand well and, however much I try, I can't avoid seeing something ridiculous (*du ridicule*) in the German language. In the second I found the beginning of *Izmail Bey* very good. Perhaps it seemed all the more so to me because I'm beginning to love the Caucasus with a deep, though posthumous love. That wild region in which two such completely opposite things as war and freedom are so strangely and poetically blended is really fine. In Pushkin I was struck by *The Gipsies*, which, strangely enough, I hadn't understood till now.

The motto of my diary should be '*non ad probandum, sed ad narrandum*' [not to prove, but to narrate].

11 July   Re-read *A Hero of Our Time*, read Goethe, and only wrote a very little towards evening. Why? Laziness, irresolution, and a passion for looking at my moustaches and my fistulas – for which I give myself two reprimands. Today I entrusted my application for a transfer[20] to Boborykin, who was here on his way to see the General. Another reprimand for having laughed at Olkhin in front of Boborykin.

11 July   [...] In the course of conversation with the doctor today, the stupid and unjust opinion I used to have about the Wallachians vanished – an opinion common to the whole army and borrowed by me from the fools I have hitherto kept company with. This people's fate is sad and moving. Today I read Goethe and a play of Lermontov's[21] (in which I discovered much that was new and good) and Dickens' *Bleak House*.[22] This is the second day I've been trying to write poetry. We'll see what comes of it. [...]

12 July   Since morning I've felt heavy-headed and couldn't force myself to work. Read *The Contemporary* all day. Esther (*Bleak House*) says that her prayer as a child consisted of the promises she had made to God (1) always to be industrious, (2) to be sincere, (3) to be contented and (4) to try to win the love of all around her. How simple, how sweet, how easy to accomplish and how great are those four rules. [...]

13 July   My prayer. 'I believe in one, almighty and good God, in the immortality of the soul, and in eternal retribution for our deeds; I wish to believe in the religion of my fathers and I respect it.'

'Our Father', etc. 'For the repose and salvation of my parents.' 'I thank Thee, O Lord, for Thy mercies, for this and for that' (here recall all the happiness that has been my lot). 'I pray Thee, inspire me to good undertakings and thoughts, and grant me happiness and success in them. Help me to correct my faults; save me from sickness, suffering, quarrels, debts and humiliations.'

'Grant me to live and die in firm faith and hope in Thee, in love for others and from others, with a clear conscience, and with profit to my neighbour. Grant me to do good and shun evil: but whether good or evil befall me, may Thy holy will be done!' [...]

14 July In the morning, apart from my usual reading of Goethe and some booklets that turned up, I got Zhdanov down on paper, but still haven't decided about the personality of Velenchuk.[23] They operated on my groin again today and again I had chloroform. The sensation wasn't so unpleasant, but it was so strange – I heard the sound of the instruments, but didn't feel pain. [. . .]

15 July The doctor woke me up early today, and thanks to that I wrote quite a lot in the morning – I kept revising the old material: the description of the soldiers. I also wrote a bit in the evening and read *Verschwörung des Fiesko*.[24] I'm beginning to understand drama in general. Although I take a completely opposite path to the majority as far as it's concerned, I like it as a means of providing me with new poetic enjoyment. [. . .]

21 July, Sineşti[25] Was woken up early this morning and taken to Sineşti. [. . .] Forgot to note down yesterday the pleasure Schiller gave me with his *Rudolf of Habsburg* and some minor philosophical poems. The simplicity, picturesqueness and calm, truthful poetry of the former is delightful. In the second, what struck me – or as Bartolomey says,[26] what 'was inscribed on my heart' – was the thought that to do anything great, one must direct all the strength of one's soul to a single point.

24 July, Cureşti [. . .] It's strange that I've only just noticed one of my chief defects: an inclination to show off all my superior qualities, which offends other people and arouses envy in them. In order to win people's love one must, on the contrary, conceal everything in which one stands out from the rank and file. I've come to realize this too late. I won't hand in my application[27] until I'm in a position to keep horses, and I'll employ all means to that end. Meanwhile, I won't have any other relations with people, except those required by the service. I reproach myself for laziness.

27 July [. . .] I'm satisfied with my day except for my laziness and the two wenches at my landlady's to whom I couldn't resolve to say a word, and I walked around the house for two hours. Some thoughts came into my head, but I feel that my memory is becoming blunted; love and respect for and confidence in my intelligence are disappearing and I'm falling back in the world of ideas without in consequence making progress – as should be the case – in the practical world. One of the thoughts apropos of which this reflection came into my head was actually this – that to try to win the love of one's neighbour is useless. [. . .]

29 July My improvement is progressing admirably. I feel how my relations with people of every sort are becoming easy and pleasant since I decided to be modest and became convinced that there is absolutely no need always to appear grand and infallible. I am very cheerful. God grant that my cheerfulness stems from me myself, as I think it does: from my desire to be pleasant to everyone, from modesty, slowness to take offence and being on guard against angry outbursts. If so I would always be cheerful and nearly always happy. In the morning I decided to stay at home and work, but I couldn't get on with things and in the evening I couldn't refrain from going out and gadding about. On the way back from supper Tishkevich and I stopped at a brothel and Kryzhanovsky caught us, which, I must confess, wasn't at all pleasant. [. . .]

1 August Got up late and read Schiller all morning, but without pleasure or enthusiasm. After dinner, although I was in the mood to work, I wrote very little our of laziness. Spent all evening chasing after wenches. [. . .]

12 August, Foksaný[28] Began the morning well and did some work, but the evening! God, shall I never reform? Lost the rest of my money and lost three thousand roubles which I couldn't pay. I'll sell my horse tomorrow. [. . .]

16 August Got up about 7, wrote quite well but not much, had dinner, wrote a bit more, ran after a wench, stayed a while at Stolypin's, then had a repulsive argument about original sin and so am going to bed in a bad mood. In the morning I shouted at Nikita – irritability. (1) Was lazy in Andropov's presence. (2) Ran after a wench when I'd promised myself not to embrace anyone for at least a month, and then only for love – lack of character. (3) Argued heatedly – irritability. (4) Sum total: irritability, lack of character and laziness. The most important thing in my life for me is to cure myself of these faults. From today I shall conclude my diary each day with this phrase.

17 August, Tecuciu[29] March from Fokşaný to Tecuciu; [. . .] Had a good sleep at mid-day and read the wonderful comedy *Poverty is no Crime*[30] [. . .]

24 August Rest day in Aslui.[31] Today I experienced two strong, pleasant and profitable impressions. (1) Received a flattering letter about *Boyhood* from Nekrasov, which, as usual, raised my spirits and encouraged me to continue my work, and (2) read Z.T.[32] [. . .] All truths are paradoxes. The direct deductions of reason are fallible; the absurd conclusions of experience are infallible. Today I censured Stolypin, was proud to get Nekrasov's letter and was lazy. *The most important thing for me is to cure myself of lack of character, irritability and laziness.*

29 August   I'm very ill. I think it's consumption. I've written nothing, but read *Onkel Tom's Hütte*. *The most important thing for me is to cure myself of laziness, irritability and lack of character.*

11, 12, 13, 14, 15, 16 September, Kishinyov[33]   [...] The disembarkation near Sevastopol worries me.[34] Self-assurance and effeminacy: these are the main, sad features of our army – common to all armies of states that are too big and strong. *Must cure myself of laziness, irritability and lack of character.*

Received *Childhood* and *The Raid*.[35] Found much that is weak in the former. The temporary – in the present circumstances – aim of my life is to improve my character, put my affairs in order and make a career both in literature and in the service.

23, 24, 25, 26, 27, 28, 29, 30 September, 1, 2, 3, 4, 5 October   The plan to form a society has changed into a plan for a journal[36] – for most of the seven – but not for Friede and me. I'm not going away on account of the journal, but it's making slow progress; I do little work and behave badly. Tomorrow the Grand Dukes are coming.[37] Let that be a great occasion for me. I must write an article for the specimen number. [...]

21 October   I've lived through a lot these last days. Affairs at Sevastopol still hang by a thread. The specimen number will be ready today, and I'm thinking again of moving. [...]

2 November, Odessa[38]   Since the landing of the Anglo-French troops we have had three engagements with them. The first was at Alma on 8 September in which the enemy attacked and defeated us; the second was Liprandi's action on 13 September in which we attacked and were victorious, and the third was Dannenberg's terrible action in which we attacked again and were beaten again. It was a treacherous, revolting business. The 10th and 11th divisions attacked the enemy's left flank, drove them back and spiked thirty-seven guns. Then the enemy put forward 6,000 riflemen – only 6,000 against 30,000 – and we retreated, having lost about 6,000 brave men. And we had to retreat, because half our troops had no artillery owing to the roads being impassable, and – God knows why – there were no rifle battalions. Terrible slaughter! It will weigh heavy on the souls of many people! Lord, forgive them. The news of this action has produced a sensation. I've seen old men who wept aloud and young men who swore to kill Dannenberg. Great is the moral strength of the Russian people. Many political truths will emerge and evolve in the present difficult days for Russia. The feeling of ardent patriotism that has arisen and issued forth from Russia's misfortunes will long leave its traces on her. These people who are now sacrificing their lives will be citizens of Russia and will not forget their sacrifice. They will take part in public affairs with dignity and pride, and the enthusiasm aroused in them by the war will stamp on them for ever the quality of self-sacrifice and nobility.

Among the useless sacrifices of that unfortunate action were Soymonov and Komstadius, who were killed. It is said of the first that he was one of the few honest and intelligent generals in the Russian army. The second I knew quite well: he was a member of our society and a would-be editor of our journal. His death more than anything else has impelled me to ask to go to Sevastopol. He made me feel somehow ashamed.

English ships continue to blockade Odessa. The sea, unfortunately, is calm. It is said that there was an action on the 27th – again indecisive – and that on the 3rd there will be an assault. I can't get there before the 5th, but I have a feeling that I still won't be too late.

3 November   In Odessa I was told of a touching incident. The adjutant to the general in charge went to the hospital at N, where the wounded men of the 4th corps from the Crimea were lying. 'The Commander-in-Chief Prince Gorchakov', he said to them, 'has instructed me to thank you for your brave service and to find out . . .' – 'Hurrah!' resounded feeble voices, one after another, from all the beds. A great and wonderful reward for Gorchakov for his efforts! Better than a portrait round the neck.[39]

The pilot on the ferry-boat at Nikolayev told me that on the 26th there had been an action in which Khomutov distinguished himself and allegedly captured a great number of prisoners and guns, but that of our 8,000 men only 2,000 returned on the 26th. An officer in Nikolayev confirmed these rumours. Nakhimov and Liprandi are said to have been wounded. The enemy have received reinforcements and are settling down in winter quarters. God knows what is true. The pilot also told me a story about a Cossack who caught a young English prince with a lassoo and took him to Menshikov. The young prince fired his pistol at the Cossack. 'Hey, don't shoot,' said the Cossack. The prince fired again and again missed. 'Hey, don't fool about,' said the Cossack. The prince fired a third time (these things are always done three times) and missed. Then the Cossack began to flog him with his whip. When the prince complained to Menshikov that the Cossack had beaten him, the Cossack said that he was teaching him to shoot: if he were a commander and couldn't shoot straight, the Cossacks would disown him. Menshikov laughed. Generally speaking one hears more talk among the people about the English than about the French.

4, 5 November (en route *from Odessa to Sevastopol*)   In Nikolayev I couldn't see a thing. I won't write down the rumours because they all turned out to be nonsense. Since the 24th nothing has been undertaken except siege works.

I was taken by boat from Kherson to Oleshko. The pilot told us about the transport of the soldiers: how a soldier lay down in the pouring rain on the wet bottom of the boat and fell asleep; how an officer beat a soldier for scratching himself; and how a soldier shot himself during the crossing for fear of having overstayed his leave by two days and how he was thrown overboard without burial. Now the boatmen try to frighten one another as they pass the place on the river where the soldier was thrown overboard. 'What was his company?' they shout.

At Oleshko I was detained for the night by a pretty and intelligent Cossack girl whom I kissed and fondled through a window. She came to me during the night. [. . .][40] I would have pleasanter memories if I had stayed at the window. [. . .]

Saw some French and English prisoners but didn't manage to talk to them. The mere appearance of these people and the way they walk somehow filled me with the sad conviction that they are far superior to our troops. However, I only had for comparison some army transport men who were escorting them.

The driver who brought me here said that on the 24th we should have completely overcome the English had it not been for treachery.[41] It's sad and ridiculous. 'The other day,' he said, 'they brought an iron coach and six, probably meant for Menshikov.' I also met some of our own wounded, a splendid lot; they are sorry for their commanders and say that they advanced to attack several times but couldn't hold on because their left 'flank' had been turned; they are glad to seize on to an unknown and therefore for them very significant word, in order to explain their failure. It would be too sad for them to believe in treachery.

11 November, Sevastopol I arrived on the 7th. All the rumours that tormented me on the way have proved to be nonsense. I'm attached to the 3rd light battery and live in the town itself. I've seen all our fortifications from a distance, and some nearby. To take Sevastopol is quite impossible – even the enemy are convinced of that, it seems – and in my opinion they are covering their retreat. The storm on 2 November put up to thirty vessels out of action – a sailing ship and three steamers. The company of the artillery officers in this brigade is the same as everywhere else. There is one person, very like Louisa Volkonskaya – I know that I'll soon get tired of him and so I try to see him as little as possible so that that impression will last longer. Of the commanders here, Nakhimov, Totleben and Istomin appear to be decent people. Menshikov seems to me to be a good commander-in-chief, but unfortunately he began his military career with inferior forces against an enemy three times as strong and better armed.

The troops on both sides had never been under fire, and so the numerical superiority was ten times more noticeable. Troops who have never been under fire can't *retreat*; they run away.

20 November

When shall I cease at last to lead a life without purpose or passion, or to feel a deep wound in my heart and know no means of healing it? God alone knows who inflicted this wound, but from birth I've been tormented by the bitter pledge of future nothingness, by wearisome grief and doubt.[42]   Simferopol

23 November, Eski-Orda[43]

On the 16th I left Sevastopol for our position. On the journey I became more convinced than before that Russia must either fall or be completely transformed. Everything is topsy-turvy. The enemy are not prevented from reinforcing their camps, although this would have been very easy, while we, with inferior forces, with no expectation of help from anywhere, with generals like Gorchakov who have lost their senses and feelings and energy and without reinforcing ourselves, stand facing the enemy and wait for the storms and bad weather which Nicholas the Miracle-Worker will send to drive the enemy away. The Cossacks want to plunder but not to fight; the hussars and uhlans suppose military worth to consist of drunkenness and debauchery, and the infantry – of robbery and making money. A sad state of affairs for the army and the country.

I spent a couple of hours chatting with French and English wounded. Every soldier is proud of his position and respects himself, for he feels himself to be an effective spring in the army machine. Good weapons and the skill to use them, youth, and general ideas about politics and the arts give them an awareness of their own worth. With us, stupid foot and arms drills, useless weapons, oppression, age, lack of education, and bad food and keep destroy the men's last spark of pride, and even give them too high an opinion of the enemy.

In Simferopol I lost all my money at cards, and I'm now living with the battery in a Tartar village and only now experiencing the discomforts of life.

26 November

I'm living a carefree life, not forcing or restraining myself in anything; I go out shooting, listen, observe and argue. One thing is bad: I'm beginning to put myself, or to wish to put myself, above my comrades and they no longer like me so much. Here is some almost reliable news from Sevastopol. On the 13th there was a sortie against the enemy trenches opposite the 3rd, 4th and 5th bastions. The Yekaterinburg regiment took the trench opposite the 4th bastion by surprise, drove out and killed the enemy and withdrew with the loss of three men wounded. The officer commanding that detachment was presented to the Grand Duke Nikolay Nikolayevich. 'So you were the hero of this action?' the Grand Duke said to him. 'Tell me what it was like.' 'When I left the bastion and began to approach the trench the soldiers stopped and didn't want to go on.' 'You can't mean it,' said the Grand Duke and walked away from him. 'You ought to be ashamed,' remarked Filosofov to him. 'Clear off!' concluded Menshikov. I'm sure the officer wasn't lying, and I'm sorry he wasn't more outspoken.

The sortie from the 3rd bastion was unsuccessful. The officer, on seeing the sentries, returned to the Admiral for instructions and gave the enemy time to prepare. I don't know any details about the sortie from the 5th bastion. On the whole this news is not entirely trustworthy, but it's more probable than the wild rumours about the capture of some thirty guns.

Liprandi has been appointed commander of the troops in Sevastopol. Thank God! Apart from the successes he has had in this campaign, he is well loved and popular – popular not for his foul language, but for his efficiency and intelligence. For good or ill, but to my great annoyance, lack of money keeps me here; otherwise I would now be on the south coast at Eupatoria or would have returned to Sevastopol.

7 December On the 5th I went to Sevastopol with a platoon of soldiers to fetch some guns. There is much new. And all of it encouraging. Saken's presence is apparent in everything. And not so much Saken's presence as the presence of a new commander-in-chief who isn't tired out, doesn't change his mind too much and isn't yet the prisoner of conjectures and expectations. Saken, as far as he can, spurs on his troops to make sorties (I say as far as he can, for only Menshikov can really spur them on by giving them immediate rewards – which he fails to do). Recommendations which come out three months later really mean nothing to a man awaiting death at any moment. But man is so foolishly constituted that while awaiting death he expects and loves rewards. Saken has built little trenches in front of the bastion. God knows whether it's a good plan or not, but it shows energy. It is said that one such little trench of eight men has been captured[?],[44] but the main thing is that to fetch the wounded from a trench during the day, others have to risk being wounded. These trenches are not connected with the bastions, and are further away from them than they are from the enemy's works. Saken has organized a system for removing the wounded and has set up ambulance stations at all the bastions. Saken has had music played.

It's wonderful how beautiful Sevastopol is. Two days ago I was extremely sad. I spent a couple of hours in a hospital ward for the allied wounded. Most of them had been struck off – dead or recovered – but the rest were convalescing. I found some five of them round an iron stove. French, English and Russians were laughing, chatting and playing cards, each one speaking his own language, and only the warders spoke some kind of strange jargon in their attempt to accommodate themselves to the foreign languages. [. . .] When I went down to the shore the sun was already setting behind the English batteries, puffs of smoke were rising here and there and shots could be heard, the sea was calm and small boats and dinghies were scudding past the huge masses of ships; on the Grafskaya pier music was playing, and the sounds of trumpets and a familiar tune drifted across; Golitsyn and some other gentlemen were standing by the embankment leaning on the rails. It was wonderful! [. . .]

It seems I shall soon be leaving. I can't say whether I want to or not.

1855

23 January, Position on the river Belbek[1]   I lived for more than a month in Eski-Orda, near Simferopol. It seemed dull, but now I look back on that life with regret. But then there's good reason to regret the 14th brigade when you're in the 11th. I've never seen a better brigade in the artillery than the former, or a worse one than the latter. Filimonov, in whose battery I am, is the dirtiest creature you could imagine. Odakhovsky, the senior officer, is a nasty mean little Pole, and the other officers are under their influence and lack a sense of direction. And I'm tied to, and even dependent on these people! I've been to Sevastopol, got some money, talked with Totleben, walked to the 4th bastion and played cards. I'm very dissatisfied with myself. I must go to the baths tomorrow. I must copy out my plan for the rifle battalions[2] and write a memorandum.

28 January   Played *shtoss* for two days and nights. The result is understandable – the loss of everything – the Yasnaya Polyana house.[3] I think there's no point in writing – I'm so disgusted with myself that I'd like to forget about my existence. They say that Persia has declared war on Turkey and that peace is bound to be concluded.

3, 4, 5 February   I've been to Sevastopol. Showed my plan to Kashinsky. He seemed displeased. Didn't manage to call on Krasnokutsky, who had called on me when I was out. The fleet[4] has assembled; something is under way. There's been action at Eupatoria[5] – I asked to be sent there, but in vain.

6, 7, 8 February   Played cards again and lost another 200 roubles. I can't promise to stop. I'd like to win everything back, but could get terribly embroiled. I want to win back the whole 2,000. It's impossible, but nothing could be easier than to lose another 400, and then what? It's terribly bad – not to mention the waste of health and time. Tomorrow I'll ask Odakhovsky for another game and that will be the last time. Translated a ballad of Heine's[6] and read *The Misfortune of Being Clever*. I must write tomorrow without fail, and write a lot.

12 February   Lost seventy-five roubles again. God is still merciful to me in that there has been no unpleasantness, but what will happen later? My only hope is in Him! A bad business at Eupatoria – an attack repulsed, which is being called a reconnaissance. Time, time, youth, dreams, thoughts – everything is being lost without trace. I'm squandering my life, not living. My losses are forcing me to come to my senses a bit.

14 February [. . .] The thought of retirement or of the Military Academy occurs to me more and more often. I've written to Stolypin to try and get myself transferred to Kishinyov. From there I could arrange one of these two things.

1 March Annenkov has been put in charge of the commissariat of both armies. Gorchakov has replaced Menshikov. Thank God! The Emperor died on 18 February and we've been taking the oath of allegiance to the new Emperor today. Great changes are in store for Russia. One must work hard and be brave to share in these important moments of Russia's life.

2, 3, 4 March These last few days I've twice worked for several hours at a time on my plan for reorganizing the army.[7] It's making slow progress, but I'm not giving up the idea. I took communion today. Yesterday a conversation about divinity and faith inspired me with a great idea, a stupendous idea, to the realization of which I feel capable of devoting my life. This idea is the founding of a new religion appropriate to the stage of development of mankind – the religion of Christ, but purged of beliefs and mysticism, a practical religion, not promising future bliss but giving bliss on earth. I realize that this idea can only be implemented by generations of people consciously working towards this end. One generation will bequeath the idea to the next, and some day reason or fanaticism will implement it. *Consciously* to work towards the union of mankind by religion is the basis of the idea which I hope will absorb me.

6, 7, 8, 9, 10, 11 March I've lost another 200 roubles to Odakhovsky, so that I've reached the ultimate extremes of embarrassment. Gorchakov has arrived with the whole staff: I've been to see him and was well received, but there is no news of a transfer to the Staff, which I very much desire. I won't ask, but I'll wait for him to do it himself, or for my aunt to write a letter. Was weak enough to allow Stolypin to induce me to take part in a sortie,[8] although I'm not only glad of it now, but regret not having gone with the assault column. In general this trip from the 9th to the 11th has been full of interesting events. Bronevsky is one of the nicest people I've ever met. A military career is not for me, and the sooner I get out of it to devote myself fully to a literary one the better.

12 March Wrote about a sheet of *Youth* in the morning, then played knucklebones and chatted with Bronevsky. We have a plan to set up a boarding-house.[9] He fully shares this good idea.

13 March   Got on with *Youth* and wrote a letter to Tatyana Alexandrovna. The plan for the boarding-house is taking shape. I've failed in so many things that in order to accomplish this one I'll work steadily, diligently and with care.

18 March   [. . .] My vocation, as far as I can understand from ten years' experience, is not practical activity, and so estate management is least of all compatible with my bent. Today the idea occurred to me of renting out my property to my brother-in-law. In that way I should attain three aims: I should free myself from the cares of estate management and the habits of my youth, impose limits on myself, and free myself of my debts. Today I wrote about a sheet of *Youth*.

20 March   For two days I've written absolutely nothing except the rough draft of a letter to Valeryan and two letters to Nekrasov. One is an answer to a letter received from him today in which he asks me to send him some articles about the war. I'll have to write them myself. I'll describe Sevastopol in various phases, and write an idyll of the officers' way of life.

21 March   I've done nothing. Received a delightful letter from Masha in which she describes how she made Turgenev's acquaintance.[10] A dear, wonderful letter elevating me in my own opinion and rousing me to action. But I've been morally and physically ill all day today. On the 24th we're going to Sevastopol.

27 March   The first day of Easter. Went to Sevastopol the day before yesterday; the trip was somehow particularly pleasant and successful. [. . .] Most pleasant of all for me was to read the reviews in the journals, very flattering reviews, of *Notes of a Billiard-Marker*. It's gratifying and useful because, by inflaming my vanity, it rouses me to activity. Unfortunately I don't yet see any sign of the latter — for five days or so I haven't written a line of *Youth*, although I've started writing *Sevastopol by Day and Night*,[11] and I haven't yet got down to answering the nice letters — two from Nekrasov, and one each from Valeryan, Masha, Nikolenka and Auntie. I've been offered through Neverezhky the post of senior adjutant, and after some hard thinking have accepted it — I don't know what will come of it.[12] Turgenev says quite rightly that we writers need to occupy ourselves with some one thing, and I'll be better able to occupy myself with literature in that position than in any other. I'll suppress my vanity — my desire for promotion and crosses – very foolish vanity, especially for a man who has already found his career. [. . .]

2 April   Yesterday the battery arrived. I'm living in Sevastopol. Our losses already amount to five thousand, but we're holding out not merely well, but in such a way that our defence must clearly prove to the enemy the impossibility of ever taking Sevastopol. Wrote two pages of *Sevastopol* in the evening.

3, 4, 5, 6, 7 April, morning   All these days I've been so occupied with what has been happening and partly with my duties that I haven't had time yet to write anything except for one incoherent page of *Youth*. Since the 4th the bombardment has eased up, but it still continues. The day before yesterday I spent the night in the 4th bastion.[13] From time to time a ship fires on the town. Yesterday a shell fell near a boy and a girl who were playing horses in the street: they put their arms round each other and fell down together. The girl is the daughter of a sailor's wife. Every day she has been coming to my quarters under a hail of shells and bombs. My cold is so terrible that I can't settle down to anything.

11 April, 4th Bastion   I've written very, very little of *Youth* or *Sevastopol* in recent days; my cold and feverish condition were the reason for this. Moreover, I'm irritated – especially now when I'm ill – by the fact that it doesn't occur to anybody that I'm good for anything except *chair à canon* [cannon fodder], and the most useless kind at that. I want to fall in love again with a nurse I saw at the dressing station.

12 April, 4th Bastion   Got on with *Sevastopol by Day and Night* and, I think, it's not bad, and I hope to finish it tomorrow. What a wonderful spirit there is among the sailors! How much superior they are to our soldiers! My lads are a nice lot too, and I enjoy being with them. Yesterday there was another explosion at the 5th battalion: the firing seems to have increased on our side and to have decreased on theirs.

13 April   Still the same 4th bastion, which I'm beginning to like very much. I'm writing quite a lot. Finished *Sevastopol by Day and Night* today, and wrote a bit of *Youth*. The constant charm of danger and my observations of the soldiers I'm living with, the sailors and the very methods of war are so pleasant that I don't want to leave here, especially as I would like to be present at the assault, if there is one.

14 April   Still at the same 4th bastion, where I feel splendid. Finished a chapter of *Youth* yesterday, and it's not at all bad. Generally speaking my work on *Youth* will lure me on now by the attraction of work begun and nearly half finished. Today I want to write the chapter 'The Haymaking', begin revising *Sevastopol* and begin the soldier's story of how he was hit. [. . .]

21 April　Seven days in which I've done absolutely nothing except for two rewritten sheets of *Sevastopol* and a proposed address.[14] The day before yesterday we were driven out of the lodgements opposite the 5th bastion, and driven out shamefully. Morale gets lower every day, and the thought of the possibility of the capture of Sevastopol is beginning to become apparent in many ways.

19 May, Position on the river Belbek　On 15 May I was appointed commander of a mountain platoon and moved to a camp on the Belbek, twenty *versts* from Sevastopol. There's a lot to do; I want to attend to the commissariat myself and I see how easy it is to steal – so easy that it's impossible not to steal. I have many plans with regard to this thieving, but I don't know what will come of them. The countryside is delightful, but it's hot. I've done nothing all this time.

31 May　On the 26th Selenginsky, Volynsky and Kamchatsky redoubts were captured. I was in Sevastopol the next day and I'm convinced that it won't fall. My command causes me a good deal of trouble, especially the financial accounts. I'm definitely not capable of practical activity; or if I am capable, then it's only with a great effort, which isn't worth making since my career is not to be a practical one. [. . .]

31 May　11 p.m. Finished reading *Faust* in the morning. [. . .]

2 June　Got up late. Succumbed to the effect of the sores, *and did nothing* except for reading *Henri Esmond*.[15] Went to see the doctor, who tried to reassure me, but didn't succeed.

8, 9 June　Laziness, laziness. Health bad. Reading *Vanity Fair* all day. [. . .]

11 June　[. . .] It's absurd that having started writing rules at fifteen I should still be doing so at thirty, without having trusted in or followed a single one, but still for some reason believing in them and wanting them. Rules should be moral and practical. Here are practical ones, without which there can be no happiness: moderation and acquisition. *Money*.

12, 13, 14, 15 June　Spent two days drilling, went to Bakhchisaray yesterday and received a letter and my article[16] from Panayev. I was flattered that it has been read to the Emperor. My service in Russia is beginning to infuriate me, as it did in the Caucasus. *Laziness*. Vanity, telling Stolypin about my article, and irritability, hitting men at drill. My health gets worse and worse and I think salivation is starting. It's amazing how loathsome I am, how altogether unhappy and repulsive to myself.

18 June Finished *Notes of a Cadet*,[17] wrote a letter and sent it off. After dinner I lazed about and read *Pendennis*.[18] [. . .]

24 June I'm making it a rule when writing to draw up a programme, make a rough draft and a fair copy, but not give a final polish to each section. If you read a thing too often, you make incorrect and unfavourable judgements, the charm and interest of novelty and surprise disappear, and you often strike out what is good and only seems bad from frequent repetition. But the main thing is that with this method you retain enthusiasm for the work. Worked the whole day and can't reproach myself with anything. Hurrah!

26 June Finished *A Spring Night*;[19] it doesn't seem as good now as it did before. Can't reproach myself with anything.

27 June, Bakhchisaray Went to Bakhchisaray and read *A Spring Night* to Kovalevsky, who was very pleased with it. [. . .]

30 June, Position on the river Belbek. 28 June. Use of the day. Left Bakhchisaray early in the morning, reached my lodgings, had something to eat, gave some orders, wrote a bit of the Diary and set off for Sevastopol. At Inkerman I gave some money to Yelchaninov, visited the Staff officers, who are becoming more and more repulsive to me, and finally reached Sevastopol. My first encounter was with a shell which burst between the Nikolayevskaya battery and the Grafskaya pier (next day bullets were found near the library). The second was the news that Nakhimov is mortally wounded. Bronevsky, Meshchersky and Kaloshin are all nice and are fond of me. On the way back next day, 29 June, – the morning of which I spent partly in the officers' battery and partly with Meshchersky – I came across Baron Ferzen at Inkerman and was awfully glad. I really am, I think, beginning to acquire a reputation in Petersburg. The Emperor has ordered *Sevastopol in December* to be translated into French. [. . .]

6 July I hope that today is the last day of the idleness in which I've spent the whole week. All today I've been reading a stupid novel by Balzac[20] and have only just taken up my pen. *Thoughts:* Write the diary of an officer in

Sevastopol[21] – various aspects, phases and moments of military life – and publish it in some newspaper. I'm thinking of settling on this idea; although my chief occupation must be *Youth* and *Early Manhood*, the other would be for money, practice in style, and variety. *Reproaches*: (1) Laziness (2) Irritability.

8 July   Health very bad, and I can't work. I've done absolutely nothing. I need to accumulate money (1) to pay my debts, (2) to redeem my estate and have the opportunity to free my peasants. I'll copy out rules for play, but only as a means of cutting my losses when I have to play, not of winning. As for the surplus left over from my command of the unit, I'll certainly take it and not tell anyone about it. If I'm asked, I'll say that I took it; I know that it's honest. [. . .]

12 July   Wrote nothing all day, read Balzac and have been solely occupied with the new chest.[22] I've decided that I'll keep no government money at all. I'm even surprised how the idea could have occurred to me of even taking what was completely surplus. [. . .]

17 July   Health worse. Did nothing. *Three rules*: (1) Be what I am: (*a*) a writer by aptitude. (*b*) an aristocrat by birth. (2) Never speak ill of anyone, and (3) Be economical with money.

2 August   In conversation with Stolypin today about serfdom in Russia, the idea occurred to me more clearly than ever before of writing my four stages in the history of a Russian landowner,[23] with myself as the hero in Khabarovka. The main idea of the novel should be the impossibility of an educated landowner in our times living a just life while serfdom exists. All its miseries should be exposed, and the means of remedying them indicated.

7 August, Position on the river Belbek   I've been to Inkerman and Sevastopol. Won 100 roubles from Odakhovsky and am quits with everyone in the Crimea. Sold Mashtak.[24] Was in good spirits. Decided from today to live only on my pay. I'll play with the money I get from home, and if I lose, then *nec plus ultra* [at the very most] 960 roubles. All that is owed to me and all I receive will be added to the capital I'm accumulating, also what is left from the unit, also everything I win. So far there is only 200 from Rosen. I've behaved well.

25 August   I've just been looking at the sky. A wonderful night. O God, have mercy upon me. I am a bad man. Grant that I may be good and happy. Lord have mercy. The stars are in the sky. A bombardment in Sevastopol, music in the camp. I've done no good; on the contrary I won some money from Korsakov. I've been to Simferopol.

2 September Haven't written my diary for a week. Lost a clean 1500 roubles. Sevastopol has surrendered; I was there on my birthday. Worked well today putting my description together.[25] I owe Rosen 300 roubles and lied to him.

17 September Received news yesterday that *A Night* has been mutilated and published.[26] It seems that the *Blues*[27] have got their eyes on me. It's because of my articles. But I wish Russia could always have such moral writers. I can't be a sickly-sweet one, though, and I can't write empty nothings, without ideas and above all without any aim. Despite a first moment of anger when I vowed never again to take up a pen, literature must be my chief and only occupation, taking precedence over all other inclinations and occupations. My aim is literary fame. And the good I can do by my works. Tomorrow I'll go to Karalez[28] and ask for my discharge, and in the morning I'll get on with *Youth*. [. . .]

19 September, Kermenchik [29] I've moved to Kermenchik; I'm staying with a *secret agent* – a spy. Very interesting. As for women, there seems to be no hope. Wrote a little of *Sevastopol in August*. Did no good to anyone, and no evil. I need at all costs to win fame. I want to publish *Youth* myself. I'll go to the south coast, get some money and apply to return home.

20 September Lots of pretty girls, and sensuality is tormenting me. [. . .]

21 September I'll come to grief if I don't reform. Given my character, education, circumstances and abilities, there is no middle course for me – either a brilliant or a wretched future. All my strength of character must go into reform. My chief vices: (1) lack of character – non-fulfilment of plans. Means of reform: (1) to know my general aim, and (2) to think about and note down my future activities and carry them out even if they are bad. My aims: (1) the good of my neighbour and (2) organizing myself in such a way as to be able to do this. At the present moment the second is more important than the first, so I must remember all the plans I've made, even if they are contrary to the first general aim. I must prescribe certain actions in advance, at first as few and as easy as possible, and above all ones that don't contradict each other.

My chief aim in life is the good of my neighbour, and its contingent aims – literary fame, based on usefulness and the good of my neighbour; wealth, based on work useful to my neighbour, capital turnover and play, and all devoted towards goodness; and fame in the service, based on usefulness to the country. I'll analyse in my diary what I've done each day to achieve these four aims, and how often I've failed to accomplish what I planned.

Tomorrow, for the first aim, I'll write letters to my aunts and my brother

Dmitry, and inquire about the men's food, health and accommodation; for the second I'll draft the plan of an article and write it (or else *Youth*) or as well as *Youth*; for the third I'll do the accounts and write to my headman, and for the fourth I'll study the locality.

23 September   Wrote a letter to Aunt Pelageya Ilinichna, gave advice and promised the Greeks help,[30] which I'll give. For the second aim I drafted the plan of *Sevastopol in August*; for the third, wrote to my headman; for the fourth, rode to our station. Didn't write *Youth*, didn't bother about the men and didn't do the accounts. [. . .]

10 October   I've been in a lazily apathetic, perpetually dissatisfied state for a long time now. Won another 130 roubles at cards. Bought a horse and bridle for 150. What nonsense! My career is literature – to write and write! From tomorrow I'll work all my life or throw up everything – rules, religion, propriety – everything.

21 November   I'm in Petersburg, at Turgenev's.[31] Lost 2800 before leaving, and only just managed to transfer 600 to my debtors. Picked up 875 roubles in the country. It's most important for me to behave myself well here. For that the main thing I need is: (1) to deal cautiously but boldly with people who can harm me, (2) to manage my expenses carefully and (3) to work. Tomorrow I'll get on with *Youth* and write a bit of the diary.[32]

1856–1862

THE YEARS BETWEEN Tolstoy's release from the army in 1856 and his marriage in the autumn of 1862 were difficult and unsettling ones as he sought to convince himself that he had the potential to become a great writer in spite of some evidence to the contrary. On his arrival in Petersburg he stayed first of all with Turgenev, and soon made the acquaintance of Nekrasov, Goncharov and many other established men of letters, throwing himself wholeheartedly into the life of the capital and frequenting its 'lower depths' no less eagerly than its more refined literary salons. The year 1856 was a remarkable one for him as a fledgling author, and saw the publication of five new stories. *Sevastopol in August* and *Meeting a Moscow Acquaintance in the Detachment* drew again on his Crimean experiences. *A Landowner's Morning* was based on his unsuccessful project to free his Yasnaya Polyana serfs. The light-hearted, anecdotal *Two Hussars* entertainingly exploited the 'fathers and sons' theme, while *The Snow-storm* drew on an incident which happened to Tolstoy while returning home from the Caucasus. The year 1856 was important for personal reasons too and, as was so often the case with Tolstoy, they eventually found their reflection in his novels and stories. First his brother Dmitry, a victim of tuberculosis who had rescued a woman from a brothel and taken her to live with him, died a painful and sordid death – as Levin's brother was later to do in *Anna Karenina*. Then Tolstoy's head was turned by Valeriya Arseneva, the daughter of a neighbouring landowner, an infatuation which led to many meetings and a lengthy correspondence in which Tolstoy adopted a pedagogical rather than an amorous tone and did not conceal from his prospective fiancée the fact that she fell short of his ideal. His affections soon cooled and the relationship had ended by the beginning of 1857, but it had been important in establishing Tolstoy's ideal of marriage in his own mind, and it provided the basis of his story *Family Happiness* (published in 1859).

In 1857 Tolstoy paid his first visit to Western Europe, and spent six months in France, Switzerland and Germany. Paris at first made a favourable impression on him, but after witnessing a public execution, he left hastily and in disgust for Switzerland. From Clarens on Lake Geneva he made many excursions into the mountains, and spent much time with his relation Countess Alexandra Tolstaya, for whom he cherished a deep affection and with whom he maintained a voluminous correspondence for many years. In Germany he lost heavily on the roulette table at Baden-Baden, but found time also to admire the Dresden art gallery. While abroad he worked intermittently on several stories of a topical nature, of which the tendentious and undistinguished *Lucerne* and *Albert* were published in 1857 and 1858 respectively without success.

When Tolstoy returned to Yasnaya Polyana in the late summer of 1857 he turned his attention energetically to the administration and reform of his estates. Farming and a growing interest in education were responsible for a further retreat from literature, and the school which he founded for the peasant children of Yasnaya Polyana was to occupy him on and off for the next three or four years. He published no works of fiction between 1859 and 1863, but his experience as a teacher bore fruit in his educational journal *Yasnaya Polyana*, of which twelve issues appeared in all, with contributions by himself, his teachers and his pupils.

As a direct result of this increasing interest in educational theory and practice, Tolstoy paid a second visit to Western Europe from July 1860 to April 1861. In Germany he studied modern educational methods and met Froebel's nephew. He revisited France, where he was deeply moved by the death of his eldest brother Nikolay from the illness which had killed Dmitry, and which Tolstoy feared would afflict him in turn. In Paris he spent many hours travelling on omnibuses, amusing himself by observing his fellow passengers. A fortnight in Florence was made more agreeable by the presence there of Alexandra Tolstaya. In February 1861 he paid his one and only visit to England, where, suffering acutely from toothache, he visited schools and museums, heard Dickens lecture on education and tried to understand Palmerston speaking in the House of Commons. In London he met Herzen and in Brussels Proudhon. On his return to Russia he resumed teaching at the Yasnaya Polyana school and was also appointed an Arbiter of the Peace. The authorities, however, viewed his educational activities with suspicion, and when the police raided his estate during his absence in 1862 and searched the premises for two days he was impelled to write a vehement and indignant letter of protest to the Emperor Alexander II himself.

Tolstoy's personal life during the years 1856–62 was overshadowed by the deaths of two of his three brothers, the divorce of his sister and a bitter quarrel with Turgenev which narrowly avoided ending in a duel. It was also marked by a number of tentative love affairs with women of his own class, casual relationships with prostitutes and a passionate liaison with a married serf who bore him a son. In the late summer of 1862, however, he fell in love with Sofya Behrs, the daughter of a Moscow physician and of a childhood friend of Tolstoy's, and after a very short engagement they were married in Moscow in September 1862. After his marriage Tolstoy continued his teaching for a while, but with less enthusiasm than before.

For the first time after a break of three years he resumed his literary activities. He revised and published in 1863 the long unfinished story *The Cossacks*, conceived and born in the Caucasus in 1852 and written intermittently over the intervening period. He quickly completed *Polikushka*, the first of his stories to have a peasant as its central figure, and began work on the first drafts of what was to become *War and Peace*. With the birth in the same year of the first of his thirteen (legitimate) children, his life now took on the pattern which it was to retain until well after the completion of his longest and greatest novel.

1856

9, 10 January   I'm in Oryol. My brother Dmitry is at death's door. How the evil thoughts I used to have about him have crumbled to dust.

2 February   I'm in Petersburg. My brother Dmitry is dead; I learned about it today.[1] From tomorrow I want to spend my days in such a way that it will be pleasant to recall them. Tomorrow I'll put my papers in order, write to Pelageya Ilinichna and to the headman, do a fair copy of *The Snow-storm*, have dinner at the Chess Club and go on copying *The Snow-storm*; in the evening I'll call on Turgenev[2] and in the morning I'll walk for an hour. [...]

7 February   Quarrelled with Turgenev,[3] and had a wench at my place.

10 February   Wrote little yesterday. Gymnastics takes up a great deal of time. Was stupid enough to agree to go to the theatre; went to Krayevsky's.[4]

11, 12 February   Finished *The Snow-storm*. I'm very pleased with it.

13, 14, 15, 16, 17, 18, 19 February   Did nothing. Went for a walk today and enjoyed seeing the crowd round the booths and studied the character of a Russian crowd listening to a speaker. Had dinner at Turgenev's; we've made it up again. Evening at Gordeyev's – *demi-monde*. My girl Peyker is extremely gifted; she laughs well, but in an affected way. Another one has an excellent voice, but uses too much vibrato. Volkonskaya wants to be in love, but she thinks she wants someone to fall in love with her. Tomorrow I'll work for six hours and promise myself not to go to sleep till I've done so. First I'll write *Yepishka* or *The Fugitive*. Then the comedy,[5] then *Youth*.

12 March   Haven't written my diary for a long time and have been in a fog for some three weeks now. Besides, I'm unwell. The plan for my comedy wearies me. Peace has been concluded. I think I've parted with Turgenev for good. Sazonova came and filled me with inexpressible disgust. I've thought up a story, *Father and Son*.[6]

21 March   The day before yesterday I accidentally read Longinov's letter and have sent him a challenge.[7] God knows what will come of it, but I'll be firm and resolute. On the whole this business has had a good influence on me. I'm making up my mind to go to the country, get married as soon as possible and not write any more under my own name. But the main thing is always to be cautious and reticent with everyone in conversation. [. . .]

4 April One of the chief evils which grow worse with time in every conceivable manifestation is belief in the past. Geological and historical revolutions are essential. Why build a house in 1856 with Grecian columns which support nothing?

19 April I've finished *Father and Son*, even the corrections, and on Nekrasov's advice have called it *Two Hussars* – that's better. I've put my papers in order and want to settle down to a serious work, *Punishments in the Army*.[8] [. . .]

21 April Behaved disgustingly after dinner with Nekrasov, roamed up and down the Nevsky and ended up at the baths. It's terrible! But it's the last time for sure. It's not passion, it's debauchery as a habit. I set myself the rule not to drink more than half a glass of vodka, a glass of strong wine or a tumbler of light wine.

22 April I'm not writing anything. My attitude to the serfs is beginning to trouble me greatly. I feel the need to learn, learn and learn.

23 April Called on Medem in the morning. Dinner at Bludov's. Evening at Kavelin's.[9] A delightful mind and temperament. The question of the serfs is becoming clearer. I came back from his place, cheerful, hopeful and happy. I'll go to the country with a project ready written.

25 April [. . .] Wrote down for myself a draft project and memorandum.[10] Paid a pleasant visit to Turgenev. Must invite him for dinner tomorrow.

5 May Dinner at Turgenev's, at which I was foolishly offended by a verse of Nekrasov and said unpleasant things to everyone. Turgenev has gone. I'm sad, especially as I'm not writing anything.

8 May Learned yesterday that my leave won't be granted for a very long time.[11] Dined at Bludov's. Dull. Went to the islands with Shevich. Pleasant. Spent the evening at Obolensky's with Aksakov, I. Kireyevsky and other Slavophiles.[12] [. . .] Their aims, like those of any intellectually active people brought together by means of discussions and polemics, have changed considerably, broadened and become based on serious truths such as family life, the commune and Orthodoxy. But they discredit them by the bitterness with which they express their views, as though expecting them to be contradicted. More calmness and *Würde* [dignity] would be more profitable. That is especially so with regard to Orthodoxy, first because, while recognizing the justice of their opinion about the importance of the part this element plays in the life of the people, one cannot help also recognizing, from a higher standpoint, the monstrosity of its expression and its historical bankruptcy, and secondly because the censorship stops their opponents' mouths.

The day before yesterday I called on Nikolay Milyutin. He promised to take me to see Lyovshin.[13]

11 May Yesterday morning I wrote a letter to Tatyana Alexandrovna, and the memorandum. At 2 o'clock I called at the Ministry of Internal Affairs. Lyovshin gave me a chilly reception. Whatever you turn your hand to now in Russia, everything is in a state of change; but the people are old, and therefore unfitted to make changes. Dined at Shevich's, wrote my project at Nekrasov's and sent it off. Vile music at Shostak's in the evening; supper at Dusseau's and on to a brothel. Restrained myself.

12 May [...] Dined at Nekrasov's. Fet[14] is a dear, and wonderfully talented. I enjoyed myself. Spent the evening with the Tolstoys[15] and read *The Two Hussars*. Maltsova[16] was there – a nice, but somehow ridiculous woman with the ingenuous naiveté of a thirty-five-year-old, wrinkles like an old woman and curls. On my return home I found a note from Vaska and Apoloshka[17] and was awfully glad, like a man in love. Everything seemed to brighten up. Yes, the best way to true happiness in life is to have no rules, but to throw out from yourself in all directions like a spider a prehensile web of love and catch in it everything that comes along – an old lady, a child, a woman or a policeman.

13 May Got up at 9. Went to gymnastics. It was dull without friends. Read *The Naval Miscellany*. I could have slapped Pogodin's face with pleasure. Base flattery, seasoned with Slavophilism.[18] A new trick. All these Moscow celebrations – what an un-Russian feature. Lyovshin said he had reported to the Minister, but all the same his reply was *évasif*. I'll write the project, despite that. Dined at Kokorev's.[19] Cabbage soup, fermented milk, champagne and a gold salt-cellar in the Russian style. Barbarity, tastelessness and obscurity. Kokorev's article is clever, but shameful; he touches on all our economic wounds superficially. Called on M. G. Nothing, nothing, silence![20] The Turgenevs[21] weren't at home. Spent the evening again at Tolstaya's. Old Maltsova again.

14 May Got up at 10. [...] Found Meshchersky, Skaryatin and Makarov half-way through dinner at Donan's.[22] We went to Pavlovsk.[23] Disgusting! Wenches, stupid music, wenches, an artificial nightingale, wenches, heat, cigarette smoke, wenches, vodka, cheese, wild shrieks, wenches, wenches, wenches!

Everyone tried to pretend they were enjoying themselves, and that they liked the wenches, but without success. In the train I was infuriated by some drunken boisterous German civilians trying to carouse like officers.

15 May   Got up late, put my papers in order, wrote a letter to Turgenev. Alexandra Nikolayevna[24] came. Called on Fet, went with him to the stock exchange, and from there to Dusseau's for dinner with Makarov, Meshchersky, Gorbunov and Dolgorukov. From there to the theatre. A splendid woman next to me. Korolyov, author of *Career*, seems a brilliant mediocrity. From there to Dusseau's and a ball, Dolgorukov, Meshchersky, Gorbunov and I. Three wenches, not bad. Felt jaded. [. . .]

Never let slip opportunities for enjoyment and never look out for them. I make it a rule for all time never to enter an inn or a brothel. [. . .]

17 May   [. . .] Read *A Superfluous Man*.[25] Awfully affected, coquettish, clever and skittish.

18 May, Moscow   Arrived at 10 and went straight to the Perfilyevs'. [. . .]

21 May   The Koloshins and Zagoskin[26] came in the morning. Dined at Aksakov's. Met Khomyakov.[27] A witty man. Argued with Konstantin[28] about village readings, which he considers impossible. At the Gorchakovs' in the evening I argued the exact opposite with Sergey Dmitriyevich; Sergey Dmitriyevich assured me that the peasantry are the most depraved class of all. Of course from being a Westerner I became an implacable Slavophile.

22 May   Dined at Dyakova's. Didn't recognize Alexandrina Obolen-skaya,[29] she'd changed so much. I didn't expect to see her, and so the feeling she aroused in me was terribly strong. [. . .]

Yes, it hurts me terribly even now to think of the happiness that might have been mine and which has fallen to that excellent man, Andrey Obolensky. Told Sukhotin of my feelings; he understood them, all the more so because, I think, he shares them.

23 May   [. . .] Called in at Verochka's. Thank God she didn't give herself to me. At Botkin's,[30] at Kuntsevo and on the way there, I was moved to tears by the beauty of nature. From there I called in at the Perfilyevs'. Varenka was there; beautiful eyes, no smile, an impossible nose. Well built, awkward, probably intelligent and kind, although she pronounces her rs like the French – on the whole a very pleasant creature. I'd like to know her better.

24 May   In the morning I finished writing my diary and notebook, and was cruelly bored, foreseeing no possibility of meeting Alexandrine today. I've no reason to remain, but feel terribly unwilling to leave. Four feelings have taken hold of me with unusual force: love, the pangs of remorse (pleasant, though), the desire to marry (in order to escape from those pangs) and – nature. [. . .]

Learned at home that the Obolenskys would be at the Sukhotins'. Went there. Sukhotina was strumming Chopin. Alexandrine came and went as usual, and we didn't talk much. Once or twice when I spoke she was all attention. No, I'm not being carried away when I say that she is the sweetest woman I've ever known. The most refined, artistic and, at the same time, moral nature. [. . .]

25 May   [. . .] Alexandrine's daughter is ill. She told Sergey Sukhotin in my presence that when she was betrothed they were not in love. Her husband wasn't there. Was she trying to tell me that she wasn't in love with him? Later, when saying goodbye, she *suddenly* gave me her hand and there were tears in her eyes because she had just been crying about her little girl's illness; but I felt terribly happy. Then she unexpectedly saw me to the door. Certainly since Sonechka's days I've never experienced such a pure, strong and good feeling. I say 'good', because although it's hopeless, it makes me glad to stir it up. [. . .]

26 May   [. . .] Was too late to dine at Bakhmeteva's, which I was very glad about, because I went on to Pokrovskoye with Kostenka and dined at Lyubochka Behrs'.[31] The children waited on us – what sweet, jolly little girls – then we went for a walk and played leap-frog. [. . .]

28 May, Yasnaya Polyana   Mlle Vergani is the most palpable despot I've ever seen – foreigners are always like that.[32] Called in at Sudakovo; life is wonderful there. At Yasnaya it's sad – pleasant, but somehow not in harmony with my mood. However, when I compare myself with my Yasnaya memories of myself of old, I feel how much I've changed in a liberal sense. Even Tatyana Alexandrovna I find unpleasant. You couldn't ram the injustice of serfdom into her head in a hundred years. On the journey I composed some poetry – poor, I think. Today I'm arranging a meeting and will speak. Let's hope for the best.

Went to the meeting. Things are going well. The peasants understand and are glad. They see me as a speculator and therefore believe me.

Fortunately I didn't talk too much nonsense and spoke clearly. [...]

31 May, Spasskoye-Pokrovskoye[33]   Set off on horseback for Turgenev's before 5 in the morning. Arrived at 7. He was out. Chatted with Porfiry[34] and finished writing my notebook. His house revealed his roots to me, and this explained a lot, and so reconciled me to him. He returned. I had breakfast, went for a walk, chatted very pleasantly with him and lay down to sleep. I was woken in time for dinner. His uncle's family[35] are a poor lot. Insipid, moralistic German women who are probably uncomfortable, therefore, in this landowning environment. [...] I'd like to write the story of a horse.[36]

1 June, Pokrovskoye   Got up at 10, whiled the time away with the children, then with Valeryan, then with Turgenev, with whom I had a bathe, and then with Masha. Later we went boating on a raft and made a little music. I'm pleased about Masha's relations with Turgenev. He and I get on well, but I don't know whether it's because he's changed or I have. [...]

3 June, Yasnaya Polyana   Trinity Sunday. Arrived before 5 and, after walking through the house, which had a nasty smell throughout, found enormous pleasure in sitting by the window which opened on to the garden. Read Pushkin's *Don Juan*.[37] Delightful! Such truth and power, which I'd never expected in Pushkin. [...] There was no meeting in the evening, but I learned from Vasily that the peasants suspect a fraud and think that everyone will be granted freedom at the coronation,[38] and that I want to tie them down by contract – that it's a 'fiddle', as he expressed it.

4 June   Got up at 5, and went for a walk with, I confess, terribly erotic thoughts. Read Pushkin's first poems. Then sorted through my old exercise books – incomprehensible, but charming nonsense.[39] Decided to write *A Landowner's Diary*,[40] *The Cossack*[41] and the comedy.[42] I'll start on *The Cossack* first. Had breakfast, slept, had dinner, went for a walk, bathed in the Voronka, read Pushkin and went to see the peasants. They don't want their freedom.

5 June   Got up at 6, rode off for a bathe with Osip, then into the open country. Came back, read through and made some corrections in *The Cossack* and roamed round the garden with the vague, lascivious hope of catching someone in the bushes. Nothing prevents me so much from working, so I decided at all costs to install a mistress for these two months. [...] In the evening I went to Gimbut's.[43] A wonderful Russian girl – Begicheva. Gimbut's wife is as dark as a raven – not stupid, but affected and unsympathetic. Durova[44] disturbs me. Shall I never be her ...?

6 June Got up at 7 and rode to Grumant for a bathe. Terrible lust, amounting to physical pain. [. . .]

7 June Slept till 11 and woke up refreshed. Roamed round the garden, the kitchen garden and Grumant again, without any success of course. I'll go to Gimbut's tomorrow, for the same purpose. Read Pushkin, parts 2 and 3;[45] *The Gipsies* is as delightful as it was the first time, but the other poems except for *Onegin* are terrible rubbish. Talked to some peasants in the evening, and their obstinacy drove me to anger which I could hardly restrain.

8 June Got up after 9. Roamed round the garden. A very pretty peasant woman of very pleasing beauty. I'm unbearably loathsome with my feeble longing for vice. Vice itself would be better. Did gymnastics, bathed, roamed round the woods. Had a few sensible thoughts about my novel of a landowner. I think I'll start work on it. [. . .]

10 June Got up at 9. The pain in my back gets worse and worse. Read a biography of Pushkin[46] and finished it. Walked round the Zakaz Wood,[47] and thought out one or two things, chiefly that priority must be given to writing *Youth*, without abandoning the other things – *Notes of a Russian Landowner*, *The Cossack* and the comedy; for the latter particularly the main theme should be the debauchery everywhere in the country. The mistress with the footman. The brother with the sister. The father's illegitimate son with the father's wife, etc. The warden came but didn't find me in, and it was too late afterwards. Started writing a note to Durova, but I'm afraid it's too affectionate. There was a meeting in the evening. The peasants definitely refused to sign. The quit-rent will be discussed in autumn. And I'll be in the country in autumn. But now I'm free.

13 June Got up at 5, went fishing, roamed about. Was in a hair's breadth of ordering the soldier to bring me a woman. Read Nikolenka's charming story *The Chechen girl*. There's a tremendous epic talent for you. Yesterday a soldier was found hanged in the Zaseka wood,[48] and I made round to have a look at him. Met Nadezhda,[49] who's very sweet, and I can't help forgiving her her banality. The soldier seemed to be standing up, trousers tucked in boots, a dirty shirt, cap turned inside out, overcoat thrown aside, legs bent in a strange way. Returned home and met Nadezhda again; she was sweet again. Had a terrible headache, suffered a long time, fell asleep and woke up at 10 before she left. All the same she's sweet. Got on better with Auntie. Alyoshka has spoken of the soldier. A reply tomorrow. Valeriya[50] has arrived. I'll call on them tomorrow. [. . .] Starting tomorrow I'll go round to all the peasants; I'll find out about their needs and try to persuade them individually to accept contracts.

14 June Got up at 9. Roamed around. Went with Natalya Petrovna[51] to Gimbut's and to Arsenyev's. During lunch at Gimbut's the inquest commission arrived.[52] I was told the Arsenyevs had gone to Tula. I decided to stay. Nadezhda Nikolayevna[53] invited me to go for a walk in the wood. Gimbut shouted that it was *inconvenable* [improper]; she pretended not to hear him; he sent M.A., and ran after us himself, urging me in the meanest and rudest manner in her presence not to compromise her. I went back with him and went to the inquest. Little yellow worms covered the dead person's clothing all over. He was a young lad of sixteen. When I got back I learned that Natalya Petrovna had gone. Nadezhda Nikolayevna was horrid. Gimbut had suddenly got into a rage with Natalya Petrovna, called her a procuress and driven her out. Back home I went fishing; the soldier came and I ran off into Chepyzh wood. She was a horrid little rascal. Dyakov arrived about 10. Chatted with him till 3. Yes, he's my best friend and a splendid one. Read Nikolenka's story and began to cry again. I did so too when reciting the Cossack song. I'm beginning to like the epic legendary manner. I'll try and make a poem out of the Cossack song.[54]

15 June Got up at 10. Roamed around with Dyakov. He gave me much practical advice about laying out the separate wing, and above all advised me to marry Valeriya. Listening to him it seems to me too that this is the best thing I can do. Is it money that holds me back? No, opportunity. Then he took me as far as the turning to Sudakovo. Valeriya put on a stern expression, probably because of the letter. I was in good spirits and calmed them down. Poor girl, her aunt seems a worthless lot. Of course the best person she knows is Mlle Vergani, but that's not saying much! A pity she has no backbone or fire – just like noodles. But she's kind. And she smiles – a painfully submissive smile. Got home and sent for the soldier's wife. Tomorrow morning I must write a letter to Bludov and get on with *The Cossack*. The soldier's wife didn't come.

18 June Dyakov came, and I persuaded him to go to the Arsenyevs' with me. Valeriya chattered about clothes and the coronation. Frivolity with her seems to be not a transient, but an enduring passion. [. . .]

24 June Went to the Arsenyevs' with my aunts. Valeriya was awfully bad, and I've quite calmed down.

25 June [. . .] Read *The Newcomes*[55] and made notes. The soldier's wife came in the evening, probably the last time.

26 June Got up before 9, read *The Newcomes*, copied out my notes, re-read *Youth*, tried to write but just came to a stop. The peasant has been taken away.[56] Did gymnastics, had a Lenten dinner at home and went to the Arsenyevs' with Natalya Petrovna. [. . .] Valeriya was in a white dress. Very sweet. Spent one of the pleasantest days of my life. Do I love her seriously? And can she love for long? These are two questions I would like to solve for myself and can't. [. . .]

28 June Got up at 10, and finished off the first chapter of *Youth* with great pleasure. Toothache worse. After dinner I went to the Arsenyevs'. Valeriya is terribly badly educated, and ignorant, if not stupid. One word, *prostituer*, which she said, God knows why, distressed me very much and, what with my toothache, disillusioned me.

30 June Got up at 10, finished *The Newcomes*. Wrote a page of *Youth*, played the 5th symphony.[57] The Arsenyevs came. Valeriya is a wonderful girl, but I definitely don't like her. But if we see each other so often I might suddenly marry her. That wouldn't be a misfortune, but it's not necessary and I don't want it, and I'm convinced that anything that isn't necessary and isn't wanted is harmful. [. . .]

1 July [. . .] Spent the whole day with Valeriya. She had a white dress on and bare arms, and they aren't attractive. This upset me. I began to tease her in a moral tone and so cruelly that she broke off smiling. There were tears in her smile. Then she played. I felt all right, but she was already distraught. All this I'm now aware of.

2 July [. . .] Had dinner and went to the Arsenyevs'. Valeriya was writing in a dark room and again wore a horrid flashy house-coat. She was cold and self-contained, and showed me a letter to her sister in which she said I was an egoist, etc. Then Mlle Vergani came in and recriminations began, first bantering then serious, which hurt and depressed me. I had seriously hurt her yesterday, but she spoke out frankly, and after the brief sadness I felt, it all passed over. She said several times: 'Now let bygones be bygones.' She was very sweet.

5 July Woke early and had a bathe. A young girl ran up to me, but I was in a good frame of mind and sent her packing. Played with the children, dined and made music. Turgenev came. He's definitely an uncongenial, cold and difficult person, and I'm sorry for him. I'll never get on with him. Walked about at night with vague sensual desires till 2 o'clock.

7 July, Spasskoye [. . .] Went to Turgenev's and am there now. On the way I experienced a religious feeling that moved me to tears.

8 July, Pokrovskoye Got up late and came back. [. . .] Spent the day in a muddle. Turgenev has organized his life stupidly. You can't organize it in such an extraordinary way. His whole life is a pretence of simplicity. I find him decidedly unpleasant. [. . .]

12 July, Yasnaya Polyana Got up late with a sore throat. Did nothing. The Sudakovo folk came. Valeriya was better than ever, but her frivolity and lack of concern for anything serious are terrifying. I'm afraid she has the sort of nature that can't even love children. But I spent the day very pleasantly all the same.

13 July Got up early. Throat better but my back still aches. Rode to the oatfields through Baburino to Myasoyedovo. The estate has been escheated and the peasants are free. The household serfs have settled on the land. I had a long talk with one of them. They go more often to the inn, and have cut down the orchards. Some are worse off, but they all say that they're contented, that they are free, and can lie on the grass as much as they like. I want to go to the Arsenyevs' and have a talk with Mlle Vergani.
  Didn't speak to Vergani. Met Zavalevsky there, and then Spechinsky. He seems a good fellow. They teased Valeriya to tears about the coronation.[58] She wasn't to blame at all, but I found it unpleasant, and I won't go there again for a long time. Or perhaps it was that they have shown me too much friendship. I'm afraid of marriage and of baseness – that's to say of amusing myself with her. But to marry – much would need to be changed, and I'll need to work more on myself. Got back late.

25 July Got up at 12 and read *Dead Souls* with pleasure; had many thoughts of my own, but wrote nothing. The weather is fine. At dinner I managed to rouse Masha by means of an argument, and then had a pleasant talk with her. After dinner I went with Natalya Petrovna to see Valeriya. For the first time I found her without her *gowns*, as Seryozha puts it. She was ten times better – above all, natural. She had put her hair behind her ears, knowing that I like it like that. [. . .] Spent the evening *happily*.

27 July [. . .] Argued irritably with Masha at dinner. Auntie stuck up for her. She said that Turgenev says it's impossible to argue with me. Do I really have an evil nature? I must control myself, and the cause of it all is pride – Valeriya was right. [. . .]

28 July [. . .] It's strange that I'm beginning to like Valeriya as a woman, whereas before it was just as a woman that she repelled me. Even so it's not always the case, but only when I make up my mind to. Yesterday for the first time I noticed her *bras* [arms], which used to repel me.

30 July [. . .] Found Valeriya and Mlle Vergani in tears. A letter from Olga;[59] she's apparently getting married. Valeriya entirely in negligé. Disliked her very much. She said something stupid about David Copperfield having to put up with a lot of misfortunes, etc. [. . .]

1 August [. . .] The Arsenyevs came. Valeriya was in a confused state of mind, cruelly affected and stupid. [. . .]

10 August Wrote in the morning, and went to the Arsenyevs' in the evening. They were just going to the bath-house. Valeriya and I spoke of marriage; she's not stupid, and is exceptionally kind.

12 August Went to the Arsenyevs' at 10 to see them off. She was exceptionally simple and nice. I'd like to know whether I'm in love or not. [. . .]

14 August [. . .] Had a discussion with Auntie about religion – it's useless. I must remember this with my future wife. [. . .]]

25 August [. . .] All I did was to tidy up my notes and read a bit of *Little Dorrit*.[60]

5 September A nightmare during the night about being impotent. Dictated three chapters and corrected three. Had a very pleasant chat with Auntie. Health still bad. The thought that I'm almost impotent torments me.

13 September Corrected *Youth*. Much worse again. I think I'll die.

24 September Health getting better and better. Mlle Vergani came. From what she says, Valeriya disgusts me. Finished *Youth*; poor, but sent it off.

25 September In the morning, some thoughts about the estate. Did nothing. Went to the Arsenyevs'. Valeriya is sweet but, alas, simply stupid, and that's where the shoe pinched.

26 September Valeriya came. She's sweet, but limited and impossibly trivial.

29 September, Sudakovo Woke up at 9 in a bad temper. Valeriya is unfitted for either a practical or an intellectual life. I told her only the unpleasant part of what I wanted to say, and so it had no effect on her. I was angry. The conversation was steered round to Mortier,[61] and it turned out that she's in love with him. Strange; it offended me, and I felt ashamed for myself and for her, but for the first time I experienced something like feeling for her. Read *Werther.*[62] Delightful. Auntie didn't send for me, and I stayed another night.

1 October, Yasnaya Polyana Woke up, still out of spirits. After midnight my side began to ache again for no apparent reason. Did nothing, but thought less about Valeriya, thank God. I'm not in love, but this relationship will always play a big part in my life. And if I haven't yet known love, then judging by the small beginnings I feel now, I shall experience it with terrible force, and God forbid it should be for Valeriya. She is terribly shallow, without principles and cold as ice, as a result of which she is constantly being distracted. Wrote a letter to Kovalevsky yesterday and sent in my resignation.[63]

8 October Went to the Arsenyevs'. I can't help taunting Valeriya. It's from habit, not feeling. She's nothing to me but an unpleasant memory. Was on the point of beginning to write a comedy.[64] Perhaps I'll get down to it.

11 October, Lapotkovo[65] Woke up before 9. Went hunting at Masha's. Reached Lapotkovo at 5, having shot only one hare. Read *Le Bourgeois Gentilhomme*, and thought a lot about a comedy based on Olga's life.[66] In two acts. I think it could be pretty good. Read through the whole of this diary. Extremely pleasant.

14 October, Pokrovskoye Got up early. Porfiry abused Nikolay Nikolayevich Turgenev to me for a couple of hours with great satisfaction. And Turgenev[67] is entirely to blame. No artistic bent can exempt one from taking part in the life of the community. Which is better when you see a man with his throat cut – to turn away from him in disgust or to give him at least some clumsy assistance?

Did nothing all day. Got a letter yesterday from Ivan Turgenev which I didn't like. Valeryan came in the evening. I don't want to go to Moscow. Read *The Pickwick Club*[68] and, on the journey, Molière.

19 October Went to Tula. [. . .] Spent the evening and the night at the Arsenyevs'. Looked more calmly at Valeriya. She's grown terribly stout and I definitely have no feelings for her. Gave her to understand that we must have a serious talk; she was glad, but *distraite*. Olga is intelligent. Spent the night there.

22 October, Sudakovo Spent the morning at home reading. Auntie is still sulking. I couldn't stand it and rode to the Arsenyevs'. [. . .] Pavlov was with them, so I couldn't find an opportunity to tell Khrapovitsky's[69] story and therefore stayed the night. We talked a little and I promised to tell it in the morning.

23 October Before Valeriya was up the Gimbuts came and I was again prevented from telling the story. After dinner we enjoyed ourselves very much. When the Gimbuts had gone we struck up a pleasant conversation the four of us at supper, and I told Khrapovitsky's story to Mlle Vergani in the study, and she told it to Valeriya. A pity I didn't tell it myself. I went to sleep almost at peace, but very far from in love – at their house.

24 October, Yasnaya Polyana Valeriya appeared, embarrassed but pleased. I felt glad and ashamed. I left. Made my peace at home with Auntie.
     Went to a ball. Valeriya was charming. I almost fell in love with her.

27 October Ill in the morning, went for a walk; can't write anything. Valeriya came. I didn't like her particularly, but she is a very nice girl, and she said honestly and frankly that she wanted to prepare herself for communion after the Mortier affair. I showed her this diary; the entry for the 25th ended with the words 'I love her'. She tore out that page.

28 October Rode to Gimbut's with the dogs and dined with him. In the morning I wrote letters to Daragan and Arsenyev, and went to Valeriya's. She had some terrible hair style and was wearing purple *for my sake*. I felt hurt and ashamed, and spent the day sadly. Conversation didn't flow. But quite involuntarily I've become a sort of fiancé. This vexes me. Found Seryozha in. Read Turgenev's *Faust*[70] at their house. It's delightful.

29 October Chatted all morning with Seryozha. Went with him to the Arsenyevs'. She was simple and nice. We chatted in a corner.

31 October, Tula Spent the night at the Arsenyevs'. She's not pretty. The constraint of my position vexes me more and more. Went to a ball, and she was very nice again. A pained voice and a desire to compromise herself and sacrifice something for me. Went to the hotel with them; they saw me off and I was almost in love.

1 November, Moscow Thought only of Valeriya on the journey. Was not quite well. Reached Moscow during the night and stayed at Shevaldyshev's.

2 November Wrote Valeriya a long letter.[71] Went to Masha's. She is nice, and in good health. I told her about Valeriya; she is on her side. Spent the evening at Botkin's very pleasantly, and at Ostrovsky's.[72] He's dirty, and although a kind man, he's a cold egoist. Terrible migraine.

4 November Finished reading *The Polar Star*.[73] Very good. Wrote my diary. [. . .]

5 November Wrote a little in the morning, dined again with Masha; *The Misfortune of Being Clever* at the theatre[74] – excellent. [. . .]

8 November Wrote an irritable letter in the morning to Valeriya; didn't send the first version, but a second one.[75] [. . .]

10 November [. . .] Bought a book, dined at home and read all Turgenev's stories. Poor. Dictated a little. Went to Olga Turgeneva's[76] with Druzhinin. Druzhinin was ashamed on my account. Olga Turgeneva, it's true, is worse than Valeriya, except for her beauty. I think about her a lot. I've found a flat. I'll move tomorrow, and go to the Law Council. Dreamed of a waltz with Valeriya and a strange happening.

11 November Began moving in the morning, read some rubbish, was tempted to join the service but refrained. Went to Davydov's, read a review of *Sevastopol in August* and *The Snow-storm* – a clever and sensible one[77] – and went to my flat. They hadn't brought my boots – I was angry. Wrote a tiny letter to Valeriya. I think about her very much. [. . .]

13 November Got up before 11, wrote the second scene of the comedy,[78] went to gymnastics, met an aristocratic boy there. Went to Druzhinin's between 3 and 4. Goncharov and Annenkov were there. They all disgust me, especially Druzhinin, and they disgust me because I want to love, I want friendship, and they're incapable of it. Followed them in a cab towards Kushelyov's and then dropped behind them; I was very glad I did. Dined at Kles's[79] – rather expensive. From there I called on A.P., but God saved me. Even called on F. and also escaped unsullied, thank God. [. . .] Read through the fair copy of *The Novel of a Russian Landowner*. It may turn out to be good. Dictated a very little of *Reduced to the Ranks* and finished a letter to Valeriya – very coldly.[80]

14 November Got up early. Wrote a little of *Reduced to the Ranks* in the morning. Went to Panayev's.[81] Was bored. I'm terribly sensitive to praise and blame. [. . .]

15 November Did nothing of what I'd planned. Got up in the morning and corrected *Reduced to the Ranks*, read *Henry IV*[82] and was angry with *The Contemporary*.[83] Gymnastics. Dined at Botkin's. *The Contemporary* affair. I expressed my opinion in part. Read *Reduced to the Ranks*. Coldly received. From there Druzhinin and I went to Annenkov's and found him playing the organ. Then to Bezobrasov's. A meeting of writers and scholars is offensive to me, and it doesn't come off without women. Then we had supper with Annenkov and talked a good deal. He's very intelligent and a good man.

16 November [. . .] Finished reading *Henry IV*. No! [. . .]

17 November In the morning revised *The Novel of a Russian Landowner*, it's dreadfully diffuse. Gymnastics. Dined at home and worked at the same thing till 9. Went to Botkin's, found Druzhinin there, and spent a pleasant evening; I was kind and modest, and that made it nice. [. . .]

20 November Got up at 10 and wrote a little. Gymnastics. Dined at Druzhinin's. Pisemsky was there. Obviously he doesn't like me, and this hurt me. Druzhinin refused to listen to me, and that jarred on me. Found a letter from Valeriya at home. There's nothing new in her letters. An immature, loving nature. Answered her and went to bed at 3.

21 November Got up at 1. Maykov came. Gymnastics. Dined at Stolypin's and was rude to his wife. At Botkin's all evening. Read *The Novel of a Russian Landowner*. It's definitely poor, but I'll publish it. I must cross things out. Called on Alexandra Petrovna, and felt disgusted as a result.

22 November Got up at 11. Wanted to write, but it was no good. Gymnastics. Dined at Panayev's. Then at Krayevsky's till the evening. The literary atmosphere disgusts me to a greater extent than anything ever before. Wrote a letter to Valeriya. Thought about her a lot. Perhaps it's because I haven't seen any women all this time.

23 November [. . .] Received a nice letter from Valeriya and replied to her.[84] Thought about Alexandra Petrovna and at the same time very, very much about Valeriya. How I long to have done with the journals as soon as possible, in order to write in the way in which I'm now beginning to think about art – a terribly pure and exalted way.

25 November   Got up at 9. Slept badly again. Went to the menagerie early. Went to Kovalevsky's. He was nice. They played some rubbish at the University. The Emperor has read *Childhood*. A lady with sensual eyes at the menagerie. [. . .] The sensual lady's expression made me think with horror about Valeriya.

27 November   Got up at 10. Received a stupid letter from Valeriya. She's fooling herself and I can see through it – that's what's tiresome. [. . .] Roamed around with sensual aims. A drunken wench on the Nevsky. Went to the bath-house. Wrote a cold letter to Valka.[85]

29 November   [. . .] My thoughts about Valeriya are few and unpleasant.

30 November   [. . .] Called on Alexandra Petrovna and found Yakovlev there. Fate saved me – I was within a hair's breadth. Received a registered letter, a nice one, from Valeriya. The Emperor read *Childhood* and wept.

1 December   Got up at 11, wrote yesterday's diary and played till it was time for gymnastics. Arm very sore, dined at home, finished reading *Carmen*[86] – feeble, French; received a letter from Turgenev and sent him one. [. . .]

3 December   I'm writing nothing. Read Mérimée – good – and thought about the comedy.[87] Gymnastics; it's good that there's no pain.

5 December   In the morning read *A Commonplace Story*[88] and sent it to Valeriya. [. . .]

7 December   Got up late, wrote a letter to Valeriya,[89] gymnastics, dined at home, read *The Poor Bride*[90] – it's simply feeble. His mistress is good. Went to the circus. Had supper at Dusseau's, I don't know why. Read Druzhinin's second article.[91] His weakness is that he never doubts whether it mightn't all be rubbish.

11 December   Read *Lear*,[92] it had little effect on me. [. . .]

12 December   [. . .] Feel very sad. Dreamed about a blood-bath on the floor. Also a brown woman on my chest, bending down naked and whispering something.

15 December   Was woken up by Alexandra Nikolayevna. I —ed her, and she went off with twenty-five silver roubles. Very late for gymnastics. [. . .]

28 December Got up late. Kept thinking about the comedy. It's nonsense. Gymnastics. I've received my discharge certificate. Dined at Shevich's.[93] Bludov is a swine. Vyazemsky has censored the last chapter.[94] [. . .]

29 December Got up late. Received a long letter from Valeriya, which I found unpleasant. Gymnastics. Was angry at home. Dined at Botkin's. The stupidity and the ignorance of the censors is awful. [. . .]

30 December University concert. *Meeresstille.*[95] Excellent. [. . .]

1857

1 January [Petersburg] Slept badly all night. I've heard too much music these last few days. Woke up after 11; received a dry but nice letter from Turgenev. Wrote a letter to Valeriya, short and dry, and one to Nekrasov which I was advised not to send. Translated a fairly tale by Andersen.[1] Read it over dinner at Botkin's but they didn't like it. Botkin had received a letter from Nekrasov in which he spoke of me in flattering tones. We had a pleasant chat. I went to Olga Turgeneva's and stayed with her till after 11. I liked her better than ever. Could hardly restrain myself from going to a masquerade.

3 January Got up very late, read a delightful article about Pushkin, and went to see Bludova and Shevich;[2] the former was out, and the latter has practically refused to take part in the theatrical performance.[3] Gymnastics. Dinner at Botkin's. From there to Tolstoy's.[4] He has a sweet, rather shallow, childishly poetic nature. From there to Krayevsky's before 10, and to the masquerade before 12. At first it was very dull, then at supper with Stolypin and Stakhovich a sweet mouth approached me. I solicited it for a long time; it drove off with me, agreed reluctantly and took off its mask at my house. As like Alexandrine Dyakova as two peas, only older and with coarser features. I took her back home, and all night and the next day felt my old happiness again.

4 January Got up after 1. The article on Pushkin[5] is wonderful. Only now have I understood Pushkin. Gymnastics. Dined at Botkin's just with Panayev. He read Pushkin to me, I went into Botkin's room, wrote a letter there to Turgenev, and then sat down on the sofa and wept groundless, but blissful poetic tears. I've been decidedly happy all this time. I'm intoxicated by the speed of my moral progress forward. [. . .]

7 January [. . .] Kiesewetter's story[6] greatly attracts me.

8 January People will remember my words that in two years' time the peasants will rise in revolt unless they are sensibly emancipated before then. [. . .]

10 January Gymnastics. Received my passport and decided to go.[7] [. . .]

12 January, en route for Moscow   [...] Must write every day, without interruption: (1) *The Hunting Ground*, (2) Second half of *Youth*, (3) *The Fugitive*, (4) *The Cossack*, (5) *The Lost One*, (6) *A Woman's Story* – 'Nuts for the squirrel when it has no teeth'. She loves and feels she has the right to, just when she has too little left to give.[8] (7) The comedy *A Practical Person*; a George Sand woman[9] and a Hamlet of our times, a clamouring, sick protest against everything; but lack of character.

20, 21, 22, 23, 24, 25 January   A reading at S. T. Aksakov's. His *Childhood* is delightful![10] A ball at the Naryshkins', danced two quadrilles, was bored. A ball at the Voyeykovs'. Muromtseva is consumptive – enjoyed myself. Ostrovsky's *A Lucrative Post* is his best work and satisfies the need to portray the world of bribery. But his vanity is impossible. Mengden[11] is a remarkable woman. Evening at the Sushkovs'. Tyutcheva[12] is nice.

9/21 February, Paris   All this time on the journey. Confusion in my head and in my notes. Arrived in Paris today.[13] I'm alone, without a servant, doing everything myself; a new city, a new way of life, no ties, and the spring sunshine which I caught the feel of. Undoubtedly a new era. Regular habits, and *above all* at least four hours' solitude and work each day. Couldn't get on with Turgenev and Nekrasov. I've spent a lot of money and seen absolutely nothing. [...] Turgenev is suspicious and painfully weak. Nekrasov is gloomy.

10/22 February   Got up late, a noise in my ears all the time, cold in the rooms; but wrote three letters, though short ones, then went for a stroll. Turgenev and Nekrasov went off to a shooting gallery for some reason. It made me feel sad. [...]

11/23 February   Got up late, dawdled a long time at home tidying up, went to the bank, drew out 800 francs, made some purchases and moved my quarters.[14] Called on the Lvovs; she's nice – a Russian.[15] Read Napoleon's speech[16] with indescribable revulsion. Made a start on the journey[17] at home and had dinner. A lively woman; I was struck dumb with confusion. The theatre. *Précieuses ridicules* and *L'Avare*[18] – excellent. *Vers de Vergile*[19] – an intolerable abomination.

12/24 February   [...] The theatre. Marivaux's *Les fausses confidences* – a delightful piece of elegance. Plessy.[20] *Le malade imaginaire*[21] – delightfully acted.

16/28 February   Got up at 10; I'm sleeping better. My English teacher arrived at once.[22] Lessons with him are going badly. I'll get rid of him.

Then Orlov[23] came; read *Honorine*,[24] an immense talent. Went to the Sorbonne.[25] Superficial. Witticisms about Pliny. Went for a walk. Dined at home. Fitz James nothing special, but the Spanish countess is delightful. [. . .]

19 February/3 March Morning at home till 2. Received a letter from Valeriya. Visited Garnier – a philosopher and follower of Descartes. Roamed around till 5. Dined at home. A disgusting Englishman. Went to a concert with Turgenev: a delightful trio,[26] and Viardot.[27] Delsarte.[28] Picked up . . . on the streets. It's sad at Turgenev's.

23 February/7 March My Italian teacher. Late for Rigault.[29] Hôtel de Cluny – interesting;[30] I've started believing in chivalry. Dined with Turgenev upstairs at Durand's. Went to the Khlyustins – spiteful people. Roamed around. An *accosteuse*.[31] I ruined my evening and felt morally agitated and tormented.

24 February/8 March Turgenev called in the morning and I went for a drive with him. He's kind, and terribly weak. Fontainebleau château. The forest. In the evening I wrote too impetuously. When I'm with him I keep an eye on myself. It's good for me. Although it's a bit hurtful to feel someone else's sharp gaze always on one, one's own becomes more effective.

25 February/9 March, Paris–Dijon Slept badly. We set off at 8;[32] played chess on the journey. Turgenev doesn't believe in anything, that's his trouble; he doesn't love, but loves to love. Went to the baths – disgusting. [. . .]

26 February/10 March, Dijon Slept splendidly. In the morning I wrote a wonderful chapter. Went round the churches with Turgenev. Had dinner. Played chess at a café. Turgenev's vanity, as the normal habit of an intelligent man, is nice. At dinner I told him something he didn't suspect, that I consider him to be my superior. [. . .]

1/13 March Got up late. Turgenev is a bore: I want to go to Paris, but he can't be alone. Alas! He's never loved anyone. Read *The Lost One* to him. It left him cold. We almost quarrelled. Did nothing all day.

2/14 March, Dijon to Paris Went to Paris. Railways a disaster. Dinner. Mme Fitz James. Calves. Trubetskaya. 'Nothing, nothing, silence.' Stupid ball. Unclothed wenches. [. . .]

3/15 March   Got up at 1. Went to the Louvre with de M. Rembrandt's portrait and Murillo. Dined at home, then *La fille du regiment*,[33] dancing and champagne alone.

4/16 March   Got up late. Went to the *Hôtel des Invalides*. Deification of a villain, it's terrible. Soldiers – animals trained to bite everyone. They ought to starve to death. Legs torn off – serve them right. *Notre dame*. Dijon is better. Fontainebleau. Terribly sad. Spent a pile of money. Late for dinner with the Trubetskoys. I've stopped liking the princess. Home succeeded and then failed.[34] I must try myself. Called on Turgenev. He's a bad man in that he's cold and useless, but he's very clever artistically and does nobody any harm. Received a telegram from Seryozha and replied. Terribly sad. Activity is the only remedy.

5/17 March   [. . .] Dined at home. Fitz James is a bore. Fortunately I saw *The Barber of Seville* instead of *Rigoletto*. Wonderful. Called on Turgenev. No, I must avoid him. I've paid tribute enough to his merits and run after him from all directions in order to be friends with him, but it's impossible.

7/19 March   Last night I was tormented by sudden doubts about *everything*. And now, although they don't torment me, they are still with me. Why? And what am I? More than once it seemed to me that I was solving these questions, but no, my life has provided me with no confirmation of that. Got up earlier, worked hard at Italian. Went for a walk to the Colonne Vendôme and along the boulevards. Turgenev called at 5, and seemed to look guilty. What can I do? I respect, value and even love him, I suppose, but I feel no sympathy for him and that's mutual. Mme Fitz James perspires, and is a dreadful flirt. Aux Variétés! *Le quadrille des Lanciers*[35] – delightful! [. . .]

12/24 March   Got up late. Went to the Louvre and the *Cour d'assises*. Dined with Lvova and argued impudently. From there to the *Café des Aveugles*, *Rigoletto* and home.

13/25 March   Went riding with Seryozha, had dinner with the Trubeskoys. It was easy for me, but difficult for him. To Turgenev's, then to a ball. With Margarita to her place. [. . .]

15/27 March   Got up late. Went to Versailles. Feel my lack of knowledge. [. . .]

20 March/1 April   [. . .] Dined. A woman disturbed me. I went to her place, but remained firm. The debauchery is terrible!

22 March/3 April [. . .] Turgenev woke me. It seems he probably has spermatorrhoea, but he still won't have treatment and gads about. [. . .]

23 March/4 April Got up at 12. Began writing in a rather lazy fashion. Read Balzac.[36] [. . .] Read *Myrrha*[37] in Italian, and had dinner upstairs. Went to see Ristori[38] – a single poetic movement makes up for the falseness of five acts. The drama of Racine and the like is Europe's poetic wound. Thank God we haven't got it and won't have. [. . .]

25 March/6 April Got up at 7 feeling ill and went to see an execution.[39] A stout, white, strong neck and chest. He kissed the Gospels and then – death. How senseless! The impression it made was a strong one and not wasted on me. I'm not a political person. Morality and art. I know, I love and I can. Feel unwell and depressed; I'm going to dinner at the Trubetskoys'. Wrote a stupid letter to Botkin. [. . .] Went to Turgenev's. He doesn't talk any more, he only chatters; he doesn't believe in intelligence, or in people, or in anything. But I found it pleasant. The guillotine kept me awake a long time and made me reflect.

26 March/7 April Got up late, felt unwell, read, and suddenly a simple and sensible idea occurred to me – to leave Paris.[40] [. . .] I called in for a moment at Turgenev's. He went to Viardot's and I to the Lvovs'. The Princess was there. I like her very much, and I think I'm a fool not to try to marry her. If she were to marry a very good man and they were very happy, I might be driven to despair. [. . .]

27 March/8 April, Paris – Ambérieu[41] Got up at 8 and called on Turgenev. Both times, when saying goodbye to him, I've cried about something as I left him. I like him very much. He has made and is continuing to make a different man of me. Set off at 11. It was dull on the train. But when I transferred to the stage-coach at night a full moon shone on the seats. Everything stood out and was suffused with love and joy. For the first time in a long while I sincerely thanked God again that I was alive.

29 March/10 April, Geneva Woke up early, felt well and almost cheerful except for the vile weather. Went to church, found no service on, was too late to prepare for communion, did some shopping and went to the Tolstoys'. Alexandrine Tolstaya has become very religious, as they all have, I think. *Le Bocage* – delightful. Read *Cousine Bette* all day, but behaved in an orderly manner. Noted down five headings.[42] At twenty-eight I'm still a silly little boy.

31 March/12 April Read the Gospels, went to the baths, caught cold.

The Tolstoys carried me off to their house. I abused Totleben – that's bad![43] Read Balzac. Alexandrine has a wonderful smile. [. . .]

3/15 April Got up late – the baths. Read the foreword to the *Comédie Humaine* there: trivial and presumptuous. Read a bit of the history of the revolution and Émile Girardin's *Liberté*[44] – shallow, though honest. [. . .] Must do three things: (1) educate myself, (2) work at poetry and (3) do good. And must check on these three things every day.

5/17 April [. . .] Went to confession. A good thing in any case. Received a letter from Auntie.

6/18 April Woke up at 9. Took communion. Read *Liberté* at home, and Balzac and a newspaper at the baths. [. . .] Read the history and constitution of Switzerland. Went out in a boat. I think *The Fugitive* is quite ready. I'll get down to it tomorrow. If I fall asleep, I won't go to church.

7/19 April Slept badly, as though afraid of being late somewhere. At 9 went to the baths, and at home read a history of France. Went to hear a sermon by Martin. Clever, but dreadfully cold. Wrote an outline.[45] Dined hurriedly and went with the Pushchins[46] to the Tolstoys'. Twice met Mariya. Not bad-looking, but superciliously polite. The Pushchins are delightfully good-natured. Meshchersky[47] may be of use to me, I'll go and see him. Was a terrible democrat – to no purpose. Flirted with an Englishwoman – also to no purpose.

8/20 April Got up early. Baths. Read *La Dame aux perles*.[48] He's talented, but the ground he tills is dreadful. Balzac's depravity is like a flower garden by comparison. Church. Felt cheerful. [. . .]

18/30 April Got up early, went for a walk, read about the disgusting behaviour of the English towards China[49] and argued about it with an elderly Englishman. Wrote a bit of *The Cossack* as poetry, which seemed better to me; I don't know which to choose. Read a history of the revolution[50] all day.

19 April/1 May [. . .] Read Tocqueville's history of the revolution all day. [. . .]

20 April/2 May [. . .] Read Sarrut's[51] history and the *Idées Napoléoniennes*[52] all day; didn't touch a pen. [. . .]

23 April/5 May Got up late. Did literally nothing all day. In the morning

I walked to Montreux and to the baths. A charming, blue-eyed Swiss girl. Wrote a reply to a letter I received from Turgenev. The English are a morally naked people and go about like that without any shame. [. . .]

25 April/7 May Wrote a little of *The Deranged One*[53] from the beginning again. At the baths the Galakhov girls tormented me. It's so dirty there, the soap *has no effect*. [. . .]

29 April/11 May, Geneva To the doctor's. A vulgar *raisonneur* [argufier]. To the Tolstoys', in a cheerful mood, went with them to Salève. Very enjoyable. I'm so ready to fall in love, it's terrible. If only Alexandrine were ten years younger! A wonderful nature. [. . .]

6/18 May [. . .] Princess Meshcherskaya is dangerous. I'm afraid I'm already to blame, and this feeling, together with the pleasure and awareness of the charm of a pretty young woman, kept me awake a long time.

12/24 May, Clarens Got up at 8, read Sarrut all day. A mass of thoughts, happy thoughts artistically, especially for the story about a Russian woman. Went to Zybina's funeral in the evening. The prayers touched me. Love is suffocating me – both physical and ideal love. Mariya Yakovlevna[54] is charming. I'm extremely interested in myself. I even love myself because there is so much love for others in me.

16/28 May, Les Avants – Gessenay Got up at 4. Set off via the Jaman pass. A pleasant walk, but the youngster[55] gets on my nerves. Reached Allières, nice and comfortable. A primitive chalet. Montbovon; 'Genevievka' disturbed me. Roman Catholic poetry! Unpacked my books, but did no writing. A pain in my chest. Set off walking to Château D'Oex; given a lift by a chaste miller. [. . .]

17/29 May. Gessenay – Interlaken [. . .] In a boat to Neuhaus. Delightful waterfalls, grottoes and castles. On foot to Interlaken; rye, milk, sweets. Health better. Drinking no wine.

18/30 May, Interlaken Unwell. Woke at 7. Walked to Böningen. Handsome people – the women especially. They begged for alms. Rain. Wrote a bit of *The Cossack*. Read about the Sevastopol campaign. The maid troubles me. Thank God for my bashfulness. Sasha bores me. Wrote a bit of *The Demented One* in the evening; went to the doctor's. Wrote to Auntie yesterday.

20 May/1 June, Grindelwald. 2 June [. . .] Some English people arrived. Sensuality torments me terribly. Couldn't sleep before midnight and paced up and down my room and the corridor. Walked along the balcony. The glaciers and black mountains in the moonlight. Pawed the downstairs maid, and the upstairs one too. She ran past several times and I thought she was waiting for me; everyone was in bed; she ran past again and gave me an angry look. I heard a noise downstairs; I'd roused the whole house; they took me for a *malfaiteur* [wrong-doer]. [. . .]

23 May/4 June, Leissigen – Bern. 5 June Left Leissigen at 7. A stone-carter gave us a lift. A little inn; terrible extortion; another pretty girl. From Spiez to Thun on foot. [. . .] Dinner in Thun with eighteen pastors. A pretty maid in the *Pinten Wirtschaft*. Reached Bern. Thought of writing to L. Karamzina[56] – must get married, must have a corner of my own to live.

24 May/5 June, Bern – Clarens. 6 June Left Bern at 8. Flat country with rye fields and woods as far as Fribourg. A 30-year-old American; he'd been to Russia. Mormons in Utah. Jos Smith, their founder, was lynched to death. Prices the same in all the inns. Hunting of *buffles* [buffaloes] and *cerfs* [stags]. I'd like to go there. Abolitionists. Beecher Stowe. Reached Vevey. Invited him to join us, but he wouldn't come. Finished the journey on foot, sad and empty. Began a letter to L. Karamzina, but didn't finish it.

26 May/7 June, Clarens [. . .] In the morning I wrote a splendid diary of my journey.[57] [. . .]

31 May/12 June, Clarens – Geneva Went up to Blonay in the morning. Delightful. A quite modern oval fountain and magnificent old terraces, splintered chestnut trees and decaying stalls. Left for Geneva. [. . .]

1/13 June, Geneva – Chambery [. . .] Set off at 6 for Chambery with a Savoyard, a playful, gentle stalwart Frenchman with a dog.

2/14 June, Chambery – Lans-le-Bourg Slept till 12. By train and on to Lans-le-Bourg with a drunken Piedmontese and a red-haired conductor with big eyes and a sardonic smile. Wanted to paw the woman next to me,[58] but was too hesitant to succeed.

4/16 June, Turin Overslept and missed Genoa. Went to two museums – arms and statues – and to the Chamber of Deputies. We all[59] had a splendid dinner together. Went for a walk. I dragged them all to a brothel

and left. Druzhinin stayed. Went to a concert to hear the Ferni sisters.
The best Sardinian society was there. [...]

5/17 June. Turin – Saint Martin Woke up early, had a bathe, dropped in
at the Athenaeum. I feel envious of this young, vigorous, free life. We went
to a café. One could live, and live well, anywhere here. [...]

7/19 June, Gressoney Couldn't sleep before 12. Terrible agitation. Rain:
we didn't go out. Offered someone five francs, but apparently she wasn't a
whore. An ugly creature, but I wanted her very much. Wrote a couple
of sheets of *The Cossack*. Read the enchanting Goethe's *Meeting and
parting.*[60] [...]

8/20 June, Gressoney – Chambave Left at 6. Ascent to the chapel. Meeting
with a handsome singer. View of the Aosta valley and the mountain range.
Descent; fragrance. Meeting with a godfather and godmother. Fragrance
of rye, nectar, grass and warm dung. Brusson. A second ascent. A poor
woman begging. Gave her half a franc. *La!* A pine forest; alone by a
stream. A second view of the Aosta valley. Chestnut trees and nuts. A
hollow basin with vineyards. St Vincent, a pretty tobacco worker, the
waters, a casino. We travelled like gentlemen. On foot to Chambave.
Ruins.

11/23 June, Evionnaz – Clarens Got up at 7. Coffee made of boot polish.
Waitress cried because I complained about the coffee. Went by stage-
coach to Villeneuve [...] Had a long trip in a boat and came back tired out.
Went by boat to Chillon. Tea at the Hôtel Byron. Good, but not complete
without women. Got back late and slept well.

15/27 June Got up at 9, still unwell; haemorrhoids. Mustn't drink wine
and must keep all the time to a diet that isn't too hot. Made some
cigarettes and had a pleasant chat with Druzhinin. Wrote a bit of *The Lost
One*. Slept after dinner, then went to Villeneuve and the Hôtel Byron. A
freckled beauty. I want a woman terribly. A pretty one.

22 June/4 July, Geneva – Bern Woke up at 9, hurried to the steamer. A
crowd, the like of which I've never seen before. [...] Different types: (1)
angular Germans with broad cheek-bones and brooches on the side of
their shirt-fronts; (2) slender Parisian Frenchmen; (3) stout, stalwart
Swiss. The railway journey. Shouts, garlands and welcomes for the
travelling lords and masters – the people. Dinner with a courier. A
travelling school of girls and boys with a ruddy, perspiring, high cheek-
boned master. Frenchmen in another carriage, wanting to *faire la noce*

[have a good time] everywhere. An enchanting moonlight night; the drunken shouts, the crowd and the dust didn't spoil the charm; a valley, moist and bright in the moonlight; I could hear the sounds of corn-crakes and frogs from there, and something seemed to draw me in that direction. But if I should go, I would be drawn further afield again. It's not with pleasure that my soul responds to the beauty of nature, but with a kind of sweet pain. It was nice as far as Bern; the people in the carriage were asleep; I looked out of the window and was in that happy frame of mind in which I know I can be no better. Found an apartment in the *Couronne*.[61] The entry of riflemen to the sound of music made me sad.

25 June/7 July, Lucerne Woke up at 9 and walked to a pension and the lion monument. At home I opened my notebook, but couldn't write anything. I've abandoned *The Hunting Ground*. A stupid and boring dinner. Went to a *privathaus*. On my way back from there at night – it was overcast with the moon breaking through – I heard some wonderful voices, two bell-towers in a broad street, and a little man singing Tyrolean songs to a guitar – it was splendid. I gave him something and invited him to sing in front of the Schweizerhof – it was no use, he went away shamefacedly, muttering something to himself, and the crowd followed him and laughed. Previously, however, there had even been a crowd of people on the balcony, listening in silence. I overtook him and invited him to the Schweizerhof for a drink. We were taken into another room. The singer was a commonplace, but pathetic person. We drank, the waiter laughed and the porter sat down. This exasperated me – I swore at them and got terribly agitated.[62] The night was wonderful. What do I want, what do I passionately desire? I don't know – only not the good things of this world. And how can one not believe in the immortality of the soul when one feels in one's own soul such immeasurable grandeur? I looked out of the window. Darkness, broken clouds and light. I could happily die!

My God! My God! What am I? Where am I going? And where am I now?

27 June/9 July Got up early and feel fine. Had a bathe. I'm more than pleased with my new apartment; got on with *Lucerne* and wrote a letter to Botkin before dinner. Got Freytag's *Soll und Haben* and Andersen's *Improvisatore* and read them,[63] went out in a boat and walked to a monastery. I'm terribly shy in the *pension*; there are a lot of pretty women. [. . .]

29 June/11 July, Lucerne – Sarnen Got up at 7 and had a bathe. Got on with *Lucerne* till dinner. It's good. One must be bold, otherwise one can't say anything except what is graceful, and I've a lot to say that is new and worthwhile. Sat with an artist at dinner, struck up a conversation with him, abused the Genevese, and he turned out to be one. What of it? I spoke sincerely. He's a nice fellow, I think, but our conversation was quietly ill-tempered. Set off for a couple of days' walking. Two Englishmen on the steamer. One was a teacher, the other his brother, an artist, I think, and I travelled with them via Stanstad to Alpnachstad. There were eleven English men and women there, for whom I acted as interpreter. *Rapacity*.[64] A bad-tempered Scotsman. A dull hotel in Sarnen, but the English and I chatted and made music. Slept badly. Here again one begins to see balding women with goitres, cretins, white-haired and self-satisfied. They wear their plaits here tied up in a bun and with an enormous pin. The people are blond and plain.

30 June/12 July, Sarnen – Beckenried Woke up at 9. Some Germans from Bern; we talked about hunting in the *Vaterland*.[65] Had a bathe. Good-natured coarseness of the Germans. Set off on foot; cretins. Nice people, good-natured in a playfully cretinous way. An old woman with a parasol. Girls. Two girls from Stans flirted with me, one of them with wonderful eyes. I had bad thoughts and was immediately punished – by shyness. A wonderful church with an organ, full of pretty women. Masses of sociable and fairly pretty ones. A wonderful eating-house, surprisingly cheap. [. . .]

2/14 July, Rigi-Kulm – Lucerne Got up at 3. A filthy bed with bugs. The same stupid view of nature and of people. Englishmen in blankets, with Murrays[66] and maps. 'Ah!' they exclaimed, when the sun appeared. [. . .] I set off with the Englishmen. I think I beat the Pole. Wonderful views below. Finished the journey by boat. The landlady's daughter struts about. She's too grand. I'm dying for lack of sleep. Had a bathe. Dozed off before dinner. Got angry at dinner with a Frenchman over something. Really, nothing can be more stupid than a *comme il faut* Frenchman. Slept, had a bathe, and went to Lucerne by boat. The Englishwoman has cleaned herself up and is nice and charming. Then I met the little one, but ran away from her. Had supper with the pastor and his family. A wonderful man.

4/16 July Got up at 7; a dog woke me up and I let it out. Wrote a bit and went to Sasha's.[67] What are we to do? It's dull. The heat is exhausting. After dinner I wrote as much as I could despite the heat, and read *Wilhelm Meister* and Miss Brontë.[68] [. . .] Roamed around in the evening; a cretin woman. Returned at night – Mendelssohn from the *pension* window. Is it possible that the tears of *Sehnsucht* [longing] which I often shed will cease as the years go by? [. . .]

11/23 July, Friedrichshafen – Stuttgart Got up at 7; had a bathe. Went to the Summer Palace. Endearing poverty, and repulsive primness and courtly atmosphere. [. . .] Had some excellent thoughts while reading. Two quite different things. *The Cossack* – as primitive and fresh as a biblical legend, and *The Hunting Ground* – very lively comedy; I must concentrate on types, all sharply defined.

Had a splendid view of the moon on my right. Very important – the idea occurred to me, clearly and forcibly, of starting a school in the country for the whole neighbourhood, and of general activity of that kind. The most important thing is constant activity. [. . .]

14/26 July, Baden-Baden Ill in the morning; roulette till 6. Lost everything. Dined at home, quite ill. In the evening, I looked on quite calmly at all this depravity and confusion, but am weak and ill. The young people in neck-ties avoid me. Went home, but the Frenchman kept me awake till 3, jabbering about his political plans, and about poetry and love. Horrible! I'd rather be without a nose, stinking and goitrous, the most dreadful cretin, the most repulsive abortion, than such a *moral* abortion.

15/27 July Borrowed 200 roubles from the Frenchman, and lost it all. [. . .]

24 July/5 August, Eisenach – Dresden Arrived at 9. Unwell. The town is nice. Went to the baths and walked back. Pushkin. He's lost much of his charm away from Switzerland. Went round to the art gallery. The Madonna[69] at once moved me deeply. Slept till 4. The theatre – a comedy by Gutzkow.[70] Germanic intenseness. [. . .]

25 July/6 August, Dresden Health still worse. Went round the bookshops and the music shops; my eyes stood out on pegs. Chose some music and books and went back to the gallery, but everything left me cold except the Madonna. [. . .]

30 July/11 August, on the steamer to Petersburg Cards again. Arrived at 2. Borrowed money in embarrassment from Pushkin. Found nobody in Petersburg except the Kolbasins. No money. Went to Nekrasov's. Disgusting stupidity – said nothing about money.

2 August, Petersburg Stayed in and read. Saltykov[71] – a talent to be taken seriously. Health poor.

6 August Decided to leave. Got everything done, for good or ill. Left at 9. Russia is disgusting. I simply don't like it. Health better.

8 August, Yasnaya Polyana [...] Delightful Yasnaya! Felt both sad and happy; but Russia disgusts me and I feel this coarse, deceitful life surrounding me on all sides. At the station Zorin was being thrashed, and I wanted to intercede. Vasily explained to me that first I would have to bribe the doctor. And he told me of many such things. Beatings and floggings. This is how I defined my purpose in life on the journey: first of all literary work, then family duties, then the estate – but I must leave the estate in the hands of the headman, and try as far as possible to lighten the load, make things better, take only 2,000 roubles for myself, and use the rest for the peasants. My chief stumbling block is the vanity of liberalism. But like Titus[72] – I'll do one good deed a day, and that will be sufficient.

9 August, Pirogovo Got up at 9. Health bad. The headman deeply despises me, and it's hard for me to do anything with him. Sashka stole some butter. I summoned him to see me. 'I don't know what happens when I've had a drink.' He said his feet were suppurating, but the headman said: 'It serves you right.' I admonished him and then gave him something. It was stupid, but what else could I do? Went to Pirogovo. The poverty of the people and the sufferings of the animals are dreadful. [...]

13 August [...] Read a bit of Brontë; wrote a letter to Turgenev. Started allowing the domestic serfs to buy their freedom.

15 August Felt all right all day. Read *The Iliad*.[73] That's the thing! Wonderful! Wrote to Ryabinin. I must revise the whole of *The Caucasian Tale*.[74] Not many of the peasants want to transfer to quit-rent. [...]

16 August In the morning, Vasily Davydkin. I gave him three roubles. *The Iliad*. Good, but no more. Went for a walk round the mill and thought about the estate. Prince Yengalychev.[75] Cunning, stupid, uneducated but good-natured. Went riding and killed a hare. At home, attended to estate business. Wrote a little note to Auntie; increased the headman's wages. Sensuality torments me; laziness again, boredom and sadness. Everything seems stupid. The ideal is unattainable; I've already ruined myself. Work, a modest reputation, money. What for? Material enjoyment – again, what for? There will soon be eternal night. I keep thinking I'll die soon. I'm too lazy to write in detail; I'd like to write all the time in fiery outlines. Love. I'm thinking of a novel of that sort.

17 August Only read *The Iliad* and intermittently attended to estate business. Went hunting, and to the Yengalychevs'. It's sad and gloomy in that house – no memories. Came back at 1. *The Iliad* is making me completely rethink *The Fugitive*.

18 August Got up late, health quite good; but in the morning I lost my temper and called someone a blockhead. It's terrible! Before you know it, you've come to grief again. Read *The Iliad*. Seryozha came; we had a pleasant chat. I've thought out *The Hunting Ground* completely, but I'm altogether dissatisfied with the Caucasian tale. I can't write without an idea. But the idea that good is good in every sphere, that the same passion exists everywhere and that the primitive state is good, isn't enough. It would be a good thing, though, if the latter work could inspire me. It's the only solution.

26 August Health so-so. Estate business in the morning. It's bad in all respects, but most of all because it's dragging me once again into the serfdom rut. I don't want the torment of introducing something new. Decided to buy land in Baburino.[76] After dinner the threshing began. Zyabrev has turned down my offer; read Koltsov.[77] Charm and immense power. Gave five men their letters of freedom. God only knows what will happen, but to make things better for people, even without getting any gratitude at all, is still something, and leaves its mark in one's soul. I'm setting off tomorrow at daybreak.[78]

28 August [. . .] Seryozha has left. He and I are becoming more and more friendly. The main thing is to find the right string to play on with a man, and to let him do the same with you. [. . .] Read the second part of *Dead Souls*; it's rather clumsy. I must write nothing except *The Hunting Ground*, and put Auntie in it. I'm going to the Gorchakovs' tomorrow.

29 August, en route from Pirogovo to Verkhoupye Started at 6. [. . .] Finished reading the *unbelievably delightful* ending of *The Iliad*. [. . .] Read the Gospels, which I haven't done for a long time. After *The Iliad*. How could Homer not have known that goodness is love! [. . .]

3 September, Yasnaya Polyana [. . .] Set off for Yasnaya but found nothing. The sale of the wood is starting. I've no money. My youth is past! I say this in a good sense. I'm calm and there's nothing I want. I even write calmly. It's only now that I've come to understand that I don't need to organize the life around me symmetrically, the way I want it, but I need to take myself apart, make myself flexible, in order to adapt myself to any sort of life.

6 September The estate again, which I've become very much involved in. Rode out with the dogs but didn't find anything, and was bored. Dined alone and tried to read Hackländer[79] – nasty, *mal fait* [badly written] and lacking in talent. As for my own writing, I've decided that my chief fault is timidity. I must be bold. Wrote two sheets of *The Lost One* in the evening. Slept badly, sensual excitement.

8 September, Sunday [. . .] Read Gogol's letters recently received. As a man he was simply trash. Terrible trash.

24 September Got up late. Bad-tempered. Scolded Yakov. Abominable! Wonderful weather. Wrote a little. I've let myself go terribly in all respects. So many unresolved problems. The charge for the use of land: should I increase it or not? etc. Rode to Gimbut's. Flirted with MN. [. . .] At home Klara – she filled me with disgust. [. . .]

5 October Worked on the estate; no labourers. A mass of expenses; I'm getting despondent. Went for a ride, wrote a bit in the evening. Expected a woman – she didn't come.

21 October, Moscow In the morning, decided about lodgings, went for a walk and dined at Fet's. He, too, is ambitious and poor. Went to the Aksakovs' with him. To the theatre and to the Arsenyevs'. Yesterday was at the Behrs'. Lyubochka[80] is awful – balding and frail. Misfortunes on all sides. And God, how old I am! Everything bores me, nothing disgusts me, I'm even fairly satisfied with myself, but everything leaves me cold. I don't desire anything, and I'm prepared to eke out this joyless existence as best I can. Only why, I don't know. What is strange is not that God ordained that a piece of bread should be His Son's flesh; 100,000 times more strange is the fact that we live and don't know why; that we love good, but that nowhere is it written: 'This is good, that is evil.'

22 October, Petersburg Set off for Petersburg; almost missed the train. [. . .] Evening at the Tolstoys'. Alexandrine is charming – a joy and a comfort. I've never seen a woman who could hold a candle to her. Alexandra Petrovna in the evening; it's too late, she's got wrinkles.

30 October, Moscow [. . .] Petersburg saddened me at first, but then quite restored me. My reputation has fallen, or is just about surviving, and I felt greatly saddened at heart, but now I'm more composed; I know I have something to say and the strength to say it forcefully; so the public can say what it likes for all I care. But it's necessary to work conscientiously and apply all one's strength – then let them spit on the altar.[81]

6 November [. . .] Alexandrine[82] is charming. She is definitely the woman who charms me more than any other. Talked to her about marriage. Why didn't I tell her everything? [. . .]

7 November [. . .] In the evening, I read *Don Quixote* and went to the baths.

11 November [. . .] Fet came to dinner. He read *Antony and Cleopatra*,[83] and by his talk kindled my ardour for art. I must begin *The Cossack* dramatically. Can't sleep.

1 December [. . .] Evening at the Dyakovs'. Wonderful sisters. Alexandrine has me on a string and I'm grateful to her for it. However in the evenings I'm passionately in love with her, and return home full of something – happiness or sadness – I don't know which.

11, 12, 13–26 December A few unenjoyable balls. A few 'Nadya'[84] soirées, pleasant but equivocal. Latterly they've been dull. Revised *The Musician*. I'll publish it. Twice went to the gipsies'.

29, 30, 31 December Ball at the Bobrinskys'. I'm beginning to like Tyutcheva in a quiet way. [. . .]

1858

2, 3, 4, 5 January   Efforts to found a music society.[1] [. . .]

6 January   To the Aksakovs'. Argument with the old man. Aristocratic feeling means a lot. But the main thing is – I feel myself a citizen, and if we are to have authority I want that authority to be in hands I respect. [. . .]

7 January   [. . .] Tyutcheva – nonsense!

8 January   No, not nonsense! Slowly but surely, she's taking a complete hold of me.

15 January, Sogolevo[2]   [. . .] Made a good start on *Death*.[3]

19 January, Moscow   Tyutcheva. She occupies my thoughts persistently. It's even a nuisance, especially since it's not love; it doesn't have love's charm. Got up at 8. Wrote letters, read a chapter. Nikolenka advised me to leave the tree in. Went for a walk with Nikolenka. Crowds. The Kremlin. The Behrs. At home with Chicherin.[4] All philosophy, including his, is the enemy of life and poetry. The more true it is, the more generalized and cold; the more untrue, the sweeter it is. I'm not a political person, I say that to myself a thousand times. To the theatre. *A Life for the Tsar*.[5] Chorus beautiful. To the club. *Asya*[6] is rubbish.

20 January   Got up early. Thought and re-thought *Three Deaths* and wrote *The Tree*. It wouldn't come out right at once. Went to gymnastics. Not bad. Spoke to M. Sukhotin sarcastically about K. Tyutcheva. Yet I think about her incessantly. What rubbish! Still I know that I only desire her love passionately, but have no pity for her. [. . .]

24 January   Got up late. Finished *Three Deaths*. Gymnastics. [. . .]

25 January   [. . .] To Fet's. Felt glad and envious at observing his family happiness. A musical evening – delightful! Weber delightful. Tyutcheva, Sverbeyeva, Shcherbatova, Chicherina, Olsufyeva, Rebinder – I'm in love with them all. [. . .]

26 January Dear Pushchin came. Had a walk; went to the puppet theatre with the children. Dined at Kireyeva's.[7] Went to Tyutcheva's prepared to love her. She's cold, petty, aristocratic. Rubbish! Chicherina is nice; very immature, I think. Kireyev is a good friend. *The Government Inspector.* Shchepkin[8] is an austere actor. Drank with Pushchin. Went to a masquerade. Two masks. One from Samara [?]. 100. I knew her. Revolting. [. . .]

10, 11, 12 February Chicherin said he loved me. It was after we'd had a drink at Chevalier's. I'm grateful to him and proud of the fact. He's very useful to me. But I still feel no strong attraction towards him.

13, 14, 15 February, Yasnaya Polyana Spent the night at Chevalier's before leaving. For half the night I had a wonderful talk with Chicherin. The other half I didn't see, since I spent it with the gipsies till morning and in Goryachy. Went to Tula. Teeth still falling out. Worked yesterday on *The Lost One*. It's beginning to take shape. Love – no!

16 February Seryozha arrived yesterday. What a remarkable thing that my love of ideas is becoming a barrier between me and old friends. It's a good arrangement for people to marry at thirty. All my people know me too well to love me. [. . .]

17–18 February Revised *Albert* a bit. And jotted down some ideas about punishments. Then did some reading. [. . .] *Midsummernight's Dream* in English and Russian[9] [. . .] Thoughts of approaching death torment me. I look at myself in the mirror for days on end. I'm working sluggishly. Must grit my teeth when it comes to physical *and* mental work.

19, 20, 21, 22, 23, 24 February, Moscow Another three days in the country; spent them very well. The old beginning of *The Cossacks* is good; I got on with it a bit. [. . .] *I'm an emancipator!!!* Through a snow-storm to Moscow. Gymnastics. The baths. Overate.

25 February Got up early, read the journals – about Lord Grey.[10] [. . .] Read Chicherin on the emancipation and Korsh[11] on the reform. [. . .]

8, 9, 10 March Went to Tyutcheva's; neither one thing nor the other, she's shy. Saw Shcherbatova at a concert and spoke to her. She's nice, but less so. [. . .]

13 March, Petersburg [. . .] I respect and love science. Health better. Nothing to do in Petersburg.

14 March [. . .] In the Hermitage – Ruysdael. Rubens'[12] prodigal son with the rough back of his neck is good, also *The Descent from the Cross.* The Murillo not very. Steen's composition is charming. [. . .]

17 March, Petersburg – Moscow Saltykov came and read. *The Idealist* is good. His is a wholesome talent. [. . .]

19 March In the morning I got on with *The Cossacks.* Toothache yesterday and today. Read St Beuve. Gymnastics. Fet. Wrote a little after dinner. Baths. Had supper with Nikolenka at Pechkin's.[13] The talk was about my being an egoist. Unpleasant and sad. But I'm to blame to some extent too.

20 March Wrote a little, but continuing toothache distracts me. Read Chicherin's article about British industry.[14] Terribly interesting. For some time now every question has assumed enormous proportions for me. I'm much indebted to Chicherin. Nowadays with every new object or circumstance – apart from the specific conditions of that object or circumstance – I can't help looking for its place in the eternal and the infinite, in history. Walked till 4. Did some writing at Mashenka's and read half of *L'oiseau* and *L'insecte* by Michelet.[15] Terribly profound in some places, and rubbish in others.

21 March [. . .] The political excludes the artistic, because the former, in order to prove, must be one-sided. [. . .]

24 March [. . .] Finished reading *L'insecte.* Maudlin and affected. In the *Literarisches Zentralblatt* – a poem of the future about the unification of Germany, Emerson on Shakespeare and Goethe;[16] in the *Athenaeum* – Dickens' argument over the literary fund.[17] Siege of Lucknow. Inhumanity of England.[18] Dined at 7, soup. Auntie came. Wrote to Alexandrine Tolstaya and read La Chapelle's *Voyage.*[19] Read Montluc's *Commentaries.*[20] A good old Gasconard. Health better.

25 March Wrote nothing. Read *L'asino*[21] in the *Athenaeum.* Read Marcus Aurelius, his conception of the universe. Chicherin; an argument about railways and Christianity. [. . .]

26 March Read splendid articles by Kokorev and by Solovyov – Buddhists.[22] Was in good spirits, but had a long walk, caught cold and got toothache again. Geology is a deadly science.

1 April Got up at 10. Chicherin. Ill at ease with him. Christ gave no orders, but revealed a moral law which will always remain the criterion of good and evil. [. . .]

12 April, Yasnaya Polyana   Got up, went for a walk. Scolded Yakov and was on the point of threatening some policemen. Bad – but it's all due mainly to my teeth. At home, I read Wiseman on Popes Leo XII and Pius VIII.²³ Wrote a bit. At dinner, I read *Scènes de la vie américaine.*²⁴ Would be interesting to write a general criticism of the French novel. Wrote with a wealth of content, but carelessly. The escape to the mountains won't come out right.²⁵ Went for a ride. Things are up and down on the estate. I must get used to the fact that they are up and down. Played quite a lot, but carelessly.

20 April   A lovely day; the grass is pushing through and the last snow is melting. Was sad, and also glad . . . An owl flew by, flapping its wings once or twice, then more and more often, before it came to rest.

21 April   A wonderful day. Peasant women in the garden and by the well. I'm like a man possessed. [. . .]

25 April   [. . .] In the morning I pottered about on the estate and re-read my army tales. The last ones are poor. [. . .]

26 April   Rode off early into the fields; was in a bad temper. Re-read and revised everything. Rode out in answer to a call from a soldier, but in vain. Dined, slept, walked into the fields . . . Put the finishing touches to *The Cordon;*²⁶ many new thoughts. A Christian outlook. Played for about three hours – three chords of sixths to the accompaniment of nightingales – and enjoyed myself. Received a letter from Alexandrine about *Three Deaths.*

27, 28, 29, 30 April   [. . .] I've been reading Macaulay²⁷ and the newspapers these last few days. No, history is too cold for me. Re-read my Caucasian diary yesterday. I was wrong to imagine that I was such a nice young lad there. On the contrary. But still, as something that is over and done with, it was very good. Recalled a lot that will be useful for my Caucasian novel. I've reached the second part of the novel, but it's so muddled that I'll have to begin it all from the beginning or else write another second part.

10, 11, 12, 13 May   A wonderful Whitsunday. Drooping bird-cherry in the workers' calloused hands; the choking voice of Vasily Davydkin. Caught a glimpse of Aksinya.²⁸ She's very pretty. I've been waiting for her these last few days in vain. Today in the big old wood; the daughter in law; I'm a fool. A beast. Her neck is red from the sun. Went to Gimbut's. I'm in love as never before in my life. I've no other thoughts. I'm tormented. *Tomorrow – every effort.*

Haven't written my diary for nearly a month. *Today is 12 June.* All this time I've written nothing. I've been busy with the estate, but more with running about . . . Have been to Pirogovo. Fet. Nikolenka came for the day. Dismissed Vasily. Turgenev came yesterday. Judging by him I've grown up; I feel at ease with him. Read *Three Deaths*; it's weak. I want to work, and above all I want order.

14 June All day in the fields. A wonderful night. A dewy white mist. Trees in the mist. The moon behind the birch trees and a corncake; no more nightingales.

15, 16 June [. . .] All day at work. Health seems better. Had Aksinya . . .; but I'm repelled by her.

16 June to 19 July I'm not writing, not reading, and not thinking. I'm wholly absorbed in the estate. The battle is still in full swing. The peasants are trying it on, and putting up a fight. The ones at Grumant are sullen, but say nothing. I'm afraid of myself. A hitherto unknown feeling of vengeance is beginning to stir in me; and it's vengeance against the commune. I'm afraid of injustice . . .[29] My talent is – *envy.* [. . .]

4 September Had a good clean up . . . Varicose veins enlarged. Went to Nikolenka's and Turgenev's: the first is very nice at home, the second intolerably difficult. Fet is a darling. The elections have taken place. I've become the enemy of our province.[30] Cherkassky and co.[31] are just as much rubbish as their opponents, but French-speaking rubbish. Went to Aleksin, and bought a number of horses. Turgenev is behaving badly towards Masha. He's a bad lot. Played cards. Won. Feel like work. *I'm thirty.*

15 September I've aged terribly and grown tired of life this summer. I often have occasion to ask myself with horror – what do I love? Nothing. Positively nothing. Such a situation is pathetic. There's no possibility of happiness in life; but on the other hand it's easier to be an out and out spiritual being, 'a dweller on earth, but devoid of physical needs'. I'm in Moscow. Business will keep me about a week. I've seen Korsh and Tyutcheva. I'd almost be prepared to marry her impassively, without love, but she received me with studied coldness. Turgenev's niece[32] was right. It's difficult to come across a really ugly creature. My illness is moral torture for me. I promised Korsh a description of this summer,[33] but the narrowness of the task sickens me. [. . .]

15 September　[. . .] Spent the evening at Yakovleva's with Auntie. One can't help loving people: they are all – *we* are all – so pitiable. [. . .]

17 September　Roamed about all morning with anguish in my heart. Dined at the Behrs'. What sweet girls! [. . .]

4 October, Yasnaya Polyana　Went hunting with Sukhotin. Saw Katenka!!!! Yesterday at dinner I said that it's impossible to prove magnetism. Mashenka said that I'm always changing my mind and that I used to believe in it before. I asked her to keep to the point. I always want to play the leading role, she said, and consider her a child. I asked her to hear me out. Seryozha lacks any delicacy, she said.[34] I lost my temper and said she had an evil character. She had an affected, but also a genuine *attaque de nerfs* [fit of hysterics]. I wouldn't have dared to say what I did if her husband had been there, she said. I humiliate her because she lives with me, so to speak, with no place of refuge of her own. Auntie wept for two days. I'd changed so much, she said. It was impossible to fathom my character. But really I'm only asking God for patience.

30 October　Saw Valeriya – had no regrets at all about my feeling. Things are all right again with Mashenka. Things are fine with the children. Went to Tula. Cherkassky isn't stupid, but rather narrow-minded. No Slavophiles understand music. Copied out *The Cossack*. Must do it again. No money, and the estate is in a bad way.

27 November　No, I've let myself go so much that it's impossible. Estate management is a boorish occupation. Today Rezun told lies; I flew into a rage and, following the loathsome custom, said: 'Flog him.' I waited for him to come and see me. I sent someone to stop the flogging, but he didn't get there in time. I'll ask his pardon. I'll never reprimand anyone again before 2 o'clock in the afternoon. I asked his pardon and gave him three roubles, but I suffered agonies. [. . .]

7, 8, 9, 10, 11, 12, 13 December, Moscow　Worked a little; but the estate rut which I've been drawn into has been distracting me too much. Today the 13th, I am in Moscow. Literature, which I had a sniff of yesterday at Fet's, disgusts me: i.e. I think that since I began my literary career in the most flattering conditions of general praise, sustained for two years during which I occupied almost the first place – without such conditions I don't want to know literature, i.e., literature for the public – and thank God. I must write quietly and calmly, without the aim of publishing. Wrote a note about the gentry problem, and burned it without showing it to anyone.

23 December   Came to Moscow with the children. Didn't manage to get another mortgage. Money is needed everywhere. Went bear-hunting. On the 21st – killed one; on the 22nd – was bitten by one.[35] Squandered a pile of money.

1859

1 January, Moscow   All this time I've been working, and today as well. My head still aches. I must get married this year – or not at all. [. . .]

16 February   All this time I've been working on a novel[1] and I've made a lot of progress, though not on paper. I've altered everything. A poem. I'm very pleased with what's in my head. The whole plot is ready and unalterable. I've hardly been anywhere. [. . .] My health isn't good: both stomach and *nerves*.

9 April, Moscow   Went hunting, then to Petersburg. Ten very happy days in Petersburg. Saw Lvova twice again in Moscow. My old feelings came back, but not so strongly. Things would be very good were it not for my health. Received some money and lost it at Chinese billiards. Worked. Finished *Anna*,[2] but it's not good. [. . .]

9 May, Yasnaya Polyana   A week in the country already. Things are going badly on the estate, and I'm fed up with it. Received *Family Happiness*.[3] It's a shameful abomination. I find myself revoltingly cold towards everything. Aksinya I recall only with revulsion – her shoulders. Feuillet[4] a tremendous talent. I'm sorry for myself. My heart simply doesn't respond to anything this year. I don't even feel sorrow. Only the need to work and forget – what? There's nothing to forget. Forget that I'm alive. I prayed today and want to force myself to work regularly and do even a little good. [. . .]

9 October   I've been in the country from 28 May until today. Disorganized, irritable, bored, despairing and lazy. I've been busy working on the estate, but too little and badly. Continue to see Aksinya *exclusively*. Masha has moved from my house into her own house; I almost quarrelled with her for good. I struck a man on two occasions this summer. On 6 August I went to Moscow and began dreaming about botany. Of course it's a dream – childishness. Went to the Lvovs', and when I think of that visit – I rave. I was on the point of deciding that that was my last attempt at marriage;[5] but that was childishness too. [. . .] And here I am at home and for some reason at peace and confident of my plans for gradual moral self-improvement. May God grant it. [. . .]

11 October   My moral condition gets worse and worse every day, and I'm almost back in my summer rut. I'll try and get out of it. Read *Adam Bede.*[6] Intensely tragic, although false and filled with only one idea. That's not so with me. [. . .]

12, 13 October   [. . .] Read Rabelais. Aksinya came. [. . .]

14, 15, 16 October, morning   Had a dream today. Crime is not a particular action, but a particular relationship towards the conditions of life. To kill one's mother might not be a crime, but to eat up a piece of bread might be a very great crime. How great it felt when I woke up at night with this idea!

The estate has fallen on my shoulders again with all its noisome, oppressive weight. I suffer agonies and am idle.

1860

1 February, Yasnaya Polyana Couldn't get to sleep yesterday till 5 in the morning. Read about *dégénérescence de l'espèce humaine*[1] [degeneration of the human species] and about the fact that there is a higher physical degree of mental development. I belong to that degree. Mechanically thought about prayer. But pray to whom? What sort of God is it that I can imagine Him so clearly that I can ask Him things and communicate with Him? And if I imagine Him to be like that, He loses all greatness for me. A God of whom one can ask things and whom it is possible to serve is an expression of weakness of mind. He is God precisely because I can't imagine to myself His whole being. Besides, He is not being; He is law and might. Let this page stand as a memorial to my conviction of the power of the mind.

16 February Yesterday I made a few changes on the estate. Did a little reading and teaching.[2] [. . .]

22 May Whitsunday. Rain. Read Auerbach and *Reinecke Fuchs*.[3] Read through my memorandum[4] – it makes sense. I've lost all my good spirits – I'm sad. I must love everyone. Filat and Ivan too, and be more natural with them. Cursed the headman and Matvey.

26 May [. . .] Got up at 5, attended to things myself and everything was fine – felt in good spirits. She[5] was nowhere about. I looked for her. It's no longer the feeling of a stag, but of a husband for a wife. It's strange. I try to reawaken my former feeling of surfeit, and I can't. An insurmountable indifference to work – that's what arouses this feeling for her most of all. In the evening I nearly lost my temper over the dungheap, dismounted and started to work full steam, and everything was fine again and I began to love them all. It will be strange if my worship of work proves of no avail. Couldn't get to sleep, felt unwell, wrote to Mashenka.

21 July/2 August, Kissingen I've hardly written my diary at all for two months. Today is 20 July.[6] I'm in Kissingen. I'll try to go backwards from today to the day I left.[7]

Yesterday, 19/31 July Read a history of pedagogy.[8] Luther is great. Went for a walk. Day-labourers work less than half as much as our peasant women and earn twenty copecks a day. Ignorance, poverty, laziness, weakness. Yesterday, I went to see an American pastor about schools. They're all controlled by the government, and their privileges have killed all private competition. The teaching of religion – just the Bible without explanations or abbreviations.

17/24 July   Visited a school. Terrible. A prayer for the king, beatings, everything by heart, frightened, morally deformed children.

16/28 July   Visited a school for young children – just as bad. *Lautier-methode* [phonetic method]. [. . .]

22 July/3 August   Read a history of pedagogy. Francis Bacon. Founder of materialism. Luther a reformer in religion – back to the sources. Bacon in natural science. Riehl[9] in politics. Met Fröbel.[10] An aristocrat – and a liberal. Riehl is a chatterbox. Art cannot produce anything when it is conscious art.

23 July/4 August   Read Riehl and Herzen[11] – an unbridled intelligence: morbid self-love, but breadth, cleverness and kindness, and refinement – all Russian. Went hunting. Wrote home.

24 July/5 August   Montaigne was the first to express clearly the idea of freedom of education. In education again the main thing is equality and freedom.

29 July/10 August   Met Fröbel. A Liberal chatterbox. [. . .]

30 July/11 August   Went to Haritz,[12] met a young schoolteacher interested in the question whether to write on every line or every other. An old man, a slave to routine. Hired some workers and did some mowing.

31 July/12 August   Nikolenka's situation is awful. He's terribly clever and clear-headed. And he wants to live. But he has no energy for living. [. . .]

1/13 August   Nikolenka left. I don't know what to do. Mashenka and he are in a bad way. And I'm no use. Spent all the time after dinner with Fröbel. He's begun to respect me. [. . .]

2, 3, 4/14, 15, 16 August   Got to know Fröbel better. Politics have exhausted him completely. Met Blum[13] and an economist. Not many clever people. The thought of experimental pedagogy excited me, but I couldn't restrain myself, talked about it and weakened the force of it. Did some writing.[14] [. . .]

11/23 August Dreamed that I was dressed as a peasant and my mother didn't recognize me. [. . .]

13/25 October, Hyères[15] It will soon be a month since Nikolenka died. This event cut me off from life terribly. Once again the question: why? It's not long now before I set off there. But where? Nowhere. I try to write, I force myself, and nothing comes of it only because I can't ascribe to work the importance I need to ascribe to it to have the strength and the patience to work. During the funeral itself the thought occurred to me to write a materialist Gospel, a life of a material Christ. Nothing remarkable about the journey from Soden. In Geneva – the *Collège*. History by dictation, and one person doing sums. A drunken teacher. Morally deformed children in a *salle d'asile* [infant school]. Foolish Turgenev.[16] Nikolenka's death is the strongest impression of my life. Marseille. School is not in the schools, but in the journals and cafés.

16/28 October Sunday. The one way to live is to work. To work one must love work. To love work, the work must be attractive. To be attractive, it must be half done, and well done. *Cercle vicieux* [vicious circle]. But what can one do? Fortune-telling, irresolution, idleness, melancholy, thoughts of death. I must escape from this. There's only one way. Force myself to work. It's now one o'clock and I've done nothing. [. . .]

29 October/10 November For ten years or so I haven't had such a wealth of images and ideas as these last three days. I can't write, they are so abundant.

31 October/12 November A boy of thirteen has died in agony from consumption. What for? The only explanation is furnished by belief in the compensation of a future life. If that doesn't exist, there is no justice, and no need for justice, and the demand for justice is a superstition.

1/13 November Justice constitutes the essential demand man makes on man. Man seeks the same relationship in his attitude to the world. Without a future life it isn't there. Expediency! That is the only immutable law of nature, say the natural scientists. It isn't there in the manifestations of man's soul – love and poetry, the best manifestations. It isn't there. All these things live and die, often without having found their expression. Nature has far overstepped her mark in giving man the need for poetry and love, if her only law is expediency.

1861

*1/13 April, Weimar*¹   It's difficult to write down now what has happened these last four months – Italy, Nice, Florence, Livorno. An attempt to write *Aksinya*.² Naples. The first vivid impression of nature and antiquity – Rome – Hyères – Paris – reconciliation with Turgenev – London – not too bad – a loathing for civilization. Brussels – a brief feeling of domesticity, a letter about Katenka to Mashenka.³ Eisenach – the journey – thoughts about God and immortality. God has been restored – hope and immortality. The first and second night in Eisenach – the cries of a sick child – the clocks – the babbling. Weimar – a wench. [. . .]

3/15 April, Jena   Couldn't sleep last night. I can't solve the problem of upbringing and education, but I'm taking a calmer view of German education. [. . .] Only Germany has derived pedagogy from philosophy. The Reformation of philosophy. England, France and America have imitated it.

4/16 April, Weimar Schullehrerseminar [School teachers' seminar]. Excellent. [. . .] Zwätzen.⁴ A very stupid school, showing what institutions imposed from above can lead to. Theory without practice. [. . .]
  The job of a school is not *die Wissenschaft beibringen* [to impart knowledge] but *die Achtung und die Idee der Wissenschaft beibringen* [to impart the respect for and idea of knowledge]. With this thought I dropped off to sleep peacefully. On the journey, as I was throwing pebbles, I thought about art too. Is it possible to have as one's sole aim situations and not characters? I think it is, and that's what I've done, and that's where I've been successful. Only it's not everybody's task, but mine.

5/17 April   Got up at 8. At the *Kindergarten*. Geometric drawing and basket-making are nonsense. You won't discern the laws of development of a child that way. They learn by heart when it doesn't concern their world, but you can't understand their world. A child can draw sticks, but only has a vague idea of a circle. And you can't teach perseverance when everything is new. Perseverance is the strength to reject *everything* that isn't what you want to be concerned with. Biedermann⁵ is not stupid, but he's a scholar and a writer, a part of whom is already in his book and no longer in him. But apart from *Childhood*, I exist entirely in myself, and for that reason I look down on these people so freely. [. . .]

6/18 April, Dresden[6]   [. . .] Went to evening mass. I can stand it in church. Perhaps I'll prepare for communion. [. . .]

7/19 April   [. . .] *Deutscher Disputations-Verein* [German debating society]. I spoke. On the country's education and on public opinion.

9/21 April, Berlin   [. . .] Auerbach!!!!![7] A most charming man! *Ein Licht mir aufgegangen* [He was a revelation to me]. [. . .] He's forty-nine, upright, young, a believer. No poet of negation.

12/24 April   The frontier. Well and cheerful; hardly aware of being in Russia.

6 May, Yasnaya Polyana   Haven't written my diary for about ten days. [. . .] I've been appointed an arbiter of the peace[8] and have acccepted. Went to Tula, chatted a lot and am beginning to be proud and therefore stupid. Markov has refused the co-editorship of the journal.[9] And generally speaking the idea of the journal is flagging. Chaos at Pirogovo, and Seryozha and I could do nothing. I've forgotten the pleasant day at the Behrs'; *but I daren't marry Liza.*[10]
Tomorrow morning, *Polikushka*, and read the statutes.[11] In the evening, prepare the school syllabus and a lecture.

7 May   Read the statutes with the peasants, and nothing else. I'm overcome by laziness. [. . .]

9 May   Went to mass; invited the priest to come and read. The children's explanation of the rituals is even more stupid than the one the priest gives them. [. . .]

12 May   Submitted an application about the school.[12] I'm a parish teacher. Tired myself out with gymnastics. Wonderful lectures in the garden. Came back home and was seized with the desire to write *The Cossack*. [. . .]

25 June   A remarkable quarrel with Turgenev,[13] a final one – he's an absolute *scoundrel* – but I think that in time I'll relent and forgive him. My work as an arbiter hasn't provided me with much material and has made me quarrel with *all* the landowners for good, and has ruined my health – also for good, I think. Order prevails in the school, but it lacks life, I'm afraid. I'm not going because of illness. Wrote out a syllabus.[14]

22 September, Moscow I'm in Moscow. Was right about Turgenev. I meant to write him a letter – and for some reason didn't – in which I meant to ask his forgiveness. There's a great deal of work ahead. I'll cling on to it. Liza Behrs tempts me, but nothing will come of it. Mere calculation isn't enough, and there's no feeling.

23 September [. . .] I've got consumption, but I'm getting used to it.[15] I'm bored because my circle is too restricted. *She* is probably in the place where I'm not.

8 October, Yasnaya Polyana Yesterday I received a letter from Turgenev in which he accused me of telling people that he's a coward and of distributing copies of my letter to him. Wrote back to him that it was nonsense, and sent a letter as well: 'you call my behaviour dishonourable; you wanted to punch my face before, but I consider myself to blame, ask your forgiveness and decline the challenge.'[16]

I have two students;[17] the school is getting worse. I'm beginning to get disillusioned about the journal.

28 October School and arbitration business are going well, but we haven't started on the journal yet. I feel like writing. Yesterday I opened a third school, which won't be a success. Wrote to Chicherin about students.

5 November Went to church with the singers. The teachers are poor. [. . .] Quarrelled with the headman; made a good start on *The Yasnaya Diary*;[18] Interrupted by the schoolchildren. [. . .]

6 November Wrote my diary[19] in the morning, pretty well. A mass of material. Worked at the school; feeling my way with analysis.

Pyotr Vasilyevich[20] was drunk. Gymnastics. Read Perevlessky[21] – he's not right. [. . .]

1862

20 *May*   On the steamer.[1] I seem to be coming back to life and to the awareness of it.

Since Moscow I've been thinking over things. The idea of the folly of progress haunts me. With the clever and the stupid, the old and the young, I talk only about this one thing. Wrote an article in this spirit for the 6th number of *Yasnaya Polyana*.[2] [. . .]

23 *August, Moscow*   In Moscow. Haven't eaten for two days, had awful toothache, spent the night at the Behrs'. A child![3] It could be! But what terrible confusion! Oh, if only I could manage to reach a clear and honourable position. [. . .] Submitted a letter to the Tsar.[4] [. . .] I'm afraid for myself – what if this is the desire for love, and not love? I try to look only at her weak sides, but nevertheless. A child! It could be!

24 *August*   Got up feeling well and with a particularly clear head; the writing went well, but the content is poor. Then I felt sadder than I've been for a long time. No, I haven't any friends at all! I'm alone. I used to have friends when I served Mammon, but not now that I serve the truth. Went to Auntie's. Living isn't so simple for old ladies either, and life pulsates for them with all its subtle complexities. [. . .] I think less about Sonya, but when I do, it's good.

26 *August*   Walked to the Behrs'; it was quiet and cosy there. Girlish laughter. Sonya was plain and vulgar, but she interests me. She gave me a story to read.[5] What force of truth and simplicity! The uncertainty torments her. I read it all without a sinking heart, and without a sign of jealousy or envy, but 'unusually unattractive appearance' and 'fickleness of opinions' touched me on the raw. I've calmed down now. All this is not for me. Work, and just the satisfaction of my needs.

28 *August*   I'm thirty-four. Got up with my usual melancholy. [. . .] Worked a bit; wasted my time writing to Sonya in initial letters.[6] Wasted my time dining at Pechkin's, had a nap at home. To the Sushkovs' (lied about the 1,000 roubles). A pleasant evening at the Tyutchevs'. A sweet, reassuring night. You ugly mug, don't think about marriage; your vocation is different, and for that you have been well endowed.

29 August   [. . .] Wrote badly. If you avoid the essential, the result is tittle-tattle. Dined at home. Called on Behrs and went with him to Pokrovskoye. Nothing, nothing, silence . . . Not love, as before, not jealousy, not pity even, though rather like it, but something sweet, a bit of hope (which there shouldn't be). You swine. A bit like pity and sorrow. But a wonderful night, and a good, sweet feeling. She made me decipher the letter. I was embarrassed. So was she. There was a scene. It's all unnatural. [. . .]

30 August   [. . .] Dined at home, had a sleep, then to the Behrs'. I'm not jealous of Sonya because of P.;[7] I can't believe that it's not me. It seemed the right moment, but it was night-time. She spoke in the same way; sadly and calmly. A walk, the summer-house, supper at home, her eyes – and the night-time! You fool, it's not meant for you; but still I'm in love, as never before except with Sonechka Koloshina and A.[8] Spent the night at their house, couldn't sleep; nothing but her. 'You've never loved,' she said, and it was so funny and I was so glad.

31 August   In the morning, too, the same sweet feeling, and the fullness of a life of love. Did some writing. Two fools – Plescheyev and Yakushkin – interrupted me; a foreword and insertions to *Mohammed*.[9] To the Tyutchevs'; died-in-the-wool blue stockings. How offensive they are to me. Someone spoke and it seemed like her voice. This third and last love is deep-seated. It's not for you, you old devil – go on writing critical articles! Began to write to her and was interrupted – a good job. I can't leave now – and that's that. Kokhanovskaya[10] is nauseating; they're all nauseating – shrivelled up in their crinolines.

3 September   At their place; nothing special at first, then a walk. 'He's ugly; you look well.' Lorgnettes. 'Please come again.' I've calmed down! On the way back I thought: either it's all unintentional, or her feelings are unusually subtle, or it's the basest coquetry – one man today, another tomorrow – and where does the person leaving fit in?[11] – or else it's unintentional *and* subtle *and* coquettish. But on the whole nothing, nothing, silence. Never has my future life with a wife presented itself to me so clearly, joyfully and calmly. [. . .] Above all, I think, it would be so simple, to timely, with neither passion, nor fear, nor a moment's regret.

7 September   [. . .] Today I'm on my own at home and can reflect on my own situation as it were at leisure. I must wait. Dublitsky, don't intrude where youth, poetry, beauty and love are – leave that to cadets, my friend. Vasenka[12] and I gorged ourselves today and lay facing each other, breathing heavily – that's the thing for you. Nonsense. A monastery, work

– that's your vocation, and from its height you can look down calmly and gladly at other people's love and happiness. I've been in that monastery and I'll go back again. Yes.

My diary is insincere. *Arrière-pensée* [ulterior motive] that she is with me, and will sit beside me and read and . . . and this is for her.

8 September In the morning Auerbach came with his wife's article. Vasenka, Suvorin. Sasha Behrs. Went round to the Behrs' for dinner all the same. Andrey Yevstafyev[13] stayed in his room – it was as if I'd stolen something. Tanechka[14] was serious and severe. Sonya opened the door; she seemed to have grown thinner. She has nothing in her for me of what the others had and have – the conventionally poetic and attractive – but she draws me irresistibly. (I went to the village with Sasha – a wench, a peasant coquette, aroused my interest, alas.) Liza seems to be quietly taking possession of me. My God! How beautifully unhappy she would be if she were my wife. In the evening she wouldn't give me the music for a long time. I was seething all over. Sonya played the part of a little Tatyana Behrs, and that seemed to me an encouraging sign. We had a walk at night.

9 September She blushes and is agitated. Oh, Dublitsky, don't dream. [. . .] Started to work, but couldn't. Instead of work, I wrote a letter which I won't send.[15] I *can't* leave Moscow, I *can't*. I'm writing without any ulterior motive, for myself only, and I'm trying not to make any plans. I seem to have been in Moscow for a year already.

Couldn't sleep till 3. Dreamed and suffered agonies like a sixteen-year-old boy.

10 September Woke up on 10 September at 10, tired after a restless night. Worked sluggishly, and waited for the evening as a schoolboy waits for Sunday. Went for a walk. To the Perfilyevs'. The stupid Praskovya Fyodorovna. To the Kuznetsky Bridge and the Kremlin. She wasn't there. She was at the young Gorstkins'. She came back looking serious and severe. And I went off again without hope and more in love than ever. *Au fond* [deep down] there is hope. I must, I absolutely must cut this knot. I'm beginning to hate Liza as well as pity her. Lord! Help me and teach me. Another sleepless and agonizing night; I feel it, I, who laughed at the suffering of people in love. What you laugh at you become a slave to. How many plans have I made to tell her and Tanechka, and all in vain. I'm beginning to hate Liza with all my heart. Lord, help me, teach me. Mother of God, help me.

11 September Wrote well in the morning. My feelings are just as strong. The whole day was just like yesterday.

Didn't dare to go to their house. Walked a lot, went to Yakovleva's. Talked to Vasya. No one can help me except God. I beseech Him. Evening at the Perfilyevs'. The pretty Mendt girls. No one for me. I'm tired. A sort of physical restlessness.

12 September Roamed about all day and went to gymnastics. Dined at the club. I'm in love as I never believed it possible to love. I'm mad, I'll shoot myself if it goes on like this. Spent the evening at their house. She's charming in every respect. But I'm the repulsive Dublitsky. I should have been on my guard sooner. Granted I'm Dublitsky, but love makes me beautiful. Yes. Tomorrow morning I'll go to their house. There have been moments, but I didn't take advantage of them. I was timid; I should simply have spoken. I just want to go back now and say everything in front of them all. Lord, help me.

13 September Nothing happened. Seryozha arrived though. Every day I think that it's impossible to suffer more and at the same time to be happy, and every day I become more demented. Went out again with melancholy, remorse and happiness in my heart. I'll go tomorrow as soon as I get up and say everything, or I'll shoot myself.

14 September 4 am. I wrote her a letter.[16] I'll give it to her tomorrow, i.e. today, the 14th. My God, how afraid I am of dying. Happiness, and such happiness, seems to me impossible. My God, help me.

15 September Only slept for an hour and a half, but feel fresh and am terribly nervous. The same feelings this morning. Went to Seryozha's and we laughed there about the immortality of the soul. To the Kremlin. To the nauseating Tyutchevs' and to them. The situation has become clear, I think. She's strange . . . I can't write for myself only. It seems to me, in fact I'm sure, that soon there won't be any secrets for me alone, but secrets for two; she will read everything. We went to the Perfilyevs'. Went to bed nervously exhausted, but didn't sleep much – six hours. Yesterday the 14th – I was a bit calmer, and today I'm calmer still. Something will happen.

15 September I didn't speak, but said there was something to speak about. Told Vasenka about the death of Nikolenka and wept like a child. Tomorrow.

16 September I spoke. She said – yes. She's like a winged bird. There's nothing to write. All this can't be forgotten and can't be written down.

17 September *Fiancé, presents, champagne.* Liza is pitiable and depressed. She must hate me. She kissed me.

18 September Worked in the morning, then went to their house. Olga Zaykovskaya.[17] Met Seryozha. She was unkempt. Dinner without Liza. A talk with Andrey Yefstafyevich. Polivanov. She doesn't kiss simply, but gravely.

19 September I'm calmer. Slept through the morning. Chicherin, boredom. Roamed around aimlessly; 5.30 at their house. She was anxious. Liza looked better; in the evening she said she loved me.

20, 21, 22, 23, 24 September, Moscow – Yasnaya Polyana I can't understand how the week has passed. I don't remember anything: only the kiss by the piano and the appearance of Satan, then jealousy of the past, doubts about her love and the thought that she's deceiving herself.

Good news about the article[18] and the sale of my works.[19] On the wedding day, fear, distrust and the desire to run away. The festivities of the ceremony. She was in tears. In the carriage. She knows everything and it's simple. At Biryulevo. Her timidity. Something morbid. Yasnaya Polyana. Seryozha affectionate. Auntie already preparing to suffer. The night; a bad dream. Not her.

25 September *At Yasnaya* Morning coffee – ill at ease. The students are puzzled. Had a walk with her and Seryozha. Dinner. She was too forward. I slept after dinner and she wrote. Unbelievable happiness. And again she's writing by my side. It can't be that all this will last as long as life itself.

26, 27, 28, 29, 30 September At Yasnaya. I can't recognize myself. All my mistakes are clear to me. I love her just the same, if not more. I can't work. Today there was *a scene.* I was sad that we behave just the same way as other people. I told her she had hurt me with regard to my feelings for her, and I wept. She's charming. I love her even more. But is it all genuine?

2, 3, 4–14 October We've had two more clashes: (1) because I was rude and (2) because of her n.[20] I love her more and more, although with a different love; there have been difficult moments. [. . .]

15 October All this time I've been busy with what are called practical matters, nothing else. But this idleness is beginning to weigh on me. I can't respect myself. And therefore I'm not satisfied with myself and uncertain in my relations with others. I've decided to close the journal and the schools too – I think.[21] I'm still annoyed with my life, and even with her. *I must work . . .*

19 December Another month of happiness. The only bad thing is Stellovsky, my mistake concerning him. Now there's a period of tranquillity as far as my feelings for her are concerned. I'm working very hard, yet it seems trivial stuff. Finished the first part of *The Cossacks*.

The features of my present life are fullness, absence of dreams, hopes and self-consciousness, but on the other hand fear and remorse over my egoism. The students are leaving and I'm sorry for them. Auntie has assumed a new, elderly expression which touches me.

22 December A strange dreamy state, as my wife says, but I've lots of energy – I'm not smoking. [. . .]

27 December, Moscow We are in Moscow.[22] As always I've paid penance with ill health and a bad frame of mind, I was very displeased with her, compared her with other people, almost repented of it, but knew it was only temporary and waited, and it passed. We had words over the doll; she wanted to show off her simple tastes in front of me. Now we've got over it. We went to the theatre; it was wasted on *her* too. I'm afraid of her father. Lyubov Alexandrovna is nice. I keep looking hard at Tanya. I've seen no writers apart from Fet and I won't see any.

30 December A mass of thoughts; I just want to write. I've become terribly grown up. *I wonder if I'm envious? I can't help growing old.* A stupid evening at the Behrs'. Labord.[23] Tanya – sensuality. Sonya moves me with her fears. The mere difference [?] between us hurts me. I will always love her.

1863–1887

THE HISTORY OF the 1860s in Tolstoy's literary biography is very largely the history of writing, re-writing and publishing *War and Peace*. By the middle of the decade, with the appearance of the first collected edition of his works in four volumes, he felt himself to be at the height of his powers as a writer and took a condescending attitude to work which was not 'creative', in marked contrast to the previous few years when 'useful' activity took pride of place, and writing was subordinated to teaching and farming. during the 1860s he seldom left his country estate except for reasons connected with his novel – the need to consult books and archives in Moscow, or to visit the site of the famous battle of Borodino and talk to survivors. In the course of the decade four children were born to the Tolstoys, and life at Yasnaya Polyana was a ceaseless round of activity for both husband and wife. Writing apart, there were routine affairs of the estate to attend to: pig-farming, horse-breeding and harvesting the various crops. A lover of trees, Tolstoy planted a birch wood which was later to become very valuable. He acquired a passion for bee-keeping. He dabbled briefly with sculpture and continued to play the piano. And of course he read widely and discussed his work with poets, philosophers and historians, as well as with his wife, whose opinion he greatly valued. One event which stands out in this period is his unsuccessful defence before a military court of a private soldier who had been charged with striking an officer. The man was found guilty and executed, and the unhappy experience served to strengthen Tolstoy's growing hostility to the government's military and judicial institutions, which reached its literary climax many years later in *Resurrection*.

War and Peace was completed in 1869 and, not surprisingly, Tolstoy told his poet friend Fet that the hours seemed dead after his prolonged labours of six years. But Tolstoy was incapable of relaxing for long, and he soon began to embark on an extensive programme of reading, while slowly rediscovering at the same time his vocation, as he thought, to teach children and to write for them. He studied in earnest the language and literature of classical Greece, particularly Homer, Xenophon and Herodotus. He re-read the plays of Molière, Goethe and Shakespeare and the classics of the Russian stage. He applied his mind enthusiastically to Schopenhauer, Kant and Pascal. Despite a temporary revulsion from fiction, especially his own, he resumed work on *The Decembrists*, long since laid aside, and began a historical novel about the life and times of Peter the Great. His list of books which made the deepest impression on him during the years 1863 to 1878 included not only the *Iliad,* the *Odyssey,* the *Anabasis* and the Russian *byliny,* but also *les Misérables* and the novels of Trollope, George Eliot and Mrs Wood. His main efforts, however, in 1871 and 1872 were concentrated on writing his *Primer* for peasant children. Not only did he write many stories himself, whose narrative interest, brevity and simplicity were calculated to make a direct moral appeal; he also translated and adapted fables and folk-tales from Greek, Jewish, Oriental and Arabic sources, compiled a section on arithmetic and provided passages for reading from the natural sciences, the Russian chronicles and the Lives of the Saints. Among his own compositions for the *Primer* were *A Captive in the Caucasus* and *God Sees the Truth but Waits,* which he was later to value more highly than all the rest of his fiction. In 1873 he returned to belles-lettres and began to work on what he insisted on calling his first 'novel' – *Anna Karenina* – the final instalment of which was published in 1877.

The main events in Tolstoy's life during the 1870s were his visits to the Bashkir province of Samara, first to recover from illness, and later to spend summer holidays with his family on an estate he had bought there. He gave widespread publicity to the serious famine in the Samara province in the summer of 1873 by writing to the newspapers and setting up a Famine Relief Fund. In the following year he lectured on his educational theories in Moscow and wrote an article on the subject. As he neared the end of his work on *Anna Karenina* and Levin's spiritual crisis, he became increasingly preoccupied with Christianity and the Orthodox faith, and for a while he resumed his long-abandoned practice of going to church. He sought and achieved a reconciliation with Turgenev, visited the most important Russian monasteries and had numerous conversations on religious matters with monks and laymen. In 1879 he began writing *A Confession,* which, although completed in 1882, was not allowed to be published in Russia. It is the best introduction to the spiritual struggle he was to wage for the remaining thirty years of his life and in the words of a distinguished critic 'is one of the greatest and most lasting expressions of the human soul in the presence of the eternal mysteries of life and death'. For the next few years he published no more fiction, but wrote *A Criticism of Dogmatic Theology* and *A Translation and Harmony of the Four Gospels,* both of which, for censorship reasons, first appeared abroad, and his comprehensive statement of faith *What I Believe.*

In the course of the 1870s six more children were born to the Tolstoys of whom two died in infancy. Their tenth child was born in 1879, but by then their marriage was already showing signs of strain, which were to be seriously aggravated in the next decade, when Tolstoy made his first attempt to leave home. Two more children followed in the early 1880s, the second being his daughter Alexandra, who died in America as recently as 1979.

In 1881 the Tsar Alexander II was assassinated. Tolstoy wrote to the new Tsar, asking him to pardon his father's murderers, but to no effect. In 1882 he took part in a three-day Moscow census and made his acquaintance at first hand with the Moscow slums. His article *On the Moscow Census* was published the same year, when he also began work on the social treatise *What Then Must We Do?*, which grew out of the same experience of urban squalor and destitution. In 1884 some fragments of *The Decembrists* were published; in 1885 several popular tales including the well-known *Where Love is, God is,* and in 1886 the powerful and harrowing story *The Death of Ivan Ilich*, with its strikingly modern, existentialist flavour.

In 1882 Tolstoy was persuaded reluctantly to move to Moscow for the sake of the children's education and after first renting accommodation near the Arbat, he eventually purchased a large wooden house with an attractive garden in a quiet part of the town near the Moscow river. For most of the rest of his life the family were to move backwards and forwards between their two homes, but it was always with a sense of relief that Tolstoy returned to the house where he was born (even though the main building itself had long been sold to meet his gambling debts). It was in Moscow in 1882 that Tolstoy began to study Hebrew, and it was there in the following year that he first met Vladimir Chertkov, a wealthy aristocrat, who had been profoundly influenced by Tolstoy's religious and ethical ideas and who became the dominant figure in Tolstoy's life after 1883. The friendship and cooperation between the two men led to the establishment of a publishing house, *The Intermediary*, to provide the people with edifying and morally improving literature at a nominal cost. In the course of the 1880s Tolstoy's increasingly unorthodox beliefs became more rigid and resulted in his refusal to do jury service, his conversion (though not at first complete) to vegetarianism, his renunciation of blood sports and alcohol and his serious attempts (initially unsuccessful) to give up smoking. He also took up cobbling as a sign of his determination to live a simple and useful life, although from all accounts he never succeeded in mastering the craft.

The diaries for the period 1863–87 are disappointingly meagre, and it should be observed that the comparatively long entries for 1884 were written at a time when relations between Tolstoy and his wife were at their lowest ebb.

1863

3 January, Moscow Only today has my toothache begun to ease up a bit. She talks about jealousy: one must respect people – I'm sure that it's just talk, but one is constantly afraid. The epic manner is becoming the only natural one for me. Polivanov's presence is disagreeable to me: I must put up with him as best I can. We're alone in Moscow; I must *faire des avances* [make approaches]; but then suddenly there will be unhappiness and worse, whereas now it's so good. She kissed me while I was writing. I felt it was in earnest; I looked round and she was crying. Tatyana is getting on my nerves. I'm astonished that I don't need anybody; solitude surprises me, but doesn't inhibit me; but to her it always seems that time is passing in vain.

5 January Family happiness completely absorbs me, and it's impossible to do anything. I must do something about the journal. It often occurs to me that happiness and all its special attributes are vanishing, and nobody knows it or will know it, and that such a thing never existed and never will exist for anybody, and yet I am conscious of it. I don't like *Polikushka*.[1] I read it at the Behrs'. I love her when I wake up at night or in the morning and see her – she looks at me and loves me. And no one – least of all I – prevents her from loving the way she knows, her own way. I love it when she sits close to me and we know that we love each other as much as we can, and she says: 'Lyovochka', and stops – 'why are the pipes in the stove so straight?', or 'why do horses live such a long time?' etc. I love it when we are alone for a long time and I say: 'What are we to do, Sonya, what are we to do?' And she laughs. I love it when she is angry with me and suddenly, in the twinkling of an eye, her thoughts and words are sometimes harsh: 'Leave me, I'm tired of you'; and a minute later she's already smiling timidly at me again. I love it when she doesn't see me and doesn't know I'm there, and I love her in my own way. I love it when she is a girl in a yellow dress and sticks out her lower jaw and tongue; I love it when I see her head thrown back and her serious and frightened and childlike and passionate face; I love it when . . .

8 January In the morning – her clothes. She challenged me to object to them, and I did object, and said so – tears and vulgar explanations. Sasha Kuzminsky[2] is a nice young man, but he's in a bad situation; too weak, too young, and surrounded by temptations. We patched things up somehow.

I'm always dissatisfied with myself on these occasions, especially with the kisses – they are false patches. [. . .] Over dinner the patch came off; tears and hysterics. The best indication that I love her is that I wasn't angry, but I was depressed, terribly depressed, and sad. I went away to forget and to amuse myself. Aksakov is just the same self-satisfied upright hero with an eloquent mind. Stupid, consumptive Rayevsky. At home I felt depressed with her. I suppose a great deal has boiled up inside me unnoticed; I feel that she is depressed, but I'm more depressed still, and I can't say anything to her – there's nothing to say. I'm just cold, and I clutch at any work with ardour. *She will stop loving me.* I'm almost certain of that. The one thing that can save me is if she doesn't fall in love with someone else, and that won't be my doing. She says *I'm kind.* I don't like to hear it; it's just for that reason that she will stop loving me. [. . .]

15 January, Moscow A new diary: but there's nothing new. I'm still the same. I'm often just as dissatisfied with myself, and just as firmly believe in myself and expect things of myself . . . If only I were not happy! All the conditions for happiness have come together for me. Often the only thing missing (all this time) is the awareness that I've done everything that *I ought to* have done in order to enjoy to the full what has been given me, and to repay others, *the whole world,* by my work for what they have given me.

Got up late; we're on friendly terms. The last squabble has left some small (imperceptible) traces – or perhaps time has. Every such squabble, however trivial, is a scar on love. A momentary feeling of passion, vexation, self-love or pride will pass, but a scar, however small, will remain for ever on the best thing that exists in the world – love. I shall know this and guard our happiness, and you know it too. Corrected some proofs. [. . .] At home I suddenly snarled at Sonya because she wouldn't leave me alone, and I felt ashamed and frightened. At dinner we were in good spirits. Mamma. Tanya – the charm of naiveté, egoism and sensibility. [. . .]

23 January Somebody told me quite truly that I'm wrong not to use the time for writing. It's a long time since I can remember such a strong desire – and a calm, self-assured desire – to write. I have no subjects, that is no one specially asking to be written, but, mistakes or not, I think I could take any subject. The type of Westerner-professor who has acquired for himself by assiduous work in his youth a certificate entitling him to intellectual idleness and stupidity comes to mind in various aspects, as opposed to the man who has retained to maturity his boldness of thought and the indivisibility of thought, feeling and action.[3] And another situation: the love of a husband, which makes strict demands on itself, all-absorbing and becoming the business of his whole life, in conflict with the attractions of the waltz, outward glitter, vanity and the poetry of the moment. *Polenka*

Sachs and perhaps the present drama *Sin and misfortune.*[4] I've never experienced a stronger impression, or one so unspoiled by a single false note. Corrected the proofs of *The Cossacks* – it's terribly weak. Probably for that reason the public will be pleased with it. I've been feverish and idle all the time, and weighed down by it. Relations with my wife are the best possible. The ebbs and flows don't surprise me or frighten me. From time to time, including today, I still have the fear that she's young and can't understand or love much in me, and that she suppresses much in herself for my sake, and instinctively debits all these sacrifices to my account. Today was a day of activity; I went to Auntie's and the Gorchakovs' (Hélène is wonderful) and Fet's (he has a wife too). The main change in me during this time is that I'm beginning to love people in moderation. Before it was all or nothing, but now love's real place is occupied, and relations are simpler. Friends at the theatre. I was glad they all liked her.

25 January Morning. Yesterday we had a quarrel, allegedly over the big room but really because we [one indecipherable word] and because we are both idle. I used to think before, and now as a married man I'm more than ever convinced that in life, in all human relationships, the basis of everything is work. [. . .]

8 February, Yasnaya Polyana We're at Yasnaya. Islenyev and Seryozha interrupted us, but still I feel so well, so well; I love her so. The estate and the affairs of the journal are in good shape. Only the students are a burden because of the unnaturalness of our relations and their involuntary envy, for which I don't reproach them. How clear it all is to me now. It was the passion of youth – a farce almost – which I can't go on with now that I'm grown up. She is everything. She doesn't know and couldn't understand how she is transforming me – incomparably more so than I her. Only not consciously. Consciously both she and I are powerless. [. . .]

23 February Sent off my article[5] – it's good, although careless. I've started writing.[6] It won't do. I've been looking through my papers – a swarm of thoughts, and a return, or an attempt at a return, to lyricism. That's good. I can't write, it seems, without a set idea and without passion. *Les Misérables*[7] – powerful. [. . .]

1 March [. . .] We recently began to feel that our happiness is frightening. Death – and that's the end of it all. Can it really be the end? God. We prayed. I wanted to feel that happiness is not chance, but *My destiny.*

3 March Twice we almost quarrelled in the evening. Almost. Today she feels bored and hemmed in. The foolish seek the storm – the young, but not the foolish. I'm afraid of this mood more than anything in the world. I've been absorbed in the estate the whole day. I can't get on with *The Gelding*[8] – it's false. But I can't change it. [. . .] So-called self-sacrifice and virtue are only the satisfaction of one morbidly developed propensity. The ideal is harmony. Only art feels this. And only that is real which takes as its motto: there are no guilty people in the world. He who is happy is right! The self-sacrificing person is more blind and cruel than the others. [. . .]

24 March   I love her still more and more. Today is the seventh month, and I'm experiencing a feeling which I haven't experienced for a long time, not since the beginning – a feeling of nothingness compared to her. She is so impossibly pure and good and chaste for me. At moments like this I feel that I don't possess her, despite the fact that she gives herself completely to me. I don't possess her because I don't dare. I don't feel myself worthy. I'm nervously irritable and so not *fully* happy. Something torments me. Jealousy of the man who could be fully worthy of her. I'm not worthy.

1 April   I sat in Auntie's room today; she was asleep. I began to recall an earlier conversation with Serdobolsky; Easter is quite different this year, with tedious plans for the estate, and I began to detest myself. I'm a dissolute egoist. But I'm happy. I must work on myself here and now. Not much is needed to consolidate this happiness. (1) order, (2) activity, (3) resoluteness, (4) perseverance, (5) desiring good and doing good to everyone. I'll keep an eye on myself in these respects.

2 June   This whole time has been for me a depressing time of physical sleep and – whether for that reason or independently – moral sleep too, depressing and without hope. I've been thinking that I have no strong interests or passions (how is that possible? And why?). I've been thinking that I'm getting old and dying; thinking that it's terrible that I don't love anything. I've been horrified at myself and the fact that my interests are money or vulgar prosperity. It's been a periodic sleep. I think I've woken up now. I love her, and the future, and myself and my life. You can't go back on what has happened. What seems weakness may be the source of strength. I'm reading Goethe, and thoughts are swarming in my head.

18 June   Where am I, the I whom I knew and loved, who will sometimes come to the surface and gladden me and frighten me? I'm puny and insignificant. And I've been like that since I married the woman I love. Everything written in this book is almost a lie – deceitfulness. The thought that she is here reading over my shoulder detracts from and mars the truth of what I write. Today her evident pleasure at talking and attracting Erlenwein's attention[9] and an insane night suddenly raised me to my old heights of truth and power. You have only to read this and say: 'yes, I know – jealousy' – and to comfort me again, and to do something else to comfort me, in order to throw me back again into all the triviality of life which I've hated since I was young. And I've been living in it for nine months. It's terrible. I'm a gambler and a drunkard. In the intoxication of estate management I've ruined nine irretrievable months which could have been the best of my life, but which I made almost the worst. What do I need? To live happily – i.e. to be loved by her and myself; but all this time I've hated myself. How many times have I written: 'Today it's all over.' I won't write it now. My God, help me. Let me always live in this awareness of Thee and of my own strength. An insane night. I'm looking for some way to hurt you, against my will. This is bad and will pass, but don't be angry, I can't help loving you.

I must add something for her – she will read it; I won't write anything for her that is untrue, but, from a choice of many things, something I wouldn't have written for myself alone. The fact that she might like another man, and a very insignificant one, is understandable to me, and ought not to seem unjust to me, however intolerable it is, because for these last nine months I have been the most insignificant, weak, absurd and trivial man myself. [. . .]

I'm sitting down to write again for the third time. It's awful, terrible and absurd to link one's happiness with material conditions – a wife, children, health, wealth. The holy fool is right. One can have a wife, children, health, etc. but that's not the point. Lord have mercy and help me.

5 August I'm writing now, not for myself alone as formerly, and not for the two of us as recently, but for him.[10] On 27 June during the night we were both particularly disturbed. She had stomach-ache and was tossing about, but we thought it was the result of eating berries. In the morning she became worse and at 5 o'clock we woke up, having decided the previous evening that I should go to meet our people. She was in her dressing-gown, feverish and crying out; then it passed and she smiled and said: 'it's all right'. I sent for Anna, more in order to do what I could, but I didn't believe it was necessary. I was both anxious and calm, occupied with trivialities as one is before a battle or at the moment of approaching death. I was annoyed with myself for feeling so little. I wanted to go to Tula and do everything as properly as possible.

I travelled with Tanya and Sasha, and we felt somehow unnatural. I was calm and didn't want to let myself be so. In Tula I found it strange that Kopylov wanted to talk about politics as usual, and the chemists were sealing up their little boxes. We set off with Marya Ivanovna (Seryozha's midwife). We drove up home and there was no one to be seen. Auntie, who at first hadn't wanted me to go and was afraid, came out to meet me distraught, animated, frightened, but with kindly eyes. 'How are things?' – 'How good that you've come, *mon cher*. The pangs have begun.' I went in. The darling, how beautiful she was with her expression of seriousness, honesty, strength and emotion. She was wearing a dressing-gown which was open, and a little embroidered jacket; her black hair was untidy – with a feverish, blotchy red face and big burning eyes she walked about and looked at me. 'Have you brought them?' 'Yes. How are things?' 'Terribly fierce pangs. Anna Petrovna isn't here, but Aksinya is.' She kissed me simply and calmly. While people were swarming about, the pangs started again. She seized hold of me. I kissed her as I had done in the morning, but she wasn't thinking about me, and there was something serious and stern about her. Marya Ivanovna went into the bedroom with her and came out. 'Labour has begun,' she said softly and solemnly and with concealed joy, like an actor taking a benefit when the curtain has gone up. She kept walking up and down, pottering about round the cupboards, getting things ready and then sitting down for a bit, and there was the same calm and solemn glow in her eyes. There were a few more pangs, and each time I held her and felt her body trembling, stretching and contracting; and the impression her body made on me was quite, quite different from previously, both before and during our marriage. In between times I ran about, arranging for the sofa on which I was born to be moved into her room, etc., and I still had the same feeling of indifference, reproachfulness because of it and irritation. I wanted to think out and do everything as quickly, thoroughly and as well as possible. They laid her down and she herself began to think of . . . (I haven't finished this and I can't write any more about this present agony).

Her character gets worse each day; I can recognize both Polenka and Mashenka in her,[11] with her grumbling and spiteful taunts. It's true this usually happens when she is not so well, but her unfairness and quiet egoism frighten and torment me. She has heard from someone and got it firmly in her head that husbands don't love sick wives, and as a result has consoled herself with the belief that she is right. Or else she never loved me, but was deceiving herself. I've looked through her diary – suppressed anger with me glows beneath words of tenderness. It's often the same in real life. If this is so, and it's all a mistake on her part – it's terrible. To give up everything – not a dissipated bachelor's life at Dusseau's and mistresses like other married men, but the poetry of love and ideas and work for the people – and to exchange it all for the poetry of the family hearth, and egoism in what concerns everything except one's own family; and in place of everything to get all the worries of a tavern, worry about baby powder and preserves, as well as grumbling, and without anything that brightens up family life, without love and without a peaceful and proud family happiness, but only outbursts of tenderness, kisses, etc.! I'm terribly depressed. I still don't believe it, but then I wouldn't be ill, wouldn't be distraught all day – quite the contrary.

In the morning I come in happy and in good spirits, and see the *Countess*, who is in a bad temper and whose hair is being combed by her *maid Dushka*, and I think of Mashenka when times were bad for her, and everything goes to pieces, and like someone possessed *I'm afraid* of everything, and I can see that only in a place where I am alone do I feel well and in a poetic mood. I get kisses, tender from habit, and then the nagging begins at Dushka, Auntie, Tanya, me and everybody, and I can't endure it calmly because it's all not simply bad, but terrible, in comparison with what I desire. I don't know what I wouldn't do for the sake of our happiness, but people will contrive to sully and demean our relations and allege that I grudge giving away a horse or a peach. There's no point in explaining. There's nothing to explain . . . But the slightest glimmer of understanding and feeling, and I'm completely happy again, and believe that she understands things the way I do. People believe what they earnestly desire. And I'm pleased that it's only I who suffers agony. Like Mashenka, she has the same trait of morbid and capricious self-assurance and submission to what she imagines to be her unhappy fate.

It's already one o'clock in the morning and I can't sleep, still less go and sleep in her room, with the feeling that oppresses me; for when someone can hear her she will groan, but now she is snoring peacefully. And she will wake up in the full assurance that I'm unjust and that she is the unfortunate victim of my fickle whims – about feeding and looking after the baby.[12] Even her father is of the same opinion. I haven't given her my diary to read, but I'm not writing everything in it. The most terrible thing is that I must say nothing and sulk, however much I hate and despise the condition. To talk to her now is impossible, but perhaps all could still be explained. No, she never loved me and doesn't love me. I don't feel so sorry about it now, but why did I have to be so cruelly deceived?

6 October   All that is over now and it was all untrue. I'm happy with her; but I'm terribly dissatisfied with myself. I'm sliding, sliding down the hill of death, and hardly feel I have the strength to stop. But I don't want death, I want and love immortality. I don't have to choose. The choice has been made long ago. Literature – art, pedagogy and the family. Inconsistency, timidity, laziness, weakness – these are my enemies.

1864

16 September, Yasnaya Polyana   It will soon be a year since I stopped writing in this book. And a good year. My relations with Sonya have grown stronger and firmer. We love each other, i.e. we are dearer to each other than all other people in the world, and we can look each other in the face. No secrets, and nothing to be ashamed of. Meanwhile I've begun a novel[1] and have written about ten printer's sheets,[2] but now I'm in the stage of correcting and revising. It's agonizing. My pedagogical interests have receded into the distance. My son is very remote from me. Recently I remembered the diary I began about Sonya as a mother,[3] I must finish it for the children.

For the novel.[4]

(1) He loves to torment the person he loves – everything irritates him.
(2) Father and son hate each other. Ill at ease in other people's presence.

1865

7 March, Yasnaya Polyana   Health so-so. This is the third day I've held my ground without either relaxing or exerting my will too much. I'm writing and revising.[1] Everything is clear, but the amount of work still to do terrifies me. It's good to determine one's future work. Then, in view of the important things to come, you don't stop and revise trivial things endlessly. Sonya has been ill. Seryozha is very ill, and is coughing. I'm beginning to love him very much. A completely new feeling. All is well on the estate.

9 March   I've been writing and revising both days. Today I couldn't after tea. There's a certain coolness between Sonya and me. I wait calmly for it to pass. I've been reading Goethe's *Faust*. [. . .]

17 March   Went to Tula. Went to the funeral at Seryozha's.[2] Even for his grief man must have rails laid down to go along – weeping and wailing, requiem masses, etc. Yesterday I saw in the snow the deep footprint of a dog in the shallow footprint of a man. Why does its weight rest on so small a surface? So that it shouldn't eat up all the hares, but just as many as it needs. That's the wisdom of God; no it's not wisdom, not intelligence. It's the instinct of deity. We have this instinct in us too. But our intelligence is our ability to deviate from instinct and to understand these deviations. These thoughts came to me with frightening clarity, force, and delight. [. . .] I'm reading Raguse's *Mémoires*.[3] Very useful to me.

19 March   I've become engrossed in the history of Napoleon and Alexander. The idea of writing a psychological history of the romance[4] of Alexander and Napoleon has swept over me like a cloud of joy and the awareness of the opportunity to do a great thing. All the baseness, all the empty words, all the folly, all the contradictions of them themselves and of the people round them. Napoleon as a man – mixed up and ready to renounce the 18 Brumaire before the Assembly. *De nos jours les peuples sont trop éclairés pour produire quelque chose de grand* [In our time the people are too enlightened to produce anything great].[5] Alexander of Macedon called himself the son of Jupiter, and people believed him. The whole Egyptian expedition – vainglorious French villainy. The – deliberate – falseness of all the *bulletins*. The peace of Pressburg *escamoté* [achieved by fraud]. At the bridge of Arcole he fell into a puddle instead of seizing the standard. A poor rider. Carried off pictures and statues in the Italian war. Loved to ride round the battlefield. Rejoiced in the dead and wounded. Marriage to Josephine – success in society. Three times corrected the bulletin on the battle of Rivoli – lied each time. Still a man at first, and strong in his onesidedness; later indecisive – it must be done! But how? You are ordinary people, but I can see my star in the heavens. He's not interesting, but the crowds are who surround him, and on whom he makes an impression. At first one-sidedness and *beau jeu* [favourable conditions] compared with the Marats and the Barras, then cautiously feeling his way – self-sufficiency and good fortune – and then madness – *faire entrer dans son lit la fille des Césars* [getting the daughter of Caesars to share his bed]. Complete madness, growing infirmity and insignificance on St Helena. Lies and greatness only because the dimension was great, but when the field of action became small, his insignificance became obvious. And a shameful death!

Alexander, a clever, amiable, sensitive man, seeking from on high greatness of dimension, seeking human heights; renouncing the throne and approving of or not preventing the murder of Paul (it can't be). Plans for the renascence of Europe. Austerlitz, tears, the wounded. Naryshkina unfaithful. Speransky, emancipation of the serfs. Tilsit – intoxication with greatness. Erfurt. The period till 1812 I don't know about. Greatness as a man, vacillations. Victory, triumph, greatness, *grandeur*, which frightened him, and the search for human greatness – greatness of mind. Confusion over outward things, but lucidity of mind. And a soldierly vein – manoeuvres and stern measures. Outward confusion, but clarity of mind. Death. If it was murder, that would be best.

I must write my novel and do the work for it.

20 March Wonderful weather. I'm well. Rode to Tula on horseback. Great thoughts! The plan for the history of Napoleon and Alexander hasn't lost its appeal. An epic poem, the hero of which should rightfully be a man round whom everything is grouped, and the hero should be that man. Read Marmont. V.A. Perovsky's captivity.[6] Davoût – put him to death.[7] Markov's review[8] – poor. He thinks well of the idea, yet is cross. Well, what would you do yourself? But my powers, my powers are frightening! Yazykov said that my speeches are too explicit, too long. He's right. Shorter, shorter.

21 March Wonderful weather. Sonya is ill. I get annoyed that she's so weak when she's ill. Seryozha worries me with his illness. The livestock farming amuses me and it's going well. I'm still reading Raguse and making notes. In the evening, wrote the bridge scene[9] – poor.

23 March   Wonderful weather. [. . .] Only wrote a little in the evening, but quite well. I can. Apart from that there have been thoughts all this time about something new and more important, and a feeling of dissatisfaction with the old. I must write each day without fail, not so much for the success of the work, as in order not to get out of my routine. I must leave out more. Tomorrow I'll try a description of Bilibin.[10] [. . .] One of the most important points about writing is the contrast between the person who feels poetry and the one who doesn't.

25 March   Seryozha is with us. I'm unwell – biliousness. Told Seryozha about Napoleon. Did no writing. Read Raguse. Just like Faust – builds factories after battles and is content. The poetry of an old man's labours. I must do it.[11]

13 August[12]   Russia's national and international task is to introduce to the world the idea of a social structure without landed property.

   La proprieté c'est le vol [Property is theft] will remain truer than the truth of the British constitution as long as mankind exists. This is an *absolute* truth, but there are also relative truths – supplementary ones – which stem from it. The first of these relative truths is the Russian people's attitude to property. The Russian people rejects that form of property which is the most deeply rooted, depends least on hard work, and inhibits more than any other form the right of other people to acquire property – namely landed property. This truth is not a dream – it is a fact expressed in the communes of the peasants and the *Cossacks*. This truth is understood alike by the Russian intellectual and the peasant who says: 'Register us as Cossacks and the land will be free.' This idea has a future. On it alone can the Russian revolution be based. The Russian revolution will not be against the Tsar and despotism, but against landed property. It will say: 'Rob and steal from me – the man – anything you like, but leave us the land.' Autocracy cannot prevent this order of things, but is actually helping it to come about. (I dreamed all this on 13 August.)

20 September, Nikolskoye-Vyazemskoye[13]   Couldn't write in the morning. Slept badly. Walked a bit. Still the same feverish condition. Read Mérimée's *Chronique de Charles IX.*[14] Strange, his intellectual link with Pushkin. Very clever and sensitive, but no talent. [. . .]

23 September, Cheryomoshnya   In bed all day. A bath revived me. Read *Consuelo.*[15] What perverse nonsense, full of phrases from science, philosophy, art and morals. A pie made of stale dough and rancid butter with truffles, sterlets and pineapples.

24 September Better. Read my novel aloud.[16] They weren't interested. But it seemed to me good enough not to be worth revising. Must impart to *Nicolas* more love of life and fear of death on the bridge. And to *Audrey* – *memories of the battle of Brünn*.

26 September, Yasnaya Polyana I've begun to do gymnastics. I feel very good. Sonya and I are back home. There probably isn't more than one person in a million as happy as the two of us are together. Apropos of the schooling of dear Masha,[17] I thought a lot about my pedagogical principles. *It's my duty* to write down everything I know about the matter.

27 September [. . .] Read the stupid *Julia Kavanagh*[18] and went for a walk. [. . .]

29 September Health not good – lumbago. Wrote to Seryozha and the Dyakovs. Spent all day writing 'the battle'[19] – poor. It won't do – it's not right. Read Trollope.[20] Good, if it weren't for the *diffuseness*.

30 September Went out hunting early in the new snow, enjoyed myself and killed a hare. Wrote to Andrey Yevstafyevich.[21] Read Trollope, good. A novelist's poetry is contained (1) in the interest of the combination of events – Braddon,[22] my *Cossacks*, my future work; (2) in the picture of manners and customs based on a historical event – *The Odyssey, The Iliad, 1805*; (3) in the beauty and cheerfulness of the situations – *Pickwick, The Hunting Ground*, and (4) in the characters of the people – *Hamlet*, my future works; Apollon Grigoryev – dissoluteness, Chicherin – an obtuse mind, Sukhotin – the narrow-mindedness of success, Nikolenka[23] – laziness and Stolypin, Lanskoy and Stroganov – the honesty of dullness.

1 October Still doing gymnastics, copying up the days and not writing. Went hunting – nothing. The poetry of work and success hasn't been tackled by anybody anywhere. Reading *The Bertrams* – wonderful.

2 October Health good. Went hunting in vain. Did some writing. But I despair for myself. Trollope makes me despair with his skill. I console myself that he has his skill and I have mine. To know what is mine – or rather what isn't mine – that's the main thing about art. I must work like a pianist.

3 October Yesterday and today I worked intensively, though fruitlessly, and now today I'm liverish and feel gloomy. It disheartens me. I must curb my *volupté* [passion] for reading and day-dreaming. I must use these powers for writing, alternating it with physical work. Rode round my woods again, and found nothing. Finished Trollope. Too much that is conventional.

15 October In a bilious mood; was angry with a huntsman. The hunting is awful. Thought out two chapters in full. No success with Brykov and Dolokhov.[24] Not working much. Had words with Sonya yesterday. It's no use – she's pregnant.

16 October Killed two white hares. Read Guizot-Witt's[25] arguments for religion and wrote a first article about an idea given to me by Montaigne.[26]

17 October Before dinner an unsuccessful hunt. Didn't much want to write. And don't want to *se battre les flancs* [drive myself hard] for nothing. Out hunting I saw a place for Dolokhov, and now it's clear.

20 October I'm exhausting my strength hunting. I've been re-reading and revising. Things are getting on. I've sketched out the Dolokhov scene. Sonya and I are very friendly.

21 October The same as yesterday. Towards evening I thought about Dolokhov. Read Dickens. Bella is Tanya.[27]

1 November The same strict hygiene. Completely fit, as I seldom am. Wrote quite a lot. Put the finishing touches to Bilibin, and am satisfied. Reading de Maistre.[28] The idea of the free surrender of power.

2 November Same hygiene. At night, heavy breathing and a dry mouth and by morning a rough tongue. Very well during the day – a good *selle* [stool] in the evening. Had a modest supper today. Finished writing Bilibin. The Islenyevs have gone. Re-read *The Cossacks* and *Yasnaya Polyana* with pleasure.

5 November [. . .] Wrote in a new way – so as not to have to revise. I'm thinking about a comedy.[29] As a general rule I must try the new way, without revisions. Had supper – to no purpose, it seems.

8, 9 November A milder diet yesterday. Strict again today. Health good, especially my head. Good thoughts in profusion yesterday. Wrote the part before the battle[30] and got a clear idea of all that is to come. Took the important decision today not to publish before finishing the whole novel.

10, 11, 12 November I'm writing; health good, and I'm no longer watching myself. Nearly finished the third part. Much is becoming quite clear. Killed two hares in half an hour.

1870

2 February, Yasnaya Polyana[1]   I can hear the critics: 'the sleigh ride at Christmas, Bagration's attack, the hunt, the dinner, the dancing – all this is good; but his theory of history, his philosophy is bad; it is tasteless and cheerless'.[2]

A certain cook was preparing dinner. The offal, bones and blood he threw out or poured into the yard. The dogs stood by the kitchen door and rushed to seize hold of what the cook threw away. When he killed a chicken or a calf and threw out the blood and the intestines or when he threw the bones away, the dogs were pleased and said: 'He's cooked a good meal. He's a good cook.' But when the cook started to shell or peel eggs, chestnuts or artichokes and to throw the shells and peelings into the yard, the dogs rushed up, took a sniff and turned their noses away and said: 'He used to cook a good meal, but now he's gone off; he's a bad cook.' But the cook continued to cook dinner, and those for whom it was cooked ate it up. [. . .]

3 February   [. . .] Russian dramatic literature has two model examples of one of the many kinds of drama – the one that is the weakest and most trivial, the satirical: *The Misfortune of Being Clever* and *The Government Inspector.* The rest of the enormous field – not of satire, but of poetry – is still untouched.

14 February   One of the best examples of how the causes of people's actions which are apparent to us (and seem so to the people themselves) are not causes at all because they do not tally with the consequences, but have other causes which do tally with the consequences, is fashion. The cause of the continual change in dress fashions is the desire of the very wealthy to be different from the very poor. But it's clear that this purpose is absurd, because there are many distinguishing features apart from fashion, and the purpose is not achieved, because everything is changed again at once. But a purpose not apparent to those involved *is* achieved: the discarded clothing clothes all the poor population of London, Paris and the big cities. And this is evidently no accident, because where there is a big concentration of people, a proletariat, there are also rapid changes of fashions which provide second-hand materials cheaply for the poor. And where there are fewer proletariat, the movements of fashion are slower, and where there are more, the movements are quicker.

1873

5 November, Yasnaya Polyana   The artist of sounds, lines, colours, words and even thoughts is in a terrible position when he doesn't believe in the importance of expressing his thoughts. What does this belief depend on? Not love of his thoughts. Love is disturbing. But this belief is comforting. And sometimes I have it and sometimes I don't. Why? It's a mystery.

6 November   [. . .] As a young man I began prematurely to analyse everything and to destroy unmercifully. I was often afraid, and thought – I'll have nothing left intact; but here I am getting old, and I still have a lot intact and unharmed – more than other people. Perhaps the instrument of my analysis was sharp or perhaps my original choice was correct, but at all events I haven't destroyed anything more for a long time; and I still have intact and unshaken my love for one woman; children and everything to do with them; science and art – true science and art, without any considerations of grandeur, but with consideration for the true reality of the unsophisticated; enthusiasm for the country, and at times for Sèvres china – is that all? It's an awful lot. My contemporaries who believed in everything when I was destroying everything haven't got 1/100th part of that. [. . .]

1874

27 February, Yasnaya Polyana   *Novum organum* together with a translation.[1]

There is a language of philosophy, but I won't use it. I will use ordinary language. Interest in philosophy is common to all people and all people are judges of it.

Philosophical language was invented to counter objections. I'm not afraid of objections. I am a seeker. I don't belong to any camp. And I ask my readers not to. This is the first prerequisite for philosophy. I must object to the materialists in my foreword. They say that there is nothing except life on earth. I must object, because if that were so, there would be nothing for me to write about. Having lived for close on fifty years, I am convinced that life on earth has nothing to give, and that the clever man who looks at life on earth seriously, its labours, fears, reproaches, struggles – *what for?* for madness sake? – such a man would shoot himself at once, and Hartmann and Schopenhauer are right. But Schopenhauer gave people to feel that there is something, which stopped him from shooting himself. What that *something* is is the purpose of my book.[2] What do we live by? *Religion.*

1878

17 April, Yasnaya Polyana After thirteen years[1] I want to continue my diary. Went to matins yesterday (Easter). In the morning, read Venevitinov's notes.[2] [. . .]

5 May Yesterday I didn't help an old lady from Telyatino. Gossiped with Vasily Ivanovich.[3] Boasted about an idea of mine and quarrelled with Sonya. Was angry today with Alexey[4] and the headman for digging round the apple trees badly. In the morning, read Fonvizina's[5] memoirs. Devotion to God is right and dangerous.

22 May Had some important and painful thoughts and feelings as a result of a conversation with Vasily Ivanovich about Seryozha.[6] [3 words deleted] All the loathsome things of my youth made my heart burn with horror and the pain of remorse. I suffered agonies for a long time. Went to Tula with Seryozha and had a talk with him. Have started to get up early and am trying to write, but without success. Without success, the more so because I'm not well. But I think my head is full to the brim, and full of good things. [. . .]

Went to mass on Sunday. I can find an explanation which satisfies me for everything in the church service. But prayers for a long life and the subjugation of one's enemies is blasphemy. A Christian should pray for his enemies, not against them.

Read the Gospels. [. . .]

Started to write 'my life'.[7]

3 June Bobrinsky was here.[8] He tormented me with his talk about religion and the Word. He has a passion for talking! His self-deception is astonishing. For me he was important, in that the delusion of basing faith on the word and the word alone was terribly obviously apparent in him. Yesterday I wrote quite a lot in my little book – I don't know why – about faith.

1881

19 April, Yasnaya Polyana[1] People from Baburino came – begging. I had no money; refused them.

Two pilgrims – soldiers.

All hopeless cases – soldiers or cripples.

A peasant from Shchyokino – hard, shy, frank, small of stature. He asked for money – I refused. A peasant from Baburino with a boy. The peasant had been sharpening an elm stake when drunk, and slashed his nose. He was in hospital for twenty-two days and they charged him five roubles fifty copecks. He couldn't pay. 'Off to the police-station then.' Off he went. They took him into a room and locked him in. 'When you bring the money we'll let you out.' He left them some grain. Nikita from Salamasovo asked for money simply because he was poor; I gave him three roubles.

25 April Talked yesterday with Seryozha and Urusov. Today, a beggar woman from Kaznacheyevka, drunk. A widow from Grumant. Her boy would do the ploughing. She asked for a horse. I didn't give her one.

A crippled old man from Golovenki, a caftan rolled up across his shoulder. Seven roubles for a horse. He wept. Don't wrong people, remember God. I saw through him. Lord have mercy.

Konstantin sent a note with a young girl. He was terribly exhausted, had been ploughing, and hadn't a crust of bread. The children gave him something. Three women pilgrims.

27 April A young man from Vologda, a sick man, with icons and communion bread. He offered them for sale. [. . .]

6 May An old man from Rudakovo. Laughing eyes and a kind, toothless mouth. We spoke about wealth. Not for nothing does the proverb say – money is hell. The Saviour was out walking with two disciples. 'Go along the road and you'll come to a cross-roads; don't go left – that way is hell' – 'Let's see what hell is like,' they thought. So they went. There was a heap of gold lying there. 'You see, he said hell, but we've found treasure.'[2] They couldn't carry it themselves. They went off to fetch a cart. They went separate ways and thought – 'It will have to be shared'. One sharpened his knife, the other baked a poisoned bun. They came back, and the one thrust his knife into the other and killed him. The bun dropped out of his pocket and he ate it. Both of them perished. [. . .]

15 May   [. . .] We went to Tula.³ [. . .] The prison. One man enjoying himself ploughing. The warder on his home ground; a *party* of convicts being assembled. Shaven-headed men in irons.

A man from Vorobyovka, the husband of a dissolute wife. An old man of sixty-seven, embittered, in 'for arson', sick and barely alive. A lame boy. 114 people in *for having no documents*. 'They even exile you for being badly dressed.' Some have got three months. Some are corrupt, some are nice, simple people. A weak old man came out of the hospital. An enormous louse on his cheek. *People are being exiled by the village communes.* Two are being exiled without being tried for any offence. One – as a result of a petition by his wife – for property worth 1,500 roubles. As a boy he had been in a mental home, deformed, and prone to fits. He fell down in front of us and began to beat himself. A tall soldier in his sixth year inside. His trial lasted a year, he was sentenced to eighteen months with an extra fifteen months for passing himself off as a craftsman. The commune wouldn't have him, and since then he's been waiting for two years to join a 'party'. Two were doing hard labour for fighting – not murder. 'We're done for, for nothing at all,' cried one of them. A kind face.

The stench was terrible.

On the way back a toothless old woman. She had a copeck and so had I. I said: 'I've got one too.' She said: 'You ought to have plenty. But we're used to poverty.' [. . .]

18 May   [. . .] In the morning Seryozha made me lose my temper, and Sonya attacked me cruelly and incomprehensibly. Seryozha said: 'Christ's teaching is well known, but it's difficult.' I said: 'You wouldn't say "it's difficult" to run out of a blazing room through the only door.' *'It's difficult.'*

In the evening I said that Malikov⁴ was doing more for the government than a whole district of gendarmes. Foaming at the mouth they began to abuse Malikov – in a despicable manner; I said nothing more. Then they began to talk. Hanging is necessary, flogging is necessary, even hitting the weak in the teeth with no witnesses present is necessary, to prevent the people from rioting – that would be terrible. But hitting Jews – that's not a bad thing. Then, without rhyme or reason, they talked about fornication – and with relish.

Somebody is mad – either they are or I am. [. . .]

29 May   [. . .] A talk with Fet and my wife. The Christian teaching is impracticable. So it's stupid? No, but it's impracticable. But have you tried to practise it? No, but it's impracticable. [. . .]

26, 27 June   A great many poor people. I'm rather unwell. Haven't slept and haven't eaten anything solid for six days. Tried to feel happy. It's difficult, but possible. I'm aware of some progress towards it.

28 June   A talk with Seryozha, a continuation of yesterday's talk about God. He and the others think that to say 'I've no knowledge of this, it can't be proved. I don't need it' is a sign of intelligence and education; whereas it's really a sign of ignorance. 'I've no knowledge of any planets, nor the axis on which the earth rotates, nor any incomprehensible ecliptics, and I don't want to take it all on trust, but I can see that the sun moves and the stars move somehow.' Of course it's very difficult to prove the rotation of the earth and its path, and the mutations and the precessions of equinoxes, and there is much that is unclear and above all difficult to imagine, but the advantage is that everything is reduced to a unity. Similarly in the spiritual and moral fields – we must reduce to a unity the question what to do, what to know, what to hope for. All mankind is struggling to reduce them to a unity. And suddenly to disunite everything reduced to a unity appears to people to be a service which they boast about. Who is to blame? We teach them church rituals and scripture assiduously, knowing in advance that it won't outlast maturity, and we teach them a multitude of sciences, unconnected with each other. And they are all left without any unity, with various uncoordinated sciences, and they think this is a gain.

Seryozha admitted that he loved the life of the flesh, and believed in it. I'm glad that the question has been clearly put. [. . .]

We had an enormous dinner, with champagne. The Tanyas⁵ were dressed up. All the children had belts costing five roubles. After dinner a cart was already on its way to a picnic, surrounded by peasants' carts bringing people back exhausted from work. [. . .]

29 June   A gentle, well-to-do old man; first he wept, then he asked permission to build. He's prepared in advance to pay a fine to the justice of the peace. Pilgrims. A beggar woman from Gorodni came on to the balcony and lay down at my feet in the middle of the doorway. [. . .]

9, 10 July, Spasskoye-Lutovinovo   At Turgenev's. Dear Polonsky,⁶ quietly occupied with his painting and writing and condemning no one, is – poor man – untroubled. Turgenev fears the name of God, but acknowledges Him. But he's also naively untroubled, living a life of luxury and idleness. [. . .]

11 July, Yasnaya Polyana   Arrived home: a white-haired nobleman, in a coat with no buttons.

Two soldiers' wives from Demenka. One cheerfully asked for bread and brushwood for five children.

Sonya had a fit. I took it better, but still badly. I must understand that she's ill and pity her, but it's impossible not to try to turn one's back on evil.

A talk with Tanya[7] about education occupied me until morning. They aren't human beings. [. . .]

16 August At Ryazhk. A man killed by an engine. There's one every month. To the devil with all engines, as long as men are safe. [. . .]

22 August [. . .] Turgenev – *cancan*.[8] Sad. [. . .]

2 September Returned from Pirogovo. I often wish to die. Work doesn't absorb me.

5 October, Moscow A month has passed – the most agonizing of my life. The move to Moscow.[9] They are still settling down. When will they start to live? It's not in order to live, but to do as other people do. Unhappy people! They have no life.

Stench, stones, luxury, poverty. Dissipation. A collection of robbers who have plundered the people and conscripted soliders and judges to guard their orgies while they feast. All the people have to do is to take advantage of these people's passions and filch back from them what they have plundered. The men are cleverer at it. The women sit at home; the men scrub floors and bodies in the baths, and work as cabbies.[10] [. . .]

1881.[11] Live at Yasnaya. Give the income from Samara[12] to the poor people and the schools in Samara, under the control and supervision of the people paying. The same with the income from Nikolskoye[13] (after transferring the land to the peasants). Keep for the time being the income from Yasnaya Polyana, from 2,000 to 3,000, for myself, that is my wife and me and the young children. (Keep it for a time, but with the sole desire to give it up entirely to others, and to be self-sufficient, i.e. to restrict my needs as much as possible and to give more than I take – to direct all my strength to this end and to see in it the purpose and joy of life.) Offer the three grown-up children the choice: either to take from the poor their own share of the Samara or Nikolskoye monies for themselves, or to live there and help to see that the money is used for good purposes, or to live with us and help us. Bring up the young ones to be accustomed to demand less from life. Teach them what they are keen to learn, only not just sciences, but sciences and work. Keep only as many servants as are necessary to help us to change things and to instruct us, and then only for a time while we train ourselves to do without them. Live all together; the men in one room, the women and girls in another. One room to be a library for intellectual pursuits, and one a work room for general use. And since we are so spoiled, a separate room also for the sick. Apart from feeding ourselves and the children and teaching them, there will be work, the estate, and helping with the corn, medical treatment and instruction. On Sundays, dinners for the poor and destitute, reading and talks. Living, food and clothing all the very simplest. Sell or give away everything superfluous – the piano, furniture, carriages. Only study those sciences and arts which can be shared with everyone. Treat all people alike, from governors to beggars. The one aim is happiness – one's own and that of one's family – in the knowledge that this happiness consists in being content with little and doing good to others.

1882

22 *December*[1]   In Moscow again.[2] Suffered terrible mental agonies again.
For more than a month. But they weren't fruitless.

If you love God, and love the good (I think I'm beginning to love it) – i.e.
live by it, see happiness and life in it – then you also see that the body is an
impediment to the true good; not to the good itself, but to the possibility of
seeing it and its fruits. Once you look to the fruits of the good you cease to
do it, and moreover, by looking to the fruits, you ruin the good, you
become vain, you grow despondent. What you do will only be true good
when you are not here to ruin it. But you must lay up in advance as big a
store of it as possible. Sow, sow in the knowledge that you, *the man*, will
not reap. One man sows, another reaps. You, Lev Nikolayevich, the man,
will not reap. If you start, not only to reap but to weed, you will ruin the
wheat. Sow, sow. And if you sow God's seed there can be no doubt that it
will grow. It's now clear that what previously seemed cruel to me – the fact
that it won't be granted to *me* to see the fruits – is not only not cruel, but
good and sensible. How could I have recognized the true good – God's –
from the untrue, if I, a man of the flesh, had been able to enjoy its fruits?

But now it's clear: what you do without seeing the reward for it, and do
lovingly, is surely God's doing. Sow and sow, God will make it grow; it is
not you, the man, who will reap, but what it is within you which sows.

1884

March, Moscow [. . .] I've just read a short textbook on medieval and modern history.

Is there any more terrible reading in the world? Is there any book which could be more harmful for the young to read? And this is what they study. I read it and it took me a long time to get over my depression. Murder, torture, deceit, robbery, adultery, and nothing more. [. . .]

The Reformation is a crude, casual reflection of the mental activity which rescued mankind from darkness. Luther, with all his wars and St Bartholomew's Nights, has no place among men like Erasmus, Boethius, Rousseau, etc. [. . .]

6 March, Moscow I've been translating Lao-Tzu.[1] The result is not what I expected. [. . .]

7 March Read about Confucius. Got up very late. Rode on horseback to Aminyevo and back. Everyone is working; only I am idle. [. . .]

8 March Got up at 9, tidied my room cheerfully with the young children. I'm ashamed to do what has to be done – empty the chamber-pot. [. . .]

10 March Got up ealy, tidied my room. [. . .] Lao-Tzu says – one ought to be like water. When there are no obstacles it flows; when there's a dam it stops. The dam breaks – it begins to flow again; a square vessel – and it's square; a round vessel – and it's round. For that reason it's more important and stronger than anything.

Read Erasmus.[2] What a stupid phenomenon Luther's reformation was. A triumph of narrow-mindedness and folly. Salvation from original sin through faith and the vanity of good works are just as bad as all the superstitions of Catholicism. The teaching about the relations of Church and state (terrible in its absurdity) could only have been the result of folly. It was indeed the result of Lutheranism. [. . .]

15 March Woke up at 8, wanted to go to sleep again and slept till 11. Golokhvastov's book against Engelhardt.[3] Some things are good, but how terrible the polemical bitterness is. It's a lesson for me, and I'm disgusted by the bitterness of my last book.[4] One should write intelligibly and briefly as well. My good moral condition I ascribe also to reading Confucius,[5] and especially Lao-Tzu. I must compile a cycle of reading[6] for myself: Epictetus, Marcus Aurelius, Lao-Tzu, Buddha, Pascal, the Gospels. That is something everybody could do with too.

16 March [. . .] After dinner I went round to the cobbler's. How bright and morally refined it is in his dirty, dark corner. He works with a boy, and his wife feeds the baby. Went to my brother Seryozha's. Didn't let Kostenka finish speaking and annoyed him. (1).[7] Walked home with Tanya in silence. The silence depressed me. How remote she is from me. Yet I'm still not able to talk. Yes, and at dinner Seryozha began talking rudely and angrily, and I spoke to him ironically. (2). In the evening I began stitching boots, the cobbler came, and then Malikov and Orfano.[8] [. . .] Yes, in conversation with Orfano I said: 'You don't know my God, but I know yours', which offended him. (3).

17 March Tidying my room is becoming an agreeable habit. [. . .] Went for a ride. Was in a very bad mood at dinner, but restrained myself. Began stitching, undid it all, and Orlov[9] came. [. . .]

We talked further about holy fools and he called Lao-Tzu the holy fool's philosophy. He stayed the night. How happy I was to make his bed for him. My brother Seryozha came. I could have been nicer to him. (1). Downstairs in the morning I apparently picked a quarrel with my wife and Tanya over their bad life. (2). Boasted to myself for having provided a chamber pot for Orlov. Wrote a letter to Chertkov.

18 March [. . .] A Jew came with a letter. I read the letter. It's strange. He's the third Jew to approach me. They all have one thing in common. They feel that their faith, however mutilated, is faith, and better than the unbelief of progress. This one seems the most serious of all. But they all have a sort of burning fervour. They flare up, but don't stay alight. [. . .]

23 March Morning as usual. Settled down to Urusov's translation.[10] Uneven. Often very bad. I don't know whether it's the text or the translation? More likely the text. I must write – i.e. express my thoughts – so that they could be good in all languages. The Gospels, Lao-Tzu and Socrates are like that. The Gospels and Lao-Tzu are better in other languages. Went for a ride on horseback. Riding is boring. Stupid and frivolous. Tried to talk to my wife after dinner. Impossible. That's the one thing that grieves me. The one thorn, and a painful one. Went to the cobbler's. One only has to go into a worker's home and one's soul blossoms forth. Stitched shoes until 10. Tried again to talk to my wife, and again there was malice – lack of love. [. . .]

28 March   Didn't sleep the whole night long, got up before 6. Tidied my room; still, it wasn't unpleasant. Stitched boots, went to Lopatin's and to the post. Dozed and read Krivenko.[11] (How Russians love the fundamentals of morality, without compromises.) Also Dumas' chatter. A letter from Chertkov,[12] and wrote one to him. Fet came to order some boots.[13] I listened to him, and stopped my own attempts to make conversation. There was a moment when I felt sorry for him, as a sick man. Would it were so more often. In spite of sleeplessness and toothache I slept like a top. There is so much in my head and heart, but I can hear no definite command from God.

29 March   [. . .] Read Confucius. More profound and better still. Without him and Lao-Tzu the Gospels are not complete. And he is nothing without the Gospels. [. . .]

30 March   Went to bed at 11 and got up again early. Walked to the stocking factory.[14] The whistles mean that at 5 a boy starts work at his machine and stands there till 8. At 8 he has a drink of tea and works till 12; at 1 he works again till 4. At 4.30 he works again till 8. And so on every day. That's what the whistles mean which we hear in bed. [. . .]
    In the evening I stitched shoes – it was good. I was late – my nieces and Leonid[15] came. Joined them for tea. It was so repulsive, pathetic and degrading to listen to them, especially the poor, mentally sick Tanya,[16] that I went to bed. Couldn't sleep for a long time because of grief and doubts and prayed to God as I'd never prayed before. Teach me and save me from this horror. I know that this prayer was only expressing my excited state. Yet strangely, my prayer was heeded. [. . .]
    How surprising that for almost a month I haven't been angry.

31 March   Couldn't get to sleep till 2, but got up at 7. Went to a metal-workers' school. The best institution in Russia. If only there were no interference from government or church. [. . .]
    Said some unnecessary things about the teaching of mathematics to the school headmaster. (1). [. . .] Was alone with her.[17] We had a talk. I was unfortunate and cruel enough to touch her pride, and it all started. I couldn't keep silent. It appeared that I'd annoyed her the morning of the day before yesterday when she came in to interrupt me. She is very seriously ill mentally. And the crux of it all is her pregnancy. (2). A very great sin and shame. Read a bit of Confucius and am going to bed late. [. . .]

2 April   Got up late. The room had already been tidied. Talked to Urusov till 4. She is gentler now – morbid and submissive. Went to Wolf's.[18] Had dinner. Seryozha came – at first irritable, then gentle and kind. Stitched boots. We talked quietly over tea and I went to bed at 12.20. It's bad that I've done nothing. She has forgotten about her anger and was glad that I'd forgiven her. That's better. This senseless life is terribly pathetic.

3 April [. . .] Repin[19] at home. Had a very good talk with him over work. [. . .]

4 April Got up late. Toothache and fever. Can't do any mental work. Never mind. Read a bit and began stitching. [. . .] In the evening I worked on the boots till after 1.

It's very depressing in the family. Depressing, because I can't sympathize with them. All their joys, the examination, social successes, music, furniture, shopping – I consider them all a misfortune and an evil for them, and I can't tell them so. I can and I do speak, but my words don't get through to anyone. They don't seem to know the meaning of my words, but only that I have a bad habit of speaking that way. In weak moments – now is one of them – I'm surprised at their ruthlessness. They must surely see that for three years now I've not merely suffered, but been cut off from life. I've been assigned the role of a querulous old man, and in their eyes I can't escape from it: if I take part in their life I renounce the truth, and they would be the first to cast this renunciation in my teeth. If I look sadly, as now, at their madness – I'm a querulous old man, like all old men. [. . .]

5 April Got up late – jaded. The same sadness. Particularly now at the sight of everyone at home. The cleaners are polishing the floor; we made it dirty. I've let myself go and am less strict with myself. I'm not noting down my sins. Cheer up. A letter from Chertkov yesterday. Repin said that even Kramskoy had called him mad. Read in *Psychiatry* about a landowner, Y, who lived with his servants.[20] A letter from Mirsky and some poems.[21] Astonishing. He's a Christian. The poems are excellent in content, but their form is that of a thirteen-year-old boy. Strakhov came. He's grown thin. Still the same narrowness and rigidity. But he could wake up. Went for a walk. Dinner. Nothing all dinner time except shopping and dissatisfaction with those who serve us. Everything is more and more depressing. Their blindness is astonishing. [. . .]

7 April [. . .] I'm going to the exhibition. Kramskoy's picture is excellent.[22] Repin's didn't come off.[23] Had quite a good talk with Tretyakov.[24] At home. Strakhov. Went to Dmokhovskaya's.[25] Said what I had to. Crowds running to matins. But when will they start running, if only 100th part of them, to the business of life! I can't imagine what life would be like then. To make this transformation is the task, the joyful work of a lifetime. [. . .]

9 April [. . .] Started Mencius.[26] Very good and important. 'Mencius taught people how to *recover*,[27] how to find the lost heart.' Delightful.

Very important. Began to reprimand Tanya, and was angry. And there was Misha standing in the big doorway and looking at me questioningly. If only he were always there in front of me! *A great fault, the second in a month.* Kept hovering round Tanya, wanting to ask her forgiveness, but couldn't make up my mind. I don't know whether it was good or bad. Went to Fet's. Had a splendid talk. I told him all the things I say about him, and we spent the evening amicably. Adam Vasilyevich[28] came in the evening. Played *vint*.[29] Stupid. This filthy, idle life is getting a grip on me again.

A letter from Chertkov – splendid.[30]

10 April [. . .] After dinner I went to Armfeldt's.[31] Felt a terrible weakness on the Petrovka. It's death, and it's evil. [. . .] Read about the Armfeldt trial till 4. I understood too that the activity of the revolutionaries was an imaginary, external activity – through pamphlets and proclamations which can't rouse up anybody to revolt. And a legitimate activity. If nobody interfered with it, there would be no harm in it. But once they put a stop to that activity, the bombs appeared.

11 April Late. Read Natalya Armfeldt's correspondence. Of a high order. A light-hearted, honest, cheerful, gifted and kind type of person. *You can't forbid people to express to one another their thoughts about how to organize their lives better.* And that's all our revolutionaries did before the bombs. We've become so stupid that such an expression of our thoughts seems to us a crime. In the morning I walked to Strakhov's. Had a good talk with him and Fet. Solovyov came. I don't need him, he's tedious and pitiable. Two brothers-in-law to lunch. Petya is obnoxious, Sasha more tolerable. Went off to Seryozha's. Again a death-like weakness. At home stitched boots. But went out to have tea and sat at the table and stayed till 2. Shameful and vile. Terrible depression. Full of weakness. I must take care of myself, as though I were asleep, so as not to damage what I need when I'm awake. I'm being more and more dragged into the mire, and my convulsions are of no avail. As long as I'm not dragged in without protest! I haven't been angry. I've little or no vanity either. But these days have been full of weakness, death-like weakness. I long for real death. I don't despair. But I would like to live, and not stand guard over my life.

14 April [. . .] If only people could stop using force when they fight. It's ridiculous and pathetic that our revolutionaries (bombs apart) who have been fighting with the legitimate and immortal weapon of the light of truth should expose themselves to the charge of wanting to fight with sticks. This is something their convictions won't allow them do do anyway.

17 April   Got up earlier, wrote a letter to Tolstaya.[32] Petitions to *royal and holy personages*, and dealings with Their Highnesses *are no longer possible for me*. Fancy asking a holy personage to stop torturing a woman!

At tea she[33] seemed to want to say something, but I was afraid of her. And I immediately said the wrong thing. Truly death is now something for me to be glad about. [. . .]

18 April   Late. Read through the manuscripts, then my own manuscript on the census.[34] I want to publish it in aid of the unfortunate. I used to doubt whether it was necessary to help political prisoners. I didn't want to, but now I understand that I haven't the right to refuse. [. . .] Dined in peace, had a sleep. Went for a walk. Lvov told me about Blavatskaya,[35] the transmigration of souls, the powers of the spirit, the white elephant and the oath of allegiance to the new faith. How can one keep sane when exposed to such impressions? Stitched boots, drank tea and went to Seryozha's until 2. An unimportant, but amicable and smutty conversation. Got a letter from Chertkov, and replied to his honest confession.[36]

I'm less strong where frankness is concerned – a sign that I'm less strong morally.

21 April   Late. Found the article (it was in draft). Revised it a bit, and took it to the printer's.[37] I don't myself believe in the article. [. . .]

22 April   Late. Had a good sleep. And seem to have woken up. I've slept for over a month. All is clear and firm again. Tried to remember whether I did anything bad when asleep. Not much. Got down to the article. Revised it a bit, but got no further than the description of the house. I must jump ahead to the conclusion. I still don't believe in this work. But it might seem good to others. The cheerfulness of the children is pathetic. I'm going for a walk, aimlessly. I'm drawn towards Rzhanov's house.[38] [. . .]

23 April   Very late. Tidied my room briskly. Read the paper. Then settled down to work – no good. [. . .] Dinner at home. It's absolutely impossible to talk to my family. They don't listen. They're not interested. They know everything. [. . .] Stitched boots all evening. The Dmokhovskys definitely want to make a revolutionary out of me. [. . .]

24 April   [. . .] Why can't I talk to the children; to Tanya? Seryozha is impossibly obtuse. The same castrated mind that his mother has. If you two should ever read this, forgive me; it hurts me terribly.

26 April   [. . .] At home I read the holy Sermon on the Mount and tried to write an introduction to it. Impossible. Set off for the book shop, but didn't get there. Nobody on the tramcar could change ten roubles. They all thought I was a swindler. [. . .]

30 April [. . .] Tried to write – couldn't get on. Took up *The Death of Ivan Ilich* – it's good; I'm better at that. [. . .]

1 May Earlier. Began to revise *Ivan Ilich* and worked well. Probably I need a rest from the other work, and that's what this work of fiction is. [. . .] I'm trying to give up smoking.

3 May Was expecting a letter from Pamyatka, and found one from my wife. Poor woman, how she hates me. Lord, help me. If this is my cross, so be it; let it weigh me down and crush me. But this harassment of my soul is terrible, not just depressing and painful to endure. [. . .] Went to Usov's.[39] A good conversation about town and country. One can talk about the advantages of the town as advantages, but as soon as one asks the question which is more moral, that's the end of it.

I'm depressed. I'm a worthless, pathetic, unnecessary creature, and moreover a self-centred one. The one good thing is that I want to die. [. . .]

4 May Got down to work. Once again I kept jumping from one article to another, and gave it up. [. . .] The older children were rude and I was hurt. Ilya is all right. He's spoiled by school and life, but he still has a spark of life intact in him. There's nothing at all in Sergey. All his emptiness and obtuseness are guaranteed for all time by his impregnable self-satisfaction. [. . .]

5 May Dreamed that my wife loved me. How simple and clear everything became! Nothing like that in real life. And it's that which is ruining my life. I'm not even trying to write. It would be good to die. [. . .]

7 May [. . .] How difficult my position is as a famous writer. Only with peasants am I completely natural, i.e. a real person. [. . .]

8 May Very late. Naum brought a letter from Ozmidov.[40] He had nothing to bury his mother with. It was unpleasant at first. Reminded me of the distribution of money at Yasnaya. Something wrong about it. Still I was prepared to collect. Then Olsufyev and Morozova turned up and gave five roubles each, Seuron a rouble, Nanny twenty copecks, and eighteen roubles were collected. I said that it's necessary to give to the poor. 'Very well. Perhaps it is necessary.' Still my family paid no heed. It was as if I was living at their expense. The more alive I am, the more dead they are. Ilya

appeared to take some notice. At least one person in the family came to
life! Alexander Petrovich [41] began to tell a story. They were having dinner
in the kitchen, and a beggar came. He said he was lice-ridden. Liza didn't
believe him. Lukyan got up and gave him a shirt. Alexander Petrovich
began to cry as he said this. Isn't it marvellous! I live with my family and
the people closest to me are the down-and-out Alexander Petrovich and
Lukyan the coachman. [. . .]

11 May   Read about Danton and Robespierre. Wonderful. [. . .]

12 May   Early. Tried not to smoke. I'm making progress. But it's good to
see one's rottenness. Had a peaceful journey. Didn't speak to anyone.
Read Mikhaylovsky on myself in *Notes of the Fatherland* for '75.[42]
    The town has corrupted me very much. Vanity has begun to rear its
head again. It's nice at Yasnaya – quiet – but, thank God, I've no desire for
pleasure, only demands on myself.
    Emerson is good.[43] The journey passed quite quietly.

13 May   Room tidied before 10. I told them not to tidy it. Began revising
my article. Can't get on with it. Read Emerson. Profound, bold, but often
capricious and confused. [. . .]

14 May   Went for a walk with the young children and Masha. Picked a lot
of mushrooms. It was pleasant. I stopped in the wood. Began telling my
fortune – influence enormous, great, average, so-so, small, very small,
insignificant. Twice it came out very small. I've had experience of fortune-
telling before – it's a habit. But *very small*, intrigued me. After all it's the
best thing I can wish for. The most enormous task after all is always *very
small*. For God, any task is *very small*. [. . .]

20 May   Spiritual agitation again. I suffer terribly. Obtuseness, deadness
of spirit – that I can stand, but on top of that there is rudeness and self-
assurance. I must learn how to endure that too, if not with love, at least
with compassion. I've been irritable and gloomy since morning. I'm ill.
Got up earlier. Drank coffee with the children. Read *Hypatia*.[44] Got a letter
from Chertkov. A ray of light in the darkness that has thickened even more
since the arrival of Tanya.[45] Petitioners: Kubyshkin in tears. His horse has
been sold for one and a half roubles. He's in tears. There's no justice. An
old widow with four children, her land is being seized. Taras and
Konstantin have come to blows with Osip. The steward wants to flog
them. Mikheyev is complaining that he's been done out of his share. And
Nikolay Yermishkin brandishes his fists at the meeting – he was drunk.
Nanny says that however much you help your own people, nobody will

remember your good deeds when you're old – they'll drive you out of the house. The priest's wife says that nowadays women won't marry without money. The Kuzminskys talk about fashions and the money they need for them. How can one live here, how can one burrow through all this mass of sand? I'll go on digging. Smoked, and talked in an unpleasant tone at tea.

21 May   Earlier. Coffee with the children. Read *Hypatia*. A mass of petitioners. Widows deprived of their share of land, beggars. How depressing this is to me, because it's false. I can't do anything for them. I don't know them. And there are too many of them. And there's a wall between them and me. A talk with my wife over tea – anger again. Tried to write – couldn't get on. Went to Tula. [. . .] Got back at 6. Read a bit and stitched boots. Had a long talk with Tanya. It's impossible to talk. They don't understand. And it's impossible to remain silent. Smoked and was intemperate.

22 May   Late. Talked with the children about how to live – to be one's own servant. Verochka said: 'Well, that's all right for a week, *but surely you can't live like that.*' And this is what we bring our children to! I tried to write – but in vain. Weakness and idleness. I'll go for a walk.

Thought hard about my life as I was walking – how all that is bad is inside me – i.e. in a place where it can be removed from. [. . .]

23 May   Got up late, in good spirits. A petitioner, a peasant from Shchyokino, obviously just begging, and a stupidly bourgeois teacher afraid he has talent as a writer and that it will be buried. I told him gently, but plainly, to give it up. Sat down to write. Couldn't get on with it. Went for a walk, like a man bemused, to the Chepyzh wood. Then to the Zaseka. Thought a lot about my wife. I must love her and not get angry; I must make her love me. That's what I'll do. Hardly smoked at all. Went for a ride with Masha in the evening, and stitched boots cheerfully.

26 May   [. . .] Walked round the Zakaz. An agonizing struggle. I can't control myself. Searched for the causes: tobacco, intemperance, lack of work for the imagination. It's all nonsense. The only cause is the lack of a loved and loving wife. It began that time fourteen years ago, when the string snapped, and I became aware of my loneliness. That's still not the reason. I must find a wife in *her*. I must, and can, and will. Lord, help me. [. . .]

27 May   Earlier. Reading Augustine.[46] Walked along the main road. Suddenly felt quite calm. Thought a lot about the fact that Paul's, Augustine's, Luther's and Radstock's teachings of redemption – the awareness of one's weakness and the absence of struggle – are of great importance. Struggle – the reliance on one's own powers – weakens those powers. Don't torment yourself, don't tighten the string and don't weaken it by doing so. But feed yourself with the food of life. It's the same as redemption. It would be very interesting to find out – will temptation go on tormenting me now, once I stop struggling against it? [. . .]

A wonderful night. It became so clear to me that our life is the fulfilment of a duty imposed on us. And everything is done so that its fulfilment should make us glad. Everything is suffused with joy. Sufferings, losses, death – all this is good. Sufferings bring happiness and joy, just as work brings rest, pain the awareness of health, the death of one's near ones the awareness of duty, because this alone is consolation. One's own death is a consolation. But you can't say the reverse: rest doesn't bring tiredness, health – pain, or the awareness of duty – death. All is joy once there is an awareness of duty. [. . .]

28 May   Early. Unwell, bilious, slept badly, but still all right. Will it really go on like this? The Kuzminskys are quarrelling. I spoke to her. Spoke to their nice nanny. Did some mowing. Read my article[47] – it could be good. [. . .]

I try to be serene and happy, but it's very, very hard. All that I do is bad, and I suffer terribly from it. It's as if I'm the only person who isn't mad in a house full of mad people, run by mad people.

29 May   Early. Still unwell. Read; didn't even try to write. Mowed. After dinner went for a walk with the girls to Bibikov's. The children there clung to us. It's enjoyable being with children. The terrible thing is that all the evil – the luxury, the dissipated life which we live – is my own doing. I'm corrupt myself, and I can't get better. I could say I'm trying to get better, but so slowly. I can't give up smoking, can't find a way to treat my wife so as not to offend her and not to indulge her. I'm seeking. I'm trying. Seryozha[48] came. My relations with him aren't good either. Just the same as with my wife. They don't see and they don't know my sufferings.

3 June   Early. Didn't sleep all night and feel abominable. Tried to write. Went to court.[49] An institution for corrupting the people. And very corrupt itself. [. . .] Dinner. She shouted in a nasty way. It hurts me that I don't know what should be done. I said nothing. Went to the Rezunovs',[50] read the Gospels. At home, tea and talk with Seryozha and Kuzminsky – good. [. . .]

4 June   Late. *Esprit de l'escalier* [Wise after the event]. Thought about yesterday's conversation, and then in the morning Kuzminsky and

Seryozha joined me for coffee on their own. [. . .] I said to Seryozha that all people should carry the burden, and that all his arguments, like those of many others, were prevarications. 'I'll carry it when others do.' 'I'll carry it once it's started to move.' 'It will move of its own accord.' Anything to avoid carrying it. Then he said: 'I don't see anybody else carrying it.' And as for me, I'm not carrying it either. I only talk. This bitterly offended me. He's just like his mother, malicious and unfeeling. I was very hurt. I wanted to go away at once. But that's just weakness. Act for the sake of God, not for other people. Do as you know best for your own sake, and not to prove anything. But it hurt terribly. Of course it's my fault if it hurt. I struggle, I douse the fire that has kindled in me, but I feel that this has weighed the scales down heavily. And indeed, what use am I to them? What are all my torments for? And however hard a vagrant's life is (and it isn't hard) there can't be anything in it to compare with this heart-ache.

Read through the extract I copied out, and revised it a bit. I'll do some mowing and stitch some boots. Tomorrow I'll get up at 5. But I don't yet undertake not to smoke. Mowed for a long time. We had dinner. Then I went to stitch boots until late in the evening. Didn't smoke. All round me the same parasitic life goes on.

5 June Got up at 5. Woke the children up. Walked to Pavel's[51] and settled down to work. Worked quite hard. Didn't smoke. At 12 I went to have breakfast and encountered just the same malice and injustice. Yesterday Seryozha made the scales tip, today she did. If only I could be sure of myself, for I can't continue this barbaric life. Even for them it would be an advantage. They would come to their senses if they have anything like a heart.

Mowed. Stitched boots. Can't remember what I did. The girls love me. Masha clings to me. [. . .]

11 June Got up with an effort at 6. Scribbled some letters, went to Tula to the post. Tired. Couldn't do anything. Went for a bathe. I'm more composed, *stronger* in spirit. In the evening a cruel conversation about the Samara money.[52] I try to do what I would do in the sight of God, but can't avoid malice. This must stop.

Thought about my unsuccessful attempts at a novel about the life of the people.[53] What an absurdity?! To have the idea of writing a work in which love would take first place, while the main characters would be peasants, i.e. people among whom love not only does not take first place, but among whom there isn't that voluptuous love either, which one is required to write about. I feel like writing, and there's a lot of work to do; but at present the change in my way of life prevents me from thinking clearly.

18 June [. . .] In the evening I did some mowing near the house. A peasant came about the estate. Went for a bathe. Came back cheerful and in good spirits, and suddenly there began some absurd reproaches on my wife's part about the horses which I don't need and which I only want to get rid of. I said nothing, but I was terribly depressed. I left,[54] and wanted to leave for good, but her pregnancy made me turn back half-way to Tula. At home, bearded peasants – my two young sons – were playing *vint*. 'She's at croquet, didn't you see her?' said their sister Tanya. 'I don't want to see her.' And I went to my room to sleep on the sofa, but my grief wouldn't let me. Oh, how depressing it is! Still. I'm sorry for her. And I still can't believe that she is completely wooden. Just woke up after 2; she came in and woke me: 'Forgive me, I'm in labour, perhaps I'll die.' We went upstairs. Labour had begun – what is the most joyful and happy event in a family passed off like something unnecessary and depressing.[55] A wet-nurse has been engaged to feed the baby.

If anyone governs the affairs of our lives, I would like to reproach him. It's all too difficult and heartless. Heartless where she is concerned. I can see that she is heading with increasing speed towards destruction and terrible mental suffering. Went to sleep at 8. Woke up at 12. As far as I can remember I settled down to write. When my brother came from Tula, I told him for the first time in my life the whole gravity of my situation. I don't remember how the evening passed. Had a bathe. *Vint* again, and I couldn't help sitting down with them and staring at the cards.

June   Recapitulation. I've been trying to change my habits. I've been getting up early. Doing more physical work. And, unwillingly, talking more and more to the people round about me. I can't say that the break with my wife is any worse, but it's complete.

I don't drink any wine at all, don't put sugar in my tea and don't eat meat. I'm still smoking, but not so much.

19 June Got up before 8. Tidied my room in Seryozha's presence. A merchant came to buy a horse. I went back on my word; 250 roubles.

The falseness of my position is bad. I'm to blame for it. I must escape from it. Wanted to give the money to Tanya. It turned out that other people – i.e. Seryozha – were envious. You'll read this one day, my son Seryozha – you must realize that you are very, very bad; and that you must work hard on yourself, and above all humble yourself. [. . .]

21 June The peasant women are working, mine aren't. I worked with the peasants all day, except for the last ricks. In the evening in Masha's room we began talking about how everyone had spent the day. It's not a game.

I'd make a habit of it. Of course there's no need to compel people. Anyone who wants can tell.

22 June   Early. First the peasant women came; mine didn't go out. Then I set off, and then Masha. She had a stomach-ache. I worked all day. Over tea the girls and Tanya and Alexander Mikhaylovich all told about their day and their sins. Tanya told how she had been angry at breakfast, and both the Kuzminskys had been angry with Trifonovna. I wanted to tell my sins, but couldn't. Impure glances at women and malice towards my wife and Seryozha. Couldn't express either the one or the other at all.

23 June   Got up at 7, worked with Blokhin without waiting for the peasants to arrive. [. . .] Sent for Tanya. She had been busy raking. She is gentle too, but very spoiled. But she could be a very, very good woman. I worked non-stop, and was very tired. I couldn't sleep – my hands ached, but I felt very good physically and mentally. They gave me a rick to do – i.e. a big load. I didn't expect in my old age that I could learn so well and improve. The carting and storing are difficult. My wife is very calm and contented, and can't see the complete break between us. I'm trying to do what I should. But I don't know what I should do. [. . .]

24 June   [. . .] Dreamed about going to France – one can live equally well anywhere. [. . .] I demand a lot from those near me. Conscience is stirring in the best of them, and that's good. [. . .]

I've been reading over my diary for these last days, looking for the cause of my temptations. It's all nonsense. The only cause is lack of intensive physical work. I don't sufficiently appreciate the happiness of freedom from temptation after work. This happiness can be cheaply bought with tiredness and aching muscles.

25 June   Got up early. Was five rows behind the peasants, but did my stint. Worked all day. Had no dinner. A beggarwoman from Tula came. I couldn't do anything for her, but it hurt to refuse. [. . .]

26 June   Got up exhausted and ill at 7 and set off to work: mowed all day without a break. Tanya came with some coffee. Very nice. Seryozha mowed. He's impossible with his self-assurance and egoism. Some peasants came – purchasers of the Myasoyedovo estate. They had to buy to rid themselves of an evil neighbour and to have some land, but they're overstepping the mark. Talked with the peasants about Turkey and the land there. How much they know, and how instructive it is talking to them, especially when compared with the poverty of our own interests. [. . .] My wife was glad of a chance to censure and abuse me. It's difficult for me, but it seems there's been some progress. And the result is a pretty kettle of fish. Everyone helped to clear the tea away together after croquet, and so *made* the servants *laugh*. As if it wasn't funny enough already that well-fed people dying of boredom should sit and make busy people waste time on trifles.

30 June [. . .] Read Emerson's Napoleon[56] – a typical greedy, bourgeois-egoist – wonderful.

I don't notice how I sleep and eat, and I'm strong and composed spiritually. But at night there are sensual temptations.

3 July Got up at 6. They had already done four rows each. I mowed with a terrible effort. Masha brought some coffee and went away. Went to dinner early. Fell asleep. Sonya is capricious and is always talking about herself. It's a terrible torture.

6 July A bad day. Got up before 8, tidied my room, wanted to walk to Tula, but felt so weak that I rode on horseback. Before I left, Artemov came about the land. I spoke to him rudely and maliciously: he has covetous eyes. And I went off depressed. It was stuffy in Tula. Clean people in banks were rattling their abacuses and wetting their fingers on sponges, making a tapping noise as they counted out banknotes; and along the roadside peasant women were stacking the hay, and the men mowing and harrowing. Beggars and pilgrims were walking about weak and hungry. Got back crushed and exhausted, and sent the money to the post. I was dreaming as I rode back of organizing my life properly, i.e. giving up to others at least a part of what I have, and getting down first of all to running the estate. I hope I might be able to do it now, without being distracted and not forgetting that human relationships are more valuable than anything. [. . .]

7 July [. . .] Went to Artemov's to ask his forgiveness. But, fortunately or unfortunately, I didn't find him in. Came back home and had the misfortune to speak about non-stop tea-drinking. A scene. I went off. She's beginning to tempt me carnally. I'd like to refrain, but I feel I won't in present conditions. But cohabitation with a woman alien in spirit – i.e. with her – is terribly vile. [. . .]

I'd just written this when she came to my room and started a hysterical scene – the sense of it being that nothing can be changed, and she is unhappy and she must run away somewhere. I was sorry for her, but at the same time I was aware that it was hopeless. She will remain a mill-stone round my neck and round the children's until I die. Probably it has to be so. I must learn not to drown with a mill-stone round my neck. But the children? Apparently it must be so. And it only hurts me because I'm short-sighted. I calmed her down like a sick woman. [. . .]

9 July   Very hot, and I felt very unwell; itchiness, and depression, and sleeplessness. Stayed at home and read Meadows on China.[57] He's completely devoted to Chinese civilization, like any intelligent, sincere man who knows Chinese life. Nowhere is the significance of ridicule more obvious than in the case of China. When a man is unable to understand a thing he makes fun of it. [. . .]

12 July   Still getting up no later than 8. Reading Meadows, and the Gospels in Hebrew.[58] I'm still unwell and weak – weak in all respects. The whole day passed uneventfully. Conversation and interest in it subsided. Announced I would walk to Kiev. Went upstairs during the night. Had words. I don't understand how to save myself from suffering, and her from the destruction to which she is flying headlong. Prayed yesterday; that means I'm weak. People pray to gods and saints – especially saints – because they need help. And if we lived a Christian life, there would be help from people and from the Church. All that we reasonably pray for people can do for us – they can help by work, intelligence and love. Two letters from Chertkov. His mother hates me, as well she might. Dreamed about Chertkov. He suddenly began dancing, gaunt as he was, and I saw he'd gone mad.

14 July   Missed several days and tried to write everything down from memory on Wednesday. On that day, I think, I asked my wife to come, and she refused with cold spitefulness and the desire to hurt me. I couldn't sleep all night. And during the night I got ready to go away, packed up my things and went to wake her up. I don't know what was the matter with me – bitterness, lust, moral exhaustion – but I suffered terribly. She got up, and I told her everything, told her that she had ceased to be a wife. A helpmate for her husband? She hasn't helped me for a long time, but only hinders me. A mother to the children? She doesn't want to be. A nurse? She doesn't want to be. A companion of my nights? She makes a bait and a plaything even out of that. I was terribly depressed, and I felt I'd spoken uselessly and feebly. I was wrong not to have gone away. I think I shan't be able to avoid it. I'm terribly sorry for the children, though. I love them more and more and pity them.

15 July   Woke up at 10. A talk with Seryozha. He was rude without any cause. I was angry and gave him a thorough reprimand – bourgeois habits, and obtuseness, and spitefulness, and self-satisfaction. Suddenly he said that nobody loved him, and began to cry. God, how it hurt me. I walked about all day and managed to catch Seryozha after dinner and said to him: 'I'm ashamed.' He suddenly burst out sobbing, and started to kiss me and say: 'Forgive me, forgive me.' It's a long time since I experienced anything like it. There's happiness.

17 July Got up late. But had coffee with the children. Still correcting the German translation[59] in the mornings and read with surprise that it leaves people unmoved. In the evening, I went mushrooming with the children and stayed behind to mow with the mowers from Baburino. At home relations are tense again, but only with my wife. All the others love me.

26 July All day with Gay. I'm miserable without physical work. Sonya is nice, and so are Seryozha and Tanya and Masha; Ilya is the worst of all – he's rude, spiteful and egotistical. [. . .]

27 July Got up late today, felt fresh. Spoke upstairs about Gay. About the fact that with a moral man family relations are complicated, but with an immoral one everything goes smoothly. Read *Ground Ash*.[60] It's a *revivalist* work – full of pathos, but good. Walked to the plantation and went for a bathe. At home relations were friendly. Thought: we reproach God, and lament that we encounter obstacles in carrying out Christ's teaching. Well, what if none of us had discordant families? We would all be friends and live happily and colourlessly. And what about other people? Other people wouldn't even know. We want to rake the fire together into a heap, so that it will burn more easily. But God has dispersed the fire throughout all the logs. They catch light, but we are sad because they don't make a big fire. [. . .]

28 July Woke up, and there was Sukhotin.[61] What a pathetic and insignificant creature. It's particularly astonishing, because to outward appearances he's gifted. We bathed and all went mushrooming. A big dinner. I don't remember the evening. All a waste of time. To eat food and have no work to show for it, to acquire knowledge and not to pass it on – that is real onanism. You will ejaculate more and more often, and you will be more and more loathsome to yourself and to others. I'm every sort of onanist. I must stop being one.

6 August Another three days have passed, and I can't remember them. Got up late today. Feverish condition. Worry and anxiety about the translation, and about the horses, and even about going mushrooming. I want to die, both when I'm physically ill, and even more when my soul is in chaos. Re-read my article on the census. Still don't want to give it up; made some corrections to it. It's strange that what couldn't help standing out was the fact that I unexpectedly found them better than I am.[62] It must be so. In the morning, a talk with Tanya. And I came to realize that among the whole series of things that fill up our lives there are those that are real and those that are frivolous. To know which things are real and which are frivolous is to know all about life. In the evening stupid charades and then the post-box.[63] Tanya was moved by Sonya's poem.[64] The three of them – the two Mashas and she herself – started to cry. The children are gradually becoming aware of their false position. [. . .]

9 August [. . .] Came home. Sonya and I were reconciled. How glad I was. Actually if *she* were to take it upon herself to be good, she would be very good.

22 August My wife's nameday. The post-box. Shakhovskoy. I wrote about the patients in the Yasnaya Polyana hospital.[65] It was good. Something is stirring them somehow. I don't know how.

26 August A mass of people. Said something disagreeable to my brother Seryozha about his not knowing English literature. I shouldn't have done. [. . .] Went mushrooming. Urusov. My wife didn't follow me but went off, with no idea where, only not after me; it's been like that all our life.

28 August I'm 2×28 years old. Our folk have gone to Tula to see Vera Shidlovskaya off. I'm glad I'm alone: read Michelet on the ancient Persians. Some good thoughts. Unwell. Pleasant, friendly relations with my wife. Told her some unpleasant truths, and she wasn't angry. In the evening I read Maupassant. Struck by his mastery of colours; but he has nothing to write about, poor man.

31 August [. . .] Had dinner on my own and called on the Kuzminskys. They were on the point of quarrelling. In the morning, as he was dressing, he asked about Sonya. She replied: 'I can't shout.' He was offended; all the old trouble came to the surface, and he started saying that they hated each other and couldn't go on living like that. She said nothing. But in the evening she took up the conversation again and reproached him for his irritability, verging on madness. He tried to justify himself, but was gloomy. In my presence she began to tell him that *she had married him for love*. But I know she has told Sonya that that wasn't so. And it suddenly became clear to me what women's strong points are: coldness – and something which they can't be held responsible for because of their weak powers of thought – deceitfulness, cunning and flattery. [. . .]

1 September　Got up late, read some Michelet, Hercules – the deification of labour and heroic deeds. A talk with Tanya about the fact that women seldom or never love – i.e. surrender their outlook on life to their beloved. They are always cold. She was genuinely embarrassed that I had spied out their *truc* [trick]. [. . .]

2 September　[. . .] A talk; women's power – flattery – the fact that they can love. We are so convinced we deserve love that we believe them. I'm wrong to confine this to Sonya. It's a universal thought and one that is very new and important for me. [. . .]

4 September　Stitched shoes all day, made some mouthpieces and cut down some lime trees. Went to the bath-house and waited for Sonya. She came, I was tired.

5 September　A talk in the morning, and unexpected malice. Later she came down to my room and nagged me until she was beside herself. I said nothing and did nothing, but was depressed. She ran out in hysterics. I ran after her. I'm terribly exhausted.

12 September　Read about Buddhism – its teaching. Wonderful. [. . .] The only mistake is wanting to save oneself from life – entirely. The Buddha doesn't save himself but saves other people. [. . .]
　Felled trees. Walked through the woods with Sonya. After dinner I walked with all of them and stitched boots – badly. Read with the children: instead of the rubbishy *Pasynkov* read *An Outing to the Woods*.[66] It was a success.

13 September　More than a week has passed again, and I've written nothing. Incontinence today . . . I'm ashamed. In the morning the girls came to do problems. It was very enjoyable. Then I read Nekrasov in order to read him to the children. Went for a walk with everybody. Called in at Fedot's. He – a man dying of a wasting disease – eats cucumbers and mushrooms. It's impossible to live like that. [. . .]

1885

5 *April*   I think.[1] The whole business of my life (unfortunately for me, because it's a slippery and deceptive path through life) is the awareness of and the expression of truth. I often have clearly expressed thoughts which make me glad and are helpful to me, but I can find no place for them and forget them. I will note them down. They will be useful to somebody.

Today. Thought about my unhappy family: my wife, sons and daughters who live side by side with me and deliberately put barriers between me and themselves in order not to see the truth and the good, which would expose the falseness of their lives, but would also save them from suffering.

If only they themselves could understand that their idle life, supported by the work of other people, can only have one justification: that of using their leisure in order to come to their senses, to think. But they deliberately fill their leisure with frivolous activities, so that they have even less time to come to their senses than those who are crushed by work.

I thought further: about Usov, and about professors: why do they – such clever and sometimes good people – live so foolishly and badly? Because of the power of women over them. They allow themselves to drift on the tide of life, because that is what their wives or mistresses want. It's all decided during the night. They are only to blame for suppressing their awareness of their weakness.

I thought further: to do the will of Him who sent me – that is my food. What simple and profound significance. You can only be at peace and always content when you take as your purpose not something external, but doing the will of Him who sent you. I don't want to have my picture printed in my works[2] – it's offensive and disagreeable to me. If I do my own will, I shall refuse, and will cause offence and sorrow. If, however, I do the will which is not my own, I shall ask them not to do it. And if they do do it, I shall be content, because I shall have fulfilled the will of Him who sent me. [. . .]

1888–1894

FROM 1888 ONWARDS Tolstoy kept his diary fairly regularly and one important event which figures prominently during the last decade of the century is the serious famine which affected large areas of European Russia in 1891 and 1892. For the greater part of two years Tolstoy devoted much time and energy, with the active assistance of his wife and family, to the alleviation of suffering in the regions to the south of Tula and Ryazan, organizing relief programmes, soliciting contributions of food, clothing and money (not without qualms of conscience), opening 'soup kitchens' and generally alerting public opinion in Russsia and abroad to his country's serious economic plight. Working towards a common cause did something to improve the uneasy relations between Tolstoy, his wife and his growing sons at this period (a thirteenth and last child was born to the Tolstoys in 1888 when he was already sixty and Sonya forty-four), but the growing influence of Chertkov in Tolstoy's life was a constant source of domestic friction which Sonya was never really able to overcome. In 1891 Tolstoy publicly renounced the copyright of all his works published after 1881, much to his wife's annoyance. He finally gave up meat, spirits and tobacco, spent more and more of his time in the country, and turned his energies increasingly towards agricultural tasks when he was not either reading or writing.

Tolstoy's major work of fiction during this period was the notorious *Kreutzer Sonata*, which took as its text 'But I say unto you that everyone who looketh on a woman to lust after her hath committed adultery with her already in his heart.' The censors banned the story, but the Tsar Alexander III, as a result of the personal intercession of Tolstoy's wife, allowed it to be included in Tolstoy's *Collected Works*. In 1892 the Maly Theatre in Moscow gave the first production of his new play *The Fruits of Enlightenment*, which was later enthusiastically welcomed by Bernard Shaw as 'the first of the *Heartbreak Houses* and the most blighting'. Tolstoy's best-known play *The Power of Darkness*, with its sombre plot of greed, adultery, poisoning and infanticide, which had been written very quickly in 1886, was also given its first performance in Moscow in the 1890s. *The Kingdom of God is Within You*, a powerful statement of the case for non-resistance and against patriotism and war, was completed and sent abroad for translation and publication in 1893, while the articles *Why Do Men Stupefy Themselves?* (on the subject of alcohol and drug abuse), *The First*

Step (advocating vegetarianism), *Christianity and Patriotism* and his preface
to some of Maupassant's stories were all written in the course of these few
restless and extremely strenuous years.

1888

23 November, Moscow   A girl came recently and asked (such a well-known and false question!) what should I do to be of use? And having talked with her I realized that the great sorrow which millions suffer from is not so much that people live badly, but that they don't live according to their conscience, their own conscience. People take as their conscience somebody else's conscience, higher than their own (for example, Christ's – the most common case), and not, apparently, being able to live according to another person's conscience, they live neither according to that person's nor their own, but live without any conscience. I tried to persuade this young lady not to live according to my conscience, as she wanted to, but according to her own. But she, poor girl, doesn't even know whether she has a conscience of her own. [. . .]

I'm still not writing – there's no necessity of the sort which would pin me down to my desk, and I can't force myself. My state of tranquillity – at not acting against my conscience – affords me quiet joy and the readiness to face death – i.e. affords me everything in life. Yesterday evening Yevgeny Popov[1] was here; he's twenty-four and in the same state as I am. Complicated relations with his wife which only a humble life can unravel, as a knot can only be untied by patiently following the thread with the whole ball of wool.

24 November   [. . .] Thought: life – not my life, but the life of the world which with the *renouveau* [revival] of Christianity is blossoming forth on all sides like spring in the trees and the grass and the water – is becoming unbelievably interesting to me. Indeed, this alone constitutes the whole interest of my life; but at the same time my earthly life is at an end. It's as if I were reading; reading a book which was getting more and more interesting, when suddenly, at the most interesting place, the book came to an end, and it turned out to be only the first volume of a work in an unknown number of volumes, and the succeeding volumes couldn't be obtained here. It could only be read abroad in a foreign language. But it certainly will be read. [. . .]

25 November   Unwell. *Slept* badly. Hapgood[2] came. Hapgood: 'Why aren't you writing?' I: 'It's a futile occupation.' Hapgood: 'Why?' I: 'There are too many books, and the world will go on just the same, whatever books are written nowadays. If Christ came and had the Gospels printed, ladies would try to get his autograph, and nothing more. We must stop writing, reading and talking; we must *act*.' [...] Kennan's[3] pronouncements about the Russian government are edifying: I would be ashamed to be tsar of a country where there is no other means of protecting me except to send thousands of people, including sixteen-year-old girls, to Siberia. [...]

29 November   [...] Sat a while with Lyova and had a talk; went to the evening school,[4] couldn't make up my mind to go in, walked about for a couple of hours, called in after 10 and met the teachers; I'll go on Thursday. [...]

30 November   Got up early, Lyova still unwell, stoked up the stove and am now ready to write. I've written nothing except a letter to Lisitsin and a copy of the things I've begun. I'm still trying to guess from cards (patience) what to write. Of all superstitions this is the only one which attracts me – trying to guess, or asking God what to do. This or that? I can only free myself from it by not doing things for myself, but for God (then there will be nothing to ask Him). For me, one thing is better than another, but for God everything is equally good or bad because what He needs is not facts, but the motives behind them. [...]

1 December   Reading newspapers and novels is rather like tobacco – a means of forgetting. Likewise idle conversation. One ought not to do these things, so as to be able instead to sit quietly and think, or play with a child and comfort it, or talk frankly with someone and help him, or most important of all work with one's hands. [...]

1 December   continuation. [...] Went to the school in the evening. Was struck by the stupidity and lifelessness, and the discipline of mechanical teaching, and the dim, lacklustre eyes of the students: the factory, tobacco, lack of sleep, alcohol. [...]

7 December   Late. Misha ill. Sonya sent for yet another doctor. When will they understand this simple thing that if doctors charge ten roubles to save you, what must the situation of the poor be like! And how then could you prosecute a person who killed an old man in order to rob him of ten roubles to engage a doctor and save his young son? Thought yesterday: serve people? But how, and what with? Not money or even physical services – sweeping the ice rink, stitching boots, washing clothes, sitting with a sick person at night. Perhaps all this is good, and better than doing it for oneself, but perhaps it is bad too, and, in effect, useless. The only useful and necessary thing is to teach a person to live well. And how is one to do that? The only way is to live well oneself. [. . .]

9 December Slept sinfully. In the morning I finished stitching boots, went for a short walk and am now sitting down to dinner. A letter yesterday from Gay. A strange thing: my life is seemingly empty; and yet I'm completely calm. Everything that is bad is only inside me, in my lack of love. But things are improving, and for that reason I'm not depressed, but glad. Dropped off to sleep. Got up; two American women – sisters – one had crossed the Atlantic, the other the Pacific, and they met and are travelling on again, and have seen everything, and have seen me, but aren't any the wiser. She[5] asked: 'Do you find it strange that they travel like this?' I tried to say that one should live in order to be *useful*[6] to others: she said that she had expected I would say that, but she can't think any more whether it's true or not. Everyone went to bed. I sat up alone, quietly. And it was good.

12 December Chopped up wood; I'm stoking up the stove. All these days I've been living a colourless, but transparent existence; I love everyone naturally, without any effort. Read. Went for a walk. A woman, lame in one leg, but strong. At home the Behrs brothers and their relatives. Felt good even with them. Masha came to say goodbye; she's bored. The atmosphere at home is bad and depressing, and that's all the more reason for not giving in. But Tanya, poor thing, wants to get married at all costs; still her choice is better than it might have been.[7] [. . .]

Yes, and yesterday I almost started to quarrel with my wife about why I don't teach my own children. I didn't recall at the time that it's good to be humbled. Yes, there is such a thing as conscience. People either live above it or below it. The former case is painful for oneself, the latter obnoxious. Better to live according to the demands of a growing conscience, always a little above it, so that it can grow up and reach the height already occupied above it. I live above my conscience, but it doesn't catch up with me; especially over the fact that I take offence and am always sensitive and vain, and don't want to stop publishing anything more in my lifetime.

13 December, Moscow Chopped wood, tidied the room, stoked up the stove, wrote my diary for the 12th and am going to have breakfast. Read, did nothing. Went for a walk. Thought: in life we are frozen, corked-up vessels, whose purpose it is to be uncorked and poured out, to establish communication with the past and the future, to become a channel and to share in the universal life. The death of the body doesn't do this. It only decants us anew, as it were, and once again into corked-up vessels. [. . .]

15 December [...] Walked about fifteen *versts*. Got back at 5. The Behrs for dinner. [...] Sonya said at dinner: 'One must be completely stupid to believe another person, and not to have one's own thoughts.' I said: 'Nobody has his own thoughts, but it's only a question of whether to follow the thoughts of Christ or Mme Minangois.'[8] She feels the burden of her life more and more, but I doubt if she will choose another path in my life-time. I'm no longer sorry. So be it. [...]

19 December Got up early. Chopped wood; I'm going to stoke up the stove and have breakfast. [...] Read in the evening. Chernyshevsky's article on Darwin is splendid.[9] Force and clarity. Talked with Lyova about the universal scourge of onanism and the falsehood under which debauchery is concealed.

1889

2 January, Moscow   Began the new year in low spirits. Read *Robert Elsmere*[1] – good, sensitive. Masha and Posha are distraught.[2] It's getting difficult. And there's no chink of light. Death beckons me more often. [. . .]

3 January   Slept better, read *Advance Thought*,[3] gave my ideas a shake-up. Walked to Polushin's,[4] Fet's and Pokrovsky's and went to fetch wood. Love and joy everywhere. At home we began to read Leskov after dinner; a Jewess came about the theatre. Should she be baptized in order to go on the stage? [. . .]

5 January, Moscow   [. . .] Read about Ruskin. [. . .]

Took a late stroll to Gautier's.[5] At home read Kennan,[6] and felt terrible indignation and horror when reading about the Peter and Paul fortress. If I were in the country, this feeling would bear fruit; here in town Grot and Zverev came and Lopatin as well:[7] cigarettes, jubilees, anthologies, dinners with wine and professional philosophical chatter moreover. Zverev's madness is terrifying. *Homo homini lupus* [Man is a wolf to man], no God, no moral principles – only flux. Terrible hypocrites, bookmen, and harmful ones at that.

10 January, Moscow   Got up early and continued writing my article *12 January*[8] until breakfast. [. . .]

13 January, Moscow   [. . .] Read about the Mormons,[9] understood the whole story. Yes, here is a glaringly obvious example of that deliberate deceit which is a part of every religion. I even wondered whether this element of conscious fabrication – not cold-blooded fabrication, but a poetic, enthusiastic half-belief in itself – isn't an exclusive sign of what is called religion. There is fabrication in Mohammed and Paul. There isn't with Christ. It has been falsely imputed to Him. He would not have been turned into a religion had it not been for the fabrication of the resurrection, and the chief fabricator was Paul.

14 January, Moscow   Earlier. Stoked up the stove, read, did my diary and wanted to write a foreword for Yershov.[10] Wrote very diligently. But feebly. And it won't do like that. Chopped wood, walked about, met Nikolay

Fyodorovich[11] and had a chat with him. For him, as for Urusov, life and books contain not what is, but what he would like there to be. And the tone of conviction in his voice is astonishing. This tone is always in inverse proportion to the truth. [. . .]

18 January, Moscow   Early, chopped wood. A Molokan[12] from Bogorodskoye came. Read upstairs. Telicheyev and another gentleman came to ask me to intercede on behalf of a governess due to be exiled. Behaved badly towards them. No love for them, and was impatient and garrulous. Before that I'd read something about myself in an article by Shelgunov in *Russian Thought*[13] and was sad and ashamed. Yes, yes, yes – it's necessary to abandon all plans to write and to do anything for myself, and preserve one thing only: the readiness to endure offence and humiliation; humility and a concern only with the possibility of doing good to others. [. . .]

24 January, Moscow   Overslept till very late. Poor, tormented Sonya came to me and said something that hurt me – I managed to take it well. [. . .] According to the symptoms, Vanechka has tuberculosis and will die.[14] I'm very sorry for Sonya. I have a strange feeling of pity for the child, of reverential awe in the presence of this soul, this germ of a most pure soul in a tiny weak body. His soul has only just been dipped in the flesh. I think most likely he will die.

   Recently a strange and very joyful thing has begun to happen to me – I've begun to feel the possibility of the constant joy of love. Previously I was so overwhelmed and choked by the evil surrounding and engulfing me that I only used to reason about love and imagine it, but now I've begun to feel its blessing. It's as if shafts of light and warmth have begun to emerge now and then from under a pile of dry logs; and I believe, and know, and feel love and its blessing. I feel what is standing in the way and obscuring it. Now I'm conscious in quite a new way of my ill disposition towards a person – it was Tanya yesterday – and I'm afraid and feel that I'm blocking out the warmth and light from myself. Moreover, I often feel such warmth that I feel that as long as I love and have pity, nothing can disturb the state of quiet joy of the true life. [. . .]

25 January, Moscow   Woke up early. Thought, and not only thought but felt, that I can and do love those who have gone astray, the so-called bad people. At first I thought: can one point out to people their errors, sins or guilt without hurting them? Can one extract teeth without pain? There is chloroform and cocaine for physical pain, but not for the soul. This is what I thought at first, but then it occurred to me at once: it's not true, there is spiritual chloroform for the soul. Just as in everything else, the body has been thought about from every aspect, but people haven't yet begun to think about the soul. People perform operations on legs and arms with chloroform, but when they perform operations for the moral improvement of a person, they deaden the effect through pain, and through pain they cause the worse illness of bitterness. But there is chloroform for the soul, and it's been known for a long time – it's just the same as always: love. [. . .]

The doctors have been. They tried to make clear and definite what is unclear and indefinite. They almost sentenced him to death.[15] [. . .]

27 January, Moscow   Got up early, stoked up the stove, and lay in bed thinking. Yes, the whole trouble is being premature, being certain you have done something you haven't done. It's true of Christianity generally, and of slavery in particular. They got rid of slaves – papers allowing you to own slaves – but despite that we went on changing our underwear every day, having baths, riding in carriages, having five courses for dinner – we live in ten rooms, etc. – all things which can't be done without slaves. It's astonishingly clear, but nobody sees it. [. . .]

30 January, Moscow   Got up very early. The water hadn't been fetched; I was glad of a bit more work to do. It's now after 10. I'll go and have breakfast. Thought of something good when I woke up, but have forgotten it. One thing I thought was that Sonya loves her children with such a morbid passion because they are the one real thing in her life. From loving and caring and making sacrifices for her child, she goes straight to Fet's jubilee, to a ball which is not only senseless but evil. [. . .]

Had a sleep and went for a walk. After dinner Popov the poet came,[16] a young man. I surprised him by saying that his was a most ignoble occupation. Went to Fet's. Had dinner there. All terribly stupid. Ate and drank a lot and sang. Disgusting. [. . .]

1 February, Moscow   Got up at 8. Worked a lot, wrote up my diary; I'm going for breakfast. Straight after breakfast my stomach began to ache. It ached a lot, but I passed the day no worse than when I'm well. Read *Zadig*[17] – a lot of good things in it. Yes, progress means increasing the amount of light, but the light is always the same. [. . .] They've been tormenting Masha because of her vegetarianism. It's astonishing. [. . .]

6 February, Moscow   Got up early again. Very jaded. Did some work. Had a sleep. Thought of a parable apropos of the fact that people who wish to live in Christ's name want to live together. People want to live in Christ's name. They are seeds wanting to germinate and bear fruit. To feel sorry for a Christian because he is surrounded by worldly people, people not like himself, is like feeling sorry for a seed because it's surrounded by earth, and doesn't hang in space or lie with other seeds. But after all, earth is just what a seed needs in order to get nourishment and sprout. [. . .]

7 February, Moscow [. . .] I'm reading *Ben Hur*.[18] Poor.

9 February, Moscow [. . .] Yes, it's becoming clear that 'one must treat words honestly', i.e. if you speak, you must speak as clearly as you can, and not with artful devices, omissions and insinuations, the way everybody writes, and the way I used to write. I'll try not to do this. [. . .]

10 February, Moscow [. . .] Wrote the foreword in rough.[19] Went for a walk. After dinner I translated assiduously. O. A. Mamonova and Dunayev came. Read *Le sens de la vie*.[20] There are some astonishing pages about war and the state. I really must write both an appeal and a novel,[21] i.e. express my thoughts and surrender myself to the flow of life.

12 February, Moscow [. . .] Read the Gospels, my own exposition, with Ivin,[22] and there was a lot I didn't like: a lot of unnecessary strained interpretations. It would be good to revise it, but I doubt if I can now. And I doubt if it's necessary. [. . .]

15 February, Moscow [. . .] Late. Chopped wood, very tired. Must stop these exertions. Sokolov,[23] an ex-revolutionary, came. Then I read *She*,[24] played patience, and another young man came, a shallow man. He wants to be useful, to learn everything, but at the age of eighteen he already knows women. Yes, I did well to tell him that the only way to be of service to people is to be better yourself. [. . .]

20 February, Moscow Slept badly. Got up later, worked, read Matthew Arnold.[25] The foreword. Remarkably similar. Only he has also included the Old Testament in his circle of what he exalts. And that depresses it and brings it down to earth. [. . .]

23, 24, 25, 26 February, Moscow [. . .] Read Matthew Arnold, he's very good with his subtle demarcations, with no loss of clarity; but with the Church of England, the National Society for the Promotion of Goodness[26] is an influential factor, and that's a pity. Why is it necessary for the promotion of goodness to wear gowns and sing certain songs in certain houses? I thought later, but still on the same subject: in real life there are bound to be anomalies and deviations from the ideal, but in one's thoughts and ideals it's bad if there are deviations, and if a straight line in one's imagination is not quite the shortest distance between two points. In the evening Sonya brought a doctor round from Masha's, Mokrousov. It was wrong of me to be sceptical, as though trying to uphold my reputation. Oh, if only I could forget about what other people will think of me. [. . .]

26 February [. . .] Contracts and property are a lie. But how are we to escape from it? By gradual steps, income tax, the abolition of inheritances and so forth. But one must be aware, I suppose, that this is not what should be, but only an approximation to it. The worst thing is a compromise, accepted as a principle. And this always happens in government affairs.

There can be no political change of the social system. The only change can be a moral one, within men and women. [. . .]

28 February, Moscow [. . .] Thought yesterday: writing a lot is a disaster. In order to escape from it, one must establish the habit of being ashamed to be published in one's own lifetime – only after one is dead. How much sediment would settle, and how much pure water would flow! [. . .]

3 March, Moscow [. . .] Revised my notes on art – they turned out better. Began to write about Frey[27] – no good. Took my notes round to Goltsev and called in at Vera Alexandrovna's.[28] Yes, woman's kingdom is a disaster. Nobody but women (she and her daughters) can do stupid and dirty things in a clean and even nice manner, and be completely satisfied. And they have no respect for people's opinions which might cause them to have doubts. [. . .]

4 March, Moscow Got up later, wrote my diary, no work to do, I'll go for a stroll. Read M. Arnold.[29] Weak. Sophisms about the Church, which for some reason he needs. Slept. Walked to the Bible shop, it was closed. Many of our people at home. Everything was all right until the arrival of Seryozha with his conversations always on the same theme, critical of everything, despairing and self-justificatory. I spoke to him more heatedly than I should. Lyova makes me sad with his weakness for smoking cigarettes. Ate too much, had stomach-ache. [. . .]

6 March, Moscow [. . .] At home, a whole crowd of people including Fet. I'm more and more at ease with people, I say what I can about God, and what they want me to say about everything else. Fet complained of boredom and of not knowing what is good and bad, what should be done and what shouldn't. I said: 'People lived and didn't know why; Christ explained the law of life – the establishment of the Kingdom of God on earth – and gave meaning to each person's life: taking part in the establishment of the Kingdom of God.' And it's all the most precise, clear and practical philosophy. And they call it mysticism. [. . .]

7 March, Moscow   [. . .] A sculptor came to do a model of me for a group,[30] then Kasatkin[31] came with my booklet *What I Believe*, agitated, angry, with tears in his eyes and, as I realized, full of pity for himself and anger with me: 'Why did you destroy my peace, and tell me what I ought to do and can't do? You don't do it yourself. You're a fraud.' [. . .] I behaved well; I wasn't embarrassed by the presence of Klodt and tried to mollify him. [. . .]

11 March, Moscow   [. . .] Woke up as I was saying to someone: 'Don't talk about the need of the poor in a material sense, and of helping them. Need and suffering don't have material causes. If you want to help, do so only with spiritual gifts, necessary for rich and poor alike. Look at the life of the middle classes. Married men make money by means which are offensive to themselves, with loathing, stress and bitterness, while their wives get through it all inevitably, with discontent, envy of others and bitterness, and it isn't enough for them, and they console themselves in their imagination with the hope of winning a lottery, if not for two hundred, at least for fifty thousand.' Read Solovyov's *Teaching of the Twelve Apostles*.[32] How empty scholars' discourses are.

Thought: with scholarship, only the importance attached to it is wrong. They, the scholars (professors), do a certain definite and necessary job, they collect, count, compile everything of the same kind. They are, each of them, an information bureau, and their works are reference books. [. . .] A *catalogue raisonné* and extracts from books are useful, but their idea that they are increasing knowledge by these compilations, collections and catalogues is a comic delusion. As soon as they leave the field of compilations, they *always* talk nonsense, and confuse good people.

Read Ruskin all morning. [. . .]

14 March, Moscow   Got up early. Worked, read an excellent book on China.[33] The Chinese can't regard us in any other way than as barbarians, madmen, evil and base profit-loving monsters. How edifying such a view is. Revised my thoughts on art again. [. . .]

15 March, Moscow   Got up just as early, worked a lot. Read Quental.[34] [. . .]

I read some nice little things by Chekhov.[35] He loves children and women, but that's not enough. [. . .]

17 March, Moscow   Got up early, chopped wood. Behaved very well towards a petitioner. Sonya is kinder. Lord, help me. Read Chekhov. [. . .] He has the ability to love as far as artistic insight goes, but as yet no reason to. [. . .]

21 March, Moscow [. . .] Got up and, without dressing, settled down to revise my thoughts on art and sat for three hours scribbling over everything, and I still don't know whether it's worth the effort. I think not.[36]

I've just said to Sonya what I've wanted to say for a long time, that I can't sympathize with her over the edition.[37] She was very angry and said: 'You really do hate me.' She suffers and causes me pain like a toothache, and I don't know how to help her, but I'm looking for ways. Help me. [. . .]

26 March, Spasskoye, at Urusov's Got up early, had a drink of tea and began writing.[38] It went quite well. Went for a walk before dinner. After dinner had a sleep and read *Paul Ferroll*.[39] Got an angry letter from Sonya, about the 'dark people'[40] and Masha. [. . .]

28 March, Spasskoye Woke up at 8. I'm going to have coffee. Did some work, got on with the comedy (bad!). After dinner went to the Novenkoy Factory[41] with its 3,000 women workers, ten *versts* away. [. . .] Drunken, savage people in the inn; 3,000 women, getting up at 4 and leaving work at 8 at night, being corrupted, having their lives shortened and their progeny deformed, live in poverty (in the midst of temptations) in this factory so that calico which nobody needs might be cheap, and Knop might have even more money, when he's already worried because he doesn't know what to do with the money he has. The management is being reorganized and improved. What for? So that this destruction of people, and other forms of destruction, might continue successfully and unhindered. It's astonishing! Came back by sledge, a husband and wife from Spasskoye gave me a lift. Told me about their life: two horses, three cows, tea every day, their own bread. And still they're dissatisfied. Just as it is in our circle. [. . .]

30 March, Spasskoye Urusov woke me in the night with a telegram about the arrival of three Americans.[42] Couldn't get to sleep for a long time. Got up at the usual time. Wrote the end of the 3rd act. All very bad. Sat down to dinner; the Americans arrived. Two pastors, one literary man. If only they would spend a dollar buying my books *What To Do* and *Life*, and a couple of days reading them, they would get to know me, i.e. what is within me, much better. They drank vodka and smoked. And I couldn't help feeling sorry for them. Urusov was very nice to them; they stayed till 4. I said a few unnecessary things. Needlessly abused the English very much. For myself, I didn't say anything new to them, and didn't hear anything new from them. [. . .]

If I'm alive,[43] *4 April, Spasskoye* Got up early. Began to revise *The Kreutzer Sonata*. [. . .]

6 April   [. . .] Got up early. Couldn't write for a long time, but then began *The Kreutzer Sonata* again. After dinner I read it to Urusov. Leg a bit painful. Urusov liked it very much. Yes, it's true that it's new and powerful.

8 April, Moscow   Alive, in Moscow, but not entirely. [Four words erased] Got up very early, did my packing, said goodbye to Urusov and set off. At the station and on the journey I did propaganda for the temperance society. I only went on foot from the station,[44] and then I used skates. Found a boy near the house, a seminarist from Ryazan, who asked me for money and leaned on me with all the weight of his onanistic helplessness. I hurried home and wasn't able to help him at all. Talked to him and gave him some money which I had on me. It is one of the most difficult situations: a youth who has formed an exaggerated and false idea about me, and has long been obsessed with this idea and with the further one about what he considers his *undeserved* misfortune, struggles to make his way to me and expects complete salvation; and suddenly there is nothing at all. [. . .]

9 April, Moscow   Got up at 6. Nerves a bit weak, got my letters in order and read them. Read the episode about the defence of the soldier who was executed.[45]
   Badly written, but the episode is awesome in the simplicity of its description – the contrast between the depraved colonel and the officers giving the commands and bandaging his eyes, and the women and the ordinary people celebrating requiem mass and raising money. [. . .]

15 April, Moscow   [. . .] Repin's picture is impossible – it's all invented. Gay's is very good.[46] [. . .]

18 April, Moscow   [. . .] A pile of letters, which I'll read after dinner. Taneyev[47] interrupted me. Read him my article on art. He's a completely ignorant man who has adopted an aesthetic outlook that was new thirty years ago, and imagines that he is in possession of the last word in human wisdom. For example: sensuality is good. Christianity is Catholic dogma and ritual, and therefore stupid. The Greek outlook on the world is the most elevated, and so on. Gorbunov[48] came. And I couldn't talk with him. Taneyev gets on my nerves. Went to bed late.

19 April, Moscow   [. . .] Yes, in the morning a Jew from Tver came, and on the pretext of his noble behaviour towards the woman he was living with asked for my help. For three months now he's been pursuing me with letters and now he turns up himself, beaming and smiling. I spoke to him irritably. I deserve indulgence (if there can be any for it), for the pain in my liver which has been coming on. Read the charming legend of Ormuzd and Ariman[49] (fictitious). After dinner I began reading. The pain started and it was very painful until 11. Put up with it reasonably well. How strange that when one is in pain, it's harder to pray and prepare for death than when one isn't. Read *World Advance Thought* and *Universal Republic*. A new world outlook and movement is growing up in the world, and seems to require me to take part in it and proclaim it. It's as if I had been made what I am, with my reputation, specially for this purpose – made to be a bell. [. . .]

20 April, Moscow   Got up at 8. Tried to write about art and am convinced that I'm wasting my time. I must give it up, especially since Obolensky[50] writes and says he's prepared to wait. I can't write because it's not clear. When it is clear, I'll write at once. [. . .]

22 April, Moscow   Woke at 6, got up at 8. Read Noyes[51] on the communities. Reading about the Shakers[52] one is horrified at the deadly uniformity and superstitions; dances and invisible callers and gifts – spectacles, fruit, etc. Thought: withdrawing to a community, setting up a community, keeping it clean – all this is sinful and wrong. An individual or individuals can't keep themselves clean on their own; to be clean they must be together; to isolate oneself in order not to get dirty is the greatest dirtiness, like the cleanliness of ladies for which the labour of other people is responsible. It's just like cleaning or digging at the edge, where it's clean already. No, the person who wants to work must clamber right into the middle where the dirt is, or if he doesn't do that, then at least he mustn't try to escape from the middle if he should find himself there. [. . .]

23 April, Moscow   Got up very early. Tired. Didn't even try to write. Read about Saint-Simonism, Fourierism and the communities, and didn't go out anywhere. Thought: it's terrible to think what a desolate state the world is in, and how the activity of the best representatives of mankind is paralysed in it by the organizations of the Church, the state, pedagogical science, art, the press, monasteries and communities: all the forces which might have served mankind as an example and a direct challenge are put in the exceptional position in which the simple life, and abstention from vice, weaknesses, follies and luxury becomes optional, pardonable and even necessary (a bishop, a minister, a scholar is bound to have servants, a digestible dinner, a glass of wine) and nobody is left to do the simple direct work of life. It's good that the Church, the state, science, literature and art don't claim everybody, and there are still the rank and file people left. But nevertheless this defection from life's work of the people with the best powers is ruinous. St Simon says: 'What if the 3,000 best scholars were destroyed?' He thinks that everything would then perish. I don't think so. More serious is the destruction or elimination of the best people morally. This is actually going on. And still the world hasn't perished. But it would be good to be able to explain this.

After dinner, during which I was in a bad mood and kept silent, I walked to Dmokhovskaya's. Called in to see Zlatovratsky. There was a factory worker there who writes. I tried to persuade him to give up writing, and alcohol too. The former is more harmful. Had a pain in the pit of my stomach. Poor Tanya came. I was very sorry for her.

25 April, Moscow Got up late. Wrote not too badly about art. Posha came. I told him he must wait.[53] [. . .]

Masha has come. I have a great feeling of tenderness for her. For her only. She makes up, as it were, for all the rest. [. . .]

26 April, Moscow [. . .] Posha and Masha at home. What is the meaning of

my attitude to Posha, which is by no means a joyful one? I love and esteem him; but is there not a father's jealousy here? Masha is certainly very dear to me. [. . .]

30 April, Moscow Got up at 8. Wrote nothing, only looked through what I wrote yesterday. Went to see the soldiers.[54] A fraud was being perpetrated on those conscripted in autumn. They were made to take the oath in front of the standard. Priests in chasubles were singing with choristers in smart surplices, icons were carried, drums were beaten and a band was playing. On my way back I heard a sergeant-major saying: 'It's forbidden.' What a terrible word! For it didn't refer to the word of God, but to the senselessly cruel and absurd military regulations. [. . .]

As I got near the troops, the priests with the icons came towards me. I walked away from them so as not to have to take off my cap. I felt conscience-stricken at running away, but was afraid and ashamed to walk towards them. Returned home, read and wrote this up. Decided to write theses, i.e. brief propositions, about art. [. . .]

2 May, Moscow Got up at 6, got ready for the journey[55] quickly and cheerfully, but wasn't in a good frame of mind. Popov came at 10 and we drove out beyond the town gates. Walked to Syrov, four *versts* this side of Podolsk, and spent the night there. Had tea on the way. The husband was drinking, the wife working, and an eight-year-old girl was washing the floors and making cigarettes for a rouble a week. [. . .] Walking with Popov was pleasant and easy.

5 May, on the road (Bogucharovo village?) Everywhere the scourge of alcohol; we read from *The Distiller.*[56] A woman from Voronezh wanted to buy the book from me – a remedy against a drunken husband. The cold is terrible. We're frozen and I even began to be afraid. We had a rest opposite the police station, without going in, and then in an inn. A father with his young girls. I gave them some books. Got as far as Bogoroditsk, thirty-four *versts* from Tula, for the night. A lot of people: an old and young soldier, women, young metal-workers. I talked about war. They understood. Slept well. We'll go on further.

6 May, on the road Walked briskly without stopping for sixteen *versts*. Had dinner in the inn at Seryukovka, where I exhorted them earnestly about drunkenness. A kind old inn-keeper, his wife and son. The church clerk, a smart young lad, was drinking and reading, and gave me five copecks for my book – *Time to come to our senses*. An ex-sergeant-major who had seen better days came with us. Got as far as Tula. [. . .]

10 May, Yasnaya Polyana Woke up later, that's a weakness too. Began to write about art – couldn't get on. Went into the woods with my notebook. Tried to express my ideas in theses – couldn't formulate them clearly. [. . .] The cutting down of oak trees is an unpleasant business. I don't know what to do. [. . .]

13 May, Protasovo[57] Still alive. Got up at 4, got ready, said goodbye to Popov and drove to Kozlovka, where I wasted about an hour. [. . .] Set off in the heat of the day and was exhausted. Got to the house and dear Masha ran out to meet me, always ready to do a kind deed, and – just as ready – his Sonya,[58] a wonderful mother. Ilya is much inferior to her, as a man. He buries himself in trifles, and then there's his luxurious living and lack of any spiritual life. He is a kind man, but very weak. [. . .]

14 May, Protasovo (and Yasnaya Polyana) Got up very early, went for a walk through the woods. Wrote down my thoughts about Ilyusha.[59] I wanted to pray for him and show him the error of his ways, and sought an opportunity all day but didn't find one. Spoke in snatches; it was difficult. The main thing is he doesn't want to listen and won't listen. [. . .]

Masha is worth a lot; serious, clever and kind. People reproach her for not having any exclusive attachments. But it's this that shows her true love. She loves everyone and makes everyone love her – not just as much as, but even more than, people who love their own family exclusively. [. . .]

20 May, Yasnaya Polyana [. . .] Read Lecky[60] on the aesthetic development of art . . . Yes, art, in order to be respected, must bring forth good.

And to know what is good, one must have a world outlook, a belief. The good is a sign of true art. The signs of art in general are that it says something new, clear and sincere. The sign of true art is a new, clear and sincere good. [. . .]

23 May, Yasnaya Polyana Yesterday it was very depressing to hear Sonya's complaints about the work to do with the estates. She has bought more and more,[61] poor woman, without knowing why, and doesn't know what to do. Got up very late and went to cut beams for a Yasnaya peasant. It was very pleasant. [. . .]

25 May, Yasnaya Polyana Early. An undefined quantity of food does harm, I think. I must have two cups of tea and nothing more. Dreamed that I was conscripted into the army and obeyed the rules for dress, reveille, etc., but felt that before long I should be required to take the oath and would refuse, and I thought there and then that I would have to refuse to do drill as well. An inner struggle followed: a struggle in which conscience got the upper hand. [. . .]

Tanya. I did wrong in objecting even to Misha Islavin.[62] [. . .]

28 May, Yasnaya Polyana Health worse. Went for a walk in the morning. Read about Jean Paul Richter. The purity of his morals and his Platonism are astonishing. His sayings are also excellent. He is the best sort of writer. On a par with the egoist Goethe. A good story about a father who brought his children up under the ground. They had to die in order to come out into the light. And they terribly wanted to die. I must follow it up when I've read some Jean Paul. [. . .]

29 May, Yasnaya Polyana [. . .] In the morning I talked to Tolstaya about faith; it seems strange, but it's impossible to say anything else except that the Graeco-Russian faith is one of the most superstitious and harmful heresies. As I was walking through the wood, where I chased and pitilessly dispatched a wounded hare, I thought how innocent murderers must be. They think about something else, and kill without a struggle. But we must come to our senses. How good a story one could write about a murderer who repented of the murder of a woman who wouldn't defend herself.[63] There's so much I want and need to write, and I haven't the strength.

1 June, Yasnaya Polyana Got up early, went to talk to Vasily Yakovlevich about the estate, and explained the Lord's Prayer to Masha's school-children. Read *Le peuple d'Israël*.[64] [. . .]

6 June, Yasnaya Polyana A young monk and an actor came begging; I gave them some money and booklets – pathetic people. Then a young student from Kiev. He said he was nervously distraught and wanted to live according to Christ's law. [. . .] Had a frank talk with him. [. . .]

One man is no better than another man, just as a place in one river is no deeper or cleaner than a place in another. Man is in flux, like a river. And a man between fifteen and sixteen years of age, and another between twenty-five and thirty, and a third between forty and fifty and a fourth between the 4th and 5th hours of the last day of his life, etc. – are all incommensurable quantities. And you can't say: this one is better or worse. [. . .]

7 June, Yasnaya Polyana   [. . .] Lyova came. Not a bad lad. He could turn out very well. There's a long way to go yet. [. . .]

11 June, Yasnaya Polyana   [. . .] A German newspaper, anti-drink and vegetarian, with my article in. I was pleased. Received some books: Whitman, some stupid poems, and De Quincey.[65] Went to bed late. Oppressed very much by life.

15 June, Yasnaya Polyana   [. . .] Thought: aren't the bad feelings children have for their parents due to the contempt they feel for their parents because of their sensuality? They feel it somehow. Verochka K.[66] hates her parents. [. . .]

Today I read an excellent adaptation of *L'homme qui rit*[67] and thought: people always describe how heroes give up their lives for others, but it's all nonsense. You need to give up your job like Semyonov's yardman[68] or, more difficult still, give up porridge when you're hungry. [. . .]

16 June, Yasnaya Polyana   [. . .] Behaved quite well with Sonya; reconciled her and Tanya. The main thing is, she seems to be beginning to understand that I need peace and love. [. . .]

20 June, Yasnaya Polyana   [. . .] Read Adin Ballou's *Non-resistance*.[69] Gave it to Lyova to translate. Excellent. [. . .]

23 June, Yasnaya Polyana   [. . .] Over dinner I took offence at Sonya for pestering me about food. Thank God I went to apologize immediately after dinner. An example of female reasoning: *I.* 'What wonderful articles about non-resistance.' *She.* 'Yes, but it's all talk. Everyone knows it and no one does it, because it doesn't pay.' *I.* 'That's because people don't drum it in.' *She.* 'However much you drum it in, they won't do it.' *I.* 'Why not, if it's drummed in in the same way as, say, the holiness of the sacrament? After all no one would spit out the sacrament, even under threat of execution.' *She*. '*Yes, but that's nothing, it's easy, any one can do it; but the other thing isn't.*' *I* (perplexed). 'But I said that despite the fact that it's nothing, people still won't do it. You don't understand.' *She*. 'What is there to understand? I understand already what you're going to say next. You just keep on and on about the same old thing.'

25 June, Yasnaya Polyana   [. . .] Thought later about a story of a man who spends all his life searching for the good life in science, in the family, in a monastery, in hard work, in *yurodstvo* – and who dies in the consciousness of a ruined, empty, unsuccessful life. Yet he is really a saint.[70] [. . .]

28 June, Yasnaya Polyana   [. . .] Saw Feinermann[71] off. He's young, and not exactly a revolutionary, but the socialist ideal stifles everything else in him. [. . .]

29 June, Yasnaya Polyana   [. . .] I'm ready to die. Dreamed in the night of a frog as big as a man, and was terrified. It seemed to be death I was terrified of. But no, it was terror pure and simple.

1 July, Yasnaya Polyana   Hardly slept at all. Very weak. *Looking Backward*[72] is excellent. Only one thing is bad: the socialist, Marxist idea that if you do something that's wrong for a very long time, it will come right of itself. Capital is concentrated in a small number of hands; eventually it will be concentrated in one. Workers' unions will also merge into one. And capital and the labour force will be separated. Then the power of the state or revolution will unite them, and all will be well. And the main thing is that our civilization will in no way be curtailed or be put into reverse: there will be the same palaces, gastronomical dinners, sweetmeats, wines, carriages, horses – only everything will be available to everyone. What is incomprehensible is that they don't see that this is impossible. Just take the luxury of the Yasnaya Polyana house and share it among the peasants. It can't be done. It wouldn't be any use. (One must give up luxury.) While oppression exists, the force of capital and inventive genius is not being directed to where it is needed. For that to happen, the masses must be able to try everything themselves. But the main thing is for us to be prepared to give up all the refinements of our civilization, simply in order to get rid of the cruel inequality which is our curse. If it's true that I love my brother, I don't think twice about depriving myself of my drawing-room in order to give him shelter if he is homeless. But as it is, we say that we want to give shelter to our brother, but only on condition that our drawing-room remains free for receiving guests. We must decide who to serve – God or mammon. We can't serve both. If God, then we must give up luxury and civilization, and be prepared to rebuild it tomorrow, only for all people equally.

2 July, Yasnaya Polyana   A bit better. The Hapgoods have left.[73] I walked to the village and the haymaking. Nothing is going well. Everyone is quarrelling. Got on with *The Kreutzer Sonata*. Not bad. Finished it all. But now I must revise it all from the beginning. Forbidding her to have children must be made the central point. Without children she is reduced to a state where she is bound to fall. More about the mother's egoism. The mother's self-sacrifice is neither good nor bad, just like work. Both are good only when there is understanding and love. But work for oneself and self-sacrifice exclusively for one's children are bad. Went to bed early.

4 July, Yasnaya Polyana   Got up at 6. Mowed, it's now 11.30, I'm tired. This morning and yesterday evening I thought hard and clearly about *The Kreutzer Sonata*. Sonya is copying it out; she's upset, and she talked last night about the disillusionment of a young woman, the sensuality of men, alien to her at first, and the lack of sympathy for children. She's unfair because she wants to justify herself, but in order to understand and speak the truth it's necessary to repent. The whole drama of the story, which I haven't been successful with all this time, is now clear in my head. He cultivated her sensuality. The doctors forbade her to have children. She is well fed, and well dressed, and there are all the temptations of art. How can she help falling? He must feel that he himself brought her to it, that he had already killed her before when he hated her, and that he was only looking for a pretext and was glad of it.

Yes, yesterday the peasants asserted that it's only women, not girls, who get hysterics. Therefore it's correct that it's the result of sexual excess. [. . .]

6 July, Yasnaya Polyana   Got up very early and walked to Prudishche meadow. Did some mowing there with Fomich and Andrey. Came home for breakfast. More mowing. Vanya is still ill at home. Went to sleep. Was woken up by Ilya and Treskin. A conversation over breakfast about the person who says and doesn't do. What a muddle! A person like Sonya says: 'Others say, but don't do. But I don't say and don't do. That's more honest.' 'What nonsense! Do you know what to do?' 'Yes.' 'Well in that case it's better to say so. Saying at least something imposes an obligation.' Sverbeyev came to dinner. I argued with him about the temperance society. Very tired, stooked the hay. [. . .]

11 July, Yasnaya Polyana   Didn't get up early because off the rain. Set off at 7. They were already mowing. Sharpened Rugin's scythe and spent all day mowing energetically. Finished all the mowing. Enjoyed it. [. . .] Went to bed at 11 and today is 12 July. Got up at 8 and saw Dyakov off. A letter from Feinermann which Sonya read and which distressed her very much.

He writes about my cross and foresees the torture I will suffer living in conditions which are offensive to me and which I want to, but hesitate to break out of. Offensive, yes, but there's no hesitation about breaking out, because I know that they are like idleness, old age or death, the favourable conditions of my life, and so their offensiveness isn't painful, but a cross whose importance he doesn't understand. A cross means something unpleasant, painful, heavy, being carried as something necessary and inevitable sent from God, and for that very reason not unpleasant, not painful, not heavy, but something without which it would be unpleasant, uncomfortable and unnatural.

15 July, Yasnaya Polyana [...] They struck up the same everlasting conversation about the estate again – despondent, despairing and censuring one another and everybody else. I tried to tell them that the solution was not at the other end of the world, but here under their noses, and that they must work to find it, try it out and then pass judgement. Lyova began to argue. It began with the orchard. They argued obstinately and rudely, saying: 'It's impossible to talk to you, you get angry at once', and so on. I was very hurt. Of course Sonya attacked me at once, harrowing my tormented heart. It was very painful. Sat up till one and went to bed ill.

16 July, Yasnaya Polyana [...] Thought: what an astonishing thing – lack of respect by children for their parents and elders in all classes of society has become an epidemic! It's an important sign of the times: respect and obedience from fear is finished, it's had its day, and freedom has appeared. And on the basis of freedom one ought to cultivate living relationships, which include everything that fear was responsible for, but without fear. With me it's only so with Masha. I'm afraid to say and write this. [...]

18 July, Yasnaya Polyana [...] Received some letters and a newspaper cutting: 'The world has of Tolstoy as much as it can digest.' It's flattering. The bad thing is that people pay attention to it. [...]

21 July, Yasnaya Polyana [...] After dinner Sonya declared that she had been faithful and was lonely. I said: 'One must always be calm, gentle and considerate.' I couldn't say anything more. And I regret it. [...]

22 July, Yasnaya Polyana Got up late. Useless chatter in the morning – they wouldn't let me work. After breakfast I went mowing. Everything had already been gathered in, only the blind man's strip was left. I mowed it till dinner. Dinner at the Kuzminskys', sad and disgusting gluttony. How pathetic they are. I can't help them. However, were I to go out begging, I

could help them even less than now. Sonya locked up Bulka, who had
bitten the dogs, and this led to an insoluble muddle: let her out? Keep her
locked up? Kill her? *Le non agir* [Non-action]. Lao-Tzu. In the evening I
played bat and ball, and was bored.

24 July, Yasnaya Polyana   [. . .]   Thought: (1) I'm writing *The Kreutzer
Sonata* and even *On Art*, and both are negative and evil, and I want to write
something good; and (2) in ancient times the Greeks had only the one
ideal of beauty. But Christianity, in proclaiming the ideal of the good, has
removed or displaced that other ideal, and made of it a condition of the
good. Is that true? I feel that in the confrontation, in the substitution of one
of these ideals by the other, lies the whole history of aesthetics, but how it
is I can't think properly. Our way of life and my ill health prevent me from
thinking. [. . .]

Slept during the day. Worked a bit on *The Kreutzer Sonata*. Finished it in
rough. I realize now how I must reorganize it all, bringing in love and
compassion for her. [. . .]

27 July, Yasnaya Polyana   Got up before 8, went for a bathe, had some
good thoughts, namely: it was a great good fortune for Masha that her
mother didn't love her. Tanya not only didn't have the incentive to seek
the good along the path I indicated, but she was led astray directly by love,
and over-indulgence. [. . .]

28 July, Yasnaya Polyana   Got up before 8, went for a bathe, got on with
The Kreutzer Sonata before breakfast; I'm now feeling sleepy and want to
work well. Went mushrooming. A sort of quiet joy. It's so good. A feeling
of happiness. Only a little something is missing. In the evening I played
chess with Tanya. Slept badly all night, dreamed, felt and thought in my
dreams that one must maintain a loving attitude towards people: I kept
dreaming of the various situations in which I had renounced a loving
attitude, and had tried to reform. It makes me very glad; it means I'm really
aware of this and am beginning to introduce it into my life. I've actually
been living like this.

30 July, Yasnaya Polyana   [. . .]   Lyova looked at me and said:
'Mushrooming – that's hunting too. One feels sorry for the little
mushrooms too, just as one does for the snipe; there's only a little
difference.' I kept silent and then thought: yes, a little difference; but just
as Bryullov, when asked how it was that in improving his picture he only
changed a little bit but the result was quite different, replied that art is only
a matter of 'the little bit',[74] so one can say with even greater justice that the
good life begins where the little bit begins. [. . .]

31 July, Yasnaya Polyana [. . .] At home read Keats,[75] the English poet. [. . .]

1 August, Yasnaya Polyana Got up late, went for a bathe. Made some notes for *The Kreutzer Sonata*. At home I wanted to settle down to my comedy, but was disgusted and ashamed. Unwell. Rain. Hardly went out at all. Before I knew where I was, I was caught up in the idle occupation of chess – problems and playing. Still thinking about art and reading about it. Received a letter from Strakhov full of subtle flattery. As the Buddha rightly said, there are ten sins: three bodily, four verbal and three mental. The first three are murder, theft (I would say the appropriation of property) and lust (fornication); the four verbal ones: equivocation,[76] slander, lying and flattery; and three mental ones: envy, anger and deceit (delusion). Received *World Advance Thought* again and, as always, experienced a great spiritual élan. Some wonderful thoughts, for example: death is the awakening from the delusion of the reality of material life. I must write to them. Without fail. Also received a letter from Alyokhin with the news that they had been searched and that all my writings and their letters have been confiscated.[77]

2 August, Yasnaya Polyana [. . .] At breakfast I lost my temper with Lyova. Mutual animosity leapt forth like a wild animal that had broken loose from its chain. I was very sad and ashamed. Why didn't I remember that I wanted his humiliation? Consoled myself with the fact that it's just that humiliation that I need. [. . .]

6 August, Yasnaya Polyana [. . .] Thought: what if there should be another child? How ashamed I should be, especially before the children. They will reckon up when it was, and will read what I'm writing. And I felt ashamed and sad. And then I thought: there's no need to be afraid before people, but only before God. I asked myself how I stood in this respect before God, and at once felt more at ease. [. . .]

7 August, Yasnaya Polyana Went down to empty the chamber pot – a Polish lawyer was there, wanting to see the famous man. I found it very unpleasant that I couldn't get through to the man in him. [. . .]

9 August, Yasnaya Polyana Saw off Urusov and Lyova. I've become very weak. Shameful indulgence over food. Read Plato on art and thought about art. Plato connects beauty and goodness together – that's wrong. In *The Republic* he speaks of the immorality or amorality of poets and so rejects them. At that time, as at present, poets were below Plato's level and were a diversion. I feel that something is missing in my thoughts about art, and that I'll find what it is that's missing. [. . .]

16 August, Yasnaya Polyana   Did nothing all day except read Schopenhauer on art.[78] What flippancy and what trash. Yet someone assured me that his is the prevailing theory of aesthetics. [. . .]

19 August, Yasnaya Polyana   [. . .] Thought of something for *The Kreutzer Sonata*. 'Fornicator' is not a term of abuse, but rather denotes a condition (the same is true of a woman fornicator, I think) – a condition of restlessness, curiosity and the need for novelty which comes from intercourse for the sake of pleasure, not with one person but with many. Likewise 'drunkard'. One can try to abstain, but a drunkard remains a drunkard and a fornicator a fornicator – at the first lapse of concentration he falls. I am a fornicator.

22 August, Yasnaya Polyana   [. . .] In the evening Sonya talked to Nikolay Nikolayevich about Posha and Masha[79] and about life as usual. She doesn't need to persuade others, but in opposing the arguments of the person she is talking to, to persuade herself and herself only, that she is right. When you know and see this clearly, how can you argue? Then Vanya went down with suspected croup. How terribly pathetic she was! The whole of her life, a good life, is concentrated in and on him. And she has cut herself off from the possibility of any other good life (with the youngsters it's no longer the same – or I doubt it), and that's why she's so frightened. [. . .]

23 August, Yasnaya Polyana   [. . .] At dinner I couldn't restrain myself when Sonya began to compare me with her father with regard to fastidiousness about food. [. . .]

28 August, Yasnaya Polyana   Got up early and immediately settled down to work and got on with *The Kreutzer Sonata* for about four hours. Finished it. It seemed good, but I went out mushrooming and I was dissatisfied again – it's not right. [. . .] Sonya moved me yesterday. Arguing that she loved Vanechka because of his likeness to me, she said: 'Yes, I loved you very much, only nothing came of it.' [. . .]

29 August, Yasnaya Polyana   [. . .] Thought about the fact that I'm fussing over my writing of *The Kreutzer Sonata* out of vanity; I don't want to appear in public as not fully finished, clumsy, even poor. And that's bad. If there's anything useful or necessary to people there, they will pick it out from what is bad. A perfectly finished story won't make my arguments more convincing. I must be a holy fool [*yurodivy*] in my writing too. [. . .]

29 August, Yasnaya Polyana [. . .] I lay down for a while. Sonya came in and said: 'How bored I am!' I'm sorry for her, sorry. [. . .]

30 August, Yasnaya Polyana [. . .] Thought little; it's impossible in company. And I prefer to be alone. But I'm not alone when Sonya is with me. [. . .]

Today is 1 September, Yasnaya Polyana Woke up early despite going to bed late; woke up early and thought about Lyova, and the fact that I did wrong in not telling him what is my, or rather their, misfortune, that they are all like hard-mouthed horses and I am the opposite, and that they don't feel my movements, and I can't pull them. [. . .]

I don't remember what I did yesterday. In the evening I read *The Kreutzer Sonata* to Nikolay Nikolayevich and Lyova, who is leaving tomorrow. It made a great impression on everybody, and most of all on me; all this is very important and necessary. [. . .]

7 September, Yasnaya Polyana [. . .] Yesterday Sonya read aloud *The Kreutzer Sonata* and Tanya made some just observations: (1) that one isn't sorry for her, (2) that she won't repent and ask for forgiveness. Her sin is so small compared with her punishment. [. . .]

11 September, Yasnaya Polyana Still unwell. In the morning wrote an introduction to my article on art[80] – not good. There was a terrible storm during the night. Went to look at the fallen trees. I don't remember the evening. One joyful thing I do remember is that the awareness of life through the recovery of my talent has been restored to me. And I continually remember that. And every time I do, every difficulty is joyfully resolved. It's as if something were to expand and get trapped, and then resume its proper shape again at once and continue on its way without hindrance.

Sonya keeps talking about moving to Moscow, which she terribly wants – and needs. Again it will be annoying; I'll be sorry to lose my solitude, sorry for the children – I shall be trapped; then, I remember that my occupation is my soul, and all becomes clear and is set free again and continues on its way. My concern for my soul doesn't mean that I'll agree to go – not at all; it's very possible that, on the contrary, it will force me not to go; but my interest is shifting from what is not in my power (according to Christian teaching) to what is necessary and important to me and therefore in my power.

15 September, Yasnaya Polyana [. . .] Thought: Rejoice! Rejoice! The business of life, its purpose, is joy. Rejoice at the sky, the sun, the stars, the grass, the trees, animals, people. And take care that nothing disturbs this joy. If this joy is disturbed it means that you've made a mistake somewhere – find that mistake and correct it. This joy is most often disturbed by greed and ambition, and both are only satisfied by toil. Avoid toil for your own benefit, wearisome and oppressive toil. Activity for someone else's benefit is not toil. Be like children – rejoice always. How terrible is the delusion of our world which sees work – toil – as a virtue. It's nothing of the sort, but rather a vice. Christ did not toil. This needs to be explained. [. . .]

24 September, Yasnaya Polyana [. . .] A wonderful book compiled from Tikhon Zadonsky.[81] All this is bound to have consequences. I sometimes think that I am present at the lighting of chips of wood. Once they have caught fire, everything else will no doubt catch fire. The logs are still quite cold and untouched, but they will all undoubtedly catch fire. The children and Ilya came. After breakfast I read *Tikhon*, and then went to the wood to do some sawing. After dinner I wrote some letters to strangers. At dinner Sonya spoke about how she had watched a train approaching and wanted to throw herself under it. And I felt very sorry for her. The main thing is, I know how much I'm to blame. I remember for example my loathsome feeling of lust after Sasha was born. Yes, I must remember my sins. [. . .]

28 September, Yasnaya Polyana [. . .] Sonya was angry that I hide my diary from her, but we patched things up smoothly.[82] [. . .] Went to bed late, engrossed in reading *The Gardenins*.[83] Excellent, wide-ranging, truthful and noble. Lyova came.

29 September, Yasnaya Polyana [. . .] A thought occurred to me and then I forgot it. Well, never mind, it's only a thought. If it were, I won't say a million roubles, but merely a stone, a pearl or a diamond, I would have dug everything up until I found it, but it's only a thought. Only fallow ground, only a seedling, only a thought! But a seed produces an oak tree, a thought produces an entirely different activity by the very strongest of creatures, man, and it seems to us that it's nothing. [. . .]

9 October, Yasnaya Polyana [. . .] Went and did some sawing with Rakhmanov and Danila, then some stitching, and we read *Oblomov*.[84] The ideal is a good one.

10 October, Yasnaya Polyana Got up later. A bit better. Looked through and revised everything from the beginning. I'm feeling disgusted with this whole work.[85] Great depression. Worked till 4 and slept. After dinner I stitched boots, and continued *Oblomov*. The love story and the description of Olga's charms are impossibly banal. Went to bed late.

11 October, Yasnaya Polyana [. . .] On the way back I continued to think about the same thing. The question is: may one, for the sake of a great and very probable good, do a small but certain evil? No, because the greatest and most probable good may turn out to be harmful; it's always possible to find two opposite opinions about any event; but a certain evil will always remain an evil. [. . .]

16 October, Yasnaya Polyana Despondency, grief, remorse; if only I could avoid hurting myself and others. Wrote a lot in revising *The Kreutzer Sonata*. Haven't experienced such a state of depression for a long time.

20 October, Yasnaya Polyana [. . .] Wrote a useless letter to Sonya about visitors being a burden to me. A talk with Zhebunyov. I began by provoking him, he didn't retaliate, I even challenged him to an argument, began to 'be ironical', as he put it, and hurt him. In the evening, when talking to him again, I learned that he had been in exile and in prison, and had been so morally exhausted that he had lost the habit of reading when in exile, and didn't read now and was suffering from apathy. Moreover he spoke with great love about Boulanger, thereby demonstrating that he is good himself. He is a good, sick, suffering, exhausted, broken man; but I went for him in a boastful, swaggering manner, and tried to show off to the gallery what a splendid fellow I am. I was so sorry and ashamed that I began to cry when taking leave of him.

21 October, Yasnaya Polyana A talk with Chistyakov[86] about his marriage. There's something unnatural in the role of teacher and adviser which they make me play. An argumentative and ironical talk with Novikov.[87] I've only just covered myself with shame and ignominy, and I go and do the same again. If only I could say the same things with love. How far I am from that.

23 October, Yasnaya Polyana Was late in the morning. Sonya arrived. Her first word was one of gratitude for my kind letter and the acknowledgement that her letter had been bad. [. . .]

27 October, Yasnaya Polyana Got up earlier, wanted to sleep badly.[88] Disgusting. [. . .] (2) Re-read the Walt Whitman that had been sent to me. There's a lot that is pompous and empty, but I found some good things here and there, for example, *The Biography of a Writer*.[89] The biographer knows the writer and can describe him! But *I* don't know what I'm like, I have no idea. Throughout my long life it's only very, very seldom that anything of me has been visible to me. (3) Recalled how I, as a young man, lived in the name of the ideals of the past, to be like my father and grandfather, to live as they lived. My children – my Misha – lives by my instincts of the 40s. He doesn't imitate the present me whom he sees, but the past me of the 40s. Why is this? Isn't it due to what I thought before, that a child doesn't live entirely here, but a part of him is where he came from, at a lower stage of development; I on the contrary already live in the place where I'm going to, at a higher stage of development; but in that place I am still backward, still a child. This is very naive. But I can't help recognizing it to be so. [. . .]

28 October, Yasnaya Polyana [. . .] Thought: (1) For a novel or drama: 'Spiritual Birth'. He discovers the falseness of his life and the truth of the true life, and he chooses the first path he comes to: giving to beggars, looking after the sick, founding a community, preaching – and he goes wrong. And then everyone attacks him and the truth with relish.[90] [. . .]

31 October, Yasnaya Polyana Got up early. Sad. Yes, I didn't write down yesterday that I was angry with Fomich for drinking the coffee which I wanted, and made scathing remarks to him and, worse still, didn't want Alyokhin to hear. How petty and nasty; I mustn't forget it. Yes, and yesterday I got a long letter from Chertkov. He criticizes *The Kreutzer Sonata* very justly;[91] I wish I could follow his advice, but haven't the inclination. Apathy, sadness, dejection. But things aren't bad for me. Death is ahead of me, i.e. life, so why should I not be glad? It's just because I feel I have lost interest in – I don't say my own person or my own joys (they are dead and buried, thank God) – but in other people's good; in the good of the ordinary people, that they should be educated, not drink, not live in poverty; I feel my interest is cooling even towards the general good, the establishment of the Kingdom of God on earth; and I thought apropos of this cooling of interest:

Man lives through three phases, and I'm now living through the third. The first phase: man lives only for his own passions, eating, drinking, enjoyment, hunting, women, vanity, pride – and his life is full. It was so with me until I was thirty, until I had grey hair (with many people it's much earlier), then I began to take an interest in the good of people, all people, mankind (this began in a decisive way with my school activities, although my efforts were becoming apparent and intervening here and there in my personal life even before that). This interest died down in the first period of my family life, but then reappeared with new and terrible force with the awareness of the vanity of my own personal life. All my religious awareness came to be concentrated in my efforts directed towards the good of the people, in work for the realization of the Kingdom of God. And these efforts were just as great, and filled my whole life just as much, as the efforts directed towards my own personal good. But now I feel these efforts weakening: they don't fill my life, they don't attract me directly; I have to argue to myself that the work is good, the work of giving material help to people, or combating drunkenness and the superstitions of the government and the Church. I feel within myself a new basis of life growing up – not growing up, but rather detaching itself, freeing itself from its wrappings – a new basis which will replace, by including within itself, my efforts directed towards other people's good, just as my efforts directed towards other people's good included within themselves efforts directed towards my own personal good. This basis is the service of God, doing His will in respect of that part of His being which has been entrusted to me. [. . .]

3 November, Yasnaya Polyana   [. . .] Thought: it's a great mistake to think that the Kingdom of Heaven is out there beyond the grave, and just as great a mistake to think that it's here. It's within one, and when it's within one, then here and there are inseparable. [. . .]

5 November, Yasnaya Polyana   Slept better, but I'm still having dreams. Spent all morning reading a novel in the *Revue des Deux Mondes*,[92] and played games of patience on the subject of art. Yes, the most important thing yesterday was that science and art without a religious basis are a nonsense and an evil. I must show how science and art are evil: science is the theory of infections, the theory of heredity, of hypnotism; art is the inflaming of lustful desires. I want to begin writing articles without corrections in a new notebook. A cigarette-free notebook. Would also like to write an article for Tatyana's day[93] about people celebrating it by founding a temperance society, and taking all taverns and inns into their own hands as in Sweden. [. . .]

7 November, Yasnaya Polyana   [. . .] Finished reading *Oblomov*. How paltry! I'm getting news that *The Kreutzer Sonata* is making an impact, and I'm glad. That's not good. [. . .]

Upstairs I talked to Alexey Mitrofanovich.[94] He raised the objection that science can indicate a moral law, that electricity somehow indicates the need for reciprocity. He's been reading *On Life* all this time. He reads it and doesn't see that he's saying the same thing (only badly) that I expressed well and tried my hardest to refute in that book, namely the idea that you can turn away from an object and study it from the shadow it casts. Yes, you can't prove anything to people, i.e. you can't actually refute people's delusions; everyone who is deluded has his own special delusion. And when you try to refute them, you gather them all together into one typical delusion, but each person has his own one, and because he has his own special delusion, he considers that you haven't refuted it. He thinks you're speaking about a different one. And indeed, how can you keep up with them all! And so it's never necessary to try to refute or to polemicize. Only through art can you influence those who are deluded, and do what you wished to do by polemics. Through art you can take hold lock, stock and barrel of a man who is deluded, and entice him in the necessary direction. You can expound new conclusions from an idea by logical reasoning, but you mustn't argue or refute, you must entice. [. . .]

8 November, Yasnaya Polyana   Got up late. Tried to write about art, but it's no good. Played patience – a sort of madness. Read. A talk with the children about servants, a letter from Lyova and our entire way of life made me think: our life with its slave workers for our convenience, with our servants, seems natural to us . . . We even think, as the children said, 'After all nobody makes him, he became a man-servant of his own accord'; and as the teacher said, 'If a man feels no humiliation at emptying my slops, then I'm not humiliating him'; and we think that we're quite liberal and justified. But this whole position is something so offensive to the nature of man that it would have been impossible not only to establish, but even to imagine such a position, had it not been the consequence of a certain, very definite evil which we all know about, and which, we assure ourselves, has long since disappeared. Had it not been for slavery, nothing like this could possibly have been invented. [. . .]

10 November   [. . .] After dinner I unexpectedly began to write the story of *Friedrichs*.[95] [. . .]

14 November, Yasnaya Polyana   [. . .] Thought again: people need to feel themselves in the right in their own eyes; without that they can't go on living, and so if their lives are bad, they can't think rightly (it's here that our ideas are ruined by the inertia of slavery), and that is the cause of the confusion in our heads. The main rule for life is to pull the trace of self-improvement (progress forward) evenly from both ends, both the improvement of our thoughts and of our lives, so that the one should not lag behind the other, nor overtake it. As it is we have exalted ideals before us, but our lives are base, while the people lead exalted lives, but their ideals are base.

19 November, Yasnaya Polyana   Alive, and very much so. Wrote all morning, finished *Friedrichs* more or less. In the evening I read Ibsen's *Comedy of Love*. How bad! Clever Germanic witticisms – awful. Didn't note down that Sonya was offended yesterday because we didn't wait for her to read. It turned out that she is seething with resentment at Tanya, who has given up her music. She says: 'I'm quite alone in the family.'

Perhaps I'm to blame. I was very sorry, lovingly sorry for her. How good that I wasn't offended, but told her it was true I was sick at heart. And she relented and was sorry for me. Went for a walk in the morning and thought about her, and about writing her a letter which she could read after my death. I want to tell her that she must *seek, seek* faith, the basis of a spiritual life, and not live, as she does, by her instincts (all of which – no, not all – are maternal and good), and by what others do. [. . .]

20 November, Yasnaya Polyana [. . .] Read in the paper this morning how the German Emperor has arranged a jubilee celebration for Moltke *pour le mérite*, and the idea occurred to me very vividly of contrasting the refusal to do military service by the slovenly Khokhlov, and the artillery celebrations,[96] the Emperor's speech, the manoeuvres, etc. When I'm in a self-assured mood, I think that the themes of my writing are like bottles of *kefir*: one bottle gets drunk – the writing gets done – and the others go sour. God grant that these two themes – of servants and slavery, and of war and the refusal to serve – may ripen and that I may write about them. It seems as if they are going sour.

28 November, Yasnaya Polyana It's now morning; after work and coffee I sat and thought over a game of patience: a pilgrim came today, I gave him fifteen copecks, he then asked for some trousers, and I refused although I had some. Thought about what I'd read yesterday in Evans' book[97] that life is love, and when life is love, it's joy and goodness. And so all that is needed, the only thing that is needed, is to love, to be able to love, and to acquire the habit of loving all people always, to break the habit of not loving anyone, whether he is there or not. Thought: surely I know this, surely I've written about it, surely I'm supposed to believe in it. Then why don't I do it – why don't I live only by it? The whole life which I lead is only a *tâtonnement* [feeling my way], whereas I must put it firmly on this basis – namely to seek, desire and do one thing – good to people – to love them and increase the love in them, and to decrease the lack of love.

Good to people? What good? One thing only – love. I know this from my own experience, and so I desire this one thing for other people, and work for this one thing. To live, not tentatively, but boldly in this way means to forget that you are a Russian, a landowner, a peasant, a married man, a father, etc. and to remember only one thing: before you is a living human being; as long as you are alive you can do what will bring good to you and him and will fulfil the will of Him who sent you into the world, you can bind yourself to him by love. This is what I wrote in a fairy tale, only better.

I thought like this very clearly and went upstairs with the idea of putting it into practice there. Stood a while in the dining-room – the children were there, there was no opportunity, I went into the drawing-room. Tanya was lying on the sofa and Novikov was reading aloud to her, and it seemed to me embarrassing and not good, and instead of putting my thoughts into practice I turned round and went away. But I don't despair, I'm working downstairs here within myself in order to understand, pity and love them. Yes, that's the one thing that's needed. It's now gone 12. I doubt if I'll do any writing.

1 December   As expected, I've done no writing. I don't remember exactly what I did, not only on the 28th, but also on the 29th and 30th. Today is 1 December, Yasnaya Polyana. Yes, the day before yesterday, a day after I last wrote, the devil assailed me – assailed me above all in the form of a proud passion, a desire that everyone should immediately share my views; in the evening of the 29th I began arguing again with Novikov about science and about servants, and argued angrily. Next morning, the 30th, slept *badly*. It was so disgusting, I felt I'd committed a crime. [. . .] All this after what I'd written on the 28th. I see, I see with my reason, that this is so, that there is no other life except love, but I can't conjure it up in me. [. . .]

Received a good letter from Biryukov. Read a beautifully written novel by Maupassant[98] – though the theme is sordid. This morning I thought about Domashka:[99] so then we heal her body, but don't think about her soul, we simply don't comfort her as we could. And I began to think. It's just here that the comforts of the Salvation Army come in, comforts which consist of raising the spirits and arousing hopes beyond the grave by acting on the nerves by means of singing and by solemn speech and intonation. I understand how they succeed, and how it seems important to them themselves when a dying person is cheered up and passes his last moments in ecstasy. But is it good? I feel it isn't. I couldn't do it. If I did, I would die of shame. But surely that's because I don't believe. But they believe. I can't do this, but what I can and must do is to do what I would want others to do to me; I would want them not to leave me to die like a dog, alone, with my grief at leaving the world, but to take part in my grief, to explain to me what they know about my situation. This is what I must do. And I went to see her. She was sitting there swollen up and pathetic – and spoke – quite simply. Her mother was weaving, her father was busy dressing the little girl. I sat a long time, not knowing how to begin, and finally asked was she afraid of death, did she not want to die? She said simply: 'Yes.' Her mother began to laugh and tell me that the twelve-year-old girl, her sister, said she would set up a cheap candle when Domashka died. '"Why?" – "Her nice clothes will be left to me," she said. And I said: "I'll make you work hard, you'll have to work for her." – "I'll work as much as you like," she said, "as long as the clothes are left to me."' I began to say: 'You'll be all right there, there's no need to be afraid of death. God won't do us any harm in life or death.' I spoke badly and coldly, but it was impossible to tell lies and feign pathos. Her mother was sitting there weaving and her father listening. But I myself know that only just now I was angry, because the view of a garden which I don't consider my own had been spoiled for me. [. . .]

After dinner I played chess, was ashamed and bored, then went off to stitch boots. [. . .] Then I went upstairs and had tea. All would have been well, but Sonya had had a letter from Mengden with a request from Vogüé to translate *The Kreutzer Sonata*.[100] I said there was no need to. She began to say people suspected her of being mercenary, but she was quite the opposite. I said something. She began to be sarcastic and I got angry again, forgot that she is right after her own fashion and she needs to be right, and said I would go and sleep downstairs. She was quite prepared for a terrible scene, poison and everything. I collected myself, went back and asked her to calm down, but she wouldn't, and I went for a walk round the garden. I walked and thought: how terrible it is that I *forget*, actually forget the main thing, that if one doesn't regard one's life as a mission, there is no life, only hell. [. . .]

6 December, Yasnaya Polyana   [. . .] Looked through the whole of *The Kreutzer Sonata*, made deletions, corrections and additions. I'm awfully fed up with it. The main thing is that it's artistically wrong and false. I'm having clearer and clearer thoughts about Koni's story.[101] [. . .]

10 December, Yasnaya Polyana   Received a letter yesterday from Ertel and Gaydeburov to say that *The Kreutzer Sonata* will be banned. It only made me pleased. Also Hansen's translations[102] and *Paris illustré* with an article on Bondarev.[103] It made me think: they get me all wrong. I ought to expound briefly and clearly what I think, namely: non-participation in government, military and judicial violence, (2) sexual abstinence, (3) abstinence from narcotics, alcohol and tobacco, (4) work. All without fine words, but briefly and clearly. [. . .]

13, 14, 15, 16, 17 December, Yasnaya Polyana   For five days I haven't written or done anything. I've read, and suffered pain. [. . .] Got a pleasant letter from Suvorin about *The Kreutzer Sonata* and a depressing one from Khokhlov senior, reproaching me for being responsible for the ruin of his sons.[104] I'm vaguely collecting facts for an exposition of my teaching and for Koni's story. [. . .] Lyova came the day before yesterday. It pained me to see him ordering someone to take his boots off when he came back from hunting, and also scolding the youngster for not taking them off properly. [. . .]

22 December   Alive. Today is the 22nd. All these last three days I've been revising my comedy. I've finished. It's bad. A lot of people came; they're giving a performance.[105] It makes me depressed and ashamed sometimes, but the thought of not obstructing the manifestation of the divine in me is a help. I must write (1) about the coat. Sonya made me a new coat. I don't need it. But it's mine, and now Lyova wants to wear it and I'm sorry. He came back from hunting and I was disturbed by the thought that he'd spattered it with blood. I was almost angry with him. Previously I would certainly have been angry, even have quarrelled. A good example. [. . .]

27 December   [. . .] Wrote a bit of Koni's story. Depressed by the falseness of the life around me, and the fact that I can't find a way of showing them their errors without offending them. They're performing my play, and I really think it's having an effect on them and that in the bottom of their hearts they are all conscience-stricken and therefore dejected. But I'm ashamed the whole time, ashamed at this foolish expense in the midst of poverty.

Today on my walk I thought: those who maintain that this life is a vale of tears, a place of trial, etc., while the other world is a world of bliss, are, as it were, maintaining that all God's infinite world is beautiful, or that life is beautiful in all God's world, except for one place and time, namely the one in which we live.

That would be a strange thing to happen!

29, 30, 31 December, Yasnaya Polyana   These last days I've been trying to write Koni's story. I've revised a bit, but haven't made any progress. All the time there have been rehearsals, the play, fuss and bother, a mass of people – and all the time I've felt ashamed. The play isn't bad perhaps, but I'm still ashamed. Got another letter from Chertkov. But the main impressions of these days are: (1) I'm sorry for Tanya. She even flirts with Zinger, and she's unhappy. (2) They read *The Kreutzer Sonata* the day before yesterday, and I listened. Yes, it made a terrible impression. Stakhovich doesn't understand a thing. But Ilya understands. [. . .]

1890

Today, 3 January, Yasnaya Polyana [. . .] A prophet, a real prophet, or still better a poet ποιητης [a doer], is a person who thinks and understands in advance what people including myself will feel. I am this sort of prophet for myself. I always think what I don't yet feel, for example the injustice of the lives of the rich, the need for hard work, etc. and then very soon begin to feel these things myself.

Read: Emerson was told that the world would soon end. He replied: 'Well, I think I can get along without it.' Very important.

10, 11, 12, 13, 14, 15 January, Yasnaya Polyana [. . .] I've felt a strange indifference recently towards expressing the truth about life – it's so hard to accept. [. . .]

Thought: (1) The sexual act is so attractive because it removes responsibility from oneself, it releases one, as it were, from fulfilling the law and transfers it, the responsibility, to others. It won't be I who will attain the kingdom of God, but my children. That's why women are so engrossed in their children. [. . .]

I'm sexually disturbed. Thought about the attitude of certain people towards *The Kreutzer Sonata*: Samarin, Storozhenko and many others, Lopatin; it seems to them that it's about a special person, whereas, they say, 'there's nothing like that about me'. Can't they really find anything? There's no remorse because there's no progress, or else there's no progress because there's no remorse. Remorse is like the breaking open of an egg shell or a grain of corn, as a consequence of which the seed begins to grow and is exposed to the influence of air and light, or else it's the consequence of growth, as a result of which the egg shell is broken. Yes, there's also an important and very vital division of people: people with remorse and people without it.

18 January, Yasnaya Polyana [. . .] Work was interrupted by Butkevich,[1] who arrived from the country. Had a talk with him. He told me that many people hated *The Kreutzer Sonata*, saying that it was a description of a sexual maniac. This distressed me at first, but then I was pleased that at least it had stirred up something that needed stirring up. Of course it could have been better, but I did the best I could. [. . .]

21 January, Yasnaya Polyana Revised the comedy and read. Sledged with the children on benches. Sonya still very agitated and restless.

A strange thing, this concern for perfection of form. It isn't wasted. But only as long as the content is good. Had Gogol written his comedy crudely and feebly, it wouldn't have been read by one millionth part of the people who have now read it. A work of art must be sharpened for it to penetrate. To sharpen it means to perfect it artistically – then it will break through indifference and make itself felt by repetition. [. . .]

22 January, Yasnaya Polyana Got up early and revised the comedy all morning. Hope I've finished. Walked to the school.[2] Masha is sick; she has written a good letter to Posha. Tanya is good, simple, cheerful and kind. Before that, I read another book of sayings of Indian wisdom. There's much in it that is good and universal. Thanks to the comedy and the playing of *The Power of Darkness* in Petersburg and Berlin,[3] I've begun to succumb to the pleasure of praise. [. . .]

5 February, Yasnaya Polyana Wanted to sleep badly; struggled all morning with the afterword.[4] Began by chopping logs and went to Tanya's school. Dozed off after coffee. I must try to write in the morning on an empty stomach. After dinner I read and thought; wanted to write, but had no energy. Thought about a drama on the subject of life:[5] the despair of a man who has seen the light, and has brought this light into the darkness of life with hope, and the assurance of lightening this darkness; and suddenly the darkness becomes darker still. [. . .]

11 February, Yasnaya Polyana Strange – a voluptuous dream. I'm not sleeping much. Weakness. I want to write, but haven't the strength. Thought today: about the letter I began to write to Kolechka;[6] the main temptation in my situation is the fact that life in abnormal conditions of luxury, tolerated at first so as not to destroy love, later takes hold of one with its temptations, and you don't know whether you live like that for fear of destroying love, or from having yielded to temptation. A sign of the fact that it's the former – i.e. that you tolerate temptation only for fear of destroying love – is that not only are the earlier demands of one's conscience not relaxed, but new ones appear.

I also thought that there's no need to write an afterword to *The Kreutzer Sonata*. There's no need to, because it's impossible for people who think differently to be convinced by arguments. It's necessary first of all to drive their feelings in a different direction while letting them argue that they are right. They will feel themselves wrong, but they will still argue that they are right. It's not that people need to argue, but they can't live without doing so. Reason is a lantern hung on each man's chest. A man cannot walk or live except by the light of that lantern. The lantern always lights up the road ahead for him – the path he is walking along. And arguments about my lantern lighting up my path for me when my path is different from his (although my path is right and his is wrong) cannot make him see anything different, or fail to see what he does see on the path he is walking along. He must be driven off the road. And that's not the job of reason, but of feeling. Even when he has been driven off the wrong road and is walking in the right direction, he will go on seeing for a long time what is lit up by his lantern on the wrong path. On my walk, I thought a great deal about Koni's story. Everything is clear and very good. (1) He didn't want to possess her, but did so because that's what one has to do – so he thought. In his imagination she is charming. He smiles, and he feels like crying. (2) A drive to church, darkness, a white dress, a kiss. (3) The old chambermaid takes the money, but looks on sadly. (4) The old chambermaid is a fatalist, Katyusha is lonely. (5) When she sees him passing through, she wants to throw herself under the train, but gets on and feels the child in her womb. (6) He asks his aunt where she is. A chambermaid at a landowner's. She is leading a bad life, having a liaison with a man-servant. And she can't help having the liaisons, her sensuality has been aroused. (7) He is agitated and asks: did you drive her out? And did she cry very much? And am I to blame? etc. (8) He tried *ambition* – bad, not in keeping with his character – went abroad – Paris – dissipation – bad. Only left with reading, elegance, hunting, cards, first nights. Hair going grey – boredom.

28 February, Optina[7]   [. . .] Went to Leontyev's.[8] Had an excellent talk. He said: 'You are without hope.' I said to him: 'And you are full of hope.' That fully expresses our attitudes to faith. [. . .]

9 March, Yasnaya Polyana   [. . .] Yesterday I read in *New Christianity: Christ must be in social life, in politics, in business.* Just fancy *Christ in business*! It's the same as saying *Christ in kicking* or *killing* (war). Yes, these people must be made to understand that all positions in society from that of landowner to hangman are ranked according to their moral nature, and therefore it's not enough to be good in the position you occupy; you must choose one position rather than another. [. . .]

Read Tanya's diary and loved her tenderly as I looked into her weak, restless soul. She writes: 'I'm not a bad person really.' She said that herself, and there was the chance to see it. But after all Pobedonostsev, and Nikanor, and Skabichevsky[9] and others all say just the same. One needs to establish if their view of themselves is right, and one can. [. . .]

17 March, Yasnaya Polyana   [. . .] Gaston Boissier[10] writes that Christians in the first century only took a stern and hostile attitude towards Rome, towards the state, to begin with, but then began to accommodate themselves to the state, and Christianity did no harm to it. He should have said that people appeared, calling themselves Christians and living in harmony with the state – bishops and churchmen. But Christians both were, and still are, not just enemies of the state, but advocates of a doctrine incompatible with it. One of the most terrible and pernicious delusions is that people baptized by Constantine, Charlemagne or Vladimir are themselves Christians. There never were and never are Christian peoples, only Christian people, and such people can be found among Turks, Chinese and Indians. [. . .]

18 March, Yasnaya Polyana   Yesterday Ilya arrived. Begrimed, hardened, and grown older without having been employed. I've done nothing. Liver still painful. Probably a fatal illness. It's neither frightening nor disagreeable to me. Only I haven't got used to it. I still want to work as I used to. Went to Yasenki. Pains began on the way. Tried to write. No good. In the evening I read Sienkiewicz.[11] Very brilliant. Sonya came and started talking about the sale of new works,[12] and I got angry. I'm ashamed.

19 March, Yasnaya Polyana   Got up early, went for a walk. Drank coffee, the pains began. Can't write, although my thoughts seem clear while I'm thinking: no memory, no spark of life. An inspector came.[13] I didn't receive him, it was wrong of me. The inspector was a sort of policeman, carrying out a cross-examination. Masha had a narrow escape. They'll close the school down, and I'm sorry for the girls. Ilya is here and I still can't talk with him. I'd very much like to, but I haven't been able to approach him, especially since he keeps aloof. Everything about him, his talk and his jokes, are seasoning for the essential thing which isn't there. [. . .]

28 March, Yasnaya Polyana   [. . .] Went for a walk in the evening and prayed. Our Father, hallowed be Thy essence, love, that the kingdom of love may come; Thy will – that all should be ruled by love (by Thee) – be done here on earth as it is, I believe, in heaven. And give me life, i.e. a part in bringing this about here and now. And eliminate the consequences of my mistakes which could be a hindrance to me, just as I eliminate in my own consciousness the consequences of the mistakes of other people which are apparent to me, and which could hinder me from loving them. And lead me not into temptation – physical suffering, clouding of the mind, desire – which are obstacles to the realization of love, and above all save me from the main obstacle within myself – from the evil in my own heart. Yes, only one thing is necessary for this life, and for all life, one thing – love – and its increase. [. . .]

8 April, Yasnaya Polyana   Slept badly. Unwell. Couldn't write. And so much needs doing. A letter from Chertkov. Wrote a few bad letters. While reading Lyova's story,[14] some thoughts occurred to me: the upbringing of children, i.e. the ruining of them, the egoism of parents, and hypocrisy. A story like *Ivan Ilich*.[15] Yes, I thought: its not good to come and fill people's rooms with smoke. But is it any better to come to joyful and happy people with a gloomy face and spoil their pleasure?

10 April, Yasnaya Polyana   Went for a walk, thought a lot yesterday and today, namely: [. . .]
(2) To express in words what you understand so that another person will understand you as you do yourself is a very difficult thing: and you always feel that you are very, very far from having achieved what you can and should. And then to go and set yourself the further task of arranging the words in a definite order so far as metre and endings are concerned – surely that's madness! But they are prepared to assure you that the words take shape of their own accord into 'And love . . . stirs the blood.'[16] *A d'autres* [Tell it to the marines]!
(3) The socialists say: 'It's not we, who enjoy the good things of civilization and culture, who need to be deprived of these good things and reduced to the level of the vulgar crowd, but the people who have been deprived of their share of earthly goods need to be raised to our level and made to share the good things of civilization and culture. The means for that is science. It teaches us to conquer nature, it can increase productivity endlessly, it can make Niagara falls, rivers and winds work for us by producing electricity. The sun will work for us. And there will be plenty of everything for everyone.'

Now only a small part of the people, the part which exercises authority, enjoys the good things of civilization, while the great part is deprived of these good things. Increase the good things and then there will be enough for everyone. But the thing is that the people who exercise authority have for long been enjoying, not what they need but what they don't need – everything that they can. And so however much the good things are increased, those who are at the top will use them all for themselves. One can't use more than a certain quantity of what is necessary, but to luxury there are no limits. One can feed thousands of quarters of cereals to horses and dogs, convert millions of *desyatins* into parks, etc. And that's what is happening. So no increase in productivity and wealth will increase the goods of the lower classes by one iota as long as the upper classes have both the power and the desire to use their surplus wealth on luxury. Quite the contrary, an increase in production, a greater and greater mastery of the forces of nature, gives more power to the upper classes, to those who are in authority – the power to hold on to all the good things and the authority they have over the lower, working classes. And every impulse on the part of the lower classes to force the rich to share things with them (revolutions, strikes) produces strife; and strife is a useless waste of wealth. 'No one shall have anything if I can't,' say those engaged in strife.

The conquest of nature and the increase in the production of earthly goods in order to fill the world full of goods so that there should be enough for everyone is just as senseless an act as increasing the quantity of logs and throwing them into a stove in order to increase the heat in the house in which the stoves are left open. However much you put in the stove, the cold air will be warmed and rise upwards, and fresh cold air will immediately take the place of the air that has risen, and there won't be an even distribution of heat, or even any heat itself. As long as there is access for cold air, there will be an outlet for warm air, which has the property of rising upwards. And it will be like that as long as there is a draught from below to above.

Up to now three remedies against this have been thought up, and it's difficult to decide which of the three is more stupid: so stupid are all three. One remedy, that of the revolutionaries, consists in destroying the upper classes through whom all wealth escapes. This is like a man breaking a chimney pipe through which heat is escaping, thinking that if there is no chimney the heat won't be able to escape. But the heat will escape through the hole, as it would through the chimney, if the draught is the same, just as wealth will escape back to the people who exercise authority, as long as their authority exists.

The second remedy consists in doing what Wilhelm II is now doing[17] – taking a small part of the wealth away from the upper classes who have wealth and authority and throwing it into the bottomless pit of poverty, without changing the existing social order; fixing fans on top of the chimney which is drawing off the heat at the point where the heat is escaping, and waving these fans at the heat and forcing it back down to the cold layers. This is obviously an idle and useless occupation, because when the draught is coming upwards from below, however much you force the heat downwards (and you can't force much of it), it will immediately escape again and all the work will be wasted.

And finally there is the third remedy, which is now being advocated with special force in America. This remedy consists in replacing the competitive, individual principle of economic life by a communal, *artel*, cooperative principle. The remedy, as it's expressed in *Dawn* and *Nationalist*, is to advocate cooperation in word and deed – to suggest and explain to people that competition, individualism and struggle waste much power and therefore much wealth, and that the cooperative principle is far more profitable, i.e. for each person to work for the common good, and then receive his own share of the common wealth. That way will be more profitable for everyone. That's all very well, but the trouble is that in the first place nobody knows what portion each person will get, if everyone gets an equal share. But the main thing is that, whatever that portion might be, it will seem inadequate to people living as they do now for their own good. 'Everyone will be all right, and you will be like everyone else.' But I don't want to live like everyone else, I want to live better. I've always lived better than everyone else, and I'm used to it.' 'But I've lived worse than everyone else for a long time, and I want to live like the others lived.' This remedy is the most stupid of all, because it presupposes that given the existing draught upwards from below, i.e. the motive for striving towards what is best, it is possible to induce particles of air not to rise higher as they get warmer.

There is only one remedy – to show people their true good, and the fact that wealth is not only not a good, but is a distraction which conceals from them what their true good is. Only one remedy exists – to block up the hole of worldly desires. Only that will give an even heat. And that is the very opposite of what the socialists say and do, by trying to increase productivity and therefore the general mass of wealth. [. . .]

11, 12, 13 April, Yasnaya Polyana   The day before yesterday I wrote about narcotics again.[18] Not bad. Yesterday: had some excellent thoughts in the morning and wrote them down in my notebook, but couldn't write. Set off for Tula after dinner and went to the rehearsal.[19] Very bored; the comedy is poor – trash. The day before yesterday, while talking with Stakhovich, I cursed the Tsar for having restored the death penalty. Got up late today, couldn't write, stitched boots. Had a walk in the evening. Lyova is sad. Tanya is sweet. It's now getting on for 1 o'clock. Thought: [. . .]
(2) People say: thanks to the luxurious way of life of the upper classes, thanks to their leisure, which is the result of the inequality of the classes, outstanding people appear on the scene, indifferent to the good things of the world, and with only spiritual interests. That's just like saying that in a field trampled by cattle the surviving ears of corn are particularly good. It is the inevitable compensation which goes with every evil, and so cannot be used to justify the doing of evil. [. . .]

18 April   [. . .] Thought for a future drama how peasants pretend that they believe, for their masters' sake, and the masters pretend for the peasants' sake. [. . .]

9 May, Pirogovo   Still ill. Not getting better. Thought today:

(1) Many of the ideas which I've been expressing recently don't belong to me, but to people who feel an affinity with me, and turn to me with their problems, quandaries, ideas and plans. Thus the basic idea, or better to say feeling, of *The Kreutzer Sonata* belongs to a certain woman, a Slav,[20] who wrote me a letter, comical for its language but remarkable for its content, about the oppression of women through sexual demands. Later she came to see me and left a strong impression. The idea that the verse in Matthew: 'If you look on a woman with lust, etc.' refers not only to other people's wives but also to your own was handed on to me by an Englishman who wrote about it.[21] And there are so many other examples. (2) There is an astonishing contrast between the attitudes of people to the two branches of knowledge: the one called moral teaching, religion even, and the one people like to call science. People who are far advanced in the first category of knowledge – moral teaching – for the most part take as their models teachers of the past: Mencius – Confucius; Plato – Socrates; Buddha – the Brahmins; Christ – Isaiah. These teachers always consider they know nothing themselves (Socrates said so directly). They consider their wisdom to have been handed on to them by their ancestors; their own they consider insignificant. A completely opposite view is taken by people of so-called science: they always think that nobody before them knew anything – that only now is science in the possession of, if not all, then a part of the truth which their predecessors never dared to dream of. If a man of science recalls how previous men of science looked at the universe, the organization of the human body, the origin of the world and what fills it, etc. he is so sure that all his predecessors were wrong, but not he, that he cannot help despising all scientific activity except his own, and that of his own time. [. . .]

11 May, Pirogovo [. . .] Everybody needs a strict diet. A book is needed about food.[22]

18 May, Yasnaya Polyana [. . .] I've been thinking all this time: [. . .] (5) The anarchists are right about everything – the rejection of what exists and the assertion that anything worse than the oppression of authority, with its existing rights, would be impossible in the absence of that authority. They are only wrong in saying that anarchy can be established by revolution – *that anarchy can be set up!* Anarchy will be established; but only by there being more and more people who don't need the protection of government authority, and more and more people who are ashamed to wield that authority. [. . .] (10) We go on writing our novels, although not as crudely as before – when a villain was just a villain and Mr Dogood a do-gooder – but still terribly crudely and colourlessly. But people are all just the same as I am, i.e. skewbald – bad and good together – and not as good as I want people to consider me, or as bad as I think the people are whom I'm angry with or who have offended me. [. . .]

[25 May.] [. . .] *22 May*   The same weakness. The foreword. Chistyakov came. All about the diaries. He, Chertkov, is afraid that I'll die and the diaries will be lost. Nothing can be lost. But they can't be sent – it would give offence. Masha has copied out the parts I marked.[23] [. . .]

2, 3, 4, 5, 6, 7, 8 June, Yasnaya Polyana   A whole week as passed. I'm in a very bad and gloomy frame of mind. [. . .] Began *Father Sergey* and pondered over it. The whole interest is in the psychological stages which he goes through. [. . .] An unpleasant talk today with Sonya apropos of a letter from Biryukov which Gay brought. (She was beside herself and gave herself full rein.)[24] In *The Newcomes*[25] Clive's mother-in-law is good – she torments them both, only she is more tormented herself. Thought: (1) I avoid people, people are a nuisance to me. But surely you live only by people and only for them. If people are a nuisance to you there's no point in living. To escape from people is suicide. [. . .]

9, 10, 11, 12 June, Yasnaya Polyana   [. . .] Masha wrote to Biryukov and approved of my letter to him.[26] I was frightfully distressed by what Andryusha said today. I said to him that it was bad to drink strong coffee. He turned away with that familiar contempt the children have for me. Gay began to say it was for his own good. He said: 'It's not only about coffee, it's about everything; surely one can't do everything Papa says.' He said just what all the children think. I'm terribly sorry for them. I dilute for them what their mother says. Their mother dilutes what I say. Whose fault is it? Mine. It's now 11 in the morning. I want to get on with Koni's story. [. . .]

14 June, Yasnaya Polyana   [. . .] I'm well. Did some work, chopped wood and sawed.

17 June   [. . .] I've thought much and often in recent days, and prayed about something I've thought of hundreds and thousands of times, only differently – namely, that I would like to serve God by actually spreading his truth abroad, not in word but in deed, by sacrifice and the example of sacrifice; but nothing comes of it. He doesn't let me. Instead of that, I live attached to my wife's skirts, subservient to her, and I and all my children lead a squalid and ignoble life which I falsely justify on the grounds that I can't destroy love. Instead of sacrifice and a triumphant example, a nasty, ignoble, pharisaical life which alienates me from Christ's teaching. But Thou knowest what is in my heart and what I want. If that is not destined to be, if Thou dost not need me for Thy service, but only for dung, so be it according to Thy will. [. . .]

18 June, Yasnaya Polyana [. . .] A letter from Seryozha with a request for money. Sonya is overcome by requests for money from her sons. It will get even worse. Surely it would be better if she were to renounce her literary possessions at least. How restful for her, how morally good for her sons and how joyful for me, how useful to men and pleasing to God.

22 June, Yasnaya Polyana [. . .] At work, while mowing, I envisaged to myself the outer form of Koni's story. *Must begin with the court session. And then the falsehood of the law, and his need for truthfulness. And further: – the state: the story of the colonists.*[27] [. . .]

24 June, Yasnaya Polyana [. . .] Yesterday I read *Without Dogma*. Love for a woman is very delicately described – tenderly and far more delicately than with the French where it's sensual, or the English where it's pharisaical, or the Germans where it's pompous – and I thought: I must write a novel about a love that is chaste and affectionate, like my love for Sonechka Koloshina, the sort of love in which there can be no transition to sensuality, which is the best defence against sensuality. Is it not indeed the only salvation from sensuality? Yes, yes, it certainly is. That is why human beings were created man and woman. Only with a woman can one lose one's chastity, and only with her can one retain it. Loss of chastity begins with the transition to sensuality. It would be good to write about it.

25 June, Yasnaya Polyana Another thought: I ought to write a book *Gluttony*.[28] Belshazzar's feast, bishops, tsars and taverns. Meetings, partings, jubilees. People think they are occupied with various important matters, but they are only occupied with gluttony. And what goes on behind the scenes? How do they prepare for it? Yesterday Holzapfel[29] left. The children jumped out of bed earlier than usual, and Andryusha was going to set off for the village. I asked him why. To buy eggs. Why? Mamma told me to. And I thought: who is looking after their upbringing? A woman without convictions, weak, good, but *journalière* [inconstant], fickle, and exhausted by the unnecessary cares taken upon herself. She torments herself, and the children are being ruined before my eyes, piling up sufferings for themselves which will be millstones round their necks. Am I right to allow it without waging a struggle? I pray, and I see that I can't do otherwise. Not my will, but Thine. On the one hand the ruin of the children and vain sufferings, on the other – struggle and bitterness. Better let it be the first. The second is certain, the first isn't. It's not for my own family that I was born and must live, but for God. [. . .]

3 July, Yasnaya Polyana Went downstairs to sleep. Got up late. Depressed and bored; idleness, luxurious living, useless talk. Its as if cog wheels are swimming in grease, get clogged and won't engage. Sometimes the wheels don't go for lack of oil, sometimes because they are full of slush. Should one write for people like that? Why? I've a strange reluctance to write. Yesterday I thought vividly about women. A woman holiday-maker came to question me when I was mowing. The main feature about women is their lack of respect for thought, lack of trust in what it – thought – will lead to. Hence falsehood, distortion of the truth, making play with ideas and spiritual gifts generally. If men were not so bound to women by sexual feeling and the indulgence which results from it, they would see clearly that women (for the most part) don't understand them, and they wouldn't talk to them. Except for virgins. You begin to get to know women from your wife, and you get to know them completely from your daughters. These are the women whom you can look at quite freely.

Mowed a lot. Still the same melancholy.

4 July, Yasnaya Polyana Got up late. I'm drinking too much *kumys*. Wrote nothing. Mowed all day. It's the one salvation. Articles and letters all about the *Afterword* and *The Kreutzer Sonata*. It's astonishing what contempt there is for the word, what abuse of it! It's the same with the women's conversations that go on all round me. The lower the subject of these conversations the better. At least it's sincere about eyes and paws. But the higher the subject, the less sincere. [. . .] It's very important for a woman that there should be more or less sugar or money, but that there should be more or less truth, she is sincerely convinced is of no importance at all.

I suffer from the fact that I'm surrounded by people with deformed brains, with such self-assured, ready-made theories that it's folly to write anything for them; there's no way of getting through to them at all. [. . .]

5 July, Yasnaya Polyana Got up in good spirits, although didn't sleep much. Found Mme Helbig[30] and Strakhov talking about whether one can purify everything by love, without changing one's life. I joined in and spoke warmly, the more so since the young people had arrived. But of course I convinced nobody. The place I'm aiming at is too tender, and so they protect it carefully, promptly and opportunely, as the eyelid the eye.

Thought: I like Schiller's *Räuber* so much because it's profoundly true and accurate. A man such as a thief or a robber who takes away the fruits of another man's labour knows he is doing wrong; but a man who takes them away by lawful means which are acknowledged by society doesn't acknowledge his life to be bad, and so this honest citizen is incomparably worse morally than the robber. [. . .]

6 July, Yasnaya Polyana   Went to watch the harvesting of the rye. In the evening I'll go and cut the rye. [. . .]

Had a rest, walked through Masha's room. Sonya had read in her diary there about Posha's letter and was beside herself. I couldn't console her. She's ill all the time and afraid of being pregnant. And I think of it with fear and am ashamed of myself. This is where I need to face God, not people. Yes, just as illness is necessary to kill sexual desire, so are humiliation and shame necessary to kill vanity.

Harvested the hay. Then the Zinovyevs came. I feel depressed with dead people. And they are so consciously, deliberately dead. Slept badly in the evening.

10 July, Yasnaya Polyana   [. . .] Still just as weak. Sonya is distressed by the fear of being pregnant. This is where the attempt must be made to transfer the case to the court of the one God.

Went for a bathe. Came back; the table was set for thirty people. The Ofrosimovs and Figners. Then music and singing. Terrible, pointless, it got on my nerves. Two pathetic machines and trumpets – people eating and making a nasty smell. Couldn't sleep till 5. Very unwell. Sonya in distress and in low spirits.

11 July, Yasnaya Polyana   [. . .] In the evening an argument with Strakhov about the Russian question. 'One of two things: Slavophilism or the Gospels.' We are going through that terrible time that Herzen spoke about. Ghenghis Khan, no longer with telegraphs, but with telephones and smokeless powder. A constitution, certain forms of freedom of the press, assembly and religious beliefs are all brakes on the increase of power as a consequence of telephones, etc. Without them something terrible is happening, and something that is only true of Russia. [. . .]

15 July, Yasnaya Polyana   Got up late. After coffee I set to work at once on the boots; finished them and went for a bathe. After dinner I had a nap. Sonya came with the news that she wasn't pregnant. I said we must sleep separately and that I didn't like that. What will happen? Was cross with Seryozha, but things are better now. I'm not angry at all with Sonya. Nor should I be. Walked a lot in the evening. A cook came, whom a doctor had sent to me from Moscow to ask my advice about his wife's unfaithfulness. [. . .]

20 July, Yasnaya Polyana   [. . .] Had a talk with Sonya. She said she's glad. But she doesn't want to sleep separately. [. . .] The Sissermans were just about to arrive some time after 2. The conversation turned to Verochka Kuzminskaya grumbling at her father for not giving her her aunt's money.

Sonya began to talk about how her children demanded the same thing, how there were quarrels over money. I began to say that it was all to do with the need for money. If there's a need, then by hook or by crook they will get the money, but it can't be got otherwise than by sinning, because acquiring it is a sin. Nobody listened to me, and everyone was cross with me for talking such nonsense or uttering truisms. At which point the Sissermans arrived, and everyone was cross.

Today is the 24th. Löwenfeld came,[31] he's writing a biography of me. Unpleasant titillation. Walked about and thought and prayed.
21. [. . .] Thought about my old diaries, about how disgusting I appear in them, and about how I don't want people to know them – i.e. I'm concerned about worldly fame even after my death. How terribly difficult it is to renounce worldly fame, not to be concerned about it at all. And not to suffer at the thought of being taken for a scoundrel. Difficult, but how good! How joyful when you cast aside your concern for worldly fame, and fall at once into God's hands, and how easy and secure you feel. It's like the boy who fell into a well and hung on by his hands, suffering pain, when he had only got to stop holding on and he would have stood on the firm ground right beneath his feet, would have fallen into God's hands. [. . .]

3 August, Yasnaya Polyana [. . .] Thought again: what a bad mistake I make in entering into conversations about Christianity with Orthodox believers, or talking about Christianity apropos of the activity of priests, monks, the Synod, etc. Orthodoxy and Christianity have only the name in common. If churchmen are Christians, then I'm not a Christian, and vice versa. [. . .]

4 August, Yasnaya Polyana If I'm alive.
Alive, Got up early, had a bathe. Prayed. Had some good thoughts about *Father Sergey*, noted them down and lost the notebook. Read Urusov's article,[32] did some translating with Tanya, repaired some boots and drove to a fire at Kolpna. [. . .]

6 August, Yasnaya Polyana Went for a bathe, and from there to the fire: [. . .] Sonya was there with money. I was very glad. [. . .] Found my notebook.
I'd made a note for *Father Sergey*. She explains her reason for coming, talks nonsense, and he believes it because she's beautiful. She is full of desire.
He doesn't see anything great about it, on the contrary he's ashamed at having succumbed. Eventually she goes into a monastery. He's not handsome, just an ordinary face, plucks at his beard, but his eyes . . . that's what arouses her. [. . .]

7 August, Yasnaya Polyana [. . .] Thought again: questions of a life after death. Why don't we know what will happen to us? Even now, when we don't know, we're inclined to despise this life for the sake of the future one, so what would happen if we did know? It wouldn't have been possible to reveal to us what would happen to us after death: if we knew something bad was in store for us, there would be additional suffering; if we knew something good was in store for us, we wouldn't go on living here, but would try to die. Only if we knew there was nothing there would we live happily here. That's almost the way it is. The most probable assumption is that there is no life of the sort we can express by means of our instruments of thought and speech. [. . .]

There's a splendid story in Vasily Ivanovich's letter about a good peasant who, when asked by the priest at confession 'Do you believe in God?', replied: 'No, I don't: I drink, and smoke and swear.' Delightful. [. . .]

10 August, Yasnaya Polyana [. . .] For *Father Sergey*. I must describe the new state of happiness – the freedom, the security of a man who has lost everything, and can't lean on anything but God. For the first time he gets to know how secure that support is.

15 August[33] [. . .] I got up very late. Went for a bathe. Prayed and thought. Drank coffee and talked frankly with Sonya for almost the first time for many years. She spoke about prayer sincerely and intelligently – namely that prayer ought to be expressed in deeds, and not by people saying: 'Lord, Lord.' [. . .]

18 August [. . .] For *Father Sergey*. A detail which should establish a level of reality. *The lawyer inhales the drops from his running nose in the frosty weather. And he smells of perfume and tobacco, and bad breath.* [. . .]

20 August, Pirogovo Got up late, weak, read Ibsen's *Wilde Ente.*[34] Not good. Seryozha is very worried about his losses. I left on horseback at 6. A splendid ride. Prayed joyfully. I think it gives me strength. [. . .]

21 August, Yasnaya Polyana Got up early, tidied my room, had a bathe, revised the conclusion. Read Ibsen's *Rosmersholm*. Not bad so far. It's now gone 2. I'll go for a rest.

After dinner I chopped wood on my own. Very depressed about the absurdity of life.

22 August, Yasnaya Polyana Early; everything as usual. Prayer comforts me. A good letter from Chertkov. Rugin[35] came. Had a very good talk with him. Sonya was awake and received him with composure, but then Ilya upset her by saying that he couldn't eat in his presence. Sonya behaved very well. She didn't do what she should have done, but she endeavoured with love to do her best. And how I valued that. And how glad I was. I was feeling depressed. She told him so. He took it well, like a peasant and a Christian, and left. The egoism and dissoluteness of our life, of all our lives, the guests included, frighten me. It seems to me to be getting worse all the time. [. . .]

28 August, Yasnaya Polyana   It's my sixty-third year. I felt ashamed that because $1890 \div 63 = 30$ and because I've been married 28 years – that these figures seemed to me in some way significant and I had been looking forward to this year as an important one. [. . .]

Thought: Masha told me how Lyova and Stakhovich were saying that one shouldn't mix philanthropy with estate management: 'In estate management justice rules, but philanthropy is quite a different matter.' People talk like that with the conviction that it's clever and nice, but in fact it's nothing else but marking out for yourself an arbitary field in which you rid yourself in advance of all human feeling, and in which you allow yourself to be cruel. This is how people talk about military service, discipline, the state. What an excellent work of art could be written on this theme! And how necessary! And how I would like to do it. [. . .]

Someone is coming. Help me, Father!

It was the mail coach from Tula. An abusive letter from America.[36] Why did I write those rude things about doctors? I'm unhappy with the older children. Worries about money and organizing their lives; and self-assurance and absolute self-satisfaction. I haven't much love for them. And I can't summon up more. Went for a walk to Kozlovka. Sonya complained about our sons.

3 September   [. . .] Thought today: I'm angry at the moral obtuseness of the children except for Masha. But who are they? My children, my own creation from every aspect, carnal and spiritual. I made them what they are. They are my sins – always before me. And there's nowhere for me to go to escape from them, it's impossible. I must enlighten them, but I can't do it, I'm bad myself. [. . .]

6 September, Yasnaya Polyana   Everything as usual. A pain in the pit of my stomach – apathy. I sleep. And I have evil thoughts. But I stand firm and pray. Chopped wood, went for a walk late on and took a letter for Sonya[37] to Kozlovka. It's now gone 10, I'm going to have a drink of tea. Yesterday I read Rousseau's *Émile*.[38] Yes, I've managed my family life badly. And this sin lies upon me and all around me. [. . .]

13 September, Yasnaya Polyana Got up early, went to saw and chop wood with Masha. Very tired. Sat down at home and was at once aware of my feebleness again. Was sad – and sad that I was sad. If I'd remembered – humility, obedience and love – I wouldn't have been sad. A pain in the pit of my stomach all morning. Read Coleridge.[39] A writer very sympathetic to me – precise, clear, but unfortunately timid – an Englishman – the Church of England and redemption. Impossible. [. . .]

Thought yesterday about the fact that war (everyone is talking about sending troops to the Prussian frontier and about war) isn't so dreadful in the sense that either bloodthirsty beasts or animals that roam in herds will be fighting, and that if they slaughter each other there will be fewer of them left – and I said so. How they attacked me! But it is so. To express it exactly, one should say: people, unfortunately, only learn from experience – and so they need the experience of the calamity of war. That's one thing. But the other thing is that people who are on the level where they can kill each other at somebody's command aren't to be pitied, as reasonable people would be. That's a consolation. [. . .]

Thought yesterday: I walk through the village and see various peasants digging. Each one digs a potato trench for himself and each one roofs his own house, and much else of the same sort. How much unnecessary work! What if all this were done together and shared? It wouldn't seem to be difficult: bees and ants and beavers do it. But it is very difficult. Man is very far from doing it precisely because he is a reasonable, conscious creature. Man has to do consciously what animals do unconsciously. Before man aims at the communal life of bees and ants, he must first consciously try to reach the level of cattle, from which he is still a long way away: not fight (wage war) over absurdities, not overeat, not fornicate, and then he can consciously aim at the life of the bees and ants as they are beginning to do in the communes. First the family, then the commune, then the state, then mankind, then all living creatures, then the whole world, like God. [. . .]

14 September [. . .] Read Coleridge. Much that is excellent. But he suffers from the English disease. It's clear that he can think clearly, freely and powerfully; but as soon as he touches on anything that is respected in England, he becomes a sophist without noticing it. Read to the girls. [. . .]

19 September, Yasnaya Polyana Unwell. Read. Chopped wood. Rugin came. I walked back with him. How inaccessible peasants are to the teaching of the truth. They are so full of their own interests and habits.

But who is accessible? The one whom the Father leads to it – a secret. Read Pressensé.[40] How insignificant! [. . .]

It's now 12 o'clock. I'd like to write a novel *de longue haleine* [on a big scale] in the evenings.

6 October, Yasnaya Polyana   Woke up early and thought with gladness about the need to write down the whole sober truth about what is considered to be belief, the madness which is accepted and repeated: redemption, the creation, the sacraments, the Church, etc. I imagined it very clearly, but not the form of it. Of course something literary would be more powerful than anything.[41] [. . .]

14 October, Yasnaya Polyana   [. . .] Got on yesterday with a conclusion to Ballou, and I'm continuing it today for the first time with enthusiasm. It looks as if it will get finished now. The day before yesterday Doctor Bogomolets came, and he and I translated *Diana*,[42] a very good article on the sexual question. Yesterday I wrote it out and revised it today during a sitting with Gay.[43] [. . .]

15 October, Yasnaya Polyana   If I'm alive. [. . .] terrible to say – 23 October. Eight days. My only occupations during these days were writing out *Diana*, revising an article on hunting,[44] and a story by Guy de Maupassant[45] – a wonderful story which Alexey Mitrofanovich translated. Got on yesterday with *Sergey*. I've made some progress. My thoughts are sluggish. [. . .]

24 October.   [. . .] In the morning I revised and wrote down the stories by Guy de Maupassant[46] while sitting for Gay. After that I couldn't write. In the evening I read a history of the church with the girls. Don't remember whether I noted down: *We can't know anything of what is, but we can know for sure what ought to be.* There are many different sorts of knowledge, but the one which is the most important and reliable of all is the knowledge of how to live. But it's just this knowledge which is despised and considered both unimportant and unreliable.

12 o'clock. I'm going to bed. I'm sad. The one joyful thing is that I feel the very best kind of love for Sonya. Her character is only now becoming clear to me.

26 October, Yasnaya Polyana   Got up early. Revised Maupassant again and didn't manage to write anything. I was wrong to praise him the day before yesterday. Such restlessness, agitation and fuss and bother that I get depressed. Generally speaking I'm in low spirits. I'm glad to be with Lyova. He's struggling against the desires of the flesh and seems about to succumb. In the evening read Pisemsky's drama *A Hard Lot*.[47] Not good. [. . .]

Yesterday, 30 October, Yasnaya Polyana. [. . .] The *Diana* article has been published.[48] I somehow fear for it. And that's bad. It's proof that I didn't do it entirely for other people's sake. [. . .]

7 November, Yasnaya Polyana Got up early, had a walk. A keen frost. Continued writing just as badly.[49] I sometimes think that I've lost the power and ability to express my thoughts as I expressed them before, and so I'm dissatisfied with their feeble expression now. I must give up. It's not important. I'm not sorry. And things are very good as they are. (Prayer fortifies and purifies me, it makes me glad.) But doubts trouble me: perhaps I ought to write. And so I try, and will go on trying, to serve people in this way, since I don't know any other way of serving them so usefully. [. . .]

18 November [. . .] In the evening I read Homer to the girls. [. . .]

Thought about the corruptness of the newspapers: read in *The Week* an account of my story in the *Fortnightly Review*,[50] where it says that the young man went off with her and that was the end of it, and that the whole story is written on the theme of married life. Of course I know it's all nonsense, but then 0.99 of news and information is the same sort of nonsense which nobody corrects – there's no time: tomorrow there will be fresh news and one mustn't miss the dead-line – the month's, the week's, or the day's. One must think with the dead-line in view. It's really surprising how strong the devil is, i.e this retrograde force. A thought is only a thought and fruitful when it isn't bound by anything: that is its strength compared with other things of the flesh. But no. They've gone and shackled it in bonds of time, in order to emasculate it and deprive it of its individuality. And it's just this emasculated form that is eager to devour everything. Philosophers and sages express their thoughts for the first of the month, and prophets too. [. . .]

Thought for my article on non-resistance: the critics of my book[51] attacked the metaphysics and said nothing about the moral teaching. It's just the same with all opinions about heresies: people tell you in detail how the Montanists and others made such and such a wrong judgement about divinity (probably describing the teaching of the Montanists and others just as correctly as missionaries described the teaching of Buddhists), and then say in two words that they lived morally without resorting to violence.

Today, 21 November, Yasnaya Polyana. It's getting on for 12 o'clock at night. Sonya has gone to Moscow. I read *The Odyssey* with the girls. [. . .]

Yesterday, the 27th, at Krapivna.   Got up very early, went for a walk, went to the police station and then to the gaol. Tried again to persuade the accused to be unanimous; we drank coffee and then I went to court. Heat and a shameful comedy. But I noted down what I needed for a realistic scene.[52] Then we travelled back by night. A snow-storm, it was frightening. Arrived safely.

Today, 15 December.   Haven't written my diary for eleven days. Lived roughly the same: walked and prayed just the same, and made the same slow progress in writing my article. Visitors: (1) Rusanov and Boulanger.[53] Left behind a very joyous impression. Then Anatoly and Andrey Butkevich.[54] News that a policeman was coming to see me about the dispatch of some hectographed articles by Butkevich. Then Anatoly Butkevich and his wife. Very good and joyous people. Before them too, an old man, Panov, a coachmaker from Samara, an Orthodox renegade, an original, free-thinking Christian. Too occupied with negation. Then Dillon.[55] He only left today. I was depressed, partly because I felt I was material for him to write about. But intelligent, and apparently with newly awakened interest in religion. I've just seen Bulygin off. I must help him spiritually, and I tried as best I could. Went out this morning and was met by Ilya Bolkhin begging for forgiveness: they've been sentenced to six weeks in gaol.[56] I was very depressed and my heart ached all day. Prayed, and will pray and go on praying that God will help me not to destroy my feeling of love. I must go away. Forgot to make a note of a dear and wonderful visitor – Posha. He's very good, serene, open, truthful and pure, and so is Masha, and I'm glad. [. . .]

Yesterday I began Koni's story from the beginning.[57] Enjoyed writing it very much. [. . .]

16 December, Yasnaya Polyana   [. . .] Yesterday I went to bed and couldn't sleep. My heart ached, and above all I felt loathsome self-pity, and anger against her. An astonishing condition! And with it all, nervous excitement and clarity of thought. With these stresses and strains I could write something splendid. Got out of bed at 2 and went into the drawing-room to walk about. She came out and we talked till after 4. The same as usual. A bit gentler on my part. Spoke my mind about one or two things. I think I must declare to the government that I don't recognize property and royalties, and let them do what they will. [. . .]

Still can't adopt a simple, kindly, affectionate tone, not just with her, but with any of them. That's proof that I'm to blame. My last words yesterday were: 'Don't judge me; I judge myself for not being affectionate enough – you try and find the same judgement in yourself.' [. . .]

25 December 8 o'clock in the evening. They've just been doing the Christmas tree. I sat downstairs and read Renan. Remarkably clever. Before dinner I went for a walk, had a sleep and asked Lyova's forgiveness for having offended him. During tea, with Dunayev present, a conversation began about our way of life and the times of *repas* [meals]; he blamed his mother, and I said that he was just the same as she was. He said that everyone said (and this was the astonishing thing) that there was no difference between Masha, Chertkov and himself, and I said that he didn't even understand what it was all about, – said that he knew nothing about humility or love, and mistook hygienic concerns for moral ones. He got up with tears in his eyes and went out. I was very hurt and sorry for him, and ashamed. And I felt love for him. Spoke to him, but was sorry it had happened. And so did no writing. Slept badly all night. [. . .]

These last days I've been receiving abusive letters. The Yasnaya Polyana Tartuffe. Was hurt at first and then felt good. Good letters from the Shakers. [. . .]

26 December Got up early. Asked Vasya to tidy my room. And when I came back after coffee and it wasn't done, was shamefully offended and angry. Pride! Abomination. I'm still writing about the Church. Seem to have made progress. But not much.

In the morning I wrote down: the Church, by teaching people to know the truth and not do it, has atrophied their moral nerve. [. . .]

Well now. 1891, *January 1*, if I'm alive. I've kept waiting for something to happen while I'm still sixty-three – which goes thirty times into 1890. Nothing has happened.[58] As if I didn't know that anything that can happen from without is nothing compared with what can happen within.

1891

Today, 15 January, Yasnaya Polyana [. . .] Thought: to think you can change your life by changing its outward conditions is just like thinking, as I did as a boy, that by sitting on a stick and taking hold of it at both ends I could lift myself up. [. . .]

Today, 25 January, Yasnaya Polyana Haven't written my diary for nine days. All this time I've been writing my article bit by bit.[1] [. . .] Two days, yesterday and today, I wrote nothing. During this time I've been reading the journals, and above all Renan.[2] The self-satisfaction of the infallible scholar is astonishing. [. . .]

No visitors of note. Seryozha and Ilyusha. Things are just as difficult with Seryozha. He is becoming more and more remote with his employment, which he regards as work. Ilya, whom I drove back, said to me: 'Why do you persecute Seryozha so?' And these words of his sound to me as a constant reproach, and I feel myself to blame. I still pray, but more and more coldly. All the time lately I've been in a moral stupor. [. . .]

Today, when walking and thinking about thieves, I clearly imagined how a thief, lying in wait for the person he wants to rob and discovering that he wasn't travelling that day or was travelling by a different route, would be angry with him, would consider himself to have been offended by him and, feeling conscious of being in the right himself, would prepare to take his revenge on him for it. And as I vividly imagined this to myself, I began to think how I could write it down, and then began to think how good it would be to write a novel *de longue haleine* [on a big scale], illuminating it with my present view on things. [. . .] But I came back home, got down to science and art, crossed things out and stumbled to a halt. And I did nothing all day. [. . .]

26 January, Yasnaya Polyana I.I.A.[3] How happy I would be if I'd written in my diary yesterday that I'd begun a big work of fiction. Yes, to start now and write a novel would make so much sense. My first, early novels were unconscious creations. Since *Anna Karenina*, for more than ten years I think, I've been dissecting, separating, analysing; now I know what's what and I can mix it all together again and work in this mixture. Help me, Father.

11 February Five days have gone by again. Today is the 11th. Yesterday I wrote about science and art. Made little progress; but it's all clear. I've no energy. These last few days abusive articles have kept appearing in the papers. On the *Afterword* – by Suvorin.[4] On *The Fruits of Enlightenment* in Berlin, saying that I'm an enemy of science.[5] The same in Beketov.[6] And yesterday the *coup de grace* [final blow] – the more so because I was out of sorts (and how glad of it!) – articles in *Open Court* about Booth and myself[7] as examples of pharisaism – saying one thing and doing another – saying one should give everything to the poor and increasing one's property by the sale of this very sermon. And referring to my wife. Like Adam – the woman gave it me, and I did eat. It hurt me very much, and it still hurts me as I write. But it shouldn't hurt me, and I can't put myself in such a position that it doesn't hurt; but it's very difficult.

I am a pharisee: but not in what they reproach me with. In that I'm innocent. And this is a lesson for me. But in the fact that while thinking and asserting that I live in God's sight, for the sake of the good, because it is good, I really live by worldly fame, and have so choked up my soul with wordly fame that I can't get through to God. I read newspapers and journals, looking for my name, I listen to a conversation and wait for it to be about me. I've so choked up my soul that I can't dig through to reach God, and a life of good for the sake of good. But I must. I say every day: I don't want to live for my own personal desires now, for worldly fame here, I want to live for love always and everywhere; but I live for my desires now and for fame here.

I will cleanse my soul. Once I have cleansed it and dug down to firm ground, I shall feel the possibility of living for the good, without the thought of worldly fame. Help me, Father. Father, help me. I know there is no Father as a person. But this form is natural to the expression of passionate longing. [. . .]

Another week. *Today is 14 February, Yasnaya Polyana.* On the same day, I think, as I wrote my last diary entry, I began once more to read the diary which Sonya is copying out.[8] And it hurt me. And I began to talk to her irritably and infected her with my anger. And she grew angry and said some cruel things. It lasted no more than an hour. I stopped settling accounts and began to think about her and made it up lovingly. 'We've sinned a lot.' Tanya and Masha are ill. Tanya is hysterical – sweet and pitiable. [. . .]

I've just been thinking about the critics:

The business of criticism is to interpret the works of great writers, above all to single out from the great quantity of rubbish written by all of us – to single out what is best. And instead of this, what do they do? Force out of themselves, or more usually fish out from the works of a bad but popular writer, some little platitude, and start to string their thoughts on to this platitude, mangling and distorting the writers in the process. And the result is that in their hands great writers become small, profound ones shallow and wise ones stupid. This is called criticism. And this partly meets the requirements of the masses – the limited masses – who are glad that a writer is pinned down by something at least, if only something stupid, and is notable and memorable for them; but this isn't criticism, i.e. making a writer clear; it's making him obscure. [. . .]

Reading *Our Destiny* by Gronlund.[9] Much in it that is good; for example, he says that if people had absolute free will it would be the greatest calamity. Man may not steal, just as he may not fly. It's good, too, that equality, as he says, must be economic equality as far as consumption is concerned, but not equality as far as production. But under the present system, on the contrary, equality has been established as far as production is concerned – a brilliant musician or poet can weave in a mill; but, economically, two completely equal nonentities are divided by a chasm – the one on the peak of luxury, the other in the depths of poverty.

Good too is the assertion, as I think I wrote somewhere myself long ago, that it's foolish to talk about equality of obligations when one side pays 0.00001 of its wealth (say a day's pay), while the other side pays an entire fourteen-hour day's labour, i.e. the whole life of a day. I wrote and said[10] that a government which requires equal fulfilment of obligation from both sides and punishes non-fulfilment equally is in direct violation of true justice, while observing its outward appearance.

Gronlund polemicizes with Spencer and with all those who reject government or see its purpose only in the protection of the individual. Gronlund supposes the basis of morality to be in communal association. As an example, or rather an embryo, of a real socialist government he puts forward the trade unions which, by constraining the individual and forcing him to sacrifice his own interests, subordinate him to the service of common aims. I think that's wrong. He says that government organizes labour. That would be good; but he forgets that government always coerces and exploits labour under the guise of organizing it. It would be splendid if government organized labour; but to do that it would have to be disinterested, have to be saintly. But where are they, these saints? It's true that individualism as they call it, meaning by that the ideal of the personal good of each individual, is a most pernicious principle; but the principle of the good of many people collectively is just as pernicious; only its pernicious nature is not immediately apparent. [. . .]

16 February   Still the same tiredness and indifference. Began to stitch boots. A talk with Pavel[11] reminded me of real life: his boy and the boy's master stand and make six pairs of boots a week, for which he works six days, eighteen hours a day, from 6 to 12. And that's true. And we wear these boots. [. . .]

17 February, Yasnaya Polyana   Was intending to go to Pirogovo yesterday, but changed my mind. Read Montaigne and Ertel.[12] The first is old, the second bad. Very much out of spirits, but had a good talk with the children and with Sonya, despite the fact that she is very disturbed. Gay came today with his wife and a picture.[13] The picture is good. What an extraordinary thing this irritability is – this need to contradict one's wife. [. . .]

5 March, Yasnaya Polyana   [. . .] Was very depressed today. Sonya talked about the printing,[14] not understanding how this depresses me. Yes, I feel it particularly painfully, because I'm depressed at heart. Depressed by the evil life of the gentry of which I'm a part. Wrote nothing. And didn't try to. I'm reading Gronlund. Not bad, but old and trivial.

Thought: I read Kozlov's article against me,[15] and I wasn't at all hurt. And I think it's because in recent times I've had a lot of lessons, a lot of pricks in this place: it's become numb and hardened, or rather I've grown a bit better, become less vain. And I think how beneficial, not only physical, but moral pain is. It alone teaches. Any pain – repentance for an evil deed – how necessary it is; if not for me myself, then for other people whom I tell about it. That's how it is with me. All moral sufferings I can and will tell people about. Thought about myself that in order to escape from my difficult situation of being party to an evil life, the best and most natural thing is to write what I am writing and want to write, and to publish it. I want to suffer. Help me, Father. [. . .]

Today, 9 March, Yasnaya Polyana   All three days I've been writing, and although it's not much, it's sensible, and I'm making progress. I think I'm at the end of the fourth chapter. Lyova has been; he left yesterday. On the eve of his departure we talked about heredity. He insisted that it's true. For me the admission that people are not equal in their *valeur intrinsèque* [intrinsic worth] is the same as for a mathematician to admit that figure ones are not equal. The whole science of life would be destroyed. Felt sad, depressed and ashamed the whole time. [. . .]

(3) Read a wonderful definition by Henry James (senior) of what true progress is. Progress is a process like the modelling and carving of a statue from a block of marble, the *elimination* of all that is superfluous. The marble, the material, is nothing. The important thing is the carving, the trimming off of the superfluous. [. . .]

This morning I told Sonya with difficulty and with trepidation that I would announce that everyone would have the right to print my writings. I saw she was distressed. Then when I came back she began to say, all flushed and angry as she was, that she would print anything at all just to spite me. I tried to calm her down, but not well; I was excited myself and went out. After dinner she came up to me, started to kiss me, saying she would do nothing to oppose me, and began to cry. I was very, very glad. Help me, Father. [. . .]

13 March   Today is the 13th, night-time. Sonya has just left for Moscow with Davydov.[16] [. . .] Things are going very well with Sonya. Today, I see, she has put out photos of all the children except Vanechka, and is proudly admiring them. It's touching. [. . .]

18 March   Got up very early. Fell asleep. Can't say I did any writing, only re-reading and revising. Astonishing weakness of thought – apathy. Temptation, as the monks say. I must resign myself to the thought that my career as a writer is finished – and be glad without it. The only thing is that without it my life of luxury is so hateful to me that I never cease tormenting myself.

Today, 24 March, Yasnaya Polyana   [. . .] Thought during this time: [. . .] (6) Yesterday, on my way to Tula, I thought – and I don't know whether what I thought was sinful – that I have a difficult life to endure. I live in the conditions and environment of a sensual life – desire, vanity – and yet I don't live in this life, I'm weighed down by it all: I don't eat, don't drink, don't live in luxury, don't boast – or at least I hate all this – and this unnecessary, alien environment deprives me of what constitutes the meaning and beauty of life: association with the poor, spiritual exchange with them. I simply don't know whether I'm doing right resigning myself to it and ruining the children. I can't; I'm afraid of evil. Help me, Father.
(7) How easily we say we will forgive insults. The day before yesterday Vanechka hit Kuzka. I said he was a bad boy. He was hurt and was in a bad temper and began to avoid me and say he wouldn't go for a walk with me and wouldn't let me into his room. And what happens? I was offended, and unkind feelings towards him rose up in me, a wish to break his will. I pretended to ignore him and deliberately walked into his room which he didn't want to let me into.

No, it's difficult for us, corrupt and proud men, to forgive an insult, to forget it, to love our enemies, even those like dear three-year-old son Vanechka.
[. . .] (10) Travels, reading, friendships, new impressions are necessary as long as these impressions are assimilated by life, as long as they leave their mark on a more or less clean surface; but as soon as there are so many of them that some are not digested before others are taken in, they are harmful: the result is a hopeless state of mental diarrhoea – all sorts of impressions slip right through without leaving any trace. [. . .]

25 March, Yasnaya Polyana Slept badly. I must stop it. Got up very early. Went for a walk and imagined very vividly, as I seldom do, a work of fiction on the subject of upbringing. Lopukhina. The mother. The problem of the mother. *Notes of a Mother*.[17] Much that is good artistically speaking came into my head, and is still coming. [. . .]

26 March, Yasnaya Polyana [. . .] The boys have arrived.[18] It's gone 12 now, I'm going to have lunch. Sonya has arrived with Ilya. And all the time they have been quarrelling about money. I was very sad. Talk about horses, money, the sale of my works, volume 13 and other unpleasant things. I was depressed and sorry for myself: it's bad. At least I didn't blame others and could see my own guilt.

Today, 9 April, Yasnaya Polyana Nothing special. Sonya is still in Petersburg,[19] her visit sometimes distresses me, but last night I woke up, began thinking and feeling annoyed, but said to myself: it's good, it's good for me, it's a trial. [. . .]

Yesterday began writing *Notes of a Mother*. Wrote a lot, but it only served to convince me that I mustn't write that way.[20] It's too impoverished: I must write in the first person. [. . .]

18 April, I think, Yasnaya Polyana Sonya came back about three days ago. I found it unpleasant, her ingratiating herself with the Tsar and telling him that manuscripts were being stolen from me.[21] I couldn't restrain myself at first and spoke to her in an unfriendly manner, but then things turned out all right, especially because wicked feelings of mine made me glad of her return. She is impulsive, but well disposed towards me, and I wish I could always remember that that thing, and not she herself, is the obstacle, and that one shouldn't be angry or wish it to be otherwise. Got on with *Notes of a Mother* a second time, the next day, but since then I've left it. I'm busy again with my article, but I'm still revising everything unfortunately, revising the 3rd and 4th chapters again. Ilya has arrived with Tsurikov and Naryshkin, and also Seryozha and Lyova, and they've been dividing things up.[22] I have to abandon my previous intention – to renounce my property rights – and have to grant deeds of gift. Masha refused hers, naturally, and is displeased that her refusal isn't taken seriously. [. . .] How can I be oppressed by life when Masha is with me! Lyova and Tanya are nice too, but they lack that moral, religious lever which controls us. Alexey Mitrofanovich has been demonstrating the differential calculus to me. I understood it, very well. No letters in particular. Everyone asks me to send them my works that are banned. [. . .]

Haven't written in my diary for ten days. Today is *2 May, Yasnaya*

Polyana   [. . .] Lyova wants to leave the university; I'm sorry for him. [. . .]
Sonya is ill. I'm praying. Reading *Ethics of Diet*,[23] excellent, and have read
Plato's *Les lois*.[24] Noted down: [. . .] (4) Talked yesterday about education.
Why do parents send their children away to school? It suddenly became
clear to me. If parents kept them at home, they would see the
consequences of their immoral lives in their children. They would see
themselves in their children, as though in a mirror. The father drinks wine
at dinner with his friends, the son in the tavern. The father goes to a ball,
the son to a party. The father does nothing, neither does the son. But
send him to school, and the mirror in which parents see themselves is
covered up.
(5) I walk along a hard road, and nearby gaily dressed women are coming
back from work singing lively songs. A pause between the songs, and I can
hear the measured tread of my feet on the road, then a song again, then
silence again and the tread of my footsteps. It's good. When I was young,
something always used to sing inside me, or often did, without any
women's songs. And everything – the sound of footsteps, and the sunlight
and the swaying of the hanging birch branches – everything seemed to be
accompanied by music. [. . .]

Today, 10 May, Yasnaya Polyana   [. . .] Thought:
(1) When a person dies, his consciousness is separated from him, and, like
a seed that has ripened and fallen to the ground, it looks for something to
catch hold of, somewhere to strike root in the soil it needs in order to begin
to live again. If a seed, in the process of shrivelling up and falling, could
feel, it would feel the cessation of life. Isn't this the same as a person feels
when he is dying? [. . .]

Today, 22 May, Yasnaya Polyana   [. . .] Thought:
(1) An afterword to the afterword: whether I explained properly or not
why the greatest sexual continence is necessary, I don't know. But I do
know for certain that copulation is an abomination which can only be
regarded or thought about without revulsion under the influence of sexual
desire. Even in order to have children you wouldn't do this to a woman you
love. I'm writing this at a time when I'm possessed myself by sexual desire,
against which I can't fight. [. . .]
(9) For a work of fiction: I not only eat and drink, I practise art, play the
piano, draw, write, read and study, and all of a sudden some poor people,
people in rags, victims of fires, widows and orphans turn up, and I can't go
on in their presence – I'm ashamed. Why the devil did they come?; if only
they had stayed where they were they wouldn't have bothered me.
   Such an occurrence in the midst of food, lawn tennis and artistic and
scientific pursuits *is better evidence than any rational arguments*.[25] [. . .]

2 June, Yasnaya Polyana   Haven't done much work all this time, though
I've made some progress. I'm beginning to doubt the importance of what I
write. There's been a mass of visitors. [. . .] Walked to Tula, went to the
abattoir but didn't see any slaughtering.[26] But I saw a woman in Tula: eyes
close together and straight eyebrows, seemingly on the point of tears, but
plump, nice-looking, pitiable, and arousing sensuality. That's what the
merchant's wife who seduces Father Sergey should be like. [. . .]

I'm very depressed because of Sonya. All this worry about money and
property, and the complete failure to understand. We were just talking
about whether a person can sacrifice his life rather than do something
which harms nobody, but is offensive to God. She objected, [indecipher-
able word] – words of abuse. I had evil thoughts of going away. I mustn't. I
must endure it. [. . .]

7 June   Yesterday evening Lyova and Andryusha returned. All my sons
are arriving – for the division of the property. It's very depressing, and it's
going to be unpleasant. [. . .]

Got up early, went to Tula by train with Petya Rayevsky. Went to the
abattoir. They drag the animal by the horns, screw up its tail so that the
cartilages crunch, don't hit it properly first time, but when they do, it
struggles and they cut its throat, let the blood flow into basins and then flay
the skin from its head. The head, bare of skin and with the tongue
clenched between the teeth, faces upwards, while the belly and legs writhe
about. The butchers are angry because the animals take a long time to
die. The cattle-dealers scurry about with anxious faces, making their
calculations.

Visited the prison[27] – a wonderful house with ornate carving for the
warder, a wonderful office, wonderful tables, officials, the one in charge
with his breath smelling of alcohol. [. . .]

9, 10 June, Yasnaya Polyana   High summer. Heart's ease, a smell like
rotting honey from the camomile, cornflowers, and silence in the woods,
only the incessant hum of bees and insects in the treetops. Did some
mowing today. Good. My writing is going badly. I'm thrashing about on
the spot. But there are plenty of artistic impressions. [. . .]

(2) *For Koni's story*. He plays catch with Katyusha and they kiss behind a
bush. *And for the same story*: the first part – the poetry of material love; the
second – the poetry, the beauty of true love. [. . .]

(5) *For Father Sergey*. He discovered what it means to trust in God only
when he was utterly and irrevocably ruined in people's eyes. Only then did
he discover that strength which is full of life. The result was complete
indifference to people and their actions. They can take him prisoner, put
him on trial, cross-examine him, reprieve him – it's all the same to him.

Two states: the first – worldly fame – disquiet; the second – devotion to the will of God – complete tranquillity. [. . .]

*Today, 18 June,*²⁸ *Yasnaya Polyana* [. . .] It's miserable at home – the division. Vera had a row with her mother, Tanya quarrelled witth Masha, Marya Fyodorovna²⁹ gets in the way. It's miserable.

15 June, Yasnaya Polyana Got on well with the last chapter, and decided to go for a walk with Alyokhin and Khokhlov. We set off, and walked happily as far as Bulygin's. Bulygin was reading Dostoyevsky's *Dream of a Ridiculous Man.* Well conceived, badly executed.

13 June, Yasnaya Polyana [. . .] Thought [. . .]
(3) The intellectual fashion of exalting women, of asserting that they are not only equal to men in their spiritual capacities, but higher than them, is a very bad and harmful fashion.

The fact that women's rights should not be restricted in any way, that people should behave towards a woman with just the same respect and love as towards a man, that she is the equal of a man as far as rights go – of that there can be no doubt; but to assert that the average woman is endowed with the same spiritual strength as a man, to expect to find in every woman what you expect to find in every man, is to deliberately deceive yourself, and to deceive yourself to the detriment of woman. If we expect of a woman what we expect of a man, we shall require it, and when we don't find what we require, we shall be irritated, and ascribe to ill will what is the result of impossibility.

So to regard women as what they are – weaker creatures spiritually – is not cruelty to women; to regard them as equals is cruelty. By weakness or less spiritual strength I mean less obedience of the flesh to the spirit, and especially – the main characteristic of women – less trust in the dictates of reason. [. . .]

25 June, Yasnaya Polyana [. . .] Yesterday Ilya came. There's still the same conflict with his mother. I'm not angry at their obtuseness. Living in such proximity, how can they help being infected by one another at least a little bit? [. . .]

Got up at 8. Pouring with rain. Drank coffee on my own. Still weak – though I'm a bit better today. Thought again in the night about the foreword to the vegetarian book, i.e. about abstinence, and wrote not too badly all morning. Then went for a walk and a bathe. It's now 5 o'clock. Still weak. I sleep badly. And I'm unbelievably vile to myself. This is the devil that God has sent me, as Paul said. [. . .] Thought: [. . .]
(3) Everyone is talking about the famine,³⁰ everyone is worrying about the

starving people, and wanting to help them and save them. Yet how disgusting it is! People who have never thought about others, about the ordinary people, suddenly for some reason are burning with the desire to serve them. It's either vanity – wanting to show off – or fear; but there's nothing good about it. [. . .]

(4) You can't begin to do good today because of some particular event, if you didn't do so yesterday. People do good, but not because there's a famine, but because it's good to do it.

14 July, Yasnaya Polyana   I.I.A. Still the 13th; a talk with my wife, still on the same subject of renouncing the copyright of my works;[31] again the same failure to understand me: 'I'm obliged to do it for the children's sake.' She doesn't understand, and the children don't understand as they spend money that every rouble expended by them and obtained from books is shame and suffering to me. Never mind the shame, but why weaken the effect which the propagation of the truth might have? Evidently it must be so. And the truth will do its job without me. [. . .]

Today, 22 July, Yasnaya Polyana   [. . .]
(1) For *Father Sergey*. When he has sinned with the merchant's daughter and is tormented by it, it occurs to him that if he is going to sin, then better to sin with the beautiful A., and not with this disgusting creature. And he is seized with disgust once more. [. . .]

Today, August 12 Yasnaya Polyana   [. . .] Thought during this time: [. . .]
(4) The absurdity of our lives is the result of the power of women; but the power of women is the result of the incontinence of men; so the cause of the ugliness of life is the incontinence of men. [. . .]

28 August, Yasnaya Polyana   I.I.A.
   Was alive, am alive, and today is *13 September*. During this time I've written quite a lot. [. . .] Also during this time, Sonya and the boys left for Moscow, and then Lyova. She left on the 3rd, I think. I wrote a letter to her yesterday, asking her to send my letter about renouncing my royalties to the editor. I don't know what will happen. [. . .] Thought during this time:
(1) Another person, and another and another. All new and special, and you keep thinking that this one really will be new and special, and know something the others don't know, and live better than the others. And it's always just the same, the same weaknesses, the same low level of thought.
(5) There is an enormous advantage in expressing one's thoughts outside an integrated work. In a work, the thought often has to be compressed from one side and expanded from another, like grapes ripening in a solid

bunch; but expressed individually, it has its own centre in itself, and develops evenly in all directions. [. . .]

18 September, Pirogovo   Sonya has come back. The Bobrinskys were here last night. Not much of interest. Sonya had a good journey back. I was tormented by her silence about the letter, but it turned out that she agrees. Sent off the letter on the 16th.[32]

Lvov came and spoke about the famine. Slept badly during the night and didn't get to sleep till 4 o'clock, still thinking about the famine. I think it's necessary to set up soup kitchens. And with this purpose I set off for Pirogovo. On the same day I had an unpleasant talk with Sonya. Because she didn't want me to go, she began to say something quite different. I was angry. And I was angry with Seryozha today. He was cross yesterday.

So far nothing has come of the soup kitchens. I'm afraid I made a mistake. One shouldn't seek, but only answer requests. [. . .]

25 September, Klekotki[33]   A whole week has passed. On the 19th I set off on horseback for Uspenskoye with Tanya and Vera. Bibikov is very kind-hearted, he gave us a bed for the night and took us next day into the heart of the province. We looked round the village of Ogaryovka. An intelligent headman – he had made a list of all the houses. The poverty is not so great because there are potatoes. I began to console myself. But then it got worse. [. . .]

22. Back home; Sonya unwell and out of sorts, and so was I. Hardly slept all night. In the morning I said there was work to do here, feeding the starving. She understood that I didn't want to go to Moscow. A scene began. I said some venomous things. Behaved very badly. The same evening I went to Tula to Zinovyev's. Didn't find out much from him. But we had a friendly talk. Returned home and found a willingness to make it up, and we made it up. On the 23rd I decided to go to Yepifan. Tanya accompanied me. Picked up Masha in Obolenskoye. [. . .] On the 24th we walked to the village of Meshcherki. The run-down state of the people is dreadful: ruined houses – there was a fire last year – they don't have anything, but they still drink. They are like children who laugh when they get into trouble. Towards evening Bogoyavlensky and Rayevsky came. I decided to settle in with Rayevsky. It would be good if Sonya doesn't object. I even left ninety roubles to buy potatoes and beet.

8 October, Yasnaya Polyana   [. . .] I'd only just written Zolotaryov a recipe on how to establish loving relations with the people you live with when on going upstairs, I succumbed to the teasing of Sofya Andreyevna, who asserted that people who try to live a moral life have ceased to be natural. [. . .]

Today is 24 October, 1891, Yasnaya Polyana. Fifteen days have passed. And a lot has happened. Yesterday, the 23rd, I was unwell, a sort of influenza; Mitasha Obolensky and Bulygin came. In the morning I got on with the 4th chapter. In the evening I sent Grot a supplement to the article on the famine.[34] On the 22nd Sonya left. I was already unwell. Before she left, she talked with me so joyfully and well that I couldn't believe it was the same person. Wrote about the famine all day; Grot came and I felt very tired in the head. Grot left in the evening. [. . .]

(3) Sonya said that her daughter-in-law Sonya was a bad mother. 'You see,' she said, 'she doesn't do what you condemn in *The Kreutzer Sonata*. She doesn't poison her husband's life with children. But if you love children and look after them you cease to be attractive.' And I thought: what a necessary flavouring for everything kindness is. The very best virtues are worth nothing without kindness; while with it the very worst vices are forgiven. What a good type for a work of fiction – a weak, corrupt, but kindly person. I think there have been such already, but I can sense such a type in a new way. [. . .]

Popov is still here. We are quite ready to go. Still no money.[35] I don't know what we'll do. But the motive is good, I think. To be sure the wretched desire for worldly fame is mixed up with it. But I'll try to do it for the sake of God. [. . .] Today, Begichevka. At Rayevsky's. This is our fifth day here. We are well. There's work to do. Wrote an article: 'Is there enough bread?'[36] There's plenty to note down but it's late now. [. . .]

Today, 6 November, am, Begichevka Our three soup kitchens are now organized. I wrote to the paper about whether there's enough bread, and began a story *Who is Right?*[37] The girls are well occupied. I also revised the 7th and 8th chapters. I'm well. A letter from England with an offer to be an agent for relief contributions.[38] Two letters from Sonya. I never cease to be sad for her and because of her. Yesterday, when praying to God for deliverance from the temptation of pride and for humility, I thought that if I want humility, I must want the things that humiliate, and began to pray with diffidence for humiliation to be sent me. [. . .] A thought today for *Sergey*.

It's necessary for him to struggle against pride, to get into that false circle where humility turns out to be pride, to feel the hopelessness of his pride, and only after his fall and shame to feel that he has escaped from that false circle and can be truly humble. And then comes the happiness of escaping from the arms of the devil and feeling himself in the embraces of God.

Today, 17 November, Begichevka Twelve days have passed, full of events, full of active life, but seemingly empty in the sense of spiritual life. I've written nothing in my notebook except the names of peasants asking to use the soup kitchens, etc. [. . .]

Today, 17   We got up early and saw Lyova and Rayevsky off to Moscow. Then I wrote a short article for the paper.[39] Didn't finish it and didn't send it off. [. . .]

Five days have passed. *Today, 24 November, Begichevka.* Got on with chapter 8 quite well. After dinner I rode to Pashkovo and visited four soup kitchens; a very joyful impression. We invited a beggar boy for supper. The children came running in. 'We're going to have supper.' – 'Me too – here's my spoon.' [. . .]

Today, 18, actually 19 December, Begichevka   Haven't written my diary for almost a month. I've been in Moscow during this time. Joy. Relations with Sonya have never been so cordial. I thank Thee, Father. This is what I asked for. Everything I asked for has been granted me. I thank Thee. Grant that I may merge more closely with Thy will. I don't want anything except what Thou wantest. Great work is in progress here. It's catching on in other parts of Russia too. There are many good people. I thank Thee. [. . .]

1892

Begichevka. Alive. A month has gone by. *Today is 30 January, 1892.* To remember each day in turn is impossible. I've been to Moscow, where I spent three weeks, and it's now a week since I've been back here. The main features and events of this month: dissatisfaction with Lyova and a depressing feeling of uncharitableness towards him. The hustle and bustle, idleness and luxury, vanity and sensuality of Moscow life. Went to the theatre. *Fruits of Enlightenment.* I'm still writing chapter 8.[1] [...] Returned here and found disorder and confusion. The distribution of materials and firewood has caused greediness. I've felt ill nearly all the time – my stomach – and I feel weak generally. I think more and more often of death and free myself more and more from desire for worldly fame. But I'm still very far from complete freedom. Wanted to copy out my notes into my notebooks – I've lost them, and am sad and jaded, and don't feel like thinking or doing anything. Father, help me to love always.

3 February, Begichevka Sonya left today.[2] I'm sorry for her. Relations with the people are very bad. I realized today that all this begging, envy, deceit, dissatisfaction and the poverty that lies behind it all is an indication of an exceptional situation and of the fact that we are in the middle of it. [...]

Today is 29 February, Begichevka There has been a terrible snow-storm these past days. Set off again yesterday for Rozhnya, and didn't get there again. I've been to Kolodezi and Karatayevo, to see about firewood and children's soup kitchens. [...]

The day before yesterday an astonishing thing happened: I was going out of doors in the morning with my chamberpot, and there was a big, healthy-looking, agile peasant getting on for fifty with a twelve-year-old boy with beautiful, wavy fair hair curling up at the ends. 'Where are you from?' 'Zatvornoye.' That's a village where the peasants live by begging. 'What do you want?' As always the tedious answer, 'Help us, your Honour.' 'What do you need?' 'Don't let us die of hunger. We haven't eaten for two days.' I was depressed. All familiar words and all learned by heart. 'Just a moment.' And I went in to fetch five copecks to get rid of them. The peasant went on talking and describing his situation. No heat, no bread. They go begging, nobody gives them anything. Outside, the snow and the cold. I went in to get rid of them. I looked round at the boy.

His beautiful eyes were full of tears, and big glistening tear-drops were running down from one eye.

Yes, this wretched officialdom and the money make you hardened.

Today is 26 May, Yasnaya Polyana   The day before yesterday I came back from Begichevka.[3] The time there passed like a single day. Everything is just the same. More depressing relations than ever with the 'dark people', Alyokhin, Novosyolov, Skorokhodov. The childishness and vanity of Christianity, the lack of sincerity. The work is just the same. Just as depressing and just as impossible to escape. I'd just begun to live freely there when Yevdokim[4] arrived and brought chapter 8, which was in a hideous condition. Began to revise it and worked every day for a month, continued revising it and am still revising it now. I think I've almost reached the end. [. . .]

Today is 5 July, Yasnaya Polyana   I've hardly written anything for a month and a half. I've been to Begichevka during this time and come back again, and now I've been at Yasnaya for more than two weeks. I'm staying on for the division of the property.[5] It's depressing, terribly painful. I pray that God will rescue me. But how? Not as I will, but as He wills. If only He could suppress the uncharitableness in me. Yesterday there was an astonishing conversation among the children. Tanya and Lyova were suggesting to Masha that she was playing a *mean trick* by refusing her property. Her conduct makes them feel the wrongness of their own, but they must be in the right themselves and so they are trying to invent reasons why her conduct is bad and a *mean trick*. It's terrible. I can't write. I wept, and I could weep again. They say: 'We would like to do it ourselves, but it would be wrong.' My wife says to them: 'Leave it to me.' They don't say anything. It's terrible! I've never seen lies and the motives for them so palpably obvious. I'm sad, sad, and sorely depressed. [. . .]

When leaving Begichevka I was struck, as I'm often struck now, by pictures of nature. 5 o'clock in the morning. Mist, people washing in the river. Everything shrouded in mist. Wet leaves glistening nearby.

Thought during this time: [. . .]

(2) When you have lived a long time – as I've lived forty-five years of conscious life – you understand how false and impossible are all attempts to adapt yourself to life. There is nothing stable in life. It's like trying to adapt yourself to running water. Everything – individuals, families, societies – everything changes, melts away and reshapes itself, as clouds do. And there's no time to get used to one state of society before it no longer exists and has changed into another. [. . .]

Today is 6 August, Yasnaya Polyana   I've been to Begichevka again.

Finished things there. I'll carry on from here. Apathy; great weakness. Chapter 8 is finished, but I'm still toiling away on chapters 9 and 10. And I'm beginning to think I'm thrashing about on the spot. The division of the property is finished.

Thought: (1) I remembered just now sitting in a steam bath and a shepherd boy coming into the anteroom. I asked: 'Who's there?' 'Me.' 'Who's me?' 'It's me.' 'Who are you?' 'I've said, me.' For him, the only person living in the world, it was so incomprehensible that anyone could fail to know the only thing that exists. And everyone is the same. [. . .]

Today is 9 August, Yasnaya Polyana   Wrote a bit better yesterday. I'm still as dissatisfied with myself: no love for anything. Least of all for myself, it's true, but still – no love. At dinner yesterday a trivial episode about mushrooms and a prohibition on picking them grieved me very sorely. I ought to be ashamed of it. [. . .]

Today is 21 August, Yasnaya Polyana   [. . .] Thought during this time: [. . .] (5) This isn't a thought, but on 13 August I made a note that it had become clear to me – not in a moment of anger but in a very peaceful moment – that I might, and probably will, have to leave home.
(6) Spoke about music. I said again that this pleasure is only a little superior in its kind to eating. I don't want to offend music, but I do want clarity. And I can't accept what people say with such obscurity and vagueness, namely that music somehow elevates the soul. The point is that it isn't a moral thing. It's not immoral, any more than eating – it's neutral, but not moral. I stand by that. And if it isn't a moral thing, one's attitude to it is quite different.

Today is 15 September, Yasnaya Polyana   It's two days since I returned from Begichevka, where I spent three good days. Wrote a draft report and conclusion. A depressingly painful impression made on me by a train full of officials and soldiers, going to put down a riot.[6] [. . .]

1 October, Yasnaya Polyana   Everything the same: the same persistent work, the same slow progress and the same dissatisfaction with myself. However, things are a bit better. Went to Kozlovka today and thought for the first time: however terrible it is to think so and say so, but the purpose of life is just as little the reproduction of the likes of us, the continuation of the species, as it is the service of other people or even the service of God. The reproduction of the likes of us. Why? To serve people. But what are they to do, the people we serve? To serve God? But surely He can do what He needs to without us. And anyway He can't need anything. If he bids us serve Him, it's only for our own good. Life can't have any other purpose except good, except joy. Only this purpose – joy – is fully worthy of life. Renunciation, the cross, giving up life – it's all for the sake of joy. And joy exists, and can be permanent and indestructible. And death is a transition to a new, unknown, completely new, different and greater joy. And there are sources of joy which never dry up: the beauty of nature, animals and human beings which is never absent. In prison – the beauty of a sunbeam, of a fly, or of sounds. And the main source is love – my love for people and their love for me. How good it would be if this were true. Am I discovering something new? Beauty, joy – simply as joy, independently of good – is disgusting. I found this out and gave it up. Good without beauty is painful. It's only the combination of the two; and not the combination, but beauty as the crown of good. I think that's something like the truth. I'm reading Amiel[7] – not bad.

Today is 7 October, Yasnaya Polyana Everything the same. The same persistent work and slow progress. During this time my elder sons came. It was nice and good to be with them. But they're very weak. A talk with Lyova. He's closer to me than the others. The main thing is, he is good and loves the good (God). Amiel is very good. [. . .]
(2) I'd like to write a foreword to Amiel,[8] in which I could express what he says in many places about what a new Christianity should consist of, what religion should be like in future. And meanwhile he lives partly by Stoicism, partly by Buddhism, partly – mainly – by Christianity as he understands it – and dies with it. Like the *bourgeois gentilhomme*, he *fait de la religion sans le savoir* [practises religion without knowing it].[9] That's probably the best religion. He isn't tempted to hold it up for admiration.
(3) If I were given the choice whether to people the earth with the best saints imaginable, but with no children, or with people as they are now, but with children constantly arriving fresh from God, I would choose the latter.

6 November Haven't written my diary for almost a month. [. . .]
During this time a student from the medical academy, Sobolevsky, has been to try and reform me and to suggest to me that the concept of God is a vestige of barbarism. I got shamefully worked up over his stupidity, and said a lot of rude things and distressed him.

1893

5 May, Yasnaya Polyana Terrible to think I haven't written my diary since 6 November 1892, i.e. six months except for a day. All this time I've been strenuously occupied with my book: with the last chapter,[1] and I still haven't quite finished.

Yesterday, 4 May, we arrived at Yasnaya from Moscow, where I spent all winter, with a break. Owing to my strenuous work (I don't think I missed a single day) I seem to have let myself go in my physical life – actually in physical work. But in many respects, especially in the demands on myself not to take part in the evil of the world, I've become more resolute. Much has become clear during this time in the course of work; the problem of free will: man is free in the spiritual world, in that which sets the physical world in motion.

We've been to Begichevka during this time. Indifference to the vulgar business of aid, and disgust with hypocrisy. The sympathy people expressed for my activity was joy at the transformation of the critic of hypocrisy into a party to it.

Events during this time: Lyova's return from Petersburg and his illness.[2] My relations with the other members of the family are just the same. The two boys, Andryusha and Misha, especially Misha, are in a very bad and aloof frame of mind. Masha has been infatuated, and has come to her senses again.[3] Now Bulygin is here. He and Rayev have been on trial, and are waging a struggle.[4] Generally speaking I think that in our country the struggle between Christianity and paganism is beginning, *éclate* [is breaking out]. One must know this and be prepared. Today is the first day that I haven't got on with my book. I still don't know what I shall write. I've had many thoughts during this time which have come to nothing. I remember:

(1) A work of dramatic art, which reveals most evidently the essence of any art, consists in presenting people of the most diverse characters and situations, putting before them and confronting them all with the need to solve a vital problem not previously solved by people, and making them act and observe in order to find out how this problem can be solved. It's a laboratory experiment. I would like to do this in my next drama.[5] [. . .]

14 May, Yasnaya Polyana I've missed a week. I haven't noticed how it passed. Sent it off yesterday and had done with it.[6] If it's bad, it's bad. I was ill, and that particularly spurred me on to finish it: I'm free. I'm re-reading things begun earlier. I don't know yet what to start on. [. . .]

23 May, Begichevka[7]   [. . .] Thought during this time: [. . .]
(4) The first leaves have just appeared on the birch trees, and are rippling gaily in the warm wind. Evening. It's growing dark after the storm. The horses have just been let out, and are nibbling the grass greedily and waving their tails.
(5) Tried to remember: what has marriage given me? It's terrible to say. It's probably the same for everybody.
(6) Two conventions are equally strong: for a man – putting up with a box on the ears without a duel; for a woman – marriage without the Church's blessing. [. . .]

5 June, Yasnaya Polyana   [. . .] I'm going to Tula now. Thought during this time:
(1) I was struck by the thought that one of the main causes of hostile feelings between husbands and wives is their rivalry over the business of managing the family. A wife mustn't admit that her husband is reasonable and practical, because if she did, she would have to do his will, and vice versa. If I were writing *The Kreutzer Sonata* now I would introduce this idea. [. . .]
(3) The Chicago exhibition, like all exhibitions, is a striking example of imprudence and hypocrisy: everything is done for profit and amusement – from boredom – but noble aims of love of the people are ascribed to it. Orgies are better. [. . .]

10 June, Yasnaya Polyana   All this time I've done nothing definite. Began the afterword, then the articles on science and art,[8] and now something on Zola's letter and Dumas.[9] Popov left, Posha came. My relations with people are just the same. Thought during this time: [. . .]
(9) Religion is not what people believe in, and science is not what people study, but religion is what gives meaning to life, and science is what people need to know.

21 June, Yasnaya Polyana   The day before yesterday I sent off with Kuzminsky an article about Zola's and Dumas' letters to the *Revue de Famille*.[10] All this time I've amused myself dividing my thoughts between *On Art*, the afterword and this article. Tried to work – I've grown too weak. Masha came. I was very glad to see her. Yesterday there was an unpleasant conversation with Sonya – something that hasn't happened for a long time. 'They are suffering, the poor people.' 'One ought to be sorry for them, but you get too excited.' However, it was all so quiet that nobody noticed it. It just hurt me very much. [. . .]

Today is 18 July, Begichevka [. . .] I've been winding up the business.[11] Had many good thoughts and kept forgetting them. I'll note down a few things: [. . .]

(2) Mankind has always lived in such a way that woman has been ruled by man; suddenly it transpires that women ought not to be ruled, but are themselves the rulers. [. . .]

(5) The form of the novel is not only not everlasting, but is already dying out. One is ashamed to write untruths, to say something happened that didn't happen. If you want to say something, say it frankly.

19 July I continue:

(9) Millions of people have existed for thousands of years and have not lived on meat and have rested regularly on the 7th day. And now science has discovered on the first question that one can't live on vegetable food without meat; but on the second, it has come to the conclusion, after making a series of experiments (putting a man in a cage and making him rotate a stone), that rest on the 7th day is necessary. If they hadn't amassed money by robbery to buy meat with, and if they had had to work themselves, they would long since have come to the undoubtedly correct solution of the first problem, and would have discovered without experiments in cages how necessary it is to rest on the 7th day. [. . .]

(10) Women, like Jews, pay for the slavery in which they have been kept by enslaving men. And serve us right. But we oughtn't to submit, but ought to eliminate in ourselves that weakness by which they try to capture us. [. . .]

(11) Art, they say, cannot abide mediocrity. Nor can it abide being too deliberate. I am a singer, I have greased my hair, put on a frockcoat and necktie and am going to stand on a platform and sing to you. And I am quite cold and feel repelled. But a wet-nurse and a nanny go for a walk in the garden and one sings a folk song in a quiet voice and the other echoes it. Besides, it's terribly difficult to sing loudly and well.

Today is 16 August, Yasnaya Polyana Almost a month. And I've lived through a great deal. Firstly, I've finished my work with the famine victims. Secondly, Chertkov and Posha have been. I finished and sent off an article *Non-action* both in French and Russian;[12] and thirdly, and most important, an excerpt from my book appeared abroad about the Oryol affair, and sparked off a lot of fuss and bother and reactions and misunderstandings and slanderous remarks.[13] Yesterday Sonya and the Kuzminskys read it and pointed out to me some inaccuracies: [. . .]

Telegrams were sent off today asking all the translators to stop publication.[14] I think it's too late. Woke up last night and began to have painful thoughts. Had the same painful thoughts in the evening too.

And I felt worse and worse, and was on the edge of a nervous break-down. [. . .]

The most important event during this time was the business that started between Masha and Zander.[15] She was very pitiable. Now she has recovered and, it seems, has refused him, but the unpleasantness and the tangle of lies over the whole business isn't over yet. [. . .]

Thought: [. . .]

(5) A conversation with social democrats (young men and women). They say: 'The capitalist system will pass into the hands of the workers, and then there won't be any more oppression of the workers and unfair distribution of wages.' 'But who will set up the works and manage them?' I asked. 'That will come of its own accord, the workers will run things themselves.' 'But surely the capitalist system was only established because managers with authority are needed for any practical job. Once there is a job there will be leaders, there will be managers with authority. And once there is authority, there will be abuse of it, – the very thing you are fighting against now.' [. . .]

(8) *August 11, morning*   A blue haze; the dew seems to be sewn on to the grass, bushes and trees to a height of a *sazhen*. Apple trees are bowed beneath their weight. From a log cabin comes the fragrant smoke of fresh brushwood. And over there, in a bright-yellow field, the dew is already drying out on the fine oat stubble and work has begun, binding, carting, scything and, in a violet-coloured field, ploughing. Everywhere along the roads and caught in the branches of trees are torn off broken ears of corn. Gaily dressed young girls are weeding a dewy flowerbed and quietly singing, and man-servants in aprons are bustling about. A lap dog is warming itself in the sun. The gentlemen haven't got up yet. [. . .]

23 August, Yasnaya Polyana   Missed five days. Strakhov and Salomon[16] have been. My restlessness has subsided. But my idleness hasn't ceased. I'm trying to write about religion, but it's no good. [. . .] Thought during this time: [. . .]

(3) I imagined to myself a prosecutor or policeman demanding from me a signed undertaking not to write any more, or something similar, and saying 'I am acting on the highest orders.' There can't be any highest orders, because mine are the highest – to defend my brothers and to denounce their persecutors. There are only two ways of forcing me to be silent: either to stop doing what I denounce, or else to kill me or imprison me for life; in actual fact only the first; and so tell the people who sent you to stop doing what they are doing. [. . .]

Today is 5 October, Yasnaya Polyana   What has happened during this time? Lyova is still not better. A struggle with Masha. I wrote to Zander; he wrote to me. Masha wrote him a bad letter. This grieved me very much. One mustn't prevent them from living, prevent them from making mistakes, prevent them from suffering and repenting and so making progress. Tanya has gone to Moscow to take Sonya's place. Sonya is now on her way here. Popov is here. He and I have been translating Lao-Tzu from Strauss' German version.[17] How good it is! I must make a book out of it. All the time I've been writing the article on religion. I think I've finished. Also wrote in rough an article about Maupassant.[18] That's all. Few thoughts and few notes. Here they are: [. . .]

(2) There are two sorts of minds: one mind is logical, egotistical, narrow and long, and the other is sensitive, sympathetic, broad and short.

(3) There are two methods of knowing the external world: one is the very crude and unavoidable method of knowing it through the five senses. We would be able to piece together a picture of the world that we know from this method of knowing, but the result would be chaos, affording us various sensations. The other method is to know yourself through love of yourself, and then to know other creatures through love of these creatures: to transfer oneself in thought into another person, animal, plant or even stone. By this method you will know from within and form a picture of the whole world as we know it. This method is what is called the poetic gift; it is in fact love. It is the restoration of the seemingly broken unity between creatures. You go out of yourself and enter into another person. And you can enter into everything. *Everything* – you can merge with God, with *Everything*. [. . .]

(15) It is actually their wives that husbands hate, as Lessing said: there is only one bad woman, and that is my wife.[19] Women themselves are to blame for this because of their deceitfulness and their play-acting. They all perform a comedy in front of others, but can't go on performing it behind the scenes in front of their husbands, and so a husband knows that all women are reasonable and good, but he knows that his wife alone is not. That's all. Other things that have happened are that the *Revue des Revues* printed a foul translation of *Non-action* and that distressed me, and also that for about three weeks now I've completely given up tea, coffee, sugar, and above all milk, and I only feel healthier for it. 10 o'clock at night.

Today is 22 December, and I've been in Moscow more than a month. And I haven't written my diary once. I'm depressed and disgusted. I can't get the better of myself. I want to do something heroic. I want to devote the rest of my life to the service of God. But He doesn't want me. Or doesn't want me to go the way I want to. And I grumble. This luxury. This sale of books.[20] This moral filth. This fuss and bother. I can't overcome my melancholy. The main thing is I want to suffer, I want to shout out the truth which is burning me.

During this time a lot has happened. First, the fact that I've been dragged here. Sonya was suffering and pining so much, it was obvious from her letters, that I came. Secondly, the fact that I wrote a foreword to Amiel. Thirdly – the hard and unending work on *Toulon*[21] which I can't give up. I've also written some fables[22] – haven't finished them. Some good letters from Lyova. A new joy. With the girls it's neither one thing nor the other. Masha – medicine. Tanya – painting.[23] The other day the musician Shor[24] was here. I had a good talk with him about music, and for the first time the true importance of art, even dramatic art, became clear to me. That will be the first of my thoughts during this time.

Other things that have happened during this time: Sabatier's book on St Francis.[25] It awakened memories in me of my former passion for the good, for the full, active, living fulfilment of the truth. Then Amiel, whom I re-read, and now Williams' new book *True Son of Liberty*.[26] Excellent. Made me want to write a drama. I sometimes think that I'm finished, and am no longer able to write. And I'm sad, as though I could go on writing on my death bed or even after death. It was wrong of me to have written in my notebook soon after arriving in Moscow that I had forgotten God. How terrible it is to forget God. And it happens imperceptibly. Things done for God are replaced by things done for people, for fame, and then for oneself, for one's own nasty self. And when you stumble over such nastiness, you want to pick yourself up again.

(1) The vagueness of the definition of art or music, for example, arises from the fact that we want to ascribe to them an importance corresponding to the uncharacteristically high position we have placed them in. Their importance is: (1) their help in transmitting one's feelings and thoughts by word; the summoning up of a mood appropriate to what is being transmitted, and (2) the fact that they are harmless, and even useful, in comparison with all other pleasures, and consequently are the most useful of all pleasures. [. . .]

(8) I look at women students with their books and notebooks running from lecture to lecture. Women painters, women musicians. They can do everything. And, like apes, they have copied everything from men. The one thing women can't do (girls still can) is to provide moral impetus. [. . .]

1894

[*24 January*] *Grinyovka*   Again a month and two days without writing my diary. *Today is 24 January, Grinyovka.* At Ilyusha's. He's abroad. This month has been hard. I've only been writing *Toulon*. I've made some progress. But generally it's poor. Things that have happened during this time: (1) About three weeks ago I wrote a letter to the Tsar about Khilkov and his children.[1] I've been waiting for a reply and rejoicing in my freedom. The letter wasn't good. There was more awareness of my own independence than love. (2) While working – fetching water – I over-trained myself in the frosty weather, and something happened to my chest. Since then I've felt weakness and the nearness of death much more keenly. (3) A stupid situation at the congress of naturalists, which I found very unpleasant.[2] (4) The weight of the empty, luxurious and false Moscow life and of the difficult or rather non-existent relations with my wife has been particularly burdensome to me. She couldn't and then didn't wish to understand, and this sin torments her – her and me, but chiefly her. The girls are good. They and Lyova bring me joy. Lyova's latest letter. He's angry with me for tolerating this ugly life which is ruining the children growing up. I feel I'm to blame. But I was to blame before. Now I can't do anything more. My daughter-in-law Sonya has been left alone, and we decided to visit her. Again the same friction and pain. [One and a half lines erased.]

Lord, help me. Teach me how to bear this cross. I am constantly preparing myself for the cross I know, for prison or the gallows, but this is a completely new and different one, and I don't know how to bear it. Its main characteristic and novelty is that I've been placed in this enforced, involuntary, crazy situation of being bound by my life to destroy the one thing I live for, am bound by this life to repel people from the truth, the elucidation of which is dearer to me than life. What a worthless creature I must be. I can't tear apart all these nasty cobwebs which hold me fast. And not because I haven't the strength, but because I'm morally unable to; I'm sorry for the spiders which spun these threads. No, the main thing is I'm no good: I've no true faith or love of God – the truth. But what then do I love if not God – the truth? [. . .] Thought during this time:

(1) One can't get rid of the illusion that acquaintance with new people brings new knowledge; that the more people there are the more intelligence and goodness there is, just as the more hot coals there are, the

more heat. With people it's not like that at all. They are always the same everywhere – in the past and in the present, in the country and in the town, one's own people and foreigners, Russians, Icelanders and Chinese. And the more there are of them together, the sooner these coals burn out, and the less intelligence and kindness there is in them. [. . .]

(5) We went to Ilyusha's. In the morning I saw peasants walking about in a snow-storm in bast shoes and driving about bringing fodder for Ilyusha's horses and cows. In the house an old cook and a little girl were working for him and his family. And I became so clearly and terribly aware of the universal enslavement of this unfortunate people. Both here and at Ilyusha's – Ilyusha who was recently a child, a boy – even at his house the same people, turned into slaves, are working for him. How can these chains be broken? [. . .]

Today is 9 February, Yasnaya Polyana   Still the same physical and mental weakness in me. The work on *Toulon* is going just as badly. A lot of mediocre endings, but no really forceful one. Perhaps it's because the beginning is so superficial. For me it continues to be serious and important. [. . .] Thought: [. . .]

(3) A clear idea occurred to me for a story in which I could present two men: the one a dissipated man who has gone astray, and had fallen into contempt merely out of kindness; the other – outwardly unblemished, honoured, and respected out of coldness, not love.[3] [. . .]

23 March, Moscow   And I'm alive. I haven't written in this exercise book for nearly six weeks. All that time I've been writing *Toulon* and finished it about five days ago and decided not to have it translated or printed.[4] And this was a relief to me. Posha has returned. Khilkova has been. The letter had no effect – or rather a harmful one.

An important and painful event – the relations that have developed between Tanya and   .[5] The most pure, good and friendly relations, but exclusive ones. It was a secret falling in love. She told me, and I spoke with him. They decided to discard all that was excessive and exclusive about it. He went away. This aroused in me a painful and nasty feeling – of humiliation for her. Tanya went to see Lyova in Paris, and it's a week since they returned. He is a good, moral person, but his illness oppresses him all the time. Relations with Sonya are good, but . . . I'm getting ready to go to Chertkov's. Busy again with the theory of art, apropos of the foreword to Maupassant. The foreword isn't a success either. There's a lot I want to write, but I don't seem to have the strength. I must try something purely literary. Thought during this time: [. . .]

(2) A work of art is something which infects people, and brings them all round to the same mood. Nothing exercises such a powerful influence in

subordinating all people to one and the same mood as the business of life and, ultimately, the whole life of mankind. If only enough people could understand the whole significance and force of that work of art which is their life! If only they could cherish it carefully enough, apply all their powers to prevent it from being spoiled by anything, and to bring it forth in all its beauty. But as it is, we cherish the reflection of life, while life itself we despise. But whether we wish it or not, life is a work of art, because it influences other people and is contemplated by them.

(3) Lose people?! We say: I have lost my wife, husband or father, when they are dead. But it's very, very often the case that we lose people who are not dead: we move so far apart from them that they are worse than dead. And conversely, it's often only when people are dying that we find them and draw near to them. [. . .]

21 April, Moscow   Haven't written my diary for almost a month. During this time I've been to Chertkov's with Masha. A splendid journey. Visited both the Chertkovs and the Rusanovs. The journey was poisoned by trying to unravel Tanya's difficult affair.[6] How weak they are, poor people! (Just as we are too.) I read their diaries. It was painful and also good. This has drawn me still closer to Tanya. She has impressed me by her attractiveness and grace. And she is such a small, insecure, weak, but nice young girl. Both of them have somehow let themselves go. However, we're all just the same. [. . .]

Lyova is getting better. We are just as close, but for some reason not in the same way as I am with the girls. Seryozha has been. I had a very difficult talk with him. He is angry with me and also with the girls because they are making progress and he isn't. [A few words erased.] He's self-assured, with an incommensurate denominator.[7] But on the other hand what joy it would be if he were to come to his senses! Ilyusha is a child, but one who deliberately persists in his crazy ways – unfortunately he still has the means to. With Sonya relations are good. Thought yesterday, as I observed her attitude towards Andryusha and Misha: what a wonderful mother and wife she is in a certain sense. I suppose Fet is right that everyone gets the wife he needs. Andryusha is jolly and kind, but stupid, imitative and vain. Misha I found very unpleasant because of his egoism, but things are better now.

All this time I've been writing a foreword to Maupassant which I think is quite clear now, and also a catechism which I was wrong to undertake before finishing what I'd started.[8] And then I also have the article on art which Chertkov game me[9] and which I approved, but I've not begun to revise it again. *Toulon* I've decided to send to the translators. Everyone approves of it. [. . .]

3 May, Yanaya Polyana Read an astonishingly naive article yesterday by a professor at Kazan University, Kapustin, about flavouring substances.[10] He wants to show that everything that people use – sugar, wine, tobacco, even opium – is necessary in a physiological sense. This stupid, naive article was highly useful to me; it showed me clearly what the hypocrites of science suppose the business of science to be. Not what it ought to be – a definition of what should be – but a description of *what is*. A complete perversion of science has taken place since the time *experimental* science began, i.e. science which describes what is, and therefore *not science*, because one way or another we all know what is, and nobody needs a description of it. People drink wine and smoke tobacco, and science sets itself the task of justifying the use of wine and tobacco physiologically. People kill each other, and science sets itself the task of justifying it historically. People deceive each other, and for the sake of a small number deprive all other people of land or the implements of labour, and science justifies it economically. People believe in nonsense, and teleological science justifies it.

The task of science ought to be the knowledge of what should be, and not what is. But present-day science, on the contrary, sets itself the main task of diverting people's atttention from what should be, and directing it to what is, and what nobody therefore needs.

Today is 15 May, Yasnaya Polyana. I've been unwell for a whole week or more. It began, I think, on the day when I was upset by Sonya's dismal escapade over Chertkov.[11] It's all understandable, but it was very painful; the more so because I've become unaccustomed to it, and was glad of my restored – even newly established – good, strong, loving feeling for her. I was afraid it would be destroyed. But no, the thing blew over, and the same feeling has been restored. [. . .] The American Crosby has been.[12] I don't know how to define him. Kenworthy's books are good.[13] I wrote him a foolish letter, and wrote many other letters too. [. . .]

Today is 2 June, Yasnaya Polyana [. . .] Still writing the Catechism; still weak. Chertkov came. We got on well. Thought little during this time. One thing: (1) Women are people with sexual organs over their hearts.

14 June, Yasnaya Polyana Wrote an exposition of Henry George's project.[14] [. . .] In the morning I went mushrooming and bathed. Decided to stop my writing. Read through all the works of fiction which I've begun. They're all bad. If I'm going to write, I'll have to start everything again, more truthfully, without invention. [. . .]

(2) Looked at the wonderful sunset as I walked towards Ovsyannikovo. A gap in the heaped up clouds, and through it, like an unevenly shaped piece

of coal, the sun. And all that above the woods and the rye. I felt joyful. And I thought: no, this world is not a joke, not just a vale of trial and tribulation and a transition to a better, everlasting world, but is itself an everlasting world which is beautiful and joyful, and which we not only can, but must, make more beautiful and joyful for those living with us, and those who will live in it after us.

Today is 25 June, Yasnaya Polyana [. . .] Coldness with Lyova, which pains me. He's constantly preoccupied with his illness, looking into himself and therefore seeing nothing and not living.

I've been depressed during this time by the dissipation of the young boys, Andryusha and Misha, especially Andryusha. Misha is still unharmed for his years, but with spoiling and the lack of moral authority the same thing will happen to him. About a week ago he (Andryusha) was out dancing till one o'clock; I said to him that he would be another Bibikov, and that it would be better for him to leave home and live in the village; yesterday, when there wasn't any dancing, it was just the same: he went off to the village and wasn't home before one. I was very worried about him, but overcame my personal annoyance, and when he came back I went out and told him that he mustn't think we were asleep, but should know we were waiting for him and were worried. I wanted to speak gently to him. Our children's situation is very bad; there isn't any moral authority. Sonya deliberately destroys mine, and in its place puts her own comic demands for propriety, which it's easy for them to meet. I'm sorry both for them and for her. It's her I've been particularly sorry for recently. She sees that everything she was doing was wrong and had led to no good. But to confess that she was wrong not to have followed me is almost impossible for her. The remorse would be too terrible.

I'm continuing to think about the exposition of my teaching, and it seems quite clear to me, but I still can't get on with the writing. [. . .]

26 June, Yasnaya Polyana [. . .] Yesterday I spoke to Andryusha and told him everything he had done wrong. I didn't speak angrily, but not lovingly either, not as I should have done. He remained silent. A perfect example of the fact that *only one thing is needful*: the only thing needful is to summon up love for him in myself, and in the degree to which I achieve this, I have a good influence on him too. [. . .]

Walked to the sand pits. The peasants there were climbing into the pits and risking their lives as they worked. I said at dinner that we must have a proper quarry made. Sonya said at first that she wouldn't give the money. There was a moment's anger. You want to offer the other cheek when somebody hits you on one, but when a real opportunity occurs, as now, you don't want to offer it, but to withdraw it. After dinner I went for a walk with Vyacheslav and decided to have a quarry made. [. . .] A talk with Lyova in the evening. He reproached me for not believing much in his illness. Could have been gentler and kinder with him.

Today is 27 June, Yasnaya Polyana Got up in the morning with *bad* thoughts, wrote nothing. Read Schopenhauer.[15] *Karma* for him exists only in the sense of the preparation in a former life of a person's character for this life, and not in the sense of a struggle in this life between light and darkness. He denies this and is inconsistent.

A talk with Vladimir Fyodorovich about criticism.[16] Recalled Kolechka's famous saying that criticism is when the foolish talk about the clever. [. . .]

6 July, Yasnaya Polyana I've been working these last days haymaking. I'm well. Only I had a pain in the liver yesterday from the heat. [. . .] I wrote a letter to Kenworthy. Added to it yesterday. Miss Welsh is translating it.[17] *Toulon* has come out in English.[18]

Thought: [. . .]

(2) 3 July. Before dinner. A bright, warm day. Near the house, in the shadow of the fence, flies are buzzing continually above the manure, and out there in the steppe the burning hot air shimmers and sparkles in the sun.

(3) Recalled my own depravity and corruption. I was corrupted by my early dissipation, by luxury, gluttony and idleness. Had it not been for that, I would now, at the age of sixty-five, be young and fresh. But surely this corruption hasn't been in vain. All my moral demands have grown out of this corruption. [. . .]

8 July [. . .] In the evening an American Jew came.[19] It's difficult to love a Jew. I must try hard. 7. I worked, carted hay, and felt terribly depressed. At 3 Turner came.[20] Talked to him about the translation and the foreword. Revised the letter to Kenworthy and sent it off. [. . .]

19 July, Yasnaya Polyana Yesterday, the 18th. Did no writing. Still the same weakness. Even worse today. And my back hurts. Yesterday morning some petitioners – then a lady, Przewalska[21] – a completely useless creature. She doesn't need me, and I don't need her. Wrote a little this morning. The Dietrichs are tedious. I keep remembering that I live in the sight of God, but my life is very feeble. A mere trickle. If only it were pure. Made no notes. It's now nearly 12. I've missed out a day. Went with Kasatkin to Gill's works in the morning.[22] Not much of interest. Very tired. In the evening I went to Chertkov's. Yesterday went for a bathe. Very weak. Strakhov has read all the things I've begun, and encourages me to continue. Went with Sonya to Chertkov's. On the way I talked a bit about the meaning of life. She and I are talking a bit better. In the evening Andryusha disappeared again to the village. A difficult conversation with Sonya. He, Andryusha, had been telling her that the peasants in the hayfield had told him that Timofey was my son.[23] I'm sorry for the children. They have no authority under whose shelter they can grow up and be strong. Wrote quite a lot yesterday. But badly.

9 August [. . .] During this time MacGahan and her son visited me and brought some books from Henry George.[24] Read *A Perplexed Philosopher* again. Excellent. Became very vividly aware again of the sin of owning land. It's astonishing that people don't see it. How necessary to write about this – to write a new *Uncle Tom's Cabin.* [. . .]

Thought during this time: (1) something unimportant: for harmony between a husband and wife, it's necessary, if their views of the world and life don't coincide, for the one who has thought less about it to give way to the one who has thought more. How happy I would be to give way to Sonya, but it's just as impossible as it is for a goose to go back into its egg. She ought to give way, but she doesn't want to – she has no understanding, no humility and no love. [. . .]

Today is 27 August, Yasnaya Polyana [. . .] Yesterday Tanya went to Ovsyannikovo to make an agreement with the peasants.[25] [. . .]

28 August, Yasnaya Polyana [. . .] Talked with Tanya. She just wants to get rid of her property. I'll try to arrange it for her in the best possible way. Read *Labour Prophet* in the evening.[26] [. . .]

Today is 30 August, Yasnaya Polyana Made no notes yesterday. In the morning I reprimanded the boys for their dissoluteness. Wrote little, or hardly anything. I'm still turning round on the same spot. Felled timber with a peasant from Kolpna. In the evening I went to Ovsyannikovo, but didn't talk to the peasants. They were drunk. Thought this morning: [. . .]

Novels end with the hero and heroine getting married. They should begin with that and end with them getting unmarried, i.e. becoming free. Otherwise to describe people's lives in such a way as to break off the description with marriage is just the same as describing a person's journey and breaking off the description at the point where the traveller falls into the hands of robbers.

Today is 6 September, Yasnaya Polyana It's now gone 4 in the afternoon. In the morning I worked on the Catechism. I'm afraid to say that I'm making progress because it's so imperceptible, but still I'm not dissatisfied, and every day there is something new and it's all becoming clearer. In the morning I thought up in bed after a bad night a very vivid story about a master and his man.[27] After breakfast I sawed up some oak trees with Andriyan.

Yesterday, the 5th, I went to Ovsyannikovo in the evening and concluded things very satisfactorily with the peasants. They will pay 425 roubles each for communal necessities. I explained to them the whole meaning of the business.[28] [. . .]

Missed out some days. *Today is 10 September, Yasnaya Polyana.* [. . .] Yesterday morning when I woke up I thought about a reply to the Englishman about anarchism, how to manage without a government.[29]

Read Guyard's excellent book.[30] He says: the aim of life is the good, the means towards self-improvement, and the instrument is love. Thought: to the question how to manage without a state, without law courts, an army, etc., no answer can be given because it is badly put. The question is not what form the state should have – the present one or a new one. Neither I nor any of us is in a position to solve that question. But I am competent to solve – and it isn't a matter of choice but of inevitability – the question how I should act in the dilemma with which I am constantly faced: whether to subordinate my conscience to the things that are going on around me, to declare my solidarity with a government which hangs people who have gone astray, drives soldiers to murder, corrupts the people with opium and vodka, etc., or subordinate my actions to my conscience, i.e. not take part in a government whose actions are contrary to my feelings. What will come of this, what state there will be, I don't know at all, and neither want to nor can know. I only know that nothing bad can come from following my innate superior qualities of reason and love, or reasonable love; just as nothing bad can come from a bee following its innate superior instinct and flying out from its hive with the swarm, apparently to its destruction. But I repeat, I won't and can't judge about this. [. . .]

24 September, Yasnaya Polyana Work went well this morning too. Tanya copied everything out for me. A strange thing; as soon as I think about Ovsyannikovo and of how Tanya gave it to the peasants, I have an unpleasant, uncomfortable feeling. Between 1 and 2 I walked to Kozlovka with a spade and repaired the road. Very tired. Came home and we waited for Sonya, but she didn't come; she'll be here tomorrow. I look forward to her coming with particular impatience. If only I could retain when she is here the same good feelings I have for her when she isn't here.

Thought a lot about what I wrote to Tsetsiliya Vladimirovna.[31] Talked about it with Marya Alexandrovna. This is where the true emancipation of women lies – in not considering any work to be women's work, the sort which one is ashamed to touch, in helping them with all one's strength just because they are physically weaker, and in taking from them all the work which it is possible to take upon oneself. Similarly with education too – just because they will probably bear children and so have less leisure, for that very reason we should organize schools for them which are not worse, but better than men's, so that they can build up their strength and knowledge in advance. And they are capable of doing so. I thought about my churlish and egotistical attitude to my wife in this respect. I acted like everybody else, i.e. badly and cruelly. I gave her all the hard work, the so-called women's work, to do, and went out hunting myself. I was glad to acknowledge my guilt.

Thought again: I saw Vaksa the dog, deformed, with one leg missing, and I wanted to chase him away, but then I felt ashamed. He's sick, ugly, deformed – that's why people want to chase him out. But beauty attracts, ugliness repels. What does this mean? Does it mean that one should seek beauty and shun ugliness? No. It means that one should seek that which has beauty as its consequence, and shun that which has ugliness as its consequence: seek the good, seek to help and serve all creatures and human beings, and shun that which does harm to other creatures and human beings. And the consequence will be beauty. If all people are good, everything will be beautiful. Ugliness is an indication of sin, beauty an indication of sinlessness – nature, children. For this reason it is false to make beauty the aim of art.

Masha left in a bad mood. Surely she isn't jealous of Tanya, and the Ovsyannikovo business – God forbid. I must write to her.

Today is 4 October, Yasnaya Polyana   I'm going backwards. It's now getting on for 12 o'clock at night. Sat upstairs with my son Seryozha and – what joy – I didn't have the slightest unkind feeling for him as before, but, on the contrary, a glimmer of love. Love – I thank Thee, father of love. Today is Tanya's birthday. She's thirty. She's sad, quiet and, I think, restless at heart. God help her. [. . .]

Today is 8 October, Yasnaya Polyana   Posha and Strakhov[32] came today. There had been a search at Strakhov's and they had explained to him that Tolstoy was a different person now and dangerous. I didn't want to be persecuted, they alleged. And I felt ashamed of myself because of it. Things had been very well at home with Sonya. But the whole day today, the evening as well, she tried once more to make me glad to be persecuted. The whole day: first stolen apple trees and prison for the woman, then condemnation of what is dear to me, then joy that Novosyolov has been converted to Orthodoxy, then talk about money for *The Fruits of*

Enlightenment.[33] I felt weaker, and my little flame of love which had lit up my life so joyfully began to grow dim. I mustn't forget that life is not to do with the works of this world, but only with this light. And I think I've remembered. [. . .]

9 October   The illness and probably early death of the Tsar moves me very much. I'm very sorry. [. . .]

Today is 13 October, Yasnaya Polyana   [. . .] Yesterday morning Masha and Vera Severtseva arrived. Masha is well and at peace. Lyova arouses pity, he and the Tsar. Chopped wood with Posha. In the evening I finished reading 'Goethe's friendship with Schiller'.[34] Thought a lot while reading both about aesthetics and about my own drama. I feel like writing. Perhaps it's God's will too. [. . .]

Thought during this time:

(1) People are now obsessed with the theory of art – one person proposing beauty as its ideal, another usefulness, a third play. The whole confusion arises from the fact that people want to continue to consider as an ideal something that has outlived its time and ceased to be one. Such is the case with usefulness and beauty. Art is the ability to depict what ought to be, what all people ought to strive towards, what gives people the greatest good. This can only be depicted by images. Mankind has already outlived two such ideals and is now living for the third. First of all it was usefulness: everything useful was a work of art, or so it was considered; then the beautiful; and now the good, the moral. The confusion arises from the fact that people want to set up what is outlived as an ideal again, as though wanting to make adults play with dolls or hobby-horses. This needs to be said clearly and concisely. [. . .]

21 October   [. . .] Some three days ago I read through my diary for 1884, and was disgusted with myself for my unkindness and the cruelty of my opinions about Sonya and Seryozha. Let them know that I take back all the unkind things I wrote about them. Sonya I value and love more and more. Seryozha I understand, and have no other feeling for him except love. [. . .]

Thought: (1) I recalled my young years and my relations with women. If a person wants to deprive himself of any possibility of free mental activity and free relations with people, he ought to do what I used to do: eat meat, drink coffee, tea, and wine, not work, but do gymnastics and read books which arouse passions. All my youth I was like an overfed, wild foal, it's strange to recall it. [. . .]

Today is the 26th   Haven't written my diary for three days. One thing that happened during this time was that I wrote to Popov, asking him to stop corresponding with Tanya. She gave in. She is very good. [. . .]

Today Pavel the cobbler[35] died. He kept asking his wife: 'Haven't they come for me?' and kept listening at the windows. During the night he cried: 'They're coming. Now.' And died. Only old men like me notice this brief, transitory nature of life. It's so clear, when people disappear one after another round about you. You're only surprised that you yourself still cling on. And is it worth it (if from no other point of view), when one is here for such a short interval of time, to tell lies, spread confusion and do foolish things in that short interval? It's like an actor who has only one short scene, who has prepared for that scene for a long time and is dressed and made up, and then suddenly goes on to the stage, forgets his lines, disgraces himself and ruins the whole play. [. . .]

Today is 4 November, Yasnaya Polyana [. . .] Seryozha came today. I got on well with him. He feels again that I'm going to meet him, and he's drawing closer. [. . .] There's nothing more for me to do. Tanya complains that her life – she is thirty – has passed uselessly by, and that she has ruined things for herself. It's good that she thinks so. Masha is being sent abroad. Tomorrow.

10 November Haven't written my diary for five days. *Today is 10 November, Moscow.* Nothing special in my outer life has happened during this time. We moved to Moscow, Bulygin came to see us, there was the same folly and baseness on the occasion of the death of the old Tsar and the accession of the new. I'm depressed by the multitude of people in Moscow. Internally, it's good that work seems to be progressing and becoming clearer, but it's bad that I no longer have that fresh awareness of the presence of God and that loving feeling which I had before. I feel that in my relations with Sonya and Lyova. [. . .]

Had a touching letter from a young man from Petersburg asking 'why live?'[36] I wrote to him yesterday.

Today is 20 November, Moscow [. . .] Thought a lot during this time. [. . .]
(6) To say that reason can lead us astray, that we oughtn't to trust it, that it's pride, is just the same as saying that a workman working in a pit with a lamp might get lost if he is guided by the light of his lamp, that he oughtn't to trust its light, that it's pride. But what is he to trust if that is his only light? I know that my reason is limited and weak in comparison with God's reason, and that I can't be aware of everything, but still reason is reason and my only guide, and a guide given by God and like Him. If a miner's lamp is not the sun, still it is a light, and a light like the sun and one that originates from it. [. . .]

Today is 25 December, evening   Haven't written my diary for more than a month. Among things that have happened during this time was the visit from the students; I wrote letters for them to Petersburg.[37] Another sad clash with Lyova. [. . .]

Today is 31 December   Five days have passed. All that time I've been writing the story *Master and Man*. I don't know whether it's good. It's pretty worthless. Chertkov has been. An unpleasant clash arose over a photograph. As always, Sonya acted decisively, but thoughtlessly and badly.[38] [. . .]

(2) Lyova said that he had a long talk with Vanya Rayevsky about the fact that young people of our time are sickly and suffer nervous illness because there is no field of activity for them, and the two of them said many other very clever things. But it all amounts to the *religion of the chamber pot*, as grandfather used to say – to not making other people serve you in the very basic, simple things. [. . .]

1895–1902

MUCH OF TOLSTOY'S ENERGY in the last years of the nineteenth century was concentrated on his vigorous campaign on behalf of the Dukhobors, victims of religious persecution in the south of Russia, many of whom were eventually resettled in Canada thanks largely to his efforts and the financial proceeds of *Father Sergey* and *Resurrection*. *Father Sergey* is often linked with *The Devil* and *The Kreutzer Sonata* because of their common theme of sexual passion and its evil potential, although Tolstoy was concerned to show that the struggle against pride and worldly fame was even more difficult to wage than the struggle against lust. His wide-ranging, if artistically flawed, major novel *Resurrection* was in effect a vast synthesis of all his social, political and religious ideas. To the same period belong the short story *Master and Man* with its theme of an eleventh-hour act of unselfishness in the face of death, and the stimulating, irritating and iconoclastic treatise *What is Art?* All these works were written when Tolstoy was approaching seventy, and they were written against a background of an unsettled family life, complicated by his absurd jealousy of his wife's platonic friendship with the composer Taneyev, his puritanical disapproval of his son's disorderly behaviour and his anxiety over his daughters' matrimonial intentions.

In his seventieth year Tolstoy was busy organizing aid for the starving peasants of the Tula province. Three years later he was excommunicated from the Orthodox Church for his heretical beliefs and writings, and retaliated with *A Reply to the Holy Synod's Edict*. Shortly afterwards he became seriously ill, and was persuaded to move to the Black Sea coast of the Crimea to the luxurious house of the wealthy Countess Panina near Yalta, where he and his wife lived for nearly a year until he was well enough to return to Yasnaya Polyana in the summer of 1902. Despite his serious illness he continued to work as and when he could, his most important essay being *What is Religion and What is its Essential Nature?* While convalescing in the Crimea he also wrote a long letter to Nicholas II appealing to him among other things to abolish private ownership of land. Not surprisingly there was no reply. Despite his advancing years and erratic health, Tolstoy's energy remained formidable. If his enthusiasm for bicycling and tennis waned, he continued to ride and walk long distances and he kept up an extensive correspondence. He published no more works of fiction in his lifetime, but his posthumous publications show that his creative energy was by no means exhausted. In 1902 he was still working on his late masterpiece *Hadji Murat* (eventually finished, but not published, in 1904), the theme of which took him back to his days as a soldier in the Caucasus, and seemed to accord ill with his belief in the doctrine of non-resistance to evil by force. He also returned intermittently to his drama *The Light Shineth in Darkness*, which Shaw believed was his greatest play, and in which Tolstoy appeared to be mocking all his most cherished ideas and to be hinting at the disastrous results likely to follow from becoming a 'Tolstoyan'!

1895

3 January, Nikolskoye   The Olsufyevs'.[1] We set off as planned on the 1st. I worked on *Master and Man* till the last hour. It's now respectable artistically, but still weak in content. The business about the photograph is very sad. They are all offended. I wrote a letter to Chertkov.[2] Even before that I felt unwell, and I was unwell and weak when I set off. We arrived in good shape. The next day and today I did nothing – read, walked and slept. [. . .]

Today is 6 January, Nikolskoye   I'm quite well and have begun work again on *The Catechism*: yesterday and today. It interests me very much and is very near to my heart, but I still can't find the right form and am dissatisfied. Read my story[3] the day before yesterday evening. It's not good. Both lack character. Now I know what to do. [. . .]

It's now 6 o'clock in the evening. I'll go for a walk and also see the Christmas tree. Went to the hospital today and was present at an operation.

29 January, Moscow   [. . .] An important event which, I'm afraid, won't be without consequence for me is the Tsar's audacious speech.[4] We went to Shakovskoy's meeting. We shouldn't have done so. It's all stupid, and it's obvious that an organization paralyses the powers of individual people. [. . .]

Today is 7 February, 11 o'clock in the morning, Moscow   [. . .] More than a week has passed. During this time I wrote a short foreword to the biography of Drozhzhin and continued revising my story. An unfortunate story. It was the cause of a terrible storm on Sonya's part that broke out yesterday. She was unwell, weak and exhausted after dear Vanechka's illness, and I've been unwell these last few days. It began with her beginning to copy out the proofs. When I asked why . . . [A page of the diary has been torn out here.][5] [. . .]

Thought during this time: [. . .]

(4) The situation of the majority of people educated in true brotherly love and now oppressed by the deceit and cunning of those who wield power and who force this majority to ruin their own lives – this situation is terrible and seems to offer no way out. Only two ways out present

themselves and both are barred: one is to break violence by violence, terror, dynamite bombs and daggers as our nihilists and anarchists did, to smash the conspiracy of governments against peoples, without our participation; the other is to enter into agreement with the government, make concessions to it and, by taking part in it, gradually unravel the net which holds the people fast and free it. Both ways out are barred. [. . .]

What then remains? You can't break violence by violence – you increase reaction; nor can you join the ranks of government – you become an instrument of government. Only one thing remains: to fight the government with weapons of thought, word and way of life, not making concessions to it, not joining its ranks, not increasing its power oneself. That's the one thing necessary, and it will probably be successful. And this is what God wants and this is what Christ taught.

(5) Looking at what goes on in all assemblies, at what goes on in society with its conventional proprieties and entertainments, I was struck very vividly by the thought which, I think, had never occurred to me before, that only evil is done by a group, or crowd or assembly. Good is done only by each individual person separately. [. . .]

15 February   God has helped me; helped me in that He has manifested Himself in me, though weakly, through love – love for those who do us evil, i.e. the only true love. And once this feeling had manifested itself, it first of all overwhelmed and inflamed me, and then those near to me as well, and everything disappeared, i.e. the suffering disappeared.

The following days things got worse. She was decidedly close to madness and to suicide. The children followed her on foot and by vehicle, and brought her back home. She was suffering terribly. It was the devil of jealousy, insane, groundless jealousy. I had only to love her again for me to understand her motives, and having understood her motives, it wasn't a question of forgiving her, but there being nothing to forgive. Sent the story to the *Northern Herald*, and it's being printed here by her and also in *The Intermediary*.[6] I finished three fables and sent them off.[7]

Today, I think, is 21 February, Moscow   These five days I've been revising the fables, revising *Master and Man*, and thinking about – I can't say writing – the *Catechism*. Sonya's health is fully restored. Snegiryov came and explained that it was the menopause which comes with old age. How good to grow old and free.

An event which astonished me very much during this time was the drunkenness and rowdyism of the Petersburg students.[8] It's terrible. This is what they have reduced the young to – by they, I mean not only the government, but also the liberals and revolutionaries, the ringleaders with no basis. Another thing: Škarvan's refusal to serve, the demand by

Alyokhin and others in Nalchik to pay allegiance without swearing an oath and Posha's fine all seem to me to be the start of a direct conflict with the government.[9] I very much want to write about this, and several times have had clear ideas about it. Clear ideas how to describe the lies amid which we live and what supports them, and to include at the same time that simple philosophy which I express in the *Catechism*.

Thought: [. . .] (4) Further clarified my ideas during this time in a conversation with the young Goryushin, a friend of Pavel Petrovich,[10] about a subject I never cease to think about – the state: we have reached the point where a merely good and reasonable man cannot take part in the affairs of state, i.e. cannot be in sympathy with it – I'm not speaking about our own Russia, but cannot be in sympathy in England with the ownership of land and exploitation by factory owners and capitalists, or with the extermination of peoples in Africa, the preparations for wars and wars themselves. And the firm ground on which a man says: 'I don't know what the state is or how it works, and I don't want to know, but I do know that I can't live contrary to my conscience' – this point of view is unshakeable, and the people of our time must adopt it in order to further the progress of life. [. . .]

It's now 12 o'clock. I'm going to send the proofs to Petersburg, and Sonya is very agitated. Poor woman. I'm sorry for her and love her, the more so now that I know about her illness.

Yesterday Ogranovich helped me to be more fair towards Lyova.[11] He explained to me that it's a latent form of malaria. And I began to understand his condition and to feel sorry for him, but I still can't summon up any vital feeling of love for him.

Today is the 26th night-time, Moscow   We've buried Vanechka.[12] A terrible – no, not a terrible, but a great spiritual event. I thank Thee, Father. I thank Thee.

Today is 12 March, Moscow   So much has been felt, thought and lived through during this time that I don't know what to write. The death of Vanechka was for me, like the death of Nikolenka – no, to a far greater degree – a manifestation of God, a drawing of me towards Him. And so not only can I not say that it was a sad, painful event but I can say outright that it was a joyful one – not joyful, that's a bad word – but a merciful event, coming from God, disentangling the lies of life, and bringing me closer to Him.

Sonya can't see it that way. For her the pain – almost physical – of separation conceals the spiritual importance of the event. But she astonished me. The pain of separation immediately released her from all that was darkening her soul. It was as if doors had been thrown open and the divine essence of love which constitutes our soul had been uncovered.

She astonished me during the first days by her amazing power of love: everything that in any way destroyed love, that was a condemnation of anyone or anything, even a gesture of ill-will – all this offended her, made her suffer and caused a painful contraction of the newly exposed shoot of love. But time passes, and that shoot is hidden once more, and her suffering ceases to find satisfaction, *vent* [relief], in universal love, and is becoming unrelievedly painful. She suffers particularly because the object of her love has gone from her, and she thinks that her happiness was in that object and not in the love itself. She can't separate the one from the other, she can't take a religious view of life in general or of her own. She can't clearly understand and feel that there are only two alternatives: either there is death, which hangs over all of us, has power over us and can separate us and deprive us of the happiness of love, or else there is no death, but only a series of changes which happen to all of us, among which one of the most important is death, and that these changes come over all of us like waves, in different combinations, some earlier, others later.

I try to help her, but I can see that I haven't helped her so far. But I love her, and to be with her is both painful and good for me. She is still weak physically: no periods for two months, and she sometimes thinks she is pregnant. Poor dear Tanya is also very weak. We are all very close to one another, as D.[13] put it very well: just as when one leaf falls, the others soon bunch closer together. I feel very weak physically and can't write anything. Worked a bit on the *Catechism*. But only in thought. Wrote a letter to Schmitt with a programme for an international *Intermediary*.[14] During this time *Master and Man* came out, and I hear praises on all sides and I don't like it, but despite that, I feel a petty, vain satisfaction.

Felt like writing something literary today. Tried to remember what things of mine were unfinished. It would be good to finish them all, namely:

(1) Koni's story, (2) *Who is Right?*, (3) *Father Sergey*, (4) *The Devil in Hell*, (5) *The Coupon*, (6) *Notes of a Mother*, (7) *Alexander I*, (8) the drama, (9) The colonists and the Bashkirs.[15] At the same time I must finish the Catechism. And now having planned all this – enough work for about eight years at least – I may die tomorrow. And that's good.

Thought during this time: [. . .]

(3) The death of children from an objective point of view: nature tried to give forth her best, and when she sees the world isn't ready for them, she takes them back again. But she has to try, in order to advance. It's an experiment. And like swallows which fly in too early, they die of cold. But they must fly in all the same. So with Vanechka. But this is an objective, foolish argument. A sensible argument is that he did the work of God; the establishment of the kingdom of God through the increase of love – more so than many people who lived for half a century and more.

(4) Sonya often said: 'He saved me from evil. Mine is a bad and harsh nature; he softened it by his love, and brought me closer to God.' As if he isn't doing so now! [. . .]

(6) Yes, one must always live as though a favourite child is dying in a room nearby. He is always dying. And I am always dying. [. . .]

(8) A few days after Vanechka's death when love began to grow weaker within me (what God gave me through Vanechka's life and death will never be destroyed), I thought that it would be good to sustain that love in myself by seeing all people as children – imagining them as they were at the age of seven. I can do that. And it's good. [. . .]

(11) Read a bad article by Solovyov against non-resistance.[16] Every practical moral injunction contains the possibility of contradicting that injunction by another one deriving from the same principle. Abstinence: well, should we stop eating, and become incapable of serving mankind? Don't kill animals: well, should we let them eat each other? Don't drink alcohol. Well, should we not take communion, or use alcohol for medicinal purposes? Don't resist evil by violence. Well, should we let a man kill himself and others?

Trying to look for these contradictions only shows that a person who spends his time at it doesn't want to follow the moral rule. It's always the same story: because of one person who needs alcohol for medicinal purposes, drunkenness is not resisted. Because of one imaginary aggressor, people kill, execute and imprison. [. . .]

Today is the 18th   Morning. Five days have passed. I've done nothing. In the mornings I've thought about the *Catechism*. Once I wrote a little more of *Father Sergey*, but it wasn't good. Masha has gone to Ilya's. Sonya is moving into a new stage of life, with painful suffering. Help her, Lord. All this time I've had headaches and felt great weakness. In the evenings there have been many visitors. And they depress me very much. [. . .]

Today is 27 March, Moscow   [. . .] With Seryozha I feel well and at ease. And I don't remember any unkind feeling towards anyone in all this time. Since I don't hear all the criticisms, but only the praise for *Master and Man*, I have the impression of a lot of fuss, and remember the anecdote about the preacher who stopped at a burst of applause which drowned a phrase of his and asked: 'Did I say something stupid?' I feel the same and know I've done something stupid: spending time on the artistic revision of a shallow story. The idea itself is unclear and laboured – not simple. The story is bad. And I would like to write an anonymous criticism of it if I had the time and it didn't mean bothering about something that isn't worth it.

During this time I've visited Izyumchenko in prison and Khokhlov in hospital.[17] Izyumchenko is very simple and cheerful. Khokhlov is very pitiable. I'd also like to write about the cruelty of this form of violence. Sonya is still suffering and can't raise herself to a religious height. Probably she needs this suffering, and it's doing its work within her. I'm sorry for her. But I believe it's necessary – necessary in order to feel the action of the hand of God, to recognize it and to love it. I was thinking yesterday about Leskov's will,[18] and thought I ought to write a similar one. I keep putting it off as though it were still far away, but whatever I do it's close at hand. It's good and necessary, not only because it saves one's nearest and dearest from doubts and uncertainties about what to do with the body, but also because a voice from beyond the grave is especially audible. And if one has anything to say to one's nearest and dearest, and to anybody else, it's good to say it in these first moments. *My will would be roughly as follows. Until I write another one it will be entirely as follows.*[19]

(1) Bury me in the place where I die, in the cheapest cemetery if it should be in town, and in the cheapest grave – as paupers are buried. Lay no flowers or wreaths, and make no speeches. If possible, bury me without a priest and a burial service. But if that should be unpleasant for those who bury me, let them do so in the usual manner with a burial service, but as cheaply and simply as possible.

(2) Do not announce my death in the newspapers and do not write any obituaries.

(3) Give all my papers to be looked through and sorted out to my wife, V. G. Chertkov, Strakhov (and my daughters Tanya and Masha) (what is crossed out I crossed out myself. My daughters need not bother about this), – to those of these people who are still alive. My sons I exclude from this commission, not because I have not loved them (I have loved them more and more in recent times, thank God), and I know that they love me, but they are not fully aware of my thoughts, have not followed their course, and might have their own particular views about things, as a result of which they might keep what ought not to be kept, and throw out what ought to be kept. The diaries of my former bachelor life I ask you to destroy, after selecting from them what is worth it, and in the diaries of my married life I ask you to destroy everything which, if published, might be unpleasant for anybody. Chertkov has promised to do this for me while I am still alive. And given his great love for me which I have not deserved and his great moral sensitiveness, I am sure that he will do it very well. The diaries of my bachelor life I ask you to destroy, not because I would like to conceal from people my own bad life – my life was the usual life of unprincipled young men, worthless from the point of view of the world – but because these diaries, in which I only wrote down what tormented me through the awareness of my sins, produce a falsely one-sided impression and are . . .

But no, let my diaries stay as they are. At least they will show that despite all the triviality and worthlessness of my youth, I was still not abandoned by God, and, if only in my old age, began to understand Him a little and love Him.

Of my other papers, I ask those who will be sorting them out not to print everything, but only what might be useful to people.

I write all this, not because I ascribe great, or indeed any, importance to my papers, but because I know in advance that in the early days after my death my works will be printed and discussed, and importance will be ascribed to them. If that is the case, then let my writings not cause any harm to people.

(4) The right to publish my earlier works: the ten volumes and the *Primers* I ask my heirs to make over to the public, i.e. to renounce copyright. But I only ask this, and I don't will it. If you do it, it will be good. It will be good for you too. If you don't do it, that's your own affair. That means you were not able to do it. The fact that my works have been sold these last ten years has been the most depressing thing of my life.

(5) Furthermore, and in particular, I ask all people near and far not to praise me. (I know they will do so because they have done so in my lifetime in the most unseemly way), but if they want to study my writings, let them look carefully at those passages in them in which I know the power of God spoke through me, and make use of them for their own lives. There have been times when I felt I was becoming the bearer of God's will. I have often been so impure, so full of personal passions, that the light of this truth has been obscured by my own darkness, but nevertheless this truth has sometimes passed through me, and these have been the happiest moments of my life. God grant that these truths should not have been defiled in passing through me, and that people might feed on them, despite the superficial and impure form which I have given to them.

In this alone lies the importance of my writings. And so I can only be reproved for them, not praised at all. That is all. [. . .]

Today is 6 April, Moscow [. . .] I'm very oppressed by this bad, idle, luxurious town life. I think I'm being useful to Sonya in her weakness. But it's unforgivable that I'm not writing, if I can't do anything else apart from that. [. . .]

Thought during this time. [. . .]

(6) A mother suffers over the loss of a child and can't be comforted. And she can't be comforted until she understands that her life is not in the vessel which is broken, but in the contents which spilled over and lost their shape, but have not vanished. [. . .]

(13) The greatest number of sufferings which arise from the association of men and women are due to the complete misunderstanding of one sex by the other. Few men understand what children mean to women, what

place they occupy in their lives, and even fewer women understand what duty to society, or to religion, means to men. [. . .]

10 April, Moscow All this time – all Easter Week – I continue to be unusually weak: I'm doing nothing and thinking little: only rarely do islands of thought suddenly emerge from the darkness and mist, and probably for that reason they seem particularly important. Sonya is still ill. She had almost recovered and unfortunately had started to adopt her former irritable and domineering tone – I was so sorry to see the loss of that loving mood which was apparent after Vanechka's death – but the day before yesterday she began to have a headache and a temperature again, though not a high one, and acute apathy and weakness. Help me, Father, to do and feel what I should.

Yesterday I walked along the streets and looked at people's faces: there were few which were not disfigured by alcohol, nicotine or syphilis. Their feebleness is terribly pitiful and offensive, when the road to salvation is so clear. Sheep jump into the water and you stand and wave them back, but they go on jumping in, and you get the impression they are doing what they should be doing, and you are getting in their way. I'm terribly tempted to write about the relationship of society to the Tsar,[20] explaining it by the false attitude towards what is old, but Sonya's illness and weakness hold me up. [. . .]

Today is 14 April, Moscow Thought further: continue to be idle and bad. No thoughts or feelings. Mental lethargy. And if any feelings emerge, they are the basest, most egotistical ones: the bicycle, freedom from family ties, etc. Am I tired after what I have experienced recently, or am I experiencing a new stage in life, having entered upon a pure old age which I have long desired? I don't know, but I'm asleep. In the mornings I don't even read, but play patience. Sonya's health is not improving, rather it is getting worse. [. . .]

During this time I've been to court.[21] It was dreadful. I never expected such incredible stupidity. I've been busy with Khokhlov. I never expected such baseness and cruelty by doctors. And Sonya's illness. I'm very sorry for her and love her. [. . .]

25 April, Moscow Yesterday Sonya left for Kiev with Tanya,[22] who came to fetch her. Her health is a bit better – she has picked up, but is quite jaded and still can't find any moral point of support. A mother's position is terribly tragic: nature has endowed her above all with irresistible desire (she has similarly endowed man, but with a man it doesn't have the same fateful consequences – the birth of children), as a result of which children appear, for whom she is endowed with an even stronger love, a physical love, since carrying, and bearing and nursing and looking after children is a physical thing. A woman, a good woman, gives her entire soul to her children, devotes herself entirely to them, acquires the habit in her soul of living only for them and by them (a most terrible temptation, especially since everybody not merely approves, but praises it highly); the years go by and these children begin to depart – into life or death – in the first case slowly, paying back love with anger, as against someone who had been a millstone round their necks, interfering with their lives; in the second case – through death – which momentarily causes terrible pain and leaves behind emptiness. The woman must live, but there is nothing to live by. She lacks the habit of, lacks even the strength for, a spiritual life, because all her strength has been expended on her children, who are no longer there. That's what I must write about in a novel about a mother.

During this time I began learning to ride a bicycle in the riding-school. It's very strange why I should be drawn to do this. Yevgeny Ivanovich[23] tried to dissuade me, and was distressed at my riding, but I'm not ashamed. On the contrary, I feel that it's a natural folly, that it's all the same to me what people think, and that it's quite harmless and amuses me in a childish way.

Sonya's spiritual condition is not good – she can't raise herself above personal interests, in her case family ones, and find meaning in a spiritual life. Masha[24] has gone to Kiev. Poor girl, she is thin and weak. Something is happening between Seryozha and Manya.[25] It will be difficult for him, and he will need to change himself in many ways. If he does so, he will be all right. [. . .]

It's now 11 o'clock, 26 April, Moscow [. . .] Saw my photograph yesterday, and was astonished how old I looked. There's not much time left. Father, help me to use it to do Thy work. It's terrible that as you get older, you feel that the life force within you becomes more valuable (in the sense of its influence on the world), and it's terrible not to expend it on what it was intended for. It's as if life has been brewing and brewing (in youth one can spill it – it hasn't yet brewed), and towards the end it is all one thick brew. [. . .]

28 April, Moscow [. . .] What should one say to one's son who is entering the age of struggle? I talked about it yesterday with Sinitsyn. All life is a struggle between the flesh and the spirit, and gradually the flesh triumphs over the spirit.

The sexual struggle is the most intense, but on the other hand it always ends with the victory of the spirit. One should say to one's son that this struggle is not a casual or exceptional phenomenon, but the business of one's whole life, that one should know about and prepare for this struggle

– like athletes; one should always be on guard, not despair or lose heart when beaten, but pick oneself up and prepare for the struggle anew. There is the casual fall, the fall with women who don't want to tie their lives to one person, and there is the fall of marriage which may last, like mine, for thirty-two years, but a fall is still a fall, and still one mustn't lose heart, but wait for the release which will come and which, I think, has come to me. [. . .]

4 May, Moscow Still the same apathy and laziness. I'm doing no work. The bicycle. Lyova came, and left with Andryusha for Hangö. He [one word erased] a difficult ordeal. I'm trying hard and seeking, not with the confidence of success which brings either success or failure, but not without hope either; but rather like water, which is constant, and which changes its shape but not its force. Thank God I can't see spring yet, and I've no wish to. I seem to be ready to do God's work, but am still not doing it. Help me, Father. Sonya returned from Kiev no better. If only one could contrive not to get angry about mental aberrations and deformities as one can about physical ones, but not to disregard them either, and if one can't cure them, at least patiently help people either to gain relief from them or to live with them. [. . .]

13 May, Moscow Medical treatment and the bicycle and the collapse of my spiritual life. Was even angry the other day because the bicycle wasn't ready, and was rude to the man. I don't remember such depression for a long time. I've withdrawn into myself, and sit and wait. Just as little of the egotistical as of the godly.

Today is 15 May, Moscow Everything just the same. My head is a bit clearer and more alert. Slept only four hours during the night. Was tired on the bicycle yesterday. Went for a ride with Strakhov. Even my enthusiasm for the bicycle is waning. Tomorrow we're expecting Manya from London. I think Seryozha's marriage will take place. That's good, as a school for Seryozha and a distraction for Sonya. I want to finish my treatment today and go to the Olsufyevs' tomorrow.

Thought during this time. [. . .]
(4) Sonya began to talk last night about the fact that Vanechka's death was a very great misfortune and suffering, and that his death was the work of God. People often talk about the evil which God does to people. And when they speak and think like that, people imagine that they believe in God, and pray to Him. God do evil! If God were to do evil, He would not be good, would not be love, and if He is not good he is not God. [. . .]

Today, I think, is 18 May, Moscow Life is very depressing. Still no desire to work or write, still the same gloomy mood. The day before yesterday Andryusha said some very rude things to me for no reason at all. I couldn't forgive him. First I didn't want to say hello to him, then I started to reprimand him, but he began again to say even worse things and I couldn't stand it and went out, saying he was alien to me. All this is bad. I must forgive him, forgive him entirely and then help him. [. . .]

Probably 20 May. Nikolskoye, at the Olsufyevs'[26] [. . .] The newspaper I received yesterday with the article about the libels and stupidities of Seuron's book distressed me, to my shame.[27] But not much. The journalist proposes I should refute them. I've made no statements about myself and so there is nothing for me to refute. I am what I am. And what I am, only I know and God. Never do recollections manifest themselves with such force as when one is in a mentally weak condition, as I am now. Thought of writing at the Olsufyevs', but it's 12 o'clock and I haven't sat down yet.

Today is 26 May, Nikolskoye [. . .] Didn't write during the day, and then wrote in the evening again, and quite a lot, so that more than half has been sketched out. It's turning out in a strange way: Nekhlyudov must be a follower of Henry George and must bring this in, and he must weaken as he pits his strength against the daughter of the refined lady lying there (Mary Urusova).[28] Sonya has been here. She was very excited as a result of the quinine. Thank God, all ended well and amicably. She left early this morning. I'm better today. [. . .]

Today is 29 May, Nikolskoye The day before yesterday I began to feel better. No fever today either, and were it not for my leg, which has not quite healed up yet, I would consider myself quite well. Only wrote a little today and wrote badly – no energy. But I got a clear picture of Nekhlyudov while committing the crime. He should have wanted to marry and simplify his life. I'm only afraid *que cela n'impiète sur le drame* [that it will be to the detriment of the drama]. I'll decide when I feel stronger. I've just been for a ride, on horseback and on my bicycle. I'm reading Poltoratsky the whole time. I love these memoirs.[29] Relations with Sonya are not cordial, and this hurts me. Nothing stimulating in my letters or outward life. Thought: [. . .] (4) They say: 'She[30] can't understand.' But if she can't understand, why doesn't she listen to others? As it is, without understanding life or knowing that this life is to be condemned, she wants to dominate it. [. . .]

4 June, Moscow Had an operation in Nikolskoye on Tuesday, and by mistake Pyotr Vasilyevich used oil with a 3 per cent solution, so that I . . . became ill. Left the next evening, however. I was quite ill. Arrived in Moscow, and found Tanya, Seryozha and Manya there. The same evening

I had a bad attack of gall stones. During the attacks I couldn't think of anything except to wish that the pain would stop. The cause of the pain, probably, was getting too hot in the sun the day before. Since then, I've been ill for five days and done nothing but read. Read Castellion's wonderful book.[31] He was a true Christian of the sixteenth century. Also a translation of Matthew Arnold.[32] [. . .]

Oh, how well Koni's story could turn out. How I think about it sometimes. It will have two extremes of true love with a false middle. [. . .]

Today must be 7 June, Yasnaya Polyana [. . .] Did nothing all day yesterday. Started to write letters, but couldn't. Yesterday I felt the awakening of sexual desire, and was horrified. Help me, Father.

I've just been playing patience and thinking about my catechism. [. . .]

Moscow in summer: unpolished windows, covers on the chairs, freedom for the yardmen and those left behind in the house and their children, tight summer clothes – thighs tightly covered by old white trousers – and houses with wonderful gardens empty, and on the streets, on boiling hot paving stones, road workers covered in dust. And outings with cigarettes and oranges, and drunken and dissolute laughter. [. . .]

Today must be 12 June, Yasnaya Polyana The days are getting fewer. Was seriously ill for two days. Had a temperature of 40.1°. My daughters, dear things, were very frightened. What a pity that by my death I shall almost inevitably be the cause of grief to them – short-lived and good, but still grief. Read the whole time. Sometimes *The Week*, sometimes *Russian Thought*. All interesting, but all unnecessary. [. . .]

13 June, Yasnaya Polyana Health still bad. I'm weak. Bile fills my stomach and makes me feel sick. I'm afraid I'm beginning to get preoccupied with my medical condition and with treating myself and observing myself, the very thing I condemned so much in Lyova. Yesterday Seryozha añ Manya came. They are very much in love, but I'm afraid that now they are married they are doing what people sometimes do when, let's say, a key doesn't open a door or the door is stuck: turn it and push it in the opposite direction. The comparison isn't accurate, but I mean to say that people may not and cannot live their lives by going their own separate ways: we must try to live by joining forces. God grant this may be a false prediction. [. . .] Thought. [. . .] (2) The concrete sciences, as opposed to the abstract ones, become less exact the nearer their subject approaches human life: (*a*) mathematics, (*b*) astronomy, (*c*) chemistry, (*d*) physics, (*e*) biology (here inexactitude begins), anthropology (the inexactitude is greater), sociology (the inexactitude reaches limits where the science itself is destroyed). [. . .]

17 June, Yasnaya Polyana Still the same stomach ailment, and hence a mood of depression and great weakness. Yesterday was a depressing day. Sonya was out of sorts. And she only spoke about what hurt me: my works and the revenue from them, the distribution of the property, theft, vegetarianism. I was outwardly restrained, but inwardly I couldn't summon up in myself the feeling of pity for her which I ought to have done, because life has been so difficult for her. [. . .]

Today is 28 June, Yasnaya Polyana [. . .] Thought during this time: [. . .] (3) *June 20*; it rained the night before. There were heavy, ragged, low, dark clouds in the sky. Their shadow raced after me across road and field. The shadow caught me up, and it grew chilly and at the same time, ahead of me, the shadow lifted from the waving rye, which had seemed almost black, and the rye became bright green. But only for a moment. The light caught up with me again, and the shadow of the cloud fell on the rye once more. [. . .] (5) Love is only real when its object is unattractive.

Today is 4 July, Yasnaya Polyana During these last days I've had a couple of good spells of writing. And I can say that I've now finished touching up Koni's story. Wrote letters yesterday and the day before – wrote more than ten, including one in English in which I said what I now think.[33] Went mowing twice. Went to Tula yesterday on my bicycle. Seryozha has been. And I didn't get on well with him. My decision always to observe my relationship to God in my relationship with people is beginning to weaken. Still I'm trying, and it sometimes helps me. [. . .]

12 July, Yasnaya Polyana Strakhov has arrived in the meanwhile. I was very glad to see him. I wrote to Veselitskaya that when we know that a man is condemned to death we are kind to him – we love him. And how can we not love anybody, when we know that we are all condemned. He – surprisingly enough – doesn't know his condition.[34] I'm writing almost every day. Things are progressing. Just as you get to know people by living with them, so you get to know your poetic characters by living with them. I've also done quite a lot of work – although I feel I've grown weak with age. I've been to see Davydov, and he's been here. Took notes from him about trial procedure.[35] Constant guests are a burden. No peace and quiet, no summer seclusion. [. . .]

5 August, Yasnaya Polyana Haven't written my diary for almost a month. This month hasn't been spent badly. I worked a little in the fields. Once mowed the rye. Wrote quite a lot of Koni's story. It's making progress. During this time I read Kidd's *Social Evolution*[36] and articles about myself in *Wahrheit* and elsewhere.[37] When you read about yourself, it might seem that what you are occupied with the whole world is also occupied with, but that's not true. A letter from Khilkov with a description of the persecutions of the Dukhobors. I wrote a letter to the English newspapers. It's being translated now.[38] [. . .]

Things have got worse with Sonya. I went for a ride and was held up in the rain; she hurt me with her sarcasm and I was offended – the old wounds. Today she demanded that I should give her the diaries to copy. I refused, saying that this always caused unpleasantness. I did wrong not to pity her. She is exhausted, mentally ill, and it's a sin to argue with her. How sorry I am for her that she is never aware of her mistakes. However, that's not my business. I need to be aware of my own, and not to compare my mistakes with hers. Everyone sins in proportion to the light that is in him. Also during this time the boys have upset me. Especially Andryusha. He is quite out of hand and has gone mad. He doesn't see or hear a thing, as though he were perpetually drunk. Thought and noted during this time: [. . .]

(4) According to Weismann,[39] the explanation of heredity consists in the fact that in every embryo there are biophors, and biophors form themselves into ids and ids into idants. What a splendid idea for a comedy.

(5) According to Weismann again, mortal creatures have continued to exist because all those which were not mortal failed to survive in the struggle against the mortals, i.e. – *the immortal ones died.* Surely I can manage to make use of this splendid idea. [. . .]

(7) We had a talk about family life. I said that a good family life is only possible given the conviction, consciously fostered in women, of the need for constant submission to their husbands (in everything, of course, except questions of the soul – religious questions). I said that this is proved by the fact that it has been so for as long as we have known human life, and the fact that family life with children is a crossing on an unseaworthy boat, which is only possible when those on board submit to one person. And this one person has always been recognized to be the man, because, since he doesn't carry or nurse children, he can be a better guide to his wife than a wife to her husband. But is a woman always inferior to a man? Not at all; as long as they are both virgins they are equal. But what is the meaning of the fact that wives now demand not only equality, but supremacy? Only that the family is evolving, and therefore its previous form is disintegrating. The relations between the sexes are seeking a new form, and the old form is breaking down. What this new form will be it is impossible to know, although there are many possibilities. Possibly more people will remain chaste; marriages might be temporary and come to an end after the birth of children, so that both spouses, having produced children, will separate and be chaste in future; children might be brought up by society. It's impossible to foresee the new form. But there's no doubt that the old one

is breaking down, and that its continued existence is only possible given the submission of the wife to the husband, as has always been the case everywhere, and as it now is where the family still holds together. [. . .]

[*7 September*]   Haven't written my diary for more than a month. *Today is 7 September, Yasnaya Polyana*. During this time I've suffered because of the bad life of the boys: Andryusha and Misha. I've tried to help them. I've been riding my bicycle and getting on with my *Resurrection*. Read it to Olsufyeva, Taneyev and Chekhov,[40] but it was a waste of time. I'm very dissatisfied with it now, and either want to give it up or revise it. These last few days I've been walking through the woods, selecting trees for the peasants. Thought during this time:

I've recently felt death very close. My material life seems to be hanging by a thread, and must very soon break off. I'm getting more and more used to this and beginning to feel – not pleasure, but the interest of expectation, of hope – as I do with the progress of *this* life.

During this time I wrote a contribution for the English newspapers about the Dukhobors, but didn't send it, and Posha went to the Caucasus[41] and ought to have come back on the 1st, but it's now the 7th and he's still not here. [. . .]

Today is 22 September, Yasnaya Polyana   During this time I've written some letters. [. . .] and have worked again on my article about the persecutions of the Dukhobors. Posha returned and brought some information, but less detailed than I would have liked. My article isn't bad. But perhaps I'm mistaken. Sent everything off today to Kenworthy.[42]

Sonya has been to Moscow and returned. She is very pitiful, and dearer than ever to me. I can see her whole character more clearly. Andryusha worries me because I can't work out a proper relationship towards him. Tanya is dear, quiet and good. Masha is in Moscow. [. . .]

(2) Recalled how often I used to argue with religious dogmatists: Orthodox, Evangelical and others. How absurd. Can one seriously reason with a person who maintains that he believes that there is only one correct view of the world and of our attitude to it, the one which was expressed 1,500 years ago by the bishops assembled by Constantine at Nicaea – the view by which God is a Trinity and sent His son into a Virgin 1,890 years ago in order to redeem the world, etc. You can't reason with such people, you can only be indulgent to them, pity them, try to cure them, but you must regard them as mentally ill, and not argue with them.

(3) Dissatisfaction with oneself is friction, the sign of movement.

(4) There is not a single believer who has not had moments of doubt, doubt about the existence of God. And these doubts are not harmful; on the contrary, they lead to a higher understanding of God. The God you

know becomes a habit and you don't believe in Him any more. You only fully believe in God when He is revealed to you anew. And He is revealed to you from a new side when you seek Him with all your soul. [. . .]

Evening of 25 September Got on with Koni's story in the morning; began revising it from the beginning. It's quite good. At least I'm not disgusted by it. Kept thinking about living for God, only forgot twice, with regard to Andryusha. In the morning, when I heard him getting up, I didn't go in to see him, and again in the evening when he came back. He hadn't been home for two days, and must have been depressed himself. The nastier he is, the more I need to love him. And that's just what I haven't done. After dinner I went off with Gastev to fell trees for Filipp and Andriyan, and then for a ride on my bicycle. [. . .]

26 September A depressing day. Woke up early, couldn't sleep, and did some thinking. After breakfast I waited for Andryusha to get up. Worried about whether to go in or not. I went in, he had his head under the bedclothes; eventually I saw he wasn't asleep and began to speak to him. I spoke gently and kindly, but unconvincingly; felt shy and suffered anguish. He remained silent. Not a sound. I went out to work and before an hour had passed I heard the incessant noise of an accordion in the kitchen. I couldn't believe my ears, and looked through the kitchen window. He moved away. I couldn't bear it and said: 'You're worse than Khokhlov.' At dinner he didn't answer me and went off in a rage. I was ashamed that I couldn't control myself. Very ashamed. In an egotistical fashion I was distressed that my words had had no effect, and forgot that one can and must live only for God. Had no success with my writing either. Made too many changes and got muddled. And I felt ashamed to write down all these fabrications. [. . .]

Today is 29 September, Yasnaya Polyana 8 o'clock in the evening. The day before yesterday I came across Andryusha at tea and made an effort to talk to him. And I was rewarded. He was contented enough, and willing to talk to me, but yesterday he came home to dinner with his breath smelling of alcohol, and I couldn't suppress a feeling of annoyance – I said nothing. Yesterday and the day before I got on with Koni's story. [. . .]

I dreamed today that I had been struck in the face, and was ashamed that I hadn't challenged the person to a duel, and then I realized that I needn't challenge him, since that would prove the consistency of my non-resistance. Generally speaking, thoughts that occur in dreams are only of the lowest kind. When one is dreaming the mind is active, but reason, the force behind moral progress, is missing.

Today is 6 October, Yasnaya Polyana   I've had letters from Popov, Posha, Chertkov, Schmitt and Kenworthy. Yesterday I answered them all. [. . .] Ilya has been. There's little of the spiritual in him. Andryusha has arrived. I can see him soon getting consumption and dying. [. . .]

Today, I think, is the 9th   [. . .] I felt depressed with Sonya. But of course I'm to blame. I'm reading the Gospels in Italian [. . .] Went for a walk and thought about the duality of Nekhlyudov. I must express it more clearly.

12 October, Yasnaya Polyana   I'm alone with Sonya and Sasha. I'm reading Italian. Andryusha distresses me. Talked with him a lot yesterday. I feel it's in vain. Marya Alexandrovna[43] is here. Arsenyev has been. I've received an Italian book. It's about the teaching of Christianity in school.[44] An excellent thought that the teaching of religion is coercion – that corruption of children which Christ spoke about. What right have we to teach what is disputed by the enormous majority of people? The Trinity, the miracles of Buddha, Mohammed, Christ? The one thing that we can and must teach is moral instruction. An excellent thought. Just now as I was playing patience I thought how Nekhlyudov must take a touching farewell of Sonya.[45]

13 October   All these last days I've seen that something has been distressing Sonya. I caught her writing a letter. She said she would speak to me later. This morning came the explanation. She had read my angry words about her, written at moments of exasperation. I had got exasperated about something, and immediately wrote it down and forgot it. I felt in the bottom of my heart that I had done something wrong. And now she has read it. And, poor woman, she suffered terribly, and, dear woman, instead of being angry with me she wrote me this letter.[46] Never before have I felt so guilty and so full of emotion. Oh, if only this were to bring us still closer together. If only she could rid herself of her belief in trivialities and come to believe in her own soul, her own reason.

When reading through my diary I found a passage – there were several of them – where *I repudiate those angry words which I wrote about her. These words were written at moments of exasperation. I now repeat this once more for the sake of everybody who should come across these diaries.* I was often exasperated with her because of her hasty, inconsiderate temper, but, as Fet used to say, every husband gets the wife he needs. She was – and I can see now in what way – the wife I needed. She was the ideal wife in a pagan sense – in the sense of loyalty, domesticity, self-denial, love of family – pagan love – and she has the potential to become a Christian friend. I saw this after Vanechka's death. Will this be realized in her? Help her, Father. What happened today really made me glad. She has seen, and will see, the power of love – of her love for me. [. . .]

24 October I've missed many days. Sonya has been to Petersburg and come back. Relations continue to be better than good. *The Power of Darkness* is a success.⁴⁷ Thank God, it doesn't make me glad. 'Seek that your names may be written in Heaven.' Wrote a letter to Andryusha, who distressed me very much. And fortunately this letter had at least some effect. Wrote a letter to Misha – long and too rationalizing.⁴⁸ Took up *Resurrection* again, and was convinced that it's all bad, that the centre of gravity is not where it ought to be, that the land question is a distraction and a weakness, and will turn out to be weak itself. I think I'll give it up. And if I do go on writing, I'll begin it all again from the beginning. [. . .]

Yesterday was 24, today is 25 October, Yasnaya Polyana Sonya and Sasha have just left. As she sat in the coach I felt terribly sorry for her; not because she was leaving, but sorry for her, for her soul. And now I'm so sorry that it's an effort to hold back my tears. I'm sorry that she's depressed, sad and lonely. I'm the only person she has to hold on to, and at the bottom of her heart she's afraid I don't love her, don't love her as much as I can, with all my heart, and that the reason for this is the difference in our views of life. And she thinks that I don't love her because she hasn't come to me. Don't think that. I love you still more, I quite understand you, and know you couldn't, couldn't come to me, and so are left alone. But you aren't alone. I'm with you, just as you are, I love you, love you to the very end with a love that could not be greater. [. . .]

28 October, Yasnaya Polyana [. . .] There's only a short time left for me to live, and there's so much I terribly want to speak about: I want to speak about what we can, must and are bound to believe in, and about the cruelty of the deception which people subject themselves to – economic, political and religious deception – and about the temptation to stupefy themselves with alcohol, and with tobacco, which is considered so innocent, and about marriage and about education. And about the horrors of autocracy. Everything has come to a head, and I want to speak. And so there's no time to go on turning out that literary nonsense which I had begun to do in *Resurrection*. But I immediately asked myself: can I write when I know nobody will read it? And I felt a sort of disappointment – but only for a while – that I can: that means there was something of the desire for fame in me, but also the important thing – the need to serve God. I've received a wonderful letter from Sonya. Help me, Father, to follow the same path of love. I thank Thee. Everything comes from Thee. [. . .]

5 November, Yasnaya Polyana I've missed six days. I don't think I've done much during that time: wrote a little, chopped some wood and felt ill, but I've lived through a lot. And I've lived through a lot because in fulfilment of a promise to Sonya I read through all my diaries for seven years.[49] I seem to be approaching a clear and simple expression of what I live by. How good that I didn't finish the *Catechism*. Probably I'll write it differently and better. If the Father wills it so. I understand why it's impossible to say these things quickly. If they could be said all at once, what would one live by in the realm of thought? This task is the most I can undertake just now.

I've just been for a walk and clearly understood why I'm not getting on with *Resurrection*. The beginning was wrong. I understood this as I thought about my story about children – *Who is Right?*; I understood that I should have begun with the life of the peasants, that they are the subject, the positive element, while the rest is shadow, the negative element. And I understand the same about *Resurrection*. I must begin with her.[50] I want to begin now. [. . .]

7 November, Yasnaya Polyana   Got on a bit these last two days with the new *Resurrection*. I'm ashamed to recall how banal it was to have begun with him. [. . .] A cheerful letter from Sonya. Will there really be *complete* spiritual unity? Help me, Father.

7 December, Moscow   Haven't written my diary for almost a month. During this time we moved to Moscow. The weakness has passed off a little, and I'm working hard, although with little success, on an exposition of religious belief. Yesterday I wrote a short article on flogging.[51] I lay down to sleep during the day and had just dozed off when someone seemed to push me, and I got up and began to think about flogging and wrote the article. During this time I've been to the theatre for rehearsals of *The Power of Darkness*. Art both began as play and continues to be a plaything, and a criminal plaything, of adults. This is confirmed by music, of which I have heard a lot. It exerts no influence. On the contrary it distracts one, if one ascribes to it the inappropriate importance which is usually ascribed. Realism, moreover, weakens its meaning.

The boys are all behaving badly, they keep disappearing and are obtuse. [. . .] Sonya is enduring her critical period well. Wrote a few insignificant letters.

Thought a lot – in terms of importance – during this time. Much of it I can't make sense of and have forgotten. [. . .]

(6) Beautiful women smile, and we think that bcause they smile, what they say when they smile is true and good. But a smile often seasons something that has quite gone off.

(7) Education. One has only to be involved in education to see all one's own shortcomings. And having seen them you begin to correct them. And self-correction is also the best means of educating one's own and other people's children and grown-ups. [. . .]

Today is 23 December, Moscow.   Haven't written my diary for a long time. During this time the Chertkovs arrived. It's two days since Kenworthy arrived. He's very pleasant. My son Seryozha has arrived – sad and thinner. He talked about his theory today. I'm glad that I only felt sorry for him. I got on well with him. Andryusha has joined the army. Today the soldier came home. He's good-natured and unaffected. Continued to write my exposition[52] – I'm making progress. I think on and off about a drama.[53] It went round and round in my head all last night. I'm unwell – a heavy cold, influenza. Apropos of a letter to me from an Englishman I also began a letter about the conflict between England and America.[54] [. . .]

1896

23 January, Moscow Haven't written my diary for exactly a month. During this time I've written a letter on patriotism[1] and a letter to Crosby, and for about two weeks now I've been writing a drama.[2] I've written three acts very badly. I'm thinking of sketching it out in rough, to give it a *charpente* [framework]. Haven't much hope of success. [. . .]

[*13 February*] Haven't written my diary for almost a month. [. . .] A great deal of music – useless. The girls – especially Masha – are weak. Will she manage to get over it somehow? I don't give them enough guidance. They need to be helped. The boys are alien to me. With regard to religion, I've been very cold all this time. [. . .]

Today is 27 February, Nikolskoye I'm getting on with the drama. It's going very sluggishly. I don't even know whether I'm making any progress. Some moderately discontented letters from Sonya in Moscow. But I feel very well here – the main thing is the quietness. I've been reading *Trilby*[3] – poor. Wrote letters to Chertkov. Schmitt and Kenworthy. Read Corneille.[4] Edifying. I've been thinking: [. . .]
(1) [. . .] There is only one kind of art, and it consists in increasing innocent joys, common and accessible to all – the good of man. [. . .]
(2) [. . .] People who wish to show themselves to be connoisseurs of art and who therefore praise the art of the past – classical art – and abuse the contemporary only show by this that they have no feeling for art. [. . .]

Today is 2 May, Yasnaya Polyana Haven't written my diary for nearly two months. I was living in Moscow all that time. Important events: a closer acquaintance with the scribe Novikov,[5] who changed his life as a result of my books, which his brother, a man-servant, received from his mistress abroad. A spirited young man. Then his other brother, a worker, asked for *What I Believe*, and Tanya sent it to Kholevinskaya. Kholevinskaya was taken to prison. The prosecutor said they ought to have laid hands on me. All this taken together made me write letters to the ministers of Internal Affairs and Justice, asking them to direct their persecutions towards me instead. All this time I've been getting on with my exposition of religious belief.[6] Made little progress. Chertkov has been. Posha has been and gone. Relations with people have been good. I've given up riding my bicycle. I'm

surprised how I could have been so infatuated. Heard Wagner's *Siegfried.*[7]
Many thoughts about this and other things. Noted down twenty in all in
my notebook. [. . .]

5 May Andryusha and Misha are in the village again. There's the same
general mood of despair. And I'm sad. The only reason is: a high moral
demand is made. In its name, everything beneath it is rejected. But it isn't
followed. Fifteen years ago I offered to give away the greater part of my
property and to live in four rooms. Then they would have had an ideal.
Now they have none. They see that the one their mother proposes – being
comme il faut – won't stand up to criticism, and mine is made fun of in
front of them – and they are glad. The only thing left is pleasure. That's
what they live for. It's impossible to live without an ideal – even a very low
ambitious one, even a selfish ideal.

Rode past Gill's today, and thought: no undertaking is profitable with
only a little capital. The more capital, the more profitable; the fewer
expenses. But it doesn't follow at all from that that, as Marx says,
capitalism leads to socialism. Perhaps it will do, but only to socialism by
force. The workers will be compelled to work together and they will work
less and their pay will be more, but there will be the same slavery. It's
necessary that people should work together in freedom, should learn to
work for one another, but capitalism doesn't teach them that. On the
contrary, it teaches them envy, greed – egoism. And so, while the material
condition of the workers can be improved through forcible association
brought about by capitalism, their contentment certainly cannot be
guaranteed. Contentment can only be guaranteed through the free
association of workers. And for that, it's necessary to learn, to try to come
together, to improve oneself morally – to serve people willingly without
being offended at getting no reward. And this certainly can't be learned
under a capitalist, competitive system, but only under a completely
different one.

I'm sleeping alone downstairs.

Today is 16 May already, Yasnaya Polyana Morning. I can't get on with my
exposition of religious belief. It's unclear, too philosophical; and I'm
spoiling the good things that were in it. I'm thinking of starting it all over
again or making a break and working on the story or the drama.[8] [. . .]
Sonya has gone to Moscow to see about her tooth. It's difficult for her to
find any life without the children. The main thing is that I get in her
way. [. . .]

17 May, Yasnaya Polyana [. . .] (2) Read about Granovsky.[9] In our
literature it's customary to say that in the reign of Nicholas conditions

were such that great thoughts could not arise (Granovsky complains about this, and others too). But in fact there were no real thoughts. It's all self-deceit. If all the Granovskys, Belinskys and others had had anything to say, they would have said it, despite all the obstacles. Herzen is the proof of that. He went abroad. And despite his enormous talent, what did he say that was new or necessary?

All these Granovskys, Belinskys, Chernyshevskys and Dobrolyubovs who have been promoted to the stature of great men ought to thank the government and the censorship, without which they would have been the most insignificant feuilletonists. [. . .]

(14) The article about art[10] must begin with a discussion of the fact that, say, for a picture which cost the artist 1,000 working days, people pay 40,000 working days: for an opera or a novel even more. And some people say of these works that they are splendid, others that they are no good at all. And there is no indisputable criterion. There is no such disagreement about water, food, or good deeds. Why is that? [. . .]

(20) The chief purpose of art, if there is art and if it has a purpose, is to manifest and express the truth about man's soul, to express those secrets which can't be expressed in simple words. That is the origin of art. Art is a microscope which the artist fixes on the secrets of his soul, and shows to people these secrets which are common to all. [. . .]

28 May, Yasnaya Polyana   12 o'clock noon. For several days I've been struggling with my work and making no progress. I'm asleep. I wanted to finish it off somehow in rough,[11] but I just can't. I'm in a bad frame of mind, aggravated by the emptiness, the barren, self-satisfied, cold emptiness of the life around me. [. . .] Salomon was here. Also Taneyev, who disgusts me with his self-satisfied, moral and, ridiculous to say, aesthetic (real, not outward) obtuseness and his *coq du village* [cock of the walk] situation in our house. It's an examination for me. I'm trying not to fail.[12]

A terrible event in Moscow – the death of 3,000.[13] I somehow can't respond to it as I should. I'm still unwell – getting weaker. [. . .] Thought during this time: (1) It's surprising how many people see some insoluble problem in evil. I've never seen any problem in it. It's completely clear to me now that what we call evil is the good whose effect we can't yet see.

(2) The poetry of Mallarmé and others. We, who don't understand it, say boldly that it's nonsense, that it's poetry which has wandered off into a blind alley. But why, when we listen to music which is incomprehensible and equally nonsensical, don't we boldly say the same thing, instead of timidly saying: yes, maybe. It needs to be understood, one must prepare oneself, etc. That's nonsense. Any work of art is only a work of art when it's comprehensible – I don't say to everyone, but to people on a certain

level of education, the level of a man who reads poetry and judges it. This reasoning brought me to the quite definite conclusion that music lost its way and wandered off into a blind alley sooner than other arts (decadence in poetry and symbolism etc. in painting). And the person who made it lose its way was the brilliant musician Beethoven. Very important: the authorities and the people devoid of aesthetic feeling who judge art. Goethe? Shakespeare? Everything that goes under their names is bound to be good, and *on se bât les flancs* [does one's uttermost] in order to find something beautiful in the stupid and unsuccessful, and taste is completely perverted. But all these great talents – the Goethes, Shakespeares, Beethovens, Michelangelos produced side by side with beautiful things not merely mediocre, but repulsive ones as well. Mediocre artists produce mediocre quality work, and never anything very bad. But recognized geniuses produce either really great works, or absolute rubbish: Shakespeare, Goethe, Beethoven, Bach, etc. [. . .]

I think it's 6 June, Yasnaya Polyana   [. . .] The day before yesterday there was a police-spy here who admitted that he had been sent to keep an eye on me. It was both pleasant and nasty. [. . .]

19 June, Yasnaya Polyana   [. . .] I went out one evening beyond the Zakaz wood and wept with joyful gratitude – for life. I have very vivid pictures of life in Samara: the steppe, the struggle between the nomadic patriarchal way of life and the civilized, agricultural one. It draws me very much. Koni's story wasn't born inside me. That's why it's going so slowly. Thought: (1) Something very important about art: what is beauty? Beauty is what we love. *I don't love him because he's beautiful, but he's beautiful because I love him.* That's just the problem: why is he loved? Why do we love? To say that we love a thing because it's beautiful is just the same as saying that we breathe because the air is pleasant. We find the air pleasant because we have to breathe. And similarly we discover beauty because we have to love: and the person who can't see spiritual beauty at least sees physical beauty and loves it.

19 July, Pirogovo   [. . .] During this time I've made progress with *An Exposition of Religious Belief.*[14] It's far from what is needed and what I want, and is quite inaccessible to the ordinary person and the child, but still it expresses everything I know coherently and logically. During this time I also wrote a foreword to the reading of the Gospels[15] and marked off passages in the Gospels. Had some visitors: Englishmen, Americans, no one of importance.

I'll write out what I noted down:

(1) Yesterday I walked through a black-earth, fallow field which had been

ploughed up again. As far as the eye could see there was nothing but black earth – not one green blade of grass. And there on the edge of the dusty grey road was a Tartar thistle (burdock) with three shoots: one was broken, and a dirty white flower hung from it; the second was also broken and spattered with mud, black and with a cracked and dirty stem; the third shoot stuck out to the side, also black, but still alive and red in the middle. It reminded me of Hadji Murat. I'd like to write about it. It fights for life till the end and, alone in the middle of the whole field, somehow manages to win the fight.[16] [. . .]

(8) Yesterday I looked through the novels, stories and poems of Fet. I remembered our incessant piano music for four hands at Yasnaya Polyana, and it became so clear to me that all this – novels, poems, and music – was not art in the sense of something important and necessary to people generally, but the wanton play of robbers and parasites who have nothing in common with life: novels and stories about nasty love affairs, poems about the same thing, or about people dying of boredom. And also music about the same thing. But life, the whole of life, is seething with its own problems about food, accommodation, work, belief, relations between people . . . It's shameful and vile. Help me, Father, to serve Thee by showing up this lie. [. . .]

26 July, Yasnaya Polyana   Morning. Didn't sleep all night. My heart aches incessantly. I continue to suffer and can't surrender myself to God. One thing: I've overcome lust, but – what is worse – I haven't overcome pride and indignation, and my heart aches incessantly.[17] [. . .]

Yesterday I walked to Baburino and couldn't help meeting (I rather tried to avoid than sought to meet) eighty-year-old Akim ploughing, Yaremich's old woman who hasn't a fur coat in her house, and only one caftan, and then Marya whose husband died of cold and who has nobody to cart the rye away and whose child is dying of hunger. And Trofim and Khalyavka, husband and wife, are dying and their children too. And we discuss Beethoven. And I prayed that He would release me from this life. And I pray again, and cry with pain. I've lost my way, I'm stuck, I can't do anything, but I hate myself and my life.

30 July, Yasnaya Polyana   I've suffered and struggled a lot more, and still haven't overcome either the one thing or the other.[18] But it's better. Annenkova was here and expressed it well: [Five words erased.] They have spoiled my diary too; I write with an eye to the possibility of its being read by people still alive. Only the awareness that one must have pity, that she is suffering and there is no end to my guilt made me feel better. [. . .]

It's terrible to think how much time has passed: a month and a half. *Today* is *14 September, Yasnaya Polyana*. During this time I had a trip to a monastery with Sonya.[19] It was very good. [. . .] Sonya has been in Moscow since the 3rd. I waited for her impatiently today and was almost in distress. [. . .]

Thought during this time: [. . .]

(7) One of the most powerful means of hypnosis – of external influence on a man's spiritual condition – is dress. People know this well: that's the reason for monastic garb in monasteries and uniform in the army.

Today is 20 October, Yasnaya Polyana   (morning) [. . .]

(1) In a work of art the main thing is the soul of the author. Therefore in the case of average works, those by women are better and more interesting. The woman will force her way through from time to time, will express the very secrets of her soul – that's what is needed – and you can see what it is she really loves, although she pretends she loves something else. When an author writes, we – the readers – put our ears to his breast and listen and say: breathe. If there are wheezing sounds they will be heard. And women don't know how to conceal them. But a man can learn literary devices, and you won't be able to see him because of his manner of writing; you only know that he's stupid. But what there is in his soul – you won't be able to see. (Not good, spiteful.) [. . .]

(6) The Japanese sang – we couldn't refrain from laughing. If we had sung before the Japanese, they would have laughed. Even more so if we had played Beethoven to them. Hindu and Greek temples can be understood by everyone. Greek statues can also be understood by everyone. And our best painting can also be understood. And so architecture, sculpture and painting, having attained their perfection, have also attained cosmopolitanism, universal accessibility. The art of speech has also attained this in some of its manifestations – in the teachings of Buddha and Christ, in the poetry of Sakyamuni, Jacob and Joseph. In dramatic art – Sophocles, Aristophanes – it has not been attained. It is being attained in some modern works. But music has lagged behind completely. The ideal of any art towards which it must aspire is universal accessibility, but the arts, and especially music today, are getting bogged down in refinement.

Today must be 23 October, Yasnaya Polyana. It's now evening and I'm sitting down to write because I feel the special importance and seriousness of the hours of life which are left to me. And I don't know what I must do, but I feel the expression of God's will has ripened within me and is ready to bear fruit. Read *Hadji Murat* – it's not right. I can't get down to *Resurrection*. The drama[20] occupies me. A splendid article by Carpenter on science.[21] We all walk close to the truth and reveal it from different sides.

26 October, Yasnaya Polyana Still just as unwell. And I can't write. My head aches. Seryozha came yesterday. I wrote letters to Sonya and Andryusha. But I think that during this time of doubt I arrived at two very important positions: (1) the one that I had previously thought about and noted down: that *art* is a fiction. It is the temptation to amuse oneself with puppets, pictures, songs, *play*, fairy stories and nothing more. But to place art as people do (and as they do with science) on the same level as the good is a terrible *sacrilège*. The proof that it isn't so is that I can say about truth that truth is good, [. . .] and about beauty that it is good; but one mustn't say about good that it is beautiful (it usually isn't beautiful) or true (it is always true).

There is only one good – good and bad – but truth and beauty are good attributes of certain objects.

The other very important thing is that reason is the only means of making manifest the release of love. I think this is an important thought, omitted in my exposition of religious belief.

Today is 5 November, Yasnaya Polyana Morning. Yesterday was a terrible day. Already the day before yesterday I had expressed to Lyova in a heated and unrestrained manner my view about his incorrect understanding of life and of what is good. Then I told him that I felt I was to blame. Yesterday he began a conversation and said some very bad things, with petty, personal animosity. I forgot God, didn't pray and felt hurt, and I confounded my true 'I' with my evil one – I forgot God in me, and went off downstairs. Sonya came in, as she did yesterday, and was very good. Then in the evening, when everyone had gone, she began to beg me to hand over to her the rights to my works. I said I couldn't. She was distressed and said a lot of hard things to me. I was even more distressed, but restrained myself and went off to bed. I hardly slept all night, and was depressed. I've just found the *prescriptions*[22] in my diary and read them through, and felt easier; I must separate off my true 'I' from the one that is offended and angry, must remember that all this is not just a hindrance, or a casual annoyance, but the very task destined for me to do, and above all I must know that if there is any lack of affection in me towards anyone, then as long as that lack of affection is in me I am to blame. And when you know you are to blame you feel relieved. [. . .]

17 November Hardly wrote anything yesterday. I'm alone with my daughters. How good to be with them. It spoils me. It's a warm bath for the feelings. A letter from Andryusha, a very good one. A fight in the papers over Repin's definition of art as amusement.[23] How appropriate it is to my work. The meaning of art still hasn't been fully clarified. It's clear to me, and I can write about it and prove it, but not briefly and simply. [. . .]

22 November, Moscow Fourth day in Moscow. Dissatisfied with myself. No work. Was confused over my article on art and made no progress. [. . .] Read Plato: the embryos of idealism.²⁴ [. . .]

Goldenweiser²⁵ has just been playing. One piece a fantasia and fugue: studied, cold and pretentious artificiality; a second – Arensky's *Bigarrure*: sensual and artificial; and a third – a ballade by Chopin: sickly and nervous. Neither the first, nor the second, nor the third can be of any use to the people.

The devil attached to me is still with me and torments me.

Today is 2 December, Moscow. Five days have passed and very painful ones. Everything is still the same. Yesterday night I went for a walk; we had a talk. I understood my guilt. I hope she also understood me. My feelings: I discovered a terrible, purulent sore on myself. They promised me they would heal it and bandaged it up. The sore was so disgusting to me and it was so depressing to think it was there that I tried to forget about it and persuade myself that it wasn't there. But some time has passed – the bandage has been taken off and although the sore is healing it's still there. And this was agonizingly painful to me and I began to reproach the doctor, unjustly. Such is my condition. [. . .]

20 December, Moscow Five days have passed and this feeling of constraint, of the weight of my body, and then the awareness of the existence of that which is not body, has increased terribly. I want to throw off this weight, to free myself from these chains, and at the same time I can feel them. I'm sick of my body. All this time I've done no work and I feel a depressing melancholy. [. . .]

I've noted various trifles about art. [. . .]

(2) What relief everyone would feel, shut up at a concert listening to Beethoven's last works, if a *trepak* or a *csárdás* or something like that were to be played to them. [. . .]

(4) Nothing confuses concepts about art so much as the acceptance of authorities. Instead of determining according to a clear and precise concept of art whether the works of Sophocles, Homer, Dante, Shakespeare, Goethe, Beethoven, Bach, Raphael or Michelangelo conform to the concept of good art, and precisely which works do so, they define art itself and its laws on the basis of the existing works of those who are recognized as great artists. And yet there are many works by famous artists which are beneath criticism, and many false reputations, many who have acquired fame by chance: Dante, Shakespeare. [. . .]

(7) Church music was good because it was accessible to the masses. Only that which is accessible to everyone is undeniably good. And so it's true to say that the more accessible the better. [. . .]

(11) People say that music strengthens the impression of the words of an aria or song. It's not true. The music outstrips the impression of the words to an unimaginable degree. A Bach aria. What words can compete with it when it is being performed? Words by themselves are a different matter. Whatever music you set the Sermon on the Mount to, the music will be left far behind when you have penetrated the meaning of the words. Faure's *Crucifixe*.[26] The music is pathetic alongside the words. [. . .]

(13) The Scylla and Charybdis of artists: either a thing is comprehensible, but shallow and vulgar, or it is pseudo-exalted, original and incomprehensible. [. . .]

(17) Apart from the fact that the most talented representatives of the people have been won over to the camp of the parasites, the reasons for the destruction of popular poetry and music were first of all the enserfment of the people, and then – most importantly – printing. [. . .]

(19) After death in importance, and before death in time, there is nothing more important, more irrevocable, than marriage. And just as death is good only when it is unavoidable, while any intentional death is bad, so it is with marriage. Marriage is not an evil only when it is irresistible.

21 December, Moscow I.I.A. I'm still writing on the 20th I'm still just as depressed. Help me, Father. Give me relief. Strengthen Thyself in me, subdue, eliminate, destroy the impure flesh, and all that I feel through the medium of it. Just now there was a conversation about art and the opinion that one can only practise art for the sake of a person one loves.[27] And there was an unwillingness to say this to me. And I wasn't amused or sorry, only hurt. Father, help me. However, I feel better already. What consoles me particularly is the task, the test of humility, of humiliation, an entirely unexpected, exceptional humiliation. In chains or in prison one can be proud of one's humiliation, but here it is merely painful unless one accepts it as a trial sent by God. Yes, learn to endure it calmly and joyfully, and to love.

22 December, Moscow I.I.A. It's beginning to be very doubtful; my heart aches incessantly. I can hardly find rest anywhere. Only Posha cheered me up today. It's disgusting that I want to cry over myself, over what is left of my life which is being ruined to no purpose. But perhaps it must be so. Yes, it certainly must be so.

25 December, Moscow 9 o'clock at night. I feel better at heart. But I've no intellectual or literary work, and I long for it. I'm now experiencing that peculiar Christmas tenderness and emotion, the need for poetry. My hands are cold, I want to cry and love. Over dinner my sons' rudeness hurt me very much.

1897

5 January, Moscow Still nothing good to note about myself. There's no necessity to work, and the devil won't go away. I've been unwell for about six days.

Began to re-read *Resurrection*, and gave it up in disgust when I got as far as *his* decision to marry. It's all untrue, made-up and weak. It's difficult to put right something that is flawed. To put it right it will be necessary: (1) to describe her feelings and life and his alternately. And in her case positively and seriously, and in his case negatively and sardonically. I doubt if I'll finish it. It's all very flawed. [. . .]

Today is 12 January, Moscow Early morning. I can't sleep for depression. And it's not gall or egoism and sensuality which are to blame, but this agonizing life. Yesterday I sat at table and felt that the governess and I are both equally superfluous, and both equally depressed. The talk about the acting of Duse and Hofmann, jokes, fine clothes, and sweetmeats – it all goes over us and through us. And it's the same all day and every day. There's nobody to rest on. Poor Tanya would have been willing at one time, but hers is a weak nature, with weak spiritual demands. Seryozha, Ilyusha . . . In other people's lives there is at least something serious and humane – say science, the service, being a teacher or doctor, young children, not to mention earning a living or serving people, but with them there is nothing except playing all sorts of games, and eating, and senile *flirtation*[1] or even worse. It's revolting. I'm writing so that people might know it, at least after my death. It's impossible to say it now. People who shout are worse than the deaf. She's ill,[2] it's true, but it's an illness which is taken for good health, and which people help her to bear, instead of trying to cure. What will come of it, how will it end? I pray incessantly, blame myself and pray. Help me, as Thou knowest how.

15 January, Moscow Early morning. Hardly slept all night. Woke up from a dream about the same shameful thing.[3] My heart aches. Thought: it doesn't matter, I've got to die of something. If God won't let me die for the sake of His work, I'll have to die foolishly and weakly like this of my own accord and for my own self. One good thing is that it eases my passage from this life. Not only am I not sorry, I actually want to leave this nasty, humiliating life. I had the particularly painful and unpleasant thought that after sacrificing everything to do with God, a life of service to God, after the distribution of my property and the withdrawal from my family in order not to destroy love – instead of that love, I had to witness this humiliating madness. [. . .]

4 February, Nikolskoye, at the Olsufyevs'. This is the fourth day I've been here. Unspeakable depression. I'm writing badly about art. [. . .]

Sonya has read this diary in my absence, and is very distressed that people might *afterwards* conclude from it that she was a bad wife. I tried to console her – our whole life and my attitude to her of late will show what sort of wife she was. If she looks at this diary again, let her do what she likes with it, but I can't write with her or subsequent readers in mind, or write a reference for her, as it were. One thing I know is that last night I vividly imagined that she would die before me, and I became terribly afraid for myself. The day before yesterday I wrote to her that once again, and particularly by degrees (which always means particularly strongly), we had begun to grow closer together four or five years ago, and it would be good if this relationship were to grow stronger and stronger until the death of one of us – until my death – which I feel is very near. But enough of that. I'll copy out what I've been thinking during this time.

(1) Ultimately it is those people who are the victims of oppression, i.e. those people who obey the law of non-resistance, who always rule. So women seek rights, but it is they who rule, just because they are the ones subjected to force – were, and still are. Institutions are in the power of men, but public opinion is in the power of women. And public opinion is a million times stronger than any laws and armies. The proof of the fact that public opinion is in the hands of women is that not only is the organization of houses and food determined by women – they spend the money and consequently control the labour of men – but the success of works of art and of books, even the appointment of rulers, is determined by public opinion, and public opinion is determined by women. It was well said by somebody that men need to seek emancipation from women, and not the other way round. [. . .]

(10) Art is – I had written food, but it's better to say sleep – which is necessary for sustaining the spiritual life. Sleep is good, it is necessary after work, but artificial sleep is harmful – it doesn't refresh or stimulate, but leaves one weak. [. . .]

[*16 February*] Back again at the Olsufyevs' in *Nikolskoye.*[4] *16 February.* Returned on the morning of the day before yesterday and fell ill. Was better yesterday. Wrote well about art. Sonya left today after a conversation which distressed her. Women don't consider the demands of reason binding upon them and can't progress as a consequence of them. This sail is not unfurled for them. They row without a rudder.

17 February, Nikolskoye [. . .] Thought before going to Petersburg:
(1) For the appeal:[5] describe the condition of factory workers, servants, soldiers, agricultural workers as compared with the rich, and show that it's all the result of fraud. The first fraud is that of land; the second fraud is that of taxes and customs; the third fraud is that of patriotism, defence; and finally, the fourth fraud, the worst of all, is the (religious) fraud of the meaning of life, of two sorts: (*a*) that of the Church and (*b*) atheism.
(2) In the Middle Ages, in the eleventh century, poetry was common to all – to the people and the masters, *les courtois* [the well-born] and *les vilains* [those of humble origin]; then it split up, and *les vilains* began to imitate the poetry of the masters, and the masters that of the people. It must be united again. [. . .]

Today is 20 February, Nikolskoye [. . .] Received a letter from Sonya today. All this has brought us closer. And I think I'm now quite free from it.[6] Yesterday I wrote a lot of letters. Thought as I walked:
(1) There is no greater cause of errors and confusion of ideas – the most unexpected and otherwise inexplicable – than the recognition of authorities – i.e. of the infallible truthfulness or beauty of people, books or works of art. [. . .] The most striking example of such an error and the terrible consequences of it which have held back the progress of Christian mankind for centuries is the authority of the Scriptures and the Gospels. [. . .]

24 February, Nikolskoye [. . .] Read and am still reading Aristotle (Bénard) on aesthetics.[7] Very important. Thought during these days: [. . .]
(2) They tell me when I condemn religious propaganda . . . you preach too. No, I don't preach, mainly because I haven't anything to preach. I won't even preach God to an atheist (if I have done so I was wrong). I only draw conclusions from what people accept, pointing out the contradictions in what they accept, and which they don't notice.
(3) A guest here – a general – imposing, clean, correct, with thick eyebrows and an important appearance (and exceptionally good-natured, but lacking any moral impulse), suggested to me the striking thought as to how and by what means people who are most indifferent to public life, to the common good – how it is precisely these people who involuntarily reach the position of being rulers over other people. I can see him being in charge of an institution on which millions of lives depend, and just because he likes cleanliness, elegance, choice food, dancing, hunting, billiards and every kind of amusement, and doesn't have any means himself, taking up a position in those regiments, institutions and societies which have all these things, and gradually, as a good and inoffensive person, making his

way up and becoming a ruler of people – just like F – and their name is legion. [. . .]

1 March, Nikolskoye [. . .] Thought: [. . .]

(1) That death now seems to me just like a change of scene: retirement from a former post and appointment to a new one. I think that I've already retired from my former post, and am no longer any use. [. . .]

Today is 4 April, Moscow [. . .] I've prayed a lot recently that my life should be better. But I'm ashamed and depressed by the awareness of the anomalous nature of my life. Had some very good thoughts yesterday about *Hadji Murat* – that the main thing is to express in it the betrayal of trust. How good he would have been but for that betrayal. I also think more and more often about the appeal. I'm afraid that the theme of art has occupied me recently for personal, egotistical and bad reasons. *Je m'entends* [I understand what I'm saying]. [. . .]

Today is 3 May, Yasnaya Polyana Haven't written my diary for nearly a month. Not a good or fruitful month.

Worked quite hard on the article about art. It's now in a state where it's possible to understand what I wanted to say, but it's still said badly and there are many *lacunes* [gaps] and inaccuracies. Came here yesterday with Tanya. I feel physically and mentally and morally weak. The moral man is beginning to wake up and is dissatisfied. [. . .] A wonderful spring. I've just come back from Kozlovka and brought some clover and lilies of the valley.

Thought a lot and made no notes. I've done no good. Capua.[8] The hairs of the Lilliputians have bound me so fast that I soon won't be able to move a single limb unless I can break them. I'm sad, sad, and not because of any external dissatisfaction. I don't want anything from life, and don't regret the past at all,[9] but I loathe myself, I'm ashamed of myself, and am sorry for my soul. [. . .]

16 May [. . .] On the 13th Sofya Andreyevna was here. Received a letter from her yesterday. It's always the same thing. Didn't sleep all night. Never have my sufferings reached such intensity. Father, help me. Teach me. Enter into me. Grow in strength within me. I can't come to any decision. Should I stop thinking about it? That's impossible. I can't decide anything. I can't pity her, and from pity I can't oppose her. Help me, God.

17 May [*18 May*] I.I.A., which is very doubtful. My heart aches terribly. There are tears in my throat. Once I start, I shall cry my heart out.

I've got the day wrong. Today is *18 May*. My heart still aches incessantly. I haven't slept for three nights, and feel I won't sleep today either. Can't do any work. I think I've come to a decision.[10] It will be difficult to carry out, but I can't and mustn't do otherwise. [. . .]

Today is 16 July Have written nothing in my diary, not just for one, but for two and a half months. I've lived through many very hard things and many good ones.

I've been ill. Very severe pains at the beginning of July, I think. I've worked all the time on my article on art, and the further I got the better. I've finished it and am revising it from the beginning. Masha got married[11] and I was sorry for her, as one is sorry for a thoroughbred horse that is made to cart water. She doesn't cart water, but she's been broken and made useless. What will come of it I can't imagine. Something monstrously unnatural, like making pies out of children. Tanya has also saddled herself with a lot of suffering.[12] Misha is tormenting himself. There's the same trouble at Pirogovo too.[13] It's terrible! Instead of moderating and allaying passion, the source of our greatest calamities, we rouse it up by every means and then complain that we suffer. I've felt sorry for Sonya all the time recently. Good letters from Chertkov. Shidlovsky, a peasant from Kiev, has been. I feel lonely – feel that my life is not only not interesting to anyone, but that people are bored and ashamed that I go on occupying myself with such stupid things.

Thought during this time:

(1) There is a type of woman – there are men like that too, but there are more women – who are unable to see themselves, whose necks, as it were, can't turn round in order to look at themselves. It's not that they don't want to repent, it's that they can't see themselves. They live as they do, and not otherwise, because that way seems good to them. And so whatever they have done, they did because it was good. Such people are frightening. And such people may be clever or stupid, good or evil. When they are stupid and evil, it's terrible. [. . .]

(5) When you happen to think of something and forget what you thought about, but you remember and know the nature of your thoughts – sad, dismal, oppressive, gay, cheerful – and even remember their sequence: at first you felt sad, then were consoled, etc. – when you remember things that way, that's exactly what music expresses. [. . .]

17 July [. . .] Rode on my bicycle to Yasenki. I like this exercise very much. But it makes me ashamed. [. . .]

Missed three days. Today is *21 July*. I'm working quite well. I'm even satisfied with my work,[14] though I'm changing a lot. Today everything has come into focus and has gained a lot from it. I've been looking through it all again from the beginning. The life round me is very miserable. The children give me no joy. I don't know why: whether it's my stomach, or the heat or excessive physical exercise – but I feel very weak in the evenings. [. . .]

9 August [. . .] Noted down in my book: [. . .] (2) The aesthetic and the ethical are two arms of one lever: to the extent to which one side becomes longer and heavier, the other side becomes shorter and lighter. As soon as a man loses his moral sense, he becomes particularly responsive to the aesthetic. [. . .] (4) It's a common phenomenon that old people love to travel, to go far and to change places. Isn't this a preview of, and a preparation for, the last journey?

15 August, Yasnaya Polyana [. . .] Tanya has just come from seeing Sukhotin. She called me to her room. I felt very sorry for her. But what can I say to her? What will be will be. I only hope there is nothing sinful. [. . .] (5) Since I've become old, I've begun to mix people up: for example, the children: Seryozha with Andrey, Misha with Ilya, and I also mix up strangers who belong to one type, or are registered as such in my mind. And so I don't know Andrey and Seryozha, but I know a collective personality to which Andrey and Seryozha belong. [. . .]

Today is 19 September Haven't written my diary for more than a month. [. . .] The important thing during this time was Boulanger's exile.[15] My work has only been interrupted by a letter to the Swedish newspapers about the Dukhobors apropos of the Nobel prizes.[16] Sonya is afraid. I'm very sorry, but I can't help doing it. It was also interrupted by ill health: a terrible boil on my cheek. I thought it was cancer, and am glad it wasn't very unpleasant to think so. I'm receiving a new appointment, one which in any case I can't escape.

St John[17] has been, a gentleman and a serious person, but I'm afraid it's more for worldly fame than for himself or for God. [. . .]

Today is 22 September, Yasnaya Polyana Wrote a letter to Sonya yesterday to say that I can't be guided in my writing by her opinions.[18] Wrote from the heart, and with a kind feeling. And she accepted it with the same feeling. Yesterday I finished the translation with Langlet.[19] Today I've been busy with *Art*, but couldn't get on with it at all, and then disliked what I had already written. [. . .]

Today is 14 October, Yasnaya Polyana It's the third day since Sonya arrived. I'm alone with her. She's doing some copying. She helps me very much. I'm still writing about art. Revised the 10th chapter today. And clarified what was unclear. I must copy up my notebook, I'm afraid I've forgotten a lot. [. . .]

(4) Details for *Hadji Murat*: (1) the shadow of an eagle runs across a mountain slope, (2) there are tracks of wild animals, horses and people in the sand by the river, (3) as they ride into the woods, the horses snort briskly, (4) a goat jumped out from behind a holly bush. [. . .]

(7) [. . .] Generally speaking – I don't know why – I don't have that religious feeling I used to have previously when I wrote my diary just for myself. The fact that people have read it and may read it in future destroys this feeling. But the feeling was precious and helped me in life. Starting from today, the 14th, I'll begin to write again as I used to – so that nobody should read it during my lifetime. If there should be any thoughts which deserve it, I can copy them out and send them to Chertkov. [. . .]

(14) You get angry with a woman because she doesn't understand something, or she understands, but doesn't do what reason tells her. She can't do this. Just as a magnet acts on iron and doesn't act on wood, so the conclusions of reason are not binding on her, are not motive forces. Feeling and the conclusions of reason are only binding on her when they are transmitted by an authority, i.e. the feeling of a desire not to lag behind others. And so she won't believe or follow an obvious demand of reason unless it is confirmed by an authority, but she will believe and follow the greatest folly as long as everyone does so. She can't do otherwise. And we get angry. There are many men like that as well – womanish. [. . .]

(18) Rode past the out-buildings. Remembered the nights I used to spend there, and the youth and beauty of Dunyasha[20] (I never had a liaison with her), her strong womanly body. Where is it? It's long been nothing but bones. What are those bones? What relation have they to Dunyasha? There was a time when those bones formed part of that separate being which was Dunyasha. But then that being shifted its centre, and what used to be Dunyasha became part of another being, enormous in size and inaccessible to me, which I call the earth. We don't know the life of the earth and so we consider it dead, just as an insect which lives for only an hour considers my body to be dead because it doesn't see its movement. [. . .]

The letter to Stockholm has been printed.[21]

Today is 16 October, Yasnaya Polyana   Didn't write my diary yesterday. Health quite improved. Sonya still works a lot with me and helps me.[22] [. . .]

Today is 10 November, Yasnaya Polyana [. . .] Went to Yasenki today with Lyova, and he started a funny conversation about culture. He wouldn't be a bad fellow if it wasn't for this enormous denominator below a very small numerator.[23] [. . .]

Walked through the village, looking into the windows. There was poverty and ignorance everywhere, and I thought about the slavery of old. Formerly one could see the cause, one could see the chains which bound people, but now there aren't any chains – and in Europe there are only hairs, but just as many of them as the ones which bound Gulliver. In our country one can still see ropes, or anyway twine, while over there there are only hairs, but they hold them so tightly that the giant people can't move. The only salvation is not to lie down, not to go to sleep. The deception is so powerful and so cunning that you often see the very people who are being sucked dry and destroyed passionately defending their bloodsuckers and attacking those who are against them. With us it's the Tsar.

14 November, Yasnaya Polyana A disgruntled letter from Sonya. And Tanya writes that she is displeased that I'm not going. I only want one thing: to do as well as possible in the sight of God. I still don't know how. Slept badly last night – bad, evil thoughts. And apathy. No desire to work. Revised the foreword on science. Made the following notes:
(1) Read about the actions of the British in Africa.[24] It's all terrible. But it occurred to me that perhaps it was unavoidably necessary in order that enlightenment should get through to these peoples. At first I thought hard, and thought it was necessary. What nonsense! Why can't people living a Christian life not simply go and live with them, like Miklukho-Maklay;[25] why do they need to trade, make drunkards of them, kill them? [. . .]
(3) Thought as a *pendant* [counterpart] to Hadji Murat of writing about another Russian brigand – Grigory Nikolayev – in such a way that he should see the whole lawlessness of the life of the rich, should live as a caretaker of an orchard on a wealthy estate with a lawn tennis court.[26]

Today is the 17th, Yasnaya Polyana For the second day I've been thinking particularly clearly about the following:
(1) My life – my awareness of my own personality – is getting weaker and weaker, and will get weaker still and end in marasmus and the absolute cessation of the awareness of personality. At the same time, absolutely simultaneously and parallel with the destruction of my personality, the things that my life has done, the consequences of my thoughts and feelings, are beginning to live and are growing stronger and stronger: are living in other people, even in animals and in dead matter. And so I would like to say that this is what will live after me. [. . .]
(2) I also thought today quite unexpectedly about the charm – actually the charm – of awakening love, when, against the background of joyful, pleasant and sweet relationships, that little star suddenly begins to shine. It's like a sudden waft of scent from a lime tree or the first shadow falling as the moon comes out. It's not yet fully light, and there is no clear light and shade, but there is joy and fear of the new and the fascinating. It's good, but only when it's for the first and last time. [. . .]

Today is the 20th, evening, Yasnaya Polyana Got on with the foreword to

Carpenter. Thought a lot about *Hadji Murat* and prepared my material. Still can't find the right tone. Letters from Sonya, one of them unpleasant. But a good one today. I think about the journey to Moscow with horror. [. . .]

Yesterday an angry conversation with Lyova. I said a lot of unpleasant things to him, he remained silent for the most part, and towards the end I felt ashamed and sorry for him, and began to love him. There is much good in him. I forget how young he is. [. . .]

21 November   Alive. Still thinking and collecting material for *Hadji Murat*. Today I thought a lot, read, started to write, but stopped at once. [. . .]
(1) Thought about death – about how strange it is that one doesn't want to die, although nothing holds one – and thought about prisoners who have become so much at home in their prisons that they don't want to, and are even afraid to, leave them for freedom. In the same way we too are at home in the prison of this life and are afraid of freedom. [. . .]

22 November   Dreamed very vividly that Tanya fell off a horse, broke her head and was dying, and that I was weeping over her.

24 November, Yasnaya Polyana   Tanya arrived safely today. Masha is still poorly. But she wasn't distressed by my letter.[27] I love them both very much. All their weaknesses are understandable and touching. [. . .]
Thought during this time:
(1) A strange fate: anxieties and passions begin in adolescence, and you think: you'll get married and it will all pass. And it did pass for me, and there was a long period – some eighteen years – of peace. Then came the striving to change my life, and a set-back. Struggle, suffering and finally, it seemed, a haven, and a respite. But it wasn't so. The real difficulties have begun and are continuing and will probably stay with me till death. [. . .]

25 November   Alive. Tanya has gone. She's very dear – and good. I was wrong to talk to her about my situation. Revised *Art*. Wrote quite a good letter to Maude. A good letter from Galya. Thought:
(1) It always seems to us that we are loved because we are good. But we don't suspect that we are loved because those who love us are good. You can see this if you listen to what that miserable, disgusting and vain person says whom you have taken pity on with a great effort: he says that he's so good that you couldn't have acted otherwise. And it's just the same when people love you.
(2) 'Lobsters love to be boiled alive.' That's not a joke. How often do you hear it, or have said it, or say it yourself. Man has the faculty of not seeing the sufferings he doesn't want to see. And he doesn't want to see the sufferings he has caused himself. How often have I heard it said about

coachmen who are kept waiting, or about cooks, man-servants or peasants that 'they are very happy' at their work. Lobsters love to be boiled alive.

Today is 2 December, Yasnaya Polyana   A sad, melancholy, despressed state of body and spirits, but I know that I'm alive and can feel this *I* of mine, if only a little, independently of this condition. A letter from Tanya today to say that Sonya was upset by my sending the foreword to the *Northern Herald*. I'm terribly afraid about this.[28] During these last days I had an absurd, irritable letter from Grot. So far nothing has been decided.[29] [. . .] Thought: [. . .]
(2) Had a talk with Dušan.[30] He said that since he had involuntarily become my representative in Hungary, how was he to act? I was glad of the opportunity to tell him and make it clear to myself that to speak about Tolstoyanism, to seek my guidance and to ask my decision about problems was a serious and crude mistake. There is no Tolstoyanism or teaching of mine, and never has been; there is only one eternal, universal, world-wide teaching of the truth as expressed particularly clearly for me and for us all in the Gospels. [. . .]
   I think I've finished *Art*.

3 December   My work on *Art* has cleared up a lot of things for me. If God bids me write works of fiction, they will be entirely different ones. And it will be both easier and more difficult to write them. We'll see.

Today is 6 December, Moscow
   On the 4th I went to Dolgoye. The tumbledown house made a very moving impression on me. A swarm of memories.[31] I've written almost nothing for two days – only prepared some chapters of *Art* and packed my things. Very depressing letters from Sonya. Arrived on the 5th. She wasn't there. She had gone to the Troitsa Monastery in a terrible state of excitement. It was all due to my article in the *Northern Herald*. I unwittingly made a mistake. Stupid letters from Grot. He's mentally ill. Went to see Trubetskoy. I've given in to them.[32] Sonya came back in the evening, more composed. We had a talk, and felt better. Made no notes. Woke up feeling ill.

7 December   Talked more and more yesterday, and I heard from Sonya something I'd never heard before: an admission of guilt. It was a great joy. I
thank Thee, Father. Whatever should happen in future, this has already happened, and it is a great good. [. . .]

11 December   [. . .] During this time Grot's condition has become clear. He's mentally ill, like all people who are not Christians. [. . .]

Today is the 13th [. . .] Want to make a note now of subjects which can be, and deserve to be, worked up properly:

(1) *Sergey.*[33] (2) *Alexander I.*[34] (3) *Persiyaninov.*[35] (4) *The Story of Petrovich, the Husband who Died a Pilgrim.*[36] (5) The following are not so good – *the Legend of the Descent of Christ into Hell and the Rebuilding of Hell.*[37] (6) *The Forged Coupon.* (7) *Hadji Murat.* (8) *The Substitute Child.*[38] (9) Probably the drama of a Christian resurrection,[39] and (10) *Resurrection* – the trial of a prostitute. (11) Excellent – a brigand who murders defenceless people.[40] (12) *The mother.*[41] (13) The execution in Odessa.[42]

It's depressing at home. But I want to be cheerful and will be. [. . .]

Diary, 1897. 21 December, Moscow I'm beginning a new exercise book, as though in a new state of mind. For five days or so now I've done nothing. I've been thinking about *Hadji Murat*, but without enthusiasm or confidence. *On Art* has been published. Chertkov is displeased.[43] So are people here. Received an anonymous letter yesterday with a threat of murder if I don't reform by 1898. I'm only given until 1898. I'm both apprehensive and pleased. Sonya is very weak, and I'm terribly sorry for her. She is undergoing a crisis too. I've been skating. It's a sign of my inactive state of mind that I've made no notes. Have just read Chekhov's story *On the Cart*. Excellent for its descriptiveness, but rhetorical as soon as he wants to give a meaning to the story. My head is wonderfully clear, thanks to my book on art.

Alive. Today is 29 December, Moscow. Morning. Thought about *Hadji Murat*. All day yesterday a drama-comedy, *The Corpse*, was taking shape in my head.[44] I'm still unwell. Went to the Behrs' yesterday. Received letters with threats of murder.[45] A pity there are people who hate me, but it doesn't interest me much and doesn't worry me at all. [. . .]

1898

Two days have passed. *1 January, 1898.* I greet the New Year very sad, depressed and unwell. I can't work, and my stomach still aches.

Received a letter from Fedoseyev in Verkholensk about the Dukhobors,[1] a very touching one. Another letter from the editor of *The Adult* about free love.[2] If I had time, I would like to write about this subject. I probably shall write. The main thing is to show that it's all a question of guaranteeing for oneself the greatest possible pleasure without thinking about the consequences. Apart from that, they preach something which already exists and is very bad. And why should the absence of external *restraint*[3] make everything all right? I am, of course, against any regulation and in favour of complete freedom, but the ideal is chastity, and not pleasure. [. . .]

Today is the 4th already. I'm a little better. I feel like working. Yesterday – Stasov and Rimsky-Korsakov,[4] coffee, and stupid conversation about art. When will I follow the rule that much talk means much bother. [. . .]

Today is 13 January, Moscow Haven't written my diary for more than a week. And I've hardly done anything. I'm still unwell. And dejected. Sometimes good and composed, sometimes anxious and not good. The day before yesterday I felt miserable. Then some peasants came: Balakhov with Stepan Petrovich and two from Tula. And I felt so relieved and cheerful. One mustn't give in to one's own circle. One can always enter the circle of God and His people. [. . .]

3 February Still as unproductive mentally. [. . .] Noted the following: [. . .]
(8) One of the most common delusions is to consider people good, evil, stupid or clever. Man is in a state of flux and contains within himself every potential: he was stupid and is now clever, he was evil and is now good, and vice versa. That is man's greatness. And for that reason one mustn't judge a man. What is he like? You judge him and he is already a different person. And one mustn't say: 'I don't love him.' You say it, and the situation is already different.
(9) People say about the Tsar that it's not he who is to blame, but his entourage. That's not true: he alone is the cause of everything. One can and must pity him, but one must know where the cause lies. [. . .]
(13) Power resides in the working people. If they endure their oppression,

it's only because they are hypnotized. This is the whole gist of the matter – one must destroy this hypnosis.

Today is 19 February, Moscow Haven't written my diary for a long time. At first I was unwell. For about five days I've been better. During this time I've kept revising and adding to and spoiling the last chapters on *Art*. I decided to send off Carpenter and my foreword to the *Northern Herald*. I've been revising this foreword too. The general impression made by this article *On Science*, as well as that of chapter 20, is – remorse. I feel that it's true and that it's necessary, but it hurts me that I should offend and distress many good, deluded people. Obviously 999 people out of 1,000 won't understand on what account I condemn our science, and will be indignant. I ought to have done it with more kindness. And I'm to blame for this, but it's too late now. [. . .]

19 March Haven't written my diary for more than three weeks. *Today is 19 March, Moscow*. Finished all my letters. During this time I've written some important letters: (1) to the American colony,[5] (2) to the *Petersburg Gazette* about the Dukhobors,[6] (3) to the English newspapers, also about the Dukhobors,[7] and (4) a foreword to the English edition of *What is Art?* – about the censor's mutilations.[8] [. . .]

The main event during this time was the permission for the Dukhobors to emigrate. *What is Art?* is now, I think, completely finished. Sonya left for Petersburg yesterday. She is just as unstable. I haven't done much work all this time. [. . .]

Today is 21 March, Moscow I'm continuing copying out my notes. [. . .] (6) The socialists will never destroy poverty and injustice, and the inequality of talents. The most intelligent and the strongest will always make use of the most stupid and the weakest. Justice and the equality of goods can never be attained by anything less than Christianity, i.e. by renouncing the self and recognizing the meaning of one's life to be in the service of others. [. . .]

(10) For the *Appeal*. All are agreed that we don't live as we ought to and as we could. The remedy for some is religious fatalism, and, still worse, scientific, evolutionary fatalism; others comfort themselves with the fact that everything is gradually getting better and better of its own accord – the gradualists; a third group promises that everything will come right once things reach their very worst – the socialists: the government and the wealthy classes will have full control of everyone, i.e. the workers, and then power will somehow transfer itself all of a sudden not simply to the workers, but to infallible, disinterested, self-sacrificing, saintly workers who will then run everything without mistakes, and without wrongdoing; a

fourth group says that things can only be put right by exterminating villains and evil men. But there is no indication where evil people end and where harmless ones, if not good ones, begin. Either the evil people will not all be exterminated, or, as in a big revolution, the good will be caught up with the bad. Once you begin to judge people strictly, nobody will be innocent. So what is to be done? There is only one means: a religious change in people's thinking. And it is precisely such a change which is being prevented by all these imaginary remedies. [. . .]

(13) How good it would be to write a work of art in which one could clearly express the shifting nature of man; the fact that one and the same man is now a villain, now an angel, now a wise man, now an idiot, now a strong man, now the most impotent of creatures. [. . .]

(16) There is an English toy called a 'peepshow'[9] – first one thing and then another is shown underneath a glass. That's the way to show Hadji Murat: as a husband, a fanatic, etc. [. . .]

(22) Had a talk with Peshkova[10] about the woman question. There is no woman question. There is the question of freedom and equality for all human beings. But the woman question is an irritant. [. . .]

Today is 27 April, Grinyovka[11] My third day here. I'm all right. A little unwell. Sonya left this morning – sad and distraught. She's very depressed. And I'm very sorry for her and I still can't help her. All the time in Moscow recently I was finishing *Carthago delenda est*. I'm afraid I haven't finished with it, and it will come back to me again. But it's reasonably good. I've done no work here. The famine disaster isn't nearly as great as it was in 1891. There are so many lies to do with everything in the upper classes, everything is so tangled up in lies, that it's never possible to answer any question simply: for example, is there a famine? I'll try to distribute the money entrusted to me as well as possible.[12] [. . .]

Today is 29, morning, Grinyovka. I've been very weak. Felt better since yesterday. But haven't been able to write anything. Walked to Lopashino and compiled some lists.[13] Read Boccaccio.[14] The beginning of ruling-class immoral art. No letters. Seryozha has been. I'll continue: I thought: [. . .]

(8) I began to think about soup-kitchens, the purchase of flour, and money, and I felt so unclean and sad at heart. The realm of money, i.e. any kind of use of money is a sin. I accepted money, and undertook to use it only in order to have a pretext for getting away from Moscow. And I acted *badly*. [. . .]

Today, I think, is 12 June, Yasnaya Polyana [. . .] Sonya has arrived, sick herself, and terribly overcome with fear on my behalf.[15] It's about four days since I arrived at Yasnaya, and I'm making a good recovery. I've written a lot of letters. Received up to 4,000 roubles, which I can't use this year. Masha and her husband and Ilyusha are here. And the Westerlunds. Dora has had a baby.[16] Tanya is definitely going to get married. I'm sorry for her, but perhaps it's necessary for her soul. Today, quite unexpectedly, I started to finish *Sergey*.[17] No news from England. I've made a great many notes. [. . .]

(12) The sight of my children owning land and making the people work has such a strange and depressing effect on me. Like pangs of conscience. And this is not a reasoned judgement, but a feeling, and a very strong one. Was I wrong not to have given my land to the peasants? I don't know.

(13) Leskov has made use of my theme,[18] and badly at that. My wonderful idea was – three questions: what time is the most important? What person? And what act?

The time is now, this minute; the person is the one you are now dealing with; and the act is to save your own soul, i.e. to perform an act of love. [. . .]

Today is 22 June, Yasnaya Polyana On the 16th I took seriously ill. I've never felt so weak and near to death. I'm ashamed to take advantage of the care bestowed on my by those near to me. Could do nothing at all. Only read and made a few notes. I'm much better today. Ukhtomsky made a fuss of my article, but still refused to print it.[19] I telegraphed to Menshikov to ask him to try the *Herald of Europe* and *Russian Labour*. I'm afraid I'm getting on his nerves. The young folk have been sent packing. They've been forbidden to hand out the flour they bought.[20] Lyova talked about his story.[21] I told him hurtfully that what he had done was 'uncivilized' (his favourite expression), not to mention the fact that it was stupid and untalented. His very crude and uncivilized, but very good-natured *beaux parents* [parents-in-law] left today. [. . .]

Today is 28 June, Yasnaya Polyana Evening, I've only now recovered, and am experiencing the pleasure of *convalescence*. I feel nature particularly keenly and vividly, and my thoughts are very clear . . . I've written a little more of *The Appeal*. Today I've been getting on with *Father Sergey*. Both are quite good. [. . .] Noted: [. . .]

(2) It's particularly unpleasant for me when people who have lived little and thought little don't believe me, and argue about moral questions without understanding me. It's for the same reason that a veterinary surgeon would be annoyed if people not versed in his art were to argue with him. The only difference is that the art of the veterinary surgeon, the cook or the samovar maker, or whatever art or science you like, is recognized as an art or science in which only those people are competent who have studied that subject; but in matters of morality all people consider themselves competent because everyone needs to justify his own

life, and life is only justified by theories of morality. And everyone makes them up for himself.

(3) I have often thought about being in love – good, ideal love, excluding all sensuality – and I could find no place or meaning for it. But it does have a very clear place and function: to lighten the struggle between sexual desire and chastity. Being in love should be for young people unable to remain completely chaste, it should precede marriage and rescue young people in the very critical years from sixteen to twenty or more, from their painful struggle. That's the place for being in love. But when it erupts into the lives of people after marriage, it is out of place and disgusting. [. . .]

17 July, Yasnaya Polyana Morning. Nothing special happened these last eleven days. Decided to let my stories *Resurrection* and *Father Sergey* be published for the benefit of the Dukhobors.[22] Sonya has gone to Kiev. An inner struggle. I don't much believe in God. I don't rejoice at the examination, but am oppressed by it, knowing in advance that I won't pass. Didn't sleep all last night.[23] Got up early and prayed a lot. [. . .]

3 August, Pirogovo Everything is just the same again. My life is just as repulsive again. I've lived through a great deal. I haven't passed the examination. But I don't despair and want a re-examination. I did particularly badly at the examination because I had the intention of transferring to another institution.[24] I must abandon these thoughts and then I'll study better. [. . .]

I'll continue to copy out what I haven't copied: [. . .]

(4) Even if what Marx predicts were to happen, then the only thing that would happen would be that despotism would be transferred. Now the capitalists are in power, then the workers' bosses would be in power.

(5) The mistake of the Marxists (and not only of them, but of the whole materialistic school) is that they don't see that the life of mankind is advanced by the growth of consciousness, the advancement of religion and a more and more clear and general understanding of life which provides a satisfactory answer to all problems, and not by economic causes.

(6) The main misjudgement, the main error, of Marx's theory is the supposition that capital will pass out of the hands of private individuals into the hands of the government, and from the government, representing the people, into the hands of the workers. The government does not represent the people, but is these same private individuals who have power, somewhat different from capitalists, but partly coinciding with them. And so the government will never hand over capital to the workers. It is a fiction, a deception, that the government represents the people. *If only there were such a system whereby the government actually did express the will of the people, such a government would have no need of force,*

nor would there be any need for a government in the sense of an authority. [. . .]

(13) I pray to God that He might rescue me from the suffering which torments me. But this suffering is sent to me by God in order to rescue me from evil. The master whips his cattle in order to drive them out of a burning shed and save them, but the cattle pray not to be whipped.

(14) There are some common misunderstandings of my views, sometimes deliberate, sometimes not, which, I confess, irritate me: (1) I say that the God who created the world in six days and who sent His son, and also His son himself, are not God, but that God is the one incomprehensible good, the beginning of everything; but people accuse me of denying God. (2) I say that one ought not to resist violence by violence; but people accuse me of saying that one ought not to fight against evil. (3) I say that one ought to strive towards chastity, and that the highest stage on this path is virginity, the second a pure marriage and the third an impure one – i.e. not just marriage – but still marriage; but people accuse me of denying marriage and preaching the cessation of the human race. (4) I say that art is an infectious activity, and the more infectious art is, the better it is. But whether this activity is good or bad doesn't depend only on how far it satisfies the demands of art, i.e. on it infectiousness, but also on how far it satisfies the demands of religious awareness, i.e. morality, conscience; but people accuse me of preaching tendentious art, etc.

(15) Woman – the legends say – is the tool of the devil. She is generally stupid, but the devil lends her his brains when she works for him. And lo and behold, she performs miracles of intelligence, far-sightedness and constancy in order to do something nasty, but when there is no need for anything nasty, she can't understand the simplest thing, can't think beyond the present moment and has no endurance or patience (except over bearing children and looking after them).

(16) All this concerns the woman who is not a Christian, not a chaste woman – like all the women of our Christian world. Oh, how I would like to show to women the full significance of a chaste woman. A chaste woman (the legend of Mary is not in vain) will save the world. [. . .]

2 November   It's terrible to see how long I've gone without writing my diary – more than two months. And not only has there been nothing bad, but rather everything has been good. The jubilee[25] was not so repulsive and depressing as I expected. The sale of the story and the receipt of the 12,000 roubles which I gave to the Dukhobors was well organized.[26] I was displeased with Chertkov and saw that I was to blame. A Dukhobor came from Yakutsk. I liked him very much. Seryozha is very close to me in deed and feeling. I deliberately don't provoke him with words. Things are very well with Sonya. I love her more than before. Masha is to be pitied for her weakness, but she is just as close in spirit. Tanya has broken things off,[27] but is very unstable. Andryusha is going to marry Dieterichs[28] and is much closer to me. Misha and Lyova are strangers. But praise God and thanks be to Him that He has come to life and is on fire within me, and that it is natural for me either to love and rejoice, or to love and pity. What happiness!

Archer[29] came here yesterday, from Chertkov; I took a liking to him. There's very much to do, but I'm entirely engrossed in *Resurrection*; I'm saving water and only using it for *Resurrection*. I think it will be quite good. People praise it, but I don't believe them. [. . .]

14 November Again I haven't noticed how eleven days have gone by. I've been very absorbed in *Resurrection*, and am making good progress. I'm quite near the end. Seryozha and Suller[30] have been, and both went to the Caucasus with my letter to Golitsyn.[31] Sonya arrived yesterday. Things are very well. It's a long time since I've felt so hale and hearty mentally and physically. [. . .]

(15) The moral progress of mankind only takes place because there are old people. Old people grow kinder and wiser and hand on their experience of life to succeeding generations. Were it not so, mankind would not have progressed. And what a simple means! [. . .]

Today is 25 November, Yasnaya Polyana Sonya went away full of good feelings, and I promised to come on 1 December. Misha is worrying her and she is depressed. I want to join her as soon as possible. [. . .]

A DIALOGUE[32]

Last night there was a conversation and a scene which had a far greater effect on me than her last journey.[33] In order to describe the conversation it must be said that I had returned the same day after 11 o'clock at night from a journey of eighteen *versts* to inspect Masha's estate. I don't say that this was hard work for me, it was a pleasure; but still I was rather tired, having done about forty *versts* on horseback, and not having slept during the day. And I'm seventy.

Under the influence of my conversation with you, my tiredness and a good, happy frame of mind I went to bed intending to say nothing about what had happened, and hoping that it would all blow over of its own accord, as you consoled me by saying. We went to bed. We said nothing for a while. Then she began to speak.

She: Will you go to Pirogovo and abuse me in front of Seryozha?
I: I haven't spoken to anybody, not even to our daughter Tanya.
She: But you spoke to my sister Tanya?
I: Yes.
She: What did she say?

I: The same as she said to you . . . she defended you to me, and probably spoke up on my behalf to you.

She: Yes, she was terribly hard on me. Too hard. I don't deserve it.

I: Please don't let's talk about it, it will sort itself out, settle down, and, God willing, disappear.

She: I can't help talking about it. It's too depressing for me to live in constant fear. If he[34] calls now, it will begin again. He didn't say anything, but he might call.

The news that he would come – as always 'might come' meant in fact that he certainly would come – was very depressing to me. I had just intended to stop thinking about it, when this depressing visit cropped up again. I remained silent, but couldn't get to sleep and couldn't refrain from saying:

I: I was just hoping for some peace, and now you seem to be preparing me again for an unpleasant prospect.

She: But what can I do? 'It's possible,' he said to Tanya. I didn't invite him. Perhaps he won't call.

I: Whether he calls or not isn't important, even your journey isn't important; what is important, as I said to you before, as I said to you two years ago, is your attitude towards your feeling. If you acknowledged your feeling to be bad you wouldn't even have thought about whether he would call, wouldn't even have spoken about him.

She: Well, what am I to do now?

I: Repent at heart of your feeling.

She: I can't repent, and I don't understand what it means.

I: It means discussing with yourself whether the feeling which you have for this man is good or bad.

She: I don't have any feeling, good or bad.

I: That's not true.

She: The feeling is so unimportant, insignificant.

I: All feelings, and therefore the most insignificant also, are always either good or bad in our eyes, and therefore you too must decide whether this was a good feeling or a bad one.

She: There's nothing to decide, this feeling is so unimportant that it can't be bad. And there's nothing bad about it at all.

I: No, the exclusive feeling of an old, married woman for another man is a bad feeling.

She: I have no feeling for a man, only for a person.

I: But this person is a man.

She: He isn't a man for me. It isn't a question of any exclusive feeling, it's a question of music being a comfort to me after my sorrow, but there isn't any special feeling for the person.

I: Why tell lies?

She: All right. There was once. I was wrong to have gone,[35] to have distressed you. But it's over now. I'll do anything not to distress you.

I: You can't do that because it's not a matter of what you do – of going, or receiving him or not – it's a matter of your attitude towards your feeling. You must decide yourself whether it's a good or a bad feeling.

She: But there isn't any feeling.

I: That's not true. And this is just what is bad for you that you want to hide this feeling, to suppress it. But until you decide whether this feeling is good or bad, and until you acknowledge that it is bad, you won't be able to help hurting me. If you acknowledge, as you do now, that this feeling is good, then you will never be able to stop wanting to satisfy this feeling, i.e. to see him, and since you want to do so, you won't be able to help ensuring that you do see him. If you avoid opportunities of seeing him, you will be melancholy and depressed. Therefore it's all a matter of deciding what sort of feeling it is, good or bad.

She: I did wrong to hurt you, and I repent of that.

I: This is just what is bad, that you repent of your actions, but not of the feeling which controls them.

She: I know that I haven't loved and don't love anyone more than you. I would like to know how you understand my feeling for you. How could I love you, if I loved someone else?

I: Your discord is due to the fact that you haven't made clear to yourself the meaning of your feelings. A drunkard or a gambler loves his wife very much, but can't refrain from gambling and drink, and never will refrain until he decides in his own heart whether his love for gambling and drink is a good feeling. Only when that has been decided is deliverance possible.

She: Always the same old thing.

I: But I can't say anything else when it's as clear as day that it's all to do with this.

She: I've done nothing wrong.

So the conversation would keep coming back to the same point with different variations. She tried to show that this feeling was very unimportant, and therefore couldn't be condemned, and there was no reason to fight against it. I kept returning to the point that if a feeling is acknowledged in one's heart to be good there is no deliverance from it, and no deliverance from those hundreds of thousands of trivial actions which stem from this feeling and sustain it.

She: Well, what will happen if I acknowledge the feeling to be bad?

I: The fact that you will fight against it, and will avoid everything that sustains it. You will get rid of everything connected with it.

She: But it's all just in order to deprive me of my only consolation – music. I'm in a terrible *cercle vicieux*. I'm depressed. I can only get rid of this depression by playing the piano. If I play, you say that it's all connected with my feeling; if I don't play I'm depressed, and you say that my feeling is the cause of it.

I: I only say one thing: you must decide whether the feeling is good or bad. Without that our torments will never end.

She: There isn't any feeling, there's nothing to decide.

I: As long as you say that, there's no way out. But if a person has no moral judge to tell him what is good and bad, that person is like a blind man who can't distinguish colours. You don't have this moral judge, and so let's not talk any more – it's two o'clock.

A long silence.

She: Well then, I ask myself absolutely sincerely: what sort of feeling do I have, and what would I wish for? I would wish for nothing more than that he should come once a month to stay a while and play, like any good acquaintance.

I: But by these very words you yourself confirm that you have an exclusive feeling for this person. Surely there isn't any other person whose monthly visit would be a joy for you. If a visit once a month would be pleasant, then once a week or every day would be more pleasant still. By saying this you unwittingly acknowledge your exclusive feeling. And without deciding the question whether this is good or bad, nothing can be changed.

She: Oh, always the same old thing. It's torture. Other people are unfaithful to their husbands, but they aren't tormented as much as I am. Why is it? Because I love music. You can reproach people for their actions, but not for their feelings. They aren't under our control. And there haven't been any actions.

I: No actions? What about the journey to Petersburg, and to this place and that, and all this music?

She: But what is special about my life?

I: What do you mean what is special? You live an exclusive life. You've become a sort of lady of the conservatoire.

These words for some reason angered her terribly.

She: You want to torment me and deprive me of everything. It's so cruel of you.

She reached a state of semi-hysteria. I was silent for quite a long time, and then remembered God. I prayed and thought to myself: 'She *cannot* renounce her feeling, she cannot use reason to influence her feelings. With her, as with all women, feeling is paramount, and any change of feeling takes place, perhaps, independently of reason . . . Perhaps Tanya is right that it will gradually disappear of its own accord in that special way women have which is incomprehensible to me. I must tell her this, I think, and say it with compassion for her and the desire to calm her down – that perhaps I'm mistaken in putting the question so much from my own point of view, that perhaps she will come to the same conclusion in her own way, and that I hope so. But at the moment her anger has reached its peak.'

She: You have tormented me, for two hours you have been using the same phrase over and over again: exclusive, exclusive feeling, good or bad, good or bad. It's terrible. Goodness knows what your cruelty will lead to.

I: But I prayed and wanted to help you.

She: It's all lies, pharisaism, deceit. You can deceive other people, but I can see right through you.

I: What's the matter with you? I just wanted to do good.

She: There's no good in you. You're evil, you're a beast. *I will love good and decent people, but not you. You're a beast.*

Whereupon there followed nonsensical, not to say terrible and cruel words: threats, suicide, curses on everyone, on me and our daughters. And some sort of threats to publish her stories if I published *Resurrection* with a description of the chambermaid.[36] And then sobs, laughter, whispering, nonsensical and, alas, hypocritical words: my head is splitting, look here, where the parting is, cut the vein in my neck, here it is – and all sorts of nonsense which could be dreadful. I held her in my arms. I knew that this always helps, and I kissed her on the forehead. She couldn't get her breath for a long time, then she began to yawn and sigh and dropped off to sleep, and is still sleeping.

I don't know how this madness can be resolved. I don't see any way out. She obviously values this feeling of hers as dearly as her life, and won't acknowledge it to be bad. And since she won't acknowledge it to be bad, she can't be rescued from it, and will go on taking actions provoked by this feeling, actions which it is painful and shameful for me and the children to see.

1899

2 January, Yasnaya Polyana The last time I wrote my diary was on 25 November, consequently a month and a week ago. [. . .] All this time I've been working exclusively on *Resurrection*. There have been dealings to do with the Dukhobors and an infinite number of letters. Kolechka Gay is with me, it's refreshing to be with him. Things are not happy in the family: Masha has been ill (it ended yesterday, she had a miscarriage). Tanya is worried and lifeless. Misha is crazy. Andryusha is equivocal. I get on well with Sonya. I'm at peace, as old men are. [. . .]

2 January My notes. [. . .]
(3) Our art is like dressing to food. If there is nothing but dressing it tastes nice, but you won't feel full and your stomach will be upset. [. . .]

Today is 21 February Haven't written my diary for more than six weeks. I'm still in Moscow.[1] At first *Resurrection* went well, then I cooled off towards it completely. Wrote a letter to a sergeant-major,[2] and to the Swedish newspapers.[3] It's three days since I resumed work on *Resurrection*. I'm making progress. A students' strike. They keep trying to involve me. I advise them to behave passively, but I've no wish to write letters to them.[4] Tanya is weak in body and spirit. My back is better. An interesting and lively Frenchman, Sinet,[5] is staying with us. The first religious Frenchman. [. . .]

26 June, Yasnaya Polyana Haven't written my diary for four months; I won't say I've spent the time badly. I've been working intensively on *Resurrection*, and still am. There's a lot in it that isn't bad, things for whose sake it is being written. The other day I was seriously ill. I'm well now. Sonya is going to our sons' today. She has been seriously ill, and is still weak. The critical time is not over yet, I'm often very tenderly sorry for her. I felt so today when she said goodbye. Relations are difficult over the printing and translations of *Resurrection*.[6] But most of the time I'm at peace. Correspondence has been neglected. People keep sending money for the famine victims, but I can't do anything except send it on by post. Kolechka[7] is with me, helping me with the work. Seryozha makes me glad every time he comes. Tanya worries me with her frivolity; she has withdrawn into egotistical love, I hope she will come back. I'm continuing to copy things out from my notebook. [. . .]

(18) People don't obey God, they worship Him. Better not to worship, but to obey. [. . .]

(21) It seems strange and immoral that a writer, an artist, when he sees people suffering, doesn't so much sympathize as observe, in order to reproduce these sufferings. But it isn't immoral. The suffering of one person is insignificant compared with the spiritual effect which a work of art – if it is a good one – will have. [. . .]

(25) The military class is a survival which has no use – a caecum. [. . .]

(34) The press is falsehood *with a vengeance.*[8] [. . .]

28 September, Yasnaya Polyana I've been working all the time on *Resurrection.* I'm now bogged down in the 3rd part. Haven't made any progress for a long time. Sonya is in Moscow. I have evolved for myself a state of peace and quiet which hasn't been disturbed yet: not to speak, and to know that this is necessary, and that I must live in these conditions. [. . .]

Read an interesting book about Christ never having existed, that it was a myth.[9] There is as much to be said *for* the likelihood that this is true as there is *against.* Cleared up all the letters yesterday with the help of Masha. Left many unanswered. Thought during this time:

I'm still ill. There's hardly a day without pain. I'm dissatisfied with myself morally too. I've let myself go very much: I'm not working physically and am preoccupied with myself, with my health. How difficult it is to endure illness with resignation, to go to one's death without resistance, but I must. [. . .]

(3) I picked a flower and threw it away. There are so many of them that I wasn't sorry. We don't value the inimitable beauty of living creatures and destroy them without pity – not only plants, but animals and human beings. There are so many of them. Culture – civilization – is nothing else but the destruction of these beautiful things and their replacement. What by? The tavern, the theatre . . . [. . .]

(5) The most valuable thing on earth is good relations between people, but these relations are not formed as a result of conversation – on the contrary they are ruined by conversation. Talk as little as possible, especially with those people with whom you want to maintain good relations. [. . .]

(15) The only instance when a person can and should be preoccupied with himself is when he feels unhappy. Unhappiness is the best condition for improving oneself, for rising to a higher level; unhappiness is an indication of one's imperfection. One should be glad of these instances. They are the preparation of oneself for work, they are spiritual food. [. . .]

Today is 2 October, Yasnaya Polyana [. . .] Andryusha has changed strikingly for the better. Perhaps he'll get worse, but the fact remains, and will leave its mark. [. . .]

Today is 13 October, Yasnaya Polyana   I'm still not altogether well – that's as it should be. But it doesn't prevent me from living, thinking and progressing towards the appointed end. *Resurrection* is making slow progress; I've sent off four chapters, which I don't think will pass the censor, but at least, I think, I've settled on one thing, and I won't make any more changes. I never cease to think about my brother Seryozha,[10] but because of the weather and my ill health I can't bring myself to go. Tanya, I think, has finally decided to get married. Sonya has been to Moscow, and is going again today. Today is a sort of mental holiday for me, and not only today but all recent days. I've thought up some good scenes for *Resurrection*. I keep thinking more and more often and more and more clearly about that separate existence, which appears to us as matter in space and movement in time. [. . .]

There is another important, happy thought which, although an old one, came to me as a new one and makes me very happy, namely:

(1) The main cause of family unhappiness is the fact that people are brought up to think that marriage brings happiness. Sexual attraction is an enticement to marriage, and it takes the form of the promise or hope of happiness, which is bolstered up by public opinion and literature; but marriage is not only not happiness, but always suffering, which is the price one pays for the satisfaction of sexual desire, suffering in the form of lack of freedom, slavery, satiety, disgust, all sorts of spiritual and physical defects in one's partner which have to be borne – malice, stupidity, falsehood, vanity, drunkenness, idleness, meanness, greed, debauchery – all defects which are particularly hard to bear when not in oneself but in somebody else, and from which one has to suffer as if they were one's own; and similarly physical defects: ugliness, dirtiness, nasty smells, sores, insanity, etc., which are even more difficult to endure in other people. All this, or at least something of it, will always be so, and everyone has to bear these hardships. But the things that ought to compensate – care, contentment, help – all this is taken as a matter of course, while all the defects are not taken as a matter of course, and the more people expect happiness from marriage, the more they suffer from them.

The main cause of these sufferings is the fact that what is expected doesn't happen, and what always happens isn't expected. And so the only escape from these sufferings is not to expect joys, but to expect what is bad and be prepared to endure it. If you expect everything that is described at the beginning of *The Thousand and One Nights*, if you expect drunkenness, nasty smells, disgusting diseases, then stubbornness, untruthfulness, even drunkenness can be, if not forgiven, at least not a matter for suffering, and you can be glad that what might have happened didn't happen – the things described in *The Thousand and One Nights* – nor madness, cancer, etc. And then everything that is good will be appreciated. [. . .]

20 November, Moscow There's a lot I haven't written down. I'm in Moscow. Tanya has gone off with Sukhotin for some reason.[11] It's shameful and offensive. For seventy years I've been lowering my opinion of women more and more, and I need to lower it still further. The woman question! Of course there's a woman question![12] Only it's not a question of women beginning to control our life, but of their ceasing to destroy it. [. . .]

Today is 18 December, Moscow Haven't written my diary for nearly a month. I've been seriously ill. It was very painful for twenty-four hours, then a respite and weakness. And death became something more than natural, almost desirable. And so it remains now that I'm getting better. It's a new, joyful step. Finished *Resurrection*. It's not good. Not revised. Too hurried. But I'm free of it, and it doesn't interest me any more.

I'll try to copy out my notes. [. . .]

(11) People usually say: 'This is very profound, and therefore not fully comprehensible.' That isn't true. On the contrary. Everything that is deep is transparently clear. Like water, which is murky on the surface, but the deeper it is, the more transparent it is. [. . .]

Today is 20 December, Moscow Health not good. Mental condition good, I'm ready for death. A lot of people in the evenings – I'm tired. *Resurrection* didn't appear in No. 51[13], and I was sorry. That's bad. I'm thinking over philosophical definitions of life. Thought today about The Coupon – good. Perhaps I'll write it. [. . .]

1900

1 January, Moscow   I'm sitting in my room, *and everybody is here, celebrating the New Year*. All this time I've written nothing in my diary. I've been unwell. There's a lot to note down. [. . .]

(2) If it has once been instilled into a child that he must believe that God is man, that God is 1 and 3, in a word that $2+2 = 5$, the instrument of his knowledge is damaged for ever; faith in reason is undermined. And this is just what is done to all children. It's terrible. [. . .]

(4) I recalled to mind my adolescence, especially my early and late youth. No moral rules were instilled into me at all – none; yet round about me *grown-ups* were self-assuredly smoking, drinking and leading a dissolute life (especially the latter), beating people and demanding hard work from them. And I did a lot of bad things, without wishing to – simply from imitating grown-ups. [. . .]

(11) Eve tempted Adam, and it's always like that. The female decides everything. [. . .]

8 January   Evening. I've done nothing for several days. I've put aside the letter to the Dukhobors,[1] and only revised the article on the 36-hour day.[2] Got nearer the end today. Masha is here (I was just going to write about them and stopped, because they would read it).[3] I'm in good spirits, despite the fact that my health is undermined. I feel the pangs of death, i.e. of a new birth. I can't regard them in any other way, especially when ill, and the more ill I am, the more clearly and calmly I regard them. [. . .]

There's not much to note down. [. . .]

(2) I'm reading about war in the Philippines and Transvaal, and am seized with horror and revulsion. Why? The wars of Frederick and Napoleon were honest wars and therefore not without a certain grandeur. This was so even with the Crimean War. But the wars of the Americans and the British in the midst of a world where even schoolchildren condemn war are terrible. [. . .]

16 January, Moscow   [. . .] Gorky has been.[4] We had a very good talk. And I liked him. A real man of the people. [. . .]

Notes:

(1) One can't be too much on one's guard against the stimulation of one's vanity – love of praise. If an enemy wanted to destroy a man, it would be safer to praise him than to get him drunk. It fosters morbid sensitivity – which leads to idle relaxation when people praise you, and to bitterness and despondency when they blame you. Above all it increases morbidity and vulnerability.

(2) Read Chekov's *Lady with the Dog*.[5] It's all Nietzsche. Previously people who hadn't evolved for themselves a clear philosophy of life which could distinguish good and evil, used to seek anxiously; now they think they are beyond good and evil, but remain on this side, i.e. they are almost animals. [...]

(7) The best attitude to sexual desire is (1) to suppress it altogether. Next best[6] (2) to have relations with one woman only, chaste and of the same faith, and to raise children together and to help one another. (3) Next worse to go to a brothel when tormented by desire; (4) to have casual relations with various women without living with them; (5) to have an affair with a woman and then abandon her; (6) still worse, to have an affair with someone else's wife; (7) worst of all, to go on living with your own unfaithful and immoral wife.

I must tear this sheet out.

27 January, Moscow Haven't written my diary for nearly two weeks. Went to see *Uncle Vanya* and was shocked.[7] Wanted to write my drama *The Corpse*, and sketched out a draft.[8]

Was very depressed by the appearance of G.[9] Retribution still not complete. Serves him right. [...]

13 March Haven't written my diary for more than two months. [...]

Today is 24 March, Moscow Yesterday Tanya had a terrible operation.[10] I understood without any doubt that these clinics erected by merchants and factory owners who have ruined and continue to ruin tens of thousands of lives are a bad thing. The fact that these men can cure one rich person, having ruined hundreds, if not thousands of poor people, is obviously a bad thing, a very bad thing. And the fact that thereby they are allegedly learning to lessen suffering and prolong life is also bad, because the means they use for this purpose (they say 'up to now', but I think essentially) are such that they can save and alleviate the sufferings of only a few chosen people; but mainly because their attention is directed not towards prevention and hygiene, but towards healing deformities which are continually and constantly occurring.

I'm getting on at times with *Patriotism*, and at times with *The Slavery of Money*.[11] [...]

6 April, Moscow   It's evening now. Seryozha is playing, and I feel for some reason moved to tears, and drawn to poetry. But I can't write at such moments. I'm keeping fairly well; I'm still doing the same work which has stood in the way of my literary work, and I long for literary work. I crave for it very much. [. . .]

I noted in my book: [. . .]

(10) There exists a naive, popular opinion that a husband, especially if he is older than his wife and his wife is very young, can educate and mould his wife. This is a gross delusion. Women have their own traditions, their own methods of handing them on, their own language as it were. And so a man can never influence a woman except through her desire to attract him. Women live quite independently of a man's spiritual life (of course there are exceptions, although very rare ones) and never yield to the influence of men, while they themselves, by their persistence and their cunning, have an indirect influence – not a direct one since men don't understand women's language either – on the whole of life, and therefore on men as well. [. . .]

2 May, Moscow   Haven't written my diary for nearly a month. I've been busy all the time with the two articles. And I would like to think I've finished them. There have been hard things, but good things too. More good things. Apart from work I've had few thoughts. Work has swallowed up everything. Tomorrow I'm going to Masha's.[12]

I noted in my book:

(1) You sometimes get angry with people for not understanding you, not following you or going along with you, although you are standing right next to them. That's just like walking through a labyrinth (such as there are in parks) and demanding that a man standing right next to you, only on the other side of the wall, should walk in the same direction as you. He has to walk a whole *verst* in order to catch you up, and to go first of all not in the same direction, but in the opposite one, in order to catch you up. But you know that he has to follow *you*, and not you *him*, only because you have already passed the place where he is standing. [. . .]

Today is 5 May, Pirogovo   Had a good journey. I'm fully fit. The country gave me new life. Saw Seryozha. It was sad, but truly good. Tanya has left. Masha, I think, has had another miscarriage. [. . .]

I'm beginning a new notebook. *19 May, Yasnaya Polyana*. Got back yesterday from Pirogovo, where I spent a wonderful fifteen days. Finished *Slavery* and wrote two acts.[13] I feel well here too. My health was on the point of breaking down. Now it's better. [. . .]

23 June, Yasnaya Polyana Haven't written my diary for more than a month. I haven't spent these thirty-five days badly. I've had moods of depression, but religious feelings got the better of them. All this time I've been continuously and diligently writing *The Slavery of Our Times*. I've put in much that is new and clearer. I terribly want to write something literary, not dramatic, but epic – a continuation of *Resurrection*: Nekhlyudov's life as a peasant.[14] Nature moves and affects me: the meadows and woods – the corn, the ploughed fields, the meadowlands. I think – will this be my last summer? Well, never mind, that's all right. I'm grateful for everything – I've been infinitely blessed. How possible it is to be always thankful, and how joyful. [. . .]

7 August, Yasnaya Polyana Tanya is ill and is still in bed. I was seriously ill – terrible pains – and was a long time getting better. I'm better now. I feel the nearness of death and try to meet it calmly, and I think I shall meet it calmly; but while I'm well, as today, I can't readjust myself quickly to the process of transition.

Finished and sent off both *The Slavery of Our Times* and the article on Umberto's death.[15] I think I've done what I ought and what I could. [. . .]

Wrote a scene for *The Corpse* today. I'll now copy up my notes: [. . .]

(5) Our feelings for people paint them all in the same colour: if we love them they all seem white to us, if we don't they seem black. But there is black and white in everyone. Look for the black in the people you love, and especially the white in those you don't love. [. . .]

21 August, Yasnaya Polyana I've been writing the drama, and am altogether dissatisfied with it. There is no awareness that it is God's work, although it has been much revised: the characters have been altered.

Still the same examination and still the same practices. Things are a little better. The old temptation was aroused today.[16] [. . .] Read George Eliot and Ruskin, and appreciated them very much.[17] [. . .]

Noted down in my book: [. . .]

(2) Why do people remember one thing, and not remember another? Why do I call Seryozha Andryusha, and Andryusha Seryozha? A character is inscribed in my memory. It's this thing that is inscribed in the memory without a name or designation, this thing that unites various faces, objects and feelings into one – it's this that is the subject of art. That's very important, I must clarify it. [. . .]

(8) My position in the family is strange. They may love me, but I'm of no use to them, or rather I'm an *encombrant* [in the way]; if I am of use, then I'm of use to them, the same as to everyone. But it's less obvious to my family than to others what use I am to everyone. And so: a prophet is not without honour, save . . .

30 August, Yasnaya Polyana I'm seventy-two. I haven't been able to do any work all these days. I've had no desire to. I've had a few good thoughts – praise and thanks be to God – that's good. [. . .]

I once asked myself: do I believe, do I actually *believe* that the meaning of life is the fulfilment of the will of God, and that that will is to increase the amount of love (harmony) in myself and in the world, and that by increasing and uniting into one all that is loved, I am thereby paving the way for a future life for myself? And I was forced to answer that I don't believe it in such a definite form. But what do I believe in? I asked. And I answered sincerely that I believe that it is necessary to be good: to be humble, to forgive, to love. I believe in that with all my being. [. . .]

7 September, Yasnaya Polyana [. . .] Made the following notes: [. . .]
(5) The source of all the disasters which people suffer from is the fact that they want to look ahead to the future: to work for it at first each one for himself, then for his family, then for the people. Man can only do what he ought, and must let life take the course which a higher will or fate wishes. Man walks, God leads.

But why is man given the ability to look ahead to the future? I can't answer that. I see that looking ahead and working with the future in mind is a source of evil, but also that such looking ahead is necessary for life: it's necessary, when sowing seeds, to look ahead to the fact that summer and autumn will come and they will grow, etc. I'll come back to this. [. . .]
(11) Thought for my big drama[18] about how to depict a good, decent creature completely lacking in the ability to understand the Christian philosophy of life.
(12) What is now called the Christian religion is the same sort of conventional propriety as the forms of address and signature on letters: 'Dear Sir' and 'Yours faithfully',[19] etc. [. . .]

Today is 22 September, Yasnaya Polyana All this time I've been working badly. [. . .]
I've been in a very bad, unkind frame of mind the whole time. The thought that God is within me no longer helps. [. . .]
Made the following notes:
(1) It seems to me that just as there is a critical sexual age and much is decided at that age, so there is a critical spiritual age – about fifty – when a person begins to think seriously about life and to try to solve the problem of its meaning. Usually what is decided at this time is irrevocable. It's a bad thing if it's wrong. [. . .]

Today is 5 October, Yasnaya Polyana Still busy with the same thing. I've sent off one article on work on the land.[20] I'm still working on the other. The cheerful Boulanger has been. The journal hasn't been abandoned yet. We'll see what happens. Health good. I've been depressed, but was wrong to say that the awareness of God within me doesn't help. It does. I'm reading the Chinese classics.[21] Very important. Wrote ten letters. I've a few notes to write, but there's no time today.

9 October [. . .] I'm not reading much. Not much mental exertion at the moment.

During these days the important thing has been that – I don't remember on what occasion, after inwardly reproaching my sons, I think – I began to recall all the nasty things I've done. I vividly recalled all, or at least most of them, and was horrified. How much better are the lives of other people and of my sons than my own life. I shouldn't be proud of the past, or even of the present, but should be humble, be ashamed, hide myself – ask forgiveness of people. I wrote '*of God*', and then crossed it out. I'm less to blame before God than before people. He made me, He allowed me to be like this. My only consolation is that I've never been evil; there are two or three acts on my conscience which tormented me at the time, but I've never been cruel. But still I'm a disgusting, repulsive creature. And how good it is to know this and remember it. You at once become kinder towards people, and that's the main thing, the one thing necessary. [. . .]

(2) Writers and their works have an improper significance and importance ascribed to them, because the press which forms public opinion is in the hands of writers. Only this can explain these strangely serious deliberations by critics about the significance of the heroes of poems and novels . . . It also explains the exaggerated significance attached to art. They all belong to the same clique. [. . .]

(4) A terrible, insoluble problem: how can clever, educated people – Catholics, Orthodox – believe in the absurdities of the teachings of the Church? It can only be explained by hypnosis. In childhood, and later on in moments of depression, people have ideas suggested to them, and they become so firmly implanted that the people are unable to free themselves from them afterwards. When I was reading books about hypnosis last year, I could find no answer in them to the question: how is one to free oneself from hypnosis? I think there is only one way: breaking off relations with the hypnotizer, a natural way of life and, above all, an advance into the realm of spiritual self-help.

16 October, Yasnaya Polyana [. . .] In spite of good health I've done nothing outstanding during these days. I've finished *Must It Be So?* and since sending it off, I haven't started anything else. [. . .] Nemirovich-Danchenko came about the drama.[22] But my enthusiasm for it has gone.

Thou Shalt Not Kill is in all the papers, even the Italian ones, with omissions. I'm expecting visitors.[23] [. . .]

Today is 27 October, Kochety I've been at Tanya's for ten days now,[24] and haven't written my diary or anything, although my health is good. Today is not 27, but 28. [. . .]

Thought:

(1) Life is continual creation, i.e. the formation of new, higher forms. When this formation comes to a stop in our view or even goes backwards, i.e. when existing forms are destroyed, this only means a new form is taking shape, invisible to us. We see what is outside us, but we don't see what is within us, we only feel it (if we haven't lost our consciousness, and don't take what is visible and external to be the whole of our life). A caterpillar sees itself shrivel up, but doesn't see the butterfly which flies out of it.

(2) Memory destroys time: it unites things that seem to have taken place separately.

(3) I've just been for a walk and thought: there is a religion, a philosophy, a science, a poetry, an art of the great majority of the people; a religion, although covered over with superstitions, a belief in God as the origin of things, in the indestructibility of life; an unconscious philosophy: of fatalism, of the material nature and the reasonableness of all that exists; a poetry of fairy tales, of true happenings in life, of legends; and an art of the beauty of animals, of the products of labour, of carved shutters and weather-vanes, of songs and dances. And there is a religion of true Christianity: philosophy from Socrates to Amiel; poetry: Tyutchev, Maupassant; art (I can't find any examples from painting) – Chopin in certain works, Haydn. And there is also a religion, a philosophy, a poetry, an art of the cultured masses: religion – the Evangelicals, the Salvation Army; philosophy – Hegel, Darwin, Spencer; poetry – Shakespeare, Dante, Ibsen; art – Raphael, the Decadents, Bach, Beethoven, Wagner. [. . .]

12 November, Moscow (Morning.) Health very good. I'm not writing anything; I'm studying Confucius and feel very well. I'm storing up spiritual strength. I want to write down how I now understand *The Great Teaching* and *The Teaching of the Mean*.[25] [. . .]

(2) Was amazed by the news that Princess Vyazemskaya,[26] apparently the quintessence of aristocracy – horses à la Daumon and French prattle – has nineteen inns to her name in the Tambov province, bringing in 2,000 roubles each. And people say there's nothing to write about, and they write about adulteries. [. . .]

18 November, Moscow [. . .] Heard talk about Lyova's work and had a glance at his book and couldn't overcome my disgust and annoyance.[27] I must learn.

23 November, Moscow [. . .] Thought during this time: [. . .]
(1) We, the wealthy classes, ruin the workers, we keep them doing dirty, non-stop work while we enjoy leisure and luxury. We don't give them the opportunity, oppressed as they are by work, to produce the spiritual flowers and fruits of life: poetry, science, religion. We take it upon ourselves to give them all this, and we give them pseudo-poetry, 'Why did you hurry away to the fateful Caucasus', etc.; pseudo-science – jurisprudence, Darwinism, philosophy, the history of the tsars – and pseudo-religion – Church dogma. What a terrible sin. If only we hadn't sucked them dry, they would have developed a poetry and a science and a teaching about life. [. . .]

26 November, Moscow Morning. For more than a month now, since my move to Tanya's on 18 October, I've written nothing; it seems to me at least that I *can't* work; I've no enthusiasm, no thoughts, no belief in the importance of my thoughts or in the possibility of expressing them coherently. I rejoice only that this doesn't prevent me from working in the moral sphere, and, I think, not entirely unsuccessfully: I feel no ill will. *Success in being good is good for the additional reason that one can't be proud or boast about it, or even be comforted by it. Such success is only success when one doesn't notice it oneself.*
I'm reading the Gospels in Dutch[28] and many passages strike me afresh. Thus, I was awfully struck by the Sermon on the Mount. [. . .]

1 December, Moscow [. . .]
(1) What a terrible quality self-assurance, self-satisfaction, is. It freezes a man, as it were: he becomes covered with a crust of ice through which there can be neither growth, nor communication with others, and this crust of ice gets thicker and thicker. These thoughts were prompted by my relations with many people: they are all – it's a terrible thing to say – swine before whom one oughtn't to cast pearls. [. . .]

8 December During this time I received a letter from Canada about wives wanting to join their husbands in the Yakut province, and wrote a letter to the Tsar, but haven't sent it yet.[29] [. . .]
A nice letter from Masha. How ! love her, and how joyful is an atmosphere of love, and how oppressive is the opposite. [. . .]

Today is the 15th [. . .]
(2) Walked past a bookshop and saw *The Kreutzer Sonata*. And I recalled: I

wrote *The Kreutzer Sonata* and *The Power of Darkness* and even *Resurrection* without any thought of preaching to people, of being of use to them, and yet all of them, especially *The Kreutzer Sonata*, have been of great use. Will it be the same with *The Corpse* too? [. . .]

(5) Thought about the fact that Schopenhauer's *Parerga und Paralipomena* is far more powerful than his systematic exposition.[30]

I don't need to (and I've no time to) – but above all I don't need to write out a system. My view of the world will become clear from what I write down here, and if any people need it, they will make use of it. [. . .]

(7) A thought that is very important and dear to me. People usually think that morality is nurtured on culture, like a flower. It's just the opposite. Culture only develops when there is no religion, and therefore no morality (Greece, Rome, Moscow). It's like a luxuriant tree, from which an ignorant gardener expects an abundant crop of fruit because it has a lot of splendid branches. But it has a lot of splendid branches only because it hasn't, and won't have, any fruit. Or like a barren calf.

19 December, Moscow   I've been unwell these last four days and very weak. I'm better today. Lyova came and started a conversation about his writing. I offended him by speaking the truth. It was bad. I should have done it more gently and kindly. [. . .]

(2) An artist, in order to produce an effect on other people, must be a seeker, his work must be a search. If he has found everything and knows everything and teaches or deliberately amuses, he produces no effect. Only if he is seeking does the spectator, the listener or the reader join in with him in his search. [. . .]

(3) The two most terrible plagues of our time: Church Christianity, or rather the dogmatic, supernatural Christianity instilled into *people* from childhood and maintained throughout their lives by hypnosis – and materialism, physiological, anthropological and, above all, historical, i.e. the conviction that everything proceeds automatically according to the laws of mechanics, physics, chemistry, biology and even psychology (in the sense of materialistic psychology), and therefore all efforts to be good or do good are vain and pointless. And this materialism lies in wait for people once they are freed from dogmatic Christianity. No sooner are they freed from the immoral lies of the Church than they fall into the even worse lies of materialism. [. . .]

Today is 20 December, Moscow   [. . .] Read the Buddhist Suttas.[31] Very good. [. . .]

Today is 29 December, Moscow   Lyova's child has died. I'm very sorry for them. Grief always has its spiritual reward and enormous profit. Grief calls

– God has visited you and remembered you . . . Tanya gave birth to a stillborn baby, and is very good and sensible. Sonya is at Yasnaya. Ilya is here. He's astonishingly childish. [. . .]

Must note down the following: [. . .]

(2) Read Nietzsche's *Zarathustra*, and his sister's note about how he wrote it,[32] and am absolutely convinced that he was completely mad when he wrote it, and mad not in a metaphysical sense, but in the straightforward and most exact sense: incoherence, jumping from one idea to another, comparisons with no indication of what is being compared, beginnings of ideas with no endings, leaping from one idea to another for contrast or consonance, and all against the background of the *pointe* of his madness, his *idée fixe*, that by denying all the higher principles of human life and thought he is proving his own superhuman genius. What will society be like if such a madman, and an evil madman, is acknowledged as a teacher? [. . .]

31 December, Moscow I'm still not writing, and am in a very low state of morale. I've just received a letter from a gentleman who is organizing a library.[33] He seems to be reproaching me with mercenariness in selling my works: a tax on the poor, etc. . . . And I became terribly offended that he should suspect and reprove me without knowing my attitude towards this. Furthermore, I felt hatred towards him, and was at a loss how to act: whether to say nothing, or to tell him to approach my wife at the warehouse. And all this was bad. I wanted to rise above it and couldn't, until I suspected that it was all a question of my attitude towards him. I mustn't hate him, but love him: must explain his mistake to him, help him. Yes, only love unties all knots. [. . .]

1901

19 January, Moscow All this time I've been ill and weak. On the good days granted me I wrote a long letter to Serebrennikov in Nizhny.[1] Mental state quite good, if only there was less empty talk.

Noted during this time:

(1) People live by their own thoughts or other people's thoughts, their own feelings or other people's feelings (i.e. understand other people's feelings, are guided by them). The very best person is the one who lives primarily by his own thoughts and other people's feelings; the very worst sort of person is the one who lives by other people's thoughts and his own feelings. The whole difference between people stems from various combinations of these four bases and motives for doing things.

There are people who have almost no thoughts, either their own or other people's, and no feelings of their own, and who live only by other people's feelings: they are self-sacrificing fools and saints. There are people who live only by their own feelings – they are animals. There are people who live only by their own thoughts – they are wise men and prophets; there are those who live only by other people's thoughts – they are learned fools. From various permutations of the strength of these properties stems the whole complex music of characters. [. . .]

(5) A man should raise himself to the level of a woman's chastity; a woman shouldn't lower herself to the level of a man's debauchery, as happens now. [. . .]

6 February, Moscow What a terribly long time since I've written my diary. All this time I haven't been altogether well, or rather, I'm getting older and closer to death. During this time I've written nothing except some unimportant letters. I've been a little less strict in my attention to myself, but I can't complain, I maintain my composure and good-will. Tanya is due to arrive today. Misha's wedding has taken place. I'm afraid she is even more irreligious than most women.[2] But perhaps it's quite the opposite. God grant it may be so. [. . .]

Today is 8 February, Moscow [. . .] People usually say: 'Why impose your religious convictions either on adults or on children? Let everyone form his own.' What a strange confusion of ideas! To impose – i.e. to deprive a person of the possibility of seeing and knowing anything else, as churchmen do – is of course bad, but to hand on both to children and to adults all that human thought has evolved in the field of religion is not only not bad, but necessary. Why, if I teach a child or an adult that the sum of the squares on the sides adjacent is equal to the square of the hypotenuse or that electricity has two poles and acts according to such and such laws am I not coercing; but if I teach that people have a spiritual essence which is immortal, and that one ought to behave towards others as one would wish them to behave towards oneself, I *am* coercing? [. . .]

11 February, Moscow I'm alive, but very weak, and above all bad. I struggle, but can't conquer ill feelings towards people. I don't yield to them, but don't overcome them either. I'm reading Chicherin's book *Science and Religion*. The point of view is correct, but the self-assurance, opaqueness of expression and preconceived ideas make it superficial and *sans portée* [without significance]. A mass of letters which I can't answer. The one good thing about my state of mind is that I look on sufferings and the approach of death not only without grumbling, but sometimes with pleasure. [. . .]

Almost a month has passed. *Today is 19 March.* I've written nothing all this time except an appeal to the Tsar and his aides,[3] and some alterations, all bad ones, to *Hadji Murat*, which I took up again reluctantly.[4]

During this time there was my strange excommunication from the Church,[5] and the expressions of sympathy caused by it, and then the business of the students which assumed a public nature and made me write an appeal to the Tsar and his aides and a programme.[6] I tried to be guided only by the wish to serve, and not personal satisfaction. I haven't sent it yet. As soon as it's ready I'll send it. I've been ill all the time with pains in the legs and body and stomach. I'm better today.

Wrote the following in my notebook:

(1) How necessary it is to remember and not forget what was said by Coleridge [. . .] 'He who loves Christianity better than the Truth proceeds to love his Church or sect better than Christianity and ends in loving himself better than all.'[7]

This is the absolutely essential answer to those who are afraid to repudiate the divinity of Christ. [. . .]

(6) Women have only two feelings: love for men and love for children, and those which derive from these feelings, such as love of fine clothes for the sake of men and of money for the sake of children. All the rest is cerebral, imitation of men, means of attracting men, pretence, fashion.

(7) No sooner does religious feeling diminish in society than the power of women increases. In a completely religious world they are powerless; in a world without religion like ours all the power is in their hands.

(8) An atheist says: 'I don't know God, I don't need this concept.' To say this is the same as saying to a man sailing across the sea in a boat that he doesn't know the sea and doesn't need this concept. The infinity which surrounds you and on which you are moving, the laws of this infinity, your attitude towards it – this is what God is. To say that you can't see Him is to act like an ostrich. [. . .]

Today is 28 March, Moscow The day before yesterday the appeals were sent off to the Tsar and others. During this time I wrote a reply to my unknown correspondents,[8] and a bit of *Hadji Murat.* [. . .]

31 March, Moscow Morning. I think I've finished *A Reply to the Synod.* Nothing from Petersburg. Wrote a short address to the Petersburg writers.[9] Continue to receive greetings and abuse. [. . .]

Haven't written my diary for nine days. *Today is 8 April, Moscow.* [. . .]
  Noted: [. . .]
(5) The only happy periods of my life have been those when I gave up my whole life to the service of people. They were: the schools, service as a mediator, famine relief, and religious aid. [. . .]

7 May, Moscow We want to leave tomorrow. Health a bit better. [. . .]
(4) Dreamed about a type of old man whom Chekhov forestalled me in describing.[10] The old man was particularly good because he was almost a saint, but at the same time given to drink and bad language. I clearly understood for the first time the force which types acquire from boldly superimposed shadows. I'll do this with Hadji Murat and Marya Dmitriyevna.[11] [. . .]
(7) Thought about the requirements of the people and came to think that the main one is ownership of land; that if it could be decreed that there should be no private ownership of land, but that land should belong to those who cultivate it, this would be the most accurate guarantee of freedom.

11 May, Yasnaya Polyana Evening. I'm copying up what is in my notebook:
(1) Must include in my foreword to *Büttnerbauer* that Orlov has something to say and knows how to say it.[12] And what he has to say is that he loves the peasant, the person who feeds us. This is why people take notice of Gorky. We all know that tramps are human beings and brothers, but we know it in theory; but he has shown us them full-scale, with love for them, and has infected us with this love. Their talk is inaccurate and exaggerated, but we all forgive him for having broadened our love. [. . .]

Today is 8 June.   Haven't written my diary for almost a month. Health a bit better. Relations with all the family are good.

I'm writing *To the Working People.*[13] Sasha is diligently copying it out. I've noted about sixteen points. I'll write out at least a few of them now:

(1) Physical work without overtaxing one's strength produces a good-natured desire to communicate with people. I was walking past the watchman. He was ploughing, his dogs jumped up at me, but he still boasted about them in a good-natured way. [. . .]

16 July, Yasnaya Polyana   Haven't written my diary for more than a month. Was seriously ill from 27 June, and before that was unwell for a couple of weeks. My illness was one long spiritual holiday: heightened spirituality, and calmness at the approach of death, and expression of love from all sides . . .

Finished *The Only Way.* Not particularly good, too weak.

I'm noting down things noted a long time ago. [. . .]

(3) In order to be heard by people one has to speak from Golgotha, to imprint the truth by suffering, or still better by death. [. . .]

(6) The Chinese say: 'Wisdom consists in knowing that you know what you know – and that you know that you don't know what you don't know'; I would add to that: 'There is still greater wisdom in knowing what needs to be known and what can be left unknown, what it is possible not to know, and what to know first and what to know later.' [. . .]

18 August, Yasnaya Polyana   Haven't written my diary for exactly a month. During this time I've written two sets of notes – they aren't bad.[14] I also want to write about religion and the lack of it, and a letter to Nicholas.[15] Then I can relax over something literary. Although a Christian drama is certainly service to God.

During this time it's been decided we should go to the Crimea.[16] I'm rather pleased about it. My health is much weaker: my heart is weaker. But I'm improving and, unfortunately, I've lost the *élan* I had during my illness. Masha is here and so is Mashenka.[17] I'm continuing my inner work without much success, but I don't despair. 'Unless we serve God in every voluntary act of our lives we don't serve Him at all,' says Ruskin.[18] That's what one must do and remember. [. . .]

Today is 10 October, Gaspra, on the south coast[19]

My health is still just as bad. Sometimes worse, sometimes better, but not much. My old state of health has gone for good. [. . .]

Arrived here on 8 September with Boulanger, Masha and Kolya.[20] Sasha is very dear. Seryozha is here now.[21] My inner work seems to be progressing a little. [. . .]

Noted during this time:

(1) It's difficult to live for God by oneself in the midst of people who don't even understand the idea, and live only for themselves. How glad one is in such a situation to have the help of people of the same belief. [. . .]

(10) One of the most common and serious mistakes people make in their judgements is that they consider to be good the things that they like. [. . .]

(13) Life is a serious business! Oh, if only one could always remember that, especially in moments of decision! [. . .]

11 October, Gaspra   I.I.A.

Today is 24 October, Gaspra   The words I.I.A. acquire more and more significance. During this time I've been writing *On Religion*.[22] Health still *chancelante* [shaky], going downhill. [. . .]

29 November, Gaspra   Haven't written my diary again for nearly two months. I've been unwell all the time. And I'm seldom any better. The main thing is rheumatic pains and weakness. I think since the 14th I've begun to have arsenic injections. Today I feel more cheerful, and so I'm writing my diary. Tanya has had another stillborn child; she has taken it well.

I think I've finished *On Religion*. As always, I doubt the importance and goodness of this work, but with more justification now, I think, than on previous occasions.

Things are well at home. I don't see much of Masha. I'm glad that I find both Gorky and Chekhov pleasant, especially the former.[23] Good letters from a member of the court,[24] and it was pleasant to get to know Mikhaylov and the Stundists better.[25]

I've only made a few notes. This is what I noted:

(1) When a stream of water flows evenly, it seems as if it's standing still. And it seems just the same with one's own life and with life generally. But you notice that the stream isn't standing still, but is flowing, when it gets weaker, and especially when it becomes a trickle; and it's just the same with life.

(2) When I am dying, I would like to be asked whether I continue to understand life as I used to understand it, as a growing nearer to God, an expansion of love. If I'm unable to speak, I'll close my eyes if the answer is yes, and raise them upwards if it's no. [. . .]

(4) They say that women love courage and beauty, or the people who love these things. That's quite untrue. They give themselves to those who are sure they will do so. And having given themselves, they justify themselves by loving those they have given themselves to. [. . .]

Today, I think, is 1 December [. . .] Our folk have gone to Uchan-Su.[26] I'm alone at home with Tanya, and out of sorts. A wonderful chapter in Polenz's novel[27] spurred me on very much to write – but in vain. Once again I can see death, better, nearer and clearer.

26 December, Gaspra Things seemed to get better for me, then worse again. I went to Yalta for the night and was taken ill there with heart trouble. Spent a week at Masha's. I'm beginning to get well again. Dear Boulanger has been. He left today. I've finished *On Religion*. But I'll probably revise it again. I've been writing about religious tolerance for about ten days, and am bored with it. It's too unimportant. But I'm not very keen even on writing the letter to the Tsar. [. . .]

1902

Today is 22 January, Gaspra Almost the whole time I've been ill, i.e. getting closer to death. And I've lived quite well. During this time I wrote a letter to the Tsar and sent it via Nikolay Mikhaylovich.[1] Both the letter and he himself are in Petersburg today. I don't know whether he'll hand it over. An excellent book by Mazzini, and Ruskin's thoughts.[2] [. . .]

23 January Still weak. Bertenson came.[3] Of course it's nothing serious. Some wonderful verses:

> The old man started to groan,
> The old man started to cough,
> It's time for the old man to get under the shroud,
> Under the shroud and into the grave.[4]

How wonderful is the language of the people. Picturesque and moving and serious. [. . .]

5 May Haven't written my diary for three and a half months. I've been seriously ill and still haven't recovered yet. I want to write down what I thought and noted during this time:

5 February[5] [. . .] February (1) *De mortuis aut bene aut nihil* [Either speak well of the dead or say nothing] – what a false, pagan rule! Speak well or say nothing about the living. How much suffering this would save people from, and how easy it is. But about the dead, why not speak ill as well? In our world, on the contrary, there is an established rule: to speak only terribly exaggerated praises, and consequently only lies about the dead, with obituaries and jubilees. And this does terrible harm to people, blurring and rendering indistinguishable the concepts of good and evil.
(2) It's necessary to suffer a serious illness in order to be sure what life is: the weaker the body, the stronger becomes one's spiritual activity. [. . .]

21 February [. . .]
(3) Peaceful deaths under the influence of the Church's rites are like death under the influence of morphine. [. . .]

21 March. [. . .]

(3) There are three fashionable philosophers I can recall: Hegel, Darwin and now Nietzsche. The first tried to justify everything that exists; the second tried to put man on the same footing as an animal and to justify struggle, i.e. the evil in men; the third contends that what it is in human nature that resists evil is merely wrong upbringing, error. I don't know how much further one can go. [. . .]

10 April, Gaspra [. . .]

(15) In the past irreligious people were enemies of society, now they are its leaders. [. . .]

Today is 22 May, Gaspra The typhus is over.[6] But I'm still in bed. I'm waiting for a third illness and death. I'm in a very bad mood. There are a few notes to copy in but I'm putting them off. I'll pray now. And prayer, as always, helps.

23, 24 May, Gaspra Was very weak yesterday. Better today. Wrote a little of *To the Working People*.[7] It's beginning to take shape. They wanted to move me out of doors, but there's a cold wind. I'm ashamed that I behaved badly towards Tanya for trying to dissuade me from going out. Transferred to the armchair. I seem to have no legs.

25, 26, 27 May, Gaspra For three days I've been out of doors, at first for four or five, and today for six hours. I'm gradually recovering. I felt the pangs of death, i.e. of a new life, and I've been given a respite. [. . .]

Today is 3 June I'm continuing to spend the days out of doors, working. I've almost finished the appeal. It's not bad. I'm recovering, but I see it's not for long. [. . .]

1 July, Yasnaya Polyana It's three days since we arrived from Gaspra. The journey was hard physically. I was getting over it, but yesterday I was feverish and weak again. I don't resent it. I'm preparing myself for, or, rather, trying to live my last days and hours as well as possible. I've been revising *To the Working People* all the time. It's beginning to take shape and I think I've finished it. [. . .]

5 August I never expected I wouldn't write my diary for so long. On 22 July I sent off *To the Working People* and since then I've been getting on with *Hadji Murat*, sometimes enthusiastically, sometimes reluctantly and with shame. [. . .]

(1) An astonishing thing: I know myself how bad and stupid I am and yet

people consider me a man of genius. So what must other people be like? [. . .]

20 September, Yasnaya Polyana   Haven't written my diary for six weeks. I've been getting on with *Hadji Murat* all the time. Health improving. I can be satisfied with my state of mind. I've no bad feelings towards anyone. I've thought a lot. There's a lot to be copied down. [. . .]

(7) Thought about the immorality of medicine. Everything about it is immoral. Immoral is the fear of illness and death induced by medical aid, immoral is the use of the exclusive aid of doctors, available only to the rich. It is immoral to enjoy exclusive comforts and pleasures, but to enjoy the exclusive possibility of preserving life is the height of immorality. Immoral is the requirement of medicine to conceal from a patient the danger of his situation and the nearness of death. Immoral are the advice and requirements of doctors that a patient should look after himself – his bodily functions – and in general should live as little as possible spiritually, but only materially: should not think, should not excite himself, should not work.

(8) Socialists see in trusts and syndicates the realization, or the progress towards the realization, of the socialist ideal, i.e. that people work collectively and not independently. But they only work collectively under pressure of force. What evidence is there that they will also work when they are free, and what evidence that trusts and syndicates will pass into the workers' hands? It is far more probable that trusts will produce slavery, in liberating themselves from which the slaves will destroy the trusts which they themselves did not set up. [. . .]

(10) My recovery is like dragging a carriage out of a quagmire in which it is stuck, not in the direction in which one inevitably has to go, but in the opposite one. There is no avoiding going through the quagmire.

26 September, Yasnaya Polyana   Health good. Abandoned *Hadji Murat* and have no desire to continue *To the Clergy*,[8] but somehow feel like writing something literary. Wrote a letter to Schmitt and sent money, and one to a young man faced with conscription.[9]

Had some good thoughts during this time. Some of them I've forgotten. (1) I imagined very clearly to myself the inner life of each individual person. How can one describe what each individual 'I' is like? Yet I think one can. Then I thought that that is actually what constitutes the whole interest, the whole importance of art – poetry. [. . .]

(3) Ilya asked me: can women be clever? I couldn't answer, but then I understood: women can be very clever, generally speaking no more foolish if not more clever than men, but their mind is not in the right place, like a joist that is put, not under a roof, but on top of it. With a man, whatever his

mind is like, it serves as a guide to action; with women mind is a plaything, an adornment. A woman's life is guided by what you will: – vanity, motherhood, cupidity, love – only not the mind. [...]

6 October, Yasnaya Polyana   Yesterday I began to revise and continue *The Forged Coupon*. I'm still writing *To the Clergy*. It's weaker than I expected. Gorky and Pyatnitsky have been.[10] Epictetus says: 'Strengthen in yourself contentment with your lot. With it you will overcome everything.'[11]

Today is 4 November, Yasnaya Polyana   [...]There's a lot to note down. [...]
(8) Read Merezhkovsky on Euripides and understood his Christianity.[12] One person wants Christianity together with patriotism (Pobedonostsev, the Slavophiles); another with war, another with wealth, another with lust for women, and everyone arranges his own Christianity for himself according to his own requirements.

13 December
(1) Critics are wrong to think that the intelligentsia as a movement can guide the popular masses (Milyukov).[13] It would be still more wrong for a writer to think that he can consciously guide the masses by his works. [...]

1903–1910

THE LAST YEARS of Tolstoy's life were eventful ones for Russia. The disastrous war with Japan was followed by Bloody Sunday, the *Potyomkin* mutiny, the 1905 revolution and the setting up and speedy dissolution of the first Duma. Tolstoy's life continued to revolve physically round the Yasnaya Polyana-Moscow axis, but mentally he was even more involved than before with issues of world significance. He openly accused the government of complicity in the savage pogroms in Kishinyov in 1903 and wrote three stories for an anthology (published in Warsaw) in aid of the Jewish victims. In the same year he wrote *After the Ball*, a telling indictment of physical violence and brutality, and in 1904 completed his long essay *Shakespeare and the Drama* with its hostile criticism of *King Lear*. Among his numerous publicist articles of the 1900s which were widely read abroad are the pamphlet *Bethink Yourselves* on the subject of the Russo-Japanese War and the powerful onslaught on capital punishment *I Cannot Be Silent*. In a letter to the Russian Prime Minister he forcefully advocated the Henry George solution to the land problem and the abolition of private property, and his outspokenness on almost every issue of social, political and religious importance meant that he was the focus of attention of men and women throughout the world. Yasnaya Polyana became a place of pilgrimage, where Tolstoy held reluctant court. Letters poured in from many countries, from Gandhi and Bernard Shaw as well as from hundreds of obscure sympathizers and critics. Some people came to film him, others to record his voice, others again to take down all he said. It is hard to believe that Tolstoy, despite his vanity and egoism, welcomed this world-wide publicity which made the last few years of his life so wearisome and helped to aggravate the tensions of an already difficult family life. The death of his favourite daughter and disciple, Masha, in 1906 was a grievous blow to him. His wife's increasing neuroticism and hysterical outbursts (not without provocation), and the bitter wrangling over his will and the problems of copyright, brought matters to a head. At the age of eighty-two Tolstoy found his position so intolerable that he finally took the decision he had long been contemplating and left home for good. The story of his last days and his death on the railway station at Astapovo makes painful reading, and a tragic conclusion to his long, searching and restless life which his diaries and vast correspondence so brightly illuminate.

1903

6 January   I'm now experiencing the torments of hell. I'm recalling all the nastiness of my early life, and these memories won't leave me and are poisoning my life.[1] People usually regret that an individual doesn't retain his memories after death. How fortunate that he doesn't! What torture it would be if in this life I were to remember all the bad things that pain my conscience which I had done in a previous life. And if the good things are to be remembered, all the bad things must be remembered too. How fortunate that memory disappears with death and only consciousness remains – consciousness which represents a sort of total resultant of good and bad, a sort of complex equation reduced to its simplest expression: x = an equally positive or negative, big or a small number. Yes, it's very fortunate, the destruction of memory; one couldn't enjoy living with it. But now, with the destruction of memory, we enter life with a clean, blank sheet on which one can write afresh the good and the bad.

5 February, Yasnaya Polyana   Haven't written my diary for a month. I've been ill for two months and am ill now. My heart is weak. And that's good. It reminds me very vividly of the nearness of death. During this time I've been busy mostly with my own memoirs. I'm making progress bit by bit. But so far – it's not good. I've also begun to write an afterword [to the appeal] to the working people,[2] but I'm making no progress. [. . .]

20 February, Yasnaya Polyana   Health a bit better. For the second day I've been out for a drive. Can't work. I've no enthusiasm. [. . .]
(1) Supporters of socialism are people who have the urban population primarily in mind. They don't know either the beauty and poetry of rural life, or its sufferings.

14 March   [. . .]
(4) Read *Opinions sociales* by Anatole France.[3] Like all orthodox socialists and devotees of science, and therefore repudiators of religion, he says that there is no need for mercy or love, only for *justice*. That is true, but in order to have real *justice*, it is necessary for our striving and our ideal to embody self-denial and love. [. . .]

Today is 20 March, Yasnaya Polyana Wrote letters yesterday and today. Wrote twenty-six of them. [. . .]

14 April, Yasnaya Polyana Haven't written my diary for a long time. I've been weak all this time. I've been unwell for three days now: a cold and a cough. And today, weak as I was, I read Thoreau and was mentally uplifted.[4] [. . .]

I'll write in here what I noted down before 2 April.

(1) People usually measure the progress of mankind by its technical and scientific successes, supposing that civilization leads to good. That isn't true. Rousseau and all those who enthuse over the uncivilized, patriarchal state are just as right, or just as wrong, as those who enthuse over civilization. The good of people who live and enjoy the highest, most refined civilization and culture and the good of primitive, uncivilized people is absolutely identical. Increasing the good of people by science – civilization and culture – is just as impossible as making the water on a flat stretch of water higher in one place than in others. Increasing the good of people only comes from increasing love, which by its very nature makes all people equal; but scientific and technical successes are a matter of age, and civilized people are just as little superior to uncivilized people in their happiness as a grown-up man is superior in happiness to a juvenile. Good only comes from increasing love. [. . .]

I'm continuing to write on *29 April, Yasnaya Polyana*. During this time I've been working continually on the afterword.[5] I think I'm coming to the end. It's quite respectable. Wrote a letter about the Kishinyov affair and a telegram.[6] [. . .]

(14) In our age there exists a terrible superstition that we eagerly accept any invention which reduces labour, and consider it necessary to make use of it, without asking ourselves whether this invention which reduces labour increases our happiness or whether it doesn't destroy beauty. We are like a peasant woman overeating beef because there is plenty of it, although she isn't hungry and the food will probably be bad for her. Railways instead of walking, motorcars instead of a horse, hosiery machines instead of knitting needles. [. . .]

Today is 13 May, Yasnaya Polyana [. . .] Finished the afterword and sent it off.[7] [. . .]

17 May I think, *Yasnaya Polyana*. [. . .] I've been revising *Hadji Murat*. Got as far as Nicholas Pavlovich,[8] and I think it's becoming clearer. [. . .]

Today is 4 June, Yasnaya Polyana Didn't sleep much. My stomach still hurts. Yesterday I gave Misha my diaries to copy for Posha. There's a lot in them of interest to me. Settled down to work today; wanted to continue my memoirs, but couldn't: *they don't grip me.* Yesterday I read *Nicholas I.*[9] Very much of interest. I must finish reading it before going on.

18 June, Yasnaya Polyana [. . .]
   Thought up three new things:
(1) The cry of the lost people of today, the materialists, the positivists, the Nietzscheans, is the cry (Mark 1, 24): 'Let us alone; what have we to do with thee, thou Jesus of Nazareth? Art thou come to destroy us? I know thee who thou art, the Holy One of God.' (That would be very good.)[10]
(2) For the Jewish anthology:[11] a gay ball in Kazan, I'm in love with Koreysha, the beautiful daughter of a military commander – a Pole – I dance with her; her handsome old father takes her lovingly on his arm to the mazurka. And the next morning, after a sleepless night in love, the sound of a drum, and a Tartar made to run the gauntlet, and the military commander giving orders to beat him till it hurts more. (That would be very good.)[12]
and (3) A description of myself in all truth, as I am now, with all my weaknesses and follies, alternating with what is good and important in my life. (That would also be good.)[13]
   All this is more important than the stupid *Hadji Murat.*

23 June, Yasnaya Polyana Health good. I'm eating berries and riding a lot on horseback. Mental inertia.
   One thing to note:
(1) I'm a person with very bad qualities, very slow to understand good, and so I need to make great efforts not to be a complete scoundrel. Yury Samarin once put it very well when he said he was an excellent mathematics teacher because he was very slow to understand mathematics. I'm absolutely the same with mathematics, but, most important, I'm just the same with what is good – very slow – and so I'm not at all a bad teacher – no, I'll be bold and say I'm a good teacher.

25 July, Yasnaya Polyana Wrote three fairy tales.[14] Bad as yet, but they could be quite good. [. . .]

9 August, Yasnaya Polyana I've been well all this time. Wrote *Daughter and Father* in one day.[15] Not bad. Finished the fairy tales. [. . .]

20 August Only finished the tales today – and not three, but two.[16] Dissatisfied with them. On the other hand, *But You Say* isn't bad.[17] [. . .]

3 September, Yasnaya Polyana Alive, but unwell. On the 29th we went riding; my horse trod on my foot, then I had a bilious attack and feel quite unwell and my foot isn't getting any better. The 28th was a depressing day. The congratulations are frankly depressing and unpleasant – they're insincere, the words 'of the Russian land', and all that sort of nonsense.[18] No flattering my vanity, thank God. Probably there is nothing to flatter. It's high time. [. . .]

(2) About literature. We spoke about Chekhov: in a conversation about Chekhov with Lazarevsky,[19] it became clear to me that he, like Pushkin, has made an advance in form. And that's a great service. But, like Pushkin, he hasn't any content. Gorky – there's a misunderstanding. The Germans know Gorky, but they don't know Polenz.[20]

Today is 22 September, Yasnaya Polyana I've been writing for a few days (more than a week) a foreword to Shakespeare.[21] Health good. My foot is healing up. [. . .]

Yasnaya Polyana, 14 November Haven't written my diary for five weeks. All the time I've been busy with my Shakespeare, which has kept growing and growing; I think I've reached the end. I can't boast about my intellectual energy during this time, but my state of mind is good. About three days ago I had a bad bilious attack.

Thought completely calmly about death, only with a certain impatience in case I were to suffer for long. Of course that's wrong, sufferings themselves may be of use for life's eternal purpose. I partly understood that that may be so, but not with my whole being.

Went to Pirogovo. On the 9th, I think. Was very glad to be with my brother. He is disintegrating bodily, like me, and, like me, growing spiritually; only I'm particularly glad to see this in him, with his peculiar simplicity and truthfulness. When talking to me about his sorrow and illness, he said: 'God has cast His eye on me too, as the peasants say.'

I've noted in my book: [. . .]

(3) People usually think that progress consists in the increase of knowledge, in the improvement of life, but that isn't so. Progress consists only in the greater and greater clarification of the answers to the basic questions of life. The truth is always accessible to a man. It can't be otherwise, because a man's soul is a divine spark, the truth itself. It's only a matter of removing from this divine spark (the truth) everything that obscures it. Progress consists, not in the increase of truth, but in freeing it from its wrappings. The truth is obtained like gold, not by letting it grow bigger, but by washing off from it everything that isn't gold. [. . .]

Today is 24 November, Yasnaya Polyana I'm still dawdling over the forewords to both Shakespeare and Garrison.[22] I've almost finished. Health good, but I'm intellectually sluggish. I've just thought of something very important, I think, namely: (1) We are aware of two lives in ourselves: the spiritual life, known to us through our inner consciousness, and the physical life, known to us through external observation.

Normally people (myself included) who recognize the spiritual life as the basis of life deny the reality, the necessity, the importance of studying the physical life, which evidently cannot lead to any conclusive results. In just the same way, those who only recognize the physical life completely deny the spiritual life and all deductions based on it – deny, as they say, metaphysics. But it is now absolutely clear to me that both are wrong, and both forms of knowledge – the materialistic and the metaphysical – have their own great importance, if only one doesn't wish to make inappropriate deductions from the one or the other. From materialistic knowledge based on the observation of external phenomena one can deduce scientific data, i.e. generalizations about phenomena, but one should not deduce any guiding principles for people's lives, as the materialists – Darwinists for example – have often tried to do. From metaphysical knowledge based on inner consciousness one can and should deduce the laws of human life – how should we live? why are we living? – the very thing that all religious teachings do; but one should not deduce, as many people have tried to do, the laws of phenomena and generalizations about them.

Each of these two kinds of knowledge has its own purpose and its own field of activity. [. . .]

19 December, Yasnaya Polyana   Andryusha's behaviour distresses me.[23] I'm trying to do what I can. Health very good: but my mental activity is still feeble. I'm trying to accept it as right and proper, and I'm partly achieving my aim. Finished working on Shakespeare and began something on the importance of religion.[24] But only two beginnings, and both are bad. Wrote a bit of my memoirs, but unfortunately didn't continue. No enthusiasm for it. Thought about *The Forged Coupon*, but didn't write any of it.

Noted a few things down in my book: [. . .]

(2) I can put myself in the shoes of the most terrible villain and understand him, but not in those of a foolish man. Yet that is very necessary. [. . .]

(4) The artist, the poet and the mathematician, or the scholar generally. The poet can't do the scholar's job, because he can't see one thing only and stop seeing things in general. The scholar can't do the poet's job because he always sees one thing only, and can't see everything.

(5) There are machine people who work splendidly when they are set in motion, but can't set themselves in motion.

(6) A truly virtuous unmarried woman who devotes all the strength of the

maternal self-sacrifice she has been endowed with to the service of God and man is the finest and happiest human creature (Auntie Tatyana Alexandrovna).

30 December, Yasnaya Polyana   Went for a ride. 20° of frost. Health good, but haven't the strength to work, although I've thought about a lot of things. I'd like to write:
(1) A popular story for the people about an angel who killed a child;[25] (2) about a peasant who doesn't go to church;[26] and (3) about a dissenter in prison and a revolutionary;[27] (4) about my own confused weak, psychical condition; (5) Why didst Thou, Jesus, Son of God, come to torment us.[28] [. . .]

1904

3 January, Yasnaya Polyana   [. . .] I'm making a little progress with *The Forged Coupon*. But it's certainly very disorganized. I'm also busy revising the *Thoughts*.[1] Thought:

(1) Am I afraid of death? No. But at the approach of death or the thought of it, I can't help experiencing the sort of trepidation that a traveller must experience as he approaches the place where his train drops down to the sea from an enormous height or who rises to an enormous height in a balloon. The traveller knows that nothing will happen to him, that it will only be the same as happens to millions of creatures, that he will only change his method of travel, but he can't help experiencing trepidation as he approaches the place. Such is my feeling too about death.

6 January, Yasnaya Polyana   Health a bit better. Wonderful weather. I've been compiling a new calendar. [. . .]

14 January, Yasnaya Polyana   Woke up today feeling healthy, physically strong, and with an overwhelming awareness of my own nastiness and worthlessness, and of a life badly lived now and in the past. And up to now – midday – I'm still under the influence of this salutary mood. How good, how profitable even, to feel, as I do today, humiliated and vile! You don't require anything of anybody, nothing can offend you, you deserve everything that is bad. Only one thing is necessary, namely that this humiliation should not turn to dejection and despair, should not hinder the effort to free oneself at least a little from one's own stinking pit – should not hinder one from working and serving as best one can. [. . .]

27 January, Yasnaya Polyana   For three days I've had a cough and cold, and for three days I haven't written anything. And I'm weak enough to think that this is bad. [. . .]

28 January, Yasnaya Polyana   Still haven't recovered. My liver and a cold in the head. Revised a bit of the *Coupon* today. And had some good thoughts about the war that has begun.[2] I'd like to write about the fact that when such a terrible thing as war takes place, everybody puts forward hundreds of opinions about all the various meanings and consequences of the war, but nobody argues about his own situation: what should he or I do in regard to the war.³ This is the best and clearest illustration of the fact that nothing can remedy the evil that exists except religion. [. . .]

19 February, Yasnaya Polyana I'm still writing about war. It won't come right yet. Health not bad. But my heart has been weak for some time. I can't welcome death at all. I've no fear, but I'm full of life, and I just can't. I've been reading Kant, and was carried away, and am now carried away by Lichtenberg.⁴ He's very close to me. [. . .]

7 March, Yasnaya Polyana Had a very good trip to Pirogovo with Sasha. Masha, judging from her letter, is worse. I can't help feeling sorry. I'm still revising my article on war. It's quite reasonable. Not good, but quite reasonable. [. . .]

(2) An excellent saying: *the living think about life*, i.e. while a person is alive he can't help giving himself up entirely to the interests of this world. For this reason death is so terrible when a person who is full of life thinks about it. But when death is near because of a wound, or illness or old age, a person ceases to think about life and death ceases to be terrible.

(3) Death is a window through which one observed the world, and which has been slammed shut, or lowered eyelids and sleep, or a walk from one window to another. [. . .]

(5) [. . .] When asleep you often dream of things which, when you space them out chronologically, seem to be absurd, but what you find out about yourself when asleep is far more true than what you think about yourself when awake. You dream that you have the weaknesses which you consider you are free from when awake, and that you don't have the weaknesses which you are afraid of when awake, and you see what you crave for. I often see myself as a soldier, often see myself being unfaithful to my wife and am horrified by it, often see myself writing only for my own pleasure.

The dream I had today made me think about this. Dreams are really moments of awakening. In these moments we see life outside time, we see joined together in one point what has been broken up chronologically; we see the essence of our life – the extent of our growth.

16 March, Yasnaya Polyana I.I.A. Very unwell. Heart weak. Irregular heart beats and pains. Went for a walk. Cold. Wrote *On War*. Almost finished it. Read *Maine de Biran*.⁵ Very interesting to me.

[*5 April*] [. . .] Began writing *The Corner-Stone*, but couldn't continue. Alexandra Andreyevna has died.⁶ How simple and good it is. [. . .]

29 April, Yasnaya Polyana [. . .] Thought of something very important today. [. . .]

(2) A man can only know something fully from the experience of his own life. I know myself fully, my whole self from the curtain of birth until the curtain of death. I know myself from the fact that I am I. This is the highest or rather the deepest knowledge. The next kind of knowledge is knowledge acquired from feelings: I hear, I see, I feel. This knowledge is external: I know that something exists, but I don't know – in the way that I know myself – what the thing I see, hear or feel is like. I don't know what it feels or is aware of. The third kind of knowledge is less deep, it is knowledge acquired by reason; knowledge deduced from one's own feelings or transmitted by word from other people – reasoning, prediction, deduction, science.

The first kind. *I am sad, hurt, bored, joyful.* There is no doubt about this.

The second kind. *I smell the scent of a violet, I see light and shade, etc.* Here there may be mistakes.

The third kind. *I know that the earth is round and rotates, and that Japan and Madagascar exist, etc.* All that is doubtful.

Life, I think, consists in the transition of both the second and the third kinds of knowledge into the first, so that a man experiences everything within himself. [. . .]

7 May, Yasnaya Polyana   [. . .] Recently sent off *On War,*[7] and am awaiting the effect, although I know that there won't be any and I shouldn't expect any.

8 May, Yasnaya Polyana   Received a letter today from a sailor from Port Arthur.[8] *Is it God's will or not that the authorities should compel us to kill?*

This doubt exists, and I am writing about it, but I also know that an enormous number of people are in great darkness. But, as Kant says, as soon as the truth is clearly expressed, it is bound to prevail over everything. When? That is another question. We would like it to be soon, but for God 1,000 years is like a single hour. It seems to me that for wars to cease (and with wars legalized violence), the following historical events are necessary: it is necessary (1) that England and America should be beaten in wars by countries which have introduced universal military conscription; (2) that as a result of this they should introduce universal military conscription themselves; and (3) that only then will everyone come to their senses.

11 May, Yasnaya Polyana   Health better. Mikhaylov and Nikolayev have come, and the Merezhkovskys are coming.[9] I've written nothing all these days. An Englishman with a letter from Chertkov.[10] Mental state *good.* [. . .] (1) Ilya Vasilyevich the man-servant is in a bad temper as a result of the holiday and the carousing. And before I know where I am I am infected by the same bad, unfriendly mood. One of the most important rules in life is:

don't yawn when other people yawn. Don't yield to any suggestion without testing it. Only yield to the sort of suggestion you acknowledge to be good – to that of Christ and Marcus Aurelius, but not Maupassant, etc. And don't forget either that you too are able to suggest. [. . .]

4 June, Yasnaya Polyana   Haven't felt like writing for several days. Health not too good. The war, the call-up of reserves – I suffer continually. Tried to write my memoirs yesterday – it was no good. Thought: [. . .]
(2) War is the product of despotism. If there were no despotism, there could be no war; there might be fights, but not war. Despotism produces war, and war supports despotism.

Those who want to fight against war should fight only against despotism.

13 June, Yasnaya Polyana   [. . .] Saw Andryusha off.[11] It's astonishing why I love him. To say it's because he's sincere and truthful isn't true. He's often untruthful (indeed, it's obvious at once). But I feel at ease and well with him, and I love him. Why? [. . .]

18 June, Yasnaya Polyana   [. . .]
(1) Am I not deceiving myself when I praise poverty? I saw this with my letter to Molostvova.[12] I see it with Sasha. I'm sorry for them, I'm afraid for them with no carriage, no cleanliness, no riding-habit. There is only one explanation and justification: I don't like poverty, I can't like it, especially for other people, but I like still less, I hate, I can't help hating what brings wealth: ownership of land, banks, interest. The devil has so cunningly ensnared me that I can see all the privations of poverty clearly before my eyes, but I can't see the injustices which rescue people from it. All that is hidden, and it's all approved by the majority. If the question were put directly, however much it hurt me, I would resolve it in favour of poverty. I must put the question to myself directly and resolve it directly. [. . .]

20 June, Yasnaya Polyana   [. . .]
(7) Man in the present, i.e. outside time, is always free, but when we look at his behaviour in time, it always seems to be the result of a preceding cause. Every act of behaviour is preceded by some other act or state, and not only one act or state but a countless number of acts and states, and therefore every act can be related to some other act or state, or some aggregate of preceding acts or states, as a consequence of it or of them. And therefore man is free, but seems unfree. It's just the opposite of what the determinists say, when they say that man is unfree, but seems free. And Lichtenberg is absolutely right: *you say that man is unfree because we know for certain that every action has its own cause, but I say that the thesis that*

every action has its own cause is untrue because I know for certain that man is free.

22 June, Pirogovo   I've been at Pirogovo since yesterday. My brother is in a very bad state, not so much physically as spiritually. True, his condition is very serious, a stroke, mouth distorted, slobbering and pains; but it's becoming more serious because he doesn't want to give in to it. In such a condition there are only two solutions: defiance, irritability and an increase of suffering, as with him, or, on the contrary: submission, gentleness and a decrease of suffering, even to the extent of eliminating it altogether. [. . .]

Yesterday the *Russian Gazette* expressed an opinion about my article published in England.[13] It pleased me very much, pleased my vanity, and that's bad.

28 June, Yasnaya Polyana   [. . .]
(5) Called to mind military drill in the time of Nicholas Pavlovich (Rosen's *Notes*:[14] beat up three, make a soldier out of one); called to mind serfdom and the attitude I felt towards a human being, as though he were an object or an animal; a total lack of consciousness of brotherhood. That's the most important thing of all that I would like to write about Nicholas I and the Decembrists. [. . .]

2 July, Yasnaya Polyana   [. . .]
(2) There was a time when anarchy was unthinkable. The people wanted to worship and obey, and the rulers were sure of their vocation and didn't think about consolidating their authority and did nothing about it. But now the people no longer worship, and not only don't want to obey, but want freedom, while the rulers don't do what is considered necessary for their own and their people's glory, but are busy maintaining their own power. The peoples sense this, and no longer put up with power, but want freedom, complete freedom. One must first of all throw a certain amount off a heavily laden wagon in order to be able to overturn it. The time has come not to throw things off gradually any more, but to overturn the wagon. [. . .]

17 July, Yasnaya Polyana   [. . .] I've been to Pirogovo. Seryozha won't rest, he's putting up resistance. And it's painful for him and for the others. On the way there I saw a new horse-collar bound together with bast, and thought again about the Robinson theme – a migrant rural community. And I wanted to write a second part of Nekhlyudov. His work, tiredness, nascent grand seigneurism, temptation by a woman, fall, mistakes, and all against a background of a Robinson community.[15] [. . .]
(3) Socialism – apart from the immediate relief of the condition of the

workers – advocates the establishment of external forms, the *future* economic organization of human societies. And therefore *il a beau jeu* [it has a good hand]. Everything is conceived in the future, without substance and without realization in the present, apart from the struggle to improve the life of the workers. The main mistake people make in their understanding of socialism is that they confuse two things by this concept: (a) the struggle against the exploitation of capital and (b) imaginary progress towards the realization of a socialist society. The first is a useful and natural thing, the second – an impossible and fantastic concept.

18 July, Yasnaya Polyana   Was unwell yesterday and had no dinner. *I've overdone it*, as the German said. I'm all right today. I'm now sitting in my room and listening at a distance to the incessant talk, and I know that this talk has been going on since early morning and will go on until late evening, and went on yesterday as well, and the day before and before that again, and is always going on and will do so as long as the people talking have no need to work. And the main thing is that everything has been said; there's nothing more to say. The only way to pad out the talk is to say malicious things about people who are not there, or to argue in a malicious way with people who are. Idleness is a terrible calamity. People are created in order to work, but they have created slaves for themselves, and emancipated themselves from hard work, and now they are suffering, and suffering not just from boredom and idle talk, but from atrophy of the muscles and the heart, from losing the habit of hard work, from maladroitness, cowardice, lack of courage, and illnesses.

But these are only the sufferings which idle people heap upon themselves; but how many of the best joys of life are they deprived of: hard work in the midst of nature, association with fellow workers, enjoyment of relaxation, food when it goes to replenish used up energy, association with animals, an awareness of the fruitfulness of one's work . . . My life has been ruined, has been corrupted by this terrible idleness. How I would like to warn others against similar ruin.

Oh, how I would like to write a second part of Nekhlyudov! [. . .]

24 July, Yasnaya Polyana   [. . .] Things are well at home. Well, without any effort from me. What was not good was listening to *The Divine and the Human*, and being agitated. Still I think I'll finish *The Stone* today. I feel I must. It's really the awareness of my duty to say what people don't know and where they are going astray. I'll try to do it as briefly and simply as possible.

29 July, Yasnaya Polyana   [. . .] People often visit me, and three days ago I thought of noting down who they all were. They were: (1) A peasant from

Gill's who had had an accident in a mine. I sent him to Goldenblat.[16] (2)
Then a soldier's wife, about the return of her husband. I wrote her a
petition. (3) Then some lads from the railway. I selected some booklets for
them. (4) Then a lady from Tiflis about religious education. I told her
what I thought. On Monday and Tuesday too there were just as many
visitors. [. . .]

15 August, Pirogovo   I've been here three days. I've been gradually getting
worse, and yesterday was quite bad: fever, and above all severe heartburn.
It was very depressing being with Seryozha. He is suffering cruelly both
physically and morally, and won't resign himself to his fate. I couldn't do
or say anything good or useful to him. On the first day I did some
translating. Yesterday I did nothing, and today I unexpectedly hit upon a
beginning for an article on religion and wrote one and a half chapters. My
head suddenly became clear, and I realized that it had been my illness
coming on. Hence my stupidity.
   I must give it a title: *The One Cause of Everything*, or *The Light has become
Darkness*, or *Without God*. [. . .]

17 August, Pirogovo   Much better today; I'm recovering. I'm thinking of
going to Seryozha's. Sat out in the open air yesterday and went for a walk.
Made some notes. Was just thinking that I definitely must abandon the
idea of polishing up my writings. Rather I should write whatever has taken
clear shape in my head according to various sub-divisions: (1) wisdom –
religion – philosophy; (2) works of fiction: (*a*) *Resurrection*, (*b*) The
Decembrists, Nicholas, (*c*) obvious corrections to the works of fiction I
write; (3) Memoirs. I must without fail note down my memories as I recall
them; those times, conditions and feelings which I vividly recall and which
seem worthy of recording. This would be very good. I don't know if I'll
succeed.
   Note: [. . .]
(2) While out walking, I vividly recalled my state of mind when young,
especially after military service. Even before that the yearning towards
self-improvement was alive, just about alive in me. I couldn't define, and
didn't know in whose name this was necessary, but I felt there was
something. But after military service I was absolutely free of all spiritual
bonds, i.e. the complete slave of the animal in me. There was only one
thing in whose name I could still sacrifice the lusts and even the life of an
animal (war, a duel for which I was always preparing myself), and only that
one thing; otherwise everything was possible. And so it was till the age of
fifty. How I would like to save people from this! [. . .]

20 August, Pirogovo   Much better today. Received some letters yesterday.

Sonya isn't expecting me particularly. Still I want to go tomorrow, God willing. Pleasant news from Chertkov about the foreword, and from Lucy Mallory too.[17] I'm walking a lot. And I'm still reading Taine.[18] It's very important for me.

When reading the history of the French Revolution, it becomes undoubtedly clear that the foundations of the Revolution (which Taine attacks so unjustly) are undoubtedly correct and ought to be proclaimed [. . .] the only mistake was in supposing that the principles proclaimed could become reality in the same way as the previous abuses: as a result of force. [. . .]

Private people could never kill or slaughter or rob one thousandth part of the number of people killed and robbed by governments, i.e. by people who arrogate to themselves the right to kill and rob. Perhaps French society was not ready for such a revolution then; perhaps it is not ready even now; but there can be no doubt that this revolution is bound to take place, that mankind is preparing itself more and more for this revolution, and that the time will come when mankind is ready for it.

26 August, Pirogovo Seryozha has died. Quietly, without the awareness, the express awareness, that he was dying. It was a secret. It's impossible to say whether it's better or worse that way. Effective religious feeling was denied to him (perhaps I'm still deceiving myself, but I think not). But all is well with him just the same. Something new and better has been revealed to him. And to me too. The degree of this illumination is valuable and important, but it doesn't matter at what stage in an infinite cycle it comes. [. . .]

15 September, Yasnaya Polyana Haven't written my diary for two weeks. I've been busy all the time with extracts for the *Cycle of Reading*. I've collected enough material for a full year and probably for another whole year. I'm not reading the papers, but am reading Amiel, Carlyle, and Mazzini,[19] and feel very good at heart. Health not bad. State of mind – I'd like to boast about it, but I'm afraid to; still, I'll say that it's very gratifying. There are a lot of things to be noted: [. . .]

(2) A strange thing: I very often feel myself drawn more to immoral, even cruel, but single-minded people (Vera, Andryusha and many others) than to liberal people who serve other people and society. I've found an explanation for this. People are not to blame if they can't see the true meaning of life, if they are still blind – not like owls, but like puppies. The one good thing they can do is not to lie, not to be hypocritical, not to do what resembles real, humane, religious activity, but is not. But when they are hypocritical, or do things for other people's sake, not for God's, or seek to justify themselves, then they are repellent. [. . .]

(8) There's a wonderful fairy tale by Andersen about the peas which saw

the whole world as green as long as their pod was green; then the world became yellow, and then (I'm going on a bit) there was a crack and the world came to an end. And the peas fell to the ground and began to grow.[20] [. . .]

22 September, Yasnaya Polyana [. . .] Read Kant.[21] His God and immortality, i.e. the future life, are remarkable for their lack of proof. However, he says himself that he won't remove from one side of the scales his wish to prove immortality. But the basic idea of a will outside time, of the thing in itself, is absolutely correct and known to all religions (e.g. the Brahmin), only there it's more simply and clearly expressed. There remains one service he has performed, but it is an enormous one: *the conditional nature of time.* That's a great thing. You feel how much you would have missed if, thanks to Kant, you had not understood this.

Sonya is in Moscow. The weather is wonderful.

Note: [. . .]

(7) Religion is a philosophy comprehensible to everyone; philosophy is a religion to be proved, and therefore involved and systematized. [. . .]

22 October, Yasnaya Polyana Haven't written my diary for an age. All this time I've been busy with the *Cycle of Reading.* I've worked a lot and done a lot. [. . .]

(14) If we dislike people, it's not because they are evil; we consider them evil because we dislike them. [. . .]

(22) People ask 'why do children die, young people who have not lived much?' How do you know they have not lived much? It is your crude measurement in terms of time, but life is not measured by time. It's like saying: 'Why is this aphorism, this poem, this picture, this work of music so short; why was it broken off and not expanded to the length of the longest speeches and plays, or the biggest pictures?' Just as the measurement of length is not applicable to the importance (the greatness) of works of wisdom, neither is it (applicable) to life. How do you know what inner growth this soul has achieved in its short time span, and what influence it has had on others?

The spiritual life cannot be measured by physical measurements. [. . .]

Today is 24 November, Yasnaya Polyana [. . .] I must write three things. These are the most essential:

(1) *The Stone,* (2) on the form of the state, and (3) a profession of faith.[22] If I have the time and strength in the evenings, then my memoirs, in any order just as they come. I've begun to remember things very vividly. I don't know whether I'll succeed in expressing them vividly. [. . .]

11 December, Yasnaya Polyana   Health worse. Pains in the stomach, and I don't feel like work. Stopped work on the exposition of my faith, and have been translating Pascal[23] for two days. He's very good. Read Spinoza and chose some extracts. [. . .]

Today is 22 December, Yasnaya Polyana   [. . .] I'm afraid I distressed Molostvova. Worked on the *Cycle of Reading*; included Spinoza. There's much to note down, above all the joyful, steadfast, serene, almost always loving state in which I find myself. The question is: where does it come from? Why, given my vile life, do I have so much happiness? [. . .]

Today is 31 December, Yasnaya Polyana   [. . .] During these last days my letter to Nicholas II has appeared.[24] Chertkov printed it following the consent I had given via Dušan. I found it unpleasant. If any measures had been taken against me, no matter what – the harder the better – I would have been pleased, but I think I behaved indelicately towards Nicholas II and Nikolay Mikhaylovich.[25] [. . .]

Note: [. . .]

(4) The surrender of Port Arthur caused me grief and pain.[26] It's patriotism. I was brought up in it, and am just as much a slave to it as I am to personal egoism, family egoism, even aristocratic egoism. All these egoisms are alive in me, but there is in me also the awareness of the divine law, and that awareness keeps these egoisms in check so that I don't have to be their servant. And bit by bit these egoisms are becoming atrophied. [. . .]

1905

1 January, Yasnaya Polyana   A mass of people, and they make me tired. But I'm glad that, like the appearance of the letter,[1] this disagreeable congregation of people is not causing me displeasure, but is a stimulus to inner work: to behave in the best way possible towards what is disagreeable. [. . .]

20 January, Yasnaya Polyana   [. . .] Note: [. . .]
(2) Music is the stenography of the feelings. What I mean is: the quick or slow succession of sounds, their pitch, their volume – all this, in speech, embellishes words and their meaning, indicating those shades of feelings which are associated with our parts of speech. Music without speech takes these expressions of feelings and shades of feelings and combines them, and we get a play of feelings without the things that gave rise to them. For this reason music has such a particularly strong effect, and for this reason the combination of music with words is an adulteration of the music, a retrogression, a writing out in letters of stenographic signs. [. . .]

Today is 29 January, Yasnaya Polyana   I'm writing *The One Thing Needful*, and either because I have combined two different beginnings, or simply because I'm not in the mood, the writing is going badly. Posha has been here the whole time. I'm very fond of him. Sasha has gone to Petersburg. Sonya is in Moscow. Seryozha is here, and relations are difficult between us. I want to master myself, but I still can't. I'm glad that after one quarrel to begin with (not a very serious one), I didn't go any further. [. . .]

I experience various states: shame, sadness, anger, tenderness; but today my state is one where nothing is important, nothing is interesting, nothing matters.

Still, I have a lot of things to note down:
(1) I was listening to some political discussions, arguments and censure, and went into another room where people were singing to a guitar and laughing. And I clearly felt the sacred quality of cheerfulness. Cheerfulness and joy – these are one of the means of fulfilling God's will.
(2) I felt recently how far I've fallen spiritually from that moral, spiritual height to which I was raised by being in association with the best and wisest people whose works I've been reading and whose thoughts I've been pondering over for my *Cycle of Reading*. There is no doubt that you can

raise and lower yourself spiritually through the company of the people you associate with, whether present or absent. [. . .]

Today is 1 February, Yasnaya Polyana I'm still writing my article *The One Thing Needful*. It either goes badly or not at all, and I continue to be in a state of 'it's not worth it'. The vanity and folly of political interests is more and more apparent. Relations with Seryozha have been unpleasant. I was unkind. And I'm suffering for it. Lyova has been seen by the Tsar, and I'm glad of it.[2] Strange to say, this has quite freed me from the desire to influence the Tsar. [. . .]

24 February, Yasnaya Polyana Began to write *Korney Vasilyev*.[3] It's poor. I'm still weak. Busy with the *Cycle of Reading*. I'd like to start writing *about life*. [. . .]

Today is 28 February, Yasnaya Polyana I've been writing *Alyosha*;[4] it's quite bad. Gave it up. Revised Pascal and Lammenais.[5] Finished writing *Korney*. It's reasonable. [. . .]

6 March, Yasnaya Polyana I'm feeling very happy. Revised Pascal and Lamennais. Looked through *The One Thing Needful*, and I don't think I'll revise it any more. [. . .]
(2) I've been thinking about what is taught in our schools, our grammar schools: the main subjects are: (1) ancient languages and grammar – no use at all; (2) Russian literature, confined to near contemporaries, i.e. Belinsky, Dobrolyubov and yours truly. All the great literature of the world is a closed book. (3) History, by which is understood the description of the nasty lives of various good-for-nothing kings, emperors, dictators and military commanders, i.e. distortion of the truth, and (4) to crown it all – nonsensical and stupid legends and dogmas which are impudently called scripture.

This is in our secondary schools.[6] In our secondary schools everything that is reasonable and necessary is repudiated. In our colleges, with the exception of specializations like technology and medicine, they deliberately teach a materialistic, i.e. a narrow and limited doctrine which is intended to explain everything and exclude any reasonable understanding of life.

It's terrible! [. . .]

Today is 18 March, Yasnaya Polyana [. . .]
Must note one thing:
(1) Turgenev wrote a good piece, *Hamlet and Don Quixote*, and brought in Horatio at the end. But I think that the two chief characters are – Don

Quixote and Horatio, and Sancho Panza and the *Darling*.[7] The former are
for the most part men; the latter for the most part women. My sons are all
Don Quixotes, but without the self-sacrifice; my daughters are all
Horatios, ready for self-sacrifice.

30 March, Yasnaya Polyana [. . .] Had some good thoughts about death. I
continue to live in the sight of God. Wrote a letter about the overturned
cart.[8] Revised the proofs of the *Cycle*. Note:
(1) Two things above all are necessary for me: to overcome my concern for
people's opinions about me, and to overcome my unkind feeling towards
them. [. . .]
(3) How right the Slavophiles are when they say that the Russian people
try to avoid power, that they run away from it. They are prepared to offer it
to bad people rather than be soiled by it themselves. I think that if that is
so, they are right. Anything is better than being compelled to use force.
The situation of a person in the power of a tyrant is far more conducive to
a moral life than the situation of a voter, or a sharer of power. [. . .]

16 April, Yasnaya Polyana All this time I've had heart pains. I didn't
notice anything before, but now I feel it: constriction, irregular heartbeats.
It's both good, and it's serious. I haven't been able to work because of it.
And I very much want to write an exposition of my belief and also
something about Henry George, whom I read in Nikolayev's edition[9] and
was delighted by once more. [. . .]

Today is 21 April (evening), Yasnaya Polyana My heart has been better
during this time. I've begun to write *Defenders of the People*.[10] It's not bad.
And Henry George.[11] [. . .]

19 May, Yasnaya Polyana [. . .]   News was received yesterday of the
destruction of the Russian navy.[12] This news struck me particularly
forcibly for some reason. It became clear to me that it could not have been
and cannot be otherwise: although we are bad Christians, it's impossible to
hide the incompatibility between the Christian faith and war. In recent
times (meaning the last thirty years or so), this contradiction has come to
be felt more and more. And therefore in a war with a non-Christian people
for whom the highest ideal is the fatherland and the heroism of war,
Christian peoples are bound to be defeated. If Christian peoples have so
far defeated non-Christian peoples, this has only happened because of the
superiority of the technological and military advances of the Christian
peoples (China, India, the African peoples, the people of Khiva and the
Central Asians); but, given equal technology, Christian peoples must
inevitably be defeated by non-Christians, as happened in the war between

Russia and Japan. Japan in the space of a few decades not only drew level with European and American peoples, but surpassed them in technological advances. The success of the Japanese in the technology not only of war, but of all material advances as well, has shown clearly how cheap these technological advances which are called culture are. It doesn't cost anything to copy them and even to invent new ones. What is valuable, important and difficult is a good life, purity, brotherhood, love, the very things that Christianity teaches us and which we have despised. That is the lesson for us.

I don't say this in order to console myself because the Japanese have beaten us. The shame and the disgrace remain just the same. But they don't consist in the fact that we were beaten by the Japanese, but in the fact that we undertook to do something which we are unable to do well and which is bad in itself. [. . .]

6 June, Yasnaya Polyana Chertkov left the day before yesterday. My relations with him were very good, better than I expected. I had a depressing talk with S. (my son). A difficult examination. I won't pass. Shortened *A Great Sin*, and discarded a lot. I regret it. Dear Posha has come. Sonya's health is not good. I was going to write 'dubious', but was afraid she would read it. I'll leave it, because it really is dubious. [. . .]
(4) The older I become, the more vivid my recollections become. And, surprisingly, I only recall what is joyful and good, and enjoy my recollections no less than, and sometimes more than, I enjoyed the reality. [. . .]
(8) People compare me to Rousseau. I am greatly indebted to Rousseau and I love him, but there is a big difference. The difference is that Rousseau rejects every kind of civilization, while I reject the pseudo-Christian kind. What people call civilization is the growth of mankind. Growth is necessary, one cannot talk about it being good or bad. It exists – life consists of it. It's the same with the growth of a tree. But the branches, or the life forces that grow in the branches, are bad and harmful if they absorb all the strength of the growth. That's the case with our pseudo-civilization. [. . .]

29 June, Yasnaya Polyana I've had stomach trouble for over a week. I've done hardly anything. Lyova is here. I'm sorry for him with all my heart, but it's impossible to help him. Perhaps it's necessary that way. And he is happy in his blindness. Just today I've written a little of *The Pool of Siloam.*[13] The more I see Posha, the more I value him and love him. Sasha is becoming coarse. Either she has no ideals, or else very low ones. Sonya's state of health is uncertain. Most probably it's nothing bad. Relations with her are very good. Note: [. . .]

(6) I have known three attitudes to married life during my lifetime: (1) marriage is indestructible; whether it's happy or unhappy, put up with it as you do your own body, without violent outbursts, despair or love affairs; (2) harmony of souls, passion, poetic love, Werther, the sufferings of love; and (3) if you don't like your husband or your wife, separate and take a new one.

(7) It would be good to write about the attitude of uncorrupted children towards vegetarianism – how they know unhesitatingly that one shouldn't take life. [. . .]

(11) As the French were called in 1790 to make a new world, so the Russians have been called to the same task in 1905.

31 July, Yasnaya Polyana   Haven't written my diary for twenty-eight days. I'd no idea it was so long. All this time I've been quite well physically, but weak spiritually; I haven't written much. I haven't made much progress with *The End of the World*. But I think I've had quite a few thoughts, and perhaps interesting ones, during this time. I'll make a note of them now. During all this time I've suffered from great indolence, weakness and a bad mood which, thank God, has only shown itself *a little bit*. I'll copy out my notes.

(1) This is a note I made: a passive revolution has begun in Russia.

(2) In times of trouble such as now in Russia, the first thing that's necessary is to refrain from helping one side or the other; the second: to look for means of reconciliation.

(3) The intelligentsia has contributed a hundred times more evil than good to the life of the people. [. . .]

(5) The revolution now can in no way repeat what happened a hundred years ago. The revolutions of '30 and '48 did not succeed because they had no ideals, and they were inspired by what was left over from the great revolution. Now the people who are making the Russian revolution have none either; economic ideals are not ideals.

(6) The only revolution that is fruitful is the one which cannot be halted. [. . .]

Today is 10 August, Yasnaya Polyana   I've been to Pirogovo. For two or three days I felt particularly weak, but after three days the work began to get going, and I've almost finished *The End of the World*. It was very good being alone and with Masha. Came back on the 7th, and things were good here. Yesterday I sinned; I was annoyed about my works – the printing of them.[14] Of course I'm entirely to blame. I don't know whether it's good or bad, but always after such a sin the bonds of love are loosened – it's like an aching wound. [. . .] Note:

(1) The difference between a man and a woman: a man always feels lust,

but it's possible to suppress it. A woman – only from time to time – but it's irrepressible. [. . .]

27 August, Yasnaya Polyana [. . .] *The One Thing Needful* and *A Great Sin* have come out,[15] and I think that *A Great Sin* has run up against an obstacle, but is pushing on and perhaps demolishing it. I've just read a criticism by an American.[16] Obviously it rubbed him up the wrong way, and it hurts. It's the same attitude in Russia: either silence, or irritation at being hurt. That's all right.

How clear to me has the history of my attitudes to Europe now become: (1) joy that I, an insignificant person, am known by such great people; (2) joy that they value me on a level with their own people; (3) that they value me more than their own; (4) that I am beginning to understand who the people are who value me; (5) that they hardly understand me; (6) that they don't understand me; (7) that they don't understand anything at all, that the people whose appreciation I valued are stupid and barbaric. Today I received a pathetic criticism of *A Great Sin*, and a *Questionnaire* from the editor of *Echo* about capital punishment, why it is necessary and justified.[17] And the editor's name is – Sauvage. [. . .]

Note: [. . .]

(8) Living is dying. To live well means to die well. Try to die well. [. . .]

9 September, Yasnaya Polyana Bad news from Masha.[18] I'm very sorry for her, and I can't relieve the pain. All this time I've been writing *The End of the World*, and I've rarely been so satisfied with anything. I think it's good. It could and should have been much better, but it's all right as it is. Just before this I was very sad for some reason. I feel lonely and want love. Of course it's wrong. Things are very good as they are. I'm still just as often too clearly aware of the meaning of life, and this cruel, senseless life depresses me. A Jew came today, a correspondent of *Rus*. At the end of our talk, as a result of my disagreement with him, he said: 'So you even consider the murder of Plehve a bad thing?' I said to him 'I regret having talked to you', and walked out angrily, i.e. I behaved very badly. [. . .]

19 September, Yasnaya Polyana [. . .] Masha has again lost a stillborn child. Tanya is still holding her own. I'm very sorry for them. All the time I've been relatively well, and working quite well in the mornings. I'd like to find a replacement for the story *The Tsar and the Hermit*[19] for the *Cycle of Reading*. I dislike it very much. It's all invented. [. . .] I'm reading Kant. It's very good.

21 September, Yasnaya Polyana A state of depression. I began to think it's because nobody loves me. I started counting up all those who don't love

me. But then I thought, why should people love me? There's really no
reason. It's only up to me to love; what they do is their affair. And people
do love me much more than I deserve.

Then during the night I thought a lot about myself. I'm an exceptionally
bad, vicious man.

(1) I have all the vices, and to a very high degree: envy, and greed, and
meanness, and sensuality, and vanity, and ambition, and pride, and malice.
No, not malice, but bitterness, deceitfulness and hypocrisy. Everything,
everything, and to a far higher degree than the majority of people. My only
salvation is that I know it, and have been fighting – fighting all my life –
against it. For this reason they call me a psychologist. [. . .]

23 September, Yasnaya Polyana Finished *The End of the World.* Masha is
out of danger. A nice, spiritual letter. Just now – this morning – there was a
letter from an intellectual son of a peasant with a venomous reproach
against me, under the guise of praise for *A Great Sin,* for not giving up my
own land myself. I was terribly offended. But it turned out for my own
good. I realized that I had forgotten that I am living in the sight of God,
and not for the good opinion of this correspondent. And I felt relieved,
very much so. Yes, one must never forget the absolute seriousness of life.

12 October, Yanaya Polyana [. . .] I've been unwell for four days – my
liver. I've written nothing. Fyodor Kuzmich[20] engages my attention more
and more. I've been reading about Paul.[21] What a subject! Wonderful!!!
I've also been reading Herzen's *From the Other Shore*[22] and was also
thrilled. One should write about him – so that people of our time can
understand him. Our intelligentsia have sunk so low that they are no
longer able to understand him. His readers await him in the future. And,
far above the heads of today's crowd, he is handing on his thoughts to
those who will be able to understand them. [. . .]

23 October, Yasnaya Polyana [. . .] The revolution is in full swing. People
are being killed on both sides. A new and unexpected element, and one
absent in previous European revolutions, has arisen – 'the black
hundreds', 'the patriots': in actual fact men with a crude, false and
contradictory idea of the people and their demand not to use force. The
contradiction, as always, is in the fact that people want to curb and put an
end to force by force.

Generally speaking the frivolity of the people who are making this
revolution is astonishing and disgusting: childishness without the
innocence of children. I say to myself and to everyone that the main thing
for each person to do now is to look to himself, take a strict attitude to
every action of his and not take part in the struggle. But this is only

possible for a person who takes a religious attitude to his life. Only from a religious point of view is it possible to be free of involvement, free even of sympathy for one side or the other, and to further one's aim: the pacification of both sides.

I feel depressed amid the surrounding company.

3 November, Yasnaya Polyana [. . .] A few notes:
(1) Went for a ride and thought about my life: about the emptiness and weakness of the greater part of it. Only in the mornings do I fulfil my vocation – writing. That's all that is needed of me. I am someone's tool.
(2) This present revolution completely lacks any ideal. And so it isn't a revolution, but a riot. [. . .]

22 November, Yasnaya Polyana [. . .] A great event – Tanya has had a baby.[23] Masha and her husband have arrived. I'd very much like to get on with *Alexander I*.[24] Read about Paul and the Decembrists.[25] I can imagine it all very vividly. I go out riding every day. [. . .]

9 December, Yasnaya Polyana During this time I finished *The Divine and the Human*. Wrote *Freedoms and Freedom* as a separate article, and included it today in *The End of the World* and sent it to Moscow and England. It's probably too late. Let it stay as it is.[26] Continued with *Alexander I* yesterday. Wanted to get on with my *Memoirs*, but hadn't the strength. Continual strikes and riots. And I feel more than ever the need for, and the tranquillity of, a retreat into myself. The other day I prayed to God and understood my position in the world in relation to God, and it was very good. Yes, I forgot, the day before yesterday I got on with *The Green Stick*.[27] [. . .]

16 December I've written a bit of *Alexander I*. But it's bad. Tried to write my memoirs – worse still. I've written absolutely nothing for two days. My stomach is still upset, and I've been very drowsy mentally and even spiritually. Nothing interests me. I haven't yet got used to enduring such periods patiently. The horrors of brutalization are continuing in Moscow. No news, the trains are not running. I sometimes think of writing an appeal to the intelligentsia and the people, on the lines of my appeal to the Tsar and his assistants.[28] But I've no strong desire, although I know clearly what to say. [. . .]

18 December, Yasnaya Polyana Feel a bit better, but my mental weakness continues. Wrote nothing yesterday. Today I began writing *Alexander I*, but poorly and reluctantly. I must make a note of a dream I had. Someone said to me: 'Are you a good man?' I said: 'To say that I am a good man would be an immodest thing to do, i.e. would mean that I am not a good man; to say that I am bad would be an affectation. The truth is that I am sometimes a good man and sometimes a bad one.' Life as a whole goes on just like an accordion – it contracts and expands and contracts again, from the bad to the good and back again to the bad. To be good only means wanting to be good more often than bad. And that is something I desire.

23 December, Yasnaya Polyana Health better; I feel fresher mentally. Talked about the revolution and couldn't resist the temptation to write it all down in short form: *Government, Revolutionaries and the People.* I've been writing it all these days, and I think it will do. [. . .] Note: [. . .]
(2) One of the chief motives for revolution is the feeling which makes children want to break their toys, the passion for destruction.
(3) Now, in the course of the revolution, three sorts of people have been revealed with their virtues and their failings. First the conservatives – people who want peace and quiet and a continuation of their pleasant life and don't want any changes. The failing of these people is egoism; their virtues – modesty and humility. Secondly, the revolutionaries – they want change and are arrogant enough to decide what change is needed, and they are not afraid of force in order to implement their changes, nor are they afraid of hardships and sufferings. The failing of these people is arrogance and cruelty; their virtues – energy and the readiness to suffer in order to achieve an aim which appears to them to be good. Thirdly, the liberals – they haven't the humility of the conservatives or the readiness to make sacrifices of the revolutionaries but they have the egoism and the desire for peace and quiet of the former and the self-assurance of the latter. [. . .]

27 December, Yasnaya Polyana All these days I've been revising *Government, Revolutionaries and the People.* I think I've finished, but don't know what to do with it. I feel, and am, quite well. [. . .]
(6) I also have in mind a clear character sketch of Alexander I – if only I could manage to get even half way with it. The thing is that he wanted sincerely and with all his heart to be good and moral, and he also wanted with all his heart to reign at all costs. I must show the duality of desires – common to all people – which sometimes takes two completely opposite directions.

It is now the night of 31 December 1905 and the beginning of 1906 All this time I've been adding to *Government, Revolutionaries and the People.* Sometimes it seems necessary, sometimes weak. My health isn't bad. But my thoughts lack vitality. Only two things to note:
(1) When reading Stroganov on Romme,[29] I was struck by his heroism

when combined with his weak and pathetic figure. It reminded me of Nikolenka. I think that this is very often the case. Strong men, sensual people like the Orlovs, are usually cowards, while these others are the opposite.

The second thing. (2) My duality: at times in the morning and at night I'm a truly wise and good man; at times I'm a weak, pathetic creature who doesn't know what to do with himself. The difference is that the former state is the real one, while in the second state I know that I'm enveloped in delusion. [. . .]

1906

4 January, Yasnaya Polyana All these days I've been revising and altering *Government, Revolutionaries and the People*, and I still haven't finished. *The People* is bad because I tried to work into it the unsuitable *Three Untruths*. I hope it will turn out all right. And that it will be useful. I'm reading *The Thoughts of Wise People* every day, and with great profit to my soul. These last two or three days, with no people here, I've been working on myself incessantly: I don't allow myself any bad thoughts or frivolous behaviour like gymnastics or fortune-telling. And that's good. If only I can keep it up until death! [. . .]

6 January, Yasnaya Polyana Still revising *Government, Revolutionaries and the People* and I think I've finished it or am near the end. I feel very gloomy. I try to overcome it but can't. I don't give expression to my badness in any way, but feel and think bad things. Note: [. . .]
(2) The Jewish faith is the most irreligious. A faith in which the denominator is infinity. A proud faith that they are God's only chosen people. [. . .]

18 January, Yasnaya Polyana Still unwell. I'm working a little on the *Cycle of Reading*.

Thought today about what I, an old man, should do. I haven't much strength, and it's getting noticeably weaker. Several times in my life I've considered myself close to death. And – how foolishly! – I would forget, or try to forget it – forget what? That I would die, and that in any case – whether in five, ten, twenty or thirty years – death is still very close. And now, because of my years, I naturally consider myself close to death, and there's no point in trying to forget it, and I can't forget it. But what should I, an old feeble person, do? I asked myself. And it seemed that there was nothing to do, that I had no strength for anything. But today I realized so clearly the clear and joyful answer. What should I do? It's already been revealed – I must die. This is my task now, as it always has been. And I must perform this task as well as possible: die, and die well. The task is before you, a noble and inevitable task, and you are searching for one. This made me very glad. I'm beginning to get used to regarding death and dying not as the end of my task, but as the task itself. [. . .]

Today is 18 February, Yasnaya Polyana All this time, i.e. since the 10th, I've been in a (physically) depressed condition, but very well at heart. I still haven't lost the disposition to live only for God, to multiply what has been given to me (my talent). [. . .] Note: [. . .]

(13) In extreme old age other people, and frequently old people themselves, usually think that they are only living out their days. On the contrary, it is in extreme old age that the most valuable and necessary life both for oneself and for others is lived. The value of life is in inverse proportion to the square of the distance from death. It would be good if old people themselves, and those close to them, could understand this. [. . .]

2 March, Yasnaya Polyana Haven't written my diary for twelve days. I've felt both good and bad physically; more often bad. I'm just about surviving. [. . .] There is much to note down, I think, and it isn't bad. [. . .]

(4) We are so used to seeing people of our circle engaged in politics, i.e. concerning themselves with how to improve the organization of people's social life and putting all their efforts into this activity, that we are not surprised at this phenomenon. And yet it is very surprising.

People who are completely negligent about carrying out their economic, family and personal affairs put all their energy into the future imaginary organization of society and, in spite of the differences between all the parties, stubbornly defend their own position. There is only one explanation: a person needs activity, and the assurance that his activity is useful. He makes a mess of his personal, economic or family affairs, and not only lacks the assurance of behaving reasonably, but quite the contrary. And so he chooses an activity where the results are not visible, and he can comfort himself with the assurance that he is doing a useful and necessary thing. Confirmation of this is the fact that the more tormented a person's private life is, the more energetically he devotes himself to politics. [. . .]

5 March, Yasnaya Polyana [. . .]
(2) How clearly was the usual, corrupting effect of power seen in the revolutionaries when they began to seize power: self-importance, pride, vanity and above all lack of respect for man. [. . .]

10 March Was in a dull, miserable state all day. By evening this state changed to one of emotion – the desire for affection – for love. I felt, as in childhood, like clinging to a loving, pitying creature, and weeping emotionally and being comforted. But who is the creature I could cling to like that? I ran through all the people I love – nobody would do. Who could I cling to? I wanted to become young again and cling to my mother as I imagine her to have been.

Yes, yes, my dear mother, whom I never called by that name, since I couldn't talk. Yes, she is my highest conception of pure love – not a cold or divine, but a warm, earthly, maternal love. This is what attracts my better, weary soul. Mother dear, caress me.

All this is stupid, but it's all true.

11 March Haven't written my diary for about four days. Yesterday I was in a particularly depressed state. I feel everything unpleasant particularly keenly. That's what I tell myself; but in actual fact I seek out what is unpleasant, I am receptive to, and not impervious to, what is unpleasant. I wasn't able to get rid of this feeling at all. I tried everything: prayer and the consciousness of my badness. And it was no good. Prayer, i.e. the vivid conception of my situation, doesn't reach down to the depths of my consciousness, and the recognition of my worthlessness and rottenness doesn't help. It's not that I want something particular, but I'm painfully dissatisfied with something, and I don't know what. I think it's life; I want to die.

By evening this state changed into a feeling of loneliness and the emotional desire for affection and love: I, an old man, wanted to become a child, to nestle up against a loving creature, to snuggle up, to complain, to be caressed and comforted. But who is this creature I could nestle up against and in whose arms I could weep and complain? Nobody now alive. So what is this feeling? It's the same old devil, egoism, who in this new crafty guise wants to deceive and take possession of me. This latest feeling explained to me my previous state of melancholy. It was only a weakening, a temporary disappearance, of the spiritual life and egoism asserting its rights (egoism which, once aroused, can find no food for itself and turns to melancholy). There is only one remedy against this: to serve somebody in the simplest way, the first way that occurs, to work for somebody. [. . .]

19 March, Yasnaya Polyana Still in the same bad, depressed state. I'm struggling against it. I think I've overcome the feeling of unkindness and reproachfulness towards people, but my apathy is just as bad. I can't do any work at all. Went riding yesterday and argued with myself all the time. The weak, worthless, physical egotistical man said: 'Everything is vile', while the spiritual man said: 'You're lying, everything is fine. What you call vile is the whetstone without which the most precious thing in you would be blunted and grow rusty.' And I told myself this so insistently and convincingly that in the end I convinced myself and returned home in a very good mood. [. . .]

(1) Thought about the fact that I'm not writing my diary for myself but for other people – primarily for those who will be alive when I am not here physically – and that there's nothing bad about that. It is, I'm inclined to think, what is required of me. Well, but what if these diaries are burnt? Well, what of it? Perhaps they are necessary for other people, but for me

I'm sure they are not just necessary – they are me. They are a good thing *for me*. [. . .]

2 April, Yasnaya Polyana [. . .] Note:

(1) It has become absolutely clear recently that an agricultural way of life is not merely one of various ways of life, just as a book – the Bible – is not one of various books, but *is* life, life itself, the only human life which alone makes possible the manifestation of all the highest human qualities. The chief mistake in the organization of human societies and one which eliminates the possibility of any reasonable organization of life is that people want to organize society without agricultural life, or with the sort of organization in which agricultural life is only one form, and the most insignificant form, of life. [. . .]

(17) People write pompously in books that where there are rights, there are also obligations. What audacious nonsense – what lies. Man has only obligations. MAN HAS ONLY OBLIGATIONS.

(18) People talk and argue about Henry George's system. It isn't the system which is valuable (although not only do I not know a better one, but I can't imagine one), but what is valuable is the fact that the system establishes an attitude to land which is universal and the same for everybody. Let them find a better one if they can.

17 April, Yasnaya Polyana [. . .] There is much to note, and I think it's not unimportant. [. . .]

(2) The Western peoples have given up agriculture, and all want to exercise power. They can't exercise power over themselves, and so they search for colonies and markets.

(3) A sensible, moral life is only possible when everyone is engaged in agriculture. Agriculture points to what is most necessary and what is less so. It is the guide to a reasonable life. One must be in contact with the earth.

(4) The emotion and enthusiasm which we experience from the contemplation of nature is a recollection of the time when we were animals, trees, flowers, the earth. More exactly: it is the awareness of our unity with everything, an awareness concealed from us by time.

Today is 25 April, Yasnaya Polyana I am better physically, and yet I haven't felt in such a weak condition spiritually for a long time, not throughout my illness. Read in the paper about Gorky's reception in America and caught myself feeling angry.[1] Read Velikanov's arguments and criticism of my writings and felt displeased.[2] Then a printed article which had been sent to me which says that I am as good as summoning the Cossacks to Yasnaya Polyana, and I was hurt.[3] Yet it's good that I feel that it's a weakness uncharacteristic of me. [. . .]

(24) I dreamed that I was trying to drive my son away: my son – a combination of Ilya, Andrey and Seryozha. He wouldn't go. I was conscience-stricken because I had used force, but also because I hadn't gone the whole way. Stakhovich was present, and I felt ashamed. Suddenly this collective son began to edge me off the chair I was sitting on with his backside. I put up with it for a long time, then jumped up and waved the chair at my son. He ran away. I felt even more conscience-stricken. I knew that he hadn't done it deliberately. My son had gone. Tanya turned up in the hall and told me I was in the wrong. And she added that she was beginning to be jealous of her husband again. The whole psychology was exceptionally accurate, but without time, or space, or personality. [. . .]

It's already *22 May, today, Yasnaya Polyana*. All this time I've been in a poorly and weak condition. I'm still writing and rewriting *Two Ways*.[4] And it's still not quite clear. There have been many joyful things recently: an old man from Kolomna, a Jew who is renouncing military service and a young man, Ofitserov, in the grip of regeneration.[5] There have been some letters too. [. . .]

Recently I have had moments of silent despair at the lack of effect that the truth has on people. Especially at home. All my sons are here at present, and it's particularly depressing. What is depressing is the unnaturalness of conventional intimacy and the greatest spiritual remoteness. Sometimes, as today, I feel like running away and disappearing. That's all nonsense. I make a note of it to confess my weakness. It's all good and necessary and may bring me joy. I can't feel sorry for those blind people who think they can see, and strenuously deny what I can see. [. . .]

29 May, Yasnaya Polyana   Very depressed about the shamefulness of my life. And I don't know what to do. Lord, help me. [. . .] There's a great deal to be noted. [. . .]
(9) We all live by robbery and alms and hard work. The only question is what percentage of each. I live entirely by alms and robbery. And it torments me. [. . .]

6 June, Yasnaya Polyana   [. . .] I'm on good and loving terms with all my sons; with Andrey it's terribly difficult. What a plague their general self-assurance is! What a lot they lose because of it. I'm still fighting against my concern for public opinion, and am trying to establish a direct relationship with God. On rare occasions – I can. [. . .]

3 July, Yasnaya Polyana   Haven't written my diary for a long time. My stomach has been upset. I've worked spasmodically on *Two Ways*. My spiritual condition is one of great joy and freedom, and I live mostly in accordance with God's will. Note: [. . .]

(15) If the Russian people are uncivilized barbarians, then we have a future. But the Western peoples are civilized barbarians, and they have nothing more to look forward to. For us to imitate the Western peoples is just like a healthy, hard-working, uncorrupted lad envying a bald-headed rich young Parisian sitting in his hotel. *Ah, que je m'embête* [Oh, how bored I am].

Don't envy or imitate, but have pity. [. . .]

(21) The Indians have been conquered by the British, but they are freer than the British: they can live without the British, but the British can't live without them. [. . .]

Today is 30 July, Yasnaya Polyana   [. . .] There is a lot to be noted:
(1) Does God exist? I don't know. I know that there is a law governing my spiritual being. The source of and the reason for that law I call God. [. . .]

24 August, Yasnaya Polyana   Haven't written my diary for twenty-four days. I've spent the time well. And now, thank God, still better and better. During this time Chertkov arrived. I went with him to Masha's. I found Chertkov very pleasant, but I'm afraid that that was largely because he has a very high opinion of me. Menshikov has also been, and, thank God, was so pleasant for a completely different reason that I recall our relations with pleasure. I was going to write that Masha is very dear to me, but everyone reads my diaries. And it's better like that.

Worked a lot on *Two Ways* and I think I've quite finished it. I think it's necessary, and may be useful. But I can't know that. I know that it was necessary for me to write it. The consciousness of being a servant of God has not grown much weaker, although it has lost its novelty; but it has taken root and, thank God, I live by it. Often when I'm out walking, or when I put out the candle as I lie in bed, I experience a new, joyful feeling of life, gratitude and (quiet) contentment. I crossed out 'quiet', because the feeling, although not unquiet, is very vital and strong. Note: [. . .]

(14) I am counted among the anarchists, but I am not an anarchist, but a Christian. My anarchism is only the application of Christianity to human relationships. The same is true of anti-militarism, communism, vegetarianism. [. . .]

(21) Recently, as I look at people without any religion, I have begun to respect people who believe in God, although they conceive of Him in the most crude forms. Belief in the Iberian Mother of God is better than the complete absence of acknowledgement of a higher law. [. . .]

1 September, Yasnaya Polyana   Haven't written my diary for six days.

Sonya's illness is getting worse and worse.[6] Today I felt particularly sorry for her. But she is touchingly sensible, truthful and good. I don't want to write about anything else. Three of my sons, Seryozha, Andryusha and Misha, are here, and two daughters: Masha and Sasha. The house is full of doctors. It's depressing: instead of devotion to the will of God and a solemn, religious mood, I find pettiness, recalcitrance, egoism. I had some good thoughts and feelings. Thank God. [. . .]

2 September, Yasnaya Polyana   They operated today. They say it's been successful. But it was very hard for her. This morning she was very well in herself. How death assuages one! I thought: isn't it obvious that death is being revealed both to me and to her; and when she dies, it will be completely revealed to her. 'Ah, so that's what it is!' But we who are left behind can't yet see what has been revealed to the person dying. It will be revealed to us afterwards, in its own time. During the operation I walked to the fir tree woods. And I was nervously exhausted. Then I wrote a bit about Henry George[7] – not well. Note: [. . .]
(9) The Western peoples are far ahead of us, but ahead of us on the wrong path. For them to get on the right path they need to go a long way back. But we only need to turn a little way off the wrong path which we have just started on, and along which the Western peoples are coming back to meet us. [. . .]

5 September, Yasnaya Polyana   I'm terribly sad. I'm sorry for her. Her sufferings are great, and probably in vain. I don't know, I'm sad, I'm sad; but that's very good.

15 September   Sonya is well. Evidently she is recovering. She's suffered a great deal. [. . .]

24 September   I've finished all the works I've started and written a foreword to Henry George. Recently my stomach hasn't been quite right, and my thoughts are few and sluggish. Began the *Cycle of Reading*, but it's going sluggishly and not well. I even thought today I couldn't go on with it. Wrote a venomous letter in reply to an enquiry about a visit by some Englishmen,[8] and am glad I didn't send it. This is just what is lacking when one is asleep: moral effort. For example I had a long dream today and lied about something, I don't remember what, and then remembered there was no need to lie, but I couldn't restrain myself. But when one is awake it's always possible to restrain oneself. And this is the crux of our whole life and the difference between waking and sleeping.
   Must note: [. . .]
(12) How much more valuable and important than writing is the business

of living – direct relationships with people. In that case you have a direct effect on people, you can see success or failure, you can see your mistakes and can correct them, but with writing you don't know anything, perhaps you had an effect, perhaps not; perhaps you were not understood, perhaps you said the wrong thing – you don't know at all. [. . .]

30 September, Yasnaya Polyana   [. . .] I'm reading Goethe⁹ and can see all the pernicious influence of this insignificant, bourgeois-egotistical, gifted man on the generation which I encountered – especially poor Turgenev with his veneration of *Faust* (a thoroughly bad work) and Shakespeare – likewise Goethe's doing – and especially with the particular importance ascribed to various statues of Laocoon and Apollo and various poems and dramas. How much I suffered when, because of my love for Turgenev, I wanted to love what he rated so highly. I tried to with all my strength and was quite unable to. What terrible harm is done by authorities, celebrated great people, and false ones moreover! [. . .]

10 October, Yasnaya Polyana   [. . .] There's a lot to be noted: [. . .]
(6) Went for a walk. A wonderful autumn morning, still and warm, the winter crops, the smell of leaves. And in place of this wonderful nature with its fields, woods, water, birds and animals, people are creating another, artificial nature for themselves in the towns, with factory chimneys, palaces, locomotives, phonographs . . . It's terrible, and one can't do anything to improve it. [. . .]

23 October, Yasnaya Polyana   [. . .] Went to Yasenki today and brought back some letters, all unpleasant. The fact that I could find them unpleasant shows how low I've sunk. Two argumentative ladies, vague, muddle-headed and tiresome (I could and should have treated them more affectionately, as I decided after a little thought), and then a feuilleton in a Kharkov paper by that young student who lived here in the summer.¹⁰ [. . .] He condemns me for something I'm not guilty of. But if he knew all the nastiness that used to exist and still does exist in my soul, he could justly condemn me many times more severely. And I feel cross because he condemns me for something I'm not guilty of and judges me falsely, then I can only be sorry for him, as I would be sorry if he had made a mistake and told lies about another person. Oh, how good it would be never to lose that direct relationship with God which rules out all interest in people's opinions. And this is possible. One can be strong or weak, one can be idle, but one mustn't give way to the temptation of wanting people to love you. This is a terrible temptation which began with me in early childhood and still has a hold on me, or, rather, continually tries to subject me to its power. At present I'm free, thanks to the feuilleton. But will it be for long? [. . .]

Today is 26 October, Yasnaya Polyana　I've finished all my things. The *Afterword*[11] is poor, but I've sent it off. I've written all my letters, even the autographs. Yesterday Sasha upset me, and I'm still depressed because I can't bring myself to talk to her. It's evening now, and I'm in a very bad mood. I want to arouse in myself the vital awareness of my spiritual principles, and I can't. Recalled my past, and thought about the terrible blindness of youth. I censure Andryusha and Sasha. But what was I like at twenty-seven? The Caucasus, the Turkish War, Sevastopol. And what was I like at twenty-two? Gambling, Chulkovo,[12] hunting. Yes, life consists of shaping and improving oneself, and it goes on as long as it can in that form. But there is a limit. The limit is absolute self-sacrifice, but that is impossible for the human animal. And so it is necessary to die, i.e. to change into a different form. Isn't that so?

Today is 9 November, Yasnaya Polyana　[. . .] Note:
(1) Only a person who considers himself free can submit to other people. A person who does what he wants considers himself free; but a person who does what he wants is a slave of everything. The only person who *is* free is the one who considers himself a slave of God, and only does what God wants and what nobody and nothing can prevent. (Good.) [. . .]
(4) Thoughts only move our life forward when they are arrived at with one's own mind, or answer a question which has arisen in one's own soul; but other people's thoughts, apprehended only by the mind and memory, have no influence on life and can coexist with actions which are contrary to them. [. . .]
(10) A person stubbornly holds on to his ideas mainly because he has arrived at those ideas himself, perhaps very recently, after condemning his previous ones. And suddenly it is suggested that he should condemn these new ideas of his, and embrace still newer ideas which he has not yet arrived at himself. And here we have yet another of those very ludicrous and harmful superstitions, namely that it is shameful to alter one's convictions. It is shameful not to alter them, because the meaning of life lies in the greater and greater understanding of oneself and the world, and so it is shameful not to change them. [. . .]

17 November, Yasnaya Polyana　[. . .] Note: [. . .]
(7) One can understand the beliefs of Buddhism that you will always return to life (after death) until you reach absolute self-renunciation. Nirvana is not destruction, but that new, unknown, incomprehensible life in which self-renunciation is no longer necessary. Buddhism is only wrong in not recognizing the meaning and purpose of *this* life which leads to self-renunciation. We don't see it but it is there, and so this life is just as real as any other. [. . .]

23 November, Yasnaya Polyana　I'm in a very good state of mind and full of love for everyone. I've been reading St John's epistle.[13] It's wonderful. Only now can I fully understand it. Today there was a great temptation which I just couldn't resist entirely. Abakumov ran after me pleading and complaining that he had been sentenced to prison because of the oak trees. It hurt me very much. He can't understand that I, a husband, can't do as I want, and sees me as a scoundrel and as a pharisee, hiding behind my wife. I hadn't the strength to put up with it in a loving spirit, and told Abakumov that I couldn't go on living here. And that wasn't good. Generally speaking people are abusing me more and more on every side. That's good. It drives me towards God. If only I could stand firm where I am now. Generally speaking I feel at this very moment one of the biggest changes that have ever taken place in me. I feel it in my calmness and joyfulness and good feelings (I daren't say love) towards people. I dislike almost all my earlier writings of recent years, except the Gospels and a few others, for their lack of goodness. I don't want them to be published.

Masha greatly alarms me. I love her very, very much. Yes, I would like to draw a dividing line under all my past life and begin a new, very short, but purer epilogue.

27 November, Yasnaya Polyana Just now, one o'clock in the morning, Masha died.[14] A strange thing. I didn't feel horror or fear or the awareness of anything exceptional taking place, or even pity or grief. I seemed to consider it necessary to arouse in myself a special feeling of emotion, of grief, and I did so, but at the bottom of my heart I was more composed than I would have been in the case of another person's bad or improper behaviour – not to mention my own. Yes, this event belongs to the realm of the body and is irrelevant. I watched her all the time she was dying; wonderfully calmly. For me she was a creature experiencing revelation before my own revelation. I watched her revelation, and it made me glad. Now this revelation in the realm accessible to me (life) has ended, i.e. the revelation has ceased to be visible to me; but what was revealed exists. 'Where?', 'When?' – these are questions relating to the process of revelation here, and cannot be related to the true life outside space and time. Note: [. . .]

(5) In serious moments when, as now, the body of a loved one lies still unburied, one sees clearly the immorality and wrongfulness and depressing nature of the life of the rich. The best remedy against grief is work. But they have no essential work, only amusement. But amusement is unseemly, and all that remains for them is automatically false, sentimental chatter. I've just received some falsely sympathetic letters and telegrams, and met the simple-minded Kynya, who knew Masha. I said: 'Have you heard about our grief?'

'Yes, I've heard' – and then said immediately: 'Give me a copeck.'

How much better and easier that is.

29 November, Yasnaya Polyana They've just taken her away to be buried. Thank God, I'm still in good spirits, as before. Things are easier with my sons now. [. . .]

28 December, Yasnaya Polyana [. . .]
   I go on living and often recall Masha's last minutes (I don't like calling her Masha, that simple name is so unsuitable to the creature who has left me). She *sits* here, surrounded by pillows, and I hold her thin, dear hand and feel life departing, feel her departing. These quarter hours are among the most important, significant times of my life.

29 December, Yasnaya Polyana I feel weak physically, but good mentally. *What is To Be Done?* has come out. It's unpleasant and feeble, but undoubtedly true. I didn't want to write any more articles, but an article on the meaning of the revolution, a letter from an officer and a notice today about *What Is To Be Done?* requires me to.[15] The main thing is, I must write that all their historical-economic theories are only a justification for their nasty life, only tramping up and down in a blind alley from which there is no exit. Note: [. . .]
(10) Just as all the convictions of every kind of politician, socialist and revolutionary with regard to a better organization of society are futile, so too are my own futile. Do what you can for yourself in the field in which you are competent, and leave the consequences to that force on which they depend. [. . .]
(12) I am distressed by the fact that I shan't see in my lifetime the consequences of my activity, and at the same time I am distressed that I shan't find in life an opportunity for the sort of activity in which I could be completely sure that I wouldn't be guided by the desire for worldly fame. I have exactly what I need, but I still complain.
(13) In the literature of today, everything that is produced is available to us with equal power to attract. The further back one goes, the less is available: the greater part has been whittled away by time; even more, if one goes back still further. The literature that is available has the shape of a cone standing on its point. Near the point are the wisdom of the Brahmins and the Chinese, Buddhism, Stoicism, Socrates, Christianity; further away, as it gets wider, come Plutarch, Seneca, Cicero, Marcus Aurelius, the medieval thinkers, then Pascal, Spinoza, Kant, the Encyclopaedists, then the writers of the nineteenth century, and finally our contemporaries. It's obvious that even among our contemporaries there are those who will survive, but it's difficult to pick them out, first because there are so many that it's impossible to go through them all, and secondly

because only the very worst things are exposed to view, since the masses are always foolish and lacking in taste. [. . .]

(28) How difficult it is to distinguish whether you serve people for their good (to satisfy an inner striving to love), or for the gratitude and praise you will get from them. There is only one way of telling: would you do the same thing if you knew that nobody would know? With every action which is not the result of an animal impulse, ask yourself: who for? [. . .]

1907

14 January, Yasnaya Polyana I've been unwell all these last two weeks and still haven't recovered yet. All this time I've been reading: Plutarch, Montaigne and Waliszewski, yesterday a book about St Paul and today I finished the *Memorabilia*.[1] It's very interesting to compare the high state of moral understanding with the simplicity of life and the low level of technical development. Now this side has advanced so far and the moral side has fallen so far behind that it is hopeless to establish a correct relationship. I made a few notes during this time, but couldn't do any work at all. With the big new *Cycle of Reading* and also the one for children which I've started I seem to have taken upon myself work which is too much for me. There's a lot to note down, and it's quite good, I think.

(1) I was thinking today that it's impossible to live peacefully with a high opinion of oneself, and that the first condition for a peaceful and good life is what St Francis said about himself in case he should not be allowed in.[2] And today I've been busy all morning reducing my own denominator. And I think it hasn't been useless: I vividly recalled in myself all the things I now condemn in my sons: passion for gambling, hunting, vanity, dissipation, meanness ... The main thing is to understand that I am a man well below average as far as concerns morality, weakness, intelligence, and especially knowledge, a man whose mental faculties are becoming feeble, and not to forget this; and then how easy life will be. Value the estimation of God, not men. Acknowledge the justice of people's low estimation of me. [...]

22 February [...]
(2) Children need dogmatism, it doesn't hurt them.

17 March, Yasnaya Polyana Haven't written my diary for a very long time, but I've made many notes in my notebooks. During this time I've only been working on the lessons for children.[3] The further I get, the greater and greater are the difficulties I see, and at the same time the greater the hope of success. All that I've done so far is hardly any use. Yesterday I divided the children into two classes. Today I thought about what to do with the lower class. [...]

There's a great deal to note down.

(1) Something strange and quite new to me is the reason why sons don't

love their fathers (in non-Christian families, of course): it's envy on the sons' part and rivalry between sons and fathers. [. . .]

(5) I feel the blessings of old age and illnesses which release me from caring about other people's opinions. The fact that I am more abused than praised is a help in this respect.

(6) Only in the realm of consciousness is man free. But consciousness is only possible in the present moment. [. . .]

(8) Philanthropy is like a man draining off lush meadows by means of drainage ditches and then irrigating those meadows in the places where they seem particularly dry. You take away from the people everything they need, thereby depriving them of the possibility of feeding themselves by their own labour, and then you try to support the weak ones by sharing out among them a part of what has been taken away from them. [. . .]

(14) It would be good to forget one's self, but it's impossible, and so one must try at least to strike a balance: to do unto others as you would have them do unto you. [. . .]

5 April, Yasnaya Polyana Haven't written my diary for more than a fortnight. I've lived reasonably well all this time. I've had a heavy cold, and now feel very weak. The lessons for children and the preparation for them have been entirely absorbing me. I notice my physical and mental powers growing weaker, but in inverse proportion to my moral ones. There's a lot I would like to write. But there's a lot I've already left unfinished for good, or not even begun. Note [. . .]

(10) The whole difference between a man and an animal is that a man knows he will die, but an animal doesn't. It's an enormous difference. [. . .]

16 April, Yasnaya Polyana Five days have passed and I'm in quite a different mood today. I can't overcome my dissatisfaction with those close to me. I feel melancholy and want to cry. Everything seems depressing. Just now after dinner and a lesson with the children – only two came – I sat alone and thought that only now was I fully and completely entrusting myself to the will of God. Come what may. There was no point in wanting to perform any task – writing a scripture for children or whatever it may be; I had to surrender myself entirely to Him, retaining only my love for Him, privately and publicly . . . and suddenly Sonya came in and we started talking about the wood, about people stealing, and about the children selling things at half price, and I couldn't suppress my anger. As if it wasn't all the same to me. Lord, help me. Help me. I'm sorry for myself and feel disgusted with myself.

Today is 30 April, Yasnaya Polyana I've been living very well all this time. I've been busy with the same things. I'd like to write a work of fiction, but

I'm hardly capable of it now. However, the main thing is not to wish for anything for oneself. The *Cycle of Reading* for children is a sufficient service. I feel very poorly and weak today. Note. [. . .]

(2) The true life is lived above all by children, who enter life and are not yet aware of time. They never want anything to be changed. The longer they live, the more they become subject to the illusion of time. As old age approaches, this illusion grows weaker and weaker – time seems to go quicker – and finally old people enter more and more into a life without time. And so it is children and old people who live the true life most of all. But people who live the life of the flesh are preparing material for the true life rather than living it themselves.

(3) People condemn egoism. But egoism is the basic law of life. The point is what one regards as one's *ego*: one's consciousness or one's body – or rather one's spiritual or physical consciousness. [. . .]

(27) Personal egoism is a small evil, family egoism a bigger one, party egoism a bigger one still, and state egoism the most terrible of all. [. . .]

Today is 22 May, Yasnaya Polyana Haven't written anything in my diary for nearly a month. During this month, I've continued lessons with the children and preparations for them. Apart from that, almost all I've done is to jot down my thoughts about Paul as the falsifier of Christianity.[4] [. . .] Wrote yesterday about Skoworoda.[5] Something else to do: to compile biographies of Epictetus, Socrates, Pascal and Rousseau, as well as those of Buddha and Confucius. This is an old man's dispersal of effort. [. . .]

7 June, Yanaya Polyana Haven't written my diary for a long time. My previous illness is over, but a new one seems to be starting. I'm very, very sad today. I'm ashamed to admit it, but I can't summon up any joy. I'm calm and serious at heart, but not joyful. I'm sad mainly because of the darkness in which people so stubbornly go on living. Because of the bitterness of the people, and our senseless luxury. [. . .] I'm sad, sad. Lord, Help me, burn up the old carnal man in me. Yes, the only consolation, the only salvation, is to live in eternity, not time. [. . .]

I thought how harmful it is to write *articles*, to compose articles and not to express one's thoughts and feelings just as they come.

10 June, Yasnaya Polyana Physically weak. I'm well at heart. Loving relationships are becoming a habit. Oh, if only this habit could be acquired in childhood! Is it possible? I think so. A few things to note:

(1) I suffer more and more, almost physically, from inequality – of wealth and of the extravagances of our life in the midst of poverty; and I can't reduce this inequality. Therein lies the secret tragedy of my life. [. . .]

20 July, Yasnaya Polyana [. . .] People have been paying a lot of attention to me recently for some reason, and this does me a lot of harm. I look for my name in the paper. This darkens and obscures life very, very much. I must fight against it. Note: [. . .]

(2) If the proposition that the three angles of a triangle equal two right angles were opposed to people's interests, they would find ways of proving the opposite (Hobbes). [. . .]

(15) What a bad habit it is when you meet a person to start off with a joke. God is in that person, and you mustn't joke with God. When you meet a person, always talk to him in all seriousness. [. . .]

Today is 8 August, Yasnaya Polyana I feel a considerable weakening of everything, especially memory, but at heart I feel very, very good. I've finished the article,[6] and apart from letters and my diary I'll now work on the children's *Cycle of Reading*. Being with Chertkov makes me very happy. I had some very good thoughts today. [. . .]

(5) In the past we had the Saint Francises, now we have the Darwins. [. . .]

(9) Intelligence only springs from humility. Stupidity – only from conceit. However great his intellectual faculties, a humble person is always dissatisfied – always seeking; a self-assured person thinks he knows everything, and doesn't try to delve deep. [. . .]

(15) Kant is considered an abstract philosopher, but he is a great religious teacher. [. . .]

(18) There is almost no freedom of choice over physical conditions: you burn yourself and you recoil, you haven't slept for two days and you fall asleep. There is more freedom of choice over actions: shall I go or not? Shall I do this job or another one? There is more freedom of choice still over thoughts – almost complete freedom. [. . .]

7 September, Yasnaya Polyana [. . .] Being with Chertkov still makes me just as happy. I'm afraid I've been suborned by his liking for me. Had a look yesterday at *The Collected Thoughts.*[7] It would be good if they were to be as useful to people as they seem to me in my moments of conceit. During this time my state of mind has been good rather than bad. I felt just now how constrained I am in writing this diary by the knowledge that it will be read by Sasha and Chertkov. I'll try to forget about them.

For the last two or three days I've been in a depressed state of mind which I haven't been able to overcome until today, because some cabbage thieves fired shots during the night, and Sonya complained and the authorities appeared and arrested four peasants and their womenfolk and their fathers turned to me. They can't accept the fact that I'm not the master – especially since I live here – and so ascribe everything to me. It's depressing, very depressing, but it's good because it makes it impossible for people to have a good opinion about me, and drives me into the realm where people's opinion counts for nothing. For the last two days I couldn't overcome this bad feeling. [. . .]

(4) I'd like to say this to people:

Dear brothers, why do you torment yourself and other people, why do you try to change and improve people's lives, change and improve people themselves? Neither you nor anybody else can do that. By trying to change and improve people's lives you only torment yourselves and other people, damage your own and other people's lives. No person in the world has been called on to reform other people, and nobody can do so. Everybody is called on to reform and improve himself only, and everybody should and can do so. [. . .]

26 September, Yasnaya Polyana   I'm a bit constrained in my writing by the fact that Repin is painting my portrait[8] – it's unnecessary and tiresome, but I don't want to distress him. Things are well with me. For a long time now I've felt an awareness of my great blessings. There were four days or so of depression and struggle as a result of my sickly condition. Thank God, I've nothing particular to repent of.

I've been compiling a new *Cycle of Reading* all this time and have finished it very roughly. A great many visitors. I'm fashionable just now. And that's depressing.[. . .]

10 October, Yasnaya Polyana   [. . .]

(9) Man doesn't know what is good and what is bad, but he writes a research paper on a fallen aerolite or the origin of the word 'cowl'.

12 October, Yasnaya Polyana   My health is good, but in my soul is paradise – or almost paradise. It's becoming more and more second nature to live lovingly, without thinking about myself for the sake of myself (my body), or about myself in the opinion of other people. And it makes me wonderfully happy. It must be because of my age which has freed me from passion – whether in anger, lust or the desire for worldly fame; but I think it's possible for everybody. [. . .]

26 October, Yasnaya Polyana   For a long time – three weeks or so, if not more – I've been in very low spirits. I've no longer felt any *joie de vivre*, or the joyful and necessary and (for me) important thoughts and feelings that used to come crowding in before. During this time I've done nothing particularly bad. I'm still working on the *Cycle of Reading*. Decided today to change many things in it. It's about six days since I started lessons again with the children. They aren't going particularly well. Worse than I expected. Gusev has been arrested.[9] [. . .]

8 November, Yasnaya Polyana [. . .] Note: [. . .]

(4) If the brain is occupied with scientific knowledge, there can be no room in it for religious and moral knowledge. This explains the irreligious nature of our upper classes. Physical labour leaves the brain free, but it isn't so with mental labour. [. . .]

(10) The most tragi-comical thing about our Christianity is that it is introduced and propagated among the poor and the weak by the strong and the rich – the very people whose existence is repudiated by Christianity. [. . .]

22 November, Yasnaya Polyana [. . .]

All this time I've been strenuously occupied with the *Cycle of Reading*. I've finished it in rough, but the work is endless. If I compile, i.e. rewrite five or six sayings a day, there will be work for more than a year, more than four hundred days. But I'm almost certain that I won't live that long. The nearer death is, the stronger I feel the obligation to say what I know, what God says through me. And I feel that this is necessary, all the more because there is nothing personal about it, no desire for worldly fame. Note: [. . .]

(9) If a rich man has a conscience, he will be ashamed of his wealth and will want to get rid of it; but to get rid of it is almost as difficult as it is for a poor man to get rich. The main difficulty is the family. One can overcome habits – but the family . . . [. . .]

[*16 December*]   Haven't written my diary for a terribly long time. *Today is 16 December, Yasnaya Polyana*. On 29 November I fell off my horse and hurt my arm. It's getting better now. During this time much has happened. I've had more and more good letters. I don't get carried away and I don't desire publicity as I used to before, but I'm simply glad that I could and can be at least of some service to people. How strange that with goodness comes humility – modesty. I don't need now, as I did before, to pretend to be humble. As soon as my inner self gets to work, I see at once that there is not only nothing to be proud of, but nothing to be glad about. I'm only glad that I feel undeservedly well, and more and more so the nearer I approach death. [. . .]

Andrey has been with his new . . .[10] It was very difficult, although I tried my best and did nothing wrong. I get on well with Seryozha, and with everybody, even the watchmen. 'Rejoice if people revile you.' [. . .]

30 December, Yasnaya Polyana   Haven't written my diary for two weeks. The only thing of importance is that Gusev has been released.[11] [. . .]

1908

20 January, Yasnaya Polyana   Chertkov is here, and a mass of people, all welcome. However, I'm in the state of mind, thank God, when everyone is welcome to me. The Abrikosovs, Gusev, Plyusnin. Yesterday Posha came. Sofya Andreyevna is in Moscow. Andrey was here yesterday. A pitiable man, pitiable for his imperturbable self-assurance. I write it and don't regret it. Perhaps if he reads it after my death, it will pierce the armour of his self-satisfaction at least a little bit. [. . .]

31 January, Yasnaya Polyana   Began to revise my old *Cycle of Reading.* And it proved to be more work than I expected, and not bad work at that. I've almost finished eight months – I still have to re-arrange and make additions – but the main work is done. Sasha is a long time in Moscow. I try not to fear for her. Things are very well with everyone. Yesterday Mikhail Stakhovich was here. I had a good talk with him. But I can't talk about intimate matters without tears. Today I've been revising my exposition of the Gospels for children at the wish of dear Marya Alexandrovna.[1] [. . .]

Note: [. . .]

(7) I have come to know the blessing and the teaching of life only at the end of my own life, and so I can't make use of the knowledge. And therefore it's necessary and it's my duty to hand on what I know to other people. For the first time I have felt this duty keenly. [. . .]

(18) I've been reading Shaw.[2] His triviality amazes me. Not only does he not have a single thought of his own rising above the triviality of the urban masses, but he doesn't understand a single great thought of the thinkers of the past. The only special thing about him is that he can express the most banal trivialities in a very elegantly distorted, new manner, as though he were saying something new and original. His main characteristic is his terrifying self-assurance, only equalled by his complete philosophical ignorance. [. . .]

10 March, Yasnaya Polyana   Haven't written my diary for exactly a month. [. . .] People have organized a jubilee celebration,[3] and this is doubly irksome for me: both because it's stupid and the flattery is unpleasant, and because from force of habit I slip into a state of finding in it not pleasure, but interest. And that is offensive to me. Chertkov has been. I got on particularly well with him. About a week ago I felt ill. I had a fainting fit. And it made me feel very good. But the people round about me made a *fuss*[4] over it. Yesterday I read a wonderful article by an Indian in Nazhivin's translation.[5] My thoughts, unclearly expressed.

This is how I live: I get up, my head is clear, good thoughts occur to me as I sit on the pot and I note them down. I get dressed and I empty the contents of the pot with an effort but with pleasure. I go for a walk. On my walk I wait for the post from force of habit, although I don't need it. I often guess to myself how many steps it will take to get to such and such a place, and I count them, dividing each one into four, six and eight breaths: one and *a* and *a* and *a*; and two and *a* and *a* and *a* . . . Sometimes, from force of habit, I'm disposed to guess that if there are as many steps as I suppose, all will be well. But now I ask myself: what is 'well'? and I know that everything is very well as it is, and there's no need to try and guess. Then when I meet someone I try to remember – though for the most part I forget that I wanted to remember – that he and I are one. It's particularly difficult to remember during a conversation. Then my dog Belka barks and prevents me from thinking, and I get angry and reproach myself for getting angry. I reproach myself for getting angry with a stick I stumble over. Yes. I forgot to say that as I wash and dress I remember the poverty of the village and feel bad about the luxury of my clothes, but cleanliness is a habit. When I get back from my walk I start on the letters. Begging letters irritate me. I remember that they are all my brothers and sisters, but always too late. Praise is irksome. I am only glad when there are expressions of unity. I read the newspaper *Rus*. I'm horrified at the executions and, to my shame, my eyes look out for T. and L.N., but when I find them it's rather unpleasant. I drink coffee. Always too much – I can't restrain myself – and settle down to my letters.

21 March   I'll continue this description some time, but now it's *21 March, Yasnaya Polyana*. I've recently been working on a new edition of the *Cycle of Reading* (Gusev is helping so well and lovingly) and also on dear Marya Alexandrovna's favourite Gospels for children as we call it. And both the one work and the other were very pleasant, especially the work on the Gospels. I've begun working with the children in the mornings, but often miss lessons. During this time there has been unwelcome concern about the jubilee; not my concern – mine has only been about how to stop it. I've just received an abusive letter apropos of it. I want to carry out the wish of the writer – send a letter to a newspaper and use the opportunity to express my views clearly and definitely.[6]

27 March   [. . .]
(2) How good that I understood today – *vaut mieux tard que jamais* [better

late than never] – that people – Seroyozha and Sonya, and their name is
legion – disagree with me not because they can refute, or think they can
refute, my arguments (as I used to think), but because none of the
arguments interests them, and they don't know and can't know anything
concerning problems of religion. [. . .]

12 April, Yasnaya Polyana   Health – my stomach is very weak. I can't
sleep, and I'm in a bad mood, which I fight against more or less
successfully. I want to make some notes now.
(1) If men knew all women as well as husbands know their wives they
would never argue with them and would never value their opinion. [. . .]

19 April, Yasnaya Polyana   Health better. The article is progressing, but
it's weak.[7] There's a lot to note down. Just now I'll note the following,
which is very good: (1) A sure sign of the fact that all my activity is futile is
that not only am I not persecuted, but that people praise me. That's good
for humility.
   I feel the great burden of foolish outward charity combined with the
absurd luxury of my own life. [. . .]

6 May, Yasnaya Polyana   I'm still busy with the article. I've devoted about
four days to my recollections about the soldier[8] for Posha. They're not too
bad, but they're provocative. No letters today, but a conversation about the
rights to my works after my death. I found it difficult to put up with.
There is much in my notebooks for me to copy out, but at present I want to
note: [. . .]
(2) To die means to go back to where you came from. What is there there?
It must be something good, judging by the wonderful creatures, the
children, who come from there.

12 May, Yasnaya Polyana   [. . .]
   Read passages from my work *The Law of Violence and the Law of Love*
and was pleased, and I finished it. Yesterday I was particularly painfully
depressed at the news of the twenty peasants who had been hanged.[9] I
began to dictate into the phonograph, but couldn't go on. [. . .]
   A nightingale sang beneath my window and moved me to tears of joy.
I've only just remembered that on my walk before tea today I forgot to
pray. I've forgotten everything. It's amazing! I'm just reading my letter to
Anatoly Fyodorovich[10] and can't remember who he is.

14 May, Yasnaya Polyana   [. . .] Yesterday, the 13th, I wrote an appeal, a
denunciation – I don't know what it was – about the executions,[11] and
another about Molochnikov.[12] I think it's what's needed. Muravyov has

been and told me many painful things.[13] Yesterday my sons Andrey and Mikhail were here, pitiable and very remote. Sasha has come. I went for a walk and had some good thoughts. [. . .]

15 May For *Thou Shalt Not Kill*.[14] And all this is done for our sake, for the sake of peaceful citizens. Whether we want it or not, we are made a party to these horrors.

And all this is done among people and by people who say that they worship and accept as God the one who said: 'It is said unto you . . . All are brethren . . . Love all, forgive all, not seven times, but seventy times seven'; the one who said about punishment: 'Let him who is without sin cast the first stone.' This is a dreadful thing, and this most terrible, forbidden deed is done by the most respected people and with the complicity of the teachers of this faith. It is done in a country where the people consider it a duty to help the unfortunate.

I can see Europeans reading this with a smile of contempt. It's very different with us, the English and other peoples will say. It's all so organized with us that it's simply a pleasure. It's all done by a machine. You don't see anything, only the flag.

21 May, Yasnaya Polyana [. . .] This morning an old beggar of eighty-two was here. He called back after eighteen years, a gentle, peaceful man, and then two students came. One was a literary person, the other a revolutionary. The revolutionary bluntly asked the question: if I could have been the executioner at the hanging of twenty people and by hanging one could have saved nineteen, ought I to have hung that one? Obviously this question was important to him, and my opinion about it disturbed him. Then he brought up other similar examples. When I said to him that one must do what one thinks right and not do evil, he said: 'And won't the result be that this person who does no evil will, despite the sufferings round about him, walk with his head high in the air saying: "Look what a good person I am."' I said to him that every one of us has too many sins of all kinds to feel ourselves free of sin for not committing the sin of compromise. Yes, this service to the people, this doing good to others, is a dreadful evil; I must write about this particularly. All the evil of government, all the evil of the revolutionaries, all the evil of education, all economic evil stems from it.

29 May, Yasnaya Polyana [. . .] I've never felt myself so weak. But every cloud has a silver lining: at such times, when I feel my nearness to death, I rejoice at this nearness. There have been so many visitors and letters that it's impossible to find time to note everything down. I'm beginning to feel the spread of my fame which, as always, arouses both good feelings and correspondingly bad ones too. [. . .]

Before copying up my notebook I'll note down what I've just been thinking: [. . .]

The situation of a man advancing towards the good which keeps moving away from him can be compared with what people do with stubborn horses, so I'm told. They fasten on the shafts in front of them a piece of bread with salt on so that the horse can smell it but can't reach it. And it stretches forward and moves in its desire to reach the bread, but its very movement moves the bread further away and so *ad infinitum.* And it's the same with people: the good can never be reached, because in attaining one good a new one immediately presents itself. And good is infinite perfection, like God.

What is the conclusion from this?

Only that a man can and must know that the good in his life is not in attaining the goal in front of him, but in progress towards the highest goal which he can never reach. [. . .]

3 June, Yasnaya Polyana Received a letter the day before yesterday reproaching me for my wealth and hypocrisy and oppression of the peasants, and to my shame I was hurt. I've been sad and ashamed all day today. I've just been out riding, and it seemed such a desirable and joyous thing to go away and be a beggar, thanking and loving everyone. Yes, I'm weak. I can't live by my spiritual 'I' all the time. And when I can't live that way, everything irritates me. The one good thing is that I'm dissatisfied with myself and ashamed, only I mustn't pride myself on it.

Finished *I Can't be Silent* and sent it to Chertkov. Almost finished the other one, the big one, too.[15] It's good that nearness to death doesn't make me sad, but rather is something to be desired, if not enjoyed. I can think well and vigorously. I'd like to write a new *Cycle of Reading* and also something artistic – about the revolution.[16]

10 June [. . .] Note:
(1) I walked round the garden this morning and, as always, thought about my mother, my 'mamma', whom I don't remember at all, but who remains for me a sacred ideal. I never heard anything bad about her. And as I walked along the avenue of birches and approached the avenue of walnut trees I saw the imprint in the mud of a woman's foot, and thought about her, about her body. And to imagine her body was beyond my powers. Anything physical would defile her. How good my feelings were towards her! How I would have liked to have the same feelings towards everyone: women and men. And it's possible. It would be good when having dealings

with people to think like that about them, to feel that way towards them. It's possible. *I'll try.*

13 June I've hardly written anything for two days. There's a mass of people here. I can't speak about my mother without tears. Molostvov has been copying extracts out of her diaries.[17] [. . .]

17 June, Yasnaya Polyana [. . .] There was a clash at table. I'm very sorry. I can't summon up good feelings, and that's depressing. Went to Marya Alexandrovna's[18] yesterday, and corrected proofs with dear Nikolayev. I've just found Sonya in a rage over the wood that was cut down. Why, why does she torment herself? I'm sorry for her, but it's impossible to help her.

I'm more and more deeply ashamed of my position and of all the folly of the world. Is it only an illusion of my thoughts and feelings that it can't continue? No, it can't.

24 June, Yasnaya Polyana A very severe headache tormented me during the night and I found it hard, very hard to endure – I groaned and woke up Yuliya Ivanovna and Dušan. The main thing is, I haven't been able to find happiness in a life of suffering. I said to myself: it's a chance to learn to endure, and it brings me nearer to liberation, and there is happiness in everything. Still I couldn't overcome the burden of suffering. [. . .]

26 June I didn't write my diary yesterday. I passed a very good night and *regretted* that I wasn't in pain, that there was no chance to correct yesterday's weakness. [. . .]

I've just thought:

It's bad that a stone is hard if you want to break it up, but if you need a stone to sharpen something on, the harder and stronger the better. It's the same with what we call sorrows. [. . .]

30 June, Yasnaya Polyana The day before yesterday a blind man came and abused me. Yesterday I went to see him at Nikolayev's and told him I loved him (1) because he was seeking God's truth, (2) because he – as a man who hated and gave offence – ought to be loved and (3) because he might perhaps need me, and as I said goodbye I shook his hand. Before he left he wanted to see me. I was glad. He said: 'I didn't mean to shake your hand, I can't shake hands with a scoundrel, a villain, a pharisee, a hypocrite . . .' Sofya Andreyevna told him to go, but I managed to say, and say sincerely, that I loved him. Oh, if it were only so with everyone![. . .]

9 July, Yasnaya Polyana I've experienced some very painful feelings.

Thank God I've experienced them. There's been a countless number of people here, and it would all have been enjoyable had it not all been poisoned by my awareness of the folly, the sin and the vileness of our luxurious life with servants, and the poverty and excessive strain of hard work all around us. I suffer painfully and incessantly from this, and I'm on my own. I can't help wishing for death, although I want to make use of what is left as well as I can. Enough of that for now.

I think it's *11 July, Yasnaya Polyana*. More and more letters of sympathy about the article *I Cannot be Silent*.[19] It's very pleasant. I feel very well today. [. . .]

Today is 5 August, Yasnaya Polyana   [. . .] Abusive letters about *I Cannot be Silent* are increasing in number. I'm reading Dickens' *Our Mutual Friend*;[20] it's very poor. Vivekananda doesn't satisfy me much either. 'Terribly clever.' Two concerts by Sibor and Goldenweiser.[21]

I've thought a lot recently while people were playing and have tried to define every piece of music by a certain feeling or mood, and to transfer it to the realm of literary art, and it turned out that there always was one: sometimes tenderness, sometimes joyfulness, sometimes passion, sometimes alarm, sometimes tender love, sometimes spiritual love, sometimes solemnity, sometimes sorrow, and many other moods, but one thing there never was – there was never anything bad: malice, censure, ridicule, etc. Could one write works of fiction like that?

11 August, Yasnaya Polyana   I'm depressed and in pain. I've had a constant fever these last few days, I feel ill and find it hard to put up with. I must be dying. [. . .]

My attitude to death is not fear at all, but intense curiosity. More about that later, however, if I have time.

I would like to say a few things, trivial though they are, about what I would like done after my death. First, I would be glad if my heirs would make all my writings public property; if not, then certainly all my writings for the people, for example the *Primers*, and the *Readers*. Secondly, although this is the most trivial thing of all, I do not wish any rites to be performed during the burial of my body. A wooden coffin; and anyone who wishes to carry it or convey it to the Zakaz wood opposite the gully, to the place where the green stick is.[22] At least there is a reason for choosing this place rather than another.

That's all. From force of habit, which, nevertheless, I haven't got rid of, I think I could still do one or two more things – strangely enough I'm thinking first of all of a work of fiction. Of course it's nonsense, I simply wouldn't have the strength to do it well. [. . .]

17 August, Yasnaya Poyana   (For works of fiction.)

(1) The child of a wealthy, atheistic, liberal-scientific bourgeois family devotes himself to religion. Fifteen years later he is a revolutionary and an anarchist.

(2) The gentle, sincere son of a priest does well at school and theological college, and is married and ordained. The daughter of a neighbour in his parish gives his mother, a vain intellectual woman, a book to read. He reads Tolstoy and questions begin to arise.

(3) A young boy, the sixth son of a blind beggar, arouses the sympathy of the wife of a leading liberal atheist. He is taken from home and sent to school, shows brilliant ability and gets a science degree. He goes abroad, meets some of his comrades, is shocked, thinks everything out again, renounces science and sees the one truth and salvation in belief in God.

(4) One of his comrades had started up in business and made a million, and now lives on the labours of his workers, while playing the liberal.

(5) The son of an aristocratic family introduces clients to a procuress; then philanthropy; then the renunciation of everything.

(6) One son of a ruined half-aristocrat, a vain man, makes a career through marriage; another son, a reserved man, makes a career as a hangman. The second used to pander to the first; now he gives himself airs.

(7) A similar sort of aristocratic writer, the son of a bourgeois, lives by journalism, feels the vileness of it and can't go on.[23]

14 September   I'm recovering bit by bit. The jubilee brought much pleasure for the baser soul, but made it hard for the higher soul. But I can't complain much about myself. I'm continuing to pull through bit by bit. [. . .]

28 September, Yasnaya Polyana   My leg is better, but the general state of my body – my stomach – is bad. I feel well at heart. Work is progressing. Only now is it real work, only now at eighty is life beginning. And this is not a joke if one understands that life is not measured by time. I'm still working on the *Cycle*. It's not altogether good. But perhaps it's useful. Something literary and important keeps wanting to intrude. [. . .]

10 November, Yasnaya Polyana   My health isn't bad. Except for heartburn. I've felt dejected since this morning. I'm ashamed. Still ashamed. I like it. [. . .]

15 November, Yasnaya Polyana   Played cards yesterday until 12 o'clock. I'm ashamed, and disgusted, and I thought: people will say: 'A fine teacher he is, he plays *vint* for three hours on end.' Then I thought in earnest:

that's just what is needed. Therein lies real humility, which is necessary for the good life. But it will be said a general should behave like a general, an envoy like an envoy and a teacher like a teacher. That's not true. A man should behave as a man. And what is natural to man first and foremost is humility, the wish to be humble. This doesn't mean that it's necessary to play cards if you can do something else that people need, but it does mean that it's unnecessary to be afraid of people's opinions and on the contrary to be well able to put up with them *sans sourciller* [without turning a hair]. [. . .]

(4) Yesterday I got into a rage with my horse. How loathsome!

29 November, Yasnaya Polyana [. . .] Dreamed during the night that I was partly writing and composing, and partly experiencing the drama of Christ. Myself – and Christ and a soldier. I remember him putting on his sword. Very vividly. [. . .]

3 December, Yasnaya Polyana [. . .] How far I still am from being even moderately decent, how bad I am. I write this now and wonder: am I not writing it for the sake of those who will read this diary? I suppose so, partly. Yes, I must work on myself – do now at eighty what I used to do with particular energy when I was fourteen or fifteen; strive to improve myself; only with this difference that then my ideals of perfection were different: muscles, and generally speaking what was needed for worldly success. Oh, if only I could train myself to put all my energy into serving God, to drawing near to Him. But drawing near to Him is impossible without serving other people. [. . .] Note. [. . .]

(2) I've lost my memory. And surprisingly enough – I haven't once regretted it. I can regret the fact that I'm losing my hair, and do regret it, but not my memory; the loss is so obviously the consequence of something acquired which is not compatible with memory. [. . .]

Today is 6 December, Yasnaya Polyana [. . .] I'm still plodding away at the *Letter to an Indian*. I think it's rubbish and all repetition. I must finish it and tear myself away. I'd like to do something literary, but I'm not making a start because there isn't anything which I'm itching to write, which I can't stop myself from writing, in the way that one should get married only when one can't stop oneself from marrying.

I want to prepare something real and close to my heart for the phonograph.[24] [. . .]

(2) How particularly fortunate I am. If many people hate me *without even knowing me*, how many people love me more than I deserve. People who ought to hate me because of their quasi-religious views which I demolish love me for those trifling things like *War and Peace*, etc., which seem to them very important. [. . .]

Today is 14 December, Yasnaya Polyana Haven't written my diary for six whole days. Finished the *Letter to an Indian*; it's weak and repetitive. Wrote a few letters. Sonya is in Moscow. I've been weak physically the last four or five days. I haven't been too bad mentally, but today the hanging and torture of people roused me to indignation and a bad, evil feeling towards the hangmen. I'm thinking about something literary, and it seems to be germinating. [. . .]

27 December, Yasnaya Polyana [. . .] When I was out walking yesterday a young man met me with tears in his eyes, but he spoke so incoherently and incomprehensibly about what he needed that I walked away from him with unkind feelings and even unkind words. And, thank God, I immediately began to suffer, and tried to find him. Fortunately he hadn't gone away and I had a splendid talk with him. [. . .]

30 December, Yasnaya Polyana Nikolay Nikolayevich[25] has arrived. I received a touching letter from Petrova in prison. Replied to her.[26] Visits today from a peasant suppliant about the partition, then a student with an astonishing question about a woman student's demand that he should marry her. Then Andrey with money matters, then a madman, then a letter from a student demanding that life should be evil. Felt very good at heart yesterday, full of joy and love; I'm worse today but, thank God, still full of joy and gratitude. Began to write *No One Is To Blame*, but couldn't get on with it. They're getting ready for a masked ball. I'm sorry. [. . .]

Secret Diary for 1908[1]

2 July, Yasnaya Polyana I'm starting a diary for myself – a secret one.

My position would be agonizing were it not for the awareness that all this is good for the soul if one assumes that the soul has a life.

If I had heard about myself from an outsider – heard about a man living in luxury, surrounded by guards, taking everything he can from the peasants, putting them in prison, and professing and preaching Christianity, and giving away five-copeck pieces, and hiding behind his dear wife for all his vile deeds – I would have no doubts about calling him a scoundrel! And yet this is just what I need to free myself from the desire for worldly fame and to live for the soul.

I've been revising Vasily Morozov's story.[2]

My soul is sorely depressed. I know it's good for my soul, but it is depressing.

At times I ask myself: what should I do – go away from everyone? Where to? To God, to die. In a sinful way I wish for death.

After writing this there was an incomprehensibly boorish and cruel scene over the fact that Chertkov had been taking photographs.[3] Doubts occur to me whether I'm doing right in remaining silent, and even whether it wouldn't be better for me to go away and hide like Boulanger.[4] I don't do so primarily because it would be for my own sake, in order to escape from this life which is poisoned on every side. And I believe that actually enduring this life is what is necessary for me.

Help, Lord, help, help!!!!

Death is the only place one can really go away to.

3 July I'm still struggling just as agonizingly, but struggling badly. Life here at Yasnaya Polyana is completely poisoned. Wherever I go – there's shame and suffering. Either it's the Grumant peasants in prison, or the guards, or the old man V. Suvorov saying: 'It's sinful, Count, oh, it's sinful, the Countess has insulted me.' Or it's this stupidity and disgracefully selfish and unjust road.[5] It's difficult. I don't know whether it's because I'm in a bad mood, or whether I'm in a bad mood because of all these horrible things. Oh, help, help me, God within me.

4 July I'm a bit better, but still depressed. Had a good talk with Sasha. How strange heredity is: men inherit their fathers' intelligence and their mothers' character and vice versa.

6 July Agonizing and painful is the ordeal to be suffered, or the retribution to be paid for lust. The retribution is terribly painful. Chertkov has just told me of a conversation he had with her. 'He lives, and enjoys every luxury and says . . . "it's all pharisaism, etc." I'm the one who is sacrificing herself.'

Help me, Lord. Again I want to go away. And I can't make up my mind. But I haven't given up the idea either. The main thing is: shall I be doing it for my own sake if I go away? The fact that I'm not doing it for my own sake if I stay – that I do know. I must think with God. And I will do so.

7 July It was agonizing yesterday. I counted up my money and thought about how to go away. I can't see her without unkind feelings. It's better today.

How clearly one can see in her all the horrors of love of body, love of self, carried to the extent of the loss of all spiritual sense of obligation. It's terrible both for others and for herself. I must have pity. I'll try and write it down as well as I can – I can't say it.

So much for her. But I'm forgetting myself. I'm bad, very bad. I couldn't help thinking about myself yesterday, my repulsive self.

Yes, I – my body – is like a repulsive latrine – take off or raise the lid of spirituality a little, and there's a loathsome stench.

Today I'll try to live for my soul.

But she's right about asparagus.[6] I must learn to live.

9 July I'm thinking of writing her a letter. I've no unkind feelings, thank God. Only one thing is more and more agonizing to me: the injustice of this insane luxury amid the unwarranted poverty and need amid which I live. Everything is becoming worse and worse, more and more depressing. I can't forget it and I can't fail to see it.

They're all writing my biography – and it's the same with all biographies – there won't be anything about my attitude to the seventh commandment. There won't be any of that terrible filth of masturbation and worse, from thirteen or fourteen to fifteen or sixteen (I don't remember when my debauchery in brothels began). And it will be the same up to the time of my liaison with the peasant woman Aksinya – she's still alive. Then my marriage, in which again, although I have never once been unfaithful to my wife, I experienced a loathsome, criminal desire for her. Nothing of this appears or will appear in the biographies. And this is very important – very important as the vice of which I at least am most conscious, and which more than any others is forcing me to come to my senses.

14 July It's still very depressing to bear with and endure Sonya's unhappy character. Egoism that excludes everything that is not herself and which goes to comic lengths, vanity, self-satisfaction, cockiness, condemnation of everybody, irritability. I had to write it down. I'm sorry for her. No one says anything to her, and she thinks she is the height of perfection.

18 July My unkind feelings have passed. I've been distracted by other thoughts. Two runaway sailors were here yesterday. I gave them some money and regretted it. I'm having some good thoughts. Sasha is back from the wedding[7] – a dear, good woman. I love her too exclusively, it's not good. My leg hurts. And I don't care at all.

1909

3 January, Yasnaya Polyana   I've been unwell for two days, but my state of mind is calm and resolute. I think more and more often about the story,[1] but it's now morning, and I'm sitting at the table pen in hand and feeling that I shall think of something. And how necessary, how necessary it is to write, and, thank God, it's not for my own sake that I consider it necessary. During this time I've been revising the end of Stolypin.[2] I think it's quite good.

Yes, my health isn't good, but my state of mind seems to be more composed with the start of the new year. [. . .] (My diary, my attitude to the fact that people read it is doing me harm. Please don't read it.) [. . .]

10 January, Yasnaya Polyana   Yesterday I almost wrote with enthusiasm, but badly. It's not worth making the effort. I've no enthusiasm at all today, and yesterday's writing seems weak, or simply bad. The day before yesterday I had a conversation with Andrey, a very edifying one for me. It began with the fact that the brothers, all of them, are short of money.

I: How is that?

He: Well everything has got more expensive, and we live in a particular milieu.

I: You should live better, more abstemiously.

He: May I object?

I: Go on.

He: You say that people should live as follows: not eat meat, refuse military service. But what is one to think about the millions who live like everybody else?

I: Don't think about them at all, think about yourself.

And it became clear to me that there is no other guiding principle for him in life except what *everybody else* does. It became clear that that is all that matters, that with minute exceptions everybody lives like that, and can't help living like that, because they have no other guiding principle. And therefore to reproach them and advise them differently is useless and harmful to oneself, since it causes ill feelings. For thousands of years mankind has progressed by the century, and you want to see this progress by the year. It progresses because people of advanced views change the environment little by little, pointing the way to an eternally remote state of perfection, pointing the way there (Christ, Buddha, yes, and Kant and

Emerson and others), and little by little the environment changes. And these people do like everybody else again, only in a different way than before.

Intellectuals are people who do the same as 'everybody else' – as other intellectuals.

I've done nothing today and have no wish to. I'm writing this in the evening, at 6 o'clock. I woke up, and two things became especially and absolutely clear to me: (1) that I am a very worthless man. I say this absolutely sincerely, and (2) that it would be good for me to die, and that I would like to do so.

I'm very bad-tempered today. Perhaps I go on living in order to become just a little less vile. Very likely that is the reason. And I will try. Help me, Lord.

11 January, Yasnaya Polyana   [. . .] A mass of executions and murders.[3] No, they are not animals. To call them animals is to slander animals, they are much worse.

I feel the need to do something. An irresistible need, but I don't yet know what. This is the time when I say from the heart: help me, Lord! I don't want anything at all for myself. I'm prepared for sufferings and humiliations, if only I could know in my own mind that I'm doing what I should. [. . .]

12 January, Yasnaya Polyana   I feel very well today. But I did nothing before 12 o'clock except play patience. Yesterday's music excited me very much.[4] I've been to the Chertkovs'. Very pleasant – not pleasant, but much more than that – was the equality of their relations with everybody. Of course even with them it isn't complete, but there isn't the agonizing presence of 'servants', serving up sweet things to eat which they mustn't touch themselves. Life in these conditions gets more and more depressing. [. . .]

I've just been thinking a lot about work. Literary work such as 'It was a fine evening, there was a smell of . . .' is impossible for me. But work is necessary, because it's an obligation. A speaking-trumpet has been put into my hands, and I'm obliged to handle it, to make use of it. Something is asking to be done, I don't know whether it will be successful. What is asking to be done is for me to write without any form – not in the form of an article or a discourse or anything literary – but to express and pour out as best I can what I feel strongly. And I feel painfully strongly the horror and depravity of our situation. I want to write what I would like to do and how I imagine to myself what I would do. Help me, God. I can't help praying. I'm sorry that I don't pray enough. Yesterday I treated Sonya badly, today a petitioner. Yes, help, help me.

15 January, Yasnaya Polyana   Landowska[5] came yesterday. A poor impression [. . .]

16 January, Yasnaya Polyana I'm somehow ashamed about my relations with Landowska, and the music. Generally my state of mind is one of dissatisfaction with myself, but not of depression: on the contrary. *Fais ce que dois.* [Do what you must] . . . and it's all right. An important letter from the Regiment of God.[6] Today there was a visitor whom I treated badly, but I recovered myself. I can't write, but I'd like to and I'm thinking. Perhaps it will come. I want to say something very, very much, and the need is choking me. [. . .]

22 January, Yasnaya Polyana [. . .] Yesterday the bishop[7] came; I talked to him frankly, but too cautiously, and didn't express all the sinfulness of his cause. And I should have done so. Everything was spoiled for me by Sonya's story about his conversation with her.[8] He would obviously have liked to convert me, or if not convert me, then destroy or diminish my influence – pernicious in their view – on belief in the Church. What was particularly unpleasant was that he asked to be informed when I was dying. I'm afraid they'll think up something to assure people that I 'repented' just before my death. And therefore I state, or, I think, repeat, *that to return to the Church, to take communion before dying, is just as impossible for me as to utter obscene words or look at obscene pictures before dying, and that therefore anything that people might say about my repentance and taking communion on my deathbed is lies.* I say this because if there are people for whom, in accordance with their religious understanding, taking communion is a religious act, i.e. a manifestation of a striving towards God, then for me any such outward act as communion would be a renunciation of my soul, of the good, of the teaching of Christ, of God.

I repeat on this occasion also that I ask to be buried without any so-called divine service, and for my body to be interred in the ground so that it should not stink. [. . .]

24 January, Yasnaya Polyana [. . .] I've just flung a book on to the shelf; it had slipped off and fallen on to the floor, and I was angry and swore at the book. My anger with a person who doesn't do what I want must be just as obvious and just as shameful.

4 February, Yasnaya Polyana Yesterday I was very ill physically. Did nothing. Struggled against unkind feelings. Read Artsybashev.[9] He's talented, but has the usual ill-bred off-hand literary manner, particularly in descriptions of nature. Great and small talents from Pushkin to Gogol have worked this way: 'Ah, that's not right, how can I make it better?' People today say: 'Oh, it's not worth bothering, it'll do as it is.'

Artsybashev not only has talent, he has ideas too: unfortunately all these people, Artsybashev included, while knowing all the incorrect and frivolous thoughts that have been expressed about the problems of life, are astonishingly ignorant about everything that has been done by the great thinkers of the past. With an awareness of their own great boldness and wisdom, they often allow themselves – in their own fashion and very feebly – to express doubts about what is being professed by everybody in their circle, and they don't know that not only their doubts, but everything that follows from their doubts, have long since been thought about and clarified, so that there is no longer an America waiting to be discovered in these problems. But still, with Artsybashev there are thoughts at work – and original ones – which isn't so with Gorky or Andreyev. There is mere talent without content in Kuprin; in Artsybashev there is both talent and content. But still they are both incomparably higher than Andreyev and Gorky, especially Artsybashev. His story *Blood* is splendid. *Gololobov* is good too. *Kupriyan* suffers from careless descriptions of things the author doesn't know about. But enough of this.[10] [. . .]

(1) From having experienced how unpleasant it is to put up with it, I've realized – it's funny to say so, at the age of eighty – that you shouldn't talk to other people about what interests you, but try and detect what interests them and, if there is anything, talk about that. [. . .]

(3) I also wanted to note that I'm compelled to believe whether I like it or not that people have accorded me a somewhat inappropriate reputation as an important, a 'great' writer and man. And this position of mine has its obligations. I feel that I've been given a speaking-trumpet which might have been in the hands of others more worthy to make use of it, but *volens nolens* [willy-nilly] it is in my hands, and I'll be to blame if I don't make good use of it. But recently, I think, I've been making use of it for empty chatter and the repetition of old things. I'll try harder.

(4) I still hear complaints and receive letters – there are probably some in the press as well – reproaching me for not having given my land away to the peasants. I can't help admitting it would have been better not to have been afraid of the reproaches of my family and to have given my land away to the peasants (which ones? – still I could have organized it somehow), but for good or bad I didn't do so, though certainly not because I valued this property. For twenty years and more I've hated it and I don't need it and can't need it, thanks to my writings, and if not my writings, then my friends. The only advantage of not having given my land away is that I've been censured and abused, and still am censured and abused.

But now I ask my heirs to give away the land after my death to the peasants, and to make my writings freely available for general use, not only those that I have made available myself, but *all of them, all of them*. If they decide not to fulfil both my requests after my death, let them at least fulfil one; but it will be better – for them as well – if they fulfil both.

18 February, Yasnaya Polyana   [. . .] I don't know and never have known a single *woman* spiritually higher than Marya Alexandrovna.[11] She is so high that she is now beyond price. [. . .]

25 February, Yasnaya Polyana   [. . .] Read V. Hugo. The prose is splendid, but I can't stand the poetry.[12]

Answered some old letters this morning – wrote no fewer than fifteen, very cheerfully and enthusiastically. [. . .]

5 March   I'd never have thought I hadn't written my diary for four days. During these four days the pain in my legs has confined me to my armchair, and made me dependent on the help of others. I can't boast about my spiritual condition, especially in the evenings. But I'm not weakening. I know that I'm bad. I'm dissatisfied that I feel no state of joy or love. Spent all day yesterday just writing two sections of *The Wisdom of Children*[13] and reading Gogol.[14] Made some notes in my book about Gogol. Sasha will write them in here:

(1) Gogol – an enormous talent, a wonderful heart and a weak, i.e. unadventurous, timid mind.

The best product of his talent is *The Carriage*, the best product of his heart – some of his letters.

The chief misfortune of his whole activity is his submissiveness to the established, pseudo-religious teaching of the Church and the state, just as it is. It would have been a good thing if he had simply accepted all that exists, but as it was he tried to justify it, and not by himself, but with the help of Slavophile-sophists, and he was a sophist himself, a very bad sophist of his own childish beliefs. His desire to attach religious significance to his own literary work adversely affected and confused the character of his thinking still more. The letter about *The Government Inspector*, the second part of *Dead Souls*, etc.

When he surrenders himself wholly to his talent, the result is works which are splendid and truly artistic; when he surrenders himself wholly to the moral and the religious, the result is something good and useful; but as soon as he wants to introduce religious significance into his works of art the result is dreadful, disgusting nonsense. That's the case in the second part of *Dead Souls* and elsewhere.

One must add to this that it's all because he ascribes to art a significance which is inappropriate to it. [. . .]

7 March   Sad news yesterday. Chertkov is being expelled.[15] He came here sick, weak and agitated. However painful it is for me to lose him, I was sorry only for him – the ruin of all his non-personal plans. But that is his ordeal and no doubt a blessing, a true blessing. Yesterday I felt very, very weak. Wrote *nothing*, which is rare for me. Sonya has written a letter and is indignant.[16] Oh, if only she could rise above herself . . . I tried to write a comedy yesterday[17] – it's no good, and I don't feel like it.

Thought a lot about Gogol and Belinsky. A very interesting comparison. How right Gogol is in his ugliness, and how utterly wrong Belinsky is in his resplendence, with his contemptuous reference to *some* God or other.[18] Gogol searches for God in the beliefs of the Church, in the place where He is misinterpreted, but still he searches for God, but Belinsky, thanks to his belief in science, which is just as absurd as, if not more absurd than, the beliefs of the Church (it's worth recalling Hegel and his *alles, was ist, ist vernünftlich* [all that is is rational]), and undoubtedly even more harmful, doesn't need any God. What a theme for a necessary article! Note: [. . .]

9 March [. . .] The Tsar has granted Chertkov a respite at his mother's request. He is weak physically, and partly spiritually as well – he is sorry for his family and his work. But he knows himself. And that's the main thing.

10 March, Yasnaya Polyana
(1) All misfortunes are the result of tradition, the inertia of the olden days. A blouse comes apart at all the seams, we've grown out of it so much, but we daren't take it off and replace it by one that fits, and we walk about almost naked out of love for the olden days. [. . .]

16 March However ashamed I am to admit it, yesterday, *15 March*, I waited for something very probable – death. It didn't come, but my health is still poor, still feverish. Only today am I a bit better. [. . .] Note: [. . .]
(3) Fighting against sexual lust would be a hundred times easier were it not for the poeticizing of both sexual relations themselves and the feelings which lead to them, and also of marriage as something particularly beautiful and something which brings happiness (while in fact marriage, if it doesn't always ruin one's whole life, does so 9,999 times out of 10,000); if only it could be instilled into people in childhood and also when fully mature that the sexual act (one only has to imagine a being one loves indulging in this act) is a disgusting, animal act which only acquires human meaning when both parties are aware that its consequences will lead to the difficult and complicated responsibilities of bringing up children and educating them as well as possible.
(4) A peasant thinks with his own mind about what he needs to think about, while an intellectual thinks with somebody else's mind about what he doesn't need to think about at all. But a peasant only thinks like that while he is at home, in his own environment; as soon as he associates with the intelligentsia, he thinks with the mind of somebody quite different and speaks with somebody else's words. [. . .]

26 March   Didn't write my diary yesterday. Health still good. And my state of mind. Read Kant: *Religion within the Bounds of Reason Alone.*[19] It's very close to me. [. . .]

1 April   [. . .] I'm tormented by this senseless life (worse than senseless, compared with the poverty-stricken life in the village), in the midst of which I'm doomed to live out my days, I don't know how. I've obviously made progress in this awareness of injustice, if in nothing else. And the luxury shames and torments me, and poisons everything, and my sons depress me by their aloofness, and the exceptional self-assurance they share with the whole family – and it's the same with my daughters too. [. . .]

8 April   [. . .] It was nice yesterday or the day before, when I had just thought how happy I was, to tell Sonya, who had come to say goodbye to me, that I was happy, and that she was the reason for it. [. . .]

Wrote nothing today. Only re-read Confucius.[20]

20 April   I've just been out on to the balcony and was besieged by petitioners, and I couldn't sustain my good feelings towards everyone. Some astonishing words yesterday from Sergey: 'I feel and know,' he said, 'that I now have such powers of reasoning that I can discuss and resolve everything correctly . . . It would be good if I could apply these powers of reasoning to my own life,' he added, with astonishing naïveté. The whole family – but especially the men – have a self-assurance that knows no limits. But I think it is greater in him than in all the others. Hence his incorrigible narrow-mindedness. I write this on purpose, so that he should read it after my death. But I can't say it. [. . .] Wrote yesterday morning about *Landmarks* and a letter from a peasant.[21] [. . .]

23 April   [. . .] Very unwell today. Did nothing all morning. Read *Landmarks*. The language is astonishing. I must beware of that myself. Un-Russian, made up words denoting implied new shades of thought, unclear, artificial, conventional and unnecessary. These words can only be necessary when one is talking about what is unnecessary. [. . .]

Today is 26 April   The day before yesterday I began writing something literary,[22] and wrote a lot, but it wasn't good and I didn't copy it out. [. . .]

Dušan has discovered gangrene in my heels.[23] That's good, very good.

30 April   [. . .] Yesterday Sonya spoke to me in distress about how she could see in my diaries my dissatisfaction with her. I'm sorry about this, and she is right that *in the long run*[24] I've been happy with her. Not to mention the fact that all is well now. And it's good that I'm sorry that I caused her distress. She asked me to write that the deletions in my diaries were made by me. I'm very glad to do so.[25] [. . .]

1 May Pasternak and his wife came yesterday and also Mogilevsky.[26] Mogilevsky played magnificently. I wept continually. Polished up the article[27] in the morning; it's not bad, I think. Went to Galya's. All is just as well with her. When I woke up I learned that Andrey and his wife had met Olga.[28] Both women were nice and kind and friendly to one another, but Andrey was terrible. He's as pleased as Punch with himself. Nothing can pierce his self-satisfaction. It's astonishing that two good women can't share between them . . . I know that it's bad to write and think this, but I can't help it. Perhaps he'll read it one day and smell his own stench.

Wonderful weather; I didn't sleep much. Yes, I forgot that Molochnikov came yesterday. I was very glad to see him. Didn't note down the most important thing that happened yesterday: namely that dear Tanya left. I saw her off with emotion, and think about her with emotion and joyful love.

5 May [. . .] I've just been out on to the terrace. There were nine petitioners there, beggars, the most unfortunate of people, and Kurnosenkova. And I just couldn't sustain a feeling of kindness towards them all. You would think it was time I learned, but so far from learning, I'm still only making slow progress. [. . .]

9 May Woke up very early. I feel well at heart. Yesterday I revised the article[29] (it's not good, especially the ending). Saw off dear Ivan Ivanovich and Marya Alexandrovna. A Baptist peasant came, a petitioner. I restrained myself. Had a long ride with Dušan. In the evening I read the article and Kuprin.[30] It's very poor, crude and unnecessarily dirty. [. . .]

10, 11 May [. . .] Yesterday I got up very early. Wrote some trifle for Tregubov. But thought of something very, very important.

In the first place, that I must write a letter, which Sasha will deliver, asking her to think about her soul, and about the true life;[31] secondly, I mustn't give up my diary and mustn't write anything for publication during my lifetime. I make an exception now for what I write about love.[32] That is necessary. I may be wrong, but I think it's of the utmost importance. [. . .]
Note:
(5) He writes to his wife:[33] 'Forgive me. I have forgiven you, but I can't

help saying, if only from beyond the grave, what I couldn't bring myself to say when alive so as not to anger you, and therefore to lose the chance, to lose it for ever even, of helping you – namely to say that you live a bad life, a life that is bad for yourself, tormenting yourself and other people, and depriving yourself of the greatest good – love. Yet you are capable – very much so – of all that is the very best. I have seen these seeds in you many times. Help yourself, my dear. Just begin – and you will see how your own self, your best and true 'I', will help you.' [. . .]

13 May Yesterday I revised *On the State*[34] and *On Love*. [. . .]
  I wrote quite a lot on love. It's not bad, it's making progress. Sonya was dreadful at breakfast. It turned out she had read *The Devil*,[35] and the old rancour began to ferment in her, and it was very painful for me. I went into the garden. I began to write a letter to her to be given to her after my death, but I didn't finish it; and gave it up, mainly because I asked myself: 'why?' and was aware that it wasn't done in the sight of God for love. Then at 4 o'clock she spoke her mind, and, thank God, I calmed her down and began to cry myself, and we both felt better.

15 May [. . .] I've just been out: first there was Afanasy's daughter with a request for money, then Anisya Kopylova stopped me in the garden about the wood and about her son, then the other Kopylova whose husband is in prison.[36] And I began to think again about how people would judge me. 'He is supposed to have given everything away to his family, but he lives for his own pleasure and doesn't help anybody' – and I felt hurt and began to think how I might go away, as if I didn't know that we must live in the sight of God in ourselves and in Him, and not only not worry about people's opinions, but rejoice at humiliation. Oh, I am bad, bad. The only good thing is that I know it – although not always – I've only just remembered it now. Well then, I'm bad, but I'll try to be less bad. Just now I couldn't restrain myself from angrily sending Kopylova away when she caught me as I was beginning to write my diary. [. . .] Tanechka[37] is ill – they are running round to all the doctors and squandering money, while people are dying of poverty in the village. No, I mustn't go away, there's no need, but I still want to die, although I know that it's bad, very bad. Yesterday I revised the article *Revolution*[38] – it's not bad. [. . .]

16 May Yesterday evening the post came. The letters were unimportant, but the papers published my letter to the priest and to Tregubov.[39] And these letters were to me like wine to a drinker, and immediately caused me concern for people's opinions. No doubt because I no longer feel physical desires, I feel vanity particularly painfully, and can't rid myself of it.

Yesterday, knowing that these letters would make me talk about them, I thought I mustn't do so, especially in front of my son Seryozha. And so I abstained from vanity for the sake of my concern for people's opinions, for the sake of vanity. I've never suffered so much before from heartburn as yesterday evening and all this morning. Slept well and got up late. There were about ten petitioners; I refused them all without getting annoyed, but it could have been better. [. . .]

Today is 19 May   [. . .] Had a very painful conversation with Sonya about the price for the land she is giving up. I said nothing, but it was painful to listen, and all because the connection with Him has been lost. [. . .]

20 *May*   Yesterday revised *On Education, The Revolution* and the letter to an American.⁴⁰ The letter is still not what it could have been. Went to Telyatinki. The evening as usual. Read some letters. Was a great nuisance to the people closest to me. An article about me by Roosevelt.⁴¹ The article is silly, but I was pleased. It aroused my vanity, but it was better yesterday. [. . .]

22 *May*   [. . .] Got up early today. Walked round the garden. Sat down for a rest and saw a peasant woman coming towards me. I did well to remember that it was God coming in her. It turned out to be Shurayeva, poor woman; her granddaughter had died, and she was asking for money. I tried to enter into her soul, in the depth of which is the same God who is in me and everyone, and I felt so good. Help me God. May it always be so. [. . .]
(6) A man is funny when he boasts about his face and his gracefulness, and a woman about her strength and intelligence. [. . .]

26 *May*   [. . .] A painful conversation with Sonya about the estate. I'm sorry I didn't speak about the sin of owning land. At dinner too she was confused, poor woman. She's an interesting creature when you love her; when you don't love her she's too simple. It's the same with everybody. [. . .]

27 *May*   A very touching meeting yesterday evening with a student who had come from the Caucasus to see me. Gusev said that he thought he was a petitioner. He gave me an envelope and asked me to read it. I refused at first, then began to read the end of it. About monism and Haeckel. I began to speak to him unkindly. He was terribly agitated. Then I learned that he was a consumptive, a hopeless case. He was about to leave and said that the reading of *On Life* had been a great event for him. I was astonished and asked him to stay. I read his note right through. He

turned out to be a person quite close to me. And I had offended him and caused him anguish. I was hurt and ashamed. I asked him to forgive me. He stayed the night in the village. This morning he came back and we had a moving talk. A very touching case. I grew fond of him. [. . .]

28 May Lev came. It's depressing to be with him. Thank God I didn't betray the demands of love, but I can't help avoiding him, and remaining silent when listening to him. I only broke my silence twice: when he was talking about his dissatisfaction with life I said what I thought about the need to live a spiritual life, and the other time I expressed my disgust when he voiced sympathy and justification for the murders of Stolypin. [. . .]

30 May Didn't sleep much; got up early. Mechnikov came, and some correspondents.[42] Mechnikov is pleasant and apparently broad-minded. I haven't had a chance to talk to him yet. [. . .]

31 May Continuation of 30 May. Mechnikov turned out to be a very superficial person – *areligious*. I deliberately chose a time to talk to him alone about science and religion. On science – nothing, except a belief in the very status of science, the justification of which I was asking him for. On religion – silence; evidently a denial of what is considered religion, and both a failure and an unwillingness to understand what religion is. The old aestheticism of Hegel, Goethe and Turgenev. And very talkative. I let him talk, and was very glad I didn't interrupt him. As always, the talk made me depressed by the evening. Goldenweiser played splendidly. [. . .]

1 June After dinner there were three visitors: a worker from the *Union of the Russian People* who had drunk too much tried to persuade me to return to the Church, a good-natured man but completely mad; then a woman with two huge envelopes demanding that I should read what was in them . . . 'a cry from the heart'. Vanity, mania to be a writer, and greed. I was angry – I should have been calmer. Then a reporter from *Early Morning*.[43] How glad I am that my relations with Lev are no longer strained. I just couldn't manage to ask Vera about her child.[44] How could it happen?

2 June Yesterday evening I read my letters. Few of interest. Slept a lot today and am fresher than I've felt for a long, long time. A telegram from Henry George's son,[45] then someone from the *Russian Word* with the proofs of the Mechnikov article.[46] Corrected the proofs and wrote about Henry George and sent it to the *Russian Word*. They probably won't print it.[47] [. . .]

5 June Troyanovsky played very nicely yesterday. Chertkov and the Goldenweisers came. Health still bad. Did nothing today: revised *The One Commandment* and the article on George a little bit. George's son came with a photographer. A pleasant person. [. . .]

8 June, Kochety Got up early and set off. A good journey. A talk with a marshal from Mtsensk[48] – Orthodox, conservative, impermeable. Dear Tanya and Misha and, least not last,[49] little Tanechka. I felt particularly keenly the insane immorality of the luxury of the rulers and the rich, and the poverty and down-trodden state of the poor. I suffer almost physically from the awareness of being party to this madness and evil. I've been accommodated here in insane luxury together with the three others who brought me here: my doctor, secretary and servant. And unfortunately, all the *Cycle of Reading* for 9 June is on this theme. [. . .]

11 June The revises of *On Love* are poor. I must do more work on them. Wrote a prayer for Sonechka in bed in the morning. Everything is bad. I couldn't work at all. Read forty-one letters with unkind feelings. Went riding and was very tired. But the main thing is the tormenting feeling of the poverty – not the poverty, but the humiliation – the oppressed state of the people. The cruelty and madness of the revolutionaries is pardonable. Then at dinner Sverbeyeva,[50] French talk and tennis; and side by side hungry, ill-clad slaves, oppressed by work. I can't stand it. I want to escape.

Read Bakunin on Mazzini.[51] [. . .]

22 June As far as I remember, I did nothing yesterday except revise *The One Commandment* and a few letters, one of which, an appeal, I scrapped. Then I rode in the woods with the three Tanyas. Set off from there on foot and came across some reapers – the whole village. Talked with them about many things, about the land, military service and the fact that they are enslaving themselves; about how difficult it is to be rid of poverty, but even more difficult of wealth; that one should live for one's soul, and all will be well. Had dinner and read. Felt in comparatively good spirits. [. . .]

5 July, Yasnaya Polyana Set off on the 3rd, as resolved. Visited dear Abrikosov. Tanya accompanied me as far as Mtsensk. Travelled third class, and it was very pleasant – a policeman and some settlers. The very people who are treated like cattle, but who alone make life and history (if anyone is interested). All well at home. Sasha is just as good as ever. [. . .]
Note: [. . .]
(2) I can't help being amazed at why God chose such a repulsive creature as me to speak to people through.

Today is 11 July [. . .] Decided to go to Stockholm.[52] I'm well at heart.

12 July Slept very little. In the morning I behaved badly towards a silly young boy who asked for my autograph. Twice I began to talk seriously to him, and both times he interrupted me, asking for a souvenir. Yesterday evening I was depressed by Sofya Andreyevna's talk about publication and prosecution.[53] If only she knew and understood how she alone is poisoning the last hours, days, months of my life! But I can't say so, and I don't expect any words to have any effect on her. [. . .]

14 July [. . .] Note: [. . .]
(2) For Stockholm: begin by reading old letters and then recent ones by conscientious objectors. Then say that it's all said very well there, but it's just like all of us having keys to open the door of the apartment we wish to enter, and then asking people hidden from us behind an impenetrable door to open it, not using our own keys for the purpose and teaching others to do likewise. The main thing is to say that the root of everything is the military. If we take soldiers and teach them murder, we repudiate everything we can say in favour of peace. One has to tell the whole truth: how can one talk about peace in the capitals of kings, emperors and commanders-in-chief of armies whom we respect just as much as the French respect M. de Paris?[54] As soon as we stop lying we shall be expelled from there at once. [. . .]

20 July [. . .] I've just been re-reading for Stockholm both my letter to the Swedes[55] and *The Kingdom of God*. Everything seems to have been said. I don't know what more to say. I'm thinking of a few things that can and ought to be said. We'll see.

When reading these old writings of mine, I'm convinced that my present writings are worse, are weaker. And, thank God, I'm not distressed by this. On the contrary, I'll refrain from writing. There is other, more important and necessary work ahead of me. Help me, my God.

21 July In the evening Sofya Andreyevna was weak and irritable. I couldn't get to sleep till 2 or later. I woke up feeling weak. Somebody had woken me up. Sofya Andreyevna hadn't slept all night. I went to see her. It was something quite mad. Dušan had poisoned her, etc. A letter from Stakhovich[56] which I ought to have told her about because she thought I was hiding something from her made her condition still worse. I'm tired and I can't do any more and I feel quite ill. I feel the impossibility, the absolute impossibility of a reasonable and loving relationship. At present I only want to withdraw and take no part in anything. I can't do anything else, and I've already thought seriously of running away as it is. Well then, show your Christianity. *C'est le moment ou jamais* [It's now or never]. But I terribly want to go away. My presence here is hardly of use to anybody. A sorry victim, and harmful to everyone. Help me, my God, teach me. The only thing I want is to do not my will, but Thine. I write this and ask myself – is it true? Am I not putting on an act for myself? Help, help, help. [. . .]

22 July [. . .] I'm thinking more and more about going away and disposing of my property. [. . .]

23 July Decided to give up the land. Talked yesterday to Ivan Vasilevich.[57] How difficult to be rid of this nasty, sinful property. Help, help, help. [. . .]

25 July Read a little of *The Cycles*. Then began to write for the peace congress. It's better, but still weak. Came across a little volume of my letters in French.[58] Very well translated and the content is good. I've obviously grown worse mentally. I mustn't write stupid things.

26 July [. . .] My son Sergey and Buturlin[59] came to dinner, and Maklakova also came in the morning. After dinner I began to talk about the trip to Sweden, and there was a terrible hysterical outburst of anger. She wanted to poison herself with morphine. I snatched it out of her hands and threw it downstairs. I struggled. But when I went to bed and thought about it calmly, I decided to give up the trip. I went and told her so. She is pitiful, and I'm truly sorry for her. But how edifying. [. . .]

28 July Written down during the night of 28/29. There are creatures in the world who all live off the produce of the land, but in order to make it as difficult as possible for them to feed themselves, they have divided their land up in such a way that only those who don't work on it can use it, while those who do work can't use it and suffer and die, generation after generation, from the impossibility of feeding themselves off the land. Furthermore these creatures elect one or several families out of many and renounce their own will and reason for the sake of slavish obedience to everything that these elected people want to do with them. These elected people are the most evil and stupid of all. But the creatures who elected them and obey them extol them in every possible way. These creatures speak in various languages incomprehensible to one another. But instead of trying to eliminate this cause of misunderstanding and dissension, they divide themselves up further, irrespective of language differences, into various combinations called states, and as a result of these combinations kill thousands and thousands of people like themselves and ruin one another. In order to ruin and kill one another more conveniently these creatures put on special, identical and for the most part motley coloured clothes, think up ways of killing one another and teach the many who give obedience to one man alone the best methods of murder.

Moreover these creatures, in order to explain their life and its meaning and purpose, assure themselves and one another that there exists a creature like themselves, only endowed with those qualities which they would like to have, and therefore capable of doing all sorts of stupid and nasty things, and they think up various and quite unnecessary ways of gratifying this imaginary creature, and devote an enormous part of their labours to this gratification, although they need these labours for the most part to feed themselves. In order that this fabrication should never cease to deceive their children, parents assiduously teach their children all sorts of fabrications about this creature called God, about how he created the world, how he became a man, and then gave people his body to eat and then flew off to heaven, which they know doesn't exist, and suchlike things. And not only do they require their children to repeat all this, but they require it of other people too, and kill, and have killed, hundreds of thousands of creatures like themselves for disagreeing with it.

But not content with continually doing all these nasty and stupid things and suffering from them, and knowing that they are suffering precisely because of these nasty and stupid things, they not only continue to do them, but elect from among themselves people who are obliged to think up arguments from which it would emerge that it is unavoidably necessary to do all these stupid and nasty things, that it is impossible not to do them. All these arguments, very involved and incomprehensible to anybody, most of all to those who think them up, they call science. And all these justifications for nasty and stupid things and various completely unnecessary sophistries are considered a very important matter, and all children are taught these sophistries, and all parents and the young people themselves consider it a great honour to study this science.

These creatures multiply by means of such a filthy, repulsive and monstrous act that they are ashamed of it themselves, and not only do not perform it in front of others, but always do so in secret. Moreover the consequences of this act – the birth of similar new creatures – are not only painful for that species of creature from whose womb these new creatures come, helpless at the beginning of their lives, but are in the highest degree troublesome for those who beget them, and who find them a burden. Apart from that, the incessant multiplication of these creatures threatens famine disasters for everyone, since their reproduction goes on at too fast a rate for people to be able to produce food for everyone. These creatures know all this and talk about it, yet in spite of this, they not only perform this repulsive act on all occasions when they can to the detriment of their interests, health and general considerations, but actually extol it in every possible manner. Some eulogize it in incoherent and involved words called poetry; others not only eulogize but bless this loathsome act in the name of that fictitious creature they call God.

I won't speak of the millions of stupid and nasty things which are done by these creatures: how they poison themselves and consider it a pleasure; how they congregate in enormous numbers in the places which have been most infected by themselves, in the midst of enormous unoccupied expanses of land, and build houses of thirty stories on one site; or how they are not concerned about better ways of transport for everyone, but are concerned only that a few people should be able to travel and fly as fast as possible; or how they arrange words so that their endings should be the same, and having put them together, then admire this arrangement of words and call it poetry; or how they arrange other words without endings, but just as stupid and incomprehensible ones, and call them laws and as a result of these words torment in every conceivable manner, imprison and kill each other in accordance with these laws. One could go on and on.

What is most surprising of all, moreover, is that these creatures not only do not see reason, or use their reason in order to understand what is stupid and bad, but on the contrary use it in order to justify all their stupidities and nastinesses. And so far from wishing themselves to see the stupidities and nastinesses which torment them, they do not allow anyone among them to point out why they should not do what they are doing, and why they can and ought to do something quite different and not torment themselves so. It is only necessary for a person who uses his reason to appear among them and all the rest of the people become angry and indignant and horrified, and abuse such a creature in all manner of ways and beat him, and either hang him on a gallows or on a cross, or burn him or shoot him. And the strangest thing of all is that when they hang or murder this one reasonable creature among all the unreasonable ones, and he is no longer in their way, they gradually begin to forget what this reasonable creature said and begin to think up for him what he allegedly said but never did say, and when everything that was said by this reasonable creature has been well and truly forgotten or distorted, these same creatures who previously hated and tortured this one reasonable creature, the one among many, begin to extol the tortured and murdered one, and sometimes even recognize him – thinking thereby to do this creature the greatest honour – as the equal of that imaginary evil and foolish God whom they revere.

These creatures are astonishing. These creatures are called human beings. [. . .]

29 July Didn't write my diary yesterday. The day before yesterday there were a lot of people here in the evening. Sergey, Rayevsky, Goldenweiser. Had an unpleasant argument with Sergey. Of course I was entirely to blame. I said some unpleasant things to him. Yesterday I hardly slept at all. During the night I painted in my diary an imaginary picture of human beings and their life. Did nothing at all. Sofya Andreyevna's painfully excited state has begun again. I'm both depressed and sorry for her; and, thank God, I managed to calm her down. Mashenka[60] came; it was very pleasant. Did nothing today. Began the Swedish speech, but it was no good. [. . .]

2 August Yesterday I walked through the rain *d'une humeur de chien* [in a vile temper]. Did nothing bad, but I'm sick at heart and have no feelings of love. Spent the evening with everyone. Woke up today at 5 and had some good thoughts. I thought about true belief in God, belief which has no need of miracles and is not interested in nature and its study. Then I thought about the congress and made some notes before getting dressed. Then went for a walk and wrote two letters to the peasants. Read my letters. Sofya Andreyevna came in and announced that she would go,[61] but all this will surely end with the death of one or the other of us, and there will be innumerable difficulties. And so I certainly won't go in such conditions. [. . .] Note: [. . .]

(3) The company of women is useful in that you can see that you mustn't be like them. [. . .]

5 August Two days have passed without any entries. Yesterday evening the bandits came for Gusev and took him away.[62] [. . .]

Sofya Andreyevna is getting ready to go to Stockholm, and as soon as she speaks about it, she falls into despair. She takes no notice of my suggestions not to go. The only salvation is: live in the present and remain silent.

8 August Two days have passed again. 6 August was an important day. I went for a walk as usual, then settled down to work at *On War*, and Sofya Andreyevna came in and announced that the congress had been postponed.[63] [. . .]

16 August Was very bored again all evening. I'm so remote from what all those around me live by. Two workers came, well-to-do, intelligent, socialists. Terrible conceit and narrow-mindedness. No individuality – one isn't a person, one is a party member. After talking to them, I came to a conclusion that has long been suggesting itself and has only now become clear. There are two sorts of people. With some people their thoughts are

bound up with their lives. Whether they like it or not they have to do what
their thoughts demand, and they cannot go on calmly doing what is
contrary to their thoughts: their thoughts rule their lives. With other
people the transmission belt has been removed from the fly-wheel, and
their thoughts (for the most part other people's) are independent of their
lives. The driving forces of these people's lives are animal lusts and
worldly fame. To try to prove to these people something that is contrary to
their lust and desire for worldly fame is as useless as putting a belt on a
small cogwheel only. The wheel turns, and they are glad, and they even
boast that their wheel turns faster than the driving wheel. [. . .]

Thought about worldly fame. In this need for people's good opinion
about you – for their love – there is something irresistible and legitimate.
And it occurred to me now that just as the desire for the praise and love
of people in one's lifetime is false and culpable, so is the desire for the
continuation of one's life in the souls of other people after one's death
good, just and legitimate. In this desire there is nothing to indulge the
personality, nothing exclusive; there is only the desire for participation in a
common, universal, spiritual life, participation in the work of God, an
unselfish, impersonal desire. I think that is right.

20 August [. . .]Today I woke up still weak and mentally jaded. Went to
meet the horses and thought on the way about one thing only, and a very
important one in practice, namely the fact that I must bore everyone by my
incessant writings all the time on one and the same thing (at least it must
seem so to the public at large), just as Croft Hiller bores me,[64] and
that I ought to keep quiet and get on living; but if I do write, should
I want to very much, it should only be something literary, for which
I often have the urge. And, of course, not for success, but in order to
say to a wider audience what I have to say, and to say it not by
forcing my work on to people, but by offering it as a challenge. Help me,
God. [. . .]

24 August [. . .] Read the Gospels; very good. Good feelings too about
Gogol. I especially like the way he is prepared to embrace mankind, but
not man.[65] [. . .]

25 August Got up feeling quite cheerful, went out – and things went
wrong from the start. A peasant from Novosil asked for help, and I was in
a hurry to go on and spoke unkindly to him. And immediately I felt
ashamed. And I was so glad when he overtook me and I spoke to him as a
brother and asked his forgiveness. I sat down on the roadside to make a
note of something and saw a man and a young girl coming. This time I
made no mistake and welcomed him and had a good talk with him. He had

seen me on the road and wanted to meet me. He had read a few things, but set store by the Church and said that ceremony was necessary. Then I met a young man, a teacher. Also had quite a good talk. He had come to get advice. [. . .] Note: [. . .]

(2) Something very important. Although this is very immodest, I can't help writing down that I earnestly beg my friends who collect my notes and letters and note down my words not to attach any importance to what I have deliberately not committed to print. I read Confucius, Lao-Tzu, Buddha (I could say the same about the Gospels too) and see, side by side with profound thoughts linked together into one coherent teaching, the most strange sayings, either uttered fortuitously or else misquoted. Yet it is precisely these strange and sometimes contradictory thoughts and sayings that are needed by those who are unmasked by the teaching. One cannot insist on this often enough. Every man is weak at times and expresses things that are patently stupid, but people write them down and then make much of them, as though they were a most important authority. [. . .]

26 August [. . .] Note:

(1) I thought about how I used to shoot birds and animals, despatch birds with a quill in their heads and hares with a knife in their hearts without the slightest compassion, and do things which I can't think about now without horror. It's surely the same with people who now judge, imprison, sentence and execute. It's wrong to think that these people know that what they are doing is bad, but yet still do it. Somehow or other they become ignorant of the fact that what they are doing is bad. That was the case with me and the hares. [. . .]

27 August [. . .] Noted during the night:

I feel that the attitude of people – the majority – towards me is no longer an attitude towards a man but towards a celebrity, above all a representative of a party or a tendency: either complete devotion and confidence, or, on the contrary, repudiation and hatred. [. . .]

28 August [. . .] Dinner, and I felt terribly, terribly, sorely depressed. Letters from Berlin apropos of Sofya Andreyevna's letter and articles in the *Petersburg Gazette* which said that Tolstoy was a fraud and a hypocrite contributed to my depression.[66] To my shame I wasn't glad that they abused me, but was hurt. And all evening I was sorely depressed. Should I go away? I ask the question more and more often. [. . .]

Today is 2 September [. . .] The man from Kiev and Muller came again,[67] and it hurt me to listen to the Kiev man's story of how he had met a peasant woman whose horse had been impounded and who was asked to pay a rouble, and how she abused me and all of us, calling us devils and fiends. 'They just sit and stuff themselves, the devils . . .' He also spoke of the fact that the peasants are convinced that I own everything and am a crafty customer, hiding behind my wife. It hurt me very much, to my shame. I even tried to justify myself. Then I went for a ride with Sasha and made inquiries about it on the way. Yes, it's an ordeal, I must endure it. And it's for my good. However, it was only today that I felt and understood that it's for my good, and then not entirely. [. . .]

Today is 3 September [. . .] The cinephotographers came, despite my refusal.[68] I let them photograph, but without my cooperation. [. . .]

4 September, Moscow We arrived safely yesterday.[69] I've waited a long time. It would have been good on the journey if it hadn't been for the curiosity and flattery – irritating and corrupting – of the passengers. [. . .] I walked along the streets and was horrified at the debauchery – no, not the debauchery, but the obvious lack of any moral, religious, restraining principle. Yet many, many people cross themselves as they walk past churches. Note: [. . .]
(1) However arrogant and self-assured it is, I can't help thinking and noting down for myself that I need to remember in my intercourse with people that with the vast majority of them I stand on such a high point in my outlook on the world that I have to come down often and very far for any intercourse to be possible between us. [. . .]

5 September, Kryokshino We went to Zimmermann's. The music was very good.[70] Then I walked along Kuznetsky Bridge, then on the train there were demonstrations of sympathy – food for vanity – temptation. But I didn't yield too much. We arrived at Kryokshino. A great joy to see everyone. Everyone was cheerful and kind, to say nothing of their attitude towards me. I felt very unwell towards evening.

8 September Yesterday night I lost a lot of blood. At first I felt bad, but slept well and am quite cheerful. Went for a walk. Sonya is coming at 2 o'clock, which I'm very glad about. Revised my letter to the Polish lady[71] for the last time, I think. [. . .]
    Did little work. Listened to music. [. . .]

13 September Still well. Got up late. Thought about what to say to the teachers.[72] But couldn't think about that or anything else. And wrote nothing all morning. Went out, and there were many people there: Dimochka, old Solomakhin and his son, then some ladies and a man wanted to kiss my hand. Then Chertkov's cinematograph and Tapsell,[73] then a whole mass of people: Sonya Ilyushina, musicians, Goldenweiser and his wife, Sibor, Mogilevsky, Tishchenko and many, many more I didn't know. Sonya hurt her leg and is in great pain. At home a treat for the peasants, about two hundred people. Chertkov *suffit à tout* [makes up for everything] . . . (that's for him). Then more folk. Had dinner. Letters of little interest. Didn't manage to sleep before dinner. They played trios by Arensky, Beethoven and Haydn magnificently. [. . .]

17 September Got up feeling cheerful. Met the photographer and cinematographer.[74] What was also unpleasant was that this makes me aware of myself, not as a creature of God's, but as loathsome Lev Nikolayevich. Made one or two notes on the way. Talked to Chertkov about the children's intention of appropriating the works that were made public property. I simply can't believe it. [. . .]

At home the unpleasant news that Sonya was upset by the suggestion of travelling to Moscow separately. Went to see her. I'm very sorry for her; poor woman, she is ill and weak. I didn't entirely calm her down, but then she spoke so nicely and kindly, took pity and said 'forgive me'. I rejoiced and was deeply moved. [. . .]

24 September [*Yasnaya Polyana*] Didn't sleep much. Had a walk. Wrote a letter to an Indian, and received a pleasant letter from an Indian in the Transvaal.[75] The letter to the Indian is very weak.[76] Maude came.[77] This interest that people show in me is tiresome. Cinematographers. Andryusha's arguments yesterday about how profitable the ownership of estates has become astonished me by their naive insensitivity: corn and rye are twice as expensive, labour is 20 per cent cheaper. Wonderful. [. . .]

25 and 26 September [. . .] On the 25th, in the evening, I had a good talk with Maude. He's sorry about his break with Chertkov, and probably feels he's not entirely justified, but it's good that Chertkov doesn't accuse him of anything.[78] Went for a long ride – to Goryushino. Did nothing all morning. Wrote a letter to the Indian.[79] Started writing *A Conversation* but gave it up.[80] Maude is translating the letters to the Indians. That's all. [. . .]

30th Woke up early. Eight beggars. I felt they were human beings, but couldn't deal with them humanely. [. . .]

10 October [. . .] In the evening Ilya came. He has the same lack of higher interests as all my sons. But never mind.

Dušan is ill. I went to see him. He was as gentle and calm as ever. I did nothing except some unimportant letters. Went to meet Sasha. Broke some stones and had a good talk with a father and son from Yasenki. In the evening I read Andreyev. I got the same very definite impression. The early stories are good, the latest ones beneath criticism.[81] Nothing to note, I think. A tiresome petitioner came. I treated him badly at first, but managed all right later. Generally speaking I can't train myself to remember God when I'm in people's company. I remember afterwards. I'll learn.

14 October [. . .] Went for a walk. Very weak. Finished Andreyev. His denominator is disproportionately big compared with his numerator. Note: [. . .]

(2) A work of art is only real when the person perceiving it cannot imagine anything different from what he actually sees or hears or understands; when he experiences a feeling similar to recollection – that this thing has already happened, and happened many times, that he has known it for a long time but has been unable to say it, and now somebody has expressed this very thing for him. And above all when he feels that what he hears or sees or understands cannot be otherwise, but must be just as he perceives it. [. . .]

(3) There are bipartite arts: music, drama, partly painting, in which the thought – the purpose of art – and its execution are separated: in music, composition and performance; similarly in drama – the writing of a play and its performance; partly too in painting, and in plastic art generally, the intention and the performance; and entirely so with illustration. And it is in these bipartite arts that false art is most commonly encountered: false, empty thought and wonderful execution by musicians or actors or painters. It's especially so in drama and music. There are dramatists (Andreyev is one of them) and composers who, without bothering about the content, significance, novelty or truthfulness of their drama or musical composition, think only about its performance, and adapt their works to the appropriateness and the impact of that performance. [. . .]

Went for a very pleasant ride. After dinner I read the *Vedic Magazine*.[82] I ought to write a letter of thanks to the Indian for his wonderful exposition of Maya. [. . .] Late in the evening I played duets with Sofya Andreyevna. My hands won't work properly.

[. . .] *16 October* Semyonov came, and he persuaded me that I couldn't refuse the phonograph recording that I had promised.[83] It was very unpleasant for me. I had to agree. [. . .]

In the evening six people came with the gramophone and phonograph. It was very depressing. I couldn't refuse and I had to prepare something as best I could. [. . .]

19 October [. . .] Read *Russian Thought: The White Horse, The Birch Tree* and some poems. Without exaggeration: a madhouse; yet I value the opinion of these readers and writers.[84] Shame on you, Lev Nikolayevich.

20 October [. . .] Dreamed very vividly of Gusev and wrote to him. Then a quite drab and bloated peasant from the Voronezh province came specially to see me. He smokes and drinks too, and condemns everybody, and denounces the clergy, but he's original and I liked him very much. He took some books and a photograph and went away. Yes, the only hope is in them, if one can allow oneself hopes and thoughts about the future. I can't. [. . .]

21 October [. . .] I've just been talking to Sasha. She was telling me about the greediness of the children and their counting on my writings which will come to them after my death, and consequently counting on my death too. How I pity them. I gave up all my property to them in my lifetime so that they should not be tempted to wish for my death and still my death is what they wish for. Yes, yes, yes. How unfortunate are people, i.e. creatures endowed with reason and the gift of speech, when they use both the one and the other in order to live like animals. That's bad, I'm passing judgement on them. If they live like that it means they can't do otherwise. But I am passing judgement. Yes, I would like some literary work. One can express everything and unburden oneself without condemning anyone. [. . .]

22 October Woke up early. Dušan came with the news that there was a violinist and his wife here. I went downstairs. Probably a Jew; he wanted to play. I left it to my daughters to decide. They refused.[85] [. . .]

Wrote nothing. Revised the conversation[86] a little. Went for a ride with Dušan. Before dinner Sasha came in to announce that they had all returned – the musicians and Friedman. What could I do? They didn't seem very sympathetic. A Catholic priest and a Frenchman came to dinner. The Frenchman flattered me grossly. The priest, obviously, doesn't believe, but wants to convince himself. A sophist of his own traditions. And he doesn't need my opinion, but he needs to express his own opinion to me. Then the musicians began to play. Magnificent. He's of gipsy origin. I was particularly moved by a *Nocturne* of Chopin's.[87] And they turned out to be very nice people.

23 October [. . .] Note:
(1) One of the main reasons for the narrowness of the people of our intellectual world is their pursuit of the contemporary, their effort to find out about, or at least to have some idea of, what has been written recently.

'We mustn't miss anything.' Yet mountains of books are written in every field. And they are all accessible, because of ease of communication. Whatever subject one talks about people say: 'But have you read Chelpanov, Kun, Breding? If you haven't, you can't talk about it.' And you must hurry up and read them. And there are mountains of them. And this haste, this stuffing one's head with the contemporary, trivial and confused as it is, excludes any possibility of serious, true, necessary knowledge. How obvious the mistake is, you would think. We have the results of the thoughts of the greatest thinkers who have stood out from milliards and milliards of people in the course of thousands of years, and these results of the thinking of these great people have been sifted through the sieve of time. All that is mediocre has been discarded, and only the original, the profound, the necessary is left; what is left are the Vedas, Zoroaster, Buddha, Lao-Tzu, Confucius, Mencius, Christ, Mohammed, Socrates, Marcus Aurelius, Epictetus and the moderns: Rousseau, Pascal, Kant, Schopenhauer and many others. And the people who try to keep up with the contemporary don't know any of this, but go on trying to keep up with it and stuff their heads with chaff and rubbish, which will all be sifted out and none of it will remain. [. . .]

25 October   Yesterday evening I read Gorky's *Philistines*. It's worthless. Got up today feeling just as weak. Went for a walk; I can only walk with difficulty. [. . .]

26 October   [. . .] A good letter from Chertkov. He tells me more clearly what I thought myself. The conversation with Strakhov was painful on account of Chertkov's demands, because it's necessary to have dealings with the government. I think I'll decide everything in the most simple and natural way – Sasha. I want to include the earlier ones too, up to 82.[88] [. . .]

Evening. Another conversation with Strakhov. I agreed. But I regret that I didn't say that all this is very painful to me, and the best thing would be – doing nothing.

1 November   [. . .] Today Goldenweiser and Strakhov came and brought the papers from Chertkov. I altered them all.[89] [. . .]

2 November   Slept well, but I'm still weak. I think I'm played out as a writer of literary works. I can't concentrate on one thing. But there's a lot I want to do. [. . .]

4 November   [. . .] On the evening of the 2nd something very important happened. I spoke about the fact that, if I went to Kryokshino, Chertkov had promised to arrange my passage through Moscow so that no one would see me. Sofya Andreyevna suddenly lost control of herself. It was very painful. Thank God – I refrained from evil. I kissed her as I said goodbye, and very much wanted to do something particularly pleasant for her. I understand life's greatest joy – paying back evil with good – but I only understand it, and I couldn't do anything that evening or the next day. I could only restrain myself when speaking, but in my heart there was *rancune* [rancour]. [. . .]

9, 10 November   In the evening I read Gorky.[90] A knowledge of the lowest strata of the people, and wonderful language, i.e. the idiom of the people. But a completely arbitrary and quite unjustified psychology – i.e. the attribution of feelings and thoughts to his characters – which gets more and more heroic, and then an exclusively immoral milieu. And on top of that a slavish respect for science. [. . .]

At home in the evening I finished reading Gorky. All imaginary, unnatural and tremendously heroic feelings, and falseness. But a great talent. And yet, like Andreyev, he has nothing to say. They ought to write poetry, or – as Andreyev has also chosen to do – dramas. With poetry the permissible obscurity would save them, with drama the setting and the actors. It was the same with Chekhov, but there's a comic strain in him.

In the evening things were unpleasant, and I was wrong not to have spoken out about *A Captive in the Caucasus* and *Polikushka*, about making them public property.[91]

12 November   [. . .] A wonderful story by Sonya about rescuing a girl on the Khodynka.[92] [. . .]

18 November   [. . .] A peasant from Telyatinki came. His son had been conscripted as a soldier and was to be tried for saying that icons were wooden boards. I'd very much like to write about it, but I'm trying to do too much. [. . .]

20 November   The musicians came.[93] I was sorry I invited them. It's all very artificial. Even the elegantly artificial return to the past. They are all Frenchmen, very nice, flattering people, and Goldenweiser. The music excites me very much physically. Worried absurdly about my French. [. . .]

23 November   [. . .] Read about Gorky after dinner. And it's strange, I have an unfriendly feeling towards him, which I struggle against. I try to justify myself by the fact that, like Nietzsche, he is a harmful writer: a great talent and a lack of any religious convictions – i.e. convictions which comprehend the meaning of life – and at the same time a self-assurance bolstered up by our 'educated' world, which sees in him its exponent, and which is infecting this world more and more. For example his saying: 'If you believe in God, God exists; if you don't believe in God, He doesn't exist.' A vile saying, but all the same it made me think hard.⁹⁴ Does the God in Himself about whom I speak and write exist? It's true, one can say of that God: 'If you believe in Him, He exists.' And I always thought so. And for that reason in Christ's words 'love *God* and your neighbour', love of God has always seemed to me superfluous, incompatible with love of one's neighbour; incompatible because love of one's neighbout is so clear, clearer than anything can be, while love of God on the contrary is very unclear. You can accept that He exists, this God in Himself, that's true, but can you love Him? This is where I encounter what I have often experienced – the slavish acceptance of the words of the Gospel.

God is love – that is so. We know Him only because we love Him; but that God in Himself exists is a rationalization, and often a superfluous and even harmful one. If I am asked 'Does God in Himself exist?' I am bound to say and I will say 'yes, probably, but I don't understand anything about Him, this God in Himself'. But it isn't so with the God of love. Him I know for certain. He is everything for me, the explanation and the purpose of my life. [. . .]

25 November [. . .] Walked round the garden and the pond. Daniel and A. Sergeyenko came.⁹⁵ Slept heavily. Had dinner and spoke English with difficulty. Daniel is a clever, cold person. [. . .]

28 November [. . .] It was difficult with Daniel because of my lack of knowledge, or rather my half knowledge of the language. [. . .]

3 December [. . .] Walked to the skating rink. Admired Sasha (when you copy this, remember that I want to admire in you the same sort of spiritual energy). [. . .] Note:
(1) To be an artist of the word, one has to have the faculty of rising to the heights and falling to the depths spiritually. Then all the intermediate stages are known, and one can live in the imagination, live the life of people who stand on the various rungs.
(2) I don't like it, and even consider it bad poetically speaking, to treat religious, philosophical and ethical questions in a literary or dramatic manner, as in Goethe's *Faust*, etc. One should either say nothing about these questions, or only speak with the greatest caution and attention, without rhetorical phrases, and – God have mercy upon us – without rhyme. [. . .]

I don't want to be a Christian, as I wouldn't advise and wouldn't want people to be Brahmins, Buddhists, Confucianists, Taoists, Mohammedans, etc. We must all find, each in his own faith, what is common to all, renounce what is exclusive to one's own and hold on to what is common. [. . .]

13 December [. . .] Something interesting happened today, something very helpful in freeing me from my concern for worldly fame: I was sent an article from the *Russian Standard* which speaks about me being a preacher of 'materialism' (*sic*), who denies everything spiritual,[96] and in James' book it is said that I'm a melancholic, close to mental illness.[97] It's very helpful; I can feel the good influence already. [. . .]

14 December Woke up with a cold, and it got worse and worse until it became an extraordinary fit of shivering, then a temperature of 42°, and I forgot everything. During the night I dreamed about Andrey, some doctor or other and Boulanger. Was bad all night, but recovered and feel as well at heart as I could wish. I don't need to make an effort to love everyone. True, it's easy when one is surrounded only by those who love you. [. . .]

18 December Ivan Ivanovich is being tried today.[98] The craziness of our life is becoming more and more incomprehensible, and my powerlessness to express my understanding of it more evident. Got up late. Went for a walk. A teacher's wife came, a pathetic woman. I wasn't deceived by her. At home I did nothing except letters. Read Smetana.[99] It's good. A peasant from Saratov came, an old man. He'd sold his horse to come and have a heart-to-heart talk. [. . .]

19 December [. . .] Went for a walk and a ride with the visitor from Saratov. All is still well. He wants to go over to 'my' faith, and I try to explain to him that there isn't such a thing as 'my' faith. He told me a terrible story about murder and execution. [. . .]

Read *Conversation with a Passer-by* to the Saratov peasant as he was about to leave. It's good [. . .]

20 December Went for a walk. Met a wretched Cossack; he said he had been exiled for distributing my books. I gave him some books. [. . .]

25 December, evening. Yesterday evening I read Epictetus.[100] Played cards. Got up late today. Didn't get to sleep last night until 3. Letters: one reproachful one about handing over my property to my wife. Wrote a reply.

I don't think it was bad. [. . .] Read *A Sentimental Journey*. It reminded me of my youth and the demands of art.[101] [. . .]

29 December   Slept well, woke up almost in good health. Went for a walk. Some good letters. [. . .]

In the evening Landowska played. I was bored. Her flattery is particularly unpleasant. I must tell her.

30 December   [. . .] Walked around outside the house. A thaw. They're getting the Christmas tree ready. I feel very good at heart. [. . .]

1910

Missed two days. *Today is the 2nd* [*January*], *1910*. [. . .]
  Seeing the New Year in with insane luxury was very painful, both in itself and because I took part.

4 January [. . .] Very sad. Those around me are very alien. I thought about my relations with the people of our world, irreligious people. They're like my relations with animals. I can love them and pity them, but can't enter into spiritual intercourse with them. [. . .]

5 January Woke up early. Walked round the garden. It becomes more and more depressing to see slaves working for our family. [. . .]
  I'm going to dinner. In the evening I read *A Dream*¹ to the whole company. Many objections. But I think it's good. *Vint*, and I'm still sad and ashamed.

6 January Many letters, not many interesting ones. The cinematographer came.² [. . .]

13 January [. . .]
(1) It's not anarchism, the teaching by which I live. It's the fulfilment of the external law which doesn't permit violence or participation in it. But will the consequences be either anarchism, or, on the contrary, slavery under the yoke of the Japanese or the Germans? That I don't know and don't wish to know. [. . .]
  I'm going to dinner. After dinner I went to see Sasha; she's ill. If Sasha wasn't going to read this, I would write something that would please her. Borrowed Gorky from her and read it. Very poor. But the worst thing about it is that the false evaluation of him is unpleasant to me.³ I should see only the good in him. [. . .]

16 January Woke up in good spirits and decided to go to the court in Tula.⁴ Read my letters and answered a few. Then set off. First came the trial of some peasants: lawyers, judges, soldiers, witnesses. All very new to me. Then came the trial of a political prisoner. The charge was that he had read and, at cost to himself, disseminated ideas for a more just and sane organization of life than the one which now exists. Felt very sorry for him.

People gathered to look at me, but not many, thank goodness. The oath upset me. I could hardly refrain from saying it was a mockery of Christ. My heart sank, and because of that I remained silent. [. . .]

21 January [. . .]
(4) We speak about life after death. But if the soul lives after death, it must have lived before life also. One-sided eternity is an absurdity.

Today is 11 February [. . .] Sofya Andreyevna has left. I spoke to her yesterday about my wish, and the unpleasantness caused by the fact that the *Readers* are being sold at a high price; she began to say she would have nothing left, and refused outright. [. . .]

28 February [. . .] Went riding with Lena. A pleasant evening with Sasha. Read *Super-Tramp*. Poor English jokes – and in Shaw's foreword as well.[5]

7–8 March Yesterday I wrote two letters, I think. Went riding with Dušan. Read Alexandra Andreyevna's notes[6] and experienced a very strong feeling: firstly, emotion caused by happy memories, and secondly sadness and the clear awareness of the fact that she, poor woman, couldn't help believing in redemption and *tout le tremblement* [all the rest of it], because if she didn't believe, she would have had to condemn her whole life and change it if she wanted to be a Christian and have communion with God. People who are not religious can live without faith, and therefore have no need of an absurd one, but she needed a faith, but a rational faith would have shown her up. So she believed in an absurd one, and how she believed! Thirdly I also felt the awareness of how the external affirmation of one's own faith and the condemnation of others – how precarious and unconvincing this is. She insists on her own faith, with such assurance, and condemns others so resolutely. Fourthly, I also felt that I had often been wrong and not careful enough when touching upon other people's faith (if only in science). [. . .]

In the evening I read my letters to Alexandra Andreyevna again with emotion. One about the fact that life is work, struggle and mistakes is such that I wouldn't say anything different at all now.[7] Ivan Ivanovich and I have decided about publishing.[8]

10 March [. . .] Wrote a reply to the Japanese,[9] and a letter about *The Horrors of Christian Civilization*,[10] and a reply about the 15,000 roubles.[11] Went riding with Dušan. I'm going to bed. Dinner, chess, gossip, cards, the gramophone, and I felt sorely ashamed and disgusted. I won't do it any more. I'll read.

19 March   [. . .] Read my letter to the Indian and very much approved of it.[12] But the one to the Japanese is terrible. But it's good that that isn't important to me. [. . .]

23 March   Health good. Letters. Work with the booklets is very boring. Wrote a letter about suicide. I don't like it either. I'd like to write a play for Telyatinki.[13] [. . .]

25 March   Went for a long walk. Met Dunayev. Sad. My thoughts agitate me. Either I don't have the strength, or I can't find the form to express them. A powerful article by Korolenko about the death penalty.[14] Went riding. Spent a tiresome evening at cards. I must stop. I'm going to bed.

26 March   [. . .] In the evening I read Korolenko's article. It's magnificent. I couldn't help sobbing. Wrote Korolenko a letter.

[*30 March*]   Missed two days. Yesterday was the 29th. In the morning on my walk I met Strakhov and then Masaryk. I like them both, especially Masaryk.[15] On the 28th the Stakhoviches came. Rather tedious. He is very alien to me. Yesterday I had two good talks with Masaryk. Rode to Ovsyannikovo. Sketched out a comedy: perhaps it will turn out all right. Masaryk is a professor and still believes in a personal God and personal immortality. [. . .]

31 March   [. . .] Felt today for the first time and with complete clarity my success in freeing myself from worldly fame. They were all trifling matters – not being embarrassed at being censured for drinking wine, playing cards and living in luxury – but all of a sudden I felt an unexpected freedom. I think I'm not mistaken.

   Slept well today. Spilled my pot and broke it, and was very tired cleaning and wiping it up, and got out of breath. It's near, and it's good that it's near. [. . .]

7 April   [. . .] An insanely lovely spring. Each time I can't believe myself. Can this beauty really come out of nothing? Seryozha came in the evening. I've come to understand him. And I'm glad. [. . .]

10 April   [. . .] Sasha is leaving.[16] She is sad. I had a good talk with her. We both blubbered. I only copied in: [. . .]
(3) What a great wrong I did in giving the property to the children. I did harm to them all, even my daughters. I see this clearly now.

12 April   [. . .] Had no dinner. Felt a tormenting anguish from the awareness of the vileness of my life among people who are working so that they can just barely save themselves from a cold, hungry death, save themselves and their family. Yesterday there were fifteen people gorging pancakes, and five or six people with families were running about, barely managing to cook and hand round the fodder. It was agonizingly shameful and terrible. Yesterday I rode past some stone-breakers, and it was as though I'd been forced to run the gauntlet. Yes, need and envy and anger against the rich are painful and agonizing, but I don't know whether the shame of my own life isn't more agonizing.

Today is 13 April   Woke up at 5 and kept thinking how to escape, what to do. And I don't know. I thought of writing. Yet it's disgusting to write while continuing to live this sort of life. Should I speak to her? Go away? Change things gradually? [. . .] I think the latter is all I can and will do. But still it's depressing. [. . .]

14 April   [. . .] I've been reading through my books. I oughtn't to write any more. I think in this respect I've done all I could. But I want to, I terribly want to. [. . .]

15 April   I.I.A. Alive – just about. Got up in better spirits. A fuss again. Petitioners. Treated them all well, remembering to show gratitude for the joy of communion with them, except for a drunken woman whom I treated badly and refused. Letters. One to Shaw,[17] and one about a peace society.[18] Bad. [. . .]

19 April   [. . .] This morning two Japanese came:[19] primitive people in an ecstasy of enthusiasm over European civilization. On the other hand I had a book and a letter from an Indian[20] expressing understanding of all the shortcomings of European civilization, even its utter worthlessness. [. . .]

20 April   I.I.A. Still alive. Got up rather late. Walked through the young fir trees; the ants interested me. Made a few notes. The colonel came again, with apparently unkind feelings towards me.[21] Corrected the proofs of two booklets. *Sins, Temptations and Superstitions* and *Vanity*. Not bad. Went riding with Bulgakov. Few interesting letters. In the evening I read Gandhi on civilization. Very good. [. . .]

22 April   Alive. Went for a walk by myself, refused to go with Andreyev[22] and a man who had come from Archangel. Had a talk later with Andreyev. He doesn't have a serious attitude to life, but touches superficially on these questions all the same. Letters. Revised two months of *For Every Day*. I liked it very much. Went for a walk. The Goldenweisers came. I'm still struggling. Wrote a letter to Sasha.[23] I'm going to bed before dinner. A letter from Sasha which moved me very much. The music excited me greatly. He played wonderfully.

4 May, Kochety[24]   Before dinner I walked round the wood and rejoiced in life, in its 'invisible forces'.[25] Had some dreams which were amazing for their psychological truthfulness. I thought I'd write about suicide, [26] but when I sat at the desk I felt feeble-minded and disinclined. Again I feel acutely the burden of the luxury and idleness of a landowner's life. Everyone works except me. [. . .]

5 May   Sleepiness again and feeble-mindedness. Wrote nothing and didn't try to. Read the old Frenchmen: La Boétie, Montaigne, La Rochefoucauld.[27] [. . .]

6 May   [. . .] Note:
   Habit – mechanical, unconscious actions – is the basis of true life, of moral striving for improvement. [. . .]

9 May   [. . .] Sonya and Andrey have arrived. I wasn't good to Andrey, I was too abrupt. With Sonya I partly expressed for the first time what depressed me. And then, in order to soften what I'd said, I kissed her silently – she understands that language completely.

18 May   [. . .]
(4) Memory? How often people take memory for intelligence. And they don't see that memory excludes intelligence, is incompatible with intelligence – intelligence which solves problems in an original manner. The one is a substitute for the other.

19 May   My last day in Kochety. It was very pleasant except for the seignorial way of life, well organized and alleviated by a just and kind attitude to people, but still a terrible, crying contrast which never ceases to torment me.
   Revised the play[28] and nothing else. Health good. Some photographs taken. [. . .]

Today is 22 May, Yasnaya Polyana   [. . .] An unpleasant talk with Sonya.[29] I behaved badly. She did everything I asked. [. . .]

Today is the 24th   Got up early and it's now 7 o'clock. Note:
(1) People come to see a person who has acquired a reputation for the importance and clarity of expression of his thoughts; they come and they don't let him say a word, but talk and either tell him something which has been said much more clearly by him, or something whose absurdity has long ago been proved by him. [. . .]

25 May   I'm well. Walked a little. My mind is working feebly. Carefully revised and looked over the *booklets*, and they're not bad. [. . .] Yes, a young teacher came in the morning, threatening to commit suicide. I behaved badly towards him.

Today is 27 May   [. . .]
(1) For the first time I felt vividly the arbitrariness of this whole world. Why do I, such a clear, simple, rational and good person, live in this confused, complicated, insane, evil world? Why?
(2) (On the courts.) If only these wretched, stupid, coarse, self-satisfied evil-doers could understand what they are doing when they sit in their uniforms at tables covered with green cloth repeating and gravely analysing senseless words printed in vile books which are a disgrace to mankind; if only they could understand that what they call laws are a crude mockery of those eternal laws which are engraved on the hearts of all people. Some people who, without any ill will, shot at birds in a place called a church have been sent to hard labour for sacrilege, but these other people continually commit and live by sacrilege against the most sacred thing in the world: human life. The Tsar teaches his innocent son to kill. All this is done by Christians. A soldier who doesn't want to serve because he doesn't need to has deserted. Oh, how I need to and want to write about this.

29 May   [. . .] A talk with Sonya. She was agitated. I was afraid, but, thank God, it turned out all right. Trubetskoy came.[30] He's very nice. I also worked quite well. Finished all the booklets and gave them to Ivan Ivanovich. [. . .]

Today is 1 June   [. . .] I've been reading Chernyshevsky.[31] His easy way of crudely condemning people who don't think as he does is very instructive. I have a very pleasant, kindly feeling towards Sonya – a good, spiritual, loving one. I feel well at heart despite my inactivity.

4 June   Got up early. Dealt with the petitioners very well, and went for a walk. Then letters. One serious one, as an answer to the writing epidemic.[32] Began working on the comedy and gave up in disgust. Revised the foreword[33] reasonably well. Went out tired after work; there were a dozen women and I behaved badly, not towards them but towards dear, unselfish Dušan. I rebuked him. It was all disgusting. [. . .] Felt terribly depressed and really thought of leaving.

5 June And now today, on the morning of the 5th, I still don't consider it impossible.

Dear, dear Tanechka came. I sobbed as I talked to her.[34] This was vile of me. It's always me, me, my pleasure, and not my work. [. . .]

I was very poorly all day. Did no work and felt sorry for myself all day and wanted others to feel sorry for me, wanted to cry, and blamed everybody else, like a spoiled child. But still I kept myself in check. The only thing was that I said at dinner that I wanted to die. And I do want to very much, and I can't help wishing it. In the evening Goldenweiser played well, but it left me cold. I went for a ride and sat for Trubetskoy.

12 June [. . .] Had a difficult time with the two girls – they were to be pitied, but I couldn't give them any help and they took up my time.[35]

I've decided to go to the Chertkovs'. [. . .]

14 June I'm beginning a new notebook at the Chertkovs'. Walked through the fields. Worked on the foreword. Looked over my old diary. For seven months now I've been constantly busy with this and this only. Can it really all be a waste of time? Letters. Not many interesting ones. Walked to Lyubuchany[36] to see the madmen. One very interesting one: 'I didn't steal,' [he said], 'I took.' I said: '[We'll meet] in the next world.' He said: 'There's only one world.' This madman is far superior to many people considered sane. [. . .]

16 June [. . .] At three o'clock I set off on foot to Meshcherskoye to see the madmen. Chertkov drove me the rest of the way. Walked round all the wards. I haven't analysed my impressions yet and so I'm not writing anything. And the impressions are less strong than I expected.[37] Worked a little on the proofs of the booklet *Sins, Temptations and Superstitions*. I very much want to be rid of this work. Sasha is better. Uninteresting letters. Read Kuprin.[38] He's very talented. *Measles* is inconsistent, but the imagery is vivid, true to life and simple . . .

20 June Got up in good spirits. Revised *To the Slavs* and the foreword. And wrote something for *The Wisdom of Children*.[39] I want to try to win over Sonya consciously by means of goodness and love. From a distance it seems possible. I'll try to do so when she's close by as well. [. . .]

23 June   Alive. It's now 7 in the morning. Yesterday I had only just gone to bed and hadn't gone to sleep when a telegram arrived:[40] 'Beg you come 23rd.' I'll go, and I'm glad of the chance to do my duty. God help me.

[*Yasnaya Polyana*.] Found things worse than expected: hysterics and irritability. It's impossible to describe. I didn't behave very badly, but not very well either, not gently enough.

24 June, Yasnaya Polyana   A lot to note down.

Got up, not having slept much. Went for a walk. During the night Sonya came in. She still can't sleep. She came to me in the morning. She's still agitated, but is calming down.

(1) Went out for a walk after an agonizing talk with Sonya. There are flowers out in front of the house, and healthy, barefoot girls tidying up. They came back later with hay and berries – cheerful, calm and healthy. It would be good to write two scenes.[41] [. . .]

25 June   Got up early. Wrote about insanity and did some letters. And suddenly Sonya was in the same irritable, hysterical condition again. I was very depressed. Drove with her to Ovsyannikovo. She calmed down. I was silent, but couldn't be kind and affectionate, I wasn't able to. [. . .]

26 June   [. . .] Sonya was excited again, and there were the same sufferings again for both of us. [. . .]

27 June   Yesterday she spoke about moving somewhere. I didn't sleep all night. I'm very tired. [. . .]

28 June   Didn't sleep much. Sonya has been in a wonderful mood since morning. She asked me not to go.[42] But then she had a letter from Chertkov. A good letter from Chertkov. But she is still excited and angry with him. [. . .]

7 July, [*Yasnaya Polyana*]   Alive, but a bad day. Bad because I'm still out of sorts, and am not working. Didn't even correct the proofs. Went for a ride to Chertkov's. When I got home I found Sofya Andreyevna in an irritable mood and couldn't calm her down at all. Read in the evening. Goldenweiser came over late on, also Chertkov. Sonya had it out with him, and still didn't calm down. But late in the evening I had a very good talk with her. Hardly slept all night.

11 July   Alive, just about. A terrible night. Until 4 o'clock. And Lev Lvovich was worst of all. He scolded me as if I were a little boy, and ordered me to go into the garden after Sofya Andreyevna.[43] In the morning

Sergey arrived. I did no work – except for the booklet *Idleness*. Went walking and riding. I can't look calmly at Lev. I'm still ill. Sonya, poor woman, has calmed down. A cruel and depressing illness. [. . .]

14 July A very depressing night. Began writing her a letter in the morning and finished it.[44] Went to her room. She demanded the very things that I promised and granted. I don't know whether I did right, whether I wasn't too weak and submissive. But I couldn't do otherwise. They've gone to fetch the diaries. She's still in the same irritable condition, not eating or drinking. Worked on the booklets, did three. Then rode to Rudakov. I can't be kind and affectionate to Lev, and he doesn't understand or feel anything. Sasha brought the diaries. She went twice. And Sonya has calmed down and thanked me. I think it's all right. [. . .]

15 July Alive, but depressed. Commotion again in the morning: I might run away, I must give her the key to the diaries. I said I wouldn't go back on what I'd said. It was very, very depressing. Before that I finished the proofs of the booklets. There's only a part of one left. Went for a ride with Dušan. In the evening an American,[45] and Chertkov, and Goldenweiser, and Nikolayev. Sonya is calm, but one feels it's all hanging by a thread. [. . .]

17 July [. . .] Read some letters and Pascal. A talk yesterday with Lev, and today he explained to me that I'm to blame. I must remain silent and try not to have unkind feelings. [. . .]

18 July Alive, but ill. Still the same weakness. I'm doing no work except writing worthless letters and reading Pascal. Sofya Andreyevna is agitated again. 'I've been unfaithful to her and that's why I'm hiding the diaries.' And then she's sorry that she's tormenting me. An uncontrollable hatred of Chertkov. I feel an unbridgeable distance between Lev and myself. And I'll tell him *son fait* [what I think of him], as lovingly as I can. A tiresome writer gentleman came. Rode to Tikhvinskoye. Very tired. Goldenweiser and Chertkov came in the evening, and Sofya Andreyevna was almost beside herself. I'm going to bed.

19 July Slept reasonably well, but am very weak; pulse irregular. Wrote a venomous article for the Peace Congress,[46] and some letters. Sofya Andreyevna was better this morning, but worse towards evening with the arrival of the doctors. [. . .]

20 July [. . .] Note: [. . .]
(4) I can't in my heart forgive Vera[47] for her fall. And I clearly understand

at once all the cruelty and injustice of this. I only need to remember my own male sexual past. Yes, nothing shows so obviously that public opinion is formed not by women, but by men. Yet a woman should be less liable to condemnation than a man because she bears all the great weight of the consequences of her sin – childbirth, shame; while the man bears none. 'If you're not caught, you're not a thief.' As a fallen woman or an unmarried mother, V is shamed in the eyes of the whole world, or straightway becomes a member of the class of despised creatures, whores. But a man is pure and good and in the right, as long as he doesn't catch a disease. It would be good to make this clear.

22 July Slept very little. Did no work. Fell asleep before lunch. Went for a ride with Goldenweiser. Wrote it in the woods.[48] That's good. Irritability and agitation again at home. Even worse at dinner. I took it upon myself to invite her for a walk, and calmed her down. Chertkov came. It was strained, painful and depressing. Bear up, Cossack. I'm reading La Bruyère.

24 July The same again as regards health and my relations with Sofya Andreyevna. My health is a bit better. But Sofya Andreyevna's is worse. Yesterday evening she wouldn't leave me and Chertkov alone, so as not to give us the chance to talk just by ourselves. It's the same again today. But I got up and asked him whether he agreed with what I had written to him. She heard me and asked what I was talking about. I said I didn't wish to answer. And she went out, agitated and irritable. I can't do anything. It's unbearably depressing for me. I'm doing nothing: writing worthless letters, and reading all sorts of trash. I'm going to bed, unwell and restless.

25 July Sonya didn't sleep all night. She decided to go away and went to Tula, where she met Andrey, and came back quite well, but terribly exhausted. I'm still unwell, but a bit better. Did no work, and didn't try. Talked with Lev. It's no good. [. . .]

27 July The same again. But only, I think, the calm before the storm. Andrey came to ask if there was a document. I said I didn't wish to answer. Very depressing. I can't believe that they only want money. [. . .]

28 July Still the same ill health – my liver, and lack of mental activity. It's quiet at home. Zosya came. Went for a ride with Dušan. Seryozha was here. Thank God everything has been exaggerated. Yes, I no longer have a diary, a frank, simple diary. I must start one.[49]

2 August [. . .] A splendid letter from Tanya. She is suffering for me, poor girl. Rode over to get some seed-rye. Sofya Andreyevna drove over to check on me. [. . .]

3 August   I.I.A. Alive, and melancholy. [. . .]

Rode to Kolpna with Goldenweiser. In the evening there was a painful scene; I was extremely agitated. Did nothing, but felt such a rush of blood to the heart that I was not only frightened, but in pain.

5 August   Note: [. . .]

(4) 1 August. The words of a dying man are particularly important. But surely we are always dying and it's particularly obvious in old age. So let an old man remember that his words might be particularly important. [. . .]

6 August   [. . .] Korolenko has come.[50] A very pleasant and intelligent man who talks well. But still it's painful to talk and talk.

7 August   A state of despondency. Tried to write. On insanity. Couldn't do anything. Invited Korolenko to go for a walk with me in the morning and we had a good talk. He's intelligent, but dominated by the superstition of science. [. . .] For Sasha to copy:

(1) I've seldom met a person more endowed with all the vices than I am: lasciviousness, self-interest, malice, vanity, and above all self-love. I thank God that I know this, and have seen and continue to see all this loathsomeness in myself and still struggle against it. This is what explains the success of my writings. [. . .]

8 August   I'd just got up when Sofya Andreyevna ran outside, not having slept all night, agitated and really ill. I went for a walk, then looked for her. Couldn't write anything. Went riding with Bulgakov. [. . .]

9 August   [. . .] At home there was the awful Ferre, awful because of his impervious, naive bourgeois nature. Then a Hungarian. I behaved badly towards them both.[51] Sasha had another clash with Sonya. [. . .]

15 August, Kochety[52]   Woke up feeling unwell. Sofya Andreyevna is going with us. We had to get up at 6 o'clock. A depressing journey. Some insignificant letters. It's very pleasant at Tanya's. I'm just going to bed in a depressed state, physically and mentally. Read a book by Fyodor Strakhov: *The Search for Truth.*[53] Very, very good.

(1) What a strange thing: I love myself, but nobody loves me.

(2) Instead of learning to live a loving life, people learn to fly. They fly very badly, but they stop learning to live a life of love in order to learn to fly

after a fashion. It's just as if birds stopped flying and learned to run or make bicycles and ride on them.

18 August   Everything is just the same, the same mental weakness. Did nothing. Sonya was distressed by the news that Chertkov has been given permission to live at Telyatinki. [. . .]

23 August   Had a brisk walk and thought. Made up a fairy tale for children. And another one on the theme: *The Same for Everyone*, and the characters for it.⁵⁴ Sketched out the fairy tale. Walked in the park. Finished the booklets. *Vint* in the evening. I'm going to bed. Sofya Andreyevna is calm.

29 August   An empty day again. Walks, letters. I'm thinking, and thinking well, but can't concentrate. Sofya Andreyevna was very agitated, went into the garden and didn't come back. She came in after 12. And she wanted to have it out again. I was very depressed, but I restrained myself and she calmed down. She has decided to leave today.⁵⁵ Thank goodness, Sasha has decided to go with her. She said goodbye very movingly and asked everyone's forgiveness. I feel a very great and loving pity for her. Some good letters. I'm going to bed. Wrote her a note.

30 August   It's sad without her. I'm afraid for her. There's no tranquillity. Walked along the roads. Was just about to start work. Mavor came.⁵⁶ A professor. Very lively, but a professor, and a supporter of the state, and an irreligious man. The classic type of the good scholar. [. . .]

Today is 1 September   [. . .] The Mamontovs came.⁵⁷ The insanity of the rich is more and more glaring. But I played cards with them until 11 o'clock and was ashamed. I want to stop playing all games. I'm tired and going to bed.

5 September   [. . .] Sofya Andreyevna came back. Very agitated, but not hostile. [. . .]

7, 8 September   [. . .] Only wrote letters, one to an Indian,⁵⁸ and one about non-resistance to a Russian. Sofya Andreyevna is becoming more and more irritable. It's depressing. But I'm bearing up. I can't yet go as far as doing what ought to be done calmly. I'm afraid of the letter we're expecting from Chertkov. [. . .] Sofya Andreyevna kept wanting Drankov⁵⁹ to photograph both of us together. I don't think I'll work. I'm restless. Haven't written anything. Walked round the park and made a few notes. Received a letter from Chertkov, and Sofya Andreyevna received a letter from him. Just before that we had a painful talk about my departure.[60] I stood up for my freedom. I'll go when *I* want to. I'm very sad, of course, because I'm not well. I'm going to bed.

10 September   Got up early. Didn't sleep much, but am fresher than yesterday. Sofya Andreyevna is still just as irritable. I was very depressed. Went riding for a bit with Dušan. A good letter from a peasant about faith. Answered it. And a very good one from an Italian in Rome about my philosophy.[61] Sofya Andreyevna has eaten nothing for the second day. They're about to have dinner. I'll go and ask her to come to dinner. Terrible scenes all evening.

12 September   Sofya Andreyevna left in tears. She tried to summon me in for a talk; I evaded it. She took no one with her. I'm very, very tired. Read in the evening. I'm worried about her.

14 September   [. . .]
(1) I must remember that in my relations with Sofya Andreyevna the point is not my own pleasure or displeasure, but the fulfilment of the task of love in the difficult conditions in which she places me. [. . .]

15 September, Kochety   [. . .]
(6) Motherhood for a woman *is not the highest calling.* [. . .]
(10) I can't get used to regarding her words as delirium. That's the cause of all my trouble.
    I can't talk with her because neither logic, nor truth, nor the words she herself has spoken, nor her conscience are binding on her – it's terrible.
(11) Not to mention her love for me, of which not a trace remains, she doesn't need my love for her either, she only needs one thing: for people to *think that I love her.* And it's this that's so dreadful. [. . .]

22 September   [. . .] *Yasnaya Polyana.* Had a very good journey. [. . .] At home I found Sofya Andreyevna in an angry mood: reproaches and tears. I remained silent.

23 September   This morning Sofya Andreyevna went out somewhere; later she was in tears. It was very depressing. A pile of letters. Some interesting ones. Sasha was angry and unjust. Had dinner, read Max Müller's *Indian Philosophy.*[62] What an empty book. Lost my little notebook.[63] [. . .]

24 September   Walked to Nikolayev's and the Kaluga men who were making felt boots. At home – books: a German one by Schmitt on science, the letter to an Indian and the one on law. Schmitt is a scientific windbag.

Maude is also preaching at me.[64] Went riding with Bulgakov. Dear Marya Alexandrovna. Sofya Andreyevna was unpleasant. It had passed off by evening. She is sick, and I'm sorry for her with all my heart. [. . .]

26 September Slept badly; bad dreams. Got up and hung the photographs in their right place again.[65] Went for a walk. Began writing to the young Czechs;[66] continued working on the booklets *For the Soul*.[67] I'm a bit more satisfied. A student, Chebotaryov, came. He's faced with military service. He doesn't know how to act. A sincere person, I liked him. Went riding with Dušan. When I got back I found Sofya Andreyevna in an agitated state. She had burned the photograph of Chertkov. I began to say something, but stopped – it's impossible to understand her. In the evening Khiryakov[68] and Nikolayev came. I was very tired. Sofya Andreyevna tried to speak again. I remained silent. I only said before dinner that she had rearranged my photographs in my room and then burned the photograph of my friend and that I seemed to be to blame for everything. The sequel to the day was the return of Sasha and Varvara Mikhaylovna,[69] summoned by Marya Alexandrovna. Sofya Andreyevna gave them a stormy reception, so Sasha decided to leave.

27 September In the morning I saw Sasha off – she has gone to Telyatinki for good.[70] [. . .]

29 September Got up early. Frost and sunshine. I'm still weak. Went for a walk. I've just returned. Sasha came running in. Sofya Andreyevna couldn't sleep and also got up early before 8. She's very nervous. I must be more careful. On my walk just now I twice caught myself feeling dissatisfied because I had renounced my freedom of will and also because the new edition will be sold for hundreds of thousands of roubles,[71] but both times I put myself to rights with the thought that one needs only to be pure in the sight of God. And one is immediately aware of the joy of life. [. . .]

29 September, Yasnaya Polyana
(1) What terrible mental poison modern literature is, especially for young folk from the people. First of all they stuff their minds with the obscure, self-assured, empty chatter of writers who are writing for the modern reader. The chief peculiarity and harmfulness of such chatter is that it all consists of allusions to, and quotations from, the most various of writers, the most modern as well as the most ancient. Phrases are quoted from Plato, Hegel and Darwin, about whom the writers themselves haven't the least conception, and alongside them are phrases from people like Gorky, Andreyev, Artsybashev and others, about whom it isn't worthwhile having

any conception. Secondly, this chatter is harmful because by filling their heads in this way it leaves no room or leisure for them to get to know the old writers who have stood the test of time not only for decades, but for hundreds and thousands of years.

Sasha has come. Sofya Andreyevna said she is ready to make peace with Varya.[72] Then I was moved by the fact that she thanked me for my affection towards her. It's frightening, but I would like to think that even she can be overcome by kindness. [. . .]

30 September   I feel very poorly and weak. Did nothing except letters, and those badly. Went riding with Dušan – it was pleasant. In the evening I read my biography,[73] and it was interesting. It's very exaggerated. Sasha came. Sofya Andreyevna is calm. Note: [. . .]
(2) Sofya Andreyevna says she doesn't understand love for one's enemies, and that it's an affectation. She and many others don't understand it, mainly because they think that the partiality they feel towards people is love.

1 October   [. . .] Sofya Andreyevna spoke about wanting to see Chertkov. I said that there was nothing to say, that she should simply stop being foolish and behave normally. Went riding with Bulgakov. The evening with Goldenweiser. Also read Maupassant. *The Family* is marvellous. [. . .]

3 October   Yesterday I didn't finish writing about the evening. Had a good talk with Seryozha and Biryukov about Sonya's illness. Then Goldenweiser played beautifully, and I had a good talk with him. [. . .] Note: [. . .]
(2) Music, as indeed any art, but especially music, arouses the desire that everyone, or as many people as possible, might participate in the pleasure being experienced. Nothing demonstrates the true significance of art more emphatically than this: you are transported into other people, you want to feel through them. [. . .]

5 October   I've been seriously ill for two days since the 3rd. Fainting spells and weakness. It began the day before yesterday, 3 October, after my nap before dinner. A good consequence of it was Sofya Andreyevna's reconciliation with Sasha and Varvara Mikhaylovna. But Chertkov is still as far away from me. I'm particularly sorry for him and Galya, for whom this is very painful. [. . .]

6 October   Got up in better spirits, but very weak, and went for a walk. Made a few notes. Sasha will copy them out. To be noted now: [. . .]
(3) The most common reproach levelled against people who express their convictions is that they don't live in accordance with them, and that

therefore their convictions are insincere. But if you think about it seriously, you will realize that it's just the opposite. Can an intelligent man who expresses convictions with which his way of life is not in accord help seeing this discrepancy? But if, nevertheless, he expresses convictions which do not accord with his way of life, this only shows that he is so sincere that he cannot help expressing what exposes his weakness, and that he is not doing what the majority of people do – tailoring his convictions to suit his weakness.

7 October   [. . .] Sonya had a hysterical fit again; it was depressing.

8 October   Got up early and went to meet the horses which had come to take dear Tanechka away. Said goodbye to her. Sasha and Varvara Mikhaylovna also saw her off and I came back home. Revised *On Socialism*. A shallow article. [. . .] Sonya came; I told her everything I wanted to but couldn't keep calm. I was very agitated. [. . .]

9 October   Health better. [. . .]
  Spent the evening quietly and calmly; read about socialism and prisons in *Russian Wealth*. I'm going to bed.

11 October   The days fly by without work. Got up late. Went for a walk. At home Sofya Andreyevna was agitated again by my imaginary secret meetings with Chertkov. I'm very sorry for her, she is ill. [. . .] Note: [. . .] (2) One must be like a lamp, closed to outside influences – the wind, insects – and at the same time clean, transparent and burning warmly. [. . .]

12 October   Got up late. A depressing conversation with Sofya Andreyevna. I was silent most of the time. I've been busy revising *On Socialism*. Rode with Bulgakov to meet Sasha. After dinner I read Dostoyevsky.[74] The descriptions are good, although certain little jokes, long-winded and not very funny, get in the way. But the conversations are impossible, completely unnatural. In the evening there were painful speeches again from Sofya Andreyevna. I remained silent. I'm going to bed.

13 October   Still mentally lacking in vigour, but spiritually alive. Revised *On Socialism* again. It's all very insignificant. But I've started it. I'll be more restrained and economical in my work. There isn't much time left to me, and I'm wasting it on trifles. Perhaps I'll still write something useful.
  Sofya Andreyevna is very agitated and is suffering. One would think it's so simple, what lies ahead of her: to live out the years of old age in

harmony and love with her husband, not interfering in his work or his life. But no, she wants – God knows what she wants – she wants to torment herself. Of course it's an illness, and it's impossible not to pity her.

14 October   Everything is just the same. But I'm very weak physically today. There was a letter from Sofya Andreyevna on the table with accusations and an invitation to renounce something.[75] When she came in, I asked her to leave me in peace. She went away. I had a tight feeling in my chest and a pulse of over 90. Revised *On Socialism* again. A futile occupation. Before going out I went to see Sofya Andreyevna and told her that I advised her to leave me in peace and not to interfere with my work. It's depressing. [. . .]

16 October   Not quite well; listless. Went for a walk; couldn't think of anything. Letters; revised *On Socialism*, but soon felt weak and gave it up. Said at lunch that I would go to the Chertkovs'. A stormy scene commenced; she ran out of the house and ran to Telyatinki. I set off on horseback and sent Dušan to say that I wouldn't go to the Chertkovs', but he couldn't find her. I came back, she still wasn't there. Finally they found her after 6 o'clock. She came back and sat motionless in her outdoor clothes, and wouldn't eat anything. And this evening she tried to explain herself, not very well. Late at night she asked forgiveness very movingly, admitted she was tormenting me and promised not to go on tormenting me. Will anything come of it?

17 October   Got up at 8; walked round the Chepyzh wood. Very weak. Thought well about death and wrote about it to Chertkov. Sofya Andreyevna came in and behaved just as gently and kindly towards me. But she is very agitated and talks a lot. Did nothing except letters. I can't work or write, but thank God I can work on myself. I'm still making progress. Read Sri Sankara.[76] It's not right. Read Sasha's diary. Good, simple and truthful. [. . .]

18 October   Still weak. And the weather is bad. Thank God, without wishing it I feel a *readiness for death*, which is good. [. . .] Read Dostoyevsky and was astonished at his slipshod manner, artificiality and fabrication. [. . .]

19 October   During the night Sofya Andreyevna came in: 'There's another conspiracy against me.' – 'What do you mean, what conspiracy?' – 'Your diary has been given to Chertkov. It's not here.' – 'Sasha has it.' It was very depressing; I couldn't get to sleep for a long time because I couldn't suppress an unkind feeling. Had a pain in my liver. Molostvova came. I walked through the fir trees, hardly able to move. [. . .]

Did nothing again, except letters. Health bad. The change is near. It would be good to live out the rest of my life a bit better. Sofya Andreyevna said she was sorry about yesterday. I made one or two remarks, especially about the fact that if there is hatred even for one person, there can be no true love. Talked with Molostvova, or rather listened to her. Skimmed through the first volume of *The Karamazovs*, and finished it. There's much that is good in it, but it's so disorganized. *The Grand Inquisitor* and Zosima's farewell. [. . .]

22 October [. . .] Didn't go riding, but went for a walk. Talked to some lavatory cleaners. Made no notes. In the letter to Dosev[77] there is much truth, but not the whole truth.

24 October [. . .] In the morning I *made a real fool of myself.* Began doing some gymnastics, unsuited to my years, and brought down a cupboard on top of me. What a fool. I feel weak. But I've come to my senses, thank goodness. Worked a bit on *Socialism*. [. . .]

25 October Got up very early, but did nothing all the same. Walked to the school and to Prokofy's, and had a talk with his son, an army conscript. A good lad; he promised not to drink. Then a bit of *On Socialism*. Rode to the school with Almedingen[78] and then a long ride with Dušan. In the evening I read Montaigne. Seryozha came. I found him pleasant. Sofya Andreyevna still as troubled as ever.

26 October Had a dream. Grushenka, a romance it seemed with Nikolay Nikolayevich Strakhov. A wonderful subject.[79] Wrote a letter to Chertkov. Made notes for *On Socialism*. Wrote to Chukovsky about the death penalty.[80] Rode to Marya Alexandrovna's with Dušan. Andrey came. I'm very depressed in this madhouse. I'm going to bed.

27 October Got up very early. Had bad dreams all night. Had a good walk. At home – letters. Worked a bit on the letter for N.[81] and *On Socialism*, but had no mental energy. Went riding with Dušan. Dinner. Read about Syutayev.[82] A marvellous letter from a Ukrainian to Chertkov. Revised the article for Chukovsky. Nothing to note. That seems bad, but actually it's good. The burden of our relations is getting worse.

28 October, Optina Monastery Went to bed at 11.20. Slept till after two. Woke up, and again, as on previous nights, I heard the opening of doors and footsteps. On previous nights I hadn't looked at my door, but this time I did look and saw through the crack a bright light in the study and heard rustling. It was Sofya Andreyevna looking for something and probably reading. The day before she was asking and insisting that I shouldn't lock my doors. Both her doors were open, so that she could hear my slightest movement. Day and night all my movements and words have to be known to her and to be under her control. There were footsteps again, the door opened carefully and she walked through the room. I don't know why, but this aroused indignation and uncontrollable revulsion in me. I wanted to go back to sleep, but couldn't; I tossed about for an hour or so, lit a candle and sat up. Sofya Andreyevna opened the door and came in, asking about 'my health' and expressing surprise at the light which she had seen in my room. My indignation and revulsion grew. I gasped for breath, counted my pulse: 97. I couldn't go on lying there, and suddenly I took the final decision to leave. I wrote her a letter and began to pack the most necessary things, just so that I could leave. I woke Dušan, then Sasha, and they helped me pack. I trembled at the thought that she would hear and come out – that there would be a scene, hysterics – and I wouldn't be able to leave later without a scene.

Everything was packed somehow or other before 6; I walked to the stables to tell them to harness the horses; Dušan, Sasha and Varya finished off the packing. The night was pitch black, I lost my way to the outhouse, found myself in a thicket, pricked myself, bumped into some trees, fell over, lost my cap, couldn't find it, made my way out again with an effort, went back home, took another cap and with the aid of a lantern made my way to the stables and ordered the horses to be harnessed. Sasha, Dušan and Varya arrived. I trembled as I waited to be pursued. But then we were on our way. We waited an hour at Shchokino, and every minute I expected her to appear. But then we were in the carriage, the train started, and my fear passed, and pity for her rose up within me, but not doubt about having done what I had to do. Perhaps I'm mistaken in justifying myself, but I think it was not myself, not Lev Nikolayevich, that I was saving, but something that is sometimes, and if only to a very small extent, within me. We reached Optina. I'm well, although I haven't slept and have hardly eaten anything. The journey from Gorbachovo in a third-class carriage, packed with working people, was very edifying and good, although I was too weak to take it in properly. It's now 8 o'clock, and we are in Optina.

29 October, Optina Monastery – Shamardino[83] Slept uneasily; in the morning Alyosha Sergeyenko came. I didn't understand why, and welcomed him cheerfully. But the news he brought was terrible. When Sofya Andreyevna read my letter she screamed and ran into the pond. Sasha and Vanya[84] ran after her and dragged her out. Andrey has come home. They guessed where I was and Sofya Andreyevna asked Andrey to find me at all costs. And now, the evening of the 29th, I'm awaiting

Andrey's arrival. A letter from Sasha. She advises me not to despair. She has written for a psychiatrist, and is waiting for Seryozha and Tanya to arrive. I was very depressed all day, and physically weak besides. Went for a walk, and yesterday I finished a note to *Speech* about the death penalty. Travelled to Shamardino. Mashenka made a very comforting and joyful impression on me, despite her story about 'the evil one', and so did dear Lizanka.[85] They both understand my situation and sympathize with it. On the journey I kept thinking as I was travelling about a way out of my situation and hers, and couldn't think of any, but there surely will be one, whether we want it or not, and it won't be the one we foresee. Yes, I should only think about not sinning. And what will be will be. That's not my business. I found a copy of the *Cycle of Reading* at Mashenka's, and just as I was reading the 28th, I was struck directly by the answer to my situation: this ordeal is necessary for me, it's beneficial for me. I'm going to bed now. Help me, Lord. A good letter from Chertkov.

30 October   I.I.A. Alive, but not entirely. I'm very weak and sleepy, and that's a bad sign.

Read something from Novosyolov's philosophical library.[86] Very interesting – on socialism. My article *On Socialism* has been lost.[87] A pity. No, not a pity. Sasha has come. I was very glad. But also depressed. Letters from my sons. The letter from Sergey is good, business-like, short and kind.[88] Went to rent a hut in Shamardino in the morning. Very tired. Wrote a letter to Sofya Andreyevna.[89]

31 October, Astapovo   They are all there at Shamardino. Sasha and I were afraid they would catch us up, and we set off.[90] Sasha caught us up at Kozelsk; we got on the train and set off. We had a good journey, but between 4 and 5 I began to shiver, then my temperature was 40° and we stopped at Astapovo. The kind stationmaster has given us two fine rooms.

3 November, Astapovo   Had a bad night. Lay for two days in a fever. Chertkov came on the 2nd. They say that Sofya Andreyevna has too. Seryozha came during the night, I was very moved. Today, the 3rd, Nikitin and Tanya came, then Goldenweiser and Ivan Ivanovich. So much for my plan. *Fais ce que dois, adv* . . . [Do what you must, come . . .].

And it's all for the good, for the others and above all for me.[91]

1903–1910

Diary for Myself Alone

1910, 29 July, Yasnaya Polyana   I'm beginning a new diary, a real diary for myself alone. Today there is one thing I must note: namely that if the suspicions of some of my friends are right, an attempt has now begun to gain her ends by means of affection. For several days now she has been kissing my hand, something that never happened before, and there are no scenes and no despair. May God and good people forgive me if I am mistaken. And I can easily be mistaken over kindness and love. I can love her completely sincerely, which I can't say about Lev. Andrey is simply one of those people about whom it's difficult to think that they have a divine soul (but he has, remember). I'll try not to get angry and to stand my ground, chiefly by keeping silent.

One shouldn't deprive millions of people of what is perhaps necessary for their souls.[1] I repeat 'perhaps'. But even if there is the slightest possibility that what I've written may be necessary for people's souls, then one shouldn't deprive them of this spiritual food so that Andrey can drink and indulge in debauchery and Lev can daub away[2] and . . . But never mind about them. Get on with your own things and don't condemn others . . . It's morning.

The day was just like the previous one: I felt unwell, but there was less unkindness in my heart. I'm waiting to see what happens, and that's bad.

Sofya Andreyevna is quite calm.

30 July   Chertkov has involved me in a struggle, and this struggle is both very depressing and very repugnant to me.[3] I'll try to wage it *with love* (it's terrible to say how far away I am from it).

In my present situation, what I probably need above all is *to do nothing and to say nothing*. Today I have clearly understood that I need only to avoid making my situation worse, and to remember clearly that I need *nothing, nothing at all*.

31 July   Spent an idle evening. The Lodyzhenskys[4] came, and I talked too much. Sofya Andreyevna couldn't sleep again, but she isn't angry. I'm waiting.

1 August   Slept well, but am still bored, sad, listless and painfully aware of the lack of love round about me and, alas, within me. Help me, Lord! Sasha is coughing again. Sofya Andreyevna has been telling Posha all the usual things. It's all alive in her: jealousy of Chertkov and fear for the property. It's very depressing. I can't stand Lev Lvovich. And he wants to settle here. What an ordeal! Letters in the morning. Wrote badly;

corrected one proof. I'm going to bed in a depressed state of mind. I'm ill.

2 August I.I.A. I've realized my mistake very, very clearly. I should have summoned all my heirs and announced my intentions, and not kept it secret. I've written this to Chertkov.[5] He was very upset. I rode to Kolpna. Sofya Andreyevna drove over to check up and keep a watch on me; she rummages about in my papers. She's just been questioning me about who brings the letters from Chertkov: 'You're carrying on a secret love correspondence.' I said I didn't want to talk and left, but I was gentle. Unhappy woman, I can't help pitying her. Wrote a letter to Galya.

3 August I go to bed with anguish in my heart, and wake up with the same anguish. I just can't overcome it. Went for a walk in the rain. Worked at home. Went riding with Goldenweiser. Felt depressed in his company for some reason. A letter from Chertkov. He's very upset. I said 'yes', and I've decided to wait and not undertake anything.[6] It's very good that I feel how worthless I am. In the evening an insane note from Sofya Andreyevna[7] and a demand that I read it. I glanced at it and gave it back. She came in and began to talk. I locked myself in, then ran away and sent Dušan to her. How will this end? The only thing is not to sin oneself. I'm going to bed. I.I.A.

4 August Nothing depressing happened today, but I feel depressed. Finished the proofs, but wrote nothing. Lost my temper with some schoolboys, and was wrong to do so; then welcomed a student and his wife and gave them a book. A great deal of fuss and bother. Went riding with Dušan to the Lodyzhenskys'. Posha is leaving and Korolenko is coming.

5 August My thoughts were a bit clearer. My renouncing Chertkov's company is shameful, embarrassing, comic and sad.[8] Yesterday morning she was very pitiable, and without any malice. I'm always so glad of this – it's so easy for me to pity and love her when she is suffering, and not making other people suffer.

6 August Today, as I lay in bed, I had a thought which, it seemed to me, was very important. I thought I would write it down later. And I forgot it, forgot it and couldn't remember it. I've just met Sofya Andreyevna, just here as I was writing this. She was walking quickly, looking terribly agitated. I became very sorry for her. I told them at home to watch her secretly and see where she went. But Sasha said that she was not walking about aimlessly, but was keeping a watch on me. I became less sorry for her. There is unkindness here, and I'm not yet able to remain indifferent to it – in the sense of loving what is unkind. I think about going away and leaving a letter, and I'm afraid to, although I think it would be better for her. I've just read my letters, taken up *Insanity* and put it down again. I've no desire to write and no strength. It's now after 12. This constant hiding and my fear for her are depressing.

7 August   A talk with Korolenko. An intelligent and good man, but completely dominated by the superstition of science. The work I have to do is very clear to me, and it will be a pity not to write it, but I don't seem to have the strength. Everything is confused, and I don't have any tenacity or steadfastness of purpose in one direction. Sofya Andreyevna is calmer, but there is the same unkindness towards everyone, the same irritability. Read about 'paranoia' in Korsakov.[9] It's as though it were copied from her. Sasha had had the book, and passages were underlined, probably by her. Korolenko said to me: 'What a fine person Alexandra Lvovna is.' There were tears of emotion in my throat, and I couldn't speak. When I recovered I said: 'I haven't the right to say so, she loves me too much.' Korolenko said: 'Well, but I have the right.'

It's still just as difficult for me with Lev, but, thank God, I have no unkind feelings.

8 August   Got up early. Many, many thoughts, but all scattered. Well, never mind. I pray and pray: help me! And I cannot, I cannot help wishing and waiting for death with joy. My separation from Chertkov is more and more shameful. I'm obviously to blame.[10] [. . .]

The same thing again with Sofya Andreyevna. She wants Chertkov to come. Again she couldn't sleep until 7 in the morning. [. . .]

My memory has gone, quite gone, and the astonishing thing is, I've not only not lost anything, but have actually gained a tremendous amount – in clarity and strength of *consciousness*. I even think that the one is always at the expense of the other.

9 August   I'm taking a more and more serious attitude to life. Agitation once again. Talks with Ferre and Sasha.[11] Sasha is harsh. Lyova is a great and difficult ordeal.

10 August   Everything is just as depressing, and I'm unwell. It's good to feel one is to blame, and I have this feeling. [. . .]

11 August   Health worse and worse. Sofya Andreyevna is calm, but just as alien. Letters. Answered two. It's depressing with everyone. I can't help wishing for death. A long letter from Chertkov describing everything that has happened so far. It was very sad and depressing to read and to recall. He is absolutely right and I feel myself to blame towards him. Posha was wrong. I'll write to them both. All that I'm writing here.

12 August Decided yesterday to tell Tanya everything.[12] Since this morning I've felt a depressing, unkind feeling towards her, towards Sofya Andreyevna. And I must forgive and pity her, but I can't as yet.

Told Tanya. She is glad and agrees. Chertkov was very pleased with my letter according to Sasha. I didn't go out all day. In the evening Gay talked well about Switzerland. Sofya Andreyevna is very agitated, and always in this condition – she is obviously ill – I feel very sorry for her. I'm going to bed.

13 August Everything just the same, and her condition is just as depressing and dangerous. A good letter from Chertkov – telling me not to go and say goodbye if it might prevent my departure.[13] Tanechka is nice and sweet.

14 August Still worse and worse. She didn't sleep last night. In the morning she jumped out of bed. 'Who are you talking to?' Then she spoke about something terrible: sexual excitation. A dreadful thing to say [3 words crossed out].

It's terrible, but thank God, she's to be pitied and I can pity her. I'll put up with it. God help me. She has tormented everyone, and herself most of all. She's going with us. Apparently she's turning Varya[14] out of the house. Sasha is distressed. I'm going to bed.

15 August On the journey to Kochety I thought that if these disturbances and demands began again I'd go away with Sasha. And I said so. That's what I thought on the journey. Now I don't think so. We arrived peacefully, but in the evening I took my notebook from Sasha and she saw me. 'What's that?' 'My diary. Sasha is copying from it.'

16 August This morning she hadn't slept again. She brought me a note saying that Sasha was copying out my accusations against her from my diary to give to Chertkov. Before dinner I tried to console her by telling her the truth, that Sasha was only copying out isolated thoughts, and not my impressions of life. She wants to be consoled, and is much to be pitied. [. . .]

17 August A good day today. Sonya is quite well. It was good, too, in that I felt anguish. And my anguish was expressed in prayer and consciousness.

18 August Sofya Andreyevna, having learned that Chertkov has been given permission to live at Telyatinki, was reduced to a state of morbidity.

'I'll kill him.' I begged her not to talk, and remained silent. And this seemed to have a good effect. Something is going to happen. Help me, God, to be with Thee and to do Thy will. And what happens will not be my affair. Often, no not often but sometimes, I am in this state of mind, and how good it is then!

19 August Sofya Andreyevna has been begging me since morning to promise what I promised before and not to have photographs taken. I agreed, and was wrong to do so. A good letter from Chertkov. He is right in what he says about the methods which have the best effect on sick people.[15] At dinner I spoke inopportunely about Arago *tout court* [quite simply].[16] And I was ashamed. And ashamed that I was ashamed.

20 August Had a good talk with the watchman. It was bad that I told him about my situation. Went riding, and the sight of this seignorial domain so torments me that I'm thinking of running away and hiding.

Today I thought as I recalled my marriage that there was something fateful about it. I was never even in love. But I couldn't help getting married.

21 August Got up late. Feel fresher. Sofya Andreyevna is just the same. She told Tanya that she hadn't slept all night because she had seen a photograph of Chertkov. The situation is threatening. I want to speak, I want to speak, i.e. to write.

22 August A letter from Rossolimo,[17] a remarkably stupid one about Sofya Andreyevna's condition, and a very good letter from B.[18]

I'm behaving quite well.

23 and 24 August I'm reviving a little. Sofya Andreyevna, poor woman, suffers incessantly, and I feel the impossibility of helping her. I feel the sinfulness of my own exclusive attachment to my daughters.

25 August Varvara Mikhaylovna writes about the gossip at Zvegint-seva's.[19] This irritates Sasha. It's all the same to me, thank God, but it impairs my feelings towards *her*. It shouldn't do. Oh, if only I could be gentle, but firm.

26 August Sofya Andreyevna spoke heatedly with Tanya last night. She is completely hopeless, her thinking is so inconsistent. I'm glad that I kept silent in response to her provocations and complaints. Thank God, I haven't the least bad feeling.

27 August She is terribly pitiable and difficult. This evening she began to talk about the photographs, from her own morbid point of view obviously. I tried to keep out of it all. And I went away.

28 August Things are more and more difficult with Sofya Andreyevna. It isn't love, but a demand for love which is near to hatred and is turning into hatred.

Yes, egoism is madness. She used to be saved by the children – an animal love, but nevertheless an unselfish one. But when that was over, all that was left was terrible egoism. And egoism is the most abnormal condition – madness.

I've just spoken with Sasha and Mikhail Sergeyevich, and both Dušan and Sasha refuse to recognize that it is an illness. And they are wrong.

29 and 30 August Yesterday morning was terrible, for no reason at all. She went into the garden and lay there. Then she calmed down. We had a good talk. As she left she touchingly begged forgiveness. Today, the 30th, I'm unwell. Mavor. Sasha telegraphed that it's all right.[20] What will happen?

31 August, 1 September I wrote Sonya a letter which flowed from the heart.

Today – *2 September* – I received a very bad letter from her. The same suspicions, the same malice, the same demand for love, which would be comic if it wasn't so terrible and agonizing for me. Today in the *Cycle of Reading* – Schopenhauer: 'As the attempt to force people to love evokes hatred, so . . .'

3, 4 September Sasha arrived. She brought bad news. Everything is just the same. Sofya Andreyevna writes to say she will come. She is burning photographs and holding a prayer service in the house.[21] When I'm alone I'm ready to be firm with her and think I can be, but when I'm with her I weaken. I'll try to remember that she is ill.

Today, the 4th, I felt melancholy: I wanted to die and still do.

5, 6, 7, 8 September Sofya Andreyevna arrived. She was very talkative, but at first there was nothing depressing about it, but yesterday it began again, the hints, the searching for excuses to condemn. Very depressing. This morning she ran in to tell me some vile thing about Zosya. I'm bearing up, and will bear up as much as I can, and pity and love her. God help me.

8, 9, 10 September Yesterday, the 9th, she was in hysterics all day; she ate nothing and wept. She was very pitiable. But she won't accept any attempts at persuasion or arguments. I said one or two things, and, thank God, without any ill feeling, and she took them in the usual way, without understanding them. I was unwell myself yesterday – gloomy and despondent. She received a letter from Chertkov and answered it. A letter from Goldenweiser with extracts from V.M.'s diary which horrified me.[22]

Today, the 10th; still the same. She is eating nothing. I went in. Immediately there were reproaches, and about Sasha too, saying she ought to go to the Crimea. I thought in the morning that I couldn't endure it, and would have to leave her. There is no life with her. Only torture. As I said to her: 'My misfortune is that I can't be different.'

11 September Towards evening she began making scenes – running into the garden, tears, screams. It even got to the stage that when I went out after her into the garden she screamed: 'He's a beast, a murderer. I can't bear to see him', and ran off to hire a cart and go away at once. And so it was the whole evening. But when I lost control of myself and told her *son fait* [what I thought of her], she suddenly became well again, and she is still well today, the 11th. It's impossible to talk to her because, first of all, neither logic nor truth are binding on her; nor is the truthful communication of the words which are said to her, or the ones she says herself. I'm very close to running away. My health is not good.

12 September Sofya Andreyevna has left after terrible scenes. I'm gradually becoming calmer.

16–17 September But the letters from Yasnaya are terrible. What is depressing is that among her crazy ideas is one to make me out as feeble-minded, and therefore to render my will, if it exists, invalid. Apart from that there are all the usual stories about me and avowals of hatred of me. I've received a letter from Chertkov confirming everyone's advice to remain firm and supporting my decision. I don't know whether I can hold out.

It's now the night of the 17th.

I want to return to Yasnaya on the 22nd.

22 September, morning I'm going to Yasnaya and I'm terrified at the thought of what awaits me. Only *fais ce que dois* . . . [do what you must. . .]. But the main thing is to remain silent and remember that she has a soul – that God is in her.

2

24 September, Yasnaya Polyana   I've lost the little diary.[23] I'm writing in this one. The day began calmly. But at lunch they began to talk about *The Wisdom of Children*, and the fact that Chertkov, the collector,[24] had amassed a lot of things. What would he do with the manuscripts after my death? I begged her rather heatedly to leave me in peace. Things seemed all right. But after dinner she began to reproach me and say that I shouted at her and that I ought to pity her. I remained silent. She went to her room and it's now after 10 o'clock and she hasn't come out, and I'm depressed. A letter from Chertkov with reproaches and accusations. They are tearing me to pieces. I sometimes think I should go away from them all. It turns out she had been asleep, and she came out looking calm. I went to bed after 12.

25 September   Woke up early, wrote a letter to Chertkov.[25] I hope he will take it the way I ask. I'm now getting dressed. Yes, all my business is with God, and I must be alone. A request again to stand for a photograph in the pose of a loving husband and wife. I agreed, and was ashamed all the time.[26] Sasha was terribly angry. It was painful for me. In the evening I called her and said: 'I don't need your stenography, but I need your love.' And we kissed each other, and both had a good cry.

26 September   Scenes again because I had hung up the pictures where they were before. I began to say that it was impossible to go on living like this. And she understood. Dušan said that she fired a child's pistol in order to frighten me. I wasn't frightened and didn't go to her room. And really, it's better. But it's very, very difficult. Help me, Lord.

27 September   How comic is the contradiction in which I live whereby, without false modesty, I am conceiving and giving expression to very important and significant ideas, and at the same time am involved in a woman's caprices and devoting a great part of my time to the struggle against them.

In the matter of moral self-improvement I feel myself a complete child, a pupil, and a bad pupil, not very diligent.

Yesterday there was a terrible scene with Sasha when she came back. She screamed at Marya Alexandrovna. Sasha left today for Telyatinki. And she [Sofya Andreyevna] is very calm as if nothing had happened. She showed me the toy pistol, and fired it, and lied. Today she drove after me on my walk, probably spying on me. I'm sorry for her, but it's difficult. Help me, Lord.

28 September It's very depressing. These expressions of love, this talkativeness and constant interference. It's possible, I know it's possible, to love all the same. But I can't, I'm unwell.

29 September Sasha wants to go on living for a while away from home. I fear for her. Sofya Andreyevna is better. Sometimes false shame for my weakness comes over me and sometimes, as today, I rejoice in this weakness.

Today for the first time I saw the possibility of winning her over by kindness – by love. Oh, if only I could . . .

30 September Today everything is just the same. She talks a lot for the sake of talking and doesn't listen. There were some depressing moments today because of my weakness: I saw unpleasant and depressing things where they don't exist and can't exist for a true life.

1 October It's terribly depressing, my unkind feeling for her, which I can't overcome when this talking begins – talking without end and without meaning or purpose. Chertkov's article on the soul and God is, I fear, too clever by half.[27] It gladdens me that all truly original religious people have one and the same thing in common. Antoine le Guérisseur too.[28]

2 October In the morning her first words were about her own health, then reproaches and endless talking, and interruptions to the conversation. And I'm not well. I can't overcome bad and unkind feelings. Today I felt keenly the need for literary work and I can see the impossibility of devoting myself to it because of her, my obsessive feelings about her and my inner struggle. Of course this struggle and the possibility of victory in this struggle are more important than all possible works of art.

3

5 October 1910 Handed over the brochures and am beginning something new today. And it seems necessary to begin something new: on the 3rd, after my nap before dinner, I lost consciousness. They undressed me, put me to bed and gave me an enema, and I said something but don't remember anything. I woke up and came round at about 11. Headache and weakness. All day yesterday I lay in a fever, with a headache; ate nothing and felt the same weakness. It was the same at night too. It's now 7 o'clock in the morning, and my head still aches, and my liver and my legs, and I'm weak, but better. The main thing about my illness is that it reconciled Sasha and Sofya Andreyevna. Sasha especially was good. Varya has come. We shall see. I'm struggling against my unkind feelings towards her and can't forget these three months of torture for all those near to me and for myself. But I'll overcome it. Didn't sleep during the night, and while I can't say I thought, ideas wandered through my head.

7 October   Yesterday was 6 October. I was weak and gloomy. Everything was depressing and unpleasant. A letter from Chertkov. He thinks it's no use. She is making an effort and has asked him to come here.[29] Today Tanya went to the Chertkovs'. Galya is very irritated. Chertkov decided to come at 8, and it's now ten minutes to. Sofya Andreyevna asked me not to kiss him. How disgusting. She had a hysterical fit.

Today is the 8th. I told her all I considered necessary. She objected and I grew irritated. And that was bad. But perhaps something will survive all the same. It's true that it's all a question of my not behaving badly myself; but I'm also sincerely sorry for her – not always, but most of the time. I'm going to bed, having spent the day better.

9 October   She is calm, but contrives to talk about herself. I read about hysteria. Everyone is to blame except her. I didn't go to the Chertkovs' and I won't go. Tranquillity is the most valuable thing of all. I feel in a stern and serious mood.

10 October   It's quiet, but everything is unnatural and frightening. There's no tranquillity.

11 October   This morning she was saying that I'd had a secret meeting with Chertkov yesterday. She hadn't slept all night. But, thank goodness, she is struggling with herself. I behaved well and remained silent. Whatever happens she interprets as confirmation of her mania – never mind . . .

12 October   More talking this morning and a scene. It seems someone told her about some will of mine bequeathing my diaries to Chertkov. I remained silent. An empty day; I couldn't work well. In the evening the same talk again. Hints and interrogations.

13 October   It turns out that she found my little diary and took it away. She knows about some will leaving something to someone – obviously to do with my works. What torture she suffers over their money value – and she's afraid I'll interfere with her edition. Indeed she's afraid of everything, poor thing.

14 October   A letter reproaching me for some paper about royalties,[30] as if the money question was all that was important; still that's better – it's clearer; but when she speaks in exaggerated tones about her love for me, and kneels down and kisses my hands, I find it very depressing. I still can't definitely declare that I'll go to the Chertkovs'.

15 October   There was a clash with Sasha and general commotion, but it was tolerable.

16 October   Today it was decided.

I wanted to go to Tanya's, but I'm hesitating. A hysterical fit, a nasty one.

The fact of the matter is that she proposed that I should go to the Chertkovs' and begged me to do so, but today, when I said I would go, she began to rave. It's very, very difficult. Help me, God. I said I would make no promises, and I'm not making any, but I'll do all I can not to anger her. I'll hardly be able to make my departure tomorrow. But I must. Yes, it's an ordeal, and my task is not to do anything unkind. Help me, God.

17 October   Weak. Sofya Andreyevna is better and seems to be repentant, but there's a hysterical exaggeration about that too. She kisses my hands. She's very agitated and talks incessantly. I feel well morally. I remember who I am. Read Sri Sankara. The basic metaphysical idea about the essence of life is good, but the teaching as a whole is a muddle, worse than mine.

18 October   Still the same depressing relations – fear and alienation. Nothing happened today. She began to talk about faith this evening. She simply doesn't understand what faith is.

19 October   A very depressing conversation during the night. I took it badly. Sasha talked of a sale for a million.[31] We'll see what happens. Perhaps it's for the best. If only I could appear before the highest judge and earn his approval.

20 October   There is nothing bad to write down. That's bad. I'll only write one thing: Sasha is a joy to me, and she is too sweet and dear to me.

21 October   I'm bearing my ordeal with great difficulty. I keep remembering Novikov's words: 'When I used the whip she was much better', and Ivan's 'It's our custom to use the reins', and am displeased with myself. During the night I thought about going away. Sasha talked a lot with her, but I have difficulty in restraining my unkind feelings.

22 October   There's nothing hostile on her part, but this pretence on both sides depresses me. A letter to me from Chertkov, with a letter to Dosev and the statement.[32] Everything is very good, but I'm not pleased about the violation of the secrecy of my diary. Dunayev talked well. It's terrible what he told me of what she said to him and to Marya Nikolayevna.

23 October   The pretence on both sides is just as depressing as ever; I try to be natural, but it doesn't succeed. I can't stop thinking about Novikov. When I went for a ride, Sofya Andreyevna set off after me on foot, to see whether I had gone to Chertkov's. I'm ashamed to admit my stupidity even in my diary. Yesterday I began doing gymnastics – the old fool wants to get younger – and pulled a cupboard over on myself and hurt myself for nothing. There's an eighty-two-year-old fool for you.

24 October   Sasha cried because she had quarrelled with Tanya. I did too. It's very depressing; the same tension and unnaturalness.

25 October   Still the same feeling of depression. Suspicions, spying, and the sinful desire on my part that she should give me an excuse to go away. That's how bad I am. I think of going away, and then I think of her situation, and I feel sorry and I can't do it. She asked me for a letter of mine to Galya Chertkova.

26 October   I'm still more and more oppressed by this life. Marya Alexandrovna tells me not to go away, and my conscience won't let me either. I must put up with her, put up with her without changing my outward situation, but working on my inner one. Help me, Lord.

[27 October] 25 October   Dreamed all night about my painful struggle with her. I would wake up, drop off to sleep, and it would start again. Sasha told me about what was said to Varvara Mikhaylovna. I'm both sorry for her and unbearably disgusted.

26 October   Nothing special happened. Only my feeling of shame increased, and the need to take some step.

28 October, Optina Monastery   During the night of the 27–28 came the impetus which made me take this step. And here I am at Optina on the evening of the 28th. Sent Sasha a letter and a telegram.[33]

29 October   Sergeyenko arrived. Everything is the same; worse even. If only I don't sin. And don't bear malice. I don't at present.

NOTES

1847

1 Of Kazan University.

2 Catherine the Great's *Instruction to the Commission for the Composition of a Plan for a New Code of Laws*, known for short as the *Nakaz (Instruction)*, was first published in 1767. Catherine borrowed many of her ideas on enlightened despotism and on crime and punishment from Montesquieu and Beccaria, and Tolstoy had been set the task by his professor of civil law at Kazan University of comparing the *Nakaz* with Montesquieu's *De l'esprit des lois*. His detailed comments have been omitted, but his general conclusions are summarized on 26 March.

3 In the omitted passages.

4 Oliver Goldsmith's novel is not included in the list of books which Tolstoy later claimed to have made an impression on him at different periods of his life.

5 Justinian's Code of Laws (*Corpus juris civilis*).

6 Tolstoy had already requested permission to withdraw from the university, and left Kazan for Yasnaya Polyana on 23 April.

7 See pp. 7–11. These rules were written down in a separate notebook between March and May.

8 Tolstoy reached Yasnaya Polyana on 1 May.

1850

1 Tolstoy moved to Moscow from Yasnaya Polyana on 5 December.

2 V. I. Ogaryov, the son of I. M. Ogaryov, a near neighbour and close friend of Tolstoy's father.

3 The story was never finished and has not survived.

4 The Council held the mortgage of the Tolstoys' estate at the time.

5 D. A. Dyakov got to know Tolstoy in Kazan, and according to Tolstoy their friendship provided him with material for his description of the friendship between Nikolenka Irtenev and Nekhlyudov in *Youth*.

6 Both distant relatives of Tolstoy's; the former, Princess A. P. Gorchakova, was at the time a nun in the Zachatyevsky convent in Moscow.

7 S. P. Koloshin, another distant relative of Tolstoy's and a minor author and editor.

8 Prince A. I. Gorchakov, an infantry general under whom Tolstoy's father served, and also distantly related to the Tolstoy family.

1851

1 The estate of Tolstoy's brother-in-law, V. P. Tolstoy, some fifty miles from Yasnaya Polyana.

2 Tolstoy's eldest brother Nikolay, at the time on leave from the army, in which he served for most of his adult life. He died of consumption in the south of France at the age of thirty-seven (*Letters*, I, 12).

3 A card game similar to whist without trumps.

4 Countess Y. M. Tolstaya, a gipsy, and the widow of Tolstoy's eccentric uncle Count F. I. Tolstoy, 'the American', portrayed by him in *Two Hussars*.

5 Prince S. D. Gorchakov, a colonel who had fought in the war of 1812, and another distant relative of Tolstoy's.

6 Prince A. I. Gorchakov (1850, Note 8).

7 The first mention of *Childhood*. The last word is indecipherable in the manuscript, and the reading 'day' has been preferred to a possible alternative reading 'childhood'.

8 Tolstoy's name for the course of lectures on law which had been given at Kazan University and which he was studying with a view to taking his master's examination as an external student.

9 K. A. Nevolin's *Encyclopaedia of Jurisprudence*.

10 A Frenchman who owned a gymnasium in Moscow. Tolstoy took gymnastics and fencing lessons from him.

11 An idea borrowed from Benjamin Franklin.

12 A reference to his income and expenditure itemized in the previous day's untranslated entry.

13 From Lamartine and other authors whom he was reading at the time. See entry for March–May, 1851, p. 22.

14 Tatyana Alexandrovna Yergolskaya, a relative of the Tolstoy family who assumed responsibility for the Tolstoy children after their father's death, although not their legal guardian, and continued to live at Yasnaya Polyana after Tolstoy's marriage until her death in 1874 (*Letters*, I, 2). He wrote about her later in his *Memoirs*.

15 The first reference to Tolstoy's unfinished *A History of Yesterday*, which he wrote in 1851.

16 The estate of Tolstoy's brother Sergey, some twenty-five miles from Yasnaya Polyana, where Tolstoy had recently returned from Moscow for the summer.

17 The word 'conscience' is surprising here. There is an error in the manuscript version of the sentence, and this may have affected the sense of the passage.

18 Tolstoy's brother, brother-in-law and sister.

19 He decided to retire from his minor official post with the Tula provincial administration before leaving for the south of Russia.

20 A village which Tolstoy had received as part of his share of the family estates.

21 In April 1851 Tolstoy left for the Caucasus with his brother Nikolay, who was returning to his army unit. They stopped briefly in Moscow and Kazan, and in the second half of May travelled via Saratov and Astrakhan to the North Caucasus.

22 The village on the left bank of the Terek where Nikolay Tolstoy's battery was stationed. It is described in *The Cossacks* under the name of *Novomlinskaya stanitsa* (*stanitsa* is a large Cossack village, cf. *aul* – a small mountain village). The name of the village is printed as Starogladovskaya in the *Letters* – both spellings occur.

23 A slip of the pen for 30 May.

24 This entry for March–May is written in a separate notebook which contains quotations from Lamartine's novel *Geneviève*, his *Histoire des Girondins*, his poem *Jocelyn* and Bernardin de Saint-Pierre's *Paul et Virginie*, together with Tolstoy's reflections on what he had been reading.

25 In his *Testament*, Gogol writes of his 'farewell tale' which was 'sung from his soul' – presumably a reference to the second part of *Dead Souls*.

26 A story by D. V. Grigorovich which, Tolstoy claimed, made a very great impression on him (*Letters*, II, 485).

27 A Chechen fortified village not far from the military garrison town of Groznaya (or Groznoye) in the North East Caucasus.

28 Z. M. Molostvova, whom Tolstoy met while a student in Kazan and again on his way to the Caucasus in 1851. He refers to her in a letter of 1903 as one of his strongest childhood loves (*Letters*, II, 634).

29 Prince M. S. Vorontsov, Governor-General of the Caucasus and Commander-in-Chief of the Caucasian Army.

30 F. G. Knoring, a platoon commander of No. 5 battery. For Tolstoy's description of him see pp. 29–30.

31 Tolstoy was translating Sterne's *A Sentimental Journey*.

32 This subject is taken up again in Chapter I of *The Raid*.

33 As a volunteer in an action against the mountain tribes under Prince Baryatinsky, who later succeeded Prince Vorontsov as Governor-General of the Caucasus and Commander-in-Chief of the Caucasian Army. Tolstoy portrayed him as the general commanding the detachment in *The Raid*, and expressed his fears that Baryatinsky might recognize himself in the story.

34 *Four Periods of Growth* – the first version of the future trilogy *Childhood, Boyhood and Youth*.

35 More usually spelt Groznaya.

36 George Sand's novel.

37 The somewhat discursive story about Luka Sekhin, a young Cossack from Starogladkovskaya, whom Tolstoy used to some extent as a model for Lukashka in *The Cossacks*, has been omitted.

38 Sado Miserbiyev, a Chechen serving in the Russian army. He is portrayed as the *kunak* of Hadji Murat in Tolstoy's story of that name.

39 Yepifan Sekhin, Luka's uncle, and the prototype of Yeroshka in *The Cossacks*.

40 Tolstoy went to Tiflis with his brother on 1 November in order to join the

regular army, and stayed until 12 January 1852.

41 The two Musin-Pushkin brothers, distant relatives of Tolstoy's, who appear as the Ivin brothers in *Childhood*. Most of the other men mentioned in this paragraph were university friends of Tolstoy's. Gautier inherited his father's French bookshop in Moscow. Islavin was the son of the Tula landowner Islenyev who is portrayed in *Childhood, Boyhood* and *Youth* as the father of Nikolenka. For Dyakov see 1850, Note 5.

42 I. V. Suvorov, Tolstoy's manservant.

43 About the dead body of his brother Dmitry, who was to die of consumption in 1856. Certain of his features were ascribed to Dmitry Nekhlyudov in *Youth*, and the death-bed scene of Nikolay Levin in *Anna Karenina* has many parallels with the death of Dmitry.

1852

1 A village on the left bank of the Terek to the north of Groznaya.

2 A village on the left bank of the Sunzha to the east of Groznaya.

3 Actions in which Tolstoy narrowly escaped being hit by a shell.

4 Princess L. I. Volkonskaya, portrayed by Tolstoy as the heroine of *A History of Yesterday* and an important source for the character of Liza Bolkonskaya in *War and Peace* (*Letters, I*, 194).

5 The entries for this period which have been included here were written on separate sheets of paper and did not form part of Tolstoy's main dairy.

6 Of *Four Periods of Growth*, i.e. *Childhood*.

7 *Histoire de la Révolution française*.

8 An answer required by the Tula provincial administration in connection with Tolstoy's resignation from the minor post he held, which had to be ratified before he could enlist in the regular army.

9 An ensign in No. 4 battery.

10 Captain Khilkovsky, second in command to Alexeyev and the prototype of Captain Khlopov in Tolstoy's *The Raid*.

11 The second version of *Childhood*.

12 Possibly some thoughts on music in an article in *Notes of the Fatherland* on a journey by Dumas to Tunis, Morocco and Algiers.

13 When Tolstoy spent much time practising the piano and writing about methods of studying music.

14 Of *Childhood* – Chapters 16 ff. after Nikolenka's move to Moscow.

15 N. I. Buyemsky, an ensign in No. 6 battery who is portrayed as Alanin in *The Raid*.

16 Lieutenant-Colonel N. P. Alexeyev, commander of No. 4 battery, 20th artillery brigade, in which Tolstoy's brother was serving as a regular officer and Tolstoy as a volunteer.

17 Of *Childhood* – before Nikolenka moved from the country to the town.

18 The first mention of what was to become *The Raid*.

19 A town on the Terek not far from the Caspian Sea. Tolstoy went there to consult a doctor about suspected venereal disease.

20 A slightly inaccurate quotation (which I have corrected) from the chapter entitled 'The Conquest' in *A Sentimental Journey*.

21 David Hume's history, which Tolstoy read in a French translation.

22 Eugène Sue's novel *Le Juif errant*.

23 It is not certain what book or article Tolstoy read about Yermak, the 'conqueror of Siberia' in the sixteenth century.

24 Oreshinka or Oreshevka, a village to the north east of Kizlyar, close to the Caspian Sea.

25 On the Caspian Sea.

26 The only thoughts occur in draft versions of *The Novel of a Russian Landowner*.

27 A reference to the chapters in *Tristram Shandy* on the shapes and significance of noses.

28 *The Novel of a Russian Landowner* (eventually published as *A Landowner's Morning*).

29 The original title of *The Raid*.

30 Chapter 27 of *Childhood*.

31 *Letters*, I, 25.

32 See the first chapter of *The Raid*.

33 The fourth version of *Childhood*.

34 A seven-volume work by the Swiss poet, historian and freemason J. H. D. Zschokke.

35 Rousseau's *Confessions* made an 'enormous impression' on Tolstoy as a young man.

36 The fourth book of Rousseau's *Émile*.

37 Rousseau's novel.

38 *Letters*, I, 30. Tolstoy submitted the manuscript of *Childhood* to Nekrasov, the editor of *The Contemporary*, together with this letter.

39 A spa near Pyatigorsk.

40 The first drafts of *The Raid* contained satirical portraits of the general and some of the officers.

41 *The Novel of a Russian Landowner*. Tolstoy's purpose, as he later declared, was to show how impossible it was for an educated landowner of his time to live a good life as long as serfdom existed.

42 A young doctor in Zheleznovodsk.

43 Plato's *Politicus*, which Tolstoy read in French.

44 From Nekrasov, with flattering remarks about *Childhood* (*Letters*, I, 31, footnote).

45 Tolstoy evidently read Dickens' novel in *The Contemporary*, which serialized it in Russian translation during the course of 1851.

46 By A. I. Mikhaylovsky-Danilevsky. It was an important source book for *War and Peace*.

47 The expression 'condition of beauty' recurs in a moral context in the entry for 19 October 1852.

48 Tolstoy was considering resigning from the army, but was waiting to see whether the authorities accepted Brimmer's recommendations that he be promoted to the rank of officer.

49 The only sketch that has survived is his *A Journey to Mamakay Yurt*.
50 By the French historian J. F. Michaud.
51 See Tolstoy's letter to Nekrasov of 18 November 1852 (*Letters*, I, 33) expressing his great displeasure at the cuts and alterations in the published version of *Childhood*.
52 A very generous payment for a new author.
53 *The Raid.*
54 *Four Periods of Growth.*
55 *The Raid.*
56 The few poems that have survived from the period 1852–4 include one called *To a Trap* – about a mouse in love whose passion gets the better of him and who is caught in a mouse-trap!

1853

1 A village some twenty miles from Groznaya.
2 In a campaign against Shamil which lasted until the middle of March.
3 A word is missing in the manuscript.
4 He was recommended for promotion as a result.
5 A George cross for which he had been recommended for his part in the winter campaign of 1852 and which he had not received because his papers releasing him from his official post in Tula had not arrived in time. Tolstoy was arrested on Olifer's orders for not turning up for guard duty during an inspection.
6 A rich Easter shortcake.
7 An open-air game in which two teams, one in each camp, try to capture each other.
8 *Christmas Night*, a story about the dissipated life of Moscow youth, left unfinished.
9 His horse.
10 The incident has been fully described in Poltoratsky's *Memoirs*, and Tolstoy may have drawn on it when writing *A Captive in the Caucasus*.
11 Charles Aubrey, the hero of Samuel Warren's novel *Ten Thousand a Year* (1839), which appeared in Russian translation in *Notes of the Fatherland* in 1852 entitled *Litigation*. Nestor's speech in Act I, Scene iii of *Troilus and Cressida* ('In the reproof of chance Lies the true proof of men . . .') is paraphrased by Aubrey.
12 Probably Alyoshka (Alexey Orekhov), Tolstoy's man-servant.
13 From *Childhood*.
14 An early title of what later became *The Wood-felling*.
15 Of *Boyhood*.
16 Chapters 3 and 2 respectively of *Boyhood*.
17 Probably the novel by Paul de Kock.
18 To continue *The Novel of a Russian Landowner* and write *The Wood-felling*.
19 *The Fugitive* (the original title of *The Cossacks*).
20 The story is entitled *Reminiscences of a Billiard Marker* in the *Letters*. Tolstoy

wrote the story in a few days and sent it to Nekrasov on 17 September.

21 By Isaac Disraeli. Essays by him were published in translation in *The Contemporary* in 1853.

22 Chapter 18 of *Boyhood*.

23 M. S. Zhukova (1804–55), a minor woman author whose story *Nadenka* was published in *The Contemporary* in 1853.

24 A review of volumes 4 and 5 of D. A. Milyutin's five-volume work *A History of the War between Russia and France in the Reign of Paul I in 1799*.

25 Grigorovich's novel *Fishermen* was published in *The Contemporary* in 1853.

26 A stronghold some twenty-five miles south of Starogladkovskaya.

27 An abridged and unsatisfactory translation in *The Contemporary* of Karoline von Wolzogen's *Schillers Leben*.

28 Probably not an 'English' lady; it is possible that Tolstoy was referring to Mrs Beecher Stowe, whose book *Uncle Tom's Cabin* had just been published in *The Contemporary*.

29 In the foreword of his twelve-volume *History of the Russian State* Karamzin attempted to define his views on history and its purpose.

30 A reference to his promotion to officer rank and his impending posting to the Danube Army.

31 One of the original titles of *The Wood-felling*.

32 *The Cossacks*, which was originally begun in verse form.

33 Nothing came of this idea.

34 The original title of *Reduced to the Ranks* (later published as *Meeting a Moscow Acquaintance in the Detachment*).

35 One of the original titles of *The Wood-felling*.

36 A story abounding in rare words and neologisms. Pisemsky is best known for his gloomy novel *A Thousand Souls*.

37 N. G. Ustryalov's *Russian History*.

38 The foreword to Novikov's monthly journal was in fact written by Novikov and not Karamzin.

1854

1 A small town on the Danube in Romania; at the time the focal point of military operations between the Turkish and Russian armies.

2 To No. 4 battery of the 12th artillery brigade of the Danube Army. This brigade was part of General Liprandi's detachment, which was besieging the Turkish fortified positions at Kalafat.

3 A village on the left bank of the Terek north east of Groznaya, where Tolstoy stopped on his journey back to Yasnaya Polyana.

4 The story based on that incident was written two years later.

5 To the rank of ensign for distinguished services in the campaign against the mountain tribesmen.

6 Tolstoy arrived in Bucharest on 12 March to await a posting.

7 The commander of No. 3 battery of the artillery brigade to which Tolstoy was attached, and who had occasion to reprimand Tolstoy for prolonging

his stay in Bucharest – hence the reference to 'coming to terms with the battery commander'.

8 After a short spell of service with the artillery brigade Tolstoy was transferred on 13 April to the staff of General Serzhputovsky, Commander of the Artillery of the Danube Army.

9 A Turkish stronghold on the right bank of the Danube which had been besieged by the Russians for several weeks.

10 The word has been deleted but is not difficult to guess.

11 A village to the north east of Bucharest where the Russian troops withdrew to after raising the siege of Silistria.

12 One of the two nephews of the Commander-in-Chief of the Danube Army.

13 General Serzhputovsky.

14 One of a small group of officers, including Tolstoy, who later planned to found a society and a journal to promote the spread of education among the troops. See Note 36.

15 An attempt by the Turks to force a crossing of the Danube at Giurgevo, on the left bank, was successfully resisted by the Russians.

16 *Letters*, I. 39.

17 Referred to as 'a witty writer' in a draft version of *Childhood*, the French novelist is also mentioned in *Boyhood* and *After the Ball*.

18 Probably Dumas père's *Histoire de la vie politique et privée de Louis Philippe*, 1852.

19 The second of the *Songs of the Western Slavs*.

20 To the Crimean Army.

21 *Masquerade*.

22 It was serialized in translation in *The Contemporary* in 1854.

23 Two soldiers portrayed in *The Wood-felling*.

24 A drama by Schiller. Tolstoy mistakenly wrote *Viesko*.

25 Sineşti is to the north-east of Bucharest; Cureşti (see entry for 24 July) has not been identified and is probably an error on Tolstoy's part.

26 Evidently a young soldier who came to Tolstoy for advice on literature; reference is made elsewhere to their reading stories together.

27 For a transfer to the Crimea.

28 A town in Moldavia on the borders of Wallachia.

29 A town about fifteen miles north east of Fokşaný.

30 By Ostrovsky. He also read *Among Friends One Always Comes to Terms*.

31 Evidently a mistake for Vaslui, a town in Moldavia.

32 These initials have not been deciphered.

33 Tolstoy reached Kishinyov on 9 September.

34 A reference to the landing of English, French and Turkish forces near Eupatoria in the Crimea on 2 September.

35 Offprints of his stories.

36 Tolstoy and Friede were at first reluctant to give up the plan to found a society (see Note 14), but eventually agreed to collaborate with the other five in launching a journal. Tolstoy wrote an article for a specimen number, but the authorities refused permission for the journal to be published.

37 Nicholas I's sons, who had been sent to 'raise the morale' of the army.
38 Tolstoy left Kishinyov at the end of October and travelled to Sevastopol via Odessa, Nikolayev and Perekop.
39 A portrait of the Tsar set in diamonds; the highest possible award.
40 A passage here has been erased from the manuscript.
41 A reference to a rumour that the Commander-in-Chief Prince Menshikov had been guilty of treachery at the Battle of Inkerman.
42 A literal translation of an eight-line poem in two rhymed stanzas.
43 A Tartar village some four miles from Simferopol.
44 A conjectured reading.

1855

1   A position some six or seven miles from Sevastopol.
2   The plan has not survived.
3   The big house at Yasnaya Polyana in which Tolstoy was born, and which had to be sold, transferred and rebuilt elsewhere to pay Tolstoy's gambling losses at *shtoss* (an old-fashioned card game).
4   The enemy fleet.
5   Prince Menshikov's plan to take Eupatoria by storm, which was a failure.
6   It is not known which one.
7   Some draft notes have survived about the shortcomings of the Russian officers and men and the loss of morale in the Russian army.
8   An attack on the French positions near Sevastopol on the night of 10–11 March – the highlight of the 'trip' referred to in the next sentence.
9   Nothing came of this.
10 In October 1854. Turgenev found her very nice, attractive and intelligent.
11 The future stories *Sevastopol in December* and *Sevastopol in May*.
12 Nothing came of it, since his rank was not sufficiently senior for the appointment.
13 His first night in one of the more exposed positions in Sevastopol, where he was to remain until 15 May.
14 A memorandum Tolstoy wrote to the Commander-in-Chief apropos of an officer's proposed patriotic address to the defenders of Sevastopol.
15 Tolstoy's spelling of Thackeray's novel might suggest that he was reading it in French – although his spelling of foreign names was notoriously unreliable and he refers to it later in English as *Esmond's life*. *Vanity Fair* in the next entry is given its English title and not translated into Russian.
16 The June issue of *The Contemporary*, containing Tolstoy's story *Sevastopol in December*. Tolstoy frequently referred to his stories as 'articles'.
17 *The Wood-felling*.
18 Here the title of Thackeray's novel is given in Russian, and in abbreviated form.
19 *Sevastopol in May*.
20 *Le lys dans la vallée*.
21 A fragment of what may have been the start of this abandoned project has

survived (*An extract from the Diary of Staff-Captain A. of the L. L. Infantry Regiment*).

22 It is not clear whether this refers to the unit's money chest, or to a new type of ammunition chest which was being designed.

23 *The Novel of a Russian Landowner.*

24 A horse.

25 A report for his superior officer on the final bombardment of Sevastopol.

26 *Sevastopol in May.*

27 The gendarmes.

28 The place on the river Belbek where the left flank of the Russian army was temporarily stationed.

29 A village near Bakhchisaray.

30 'Nicholas I's legion' consisting of local Greek volunteers, to whom Tolstoy promised artillery support.

31 Tolstoy arrived in Petersburg on 21 November. He had been sent as a military courier with a report on the artillery action at Sevastopol and stayed with Turgenev, who had become acquainted with his sister and brother and to whom he had dedicated his story *The Wood-felling*.

32 Perhaps the diary referred to in Note 21.

1856

1 He died on 21 January, having been cared for by his mistress Masha and Tolstoy's aunt Tatyana.

2 Tolstoy had moved out of Turgenev's apartment and was now living on Ofitserskaya Street.

3 Apparently over some remarks by Tolstoy about George Sand which Turgenev considered crude and vulgar.

4 A. A. Krayevsky, a journalist and subsequently editor of *Notes of the Fatherland*, which published Tolstoy's story *A Landowner's Morning*.

5 One of the two unfinished comedies (or two versions of the same comedy) of which only the opening scenes have survived – *A Family of the Gentry* and *A Practical Person* – and which were evidently to concern the moral decline of a rich landowning family.

6 The first mention of *Two Hussars*.

7 The pretext for the challenge was a letter sent to Nekrasov by M. N. Longinov, a literary historian and bibliographer, which accused Tolstoy of insufficient freedom of thought. Nekrasov was able to intervene to prevent the threatened duel.

8 Two fragments survive of an article about crime and punishment in Russian army legislation.

9 All three visits may have been connected with Tolstoy's interest in the possibility of emancipating his serfs. Kavelin, a lawyer by training, had recently compiled a memorandum on the subject, which was circulating in manuscript, and Tolstoy was drafting his own plans for emancipating the Yasnaya Polyana serfs on generous terms.

10 About the emancipation of his Yasnaya Polyana serfs.

11 Tolstoy was still in the army and had applied for eleven months' leave.

12 Probably Ivan Sergeyevich, the third son of S. T. Aksakov and soon to become editor of the Slavophile journal *Russian Conversation*. Ivan Kireyevsky, who died later in the year, has been called the founder of Slavophilism.

13 An official of the Ministry of Internal Affairs who had compiled a historical account of serfdom in Russia for the Emperor and whom Tolstoy had approached in connection with his plans to emancipate his serfs.

14 The poet A. A. Fet, whom Tolstoy first got to know on his return from Sevastopol and who became a close friend (*Letters*, I, 135–6). Their extant correspondence is considerable, and Fet's memoirs contain some interesting biographical material about Tolstoy.

15 Countess A. A. Tolstaya, Tolstoy's relative and life-long friend who occupied a high position at the Imperial Court. Tolstoy described his extensive correspondence with her as 'one of the best source materials' for his own biography (*Letters*, I, 103–4). The other Tolstoys referred to here are her mother and sister.

16 The wife of the wealthy industrialist and factory owner S. I. Maltsov.

17 V. S. Perfilyev and A. N. Volkov (a translator at the Ministry of Foreign

Affairs). 'Vaska' Perfilyev was a close friend of Tolstoy's who married his second cousin and later became Governor of Moscow.

18 A reference to Pogodin's ultra-patriotic article on the Moscow celebrations in honour of the Sevastopol sailors which appeared in the May issue of the *Naval Miscellany*.

19 V. A. Kokorev, who made a vast fortune out of tax-farming and also wrote on economic affairs.

20 An expression derived from Gogol's *Notes of a Madman* which Tolstoy used to denote lack of success with women.

21 A. M. Turgenev and his daughter Olga (with whom the novelist Ivan Turgenev had a brief romance). He had a varied career as a soldier, administrator and writer.

22 A restaurant on the Moika in Petersburg.

23 The Emperor Paul's palace, a little to the south of Tsarskoye Selo.

24 Probably A. N. Zhukova, a *demi-mondaine*, with whom Tolstoy was consorting at the time.

25 By Turgenev (*The Diary of a Superfluous Man*).

26 The son of the novelist Zagoskin. He worked for many years compiling material for a major biography of Nicholas I.

27 A. S. Khomyakov, a leading Slavophile writer and religious thinker. Tolstoy was never on close terms with him, but said much later that he greatly respected him and his Slavophile views.

28 Konstantin Aksakov. He wrote to Turgenev about their conversation with Tolstoy, finding him a strange person and unsure of himself, at times talking intelligently and at other times getting stuck, repeating himself and not apparently understanding what was said.

29 The sister of Tolstoy's friend D. A. Dyakov and recently married to Prince Andrey Obolensky – a fact which Tolstoy, who was fond of her, clearly regretted. She was later to be actively involved in the cause of women's education in Russia. A. M. Sukhotin – an officer friend of Tolstoy's who had taken part in the defence of Sevastopol.

30 Botkin had a *dacha* at Kuntsevo, a summer colony near Moscow, and his friend Druzhinin was living there with him at the time. Both men were writers and critics and both were staunch advocates of 'art for art's sake', which led them to break with *The Contemporary* as it became more left-wing (*Letters*, I, 61 and 91).

31 Tolstoy's future mother-in-law and a friend of his from childhood days (she was only two years older than he was). The Behrs had a *dacha* at Pokrovskoye-Streshnevo, a few miles from the centre of Moscow.

32 Tolstoy travelled from Moscow to Yasnaya Polyana with Mlle Vergani, a French governess with the Arsenyev family, whose Sudakovo estate was some five miles from Yasnaya Polyana.

33 Spasskoye-Lutovinovo – Turgenev's estate in the Oryol province. Pokrovskoye – the estate of Tolstoy's sister's husband, about fifty miles from Yasnaya Polyana, which passed to her after her husband's death.

34 Porfiry Kudryashov, an emancipated serf – possibly the illegitimate brother of Turgenev – who accompanied him abroad as a man-servant.

35 N. N. Turgenev, who managed the novelist's mother's estates at the time.

36 The first mention of *Strider*.

37 *The Stone Guest.*

38 The forthcoming coronation of Alexander II in August 1856.

39 Perhaps the philosophical notes and essays dating from his student days. See R. F. Christian, *Tolstoy: A Critical Introduction*, pp. 6–10.

40 A diary which Tolstoy kept from 28 May to 10 June 1856, recounting his unsuccessful attempts to ease the lot of his serfs before their official emancipation.

41 *The Fugitive Cossack*, an early title of *The Cossacks*.

42 See Note 5.

43 A local forester.

44 Gimbut's wife was a Durova; the Durova mentioned by Tolstoy was one of her sisters.

45 Volumes 2 and 3 of Annenkov's edition of Pushkin's works.

46 *Materials for a Biography of Pushkin*, which was the first volume of Annenkov's edition.

47 A wood on Tolstoy's estate where he was eventually to be buried.

48 A big larch wood near Yasnaya Polyana.

49 Nadezhda Gimbut, the forester's wife.

50 V. V. Arsenyeva, whom Tolstoy seriously contemplated marrying. His letters to her, of which twenty have survived, give an illuminating picture of his views on marriage and the ideal wife (*Letters*, I, 63 ff.). Tolstoy later portrayed aspects of his romance with her in his story *Family Happiness*.

51 Okhotnitskaya, an indigent gentlewoman who lived with the Tolstoys.

52 To investigate the death of the soldier found hanged.

53 See Note 49.

54 *The Fugitive*, which Tolstoy had begun to write in verse form some years earlier and had still apparently not abandoned the idea of entirely.

55 Thackeray's novel was published in Russian translation in *The Contemporary* in 1855–6.

56 A peasant who had been drowned on the estate.

57 By Beethoven.

58 She was to go to Alexander II's coronation and be presented at court.

59 Valeriya's sister.

60 Tolstoy evidently read Dickens' novel in English.

61 A concert pianist from whom Valeriya was taking lessons, thereby arousing Tolstoy's jealousy.

62 Goethe's *Die Leiden des jungen Werthers*.

63 From the army.

64 *Uncle's Blessing*. Only a list of characters and a synopsis of the two acts remain of what appears to have been a satire directed against emancipated women.

65 A post-station less than twenty miles from Yasnaya Polyana.

66 *Uncle's Blessing*. Olga – Valeriya's sister. Molière's comedy obviously acted as a stimulus to Tolstoy.

67 Ivan Turgenev, the novelist, whose frequent absences from Spasskoye

were responsible, in Tolstoy's opinion, for the fact that N. N. Turgenev was allowed to neglect the management of the estate (for which he was eventually dismissed).

68 The first Russian translation of Dickens' novel was serialized in *Notes of the Fatherland* in 1849–50.

69 Tolstoy called himself by that name in his letters to Arsenyeva when discussing his relationship with her (he called her Dembitskaya).

70 Turgenev dedicated his story *Faust* to Tolstoy's sister.

71 *Letters*, I, 64.

72 A. N. Ostrovsky, the popular and immensely prolific dramatist. Tolstoy often commented on Ostrovsky's plays in his diaries and letters, but only four of his letters to the dramatist have survived (*Letters*, II, 403).

73 Herzen's journal, published in London. Two issues came out in 1855 and 1856.

74 Tolstoy saw Griboyedov's comedy at the Maly Theatre.

75 *Letters*, I, 67.

76 The daughter of A. M. Turgenev (see Note 21).

77 By Dudyshkin in *Notes of the Fatherland*.

78 *Free Love*, another fragment which overlaps in characters and subject matter with *Uncle's Blessing*. Two scenes and the beginning of a third scene of the first act have survived.

79 On the site of the pre-revolutionary *Hôtel de l'Europe*.

80 *Letters*, I, 72.

81 I. I. Panayev, editor-in-chief of *The Contemporary* and remembered today for his *Literary Reminiscences* (*Letters*, I, 51).

82 Shakespeare's historical drama.

83 For reprinting some poems by Nekrasov the journal got into trouble with the censors, and there were threats of a possible closure. It was felt in literary circles that the editors had acted imprudently.

84 *Letters*, I, 78.

85 I.e. Valeriya (the letter has not survived).

86 Prosper Mérimée's story.

87 Either *A Family of the Gentry* or *A Practical Person*.

88 By Goncharov, the author of the better-known *Oblomov*.

89 *Letters*, I, 84.

90 A comedy by Ostrovsky.

91 *A Criticism of the Gogol period of Russian Literature and our Attitude towards it*. In his two articles Druzhinin took issue with the aesthetic views of Chernyshevsky.

92 Druzhinin's translation of Shakespeare's play.

93 Lydia Shevich, one of the daughters of Count Bludov (portrayed by Tolstoy in *Hadji Murat*). A married woman in her forties, she was apparently attracted to Tolstoy at the time.

94 In fact the next to last chapter of *Youth*, describing the unusual circumstances of the dissipated student Semyonov's conscription as a soldier.

95 Mendelssohn's symphonic poem *Calm Sea and Prosperous Voyage*.

1857

1 *The Emperor's New Clothes*. The translation has not survived.
2 Count Bludov's daughters. See 1856, Note 93.
3 A performance intended to raise money for the Literary Fund.
4 Possibly F. M. Tolstoy, a music critic and composer.
5 Belinsky's fifth article on Pushkin, which deals particlarly with his lyric poetry.
6 A German who came to Petersburg as a professional violinist and whose life history, as recounted to Tolstoy, formed the basis of the latter's story *Albert* (originally called *The Lost One*).
7 To go abroad.
8 This plan came to nothing.
9 Panayev's wife was to be the 'George Sand woman' in the comedy.
10 A chapter from Aksakov's book (*The Childhood Years of Grandson Bagrov*), which dealt with his own childhood in fictional form.
11 The wife of the statesman Baron Mengden and a well-known hostess and close friend of the Tolstoy family (*Letters*, I, 275).
12 One of the daughters of the poet Tyutchev whom Tolstoy greatly admired. It was rumoured in 1858 that Tolstoy intended to marry her. She never married and devoted much of her life to 'good works', especially public education and health.
13 Tolstoy spent most of February and March in Paris, having travelled via Warsaw.
14 To 206 Rue de Rivoli from the Hôtel Meurice, where he had first stayed on arriving in Paris.
15 Princess Alexandra Lvova, who was staying with her uncle, whom Tolstoy had known for a long time. Tolstoy frequently visited her in Paris, was attracted to her and was even advised to marry her by his cousin Alexandra Tolstoy.
16 Napoleon III's recent speech extolling French successes achieved during his reign.
17 An account of his journey from Russia, which has not survived.
18 Tolstoy saw Molière's comedy at the Théâtre français.
19 A comedy be Mélesville, also on at the Théâtre français.
20 A French actress who had previously performed in Petersburg, and was acting at the time in Marivaux's play.
21 It would seem that Tolstoy saw Molière's play on the same day as Marivaux's.
22 Tolstoy engaged both English and Italian teachers in Paris.
23 Prince N. A. Orlov, the son of Prince A. F. Orlov, head of the Third Section and a personal friend of Nicholas I. The son held a number of diplomatic posts abroad, including Paris, and later married Princess Trubetskaya, whom Tolstoy was fond of.
24 Balzac's novel.
25 Tolstoy attended some lectures at the Sorbonne and the Collège de France

on classical literature, political economy and international law.

26 Probably Beethoven's Trio, opus 70.

27 The singer Pauline Viardot-Garcia, the great love of Turgenev's life.

28 An opera singer.

29 A professor of classical culture.

30 The collection of medieval arms and antiquities in the museum particularly interested Tolstoy.

31 Possibly a coinage of Tolstoy's to denote a woman who accosts.

32 Tolstoy and Turgenev went to Dijon at Turgenev's suggestion and spent five days there.

33 The comic opera by Donizetti.

34 Daniel Douglas Home, the Scottish spiritualist and medium, whose seance at the Trubetskoys' met with mixed success. He was in great demand in Europe.

35 A one-act comedy by Cormon and Grangé.

36 *La Cousine Bette.*

37 A late eighteenth-century tragedy by the Italian poet Alfieri, based on the Greek legend of the unnatural love of Myrrha for her father Cinyras, king of Cyprus.

38 She played the title role in the play.

39 Tolstoy wrote about it at some length in his letter to Botkin the same day (*Letters*, I, 95) and again many years later in *A Confession.*

40 For Geneva.

41 After leaving Paris Tolstoy continued his European travels for a further four months. He travelled from Paris to Ambérieu by train and from there to Geneva by stagecoach. In Geneva he renewed his acquaintance with his 'Aunt' Alexandra Tolstaya and spent a great deal of time with her, both at the villa *Le Bocage*, where she was staying with the Grand Duchess Marya Nikolayevna, and on excursions into the neighbouring countryside. Before long he moved to Clarens, not far from Geneva, where he made friends with a small group of Russians – the Pushchins, Meshcherskys and Karamzins – as he mentioned in a letter to his aunt Tatyana Yergolskaya (*Letters*, I, 100). In the middle of May he travelled on foot round Switzerland with an eleven-year-old boy, Sasha Polivanov, the son of a Russian lady he knew in Clarens. Their journey, which took them through Montreux, Les Avants, Col de Jaman, Château d'Oex and back to Clarens via Interlaken, Grindelwald, Thun, Bern and Fribourg, is described separately in Tolstoy's *Extract from a Diary, 1857: Notes on a Journey through Switzerland*, but a few entries were also made in Tolstoy's main diary and are included here. The journey lasted ten days from 15/27 May to 25 May/6 June, and shortly after his return Tolstoy set off again for Northern Italy, where his friends Botkin and Druzhinin were staying. He joined them at Turin, where they spent some time sightseeing before returning to Clarens, partly on foot, through the Aosta valley and the St Bernard Pass. After a few days' rest, Tolstoy set off for Lausanne, Bern and Lucerne, arriving in Lucerne on 24 June/6 July. It was during his stay there that the incident occurred which is described in Tolstoy's story *Lucerne*. On 7/19 July he left Lucerne for Zürich, but soon moved on to Schaffhausen,

Friedrichshafen, Stuttgart and Baden-Baden, where his heavy gambling losses and the news of the breakdown of his sister's marriage made him decide to return to Russia. The final stage of his European journey took him through Frankfurt (where he saw Alexandra Tolstaya again), Dresden and Berlin. On 27 July/8 August he boarded a ship at Stettin and four days later was back in Petersburg.

42 Of stories he intended to work on in Geneva.

43 Totleben had been in command of the defences at Sevastopol and had until the previous month been convalescing in Switzerland from a Crimean War wound.

44 *De la liberté de la presse et du journalisme.* Girardin founded *La Presse* in 1836; it ushered in the age of the cheap newspaper in France.

45 Of *The Fugitive.*

46 M. I. Pushchin and his wife Mariya. M. I. Pushchin was the brother of the Decembrist friend of Pushkin's.

47 Prince Meshchersky was married to the daughter of Karamzin and was living at the time in Switzerland.

48 A novel by Dumas fils.

49 A reference to the bombardment of Canton by the British navy in 1856 – also mentioned in Tolstoy's story *Lucerne.*

50 Presumably *L'Ancien régime et la révolution* (1856).

51 A deputy of the Constituent Assembly in 1848 and an editor of *La Tribune* under Louis-Philippe, he wrote a six-volume *Biographie des hommes du jour.*

52 Written by Louis-Napoléon in London in 1838.

53 Another tentative title of *Albert.*

54 Pushchin's wife.

55 Sasha Polivanov.

56 Yelizaveta Nikolayevna Karamzina, daughter of the historian and the sister of Meshchersky's wife. She was staying at the time with the Meshchersky family, and Tolstoy was very attracted by her.

57 *Extract from a Diary* (see Note 41).

58 A conjectured reading for the initials which Tolstoy used in his diary.

59 Botkin, Druzhinin and Tolstoy.

60 *Wilkommen und Abschied,* 1770.

61 *Die Krone,* a hotel on the outskirts of Bern.

62 See Tolstoy's story *Lucerne.*

63 The title of Freytag's novel, which came out in 1855, is written in German in the diary and Tolstoy presumably read it in the original; the title of Hans Andersen's novel is written in Russian, but it is likely that he read it in a German translation.

64 In English in the original.

65 An alternative reading is Waadtland, a canton in the Pays du Vaud.

66 Guide-books published by John Murray.

67 Alexandra Tolstaya.

68 The title of Goethe's novel is in Russian; 'Miss Brontë' is written in English and evidently refers to Mrs Gaskell's *Life of Charlotte Brontë.*

69 By Raphael.

70 Probably *Ein weisses Blatt*, a comedy by Karl Gutzkow, which had recently been revived on the Dresden stage.

71 Saltykov-Shchedrin, Russia's best-known satirical writer and author of *The Golovlyov Family* (*Letters*, II, 389). Tolstoy was probably reading Saltykov's *Provincial Sketches* at the time.

72 A reference to the Roman Emperor Titus, who, according to Suetonius, considered the day wasted unless he had done a good deed.

73 In Gnedich's translation.

74 *The Cossacks*.

75 P. G. Yengalychev was married to Valeriya Arsenyeva's sister Olga.

76 An estate very close to Yasnaya Polyana where Tolstoy opened a school in the 1860s.

77 Koltsov's poems were included, together with those of Tyutchev and Fet, in the list of works which had made a great impression on him between the ages of twenty and thirty-five.

78 For Pirogovo, to go hunting.

79 Possibly the German writer's novel *Europäisches Sklavenleben*.

80 His future mother-in-law.

81 An allusion to Pushkin's poem *To a Poet*.

82 Obolenskaya (née Dyakova). Tolstoy's infatuation for her left its mark in an unfinished fragment.

83 His own translation of Shakespeare's play.

84 Tolstoy made up a Russian noun from Nadya (*nadinstvo*) which he sometimes used to refer to women's tittle-tattle.

1858

1 A draft constitution, written by Tolstoy, has survived, but nothing came of the project.

2 The estate of Tolstoy's mother's cousin, Princess Volkonskaya, where he was spending a few days.

3 Tolstoy was undecided whether to conclude his story *Three Deaths* with the death of the lady or the tree (see entry for 20 January).

4 A distinguished lawyer, historian and liberal politician, who met and corresponded frequently with Tolstoy (*Letters*, I, 132).

5 Glinka's opera *Ivan Susanin*.

6 Turgenev's story had just appeared in the January issue of *The Contemporary*.

7 A widow whose beauty had once been the inspiration for a poem by Pushkin, and the mother of Tolstoy's friend Kireyev referred to below.

8 The famous Russian actor Shchepkin played the part of the governor of the town in Gogol's play.

9 The title appears in English. Shakespeare's play had recently been published in A. A. Grigoryev's translation, to which Tolstoy was referring.

10 In the context of an article by Y. F. Korsh on parliamentary reform in England and the First Reform Act of 1832.

11 Y. F. Korsh, a publicist, critic and translator, and a member of the Granovsky circle.

12 Not Rubens', but Rembrandt's.

13 A restaurant in the centre of Moscow.

14 In the *Athenaeum (Ateney)*, 1858.

15 Two works on natural science by the French historian Jules Michelet.

16 Gustav von Meyern's poem *Ein Kaiser*, and a note on a German translation of two articles by Emerson on Shakespeare and Goethe which appeared in different issues of the German literary weekly in 1858 (Tolstoy spells it *Centralblatt*).

17 A report in the *Athenaeum* (London) of 13 March 1858 of a speech by Dickens criticizing the work of the London Literary Fund Society, which allegedly devoted too much money to administration and not enough to writers in need.

18 March issues of the *Athenaeum* contained reviews of books about the Indian Mutiny.

19 Claude-Emmanuel Luillier, dit Chapelle – the author, with Bachaumont, of *Voyage en Provence et Languedoc*, 1656.

20 The historical memoirs (called *Commentaries* after Caesar) of the Gasconard officer Blaise de Montluc (or Monluc), who became Maréchal de France in 1574.

21 A political pamphlet *L'asino, un sogno*, 1857, by the Italian writer and member of Mazzini's Young Italy F. D. Guerrazzi.

22 The Russian historian S. M. Solvyov's *Historical Letters* branded the views of the Moscow Slavophiles as antihistorical and 'political Buddhism'.

23 Tolstoy read a review of the memoirs of the last four popes by the English cardinal and Archbishop of Westminster, Nicholas Wiseman.

24 Probably Alfred Assollant's *Scènes de la vie des États Unis*, in the *Revue des Deux Mondes*.

25 There is no such scene in *The Cossacks*.

26 The chapters in *The Cossacks* devoted to Lukashka's murder of an Abrek in 'the cordon'.

27 The first volume of Macaulay's *History of England*.

28 Aksinya Bazykina, a married peasant woman with whom Tolstoy had a liaison and who bore him a son. She was living with her father-in-law at the time; hence the reference to 'the daughter-in-law' later in this entry.

29 These comments refer to Tolstoy's unsuccessful negotiations with his peasants, who resisted his decision to transfer them to the system of quit-rent (*obrok*) and to farm his land with hired labour.

30 For signing a petition by a group of landowners on the need to free the peasants with an allotment of land.

31 The landowner Cherkassky, a publicist of Slavophile sympathies, accepted the need for the peasants to be granted freedom with land, but proposed a number of unacceptable provisos.

32 Since Turgenev did not have a niece it is thought that Tolstoy was referring to Turgenev's first cousin once removed, Olga Alexandrovna Turgeneva.

33 A fragment entitled *A Summer in the Country* has survived.
34 Probably Sergey Sukhotin, a Tula landowner and brother of Alexander (1856, Note 29). It is not clear from the text who is speaking, and I have apportioned the dialogue between Tolstoy and his sister as the sense seems to require.
35 This happened during a hunting expedition with Fet. Tolstoy described the incident in his story for children (translated by Maude as *The Bear-hunt*).

1859

1 *Family Happiness* – also referred to in subsequent entries.
2 The original name of the heroine of *Family Happiness*.
3 The proofs of the second part.
4 Tolstoy was probably reading the French novelist Octave Feuillet's *Roman d'un jeune homme pauvre* (1858).
5 A reference to Tolstoy's intended proposal of marriage to Alexandra Lvova, the exact circumstances of which are unclear.
6 There is a copy of George Eliot's novel in Tolstoy's library at Yasnaya Polyana with his markings in the margins.

1860

1 An article by the French archaeologist and psychologist Alfred Maury in the *Revue des Deux Mondes*.
2 In autumn 1859 Tolstoy had begun to give lessons to the children in the school he had opened on his estate.
3 Berthold Auerbach's *Neues Leben* (he subsequently met the German writer in Berlin in 1861) and Goethe's poem.
4 Tolstoy had some criticisms to make of new draft regulations for primary and secondary education in schools run by the Ministry of Education.
5 Aksinya Bazykina.
6 2 August is in fact 21, not 20 July, old style. There are other minor errors in dating hereabouts.
7 On 27 June Tolstoy and his sister and her children set off on a journey abroad to study educational systems and teaching methods in Europe. They travelled via Moscow to Petersburg and from there by boat to Stettin. After spending a week or so in Berlin they travelled on to the Bavarian resort of Kissingen, stopping en route at Leipzig.
8 By Karl von Räumer.
9 Wilhelm Heinrich Riehl, a distinguished professor of history and public law at the University of Munich. Tolstoy was reading his *magnum opus*, *Naturgeschichte des Volkes, als Grundlage einer deutschen Sozialpolitik*.
10 Julius Fröbel, the nephew of the better-known Friedrich Fröbel, the educational reformer and founder of the kindergarten. Julius Fröbel had

been sentenced to death for his part in the 1848 revolution, but the sentence was commuted and he went to live in America. He returned to Germany in 1857. In his memoirs he recalled his meeting and conversations with Tolstoy.

11 Probably the collection of Herzen's articles *After Five Years*, published in London in 1860.

12 A village near Kissingen.

13 A retired professor of geography and statistics.

14 Some of Tolstoy's notes on experimental pedagogy have survived.

15 Tolstoy arrived in Soden on 14/26 August to join his brother Nikolay, who was seriously ill with tuberculosis. They travelled together to Hyères, stopping at Frankfurt, Geneva and Marseilles where Tolstoy visited schools. Nikolay died at Hyères on 20 September.

16 Thought to be the Decembrist N. I. Turgenev, not the novelist, but the reference is obscure.

1861

1 Tolstoy reached Weimar on 31 March/12 April after four months travelling in Europe. He left Hyères at the end of November 1860 (old style) and spent about a fortnight in Florence, where he met the Decembrist S. G. Volkonsky, whom he intended to portray in his novel about them. In the course of January he visited Livorno, and then spent a month or so in Naples and Rome. Little is known of his stay in Paris except that he continued to visit schools and briefly resumed his friendship with Turgenev. His short visit to England is the subject of a book, *Tolstoy in London*, by Victor Lucas, London, 1979, which gives an interesting account of his educational activities, school visits and collection of pedagogical material, including essays written for him by schoolchildren in London which he took back with him to Russia. Much of March was spent in Brussels pursuing his educational interests and working on his story *Polikushka*, and from there he went via Frankfurt and Eisenach to Weimar.

2 The story *An Idyll*, or its second version, *Tikhon and Malanya*, which drew on Tolstoy's liaison with Aksinya Bazykina.

3 Tolstoy had met Princess Golitsyna and her niece Katenka the previous winter in Hyères, and his sister was on friendly terms with them both. Tolstoy was seriously attracted by Katenka and even contemplated marriage. According to his wife, the two ladies were the prototypes of Mme Stahl and her ward Varenka in *Anna Karenina*.

4 A village near Jena which had an agricultural school which Tolstoy visited.

5 A German historian and journalist, at the time editor of a Weimar newspaper. The book referred to was his *Geschichtsunterricht nach kulturgeschichtlicher Methode*, 1860.

6 Tolstoy spent three days in Dresden *en route* for Berlin to visit more schools and buy books.

7 Tolstoy's long talk with Berthold Auerbach was the highlight of his visit to Berlin.

8 He served for only one year. The posts of arbiter were created after the emancipation to adjudicate between landowners and peasants in disputes arising from the settlement of 1861.

9 Tolstoy's pedagogical journal *Yasnaya Polyana*, which began to appear in January 1862.

10 Sonya's elder sister.

11 The Act of Emancipation of February 1861.

12 An application for official recognition.

13 This was the famous quarrel at Fet's estate when Tolstoy offended Turgenev by an injudicious reference to the education of Turgenev's illegitimate daughter (*Letters*, I, 148).

14 A programme for the first issue of *Yasnaya Polyana*.

15 Unlike his brothers Nikolay and Dmitry, Tolstoy never suffered from consumption.

16 See *Letters*, I, 148. Turgenev accused Tolstoy of circulating copies of an earlier letter by Tolstoy which has not survived, and threatened to 'demand satisfaction'.

17 Students employed as teachers at his school.

18 The first version of the article *The Yasnaya Polyana School in November and December*.

19 *Yasnaya Polyana Diary*.

20 P. V. Morozov, a teacher from Tula, soon to be employed by Tolstoy at his school.

21 Author of a book of object lessons based on Pestalozzi's theories. Tolstoy criticized the book in the August issue of *Yasnaya Polyana*, 1862.

1862

1 On the Volga, en route for Samara, where Tolstoy was going to take the *kumys* (fermented mare's milk) cure.

2 *Upbringing and Education*.

3 S. A. Behrs, Tolstoy's future wife.

4 About the police search carried out at Yasnaya Polyana during Tolstoy's absence (*Letters*, I, 163).

5 *Natasha*, in which Sonya portrayed some features of Tolstoy in the person of Dublitsky (*Letters*, I, 168, fn. 2). She destroyed it before her marriage.

6 As Levin later did to Kitty in *Anna Karenina*.

7 Either N. A. Popov, a student who corrected the proofs of Tolstoy's journal, or M. A. Polivanov, both suitors of Sonya.

8 Either A. A. Obolenskaya, as Soviet commentators believe, or Aksinya, the mother of Tolstoy's illegitimate son.

9 An article on Mohammed written by Sonya's sister Yelizaveta and edited by Tolstoy for publication in his journal.

10 The pseudonym of a Slavophile authoress, referred to disparagingly in a letter to Druzhinin (*Letters*, I, 124).

11 The 'P' of Note 7.

12 V. S. Perfilyev (also Vasenka in the entry for 7 September). See 1856, Note 17.

13 Sonya's father, who was expecting Tolstoy to propose to his eldest daughter Liza, not to Sonya.

14 Sonya's sister.

15 In which Tolstoy explained what he had meant by the initials he had used in an earlier message (Note 6).

16 *Letters*, I, 168 – a revised version of the letter referred to in Note 15 which was not sent but has survived.

17 The people referred to are a friend of Sonya's, Tolstoy's brother, Sonya's sister, her father and her suitor. The last sentence is unclear in Russian.

18 Note 2. The article had just been passed by the censors.

19 A reference to negotiations with the Petersburg bookseller Stellovsky with a view to publishing Tolstoy's collected works. The negotiations came to nothing at this stage.

20 Only the initial letter 'n' appears in the original, and it is not clear what word was intended.

21 After his marriage Tolstoy gave up teaching at his school (although lessons continued for a time with other teachers). The last issue of the journal (No. 12) appeared early the following year.

22 The Tolstoys moved to Moscow on 23 December and stayed at Chevalier's hotel until early February.

23 A nickname for Tanya, who was taking lessons from the Italian singer of that name.

1863

1 The story he had begun in Brussels.
2 A cousin of the Behrs sisters, who later married Tatyana.
3 Believed to be the germ of the idea of the Koznyshov-Levin relationship in *Anna Karenina*.
4 Druzhinin's story and Ostrovsky's drama respectively. Tolstoy had just seen the Ostrovsky play a day or two before.
5 *Progress and the Definition of Education*, published in the final issue of *Yasnaya Polyana*.
6 Probably *Strider, The Story of a Horse*.
7 Hugo's novel was the one work which Tolstoy claims to have made an 'enormous' impression on him between the ages of thirty-five and fifty.
8 The original title of *Strider*.
9 A teacher at the school in Baburino. Sonya refers to her husband's jealousy of him in her autobiography.
10 Tolstoy's eldest son was born on 28 June 1863.
11 Pelageya Yushkova, Tolstoy's guardian in Kazan, and his sister Marya Nikolayevna.
12 A reference to Tolstoy's disapproval of his wife's refusal, because of mastitis, to feed her baby herself.

1864

1 *1805*, the genesis of *War and Peace*.
2 Ten quires.
3 Probably a reference to the diary entry for 5 August 1863; if Tolstoy intended to keep a separate diary about Sonya and motherhood, nothing came of the intention.
4 Both entries refer to the old Prince Bolkonsky in *1805*.

1865

1 The first three chapters of Part 2 of *1805*.
2 Of Seryozha's son, Tolstoy's nephew.
3 *Mémoires du maréchal Marmont, duc de Raguse*, published in Paris, 1856–7, after his death. A marshal in Napoleon's army, he had been jointly responsible for surrendering Paris to the allies in 1814, and in his memoirs he attempted to justify his conduct, which had made Napoleon's abdication inevitable. These memoirs provided Tolstoy with several of the details about Napoleon and Alexander in the next entry.
4 The meaning is not entirely clear; the Russian word *roman* can mean both 'novel' and 'romance'.
5 These words were spoken by Napoleon on the day after his coronation, as recounted by Raguse.

6 V. A. Perovsky was captured at the Battle of Borodino and taken to France, where he remained until the allies took Paris in 1814. His memoirs of 1812 were published in *Russian Archives*, No. 3, 1865.

7 Perovsky's account of his interrogation by Davoût and his last-minute reprieve form the gist of the scene in *War and Peace* where Pierre is similarly interrogated.

8 Of *The Cossacks* (*Notes of the Fatherland*, 1865). Markov reproached Tolstoy for his allegedly inaccurate picture of the life of the people of the Caucasus.

9 Crossing the bridge at Enns.

10 The witty Russian diplomat in post in Vienna in *1805*.

11 Tolstoy's intention of comparing Napoleon and Faust towards the end of their lives was never realized.

12 This entry is not from the diary proper, but from one of Tolstoy's notebooks.

13 The Tolstoys moved to the estate of the late Nikolay Tolstoy on 26 June and stayed there until October, with short visits to his sister at Pokrovskoye and to his friend Dyakov at Cheryomoshnya.

14 Mérimée's historical novel about the persecution of the Huguenots in France.

15 George Sand's long novel of musical life in eighteenth-century Austria and Bohemia.

16 To the Dyakovs', with whom Tolstoy was staying.

17 The Dyakovs' daughter.

18 An English authoress (1824–77) of novels and stories, especially of French society life.

19 Schön Grabern (Chapters 17–21 of Part 2 of the first volume of *War and Peace*).

20 *The Bertrams*. 'Diffuseness' (misspelt) is in English in the original.

21 Tolstoy's father-in-law.

22 Tolstoy had two of Mrs Braddon's novels in his library at Yasnaya Polyana, including *Lady Audley's Secret*, and apparently had a high opinion of them.

23 Tolstoy's late brother.

24 A scene from the draft versions of the description of the Battle of Schön Grabern which was transformed in the final version into the episode of Captain Timokhin's attack.

25 The historian Guizot's daughter, Henriette de Witt, who wrote religious works and books for children.

26 A short fragment entitled *On Religion*, which was Tolstoy's first attempt to formulate his religious views coherently.

27 The heroine of *Our Mutual Friend*, whom Tolstoy compares to his sister-in-law.

28 Tolstoy was reading de Maistre's *Correspondance diplomatique 1811–1817* (Paris, 1861), and also a book by Albert Blanc on the political memoirs and diplomatic correspondence of de Maistre. For a full account of de Maistre's influence on Tolstoy see Isaiah Berlin's *The Hedgehog and the Fox*, 1953.

29 His thoughts evidently came to nothing.
30 The camp scenes before Schön Grabern.

1870

1 The entries for 1870 are not part of a diary, but are written on separate sheets of paper.
2 The reference is probably to an article of 1870 by the critic Shelgunov, which followed earlier critics in sharply attacking the philosophical digressions in *War and Peace*.

1874

1 An entry on a separate sheet of paper, referring to Francis Bacon's *Novum organum* and a Russian translation of it which Strakhov had sent to Tolstoy.
2 As early as 1874, soon after *Anna Karenina* had been begun, Tolstoy appears to have been contemplating writing a book about religion.

1878

1 The last entry in the diary proper was 10 April 1865.
2 On the history of the Decembrist movement. Tolstoy was working at the time on his novel *The Decembrists*.
3 V. I. Alexeyev, a teacher in the Tolstoy household, who wished to settle on some land Tolstoy had bought in the Samara province.
4 A. S. Orekhov, a former valet of Tolstoy's and now an estate manager at Yasnaya Polyana.
5 The wife of the Decembrist, who accompanied him into exile, a hypothetical prototype of Pushkin's Tatyana.
6 Tolstoy's eldest son.
7 Some unfinished autobiographical reminiscences of his childhood.
8 A disciple of the English evangelist Lord Radstock.

1881

1 After an interval of three years Tolstoy resumed his diary in 1881. I have omitted many entries, which mainly concern visits from beggars and suppliants.
2 A play on the words *ad* ('hell') and *sklad* ('treasure').
3 Tolstoy made two visits to the local prison to familiarize himself with conditions there.
4 A. K. Malikov, a man of earlier socialist leanings, had been briefly imprisoned after the Populist 'Trial of the 193'.

5 Tolstoy's daughter and sister-in-law.
6 Y. P. Polonsky, a minor poet whom Tolstoy first met in 1855 and who later reacted strongly against Tolstoy's religious and philosophical views.
7 Tatyana Kuzminskaya.
8 Turgenev, on his last visit to Yasnaya Polyana, demonstrated to the Tolstoys how the cancan was danced in Paris.
9 On 15 September the Tolstoys moved to Moscow and stayed temporarily in No. 3, Denezhny Lane (the present Maly Lyovshinsky Lane).
10 Tolstoy's denunciation of Moscow life soon found expression in his book *What Then must We Do?*
11 A separate, undated entry, originally assigned to 1884, but now believed to have been written in 1881, when Tolstoy was already thinking of disposing of most of his property.
12 Tolstoy's estate in the Samara province.
13 His late brother Nikolay's estate at Nikolskoye-Vyazemskoye in the Tula province.

1882

1 The only diary entry for 1882. It mainly refers to his treatise *What I Believe*.
2 In July Tolstoy bought a house in Dolgo-Khamovnichesky Lane (the present No. 21, Lev Tolstoy Street) and the family moved there in October. It was to remain their permanent town residence for the rest of his life.

1884

1 Extracts from S. Julien's French translation *Le livre de la voie et de la vertu*, Paris, 1841.
2 *Praise of Folly*.
3 *Letters from the Country* by D. D. Golokhvastov, which was directed against the Populist writer A. N. Engelhardt's collection of letters of the same title, and advocated large-scale private, as opposed to communal, ownership of land.
4 *What I Believe*.
5 Tolstoy was reading Confucius in James Legge's three-volume English edition *The Chinese Classics*.
6 The first mention of Tolstoy's plan to compile a collection of sayings and aphorisms from the works of great writers and thinkers for daily reading (translated in *Letters* as *A Circle of Reading*). Several volumes were written in the 1900s.
7 The figures here and elsewhere refer to Tolstoy's enumeration of his daily 'sins'. The figures normally follow the particular offence.
8 A. K. Malikov – see 1881, Note 4. A. G. Orfano – a retired officer who had been tried and acquitted on a charge of maintaining contacts with Herzen

and Ogaryov in London and who later fell foul of the authorities again for building a factory run on cooperative lines. He was critical of Tolstoy's *What I Believe.*

9 V. F. Orlov, a teacher who had stood trial in the Nechayev case, on which the plot of Dostoyevsky's novel *The Devils* was very loosely based.

10 L. D. Urusov's translation into French of Tolstoy's *What I Believe.*

11 *Physical Labour as an Essential Element of Education* by S. N. Krivenko, a Populist writer and later one of the editors of *Russian Wealth.*

12 Tolstoy's most famous and dedicated disciple and the dominant figure in his life from this time onwards (*Letters*, II, 367ff.). Their correspondence extended to nearly a thousand letters.

13 These boots are now on display in Tolstoy's town house in Moscow.

14 He described the appalling working conditions there in his 'article' *What Then Must We Do?*

15 L. D. Obolensky.

16 His daughter, whose worldly way of life at the time distressed her father.

17 Sonya.

18 A bookshop on Mokhovaya Street.

19 I. Y. Repin, best known as a realist painter (*Letters*, II, 379), who painted several portraits of Tolstoy and gave painting lessons to Tatyana. Tolstoy went the following day to see his picture *They Did Not Expect Him*, but it was not yet on display at the exhibition.

20 An article in *Archives of Psychiatry* by Kovalevsky on two cases of pathological temporary aberration.

21 D. I. Svyatopolk-Mirsky had served in the Crimea and had met Tolstoy there. His letter recalled their meetings, and he enclosed some of his own poetry.

22 *Inconsolable Grief*, on view at the 12th Exhibition of 'The Itinerants' (*Peredvizhniki*).

23 *They Did Not Expect Him*, on view at the same exhibition.

24 P. M. Tretyakov, the art collector and joint founder with his brother of the Tretyakov Art Gallery in Moscow (*Letters*, II, 460).

25 A. V. Dmokhovskaya, the mother of a revolutionary who had been exiled to Siberia in 1880 and had died on his way there. She had recently sought Tolstoy's help on behalf of her son-in-law, who had also been exiled to Siberia in the aftermath of the assassination of Alexander II.

26 Tolstoy read him in James Legge's *The Chinese Classics.*

27 In English in the diary.

28 A. V. Olsufyev, a local landowner.

29 *Vint* – see 1851, Note 3.

30 On his impressions of the Petersburg aristocracy celebrating Easter.

31 Anna V. Armfeldt, the mother of Natalya Armfeldt, who had been sentenced to fourteen years' hard labour in 1879 for revolutionary activities. Tolstoy lent his support to the attempts to persuade the authorities to allow Anna Armfeldt to settle near her daughter's place of exile, and was reading the daughter's letters to her mother about her trial and her life in Siberia.

32 To Alexandra Tolstaya, asking for her help over the Armfeldt case.

33 Sonya.

34 Manuscripts brought by Dmokhovskaya about the life of political prisoners in Siberia, and his own manuscript *What Then Must We Do?*

35 Y. P. Blavatskaya, after extensive travels in America, Canada, India and even Tibet, founded the Theosophical Society in New York in 1875 and published *Isis Unveiled* (1877) with its unorthodox theories about the evolution of mankind and religion.

36 Chertkov's confession about 'the devil within him' and the sordid side of his personality.

37 The beginning of *What Then Must We Do?*

38 A house in a particularly impoverished quarter of Moscow which Tolstoy first visited in connection with the Census of 1882, and described in grim detail in *What Then Must We Do?*

39 S. A. Usov, a professor of zoology at Moscow University and a close friend of Tolstoy's at the time.

40 N. L. Ozmidov, a copyist and distributor of Tolstoy's banned books and later a collaborator on *The Intermediary* (*Letters*, II, 404, fn.1).

41 A. P. Ivanov, a copyist.

42 N. K. Mikhaylovsky's *Notes of a Layman*, in which he analysed the strengths and weaknesses of Tolstoy's ideology.

43 Ralph Waldo Emerson's essay *Self Reliance*, later published in Tolstoy's edited and abbreviated version by *The Intermediary*.

44 Charles Kingsley's novel. Tolstoy had noted on 18 May: 'I'm reading *Hypatia*. Undistinguished. Interesting how he resolves the religious problem.'

45 Tatyana Kuzminskaya.

46 Tolstoy was reading St Augustine's *Confessions* in French.

47 *What Then Must We Do?*

48 Tolstoy's son.

49 To the village of Trosna to hear the case of two old peasants thought to have been wrongly imprisoned.

50 A Yasnaya Polyana peasant family.

51 P. P. Arbuzov, who taught Tolstoy cobbling.

52 Tolstoy had suggested recovering debts owed by the peasants on his Samara estate and distributing the money to those in need there. His wife strongly protested.

53 Tolstoy had made more than one attempt between 1877 and 1879 to begin a novel about peasant colonists in Russia in the late eighteenth and early nineteenth centuries.

54 Tolstoy's first attempt to leave home.

55 The birth of Tolstoy's last child, Alexandra (*Letters*, II, 711).

56 In Emerson's book *Essays on Representative Men* (Leipzig, 1856).

57 Thomas Taylor Meadows' books *The Chinese and Their Rebellions*, London, 1856, and *Notes on the Government and People of China*, London, 1847.

58 Tolstoy had earlier taken lessons in classical Hebrew from a Moscow rabbi.

59 Frau Sophie Behrs' German translation of *What I Believe*.
60 H. W. Pulley's *The Ground Ash: A Public School Story*, 1874, which Chertkov had sent to Tolstoy from England (*Letters*, II, 374, fn.1). 'Revivalist' is written in English with a Russian ending.
61 M. S. Sukhotin, a widower and family friend who later married Tolstoy's daughter Tatyana.
62 The inhabitants of Rzhanov's house (1884, Note 38).
63 The opening and reading aloud of the notes, poems and messages of various kinds which the family 'posted' during the week for Sunday evening entertainment.
64 Sonya's poem *The Angel*, published in her son Sergey's book *Ocherki Bylogo*, about the relations between a husband and wife at Yasnaya Polyana, disrupted by the intervention of the devil and restored to harmony by the touch of an angel's wing!
65 Tolstoy wrote *A Sick List of the Mental Patients of the Yasnaya Polyana Hospital* for the 'post-box'. The list included symptoms and prescribed treatment. He himself was the first patient.
66 Both stories by Turgenev. The second story is known in the Garnett translation as *A Tour in the Forest*.

1885

1 The only entry for 1885.
2 Sonya wanted to include Tolstoy's picture in the edition of his works which she was preparing, and he reluctantly agreed.

1888

1 Y. I. Popov, a writer on agricultural themes, a collaborator on *The Intermediary* and a suitor of Tolstoy's daughter Tatyana (*Letters*, II, 469).

2 Isabel Hapgood, an American writer and translator, who corresponded with Tolstoy and translated several of his stories and articles, as well as works by other major nineteenth-century Russian authors (*Letters*, II, 451, fn. 7).

3 George Kennan, the American journalist and traveller, who wrote extensively on Russian themes. His two-volume study *Siberia and the Exile System* (1891) is a standard work. At the time Tolstoy was reading an article in the *Century* by Kennan on political exiles and common criminals in Tomsk, which was sharply critical of the Russian government (*Letters*, II, 466).

4 Tolstoy hoped to take up teaching again, and visited a local evening school for young factory workers, but the school authorities turned down his request to be employed.

5 Sonya.

6 In English in the diary.

7 The prospective bridegroom was Y. I. Popov.

8 The proprietor of a fashionable women's dress shop in Moscow.

9 In *Russian Thought*, IX, 1888. Tolstoy sympathized with the radical critic and journalist Chernyshevsky's criticism of Malthusian theory.

1889

1 Mrs Humphry Ward's novel, expressing her view that Christianity could be revitalized by emphasizing its social mission at the expense of its miraculous elements.

2 Sonya insisted that the proposed marriage between her daughter Masha and P. I. Biryukov (Posha) be postponed for a year. Biryukov ranked second after Chertkov among Tolstoy's closest friends and collaborators and wrote the first comprehensive biography of him (*Letters*, II, 413 ff.).

3 *The World's Advance Thought and the Universal Republic*, an American journal edited by Lucy Mallory in Portland.

4 N. A. Polushin, a writer of stories for the people whom Tolstoy recommended to the publisher Sytin.

5 An old-established French bookshop and music shop on the Kuznetsky Bridge.

6 An article about the Peter and Paul Fortress in the *Century Illustrated Monthly Magazine*.

7 N. Y. Grot, professor of philosophy at Moscow University and editor of the journal *Problems of Philosophy and Psychology*, which later published Tolstoy's *What is Art?* (*Letters*, II, 428). N. A. Zverev, also a professor at Moscow University and later Deputy Minister of Education and a member

of the Council of State. He wrote an essay on *Count L. N. Tolstoy as Artist* (1916). L. M. Lopatin, professor of philosophy and president of the Moscow Psychological Society.

8 *Education Day, 12 January.* This day – the anniversary of the founding of Moscow University, and also Tatyana's Day – was celebrated as a university holiday throughout Russia. Tolstoy's article was published in the *Russian Gazette.*

9 Books on the Mormon sect, founded by Brigham Young in 1830, and sent to Tolstoy by Young's daughter.

10 A. I. Yershov had served with Tolstoy in the Crimea and asked him to write a foreword to the second edition of his book *Sevastopol Memoirs of an Artillery Officer.* Tolstoy's foreword was first published in England in 1902.

11 N. F. Fyodorov, the ascetic philosopher and librarian at the Rumyantsev Library (*Letters*, II, 353–4).

12 F. A. Zhyoltov, a peasant author of stories about the life of workers and peasants and a member of the sect of Molokans (so called because they drank milk during fasts), whose members rejected Orthodox Church ritual and lived a communal existence.

13 N. F. Shelgunov's *Essays on Russian Life*, which contained a criticism of the principle of forcible non-resistance to evil.

14 Tolstoy's youngest son, who died in 1895.

15 Vanechka.

16 B. N. Popov, whose book entitled *Poems* had just been published in Moscow.

17 By Voltaire.

18 Lewis Wallace's historical novel about the early days of Christianity: *Ben Hur: a Tale of the Christ.* It was translated into Russian soon after it was published.

19 See Note 10.

20 By Édouard Rod. The author sent a copy to Tolstoy and Tolstoy later quoted from it in *The Kingdom of God is Within You.*

21 The first – an unfinished article urging people to lead a better life; the second – thought to be the first mention of *Resurrection.*

22 I. S. Ivin, a peasant who was a prolific author of novellas, short stories and poems, and provided raw material for the publishers of cheap popular literature. Tolstoy tried unsuccessfully to persuade him to work for *The Intermediary.*

23 D. P. Sokolov, sentenced in 1875 in the so-called 'Trial of the 193'.

24 By Rider Haggard (translated into Russian in 1887).

25 *Literature and Dogma.*

26 In English in the diary.

27 William Frey, a Russian who emigrated to America in 1868 to found an agricultural community on communist lines and returned to Russia in 1885 after a period in England (*Letters*, II, 401). Tolstoy never finished the article he intended to write about him after reading an English biography of Frey by Edward Spencer Beesly.

28 Tolstoy's notes were intended for Goltsev to use in a public lecture on *The*

Beautiful in Art; Vera Alexandrovna Shidlovskaya – Tolstoy's wife's aunt.

29 Matthew Arnold's *St Paul and Protestantism: with an introduction on Puritanism and the Church of England*. Tolstoy refers to it again on 4 March.

30 K. A. Klodt, whose sculpture of Tolstoy ploughing is now in the Tolstoy Museum in Moscow.

31 N. A. Kasatkin – an artist and academician who became a People's Artist of the R.S.F.S.R. after the revolution.

32 V. S. Solovyov's introductory article to M. S. Solovyov's translation, in which Tolstoy's own translation is criticized.

33 Either S. M. Georgiyevsky's *Principles of the Life of China*, 1888, or *How the Chinese Live* by A. A. Gatsuk, 1889.

34 Poems by the nineteenth-century Portuguese poet Anthero de Quental, who in later life became interested in Buddhism.

35 Probably the collection of Chekhov's stories *In the Twilight*, published in 1888.

36 Tolstoy completed his article *On Art* the following day, and it was eventually published in *Russian Wealth*.

37 The fourth edition of Tolstoy's works, which his wife was responsible for.

38 The comedy eventually entitled *The Fruits of Enlightenment*.

39 A novel by Mrs Caroline Clive (1855, Russian translation 1859). It concerns the fate of a man who murders his wife to marry the woman he loves, escapes suspicion but is later driven by conscience to confess, with disastrous results for his family

40 Sonya's name for the 'Tolstoyans' with their addiction to manual labour and a peasant way of life.

41 Knop's textile factory.

42 William Wilberforce Newton, an American Episcopalian minister, accompanied by another minister and a writer. Newton published an account of this visit in *A Run Through Russia; the Story of A Visit to Count Tolstoi*, 1894.

43 A formula frequently used by Tolstoy the night before the next day's entry.

44 Tolstoy had originally intended to walk from Urusov's to Moscow.

45 In 1866 Tolstoy had spoken at a court-martial in defence of Vasily Shabunin, a soldier accused of striking an officer. Shabunin was found guilty and executed. In 1889 a witness for the defence, N. P. Ovsyannikov, sent Tolstoy an account he had written of the episode, which was later published with Tolstoy's amendments as *An Episode from Count Tolstoy's Life*. Tolstoy himself wrote his *Memoirs of a Soldier's Court-Martial* in 1908. See W. Kerr, *The Shabunin Affair*, 1982.

46 Tolstoy visited the 17th 'Itinerants' Exhibition, where Repin's picture of St Nicholas saving three men wrongly condemned to death in Myra in Lycia and Gay's picture of Christ and his disciples in the Garden of Gethsemane were on display.

47 S. I. Taneyev, the distinguished pianist and composer. Sonya's infatuation with him later caused Tolstoy acute – and quite groundless – jealousy (*Letters*, II, 554, fn.1).

48 I. I. Gorbunov-Posadov, a writer and poet, and a close collaborator with

Chertkov and Biryukov on *The Intermediary*, of which he later became editor.

49 A Persian legend written by A. I. Apollov for *The Intermediary*, but banned at the time in Russia and first published in England.

50 L. Y. Obolensky, editor of *Russian Wealth*.

51 J. H. Noyes' *History of American socialisms*, Philadelphia, *1870*.

52 An American religious, anarchical and pacifist sect which Tolstoy read about in Noyes' book.

53 If he wished to marry Tolstoy's daughter Masha.

54 New conscripts at the Khamovniki barracks.

55 The journey on foot from Moscow to Yasnaya Polyana with Y. I. Popov.

56 Tolstoy's comedy *The First Distiller*.

57 The farmstead on the Tolstoys' Nikolskoye-Vyazemskoye estate, where his son Ilya and his family were living at the time.

58 Ilya's wife. Tolstoy had walked some twenty kilometres in the heat of the day.

59 In Tolstoy's notebook there is a 'bill of indictment' against Ilya and Sonya accusing them of leading an extravagant life with servants, horses, carriages and dogs, and alluding to the growing rift between husband and wife.

60 W. E. H. Lecky, the English historian and philosopher. Tolstoy was reading the chapter on the aesthetic, scientific and moral development of rationalism in the Russian translation of Lecky's book *History of the Rise and Influence of the Spirit of Rationalism in Europe*, London, 1865.

61 In 1888 Sonya had bought two more estates, as well as managing the Yasnaya Polyana, Nikolskoye-Vyazemskoye and Samara properties.

62 Sonya's cousin, with whom Tatyana was for a time in love.

63 The theme is dealt with to some extent in *The Forged Coupon*.

64 Ernest Renan's *Histoire du peuple d'Israël*.

65 G. Stewart, a friend of Whitman's, had sent *Leaves of Grass* to Tolstoy as well as some other poems by Whitman. It is not clear whether he also sent De Quincey's *Confessions of an English Opium Eater*, which is in the library at Yasnaya Polyana.

66 Vera Kuzminskaya.

67 A shortened version of Victor Hugo's novel, revised by Tolstoy and published by *The Intermediary*.

68 The hero of a story by S. T. Semyonov, a peasant writer of whom Tolstoy thought highly. He later wrote a foreword to a collection of Semyonov's peasant stories which were awarded a prize by the Academy of Sciences.

69 The book by the American writer Adin Ballou (1803–90,) entitled *Christian Non-resistance in all its Important Bearings, Illustrated and Defended*, Philadelphia, 1846.

70 *Father Sergey* develops this idea to some extent. *Yurodstvo* – a noun from *yurodivy*, often translated as a 'holy fool' or 'God's fool', a simpleton believed to possess divine gifts of prophecy. In certain contexts I have translated *yurodivy* as 'an eccentric'.

71 I. B. Feinermann, a Ukranian Jew, strongly influenced by Tolstoy's ideas, who came to live near him in 1885 and became a convert to Orthodoxy in

order to teach at the Yasnaya Polyana school. He wrote extensively about Tolstoy (*Letters*, II, 489).

72 A Utopian novel by the American novelist and political theorist Edward Bellamy (1888), the hero of which falls asleep in 1887 and wakes up in 2000 to find that great social improvements have taken place which have transformed capitalism.

73 They had been staying with Tolstoy since 27 June.

74 Tolstoy devoted several pages of *What is Art?* to developing these words of the Russian painter Bryullov, which he had first heard from his friend Gay.

75 It is more likely that Tolstoy read *about* Keats in an article by Henri-Joseph Texte in the *Revue des Deux Mondes*. John Middleton Murry compared the two men in his article *Keats and Tolstoy*.

76 The words 'equivocation' and 'delusion' both appear in English in the diary.

77 A. V. Alyokhin, the son of a wealthy merchant who founded a Tolstoyan commune with his two brothers, and later helped Tolstoy with his famine relief work (*Letters*, II, 470).

78 Probably the sections on art and aesthetics in the second and third books of *Die Welt als Wille und Vorstellung*, which Tolstoy read in a Russian translation.

79 With N. N. Gay about Masha's intended marriage to P. I. Biryukov.

80 The article was later called *Science and Art*.

81 Tolstoy was reading the manuscript of *Edifying Exhortations of Saint Tikhon Zadonsky*, compiled by Ozmidov and Chertkov's wife and published the following year.

82 She nevertheless read the diary surreptitiously.

83 Tolstoy later wrote a foreword to Ertel's novel at his widow's request.

84 By Goncharov, whose earlier novel *A Commonplace Story* he had recommended to Arsenyeva.

85 *The Kreutzer Sonata*.

86 N. M. Chistyakov, a friend of Ertel's, whom Chertkov invited to look after all his economic and financial affairs, which Chistyakov did until 1894.

87 A. M. Novikov taught the Tolstoy children in 1889–90 and later worked with Tolstoy on famine relief. He left some reminiscences of Tolstoy.

88 Here and in several other places (e.g. 1 December 1889, 5 February 1890 and 25 June 1891) the expression *durno spat*, which I have translated literally as 'to sleep badly', clearly seems to imply masturbation, whereas the more common *plokho spat* (also translated in the same way) has no such connotation.

89 There is a question mark after this title in the manuscript and I have been unable to trace it among Walt Whitman's works.

90 These ideas were expressed later in *Father Sergey*.

91 For example, that Tolstoy's views on sex are too closely implicated in the passenger's narrative, which is insufficiently lively and natural as a result.

92 Henry Rabusson's *Idylle et drame de salon*.

93 See Note 8. Tolstoy had written an article for Tatyana's Day (12 January) 1889, but did not write another one.

94 A. M. Novikov.

95 The original title of *The Devil*.

96 The celebrations on 8 November 1889 to mark the 500th anniversary of the Russian artillery.

97 F. W. Evans, *The Divine Law of Cure*, Boston, 1884.

98 *Fort comme la mort.*

99 Domma Makarova, a young Yasnaya Polyana peasant girl who was seriously ill and whom Tolstoy had recently visited.

100 Vicomte Melchior de Vogüé's pioneering study *Le roman russe* had appeared in 1886, and he wrote extensively on Russian literature. Neither he nor his wife (who also asked to translate *The Kreutzer Sonata* – *Letters*, II, 451) actually did so.

101 *Resurrection*, so called because the story which served as the basis for it was told to Tolstoy by the lawyer A. F. Koni (*Letters*, II, 556).

102 P. G Hansen, a Dane who had worked in Russia. He translated into Danish and sent to Tolstoy *Childhood, Boyhood* and *Youth, The Power of Darkness, The Fruits of Enlightenment* and some minor works (*Letters*, II, 482).

103 T. M. Bondarev, a peasant, religious sectarian and the author of *Hard Work and Slothfulness or the Triumph of the Farmer*, which Tolstoy greatly admired and for which he wrote a foreword.

104 A wealthy stockbroker who was concerned about the influence of Tolstoy's views on his sons, one of whom had been expelled from college and was working on a Tolstoyan agricultural community.

105 The first amateur performance, at Yasnaya Polyana, of what was to become *The Fruits of Enlightenment* was to be given on 30 December.

1890

1 Andrey S. Butkevich, a medical student at Moscow University and later a doctor in Moscow who came under Tolstoy's spell for a time and later wrote memoirs of an 'ex-Tolstoyan'.

2 The school opened by Masha in a gardener's cottage near the entrance to the Yasnaya Polyana estate for the education of the local children. Tolstoy sometimes taught there, as well as his other daughter Tatyana.

3 Privately in Petersburg and by the Freie Bühne society in Berlin.

4 To *The Kreutzer Sonata.*

5 Possibly *The Light Shineth in Darkness*, which he sometimes called 'his own' drama.

6 N. N. Gay junior. Part of the letter concerns Tolstoy's admission that he sometimes acts against his conscience in order to avoid some unpleasantness in the family.

7 Tolstoy visited the Optina Monastery with his sister (Mashenka), who was living temporarily in a nunnery nearby.

8 K. N. Leontyev, novelist and critic, who was living at the monastery at the time and became a monk shortly before his death. His major work, *On the*

Novels of L. N. Tolstoy, was written in 1890, but not published until 1911.

9 Respectively the ultra-conservative Chief Procuractor of the Holy Synod; an archbishop who had frequently spoken against Tolstoy; and a literary historian who was highly critical of his work, especially *Anna Karenina*.

10 The French classical historian's article *Études d'histoire réligieuse*, which Tolstoy read in the *Revue des Deux Mondes* and alluded to in the first draft of *The Kingdom of God is Within You*.

11 The Polish novelist's *Without Dogma* (*Letters*, II, 670–1).

12 Sonya was planning to publish a supplementary thirteenth volume to the recent eighth edition of Tolstoy's works, and this duly appeared in 1891.

13 To visit the school which Tolstoy's daughters had opened without official permission.

14 One of two stories (*Love* and *Monte Cristo*) which his son had written (*Letters*, II, 479).

15 These ideas were to some extent expressed in Tolstoy's unfinished story *Mother*.

16 The words 'love' and 'blood' rhyme in Russian.

17 A reference to certain reforms by the German Emperor in the field of labour legislation.

18 The article eventually entitled *Why Do Men Stupefy Themselves?*

19 Of *The Fruits of Enlightenment*.

20 Apparently a Czech woman who had written him an unsigned letter from a monastery.

21 Not an Englishman, but an American religious writer, Alonzo G. Hollister.

22 See the foreword Tolstoy wrote (*The First Step*) to Howard Williams' *The Ethics of Diet*.

23 Tolstoy had originally agreed to send some of his diaries to Chertkov for him to make extracts from them. Chertkov had suggested that all the diaries should be handed over to him for safe keeping, and Chistyakov had come to collect them. However, Tolstoy changed his mind for fear of offending his wife (see *Letters*, II, 458).

24 This sentence was erased, but can still be deciphered.

25 Thackeray's novel.

26 Tolstoy, while not actually opposing Biryukov's and Masha's wish to get married as his wife did, nevertheless repeated his belief that marriage was 'a fall' for people wishing to lead a good Christian life. Biryukov had written to Masha, Tolstoy and Sofya Andreyevna (see also 6 July 1890), but none of the letters has survived.

27 See 1884, Note 53.

28 See *The First Step* (Note 22).

29 A Swiss citizen and member of the Salvation Army whom Sonya had engaged as a tutor to the young children.

30 N. D. Helbig (née Princess Shakhovskaya), a pianist and pupil of Liszt's. She had come to Yasnaya Polyana in 1887 to meet Tolstoy and had returned as a guest on several occasions. She published her reminiscences of him in *Tolstoy at Sixty*, *The Bookman*, NY, 1911.

31 R. V. Löwenfeld, a German Slavist and literary critic, translated Tolstoy

and wrote a number of articles about him. He came to Yasnaya Polyana to collect material for a major book on Tolstoy's life and works – *Graf Leo N. Tolstoi. Sein Leben, seine Werke, seine Weltanschauung*, Berlin, 1892 – which appeared in Russian translation in 1904.

32 A manuscript (not published) entitled *Unknown Works of Count L. N. Tolstoy.*

33 15 August should be 14 August.

34 Löwenfeld sent Tolstoy several plays by Ibsen in German translation, of which he read *The Wild Duck* and *Rosmersholm.*

35 I. D. Rugin, an employee of *The Intermediary* publishing house temporarily attracted by Tolstoy's ideas.

36 From a Dr. F. D. Brooks of Milwaukee.

37 Sonya was now in Moscow.

38 More exactly, he re-read it.

39 Coleridge's philosophical treatise *Aids to Reflection*, a series of aphorisms and comments, which Strakhov had sent to Tolstoy.

40 E. de Pressensé's *Histoire des trois premiers siècles de l'Église Chrétienne*, 5 volumes, Paris, 1858–69. Tolstoy's copy at Yasnaya Polyana has many notes in his handwriting.

41 He wrote about it in *The Kingdom of God is Within You.*

42 In 1890 Tolstoy received from New York a brochure entitled *Diana. A psycho-physiological essay on sexual relations for married men and women.* With the aid of Dr Bogomolets he quickly produced a Russian version of it entitled *On the Relations between the Sexes.* Tolstoy availed himself of the medical knowledge of Dr Bogomolets, whom he had previously helped to obtain permission to visit his sick wife, a political prisoner in Siberia.

43 Gay was sculpting a bust of Tolstoy, now in the Tolstoy Museum in Moscow.

44 Chertkov's article *An Evil Sport*, for which Tolstoy wrote a short foreword.

45 Maupassant's *Le port*, translated at Tolstoy's suggestion by Novikov and considerably revised by Tolstoy. It was eventually published under the title *Françoise.*

46 *Le port (Françoise)* and part of *Sur l'eau* (entitled *Expensive* in Tolstoy's version).

47 He re-read the drama, which he had first read in 1859.

48 In *The Week*, 1890, No. 43.

49 *The Kingdom of God is Within You*, referred to below as his article on non-resistance.

50 *The Week*, in reporting the publication of E. J. Dillon's translation in the English journal the *Fortnightly Review* of Tolstoy's story *Walk in the Light while there is Light*, had distorted the content of the story.

51 *What I Believe*. The reference in the following sentence is to the followers of Montanus, a second-century prophet from Phrygia, who gave his name to the 'heresy' of Montanism.

52 His impressions of the murder trial he attended at Krapivna were later used in the court scene in *Resurrection* and also in the murder episode in *The Forged Coupon.*

53 G. A. Rusanov, a landowner and university graduate, who greatly admired Tolstoy's fiction and whose friendship with him dated from a visit to

Yasnaya Polyana in 1883 to discuss the problems raised by *A Confession* –
he declared in his will that it was due to Tolstoy that he became a Christian
(*Letters*, II, 442); P. A. Boulanger, a personal friend of Tolstoy's who had
been arrested in 1897 for his activities on behalf of the Dukhobors,
emigrated to England, where he lived at the Purleigh Colony, but was later
allowed to return to Russia, where he wrote extensively about Tolstoy and
his ideas (*Letters*, II, 562).

54 See Note 1. Anatoly was Andrey's brother.

55 Emile Joseph (Mikhaylovich in Russian) Dillon, an English journalist and
translator of Tolstoy and author of *Count Leo Tolstoy; a new Portrait by his
Contemporary and Critic Dr E. J. Dillon*. After the 1917 revolutions he
published *The Eclipse of Russia*, London, 1918.

56 Bolkhin and some other Yasnaya Polyana peasants had been charged, at
Tolstoy's wife's instigation, with felling birch trees on the estate.

57 The title *Resurrection* was used for the first time in this version.

58 In fact he would not be sixty-three until August 1891.

1891

1 *The Kingdom of God is Within You*, to which chapter references in 1891
entries relate.

2 Renan's *L'avenir de la science*.

3 *If I'm Alive*. See 1889, Note 43.

4 An article by A. S. Suvorin, editor of *New Times*, criticizing the *Afterword to
the Kreutzer Sonata* for advocating celibacy.

5 An unfavourable review in the *Berliner Tageblatt* of the performance at the
Residenz-Theater in Berlin of Tolstoy's play.

6 Professor Beketov's article did not attack Tolstoy, but Tolstoy disapproved of his attempt to base morality on evolution.

7 *The Open Court*, a monthly magazine published in Chicago, 'devoted to the
science of religion, the religion of science, and the extension of the
religious parliament idea'. The other target of its attack was William Booth,
founder of the Salvation Army.

8 His diary of the Crimean War years.

9 *Our Destiny, the Influence of Socialism on Morals and Religion; an Essay in
Ethics*, London, 1890, by the American Laurence Gronlund. Tolstoy wrote
very favourably of it in a letter to the author, and tried unsuccessfully to get
it translated into Russian.

10 In *What Then Must We Do?*

11 P. P. Arbuzov, who taught Tolstoy cobbling (referred to in 1884, Note 51).

12 Montaigne's *Essais* and the first chapters of Ertel's novel *Change*, dealing
with the growing tendency for landed estates to pass into the hands of
merchants and rich peasants.

13 *Judas*, later called *Conscience*; exhibited at the 19th 'Itinerants' Exhibition
and now in the Tretyakov Gallery.

14 Of volume 13 of Tolstoy's works, published by his wife, and combining *The

Kreutzer Sonata and *The Afterword* to it. Tolstoy's worries were to do with royalties on his writings, which he wished to renounce.

15 The first of a series of articles by A. A. Kozlov, professor of philosophy at Kiev University, in *Problems of Philosophy and Psychology*. It was devoted to Tolstoy's book *On Life* and criticized Tolstoy for his low opinion of European philosophy and the lack of an integrated philosophy of his own.

16 To intercede with the authorities who had just banned volume 13 of her edition of Tolstoy's works.

17 An unfinished story *Mother*, based to some extent on the life of A. P. Lopukhina, a Tula friend, and concerned with the upbringing of children.

18 Tolstoy's two youngest sons.

19 See Note 16. She had gone to Petersburg to seek an audience of the Tsar.

20 It was begun in the form of a diary by the mother.

21 Sonya had managed to obtain an audience of the Tsar Alexander III, in which she denied that her husband was to blame for the dissemination of his banned writings, which was the work of his sympathizers, who even stole his manuscripts.

22 Tolstoy's attitude to the private ownership of property necessitated the distribution of his estates and possessions between all the members of his family except himself.

23 Howard Williams' *The Ethics of Diet*, London, 1883, was later translated into Russian with a foreword by Tolstoy entitled *The First Step* – a powerful advocacy of vegetarianism on moral grounds.

24 In a French translation by Victor Cousin.

25 These thoughts were later developed by Tolstoy in *The Light Shineth in Darkness*.

26 Tolstoy visited the Tula abattoir to collect material for his article *The First Step*.

27 In order to meet the woman prisoner M. F. Simonson, who had been actively involved with a Tolstoyan agricultural commune and was being sent into administrative exile for her allegedly harmful influence on people.

28 The date should be 17 June. (Tolstoy has returned from a short journey and is retracing the events of the previous few days.) The two following dates are also wrong: 15 June should be 13 June, and 13 June should be 11 June.

29 M. F. Kudryavtseva, a doctor's wife and a friend of Marya Alexandrovna Schmidt, a devout Tolstoyan who spent much time at Yasnaya Polyana (*Letters*, II, 404–5, fn. 2).

30 At first Tolstoy had reservations about organized state aid to the victims of the serious famine of 1891–2, but soon changed his mind and threw himself into relief work with characteristic energy.

31 Sonya was upset by Tolstoy's proposal to state in the newspapers that he renounced the copyright of the works published in volumes 12 and 13 of Sonya's edition. Despite her objections he stuck to his plan. See Note 32.

32 To the editors of the *Russian Gazette* and *New Times* granting all who so wished the right to publish free of charge all works written by him since 1881, including those printed in Sonya's edition. See *Letters*, II, 483. Sonya had not at first forwarded the letter.

33 A railway station some 60 miles from Tula and 20 miles from Begichevka.

34 Tolstoy's article *On the Famine*, which had been sent to Grot for publishing in *Problems of Philosophy and Psychology*, was banned by the censor.

35 Tolstoy had no money of his own and had to rely on his wife for travel and other expenses for his journey to the Ryazan province. Sonya gave him 600 roubles to set up soup kitchens.

36 Published under the title *A Terrible Problem* on 6 November 1891 in the *Russian Gazette*, which received a second warning from the authorities as a result.

37 This story, intended for a volume in aid of the famine victims, was never finished.

38 From Fisher Unwin, London publisher and secretary of the Russian Famine Fund. For Tolstoy's reply see *Letters*, II, 488.

39 *On Ways of Helping the Population Suffering from the Harvest Failure*, published in 1892 in the volume *To Aid the Famine Victims*.

1892

1 Of *The Kingdom of God is Within You*.

2 She had been at Begichevka since 24 January.

3 During the previous two months he had been to Moscow, Yasnaya Polyana, Begichevka and back again to Yasnaya Polyana.

4 Y. P. Sokolov, a peasant who worked for Chertkov as a copyist.

5 The legal document dividing all Tolstoy's property between his wife and children had been signed on 7 June.

6 A riot caused by peasants resisting the felling of a wood belonging to them by Count Bobrinsky – an episode which Tolstoy wrote about in Chapter 12 of *The Kingdom of God is Within You*.

7 Henri-Frédéric Amiel, diarist and critic who spent most of his life as a professor at Geneva University. Tolstoy was reading his *Fragments d'un journal intime*, published posthumously, 1883–7.

8 In December 1893 Tolstoy wrote a foreword to his daughter Masha's Russian translation of Amiel's diary, which was published the following year.

9 A reference to M. Jourdain in Molière's play, who spoke prose without realizing it.

1893

1 Chapter 12 of *The Kingdom of God is Within You*.

2 Tolstoy's son was suffering from neurasthenia.

3 By P. I. Rayevsky, son of a landowner who died while working with Tolstoy on famine relief.

4 Bulygin and P. A. Rayev, a Tolstoyan sympathizer, had opened a school for local children on their farm without permission. They were sentenced to a fine or a month's imprisonment, and the school was closed.

5 *The Light Shineth in Darkness*.

6 The last chapter of *The Kingdom of God is Within You.*

7 Tolstoy and his daughter Tatyana spent a few days in the Begichevka area taking stock of the situation.

8 The various manuscript drafts on science and art which Chertkov had just returned.

9 More correctly, Zola's speech at a Paris banquet calling on the young generation to discard outworn beliefs and put their faith in science and work, and Dumas fils' letter to the journal *Gaulois* with its emphasis on the ideal of loving one another. The editor of *Revue des Revues* sent newspaper cuttings to Tolstoy about the different standpoints of Zola and Dumas, and as a result he began writing the article *Non-action.*

10 The article *Non-action.* The French journal did not publish it.

11 Of the famine relief. This was his last visit to Begichevka.

12 *Non-action* was published in Russian in the *Northern Herald*, 1893, No. 9. It came out in *Revue des Revues* in October 1893 in a bad French translation.

13 Chapter 12 of *The Kingdom of God is Within You* with the episode of the punitive expedition to quell a peasant riot referred to in 1892, Note 6.

14 Tolstoy's wife had insisted that the telegrams be sent to the translators in Paris, Berlin and Boston, followed by letters with amendments to the original text.

15 Masha had fallen in love with N. A. Zander, a young doctor temporarily engaged as a resident tutor to Tolstoy's younger sons, but Tolstoy and his wife both opposed the match, and Zander left Yasnaya Polyana at the end of July.

16 Charles Salomon, a French industrialist who translated some of Tolstoy's works into French and wrote several articles about him. They corresponded frequently and Salomon visited Yasnaya Polyana several times.

17 They used both German and French translations of *Lao-Tzu. Tao-te-king*, but never completed their Russian version.

18 A foreword to the *Works of Guy de Maupassant.*

19 Lessing's epigram *Das böse Weib* (Ein einzig böses Weib lebt höchstens in der Welt: Nur schlimm, dass jeder seins für dieses einz'ge hält).

20 By Tolstoy's wife, despite Tolstoy's letter renouncing the copyright of his works.

21 The original title of *Christianity and Patriotism*, so called because of the presence of a Russian naval squadron in Toulon in 1893 to mark the conclusion of a Franco-Russian alliance.

22 *Three Fables*, not finished until 1895.

23 Masha had wanted to enrol as a medical student; Tanya had already qualified as an artist and had her own studio.

24 D. S. Shor, a pianist and professor at the Moscow Conservatoire.

25 Charles Paul-Marie Sabatier's *Vie de Saint François d'Assise.* Tolstoy asked the author's permission for the book to be translated into Russian. This was given and a Russian translation was published by *The Intermediary* in 1898.

26 *A True Son of Liberty; or the Man who would not be a Patriot*, New York, 1893, by Frank Purdy Williams, an American writer and follower of Henry George.

1894

1 About the fact that Khilkov's mother, Princess Khilkova, in the absence of her son, who was living in exile, forcibly took his children away from his common-law wife (*Letters*, II, 499, fn. 6). D. A. Khilkov was a former Guards officer and wealthy landowner who gave up his career and most of his estates to work on the land (as a peasant) and who was exiled for his anti-clerical beliefs (*Letters*, II, 457). See 23 March entry.

2 Tolstoy was recognized while attending a congress of naturalists and doctors in Moscow and made to sit on the platform next to Timiryazev, the president.

3 Compare the characters Fedya Protasov and Karenin in the play *A Living Corpse*.

4 Tolstoy soon changed his mind and sent his article *Christianity and Patriotism* to be published abroad. Turner translated it into English for the *Daily Chronicle*.

5 Popov.

6 While at Chertkov's, Tolstoy had painful talks with Tatyana's suitor, Popov.

7 An arithmetical metaphor which Tolstoy was fond of using. The numerator of a fraction denoted a person's positive qualities, and the denominator his opinion of himself.

8 An exposition of his beliefs, originally in the form of questions and answers, which was eventually called *Christian Teaching*.

9 See 1893, Note 8.

10 An article by a professor of hygiene (subsequently an Octobrist member of the second and third Dumas) which was directed against Tolstoy's article *The First Step*.

11 Sonya objected to a photograph which Chertkov had taken.

12 E. H. Crosby, an American social reformer and 'Tolstoyan', who wrote extensively on Tolstoy. Tolstoy in turn wrote a preface to Crosby's book *Shakespeare's Attitude to the Working Class* (*Letters*, II, 511).

13 *From Bondage to Brotherhood* and *The Christian Revolt*. J. C. Kenworthy, an English lay preacher and ardent 'Tolstoyan', greatly impressed Tolstoy by his book *The Anatomy of Misery*, and went to Russia in order to meet him. He was closely associated with the *Croydon Brotherhood Church* and wrote extensively but not always reliably about Tolstoy's ideas (*Letters*, II, 533).

14 A short account of George's 'single tax' theory, written for the benefit of the peasant and religious sectarian T. M. Bondarev (*Letters*, II, 518).

15 A section of *Parerga und Paralipomena* concerning reincarnation in Eastern religions.

16 V. F. Lazursky, a literary historian and university professor, invited by Tolstoy's wife in the summer of 1894 to teach Latin and Greek to Andrey and Mikhail. During his stay at Yasnaya Polyana Lazursky kept a diary of his conversations with Tolstoy (published in 1939), mainly on literature and art.

17 Hannah Welsh – an Englishwoman who taught English and music to Tolstoy's children from 1894 to 1900.

18 In the *Daily Chronicle* (see Note 4).

19 Joseph Krauskopf, an American rabbi from Philadelphia, who was visiting Russia to explore the possibility of colonizing Jews there, and brought Tolstoy a booklet of his entitled *Homilies. Six Lectures.*

20 C. E. Turner, who had translated *Toulon* into English, came to see Tolstoy about an English edition of his *Translation and Harmony of the Gospels.* Turner held a tenured post as Lector in English at Petersburg University and was the author, *inter alia*, of *Studies in Russian Literature*, 1882, and *Count Tolstoi as Novelist and Thinker*, 1888.

21 A Polish lady, two of whose letters to Tolstoy have survived.

22 Coal mines and cement and brick works, some five miles from Yasnaya Polyana.

23 Timofey Bazykin, Tolstoy's illegitimate son by a peasant woman, who later worked as a coachman on Andrey's estate.

24 Varvara Nikolayevna MacGahan, the Russian-born widow of an American journalist, who was visiting Russia as a newspaper correspondent and brought Tolstoy a signed copy of George's book *A Perplexed Philosopher*, which dealt with Herbert Spencer's views on land ownership.

25 On Tolstoy's advice, Tatyana made a 'Henry George style' agreement with the peasants on the land she owned near Ovsyannikovo. Under the agreement the land was leased to the peasants, who undertook, instead of payment of rent, to contribute a fixed annual sum for communal necessities.

26 The journal published in Manchester by John Trevor (*Labour Prophet. The Organ of the Labour Church*).

27 The first mention of *Master and Man*.

28 See Note 25. According to Tatyana, this episode was the germ of the discussions between Nekhlyudov and the peasants about land reform on Henry George lines in *Resurrection*.

29 Tolstoy did not reply directly to the Englishman, Charles Foyster, but wrote an answer in the form of an article on the attitude to the state which was dated 15 December 1894 and sent to the *Daily Chronicle*.

30 *Des droits, des devoirs et des institutions du point de vue de la destinée humaine*, 1848, by the French Utopian sociologist Auguste Guyard.

31 Khilkov's common-law wife, who had written to Tolstoy about the unjust division of labour in the family between men and women. Marya Alexandrovna (Schmidt) – the daughter of a Moscow professor who gave up her own profession under the influence of Tolstoy's religious writings and settled near him, copying out his banned works and growing and selling produce. Tolstoy regarded her as spiritually superior to any woman he knew.

32 F. A. Strakhov, who was to edit a proposed manuscript journal, *L. N. Tolstoy's Archives*.

33 Although Tolstoy had renounced the copyright of his works he had agreed to accept a small payment for performances of *The Fruits of Enlightenment*

(and later *The Power of Darkness*), which he used for charitable purposes and referred to jokingly as his 'pension'.

34 An article in the *Herald of Europe* by V. D. Spasovich. The thoughts it prompted about his 'drama' refer to *The Light Shineth in Darkness*.

35 P. P. Arbuzov.

36 Captain Walrond, commander of the cruiser *Chesma*.

37 A student delegation from Moscow University visited Tolstoy to protest against the expulsion and administrative exile of fifty-three students for a demonstration at a lecture by Professor Klyuchevsky, thought to be unduly favourable to the late Tsar. Tolstoy wrote on their behalf to his lawyer friend A. F. Koni, and may have written other letters which have not survived.

38 She destroyed the negatives of several photographs in which Tolstoy had been taken together with Chertkov, Biryukov and other 'Tolstoyans'.

1895

1 Tolstoy and his daughter Tatyana were guests of the Olsufyevs from 1 to 18 January.

2 See 1894, Note 38. Sonya objected to Tolstoy being brought down to the level of the 'Tolstoyans' by being photographed with them.

3 *Master and Man*.

4 In a speech of 17 January 1895 Nicholas II referred to discussions about the possible participation of the *zemstva* in government affairs as 'senseless dreams', and made it clear that he intended to uphold the principle of autocracy no less firmly than his father. On the initiative of D. J. Shakhovskoy, a meeting was organized of members of the liberal intelligentsia at which Tolstoy was present, but he refused to write a statement of protest against the Tsar's speech for publication abroad.

5 The cause of the storm, which presumably led to the page being torn out, was Tolstoy's opposition to his wife's publishing his new story *Master and Man* in her edition of his works in view of his renunciation of copyright, and his offer of the story free of charge to the *Northern Herald*.

6 Tolstoy eventually agreed to let his wife publish *Master and Man*, but also to allow the *Northern Herald* and *The Intermediary* to publish it simultaneously without charge.

7 His *Three Fables* were published at the invitation of the president of the Society of Lovers of Russian Literature in an anthology issued by the Society in 1895.

8 Tolstoy had read a newspaper account of the disorderly behaviour of the students, who were celebrating the 75th anniversary of the founding of Petersburg University.

9 A. A. Škarvan, a Slovak doctor, who sympathized with Tolstoy's views, refused to serve as a military doctor on conscientious grounds, and was later imprisoned and deprived of his medical diploma. M. V. Alyokhin, a landscape painter and one of three brothers who were all 'Tolstoyans', wished to pay allegiance to the new Tsar, but not to swear an oath. It is not known why Biryukov was fined.

10 Goryushin was a university student with social democratic sympathies; Pavel Petrovich Kandidov was employed at the time as a coach to Tolstoy's young sons and also acted as his wife's secretary in connection with her edition of Tolstoy's works.

11 Tolstoy's son Lev was a patient at the time in Ogranovich's sanatorium near Zvenigorod.

12 Tolstoy's youngest son Ivan died of scarlet fever shortly before his seventh birthday.

13 Probably A. N. Dunayev.

14 Eugen Heinrich Schmitt was an Austrian writer who shared many of Tolstoy's ethical beliefs and hoped to systematize them. He translated some of Tolstoy's articles into German and wrote a book about him (*Letters*, II, 515). Tolstoy wrote to him to propose founding an international *Intermediary* which would publish, perhaps in Switzerland, a series of cheap

books and pamphlets in four European languages (see letter to Khilkov in *Letters*, II, 515). Nothing came of the project.

15 Of the stories listed, *Who is Right?* (a story about the famine), *Notes of a Mother* and the projected novel about the colonists and the Bashkirs were abandoned. *The Devil in Hell* eventually appeared as the legend *The Destruction of Hell and its Rebuilding*. *The Coupon (The Forged Coupon)* was finished in 1904. The story about Alexander I was finished in 1905 and entitled *The Posthumous Notes of the Elder Fyodor Kuzmich*. The drama referred to is *The Light Shineth in Darkness*.

16 Vladimir Solovyov's *The Principle of Punishment from the Moral Point of View* in the *Herald of Europe*, 1895, No. 3.

17 N. T. Izyumchenko, the son of a peasant, was sentenced to two years in a disciplinary battalion as a conscientious objector, and Tolstoy and his wife visited him in a transit prison in Moscow. Khokhlov was a patient in a psychiatric hospital.

18 Leskov, who had died in February 1895, left clear instructions in his will about how he was to be buried, and Tolstoy followed his example in wishing to avoid all ceremonies and speeches.

19 The subject of Tolstoy's will was later to become a major source of hostility between his wife and Chertkov.

20 He did so in his article *Senseless Dreams*.

21 The Moscow circuit court, to collect material for *Resurrection*.

22 T. A. Kuzminskaya.

23 Y. I. Popov.

24 M. L. Tolstaya.

25 Tolstoy's eldest son was shortly to marry Marya (Manya) Rachinskaya, the daughter of Professor K. A. Rachinsky, director of the Petrovsky Agricultural Academy.

26 Tolstoy and his daughter Marya were guests of the Olsufyevs from 19 to 31 May.

27 Tolstoy had received a copy of a German newspaper which referred to a booklet, *Graf Leo Tolstoi, von Anna Seuron* (Berlin, 1895). Anna Seuron, a Frenchwoman who had spent five years with the Tolstoys as a governess, had published her memoirs of that period, which were considered to be so libellous that it was suggested that Tolstoy should issue a refutation.

28 A reference to *Resurrection*, and to the daughter of Tolstoy's old friend L. D. Urusov, on whom Tolstoy modelled Missy Korchagina in the novel.

29 Major-General V. I. Poltoratsky had served with Tolstoy in the Caucasus, and his memoirs were later used by Tolstoy as a source of information on that area when he was writing *Hadji Murat*.

30 Sonya.

31 *Traité des hérétiques* by Sébastian Castellion, the Protestant theologian and professor of Greek at Basle.

32 Of his article *The Function of Criticism at the Present Time* in the *Northern Herald*, 1895, No. 6.

33 The one in English was to an Australian writer, S. A. Rosa, and reaffirmed his belief in Henry George's solution to the land problem.

34 Strakhov had just been operated on to remove a cancer. He died a few
   months later.

35 For the court scenes in *Resurrection*, which Tolstoy had in mind when he
   wrote earlier in the same entry 'things are progressing'.

36 By the English philosopher and sociologist Benjamin Kidd, author of
   Individualism and After, Principles of Western Civilization and *The Science of
   Power*.

37 C. Strempf, the editor of the Stuttgart journal *Wahrheit*, had sent Tolstoy
   three issues containing articles by him about Tolstoy's religious teaching.

38 Letters, II, 522. A letter to *The Times* on the persecution of the Dukhobors
   which Tolstoy revised several times before eventually sending it off (see
   entry for 22 September).

39 Tolstoy is believed to have read about Weismann and his disbelief in the
   inheritability of acquired characteristics in Kareyev's book *Historico-
   philosophical and Sociological Studies*, Petersburg, 1895.

40 Chekhov had paid his first visit to Yasnaya Polyana the previous month and
   read the manuscript of *Resurrection* there, after hearing Tolstoy read it.

41 Biryukov had gone to the Caucasus to get more information about the
   persecution of the Dukhobors.

42 Biryukov's article on the persecution of Christians in Russia in 1895 and
   Tolstoy's own letter (see Note 38) – both of which were published in *The
   Times* on 23 October 1895.

43 M. A. Schmidt.

44 Policarpo Petrocchi, *La religione nelle scuole* (Milan, 1895).

45 The original name of Nekhlyudov's fiancée in *Resurrection* (eventually
   Missy Korchagina).

46 In which she asked him to delete all harsh references to her in his
   diaries.

47 Sonya had been to see Tolstoy's play, which had been banned since 1887,
   and also the first performance of Taneyev's musical trilogy *Oresteia*.

48 The letters to his sons Andryusha and Misha are both translated in *Letters*,
   II, 524–6 and 527–32.

49 At Sonya's request, Tolstoy deleted 45 passages which were sharply critical
   of her.

50 With a description of Maslova, not Nekhlyudov.

51 *Shame*, published with some omissions in the *Stock Exchange Gazette* in
   1895. Corporal punishment was not abolished until 1904.

52 *Christian Teaching*.

53 *The Light Shineth in Darkness*.

54 John Manson had written to ask Tolstoy to express his views on the conflict
   between Britain and America over the frontiers of Venezuela. Tolstoy
   replied with an article which was published in the *Daily Chronicle* on 17
   March 1896 under the title *Patriotism or Peace? Letter on Venezuela*.

1896

1 *Patriotism or Peace?* See 1895, Note 54.
2 *The Light Shineth in Darkness.*
3 George du Maurier's novel about the life of artists in Paris, which Tolstoy read in Russian translation.
4 *La suite du Menteur,* Corneille's sequel to his comedy *Le Menteur.*
5 M. P. Novikov, an army clerk who wrote several stories about peasant life which Tolstoy admired. He later wrote about his relations with Tolstoy, which lasted until Tolstoy's death and which profoundly affected his life (*Letters,* II, 679). His brother wished to obtain Tolstoy's banned work *What I Believe,* and was given a letter by Tatyana Tolstaya to take to M. M. Kholevinskaya, a Tula doctor, who gave him a copy. Kholevinskaya had previously been arrested for distributing Tolstoy's banned works, and in February 1896 her house was searched by the police and Tatyana's letter discovered. She was arrested again and imprisoned, and wrote a letter to Tatyana which greatly upset Tolstoy and to which he replied at length (*Letters,* II, 535).
6 *Christian Teaching,* as it was eventually called.
7 At the Bolshoy Theatre in Moscow. The next day he wrote to his brother criticizing it severely.
8 'Koni's story' (*Resurrection*), or *The Light Shineth in Darkness.*
9 In Kareyev's book *The Historical World-outlook of Granovsky,* Moscow, 1896. Professor T. N. Granovsky was a distinguished historian and leader of the Moscow circle of pro-Western intelligentsia in the reign of Nicholas I.
10 *What is Art?*
11 *Christian Teaching.*
12 See 1889, Note 47.
13 The tragedy of Khodynka field, when crowds of people were trampled to death during the celebrations that followed the coronation of Nicholas II. Tolstoy wrote a story on the subject in 1910, based to some extent on a story by V. F. Krasnov entitled *Khodynka: The story of one not trampled to death* (*Letters,* II, 548).
14 Eventually known as *Christian Teaching.*
15 *How to Read the Gospels, and What Their Essential Nature is* (London, 1898).
16 The first mention of the story *Hadji Murat,* one of the original titles of which was *The Burdock.*
17 Another reference to Tolstoy's jealousy of Taneyev.
18 Pride or indignation (see Note 17).
19 Tolstoy, still suffering from his jealousy of Taneyev, went with his wife to Shamardino Convent to see his sister. Their trip lasted six days, from 10 to 15 August.
20 *The Light Shineth in Darkness.*
21 *Modern Science* by Edward Carpenter, included in his *Civilization: Its cause and cure and other essays* (London, 1889). Tolstoy later got his son Sergey to

translate the essay into Russian, and wrote a foreword to it himself.

22 'Prescriptions' referred to in a diary entry of 20 October (not translated here) for helping to relieve sufferings caused by various passions.

23 Repin, in a letter to *New Times* in connection with the silver jubilee of his career as an artist, had compared an artist's work with that of other professional people and said: 'We are lucky people – our work is amusement.' The letter caused an outcry, and Repin subsequently modified his view.

24 A Russian translation of *Phaedon*.

25 A. B. Goldenweiser, a distinguished pianist and composer, later for many years a professor at the Moscow Conservatoire, and for a time its Principal. His memoirs of Tolstoy, whom he knew well, were published after the revolution and have been translated into English in abridged form as *Talks with Tolstoy*.

26 Jean-Baptiste Faure, the French operative baritone and composer. He published many songs, including the very popular *Les Rameaux*. *Crucifixe* was a favourite duet of Tolstoy's.

27 An opinion expressed by Tolstoy's wife. Tolstoy no doubt attributed Sonya's piano practising to a wish to please Taneyev.

1897

1 In English in the diary.

2 Sonya.

3 His jealousy of Sonya's apparent infatuation with Taneyev.

4 The Tolstoys had been to Petersburg to see off the Chertkovs, who were leaving for England after having been exiled for publishing an appeal in support of the Dukhobors.

5 An 'appeal' directed against the existing political and economic structure of society, which eventually took the form of two articles, *Must it be so?* and *What is the Way Out?*

6 His jealousy of Taneyev.

7 *L'Esthétique d'Aristotle* (Paris, 1889) by C.-M. Bénard, quoted in *What is Art?*

8 Tolstoy often used this word to denote idle frivolity (a reference to the alleged behaviour of Hannibal's troops in Capua after their victory over the Romans).

9 A slightly inaccurate quotation of a couplet from a poem by Lermontov.

10 To leave home – a step not finally taken until 1910.

11 To her nephew N. L. Obolensky, the grandson of Tolstoy's sister.

12 She had fallen in love with M. S. Sukhotin, a married man, who was later to be her husband.

13 Tolstoy's niece Varvara (his brother Sergey's daughter) was living with a Pirogovo peasant as his common-law wife.

14 *What is Art?*

15 Like Chertkov, Boulanger was compelled to go into exile abroad for helping Tolstoy's campaign on behalf of the Dukhobors.

16 Having learned that it was intended to offer the first Nobel prize for literature to him, Tolstoy wrote to the Swedish press suggesting that the money be given to the Russian Dukhobors.

17 Arthur St John, a British army officer in Burma, who was sufficiently influenced by Tolstoy's ideas to abandon his career, and who played a big part in the Dukhobor emigration (*Letters*, II, 579).

18 She was strongly opposed to Tolstoy's sending his letter to the Swedish press because of its unrestrained abuse of the Russian government. Relations between them were particularly strained at the time – see Tolstoy's letter to her (not sent) of 19 May 1897 (*Letters*, II, 558).

19 The translation into Swedish of Tolstoy's letter to the Swedish press, done by a Swede who was at Yasnaya Polyana at the time.

20 There were apparently three Dunyashas in the Tolstoy household. It is thought that Tolstoy was referring here to Yevdokiya Nikolayevna Orekhova, a housemaid he had once been fond of.

21 Tolstoy's letter about the Nobel prize was printed in the *Stockholm Dagblad* in October.

22 Despite their strained relations, Sonya was helping her husband by copying out *What is Art?*

23 See 1894, Note 7.

24 Newspaper reports about British exploitation of the Indian population of South Africa.

25 The famous Russian explorer, geographer and anthropologist.

26 He later did so in *The Forged Coupon*.

27 Masha, who was staying with her husband in the Crimea, had written to ask whether her father felt any estrangement between them as a result of her marriage. He confessed that he did, but added that he did not wish to and would not do so in future.

28 Because of Sonya's objections, Tolstoy withdrew his foreword to Carpenter's article, but she later changed her mind and it was printed the following year.

29 Grot had had second thoughts about the simultaneous appearance of the full text of *What is Art?* in both England and Russia, and wished to spread the Russian version over several issues in his journal.

30 Dušan Makovitsky, a Hungarian Slovak doctor educated at Prague University, and a dedicated 'Tolstoyan' who had set up in Hungary a counterpart to *The Intermediary* for publishing the works of Tolstoy and other authors. He later became Tolstoy's personal doctor, lived at Yasnaya Polyana from 1904 to 1910 and kept a detailed record of his conversations, published in full in *Literaturnoye nasledstvo*, No. 90, 4 volumes, Moscow, 1979. He accompanied Tolstoy on his last journey to Astapovo in 1910.

31 The main part of the Yasnaya Polyana house where Tolstoy had been born and which he had sold to pay his gambling debts had been re-erected at Dolgoye, some twelve miles away. It was eventually demolished in 1913 and the timber and bricks were given to the local peasants.

32 S. N. Trubetskoy, coeditor with Grot of the journal which was publishing *What is Art?* Tolstoy was eventually obliged to accept their

conditions, and the work appeared in several successive issues.

33 *Father Sergey*, finished in 1898.

34 *The Posthumous Notes of the Elder Fyodor Kuzmich*, finished in 1905.

35 Nothing is known about this.

36 The basis of the story *Korney Vasilyev*.

37 A revised version of *The Devil in Hell*. It was published in England in 1903.

38 Nothing came of this.

39 *The Light Shineth in Darkness*.

40 This subject was used in a draft version of a chapter of *Resurrection* and in *The Forged Coupon*. Tolstoy also wrote a children's story, *Fedotka*, on the same theme.

41 A story of this title was begun in 1891 in the form of a woman's diary but was never finished.

42 The execution in Odessa in 1879 of three men accused of an attempt on the life of Alexander II provided Tolstoy with material for his story *The Divine and the Human*.

43 Because the first five chapters of *What is Art?* were published in Russia sooner than in England.

44 The first mention of *A Living Corpse*.

45 One anonymous letter from a secret society calling itself *The Second Crusaders* threatened Tolstoy with death as 'an enemy of our Tsar and country'.

1898

1 N. Y. Fedoseyev organized one of the first Marxist circles in Russia. Exiled for revolutionary activities, he became acquainted with some of the Dukhobors in Siberia and twice wrote to Tolstoy about the conditions they were compelled to endure.

2 George Bedborough, editor of an English pedagogical journal, had written to ask Tolstoy some questions about free love, but Tolstoy did not reply. See Bedborough, *Love and Happiness; Letters to Tolstoy written in 1897 and now first published* (Letchworth, 1917).

3 In English in the diary.

4 The two men were in Moscow for the first performance in the Bolshoy Theatre of Rimsky-Korsakov's opera *Sadko*, and called on Tolstoy the following evening.

5 To George Howard Gibson, a member of an American community called 'Christian Commonwealth'. Tolstoy's letter is translated in full in *Letters*, II, 515–17.

6 About collecting funds for resettling the Dukhobors. The letter was not published.

7 *Letters*, II, 567–70. Tolstoy's letter appeared in the *Daily Chronicle* on 29 April 1898.

8 In his foreword to the English translation Tolstoy mentioned the cuts made

by the Russian censors in the version published in *Problems of Philosophy and Psychology*.

9 In English in the diary.

10 A. N. Toliverova-Peshkova, editor of a children's magazine and the monthly journal *The Woman's Cause*.

11 His son Ilya's estate, where Tolstoy had gone to help with the famine relief – the consequence of another harvest failure, though not so serious as the one in 1891–2.

12 The money received as a result of a letter he wrote to the *Russian Gazette* on behalf of the famine victims.

13 A village in the famine area where Tolstoy made notes about the condition and needs of the famine victims.

14 Selected stories in Russian translation.

15 Fear of government reaction to Tolstoy's work for the famine victims, especially the publication abroad of his *Famine or No Famine?*

16 Lev Tolstoy's wife's first son, who died two years later.

17 *Father Sergey*, which had been left unfinished for seven years.

18 Leskov's *The Hour of God's Will*, drawing with Tolstoy's consent on the subject of his own sketch *The Wise Virgin*, a subject which Tolstoy later worked up in his story *Three Questions*, 1903.

19 *Famine or No Famine?*, which Ukhtomsky, the editor of the *St Petersburg Gazette*, refused to publish, and which only came out in Russia in a heavily censored version the following month.

20 Six young schoolchildren who had bought flour with the money they had collected were prevented by the authorities from distributing it to victims of the famine.

21 *The Chopin Prelude*, a story taking sharp issue with the views on sex expressed in *The Kreutzer Sonata*.

22 Despite his statement in 1891 renouncing his copyright on works written since 1881. The new decision only applied in fact to *Resurrection*, which was published simultaneously in English, French and German, as well as Russian.

23 Because of jealousy of Taneyev. On her way back from Kiev Sonya intended to call on some friends with whom Taneyev happened to be staying at the time.

24 In other words, to die.

25 Tolstoy's seventieth birthday.

26 Tolstoy had received an advance of 12,000 roubles from A. F. Marx, who agreed to pay 1,000 roubles a printer's sheet for the right to publish *Resurrection*.

27 A temporary rift with her future husband, M. S. Sukhotin.

28 He married Chertkov's sister-in-law in January 1899.

29 Herbert Archer, an English member of the Purleigh colony in Essex.

30 L. A. Sulerzhitsky, an artist and art school contemporary of Tatyana Tolstaya's, who later became a producer at the Moscow Arts Theatre. He had earlier been confined to a mental hospital in Moscow for refusing to do military service.

31 A letter asking Prince G. S. Golitsyn, civilian governor of the Caucasus, not to place any obstacles in the way of Sulerzhitsky and his son Sergey, who were to accompany the Dukhobors from the Caucasus to their new home in Canada.

32 Tolstoy had intended to send the following record of a conversation with his wife during the night of 28 July about her relations with Taneyev to his sister-in-law, Tatyana Kuzminskaya, and it was therefore written in the form of a letter to her. He changed his mind and did not send it, and it was found among his papers.

33 See Note 23.

34 Taneyev.

35 To her friends on her way back from Kiev (see Note 23).

36 Part I. Chapter 17.

1899

1 Tolstoy moved to Moscow on 25 November, returned to Yasnaya Polyana on 19 December and moved back again to Moscow on 10 January, where he and his family stayed until May.

2 To M. P. Shalaginin, on the incompatibility of war and Christianity.

3 To a group of Swedish pacifists who had asked him for his views about the Hague Peace Conference. Tolstoy's reply was published in England in the form of a short article, 'Apropos of the Peace Congress' (*The Free Word News-sheet, 1899,* No. 6).

4 He did in fact write an article, 'The Student Movement of 1899', on the subject of the serious student disturbances which had broken out in February at Petersburg University and spread to other parts of the country.

5 An artist who had been sent to a disciplinary battalion in Algeria for refusing to do military service, and had escaped from there.

6 The English publishers had not been able to keep abreast of their Russian counterparts, and Tolstoy had held back the next instalment to Marx's journal by a week to enable the English translation to appear simultaneously.

7 N. N. Gay junior.

8 In English in the diary.

9 I. G. Verus, *Vergleichende Übersicht der vier Evangelien* (Leipzig, 1897).

10 He was distressed by the unfortunate marriages of his daughters Varvara and Vera.

11 She had married Mikhail Sukhotin on 14 November, and immediately gone abroad with him.

12 But see 1898, 21 March (22).

13 It came out in the next issue of *The Cornfield*, No. 52, 25 December 1899.

1900

1 A letter to the Dukhobors, now settled in Canada, many of whom had allegedly succumbed to the temptation to own private property. The letter was begun in December 1899 but not finished until February 1900. Tolstoy refers to sending it off in the entry for 13 March below.

2 *The Slavery of Our Times.*

3 She and her husband were copying out extracts to send to Chertkov for his collection of Tolstoy's thoughts.

4 This was Gorky's first meeting with Tolstoy. Tolstoy allegedly called him 'a real Russian peasant'. Gorky reportedly referred to the occasion as being like a visit to Finland – 'neither home nor abroad, and cold as well' (*Letters*, II, 585).

5 Tolstoy took exception to Chekhov's treatment of the theme of adultery in the story.

6 'Next best' and 'next worse' are both in English in the diary.

7 At the Moscow Arts Theatre, where he had some disapproving things to say to Nemirovich-Danchenko, especially about the character of Dr Astrov.

8 *A Living Corpse*, which he returned to after an interval of three years but never completely finished. It was published for the first time the year after Tolstoy's death.

9 Gasha Trubetskaya, a former housemaid with whom Tolstoy had once had a liaison. She was employed by Tolstoy's sister, who was staying with him in Moscow at the time, and her reappearance there caused great distress to Tolstoy's wife. 'Serves him right': for 'him' read 'me'.

10 A trepanation of the skull.

11 *Patriotism and the Government* and *The Slavery of Our Times.*

12 To his daughter's estate at Pirogovo (where his brother's estate also was).

13 Of *A Living Corpse.*

14 Nothing came of the idea.

15 Both *The Slavery of Our Times* and *Thou Shalt Not Kill*, written on the occasion of the murder of King Umberto of Italy by an anarchist, were sent to Chertkov for publication in England.

16 To leave home.

17 Tolstoy's library contains Leipzig editions of *Adam Bede, Felix Holt* and *Romola* with marginal notes by Tolstoy, and also *The Mill on the Floss* and *Middlemarch*. It is not certain exactly what he was reading at the time, either by Eliot or Ruskin.

18 *The Light Shineth in Darkness*, as opposed to the 'little drama' *A Living Corpse.*

19 In English in the diary.

20 *What is the Way Out?*, sent to Chertkov in England.

21 James Legge's *The Chinese Classics* (London, 1875–6).

22 Like Posse, he wanted to obtain the text of *A Living Corpse* (in his case to

produce at the Moscow Arts Theatre), but permission was again refused as it was still unfinished.

23 In other words, the police.

24 He stayed with Tatyana at Kochety from 17 October to 2 November.

25 He wrote down his thoughts on the teachings of Confucius in some detail in an untranslated part of his diary entry for 12 November.

26 The wife of Prince K. A. Vyazemsky, who had become a monk on Mount Athos.

27 It is doubtful whether Tolstoy took his son's writings very seriously. Most of the copies of them in his library have not even been cut.

28 Tolstoy had begun to study Dutch in the winter of 1897, probably as a result of his friendship with Van der Veer, and could apparently read it fairly fluently.

29 Eleven wives of Dukhobors, having emigrated to Canada, wished to return to Russia to join their husbands in exile in Siberia. Tolstoy's letter to the Tsar had its effect and their wish was granted.

30 There are three editions of this collection of essays and aphorisms in Tolstoy's library.

31 Tolstoy read the Buddhist Suttas, part of the Vedas, in a Russian translation of Professor T. W. Rhys-Davids' English translation from the Pali.

32 Tolstoy read *Also sprach Zarathustra* in the original; also the article by E. Förster-Nietzsche on the genesis of the work, published in *Die Zukunft* in 1900.

33 The letter has not survived, but was presumably one of many requests for free copies of Tolstoy's works for provincial libraries.

1901

1 In fact via the book-dealer Serebrennikov to a peasant, V. K. Zavolokin, who had suffered for his religious and pacifist beliefs. There was a brief correspondence between the two men, and Tolstoy's letters to Zavolokin were published in England as a brochure entitled *On Reason, Faith and Prayer. Three Letters, (Free Word,* 1901).

2 Tolstoy's son Mikhail married A. V. Glebova, a maid of honour, and the Grand Duke Sergey Alexandrovich came to Moscow from Petersburg for the wedding. Tolstoy did not attend the ceremony.

3 On the minimum reforms needed, in Tolstoy's view, to calm the social unrest at the time. The appeal was first published in England in 1901.

4 Tolstoy worked intermittently at the novel between 1896 and 1904, but it was not published until after his death.

5 By decree of the Holy Synod in February 1901, on the initiative of the Chief Procurator, K. P. Pobedonostsev (*Letters,* II, 347).

6 The appeal to the Tsar was prompted by social unrest stemming from the decision of the authorities to impose compulsory military service on some 200 students of Kiev and Petersburg Universities who had taken part in

demonstrations; the 'programme' referred to was an unfinished article entitled 'What the Majority of the Russian Working People Want Most of All'.

7 A slightly garbled version of a saying of Coleridge's, which Tolstoy also used as an epigraph to his reply to the Holy Synod's decree of excommunication.

8 To the authors of the Holy Synod's decree of excommunication and the various people who had written to him about it.

9 A group of Petersburg writers including Maxim Gorky had protested against a police attack on a demonstration in front of the Kazan Cathedral on 4 March in support of university students who had been maltreated, as a result of which the Petersburg Union of Writers had been closed (*Letters*, II, 591).

10 The old peasant in Chekhov's story *In the Ravine*.

11 Major Petrov's mistress in *Hadji Murat*.

12 In his foreword to the Russian translation of Wilhelm von Polenz's novel *Der Büttnerbauer*, Tolstoy had intended to mention the work of the painter N. V. Orlov, who shared Tolstoy's views and painted many pictures of peasant life. He did not do so, but wrote a separate foreword to an album of Orlov's pictures of Russian peasants in 1908. For Polenz see *Letters*, II, 614.

13 An article on the labour problems, eventually called *The Only Way*, and first published in England in 1901.

14 *Notes for Soldiers* and *Notes for Officers*.

15 About the situation of the working people of Russia – eventually written and despatched in 1902 (*Letters*, II, 608–13). The Tsar did not reply.

16 For Tolstoy to convalesce after a serious illness. Countess Panina put her house and estate at Gaspra, near Yalta, at the disposal of the Tolstoy family and they lived there from September 1901 until June 1902. The house had previously belonged to Prince Golitsyn, Alexander I's Minister of Education, and was built by an English architect.

17 Tolstoy's daughter and sister respectively.

18 Tolstoy is quoting from *Selected Thoughts of John Ruskin*, translated from the English by L. P. Nikiforov.

19 For a description of Countess Panina's house at Gaspra see Tolstoy's letter to his brother in *Letters*, II, 605.

20 Kolya – Nikolay Obolensky, the husband of Tolstoy's daughter Masha.

21 Sasha – Tolstoy's daughter Alexandra; Seryhozha – his son Sergey, who joined them later.

22 The article 'What is Religion and What is its Essential Nature?' was completed in 1902.

23 Gorky, who had been arrested earlier in the year, had been released on medical grounds and given permission to reside temporarily in the Crimea for health reasons. Chekhov had his own house in Yalta, and both writers often visited Tolstoy at Gaspra. Tolstoy wrote to Chertkov that Chekhov was a complete atheist but a kind person, while Gorky had far more depth but was overpraised.

24 S. P. Polyakov, a member of Kovno circuit court who had written an article

on 'Count Tolstoy's Teaching on Life' (1900), had written to say that he intended to give up the law as a result of his sympathy for Tolstoy's views.

25 Probably M. A. Mikhaylov, a vine-grower, Tolstoyan sympathizer and brother of the artist K. A. Mikhaylov, who considered Tolstoy to be his 'spiritual father'. Tolstoy also got to know several members of the evangelical Stundist sect living in nearby Yalta and Feodosiya.

26 A famous waterfall near Gaspra.

27 Tolstoy was reading *Der Grabenhäger* at the time, which he considered to be inferior to *Der Büttnerbauer*, despite one particular chapter which, he told Chertkov, made him wish to resume writing fiction himself.

1902

1 See 1901, Note 15. The Grand Duke Nikolay Mikhaylovich, grandson of Nicholas I and a distinguished historian, made Tolstoy's acquaintance in the Crimea and visited him on several occasions. The extant correspondence between the two men amounts to more than thirty letters. The Grand Duke was murdered by the Bolsheviks in 1918 (*Letters*, II, 615).

2 Tolstoy was reading Nikiforov's Russian translations of Mazzini's *The Duties of Man* and *Selected Thoughts of John Ruskin*.

3 A well-known Petersburg doctor who had been called in to see Tolstoy at Sofya Andreyevna's request.

4 The words of a Russian folk song which Tolstoy had been reading and which, according to Dr Bertenson, he applied to himself and wept.

5 During Tolstoy's illness he occasionally dictated his thoughts to his family and later transferred them to his diary.

6 After recovering from angina pectoris, which had almost led to his death, Tolstoy was smitten with typhoid fever, but he was spared a 'third illness' and was soon well enough to return to Yasnaya Polyana.

7 An article prompted by the spread of industrial unrest in Russia, and the workers' demands for reforms. The article was finished in September and published in England later in 1902.

8 An anti-clerical treatise, finished in December and first published in England in 1903.

9 Eugen Schmitt, in serious financial straits as a result of illness, had asked Tolstoy for help, and Tolstoy sent him 300 roubles from the money received for *Resurrection* with the request to return it later. The other letter was to a young Moscow sympathizer who had written for advice about whether to serve in the army and do propaganda there for Tolstoy's ideas, or to refuse to serve and miss that opportunity.

10 K. P. Pyatnitsky had founded the influential journal *Knowledge* in 1898, and his friend Gorky collaborated with him in the enterprise.

11 A slightly abbreviated quotation of a saying by Epictetus, which Tolstoy had taken from an illustrated Russian desk calendar.

12 A speech by Merezhkovsky delivered before the performance of Euripides' *Hippolytus* at the Alexandrinsky Theatre in Petersburg, in which he spoke

against Tolstoy's views on sex in *The Kreutzer Sonata* and argued that Christianity provided a synthesis of spiritual and carnal love.

13 Tolstoy was referring to *The History of the Russian Intelligentsia* by the historian P. N. Milyukov, a founder of the Constitutional Democratic Party and later Foreign Minister in the Provisional Government.

1903

1 Biryukov had asked Tolstoy to recall what he remembered of his early years for the biography he was writing of him, and Tolstoy began to do so in his *Memoirs*.

2 It later became a separate article, *To the Politicians*, first published in England in 1903.

3 Tolstoy read France's *Opinions socialistes* (not *sociales*), Paris, 1902, and found his anti-religious and pro-socialist views distasteful.

4 Tolstoy was a great admirer of the American self-styled 'mystic transcendentalist and natural philosopher' Thoreau. One of the works he read was *The Intermediary's* publication entitled *Henry Thoreau: The philosophy of the natural life* (1903).

5 The article *To the Politicians*.

6 A letter to E. Linetsky and several prominent Jews about the anti-Jewish pogroms in Kishinyov in April 1903, and a telegram to the mayor of Kishinyov signed by Tolstoy and a group of Moscow intellectuals protesting against the actions of the authorities.

7 *To the Politicians* was sent to Chertkov in England and later published in the *Free Word*.

8 Chapter 15, with its harsh assessment of the character of Nicholas I.

9 N. K. Schilder's *The Emperor Nicholas I, his life and reign* (Petersburg, 1903).

10 An idea which led to nothing.

11 Tolstoy agreed to contribute to an anthology in aid of the victims of the Kishinyov pogroms – though not the story outlined in this paragraph (*Letters*, II, 631).

12 The basis of his story *After the Ball*. The girl's surname clearly suggests that of V. A. Koreysh, a student friend at Kazan University, and confirms the autobiographical nature of the story.

13 Nothing came of this idea either.

14 *Esarhaddon, King of Assyria, Three Questions* and *Work, Death and Sickness*, all of which were published in Yiddish translation in the anthology compiled in aid of the Kishinyov victims (Note 11).

15 One of the original titles of *After the Ball*.

16 The third tale was finished a week later than the other two.

17 Another early title of *After the Ball*.

18 Some of the messages of congratulations on Tolstoy's seventy-fifth birthday included the words 'great writer of the Russian land', first used by Turgenev in a letter to Tolstoy shortly before his death in 1883.

19 V. A. Lazarevsky, a minor author and great admirer of Chekhov, wrote to Chekhov to tell him that Tolstoy had called him the Pushkin of prose.

20 Tolstoy believed that Gorky was overestimated as a writer, and regretted that the German novelist, essayist and dramatist Wilhelm von Polenz was less well known.

21 The article, which was eventually called *On Shakespeare and the Drama*, was originally begun as a foreword to Ernest Crosby's *Shakespeare and the Working Class*.

22 A foreword to the short biography of W. L. Garrison by V. Chertkov and F. Holah, published by the Free Age Press in English, and later in Russian.

23 Tolstoy's son Andrey's relations with a married woman, Anna Leonidovna Tolmachova, led to his separation from his wife and children in November 1903 (and his eventual divorce in 1907 when he wished to remarry).

24 What he began to write (at first called *The Stone* or *The Corner-Stone*) was eventually absorbed in his article *The One Thing Needful* (1905).

25 Tolstoy wrote a story, *Prayer*, on this theme in 1905.

26 A legend Tolstoy had taken down from a story-teller and which he worked up in 1907 for his *Cycle of Reading*.

27 A story which grew out of a rough draft in his diary after the entry for 30 December, and which was eventually called *The Divine and the Human*.

28 No stories were written on the last two subjects.

1904

1 An anthology in calendar form entitled *The Thoughts of Wise People for Every Day*, published in 1903 by *The Intermediary* and revised in 1904 with a new *Cycle of Reading* in mind.

2 The Russo-Japanese War, which began on 27 January 1904.

3 These thoughts were expressed in the article *Bethink Yourselves!*, which Tolstoy began writing almost at once and which was widely read abroad.

4 Tolstoy was reading the German philosopher Georg Lichtenberg's *Vermischte Schriften*, in a four-volume edition of 1800–2. Many of his thoughts were included in Tolstoy's *Cycle of Reading*.

5 Tolstoy was reading Ernest Naville's book on the French philosopher, *Maine de Biran, sa vie et ses pensées* (Paris, 1874).

6 A. A. Tolstaya.

7 The article *Bethink Yourselves!*, which Tolstoy sent to Chertkov for publication in England.

8 The text of the letter is included in the last chapter of *Bethink Yourselves!*

9 K. A. Mikhaylov, art teacher and 'spiritual son' of Tolstoy (1901, Note 25); S. D. Nikolayev, a disciple of Henry George, who translated all George's main works into Russian. Dmitri Merezhkovsky and his wife Zinaida Gippius spent 11 and 12 May at Yasnaya Polyana, and both left accounts of their visit.

10 William Briggs, an Englishman who had originally intended to be a Unitarian minister but changed his mind because of religious doubts, was working at the time with Chertkov as a market gardener, and brought Tolstoy a letter with questions about who would be entitled to publish Tolstoy's works after his death.

11 To Tambov, where he had been posted as orderly to General Sobolev.

12 A long letter to Y. V. Molostvova, the daughter of a rich landowner who was very close to Tolstoy in her views, in which Tolstoy replied to her own letter complaining about the unsatisfactory nature of her life with his

advice on how rich people with a conscience ought to act. His letter apparently gave offence. See 22 December.

13 *Bethink Yourselves!* was published in *The Times*, and got an enthusiastic reception, especially from the *Daily News*.

14 Baron A. Y. Rosen's *Into Exile: Notes of a Decembrist, 1825–1900* (Moscow, 1900).

15 This was never done.

16 A Tula barrister to whom Tolstoy sometimes referred people in need of legal aid.

17 Lucy A. Mallory, editor of the American journal *World's Advance Thought*, had written very favourably about *Bethink Yourselves!*

18 Hippolyte Taine's *Les Origines de la France contemporaine* (1875–93).

19 Extracts from Amiel's Diary; *The Riddle of the Sphinx* (Moscow, 1900), which was a translation of extracts from Carlyle's *Past and Present*; and Mazzini's *The Duties of Man*.

20 Hans Andersen's fairy tale *Five out of one Shell*.

21 The manuscript of a Russian translation of *Selected Thoughts of Kant*, to be published by *The Intermediary*.

22 The first two items were incorporated into *The One Thing Needful*; the third took the form of an article, *Who Am I?*, subsequently entitled *The Green Stick*.

23 Extracts from Pascal's *Pensées* for inclusion in the *Cycle of Reading*.

24 The full text is translated in *Letters*, II, 608–13.

25 The Grand Duke Nikolay Mikhaylovich had personally delivered Tolstoy's letter to the Tsar. Tolstoy was concerned because what had been intended as a private communication from one man to another had been published abroad by Chertkov.

26 Port Arthur with its garrison of 15,000 men surrendered to the Japanese on 20 December 1904 after six months' siege.

1905

1 To Nicholas II (see 1904, Note 25).

2 Tolstoy's son had hoped to persuade the Tsar to convene the old *Zemsky Sobor*, the 'Assembly of the Land' in Muscovite Russia.

3 A tale Tolstoy had heard from a story-teller in 1897 and was reworking for publication in the *Cycle of Reading* about a peasant who left his wife to become a pilgrim.

4 *Alyosha Gorshok (Alyosha the Jug)*, a story Tolstoy wrote in a few days in 1905 but which was not published until after his death. Alyosha's nickname was the result of his being beaten for breaking a jug of milk.

5 Short biographies compiled by members of his family at his request for publication in the *Cycle of Reading*.

6 I have used 'secondary schools' and 'colleges' to translate *nizshiye* and *vysshye shkoly*.

7 In a much-quoted speech of 1860 Turgenev had attempted to classify the

characters of Hamlet and Don Quixote as representing the two fundamental and opposite tendencies of human nature: the former – analysis,
egoism and unbelief; the latter – belief in something eternal and
unshakeable, belief in the truth. He referred also to Shakespeare's Horatio
in *Hamlet* as a disciple in the best sense of the word, honest, loyal, self-
sacrificing, warm-hearted, but with a rather limited mind. Tolstoy put
Horatio on a par with Don Quixote, and added the character of the
heroine of Chekhov's story *The Darling*.

8 A reference to a letter from a semi-literate peasant to Tolstoy asking him
how long the down-trodden peasantry would have to go on 'dragging an
overturned cart'. Tolstoy's reply was published in article form in England
under the title *How Are the Working People to Free Themselves?* –
subsequently reworked and entitled *The True Freedom*.

9 *Selected Speeches and Articles of Henry George*, compiled by S. D. Nikolayev
and published by *The Intermediary*.

10 The original title of *A Great Sin*.

11 What began as an article about Henry George became part of *A Great Sin*.

12 On 14 May 1905 two Russian naval squadrons were routed by the Japanese
fleet off the island of Tsushima.

13 The original title of *The End of the World* (sometimes translated as *The End
of an Age*), an article devoted to Tolstoy's belief that the coming social
revolution would lead to a new social order based not on coercion but on
love. The title is a reference to Matthew, 24:3. It was first published in
England in 1905; an edition published in Russia in 1906 was confiscated.

14 More precisely, the fact that his wife objected to his articles appearing
without payment in the *Free Word* and *The Intermediary*.

15 The former in the August number of the *Free Word*; the latter in the July
number of *Russian Thought*.

16 According to Makovitsky, Tolstoy was sent a copy of an American
newspaper with a translation of *A Great Sin*, and also a review of the article
in the *Spectator* of 5 August 1905.

17 From the editor of the Paris newspaper *Echo de Paris*, to which Tolstoy did
not reply.

18 A difficult pregnancy resulting in a stillborn child.

19 Another name for the story *Three Questions*, which had first appeared in
The Intermediary in 1903 and was included in the *Cycle of Reading*, but was
later removed.

20 *The Posthumous Notes of Fyodor Kuzmich*. The biographer of Alexander
I, N. K. Schilder was inclined to believe the legend that the Elder Fyodor
Kuzmich was in fact the Emperor Alexander, who had not died in 1825 but
had withdrawn from the world.

21 N. K. Schilder's biography *The Emperor Paul I* (Petersburg, 1901) and the
diary of Paul's tutor, S. A. Poroshin.

22 Tolstoy re-read Herzen's book after V. V. Stasov had mentioned it in a
letter to him the previous month.

23 A daughter, also called Tatyana (Tatyana Sukhotina-Albertini).

24 See Note 20.

25 The first volume of *Social Movements in Russia in the First Half of the Nineteenth Century* (Petersburg, 1905) with articles and materials on some of the Decembrists.

26 It was included in the second edition of *The End of the World* (Chapter 12), published by the *Free Word*.

27 See 1904, Note 22.

28 Incorporated into the article *An Appeal to the Russian People. To the Government, the Revolutionaries and the People.* The article was finished in 1906.

29 Tolstoy was reading the Grand Duke Nikolay Mikhaylovich's book on Count Stroganov, with its description of the heroic death of Stroganov's tutor, Charles-Gilbert Romme, during the French Revolution.

1906

1 Gorky travelled to America with M. F. Andreyeva, and when it transpired that they were not married, some American newspapers and public figures gave him a hostile reception.

2 P. V. Velikanov, a teacher then living in Novgorod, who, unlike Tolstoy, whose views he shared in many respects, believed in the need for political action.

3 An article in the *Stock Exchange Gazette* which accused the owner of Yasnaya Polyana of calling in the Cossacks to stop the illegal felling of trees on the estate – a charge which Tolstoy vehemently denied on his wife's behalf.

4 It eventually became *On the Meaning of the Russian Revolution*.

5 F. D. Bykov, a carpenter who, according to Makovitsky, revered Tolstoy as a second Christ, and knelt before him, much to his embarrassment; Y. O. Dymshits, a Jewish pacifist and founder of a vegetarian society, whose Tolstoyan views did not all survive the October revolution; A. A. Ofitserov, a follower of A. M. Dobrolyubov (one of the first Russian symbolist poets), later imprisoned for distributing pacifist and anti-clerical literature.

6 She was suffering from serious abdominal pains which necessitated an operation.

7 A foreword to the Russian translation of Henry George's *Social Problems*, published by *The Intermediary*.

8 A request for Tolstoy to take part in a reception for an English parliamentary delegation which was due to visit Russia, and which he declined in rather strong language. The visit did not take place.

9 *Dichtung und Wahrheit.* Tolstoy was re-reading Goethe's memoirs since he was thinking of writing his own.

10 A scurrilous article entitled *At Yasnaya Polyana. Impressions of a Tourist* by a young student which claimed that the local peasants regarded Tolstoy as a typical serf-owner and a wolf in sheep's clothing.

11 To the article *On the Meaning of the Russian Revolution*.

12 A gipsy settlement near Tula.

13 The first epistle of St John the Divine.

14 She died at the age of thirty-five of pneumonia.

15 An article in the *Russian Gazette* took issue with *On the Meaning of the Russian Revolution* on the grounds that it postulated too great a change in human nature; the letter from an officer expressed doubts about Tolstoy's anti-militarism; and the notice about *What Is To Be Done?* (the last chapter of *On the Meaning of the Russian Revolution*, which came out as a separate article) accused Tolstoy of repeating his old views to no effect.

1907

1 Plutarch's *Oeuvres morales* (a five-volume French translation); Montaigne's *Essais*; Waliszewski's *L'héritage de Pierre le Grand*; Renan's *Saint Paul*; and Xenophon's *Memorabilia*, which Tolstoy read in a Russian translation with parallel Greek and Russian texts.

2 A reference to an incident which Tolstoy read in Sabatier's life of St Francis in which St Francis, in answer to the question 'what is perfect joy?', replied that if we were refused admission to a house when cold and wet and hungry, and were humble enough to accept that the janitor was right to refuse us, that would be perfect joy.

3 Some scripture lessons for Yasnaya Polyana children, out of which grew the *Children's Cycle of Reading*.

4 In an unfinished article comparing St Paul's teaching unfavourably with the teaching of Christ.

5 An article on the eighteenth-century Ukrainian philosopher and poet for the *Children's Cycle of Reading*.

6 *Kill No Man (Ne ubii nikogo)*, written apropos of the imprisonment of N. Y. Felten, editor of the publishing house *Renewal*, for publishing Tolstoy's article *Thou Shalt Not Kill (Ne ubii)*. He was soon released on bail.

7 A compilation of Tolstoy's thoughts by the Chertkovs which has not been published.

8 I. Y. Repin spent more than a week at Yasnaya Polyana painting a large portrait of Tolstoy and his wife seated at a table. Tolstoy had some very unflattering things to say about it in a letter to his sister-in-law, calling it 'incredibly funny'.

9 N. N. Gusev, who had worked for *The Intermediary* publishing house since 1905, became Tolstoy's secretary in 1907 and stayed with him in that capacity for the next two years. He was arrested in October 1907 and briefly imprisoned, and arrested again in 1909 and sent into exile for distributing Tolstoy's banned works. His extensive writings included *Two Years with Tolstoy*, and from 1925 to 1930 he was director of the Tolstoy Museum in Moscow.

10 Tolstoy's son had divorced his first wife and married his mistress Y. V. Artsimovich in November 1907 – a marriage of which Tolstoy strongly disapproved.

11 After nearly two months' confinement Tolstoy had campaigned vigorously for his release.

1908

1 M. A, Schmidt. (See 1894, Note 31.)

2 It is not known what Tolstoy was reading by Bernard Shaw (or Schaw as he calls him in the diary).

3 For Tolstoy's eightieth birthday.

4 In English in the diary.

5 *God and Man* by Swami Vivekananda, a disciple of Ramakrishna.

6 This letter prompted Tolstoy to write to the press asking for the preparations to celebrate his eightieth birthday to be stopped – which they were.

7 *The Law of Violence and the Law of Love.*

8 His recollections about the Shabunin case (see 1889, Note 45), which he was writing for Biryukov's biography of him.

9 In the Kherson province, for a violent assault on the estate of a local landowner.

10 A. F. Koni, who supplied Tolstoy with the germ of the story of *Resurrection*.

11 *I Cannot be Silent*, as it later became.

12 An article written in connection with the arrest and imprisonment of V. A. Molochnikov, a fitter and Tolstoyan sympathizer, for distributing banned works of Tolstoy. Molochnikov had previously written to the Russian Prime Minister urging him to come to Tolstoy for advice on how best to satisfy the needs of the people.

13 N. K. Muravyov, a Moscow lawyer who later helped to draw up Tolstoy's will, had told him disturbing details about political trials in which he had been involved as counsel for the defence.

14 Later entitled *I Cannot be Silent*, against capital punishment.

15 *The Law of Violence and the Law of Love.*

16 Two short stories involving revolutionaries were begun at the end of the year but never finished.

17 N. G. Molostvov was writing a biography of Tolstoy which was published jointly with P. A. Sergeyenko. The first part of it, which came out in 1910, was not favourably received by Tolstoy. The extracts from his mother's diaries which Molostvov copied out were included in the book.

18 M. A. Schmidt.

19 The article was published on 3 July in both the Russian and the foreign press (although the Russian version was cut by the censor) and Tolstoy received more than sixty letters of appreciation.

20 The title is in English in the diary, and presumably Tolstoy read the novel in English.

21 The recitals given by Goldenweiser and the distinguished solo violinist B. O. Sibor included – surprisingly enough in view of Tolstoy's strictures in *What is Art?* – two sonatas and a romance by Beethoven. One of the sonatas was the Kreutzer!

22 The green stick which, according to Tolstoy's brother Nikolenka, was buried there, and was a symbol of universal happiness and brother-hood.

23 Nothing came of any of these ideas.

24 Two men had been sent to Yasnaya Polyana by Edison to make a record of Tolstoy's voice. He recorded some thoughts in Russian, English and French.

25 N. N. Gusev.

26 K. A. Romanik-Petrova had written to Tolstoy describing prison life in the Butyrskaya prison in Moscow, where she was serving a sentence for provoking unrest among the peasantry. Tolstoy in reply advised her to try to cultivate loving feelings towards both her fellow prisoners and her gaolers.

SECRET DIARY FOR 1908

1 This diary 'for himself alone' was kept by Tolstoy for the short period of 2–18 July 1908. In August 1908 he gave it to Chertkov, asking him to copy out what he thought necessary and then destroy the manuscript. Chertkov copied out the whole manuscript before destroying it.

2 A story by his former pupil, the Yasnaya Polyana peasant V. S. Morozov, called *Just Because of One Word*, for which he also wrote a foreword.

3 Sofya Andreyevna was angry because Chertkov was frequently visiting Yasnaya Polyana with an English photographer, who took numerous pictures of Tolstoy.

4 P. A. Boulanger, working at the time as an accountant on the railways, had squandered a large sum of government money at cards and had disappeared after leaving a note to say that he intended to kill himself. In fact he fled to the Caucasus, but settled near Tolstoy again in 1909 after a period abroad.

5 The road to Yasnaya Polyana was being remade in such a way that the interests of the peasants living in the village had been ignored.

6 A reference to Sofya Andreyevna's taunt that while preaching simplicity Tolstoy ate asparagus.

7 The wedding of her niece (Ilya's daughter), who married N. A. Holmberg.

1909

1 The story *The Monk Iliodor (Ieromonakh Iliodor*, ieromonakh – a monk with the office of a priest), which he began to write later that month.

2 *The Death Penalty and Christianity*, an article Tolstoy wrote in response to one by Stolypin which attempted to justify capital punishment by a reference to some verses in Mark's Gospel. Tolstoy's article was finished in January 1909 and published with cuts in some Russian newspapers the following month.

3 Press reports of a spate of executions of armed robbers and revolutionaries

prompted Tolstoy to write about the subject in *The Death Penalty and Christianity.*

4 Goldenweiser's recital of Chopin at Yasnaya Polyana the previous evening moved Tolstoy to exclaim: 'It's good to be alive!'

5 The Polish pianist Wanda Landowska came to play at Yasnaya Polyana on three occasions, 1907, January 1909 and December 1909. As well as admiring her playing of Chopin, Bach, Handel and Mozart, Tolstoy claimed to have had some of his views on art confirmed. The 'poor impression' referred to below was apparently due to Landowska's overenthusiastic attitude to Tolstoy as a great writer, which he found embarrassing.

6 From the leader of a Muslim sect who wished to come to Yasnaya Polyana to meet Tolstoy and was duly invited.

7 The Bishop of Tula, who hoped to persuade Tolstoy to return to the Orthodox fold.

8 The Bishop had told Sofya Andreyevna that Tolstoy could not be given a church burial, but asked her to let him know if her husband became dangerously ill.

9 The first volume of stories by M. P. Artsybashev, published by *Life in* 1908. In Tolstoy's copy there are marks awarded by him on a five-point scale. See *Letters*, II, 685 for further comments on Artsybashev's stories.

10 Tolstoy had been highly critical of Artsybashev's sensational novel *Sanin*, which he read in 1908, and more favourably disposed towards Kuprin in 1910 when he called him a true artist who raised problems of life which were more profound than those in Artsybashev and Andreyev.

11 M. A. Schmidt.

12 Nevertheless Tolstoy had included a prose translation of the poem *Les pauvres gens* in the first volume of the *Cycle of Reading*, and did a new translation of it for his projected *Children's Cycle of Reading*.

13 A series of dialogues between children and adults on religious and moral issues, which Tolstoy began work on the following month.

14 Tolstoy was re-reading Gogol's works and Belinsky's letter to Gogol in connection with a request by V. A. Posse to write an article to commemorate the 100th anniversary of Gogol's birth on 19 March 1909.

15 The police had issued an order expelling Chertkov from the Tula province on the grounds that his presence there was liable to disturb the peace.

16 A letter to the press protesting about Chertkov's expulsion.

17 Two versions have survived of the beginning of a comedy with no title. It was never continued.

18 A reference to a phrase in Belinsky's letter to Gogol.

19 A Russian translation of Kant's *Die Religion innerhalb der Grenzen der blossen Vernunft.*

20 The chapters on Confucius in Pauthier's *Les livres sacrés de l'Orient* (Paris, 1852).

21 Gerschenson had sent Tolstoy a copy of the influential anthology of articles on the Russian intelligentsia, *Landmarks*, which had been

published early in 1909. The anthology, whose authors were mainly Orthodox believers with Marxist backgrounds, examined the roots of the Russian revolutionary movement and its prospects for the future. Tolstoy wrote a critical article about it – he particularly disliked its foreign philosophical terminology – and included a quotation from a letter he had received from a peasant, I. V. Kolesnikov. The article was published posthumously.

22 The unfinished story *There are no Guilty People in the World*, based partly on the life of V. F. Orlov, schoolteacher, former revolutionary and friend of Tolstoy.

23 A mistaken diagnosis.

24 In English in the diary.

25 The deletions made by Tolstoy at his wife's request in the diaries for 1888–95 of passages particularly critical of her.

26 The artist Leonid Pasternak, his wife, who was a concert pianist, and A. Y. Mogilevsky, a distinguished Moscow violinist. They played Bach, Beethoven and Mozart and Tolstoy was deeply moved.

27 An article which began with the words: 'Stop and think, for God's sake.' It was given various titles including *The Revolution of Consciousness* and *The Old and the New* in the course of writing, but was ultimately called *The Inevitable Revolution*.

28 Olga Konstantinovna Tolstaya, the divorced wife of Andrey.

29 *The Inevitable Revolution*.

30 Tolstoy spoke elsewhere about the 'cynical coarseness' of Kuprin's story, which dealt with the life of prostitutes, part of which was read aloud to the family.

31 Tolstoy began a letter, to be delivered to his wife after his death, but never finished it.

32 The article *On Love*, begun in May and finished in July, was eventually called *The One Commandment*.

33 In his notebook this entry is prefaced by the words 'Letter to Sonya'.

34 A short unfinished article prompted by a conversation with a policeman about his duty to the state.

35 The story reminded her of Tolstoy's liaison with Aksinya Bazykina before he was married.

36 Afanasy's daughter – the daughter of Afanasy Ageyev, a peasant friend of Tolstoy's; Anisya Kopilova – a widow whose son had been threatened by the police; Y. F. Kopylova – another Yasnaya Polyana peasant, whose husband was in prison for theft.

37 Tanechka Sukhotina, Tolstoy's granddaughter.

38 *The Inevitable Revolution*

39 To the priest I. I. Solovyov about his attitude towards the official Church, and to I. M. Tregubov about freedom of conscience, both published in the *Voice of Moscow*. Tregubov, a 'Tolstoyan' and author of numerous pamphlets and articles on the Russian sects, had earlier been arrested and exiled for his views. He worked for *The Intermediary* for a time, and corresponded frequently with Tolstoy over the years.

40 To a Russian émigré, John Sevitt, who had written to him from Redlands, U.S.A., on the subject of religious education.

41 Tolstoy read in the *Russian Word* the gist of an article by the American President Theodore Roosevelt entitled *Tolstoy* which had been published in the American journal *Outlook*, 1909, No. 2. The article was highly appreciative of Tolstoy's fiction, but critical of his social, political and religious views.

42 I. I. Mechnikov, the Russian director of the Pasteur Institute in Paris who had been awarded a Nobel prize in 1908, was visiting Russia and receiving a warm welcome. He and his wife, together with reporters and photographers, came to see Tolstoy, and he later wrote an account of his visit.

43 To talk to Tolstoy about Mechnikov's visit for a newspaper article.

44 Tolstoy's niece (his brother Sergey's daughter) had had an illegitimate child as a result of a liaison which was soon broken off.

45 Henry George's son, who had recently arrived in Russia, asked Tolstoy if he could visit him at Yasnaya Polyana. Tolstoy readily agreed and the visit took place on 5 June. George later wrote about it in an article in the *New York World*, 14 November 1909, entitled *My Farewell to Count Tolstoy*.

46 S. P. Spiro's article *Tolstoy on I. I. Mechnikov*.

47 Tolstoy's article on the land problem, *Apropos of the Visit of Henry George's Son*, was not accepted by the *Russian Word*, but was published by the *Russian Gazette* on 9 June.

48 On 8 June Tolstoy and his wife went to stay with their daughter Tatyana at Kochety, her husband's estate in the Tula province. He travelled in the same coach as the marshal of the nobility for the Mtsensk district, to whom he talked about Henry George and the land problem without success.

49 *Sic* – in English in the diary.

50 A. V. Sverbeyeva, the wife of the then counsellor at the Russian Embassy in Vienna; they owned an estate near Kochety.

51 Bakunin's *Message to My Italian Friends*, addressed to a workers' congress convened by Mazzini on 1 September 1871.

52 Tolstoy had been invited to take part in the 18th International Peace Congress in Stockholm in August.

53 Sofya Andreyevna wanted to prosecute the Petersburg publishers who had brought out *Three Deaths* and extracts from *Childhood* without her permission. Tolstoy said that if she did so, he would take away her authority to publish his works.

54 M. de Paris – a way of referring to the executioner.

55 The letter he wrote to a group of Swedish intellectuals in 1899 about the Hague Peace Conference of the great powers to discuss disarmament. He believed that only individual refusal to do military service would be effective, but that that was incompatible with a conference of governments.

56 M. A. Stakhovich had told Tolstoy that Prince Vasilchikov had been deeply offended by some remarks which Tolstoy had made in a letter to Molochnikov about the treatment of peasants on the Vasilchikov estates and which Molochnikov had quoted in a letter of his own to the prince. Tolstoy's reply to Stakhovich explaining that the remarks had been of a

general nature and not directed specifically against Vasilchikov was seen by Sofya Andreyevna, who reacted angrily against Molochnikov.

57 To I. V. Denisenko about a will Tolstoy had asked him to draw up renouncing all his property and handing over the land that used to belong to him to the peasants.

58 *Léon Tolstoi, 'Appels aux dirigeants'* (Paris, 1902).

59 A. S. Buturlin, a landowner from Simbirsk and an old friend of Tolstoy's who had at one time been imprisoned in connection with the Nechayev affair.

60 Tolstoy's sister.

61 To the Stockholm congress with Tolstoy, contrary to her previous intentions.

62 Gusev was arrested and exiled to the Cherdyn district for allegedly conducting revolutionary propaganda and circulating banned works of literature. Tolstoy wrote *A Statement about the arrest of Gusev*, which was published in the *Russian Gazette* on 11 August with the omission of a few words.

63 The congress had been postponed for a year because of a general strike in Sweden. Tolstoy believed that his decision to speak may have had something to do with the postponement.

64 H. Croft Hiller had sent Tolstoy his book *Meta-Christianity. Spiritism established, Religion re-established, Science dis-established* (London, 1903). He subsequently sent various Appendices to it, which Tolstoy refers to unflatteringly here.

65 A reference to Easter Sunday in *Selected Passages from Correspondence with Friends*.

66 Certain people in Berlin, having heard that Tolstoy was planning to deliver his paper intended for the Stockholm Peace Congress in the German capital, tried to make use of two letters by Sofya Andreyevna refusing permission for selected works of Tolstoy's to be published free for distribution to schoolchildren, in order to discredit him. An article in the German language edition of the *St Petersburg Gazette* which carried the story was reproduced in a number of German papers and prompted charges of hypocrisy.

67 A hairdresser from Kiev and a deaf mute from a wealthy German family.

68 Sofya Andreyevna gave permission for Pathé cinephotographers to visit Yasnaya Polyana. Tolstoy was uncooperative, but pictures were taken while he was on his way to the station *en route* for Moscow.

69 The Tolstoys were on their way to visit the Chertkovs on their estate of Kryokshino outside Moscow.

70 At Zimmermann's music shop Tolstoy listened to a new recording machine called the 'Mignon' which was later taken round to Kryokshino (among other things he greatly enjoyed hearing Paderewski playing a Chopin *étude*).

71 To Stefania Laudyn, author of a book on the Polish question, who had asked Tolstoy to speak out in defence of the oppressed Polish people. Tolstoy's reply took the form of an article, *A Reply to a Polish Woman*.

72 A visit was expected from a big group of teachers from the Zvenigorod district, and Tolstoy wanted to jot down some thoughts about education.

73 Thomas Tapsell, an English photographer, who was living with the Chertkovs and took numerous pictures of Tolstoy.

74 Thomas Edison had sent two Englishmen from London to Kryokshino with the latest cinematographic equipment to take pictures of Tolstoy.

75 Tolstoy replied to a letter from an Indian publicist Narain Bishen who had written to complain about the poverty-stricken condition of the people of India, and also received a letter from Gandhi (at the time in London) asking him to support the struggle of the Indian people in South Africa. For Tolstoy's letters to Gandhi see *Letters*, II, 691 and 706.

76 Gandhi had asked Tolstoy to verify his authorship of the *Letter to an Indian* and to confirm that the English translation was accurate since one of his friends wished to publish it in India. Despite Tolstoy's reservations about its weakness, it was translated into Hindi and published with a foreword by Gandhi.

77 To collect more material for the second volume of his biography of Tolstoy.

78 Maude and Chertkov had quarrelled over the publication of Tolstoy's works abroad.

79 To Gandhi (*Letters*, II, 691).

80 A conversation between a passer-by and some peasants about their oppressed condition and the means of escaping from it eventually became a dialogue involving one peasant only – *A Passer-by and a Peasant* – which Tolstoy finished in October but which was not published in his lifetime.

81 Andreyev first made contact with Tolstoy in 1901 when he sent him a volume of his collected stories (*Letters*, II, 608). The two authors corresponded from time to time, but only three letters from each have survived. Andreyev eventually visited Yasnaya Polyana in April 1910. Of Andreyev's later works, Tolstoy had serious reservations about *The Seven Who Were Hanged*, which Andreyev wished to dedicate to him (*Letters*, II, 680).

82 A journal published in India by Professor Rama Deva.

83 Tolstoy was regretting his promise to record his voice for the Society of Workers of the Periodical Press and Literature, but was persuaded to keep it.

84 *Russian Thought*, No. 1, 1909 published Ropshin's (B. Savinkov's) novella *The Pale Horse* (not *The White Horse* as Tolstoy writes), Sologub's story *The White Birch Tree* (not *The Birch Tree*), and poems by Blok, Bryusov, Bely, Gippius, Merezhkovsky, Solovyov and Sologub.

85 The violinist M. G. Erdenko and his pianist wife, both of whom went on to have distinguished musical careers, had come to Yasnaya Polyana to demonstrate their method of playing Russian music. Their offer was not accepted, but being unable to get railway tickets back to Moscow they returned to Yasnaya Polyana and were then admitted.

86 *A Passer-by and a Peasant*.

87 The recital eventually given by the Erdenkos, including some Jewish folk

melodies and several pieces by Wieniawski, as well as Chopin's Nocturne, greatly moved Tolstoy, who, according to M. G. Erdenko, danced across the room to the music of a mazurka.

88 Strakhov had brought a letter from Chertkov saying that Tolstoy's will signed at Kryokshino on 18 September 1909 whereby his family would retain the copyright only of Tolstoy's works published before 1881 was legally invalid. Tolstoy then decided to renounce the copyright on all his works and to appoint his daughter Alexandra (Sasha) as executor. He later changed his mind again.

89 The text of a new will, which Tolstoy amended and signed. This will also proved to be inadequate, since no second person was named in the event of Alexandra's death.

90 Presumably some of Gorky's early stories about down-and-outs. 'The lowest strata of the people' is a free translation of *naroda chernosotennogo* – a reference to the 'Black Hundred' anti-revolutionary groups active in Russia in 1905–7.

91 Sofya Andreyevna was contemplating legal action against publishers who had issued cheap editions of the stories mentioned, which, since they were written before 1881, were not public property – a fact which Tolstoy now regretted.

92 This story by his wife may have prompted Tolstoy to write his own story about the disaster on the Khodynka field during the coronation celebrations of 1896.

93 Members of a Paris society for performers on ancient instruments, including Henri and Mariel Casadesus, whom Goldenweiser had brought to Yasnaya Polyana together with S. Kusevitsky (Sergei Koussevitzky).

94 A remark by Luka in Act 2 of Gorky's play *The Lower Depths*.

95 C. W. Daniel, the English editor of *The Open Road*, and A. P. Sergeyenko, at the time Chertkov's secretary. A frequent visitor at the Tolstoys', his books included *How Count Tolstoy Lives and Works* and *Tolstoy and his Contemporaries*. He also published three volumes of Tolstoy's letters.

96 *The Tragicomedy of our Russian Life, Russian Standard*, 25 November 1909.

97 In William James' *Varieties of Religious Experience*, which Tolstoy was re-reading in Russian translation.

98 Gorbunov-Posadov. See 1889, Note 48. He had been accused of publishing without the censor's permission a book by Herbert Spencer, *The Right to the Use of the Earth*, which reprinted two chapters of Henry George's *The Perplexed Philosopher*.

99 Tolstoy read in German the Czech writer A. Smetana's *Die Geschichte eines Exkommunizierten*.

100 Sayings of Epictetus in the anthology *For Every Day*.

101 Tolstoy had translated most of Sterne's novel in 1851 and 1852.

1910

1 Tolstoy had noted in his diary in October 1909 that he had had a wonderful dream about himself speaking impassionedly about Henry George. After several revisions he included it as the final part of his trilogy *Three Days in the Country*.

2 A. I. Drankov, owner of a cinematographic office in Moscow, came to show the films he had recently taken and to take new ones.

3 Tolstoy read the second volume of Gorky's stories published by *Knowledge* in 1902. He spoke to Makovitsky about the falseness, in his opinion, of the language, descriptions and similes in some of the stories.

4 Tolstoy heard two cases, one involving a mail robbery, the other membership of the Socialist Revolutionary Party and possession of banned literature. The sentences were comparatively light (the first was an acquittal), which some people attributed to Tolstoy's presence.

5 Tolstoy read W. H. Davies' *Autobiography of a Super-tramp*, with a foreword by Bernard Shaw.

6 M. A. Stakhovich brought with him the manuscript of a book containing A. A. Tolstaya's correspondence with Tolstoy and her reminiscences.

7 *Letters*, I, 108–10.

8 Gorbunov-Posadov had decided to begin publishing the booklets which comprised *The Way of Life*, a new series of booklets which differed from the *Cycle of Reading* and *For Every Day* by being organized thematically and not by the calendar.

9 To the Japanese Christian pastor who had written to Tolstoy to ask about his attitude to military service and to taxation.

10 A letter to I. I. Perper, editor of the *Vegetarian Review*, asking him to publish Bruno Friedank's book *Die Greuel der 'Christlichen' Civilisation*, which had been translated by A. A. Goldenweiser. See *Letters*, II, 698.

11 Tolstoy had been asked by a teacher how to dispose in his will of 15,000 roubles; he suggested that the money should be used to publish a popular encyclopaedic dictionary.

12 A letter to the Indian writer Tarakuatta Das, editor of the *Free Hindustan*, published in North America, who had asked his opinion about the treatment of Indians by the British. Tolstoy's letter, begun in June and resumed much later in the year, grew into the article translated into English by Aylmer Maude as *Letter to a Hindu*. Tolstoy re-read his letter on hearing that it had been widely circulated in India.

13 At the request of a group of young people at Telyatinki, Tolstoy began to write a comedy – at first called *One Good Turn Deserves Another* – for them to take part in. It was not finished but the draft was used for a performance at Telyatinki after his death. It is referred to again below on 30 March.

14 *An Everyday Occurrence, Russian Wealth*, 1910, No. 3. Tolstoy wrote an enthusiastic letter about it to Korolenko the following day (*Letters*, II, 699).

15 Thomas Masaryk, professor of philosophy at Prague University and later President of the Czech Republic, who corresponded with Tolstoy and visited him on 30 March 1910.

16 Alexandra Tolstaya, who was suspected of having tuberculosis, was leaving for the Crimea for treatment.

17 Bernard Shaw had sent Tolstoy his play *The Shewing-Up of Blanco Posnet* and a letter indicating its connection with *The Power of Darkness*. For Tolstoy's reply see *Letters*, II, 700.

18 John Eastham, an English Pacifist, had sent Tolstoy an invitation to speak at a meeting in London in May and a prospectus of the First Universal Races Congress, which he was helping to organize. Tolstoy refused, mainly
on the grounds that as long as separate peoples and states existed there would always be wars.

19 A headmaster who had been educated in America and an official who had been sent to Russia for further study.

20 A letter from Gandhi together with a copy of his book *Indian Home Rule*.

21 A retired colonel who came to reproach Tolstoy for his apostasy and for his hostility towards the state.

22 Andreyev spent two days at Yasnaya Polyana, where the two writers discussed among other things the works of Gorky, Sologub and K. Chukovsky. Andreyev wrote about the visit in an article entitled *Six Months Before Death* in the *Sun of Russia*, November 1911, No. 53.

23 The doctors believed that both her lungs were affected by tuberculosis.

24 Tolstoy travelled with Makovitsky and Bulgakov to Tatyana's estate at Kochety and stayed there until 20 May.

25 A quotation from a poem by Fet.

26 He had read an article in the *Modern World*, 1910, No. 3, entitled *Modern Suicides*, by Dr D. N. Zhbankov, which he discussed with Andreyev and corresponded about with Masaryk.

27 Tolstoy was reading *Essais de Montaigne, suivis de sa correspondance et 'De la Servitude voluntaire' d'Estienne de la Boétie* (Paris, 1854) and La Rochefoucauld's *Maximes*.

28 See Note 13.

29 About some Yasnaya Polyana peasants who had been arrested by the Circassian employed by Sofya Andreyevna to patrol the estate.

30 P. P. Trubetskoy, the Russian sculptor living abroad, came with his wife to stay for a few days at Yasnaya Polyana and did a sculpture, a portrait in oils and two pencil sketches of Tolstoy. When Sofya Andreyevna asked him whether he had read *War and Peace* he amused Tolstoy by confessing that he never read anything.

31 An article about Chernyshevsky in Siberia based on unpublished letters and the family archive which Tolstoy read in *Russian Wealth*, Nos. 4 and 5.

32 A reply by Tolstoy to the letter of a peasant blacksmith who wished to take up writing. Tolstoy made it very clear which occupation he thought preferable.

33 In this and other entries hereabouts the foreword mentioned is the one to *The Way of Life*.

34 Presumably Tolstoy talked to his daughter about his wish to leave home.

35 Two girls (including one on crutches) had come a long way to ask Tolstoy's

advice on how to live a fruitful, Christian life and also to get his opinion about their writings, which they had brought with them. They had settled temporarily in the village to be near Tolstoy, and he visited them there on 12 June.

36 A branch of the Meshcherskoye psychiatric hospital.

37 Tolstoy recorded his impressions in an article, *On Insanity*.

38 Tolstoy had a high opinion of many of A. I. Kuprin's stories and often spoke of his talent and vivid imagery, but was not enthusiastic about *Emerald* and was disgusted by *The Pit*.

39 See 1909, Note 13.

40 From Sofya Andreyevna, asking Tolstoy to return urgently.

41 Tolstoy's intention of contrasting life inside and outside the house.

42 Sofya Andreyevna was going to Sergey's estate for his birthday and wanted Tolstoy to go with her. When she realized that he felt too tired to make the journey she changed her mind but Tolstoy did eventually go.

43 The terrible quarrel was largely the result of Sofya Andreyevna's determination to recover her husband's diaries from Chertkov. According to an eye-witness she ran into the garden shouting that she would kill Chertkov. Tolstoy woke up his son Lev and told him to go and look for her. In his memoirs *The Truth about My Father*, Lev Tolstoy claimed that she kept repeating 'I won't go back. He drove me out like a dog' and that he returned to the house and made his father accompany him in order to calm her down.

44 Tolstoy agreed not to give his diary to Chertkov for copying, to take back the old diaries which Chertkov still had and not to see Chertkov in future. For the full text of his letter see *Letters*, II, 700-2.

45 Matthew Gering, a friend of the American politician and Secretary of State William Bryan, who had visited Tolstoy in 1903 and corresponded with him, asked to visit Yasnaya Polyana with a personal message from Bryan. Tolstoy agreed and Gering spent two days with him.

46 Tolstoy received an invitation to the Stockholm Peace Congress which was due to open in August, having been postponed from the previous year. He wrote a short addition to the paper he had prepared in 1909 but did not send it, confining himself to a brief letter instead.

47 Tolstoy's niece, who had had an illegitimate child.

48 His will, witnessed by Goldenweiser, Sergeyenko and Radynsky, bequeathed his entire literary heritage to his daughter Alexandra or, in the event of her death, to Tatyana. Further changes were made later, clarifying points of detail to do with the disposition of his writings after his death.

49 From 29 July Tolstoy began to keep his *Diary for Myself Alone* parallel with his ordinary diary.

50 V. G. Korolenko, editor of the influential journal *Russian Wealth* and vehement opponent of capital punishment, spent two days with Tolstoy. He returned to Yasnaya Polyana for Tolstoy's funeral.

51 A neighbour of Tolstoy's (a former vice-governor of Smolensk), and a Hungarian newspaper correspondent who had not heard of Henry George respectively.

52 Tolstoy and his wife and daughter Alexandra left for his daughter Tatyana's estate at Kochety where Tolstoy stayed until 22 September.

53 A manuscript collection of articles which was published by *The Intermediary* in 1911 with an introductory letter by Tolstoy.

54 Tolstoy had made a list in his diary and notebooks of some forty types of characters he would like to depict in future, but this was the only one of the intended 'character' stories to be written.

55 To return to Yasnaya Polyana from Kochety to see her son.

56 James Mavor, professor of political economy at Toronto University, who had helped the Dukhobors to resettle in Canada and had visited Tolstoy previously in 1889.

57 Vsevolod Savvich Mamontov, son of the wealthy industrialist and art patron Savva Mamontov, and his wife.

58 A reply to a letter from Gandhi and a friend who had set up a farm near Johannesburg for Indian residents who were resorting to civil disobedience (*Letters*, II, 706–8).

59 A. I. Drankov (see Note 2). He spent three days taking pictures and showing ones he had taken previously.

60 Sofya Andreyevna wanted Tolstoy to go back with her to Yasnaya Polyana, but he refused.

61 Giulio Vitali, author of several works on Tolstoy, had written to Makovitsky outlining what he considered to be the main points of Tolstoy's philosophy of life for a book which he intended to dedicate to him. Tolstoy confirmed their correctness, and the book was published in Rome in 1911: *Leone Tolstoi: Con ritratto, bibliografia e lettera autografa.*

62 A Russian translation by N. Kolayev of Max Müller's *The Six Systems of Indian Philosophy* (London, 1899)

63 Sofya Andreyevna had found Tolstoy's *Diary for Myself Alone* with his entries for the period 29 July to 22 September in the top of his boot. She did not return it, but made her own notes in it.

64 Tolstoy received German translations by Škarvan of his three articles: *On Science, Letter to an Indian* and *On Law* with comments on them by Eugen Schmitt (the German translation of *On Science* was edited by Schmitt) and also the second volume of Aylmer Maude's biography.

65 In Tolstoy's absence his wife had moved the photographs of Chertkov and Alexandra Tolstaya which were hanging in his study.

66 The editors of a Czech newspaper, *Mladé Proudy*, had written to Tolstoy about the persecution of young socialists in their country and their wish to publish a 'Reader' containing socialist articles. Tolstoy, whose opinion and cooperation had been sought, replied with a letter which grew into an article, *On Socialism*, which he continued to work on until he left home for good.

67 Probably the proofs of the third chapter (*The Soul*) of *The Way of Life*.

68 A. M. Khiryakov, who wrote extensively about Tolstoy and edited a posthumous collection of his works, corresponded with him from prison where he had been sentenced for editing a liberal newspaper in Petersburg.

69 V. M. Feokritova, a friend of Alexandra's, who worked at Yasnaya Polyana as Sofya Andreyevna's copyist and also helped Alexandra to copy out her father's writings. She accompanied Tolstoy and his daughter on Tolstoy's last journey, and was present at his death at Astapovo.

70 Because of the very strained relations with her mother, Alexandra moved temporarily to her house at Telyatinki, from which, however, she frequently came back to Yasnaya Polyana.

71 Sofya Andreyevna's new (12th) edition of Tolstoy's works, which came out in 22 volumes in 1911.

72 V. M. Feokritova.

73 The second volume of Aylmer Maude's biography.

74 The first volume of *The Brothers Karamazov*. He had some critical things to say to Bulgakov about its unnaturalness and lack of artistry, while singling out for praise individual scenes such as those involving Father Zosima and the Grand Inquisitor. One particular reproach was that 'all the characters speak the same language'.

75 Sofya Andreyevna was alarmed that her husband, with the collaboration of Chertkov, had drawn up a will renouncing all copyright to his works, and that rich publishers would get richer while she and his children would starve.

76 A ninth-century Indian philosopher.

77 A reference to a letter Chertkov had written (and which had been forwarded to Tolstoy by Chertkov's wife) to the Bulgarian 'Tolstoyan' X. F. Dosev, trying to clarify the relationship between Tolstoy and his wife and to correct Dosev's wrong impression that Tolstoy was a slave to Sofya Andreyevna.

78 Natalya Almedingen was a journalist and editor of children's magazines in Petersburg, and also worked for *The Intermediary* publishing house.

79 Tolstoy evidently had in mind a story (never written) involving his old friend the critic and philosopher Strakhov, and Grushenka from *The Brothers Karamazov*.

80 Korney Chukovsky had asked Tolstoy and other writers to write a few lines directed against capital punishment, suitable for publication in the newspaper *Speech*. Tolstoy's reply, which he was still working on during his last day at Yasnaya Polyana, was never properly completed, but came out after his death under the title *An Effective Remedy* – a title invented by the editor of *Speech*.

81 His 'farewell' letter to Sofya Andreyevna, telling her of his final departure. For the text and Tolstoy's movements after leaving home see *Letters*, II, 710–11.

82 P. N. Gastev's reminiscences about the peasant Syutayev, whom he had met in a commune in 1890, which Tolstoy read in manuscript. Tolstoy had a high regard for Syutayev, a Christian anarchist and critic of the Orthodox Church.

83 The convent where Tolstoy's sister had lived since 1889.

84 I. O. Shurayev, a man-servant.

85 Tolstoy's sister's daughter, Y. V. Obolenskaya, who was staying with her mother.

86 A booklet by V. Kozhevnikov entitled *The Relationship of Socialism to Religion in General and Christianity in Particular*, published in Novosyolov's Religious and Philosophical Library series.

87 It had been left behind at Yasnaya Polyana.

88 Saying in effect that his father was right to do what he had done.

89 His last letter to his wife, translated in *Letters*, II, 713–14, in which he ruled out a return home or a meeting with her.

90 Tolstoy and Makovitsky.

91 Tolstoy's last written words, preceded by a shortened version of the favourite saying of his: *Fais ce que dois, advienne que pourra*.

DIARY FOR MYSELF ALONE

1 A reference to the content of his new will (1910, Note 48) making his works freely available to all.

2 Lev was learning to sculpt.

3 By encouraging him and helping him to write his secret will, which led to so much discord in the family.

4 M. F. Lodyzhensky, author of a 'mystical trilogy', discussed Indian philosophy, yoga and theosophy with Tolstoy.

5 For the text see *Letters*, II, 703.

6 Chertkov, in reply to Tolstoy's letter (see Note 5), strongly defended his position and Tolstoy acquiesced.

7 An extract from Tolstoy's diary for 29 November 1851, in which he spoke of his love for men and which Sofya Andreyevna misconstrued.

8 To please Sofya Andreyevna, Tolstoy agreed not to visit Chertkov at Telyatinki on 17 July, and Chertkov stopped visiting Yasnaya Polyana on 24 July.

9 *A Course in Psychiatry* (Moscow, 1901) by Professor S. S. Korsakov, which had been sent to Tolstoy by doctors of a Moscow psychiatric hospital.

10 At this point Tolstoy includes in his diary a number of phrases which appealed to him from the speech of a peasant woman.

11 In connection with the drawing up of the secret will.

12 About the will.

13 His departure for Kochety.

14 V. M. Feokritova.

15 Chertkov offered Tolstoy advice about the treatment of neurotic patients.

16 According to Makovitsky, Tolstoy related how the French physicist and politician François Arago stopped a speaker who kept referring to him as *Monsieur* Arago and asked to be called Arago *tout court*. The context in which Tolstoy's remark was made is not clear.

17 A neuropathologist, called in to give advice about Sofya Andreyevna's apparent neurosis. He advised her not to get agitated, to take baths and to go for walks!

18 From K. Bayromov, a former Babist, who sympathized with Tolstoy's religious and philosophical views.

19 A reference to stories, inspired by Sofya Andreyevna, about an allegedly

unnatural relationship between Tolstoy and Chertkov, which were spread by Zvegintseva, who disliked Chertkov.

20 All right for Mavor (see 1910, Note 56) to visit Yasnaya Polyana.

21 Sofya Andreyevna had invited a priest to hold a prayer service in her bedroom and then sprinkled all the upstairs rooms, including Tolstoy's bedroom and study, with holy water to exorcise the evil spirit of Chertkov.

22 V. M. Feokritova's diary contained some abusive remarks about Tolstoy attributed to his wife.

23 See 1910, Note 63.

24 The word was used by Sofya Andreyevna, who believed that Chertkov was trying to obtain more and more of Tolstoy's manuscripts.

25 For the text of the letter in reply to Chertkov's letter of the previous day criticizing Tolstoy for allowing his wife to interfere with relations between the two men see *Letters*, II, 708.

26 This last photograph of Tolstoy was taken by Bulgakov.

27 Chertkov had sent the manuscript of his article *On Free Thinking*, which was never finished.

28 *Culte Antoiniste: Révélation d'Antoine le Guérisseur* – a biography of a Belgian worker and vegetarian who left the Catholic Church, became interested in spiritualism, and acquired a reputation as a healer.

29 Chertkov came to Yasnaya Polyana on 7 October with Sofya Andreyevna's agreement.

30 See 1910, Note 75.

31 It was rumoured that Sofya Andreyevna intended to sell the copyright of Tolstoy's works to a publishing house for a million roubles.

32 A letter to Dosev – see 1910, Note 77; the statement – a draft statement to the press that Tolstoy's works were not for sale.

33 See *Letters*, II, 711–12.

INDEX

Flann O'Brien

The Third Policeman

'Wonderful. *The Third Policeman* is a great masterpiece of black humour.'
George Mackay Brown

A murder thriller, an hilarious comic satire about an archetypal village police force, a surrealistic vision of eternity, the story of a tender, brief, unrequited love affair between a man and his bicycle and a chilling fable of unending guilt, *The Third Policeman* is comparable only to *Alice in Wonderland* as an allegory of the absurd. Distinguished by endless comic invention and its delicate balancing of logic and fantasy, *The Third Policeman* is unique in the English language.

'Flann O'Brien learned from Joyce the art of tuning language to a lyrical pitch, which he could then turn to his purpose, whether it was to be plain foolery, unconcealed indignation or high comedy. The best of his contemporaries and many subsequent Irish writers have much to thank him for.'
Sunday Times

'Flann O'Brien is inventive, his storytelling is swift and sure, making the eccentric seem natural and the commonplace hilarious.'
The Times

flamingo

Simone de Beauvoir

The Mandarins

With an introduction by Doris Lessing

In wartime Paris, a group of friends gather to celebrate the end of the German occupation and to plan their future. Henri, ex-Resistance fighter, is eager to resume his life, to travel and to write a novel; Paula is convinced that she can revive her dying affair with Henri. Robert, a writer, is determined to enter politics whilst his psychiatrist wife, Anne, is deeply distracted by an affair with a young American; their daughter, Nadine feels only bitterness and disillusionment after the killing of her lover by the Germans.

Winner of the Prix Goncourt, *The Mandarins* captures the dizzying sense of promise felt throughout France after liberation. Herself a central figure in the cultural life of the Left Bank, de Beauvoir punctuates the novel with wickedly accurate portraits of the intellectual giants of the time, including Sartre and Camus.

'A remarkable book, a novel on the grand scale, courageous in its exactitude and endearing because of its persistent seriousness.'
Iris Murdoch, *Sunday Times*

'Simone de Beauvoir has given us a magnificent map of the mental terrain of French intellectualism. *The Mandarins* is a window on the world through which we see and recognize not just the facts of a situation but the truth about it. Moving and engrossing.'
New York Times

Joan Didion

The White Album

'We tell ourselves stories in order to live.'

Looking for plausible stories as the Sixties are about to implode, Joan Didion sets out, notebook in hand, on a now-legendary journey into the hinterland of the American psyche: she kills time waiting for Jim Morrison to show up, parties with Janis Joplin, visits the Black Panthers in prison, watches a campus combust, dines with Tate and Polanski, buys dresses with Charlie Manson's girls, and gravitates towards biker movies 'because there on screen was some news I was not getting from the *New York Times*'. She and her reader emerge, cauterized, from this devastating tour of the myths and realities of that age of self-discovery into the harsh light of the morning after the sixties . . .

'Demonstrates an uncanny ability to capture the insidious and pervasive infections of mind and spirit that have led to both the corruption of government and business, and the withering of the individual.'
Chicago Sun-Times

'Everything Didion writes has a land's end edginess to it – a hyperattentive eye on the dramas found at the outskirts of the human condition. She writes as someone who has come through great shudders of the earth with a fundamental understanding that everything is subject to instantaneous and complete revision.'
Village Voice

'She is the best chronicler California has.'
Vogue

'Simply an original and unexpected writer who is never banal.'
New York Review of Books

ISBN 0 00 654586 6

 flamingo

MODERN CLASSIC

Robert Tressell

The Ragged Trousered Philanthropists

With an introduction by Alan Sillitoe

The Ragged Trousered Philanthropists tells the story of a group of working men who are joined one day by Owen, a journeyman-prophet with a vision of a just society. Owen's spirited attacks on the greed and dishonesty of the capitalist system rouse his fellow men from their political quietism. *The Ragged Trousered Philanthropists* is both a masterpiece of wit and political passion and one of the most authentic novels of English working class life ever written.

'The first great English novel about the class war, *The Ragged Trousered Philanthropists* is spiked, witty, humorous, instructive and full of excitement, harmony and pathos.'   Alan Sillitoe

'Some books seem to batter their way to immortality against all the odds, by sheer brute artistic strength, and high up in this curious and honourable company must be counted *The Ragged Trousered Philanthropists*. Robert Tressell's unfailing humour mixes with an unfailing rage and the two together make a truly Swiftian impact.'
Michael Foot, *Evening Standard*

'*The Ragged Trousered Philanthropists* is a wonderful book. Its wonder comes from the raciness of its story and the passionate ethics that emerge.'   *City Limits*

flamingo

Flamingo

Flamingo is a quality imprint publishing both fiction and non-fiction. Below are some recent titles.

Fiction

- ☐ News From a Foreign Country Came *Alberto Manguel* £4.99
- ☐ The Kitchen God's Wife *Amy Tan* £4.99
- ☐ A Thousand Acres *Jane Smiley* £5.99
- ☐ The Quick *Agnes Rossi* £4.99
- ☐ The Crown of Columbus *Michael Dorris & Louise Erdrich* £5.99
- ☐ The Cat Sanctuary *Patrick Gale* £5.99
- ☐ Dreaming in Cuban *Cristina Garcia* £5.99
- ☐ Mary Swann *Carol Shields* £4.99
- ☐ True Believers *Joseph O'Connor* £5.99
- ☐ Bastard Out of Carolina *Dorothy Allison* £5.99

Non-fiction

- ☐ The Proving Grounds *Benedict Allen* £5.99
- ☐ Long Ago in France *M. F. K. Fisher* £5.99
- ☐ Ford Madox Ford *Alan Judd* £6.99
- ☐ C. S. Lewis *A. N. Wilson* £5.99
- ☐ Into the Badlands *John Williams* £5.99
- ☐ Dame Edna Everage *John Lahr* £5.99
- ☐ Number *John McLeish* £5.99
- ☐ Tangier *Iain Finlayson* £5.99

You can buy Flamingo paperbacks at your local bookshop or newsagent. Or you can order them from Fontana Paperbacks, Cash Sales Department, Box 29, Douglas, Isle of Man. Please send a cheque, postal or money order (not currency) worth the purchase price plus 24p per book (maximum postage required is £3.00 for orders within the UK).

NAME (Block letters)_____

ADDRESS_____

_____

_____